AN ENEMY WE CREATED

ALEX STRICK VAN LINSCHOTEN
AND FELIX KUEHN

An Enemy We Created

*The Myth of the Taliban-Al Qaeda Merger
in Afghanistan*

OXFORD
UNIVERSITY PRESS

Oxford University Press is a department of the University of Oxford. It furthers the University's objective of excellence in research, scholarship, and education by publishing worldwide. Oxford is a registered trade mark of Oxford University Press in the UK and in certain other countries.

Oxford   New York
Auckland   Cape Town   Dar es Salaam   Hong Kong   Karachi
Kuala Lumpur   Madrid   Melbourne   Mexico City   Nairobi
New Delhi   Shanghai   Taipei   Toronto

With offices in
Argentina   Austria   Brazil   Chile   Czech Republic   France   Greece
Guatemala   Hungary   Italy   Japan   Poland   Portugal   Singapore
South Korea   Switzerland   Thailand   Turkey   Ukraine   Vietnam

Published in the United States of America by
Oxford University Press
198 Madison Avenue, New York, NY 10016,
United States of America

Published in the United Kingdom in 2011 by C. Hurst & Co. (Publishers) Ltd.

www.oup.com

Library of Congress Cataloging-in-Publication Data
Strick van Linschoten, Alex.
An enemy we created : the myth of the Taliban-al Qaeda merger in Afghanistan / Alex Strick van Linschoten and Felix Kuehn.
p.   cm.
Includes bibliographical references and index.
ISBN 978-0-19-992731-9 (hardback : alk. paper) 1. Taliban—History. 2. Qaida (Organization)—History. 3. Afghanistan—History—20th century. 4. Afghanistan—History—2001-5. War on Terrorism, 2001–2009. 6. Terrorism—Religious aspects—Islam. I. Kuehn, Felix, 1979– II. Title.
DS371.3.S758   2012
958.104—dc23   2012006855

3 5 7 9 8 6 4 2

Printed in the United States of America
on acid-free paper

CONTENTS

ACKNOWLEDGEMENTS

Any manuscript of this size necessarily involves the input and assistance of a large number of different voices and perspectives. First and foremost, it would have been impossible to conduct our research without the support of Afghan friends and colleagues in Afghanistan, particularly in Kandahar. Unfortunately, the ongoing conflict means we cannot name individuals out of concern for their safety, but we hope they know who they are and how important they were (and are) to our ability to do this kind of work. This project would simply not have happened were it not for this help.

An Enemy We Created was originally commissioned as a study for New York University's Center on International Cooperation. Barney Rubin (as Senior Fellow and Director of Studies) was instrumental in ensuring we could get on with our research uninterrupted and was extremely patient with our late submission of the draft manuscript back in October 2010. Jake Sherman and Tom Gregg were extremely helpful with the administrative side of the project. Funding from the Center on International Cooperation was important in allowing us to translate key texts and to facilitate our research.

Our interviews for this project were conducted in several countries. In Afghanistan, these ranged from government members and tribal elders to Taliban fighters, more senior members of the movement's political cadre, as well as ordinary people, too. We spoke with journalists, analysts and researcher colleagues based in and outside Afghanistan, and humanitarian and political practitioners themselves.

These included: Abdullah Anas; Orzala Ashraf; Martine van Bijlert; Vahid Brown; Bob Churcher; Faisal Devji; Vanda Feldab-Brown; Kathy Gannon; Antonio Giustozzi; Joanna Nathan; Gretchen Peters; Ahmed Rashid; Naeem

Rashid; Michael Semple; Saleem Shahzad; James Shinn; Brendan Simms; Yaroslav Trofimov; Francesc Vendrell; and Marvin Weinbaum. There were many other encounters in Europe and in the United States. We thank them all for taking the time to talk to us. In addition, Sebastian Dietrich helped find some very useful out-of-print documents for us; Naira Antoun conducted an interview on our behalf in London as well as some background research; David Rohde generously helped find some documents left in Kabul in 2001 by Afghan Taliban and foreign fighters.

We want to express our thanks, too, to Peter and Margaret Ann McCann and the staff of Castle Craig in Scotland for hosting us for several weeks in late 2010 while we were finishing the first draft of the manuscript. Similarly, in Germany, Klaus, Inge and Peter Kuehn's continued support has been invaluable.

Our research required a fairly complex technical back-end and we were lucky to receive advice and support from Mark Anderson, Mark Bernstein, Nathan Matsias and Stacey Mason; all helped with the tricky-yet-indispensable *Tinderbox* programme.

Early drafts (partial and full) of the manuscript were read by a small group of some of the best minds working on these issues: Mariam Abou Zahab; Matthieu Aikins; Steve Coll; Gilles Dorronsoro; Jere van Dyk; Andrea Binder; Joshua Foust; Marcus Geisser; Tom Gregg; Thomas Hegghammer; Ron Neumann; William Reeve; David Rohde; Barney Rubin; Thomas Ruttig; and Farida Strickel. We are grateful for their comments and suggestions. This book is better for it, although needless to say any errors and omissions remain ours and ours alone.

Among this group a few friends went above and beyond in their help: Christian Bleuer delivered voluminous and useful criticism; Leah Farrall—one of the top 'unknown' scholars working on al-Qaeda-related issues—provided constant and dependable feedback over the course of the past year; Anand Gopal—surely the best new-generation writer researching the Taliban and their Afghan affiliates—generously offered his time and titbits from his research archive throughout; Anatol Lieven was happy to discuss Pakistan and India at length on multiple occasions; Jean MacKenzie continued to offer us a roof over our heads whenever when we were in Kabul and kept us regularly supplied with good conversation and pizza; Graeme Smith—the grandfather of post-2001 journalism and research in southern Afghanistan—patiently kept in touch and offered his advice throughout.

ACKNOWLEDGEMENTS

Larry Landrigan offered painstakingly detailed line edits of the entire text when we were going through the final proofs.

We have been very lucky with our publisher. Hurst punches well above its weight in the leagues of serious scholarship, and we are glad to be able to call Michael Dwyer our friend as well as our editor.

The authors also wish to thank O.W. and S.I..

'A history in which every particular incident may be true may on the whole be false.'

Thomas Babington Macaulay

'Human life could scarcely go on without myths. Certainly politics cannot.'

John Gray, *Al Qaeda and what it means to be modern*[1]

'There are no pure ideas and straight lines in the history of great events.'

George Packer, *The Assassin's Gate*[2]

1

INTRODUCING TALQAEDA

"'That's the thing that bothers me most,' said the SAS officer. "In 2006 when the fighting started, we called everyone who resisted us 'Taliban.' But they really weren't necessarily. They were just the community's warrior class who had always defended their community against outsiders, and were bound to do so again. The 'Taliban' in that sense were an enemy of our own creation. That was why, in 2005, we sent a memo to John Reid at the Ministry of Defence saying, 'If you want an insurgency here, you can have one.'"

James Fergusson, *The Taliban*[3]

The news had already hit the wires by the time US President Obama walked up to the podium and announced the death of Osama bin Laden at the hands of a Special Forces team in Abbottabad, Pakistan. The President's announcement came in the middle of the night in Washington—crowds gathered and cheered in the streets outside the White House in Washington D.C.—but it was early morning in Kandahar at that time.

Quite soon, dozens of emails and phone calls started to reach us from journalists with a range of questions as to the possible impact on Afghanistan and the Taliban. Afghan friends came to the office asking if the news was real, if I had heard that bin Laden was dead. 'You must be very happy,' some said. One of the first people to write was my brother who asked, in jest: 'So does that mean it's all over and you can come home?'

We called friends and contacts in Quetta, and others started to look into the reaction from the Afghan Taliban. They would have to make a statement. Such an important event could not pass without comment. Another friend walked by the office to ask about bin Laden and we looked at the headlines that were now coming from the wires. I tried to explain: 'I'm sure it's true. If the President of the United States gets up in front of the world and says something like this happened, it means he has conclusive evidence.'

'Oh, do you want to call up a commander in Helmand?' my friend replied.

A few minutes later I was talking on the phone with what turned out to be one of the senior field commanders in Helmand. He happened to be related to my friend. After introducing myself, I asked what he thought about the death of bin Laden and what it would mean for the Taliban. He hadn't heard anything about it yet, he said, but his reply was neither concerned with whether or not the news was true nor with the exact circumstances of bin Laden's death.

'We are fighting for Mullah Mohammad Omar,' he said. 'He is our amir. We have never fought for Osama bin Laden. His death does not matter to us. We will continue with our struggle.'

Talking to others, similar replies came from individuals close to the Quetta shura and from other parts of the country. Al-Qaeda and bin Laden were of little relevance to Afghanistan, and while many commentators may have a different opinion, in reality they never have been.

Since the mid-1990s, much has been written on the nature of the relationship between 'the Taliban' and 'al-Qaeda.' Journalists were often first on the scene and did much of the groundwork and interviews that would later be used by others. Academics arrived several years later and are only now starting to synthesise and digest this information; indeed, several prominent books were released that dealt specifically with this topic.[4]

The work of deciphering the relationship between highly secretive organisations in the midst of an ongoing war is extremely challenging. Our understanding of the militant groups and their relationship to each other underpins the actions taken by our governments and militaries. Much of the current discourse presented by policy-makers, journalists, researchers and commentators argues that the Afghan Taliban and al-Qaeda have merged, that they are now to be viewed as a single entity, that they represent a broad-based ideological movement, that they have shared histories, have inter-married and pose an equal if not greater threat to international security.

Public opinion offered judgement of its own on the matter: an ABC News/ Washington Post poll conducted in December 2009[5] found that 91% of Americans asked said that they were angry (to differing degrees) about the Taliban's support for bin Laden pre-September 11. Another ABC/Washington Post poll (in October 2009)[6] stated that even if it were found that the Taliban were not supporting international terrorism, 79% of Americans would still rather that the Taliban were kept out of power.

Several articles were published in 2009 and 2010 that attempted to get to the bottom of the relationship, some of which suggested that al-Qaeda and the Taliban had somehow 'fused.'[7] Much of the debate was motivated by speculation that foreign governments in Afghanistan would soon start (or had already started) serious negotiations with the Taliban in order to cut a deal that would allow for a drawdown of the foreign military presence.

That the Taliban was a threat to the West's national security became an easy mantra to repeat: what was initially characterised as a 'strong relationship' was soon a 'nexus' that involved ideological and financial ties, all of which translated into an actual threat to American and European citizens living at home. The West's past and current strategy in Afghanistan is broadly based on these assumptions and they inform the policy choices being made for the coming years.

This book aims to broaden the field of discussion regarding our understanding of the interactions and links between al-Qaeda and the Taliban by looking behind the popular discourse and challenging the assumptions that underpin it.

The organisations or groups we refer to as 'the Taliban' and 'al-Qaeda' have remained ambiguous and illusory to the outside observer. The very nature of their networks makes it difficult to reach definitive conclusions about their interaction, and indeed about the form of entity with which we are dealing. Moreover, much of the vocabulary used to describe these actors draws on popular Western concepts about how parties, groups and social organisations work. In the Afghan case, these are often a poor guide to understanding the nature of these entities or phenomena.

While common acquaintances, group affiliation, historic relationships, phone communications, meetings and at times patent cooperation may imply a transfer of ideas, common goals or a shared strategy, they do not necessarily mean that an individual is indeed part of one or another organisation or subscribes to all of its policies and/or goals in the context of the groups discussed in this book. This is especially true given the multi-layered identities and mergers of political, national and religious ideas in Afghanistan today. Much of what is often presented as hard fact is in reality blurred and amorphous.

Any assessment of the relationship between the Taliban and al-Qaeda, as well as of their affiliates, must trace their roots and evolution over decades rather than focusing on the recent past. Only the context of the groups' histories—and the histories of the individuals associated with them—and their ideological heritage, and the way these informed their sense of identity over time can provide a more nuanced picture. Neither the Taliban nor al-Qaeda are static entities; both, however, have been the focus of a wide-ranging web of interests and narratives.

In light of the ongoing conflict in Afghanistan, a more variegated understanding of the world of militant Islam—and a discussion that does not ignore details but instead dwells on them—can only help to inform policy-making. This international approach has been redrafted and fine-tuned on many occasions, yet the situation has continued to deteriorate.

A snapshot of the relationship between al-Qaeda and the Taliban as of 2011 omits arguably the most important means of understanding the status quo, namely history. Although the two groups encountered each other for the first time only in late 1996, the preceding two and a half decades offer important context and perspectives: where did the two groups draw their ideologies from? How well did the respective members know each other? How cohesive was each organisation?

For the Taliban, the 1970s contain the ideological heritage of Deobandism,[8] and the extent of symbiosis between religion and politics prior to the war precipitated by the Soviet invasion of 1979. The individuals that would come to form al-Qaeda had already embarked on their own separate trajectories, and it is instructive to compare the activities and concerns of the two from this early stage.

As of 2011, it is estimated that there are relatively few al-Qaeda members in Afghanistan—between 50 and 100 as of July 2010, according to the head of the CIA[9]—but the growing conflict and increasing fragmentation of the insurgency gives them greater freedom of movement and access to local insurgent groups. The Taliban, under the leadership of Mullah Mohammad Omar, is the driving force behind an insurgency against the forty-nine nations that have come to Afghanistan. Certain elements among the various heterogeneous groups that make up 'the Taliban' have drawn closer to the commanders and groups that have long-established relationships with Arabs from the anti-Soviet *jihad* of the 1980s, spearheaded by Jalaluddin Haqqani and his network.

The extent to which the Taliban can become part of the Afghan political system without offering refuge to al-Qaeda, its affiliates or other groups posing a threat to international security is a central condition that will determine whether or not they are invited to participate in political negotiations to end the war. Above all, this book seeks to determine whether or not the Afghan Taliban still pose a threat to the international order.

The starting point of this examination of the Taliban-al-Qaeda relationship is the 1970s, well before the groups in question were formed. This was chosen in order to shed light on the educational and socio-economic background of the actors who would later emerge in leading roles. While the names 'Taliban' and 'al-Qaeda' are useful as general organising principles, the networks and individuals associated with the two blocs are more significant as means of understanding the precise interactions between the two, and, more often than not, evade clear categorisation.

In order to examine the relationship between the groups, the authors tracked key individuals and established nodes of interaction between the two groups over time, mapping out the networks thus established to show points of interaction, cooperation or conflict between them. Attitudes and discussions concerning key religious concepts such as *takfir* and *bayat* as well as interpretations of the *Qur'an* were examined. We also looked at those events that are often referenced by analysts as having been precursors of the September 11 attacks, or moments where close cooperation between the two is alleged to have taken place.

The underlying questions that this book seeks to address are whether 'the Taliban' ever merged with 'al-Qaeda,' and whether the Afghan Taliban have ever presented a direct threat to those countries fighting in Afghanistan.

This book distinguishes between the Afghan and Pakistani Taliban; the two have separate histories, key players, geographical focuses and goals. The nature of the relationship between the two will not be explored in any detail, but the authors hold that it is myopic to present them as one and the same. This limitation is worth mentioning in the context of our conclusions: the Pakistani Taliban and their activities within Pakistan (and potential internationalist ambitions) very much need to be kept in mind when considering possible policies for Afghanistan and Pakistan. The scope of this book was intentionally limited to the specific context of the Afghan Taliban and their relationship with al-Qaeda.

This volume makes no claim to be exhaustive but instead outlines the main points of interaction as well as the key sources of information on the relationship, its aim being to broaden and deepen the discussion regarding the relationship of the Afghan Taliban with al-Qaeda in particular, and the relations between the various militant Islamist groups more widely.

Note on Sources

The subject of this book potentially has direct operational and strategic implications; its conclusions are relevant, but the historical detail and context are there to inform the reader, not to offer an intelligence briefing. To this end, all names of interviewees who have cooperated in the research for this book have been removed.

The findings presented here are based on a comprehensive review of English-language literature on the relationship that have been published to date, but the authors also sought to bring new sources to light and to include them in the discussion. In particular, first-hand, primary-source accounts of the relationship tend to be written by Arabs or affiliates of al-Qaeda.[10] Much less is available from the Taliban's perspective.[11] This disparity of resources has worked to the detriment of our understanding of the motivations among the Taliban's leadership.

Former and current Taliban affiliates have only recently started to record their own testimonies on the events that took place during their lifetimes in a systematic fashion. Other sources, such as newspapers and magazines published during the late 1990s,[12] offer more granular detail and commentary from Taliban leaders in their own words as events were happening. They present an opportunity to gather anecdotal or incidental material for context to events and trends about which we currently know very little.

It has become increasingly difficult to conduct fieldwork given the deteriorating security situation across Afghanistan—particularly in the south—and the fragmentation of the insurgency, but certain channels to current and former members of the Taliban remain open, thus allowing questions to be asked about their current relationship with al-Qaeda.

Reviewing these resources allowed us to gain insights into who the Taliban were and are, why they have acted in the ways they have in relation to bin Laden and al-Qaeda. The issue of motivation is especially important to an assessment of who the Taliban are at the moment, and what they stand for. Motivation and goals—both stated and actual—are key areas of interest when assessing the strength of the relationship.

The baseline for this book was a survey of the existing literature; this included books, reports, newspaper and magazine articles as well as official documents that have since been declassified from Western sources. The reports produced by Western monitoring centres[13] from the 1970s onwards were reviewed. This material was supplemented by original source material such as newspapers, magazines and documents published between 1994–2001, online and post-2001. Six books from Arabic and Pashtu were translated in full for this project:[14]

- Abu al-Walid al-Masri—*The Cross in the Sky of Kandahar* (published online, 2007)—313 pp. from the Arabic
- Mohammad Salah—*Narratives of the Jihad Years: the Journey of the Afghan Arabs* (published in Cairo, 2001)—220 pp. from the Arabic
- Ayman Sabri Faraj—*Memoirs of an Afghan Arab* (published in Cairo, 2002)—306 pp. from the Arabic
- Abdullah Anas—*Birth of the Afghan Arabs* (published in London, 2002)—152 pp. from the Arabic
- Mohammad Taher Aziz Gumnam—*Kandahar Assassins* (published in Kandahar, 1986) from the Pashtu
- Mohammad Taher Aziz Gumnam—*Kandahar Heroes* (published in Kandahar, 1996) from the Pashtu

Interviews were conducted with those present during the relevant periods or incidents—these were predominantly Afghan sources, some of whom were/are affiliated with the Taliban—and this eyewitness testimony was supplemented by interviews with scholars, researchers and journalists in Afghanistan as well as in the United States, France, the United Arab Emirates, Germany and the United Kingdom. Interviewees include a number of 'Afghan Arabs' who had close links to al-Qaeda during the 1980s and 1990s. They are all based outside Afghanistan now.

What follows is also based on the study of a number of key actors, interlocutors and facilitators, focused around locations, groups and organisations. The core group of individuals we traced amounted to thirty Afghans and seventy non-Afghans, while the wider networks include 276 individuals and forty-seven groups.

There are numerous obstacles in doing so, in particular the use of *noms de guerre* by foreign mujahedeen who joined the Afghan *jihad*, and the subsequent extensive use of pseudonyms by militants makes it difficult to follow the less well-known individuals. This is particularly relevant for recent developments within the insurgency that has witnessed a great influx of a younger generation who are relatively unknown and who frequently change their names/pseudonyms.

* * *

We begin by examining the ideological and socio-economic backgrounds of the different actors who make up 'the Taliban' and 'al-Qaeda.' Chapter two traces their education as well as the context and history of the time prior to their coming together as groups. The 1980s *jihad* is then taken as the backdrop for the arrival and mobilisation of both groups in chapter three: specifically, where were they located, what were their goals and to what extent can we talk of a merger between the Taliban and non-Afghan fighters during this period? Chapter four looks at what happened after Soviet troops withdrew; the security vacuum and fractures within the mujahedeen government that attempted to rule resulted in a chaotic situation in many parts of the country, one which directly contributed to the formation of 'the Taliban' as a movement in Kandahar in 1994. The period of Taliban formation and rule is the focus of chapters five and six; this is a time when many of the original attitudes towards the Taliban and claims of the relationship with al-Qaeda were formed, and we assess the major incidents and manifestations of this relationship in turn. In many ways, the September 11 attacks are at the core of why the discussion of the Taliban-al-Qaeda relationship is important; the Taliban are sometimes claimed to have had foreknowledge of the attacks, and other events that took place during the late 1990s are also held to form part of the Taliban's record of 'supporting terrorism.' Chapter seven examines all of these arguments in turn. Chapters eight and nine assesses the post-2001 environment up until 2009 and the new paradigm that saw the two groups grouped together; an assessment of the Taliban's goals (as compared to those of al-Qaeda) is included in this section. The most recent evidence and dynamics relating to the relationship are examined in chapter ten, which covers 2010 and the post-surge realities. The conclusion, chapter eleven, broadens the discussion and considers what it means for the possibilities of a political settlement in Afghanistan.

2

FOREBEARS (1970–1979)

'Every Afghan is a Deobandi.'

Rahmatullah Hashimi, Taliban Ambassador, 2001[1]

'On Friday evenings, Abu Suhail would hold classes on the theology and ideology of Sayyid Qutb, the Egyptian theologian [and] would read to us from his work, particularly *In the Shade of the Kur'an* and *Milestones*. [...] He had a profound respect for the teachings of Islam, but was able to write about it in a way that seemed modern and real. He wrote about the world I lived in, not the world of centuries past.'

Omar Nasiri, *Inside the Global Jihad*[2]

On 10 March 1963, Prime Minister Mohammad Da'ud Khan resigned and King Zahir Shah took the lead in ruling Afghanistan.[3] Da'ud had been close to the Soviet Union and had undertaken the first steps in modernising Afghanistan, inaugurating vast development projects mostly carried out with the support of foreign countries. He had been unpopular with conservative Afghans, and religious leaders and their followers hoped that the country would return to 'Islamic principles' with Zahir Shah in power. In 1959, Da'ud, along with several members of the royal family and the Deputy Prime Minister, had appeared in public with his wife and daughter unveiled. Even though no official announcement was made, the tradition of *purda*, the customary veil

11

worn by women, was metamorphosing in Kabul and in other major cities.[4] The young legal advisors of Da'ud, who had been trained at Cairo's al-Azhar[5] seminary and continued their education at universities in Switzerland, France and the United States, had concluded that the practice of *purda* could not be justified under Islamic law.[6] This public display, while welcomed by the Westernised urban middle class, was understood by rural conservatives as a direct attack on their traditional customs and religious values. A delegation of religious clergymen accused Da'ud of being against Islam and of promoting Western values. Several members of the delegation were illiterate mullahs from the countryside.[7]

As Olivier Roy has explained, the village mullahs were traditionalists for the most part.[8] The arguments put forward by Da'ud and his legal advisers drew on their foreign education and the rural clergy regarded them as atheists and Western sympathisers.[9]

Zahir Shah continued with Da'ud's reforms and disappointed much of the religious leadership.[10] The passing of a new constitution in 1964, for example, allowed a host of new media outlets to start operating.[11] This, in turn, saw an opening up of the media space, with fewer restrictions on what those outlets were allowed to broadcast or print. While the impact on rural communities of such policies was marginal, they found considerable resonance among those in the cities, and particularly in Kabul.

By the beginning of the 1970s, the relative calm present until then throughout Afghanistan had begun fraying at the edges. Both communism (and Islamism as its counter-reaction) were active political forces in Kabul and among educated urban elites. Foreign governments were increasingly engaging in domestic Afghan affairs, though Soviet influence was disproportionate; in 1970, 7,000 Afghan army officers were being trained in the Soviet Union and Czechoslovakia while only 600 were trained in the United States.[12] Financially, Afghanistan was a recipient of massive Soviet economic aid, totalling $1.265 billion by 1979.[13]

Both ideologies were subject to considerable variety and extreme positions; for some, communism was merely a vehicle to reach power while others were true followers. Among the Islamists, some advocated peaceful non-violent opposition while others took action, like Gulbuddin Hekmatyar who served time in prison for the murder of a Maoist supporter.[14]

The Islamists in Kabul had formed around new ideas brought from abroad: Afghan religious scholars educated in Egypt at the famous al-Azhar seminary now returned home to find their country to be weak and backward, with much of its political elite adopting communism. These religious clerics set up groups that would form an opposition to the communists[15]—the most famous at the time was that of Mawlana Mohammad Ata'ullah Faizani. It was, however, the group that coalesced around Ghulam Mohammad Niazi whose members would rise to prominence and shape Afghanistan's future. The early 'Muslim Youth Organisation' (*Sazmaan-i Jawanaan-i Musulmanaan*) borrowed its structure from the Muslim Brotherhood (*Ikhwaan al-Muslimeen*) in Egypt. Niazi himself had spent time in Egypt in the early 1950s, a time when the Muslim Brotherhood constituted the largest organisation in the country and was intrinsically involved with the government—and increasingly clashing with it by the mid-1950s.[16]

In 1969 or early 1970 Niazi began to form small groups of activists: he brought together men like Ahmed Shah Massoud, Hekmatyar, Sayyaf and Burhanuddin Rabbani, all of whom would later play significant roles in Afghan politics.[17]

This political debate in Kabul—one that often resulted in open hostilities at the university—was slow to reach southern Afghanistan except in a few specific instances. The spread of news about events in the capital would naturally have relied mostly on face-to-face conversation, an information flow prone to create rumours. There were only two publications in Kandahar (listed for the Islamic year corresponding to 1971–2): the daily *Tolo-ye Afghan* with a print run of 952, and a government paper that was distributed to government employees (including teachers) with an outreach into the districts of 323 copies.[18] Considering the extremely high rates of illiteracy in rural areas, print media had little reach. Broadcast news programmes were followed only by the wealthier sections of society who could afford a radio, while teashop radios were generally tuned to music shows. Wiebe, in his study of southern Afghanistan and Kandahar City during the 1970s, points out that local government was dominated by traditional structures, with many trusting more in their local landowners and leading families than in government representatives.[19] He also notes that village mullahs in Kandahar had very little contact with the actual substantive ideas of communism, an observation confirmed by interviews with Kandaharis today; many mobilised against the communists only in the light of their plans for substantive land reform.[20]

In July 1973, Da'ud seized power in a coup to replace what he claimed was ineffective leadership. In the 1950s, when he was Prime Minister, Da'ud had initially played American donors off against their Soviet counterparts; in this way, the American-funded Helmand Valley Project, a massive undertaking aimed at providing irrigation and electricity, was launched[21] in southern Afghanistan, as were similar but smaller[22] industrial and agricultural projects run by the Soviets in Nangarhar province.[23] Once firmly back in control, Da'ud pushed forward with his reforms, aiming to implement far-reaching social and economic changes, but to little effect.[24] He had come to power backed by the Parcham faction of the People's Democratic Party of Afghanistan[25] (PDPA) and regarded the Islamist movement as his enemy.[26] Local government offices in the districts advised that traditional representative systems were an obstacle to the implementation of the new edicts.[27]

Accordingly, and as people across Afghanistan still remember to this day, the 'Mullahs, Khans and Maliks' started to disappear, being imprisoned or killed.[28] This caused great consternation and resentment among the elites who immediately started to mobilise against the government.

While Da'ud continued with his reforms in Afghanistan, General Zia ul-Haq, with the help of the military, deposed the Pakistani government in 1977. Under his leadership, Pakistan would undergo a process of deepening Islamisation that lasted until his death in August 1988.[29] This was a boon for the anti-communist resistance movements in Afghanistan, the elites of which were received with open arms by Pakistan and which would receive funding and support from the United States and Saudi Arabia. The retreat of Afghanistan's opposition forces to Pakistan's tribal regions was often the norm whenever violent political change overtook Afghanistan.[30]

* * *

For the Arab world, the death of Gamal Abd al-Nasser in September 1970 signalled a watershed. Nasser had presided over the grand political experiment of Pan-Arab nationalism, uniting Egypt and Syria in the United Arab Republic and personifying an attempt to forge a greater sense of Arab identity. This intellectual project had been a feature of debate in the Arab world since the 1920s, but gained momentum after the defeat of Arab states by Israel in the 1948–49 war. For commentators like Sa'ti al-Husri, 'the Arabs lost the war precisely because they were seven states,' pointing towards the division of the Arab world.[31]

The defeat of the Arab states in the 'Six Day War' in 1967, which ended with the occupation of the Sinai Peninsula, Gaza, the West Bank and the Golan Heights by Israel, left a deep impression on many Arabs and Muslims. Fuelled by the writings of Sayyed Qutb that lamented the state of *jahiliyya* or 'ignorance' that had befallen the Arab lands, Islamists were on the rise. The humiliating defeat of 1967 was followed again, in 1973, by a rerun in the 'October War'; for many Arab Muslims this was not only a clear demonstration of the weakness and failure of their governments, but signalled that Westernisation and foreign ideologies were responsible for their backwardness and that only an Islamic state and a society that would return to the values and norms that guided the Prophet's *umma* could rise once again: *Al-Islam huwwa al-Hal* ('Islam is the solution').[32]

In the words of one prominent Egyptian Islamist:

The unfolding of events impacted the course of the jihadi movements in Egypt, namely, the 1967 defeat and the ensuing symbolic collapse of Gamal Abdel Nasser, who was portrayed to the public by his followers as the everlasting invincible symbol. The jihadi movements realised that woodworms had eaten at this icon, and that it had become fragile. The 1967 defeat shook the earth under this idol until it fell on its face, causing a severe shock to its disciples, and frightening its subjects. The jihadi movements grew stronger and stronger as they realised that their avowed enemy was little more than a statue to be worshiped, constructed through propaganda, and through the oppression of unarmed innocents. The direct influence of the 1967 defeat was that a large number of people, especially youths, returned to their original identity: that of members of an Islamic civilisation.[33]

Indeed, the re-emergence of Islamist groups was one of the most prominent trends of the 1970s, particularly for Egypt, Syria and Lebanon. In each case, the drive towards Islamisation was prompted by local political circumstances—the political and economic failures of the various ideological experiments—more than by the advocacy of careerist Islamists or recruitment drives by Islamist organisations.

In 1973, and in reaction to the United States' support for Israel, the Organization of Arab Petroleum Exporting Countries (OAPEC) declared an embargo. The resulting oil crisis had a significant impact on the United States' economy and fuelled discussions about energy security. It also massively increased revenue for the oil-producing countries, who found themselves awash with hard currency. The price of oil had risen by approximately 70% per barrel.[34]

New conditions pushed the old dreams aside. The oil boom had started to deliver unprecedented returns to the elites of certain countries—many of whom embarked on orgies of spending—and this was held up against the dire status of development and political freedoms around the region.[35]

The Taliban's Ideological Forebears

Religion and Politics in Afghan History

The groups of religious clerics that were to aggregate together in Kandahar during the 1980s to form *mujahedeen* fronts against the Soviet Union were not a new phenomenon. Afghanistan and Pakistan—and when discussing the intersection of religion with politics we must take both into account—have a long history of rallying religious students and their teachers in the service of various causes.

The Afghans who fought the two Anglo-Afghan Wars of the nineteenth century were mobilised on a religious basis. Abdur Rahman—the so-called 'Iron Amir'—ruled Afghanistan up to the turn of the century and had instituted measures to strengthen the state. He identified the legal system as the primary element requiring reform—which is to say, against the influence of the tribes who resisted the state—and to do that he needed to reform the education provided by the state.[36] Abdur Rahman sought to co-opt the clergy as part of his new government system as they had traditionally been involved in education and in previous instances of popular mobilisation.

The reign of Habibullah bore the fruit of Abdur Rahman's efforts. Internally the country was at peace, but outside influences would end the fragile balance. Habibullah invited Mahmud Beg Tarzi and his family back to Afghanistan. Tarzi, a Western orientated nationalist, gave new impetus and focus to the 'nationalist constitutional anti-colonial movement' within Habibullah's government.[37] There were also increased Deobandi[38] stirrings in the eastern provinces: the Akhund of Swat, Hadda-i Sahib and the 'Indian Wahhabism' of Shah Waliullah and Sayyed Ahmad Bareilly.

King Amanullah, who reigned from 1919 and who tried to assert Afghanistan's sovereign independence, declared a *jihad* against Britain, the colonial power, in order to cement his hold over the various tribes and clergymen; he promised full independence. His success greatly enhanced his status, in particular among the religious clergy that had originally favoured his brother Nasrullah as king. Nevertheless, Amanullah followed Habibullah and tried to introduce an ambitious reform programme—styled on and inspired by Atatürk's reforms in Turkey—throughout the country.[39] This was broadly secular in nature, and while some of the changes were sorely needed, Amanullah lacked the military clout to enforce his programme, since he no longer had British funding; Afghanistan had previously received this funding but it was cut off following the declarations of *jihad*. In the mid-1920s fatwas were issued by clerics across the country (although particularly in the east and south-east) and the religious clergy revolted. Communities in the eastern provinces received tribal support from what later became Pakistan.[40] The religious uprising was not a homogenous affair, and Amanullah's policy of patronage towards certain *pirs* and clerical families in Afghanistan and Pakistan paid off. Despite the government's eventual victory, the religious clergy had proved that they still held sway over the population.[41]

The 1930s saw an attempt to increase government control of the religious clergy. The *Jami'at al-Ulemaa'* ('The Society of Religious Clergy') was created in 1931 and this provided a formal structure through which the state could begin to rein in the clergy. Nevertheless, religious leadership remained an independent power that Nadir Shah, who ruled Afghanistan from 1929 until 1933, had to honour. The appointment of Fazl Omar Mujaddidi, from one of Afghanistan's prestigious religious families, as Minister of Justice was thus a concession to that fact.[42]

During the 1930s and 1940s the government of Nadir Shah and his son, Zahir Shah, opened madrassas in every province in an attempt to extend its control over religious education. In 1938–9, the Qadiriyya Sufi *pir* Mohammad Sadi al-Keilani was encouraged to mobilise the religious clergy in order to restore Amanullah to the throne.[43] He even secured the cooperation of the Faqir of Ipi, another Qadiriyya *pir* based in Waziristan who was waging his own campaign against the British. Al-Keilani was bought off by the British at the last moment and returned to his home in Damascus, bringing the campaign against Zahir Shah to a halt.

In 1952, a *Shari'a* faculty was established at Kabul University in cooperation with Cairo's Al-Azhar University. This was an important first step in the rise of an educated Islamist elite among Afghan clerics.[44]

The 1940s and 1950s saw a shift away from the use of religious discourse as a means for popular mobilisation. The Safi Rebellion (1945–6), the Mangal unrest (1959) and riots in Kandahar over the enforcement of taxes for landowners (also 1959) all failed to receive religious support from the prominent clerics. As Olesen notes:

> The popular religious discourse, which throughout the period 1880–1930 had been dominated by the concept of jihad, had changed after the pan-Islamic fervour had died out and the legitimacy of the ruler was unchallenged. [...] This change in religious discourse may possibly also be ascribed to a generally higher level of scriptural learning among the religious personnel as a result of the massive build-up of new government

17

madrasas. It was accompanied by a gradual replacement of the *pir*, whose position depended upon the veneration of his followers, by the *alim*, who owed his education and employment to the government.[45]

A new constitution was approved in 1964 and clashes over the progressive political stances being espoused in parliament dominated the 1960s. Attempts to emancipate women[46] were met with strong resistance from the clergy. One well-known clash between the progressives and conservatives occurred when religious vocabulary was employed in a poetic ode to Lenin.[47] Clashes of this kind became increasingly violent as members of both sides were killed (including one member of the religious clergy in 1972).[48]

Indeed, the 1970s were a key period in the establishment and fracturing of the religious opposition and political parties.[49] The debates had relatively little impact and were not as fiercely contested in southern Afghanistan as they were in Kabul. Some clerics were working together with the government, who tried to encourage others to join up, but these matters were by no means as fiercely disputed as in the capital.

The ideological debates of the capital were far from the concerns of the village *mullah*s and *mawlawi*s, and it was only the arrest and disappearance of many fellow clerics and the edicts attempting to implement land reform and changes to the educational status quo that led to the issuing of fatwas and calls for resistance against the government in 1978 and 1979. The crucial element in the mobilisation of the public of the south and its religious clergy was the arrival of Soviet troops in 1979–1980. Prior to that point there had been relatively little popular local takeup of resistance in southern Afghanistan.

The underlying dynamic of politics and power in Afghanistan, particularly in the south and the east of the country, has been characterised by a rural-urban dichotomy. Cities are drivers of development and change; in southern and eastern Afghanistan they were increasingly a place where the traditional tribal leadership, who sought better education for their children and a better lifestyle, congregated. During the 1970s and 1980s, this traditional leadership was killed, dispersed, or fled the country, and in the course of the *jihad* they were replaced by commanders and strongmen who did not represent the same governing structures as the traditional leadership did.[50] This further deepened the dichotomy, severing longstanding social links between the city and tribal communities in the countryside.[51]

The rural-urban relationship—and with it that of the population to the central state—shaped Afghanistan's history: kings had tried to modernise the country from the capital but all too often met stark resistance from the rural communities where religious leaders, *mullahs* and *mawlawis*, played a more important role than in the city. Here the real rulers were the tribal elite and landowners, not the religious clergy.

Islam and Deobandism

Islam is not a monolithic entity, and while approximately 80% of the population in Afghanistan are Sunni, the Sunni branch encompasses a wide range of different interpretations—from reformists, foreign-educated progressives, Salafists, Deobandis, Talibs, conservative judicial scholars and so on.[52] All of these can be pro-government or anti-government (or sometimes both), and pro-West or anti-West. There is no uniformity of opinion.

For southern Afghanistan, the influence of Deobandi religious teachings was omnipresent. This initially came directly from the Deoband seminary in northern India, but it was then transmitted by teachers and scholars in Pakistan and Afghanistan who had been instructed in the same way. First established in 1867, the small religious seminary at Deoband was to become one of the most influential institutions in South Asia. The religious clergy of India, Pakistan and Afghanistan would draw a rich intellectual heritage from it over the years; the 'Taliban' movement that emerged in the 1990s was also partly formed in the Deobandi image.[53]

When it was originally founded, the school at Deoband was a reaction to Hindu proselytising in the surrounding area. A revivalist trend—given impetus by Shah Waliullah[54]—sought to teach a literal and scripturalist interpretation of Islam in a school that modelled itself on the British educational system. This was so unique at the time that the school's institutional report made continual efforts to explain these innovations to parents.[55] The administrators of the school also attempted to remain independent of government influence, taking donations and endowments from private pockets but refusing to be co-opted. Metcalf quotes from one of a list of principles intended to serve as a guide for students:

First, the workers of the madrasa should, as best they can, keep in view the increase of donations; and should encourage others to share this same concern [...] The well-wishers of the madrasa should always make efforts to secure the provision of food for the students, indeed, they should try to increase the food. As long as the madrasa has no fixed sources of income, it will, God willing, operate as desired. And if it gain any fixed income, like *jagir* holdings, factories, trading interests or pledges from nobles, then the madrasa will lose the fear and hope which inspire submission to God and will lose His

19

hidden help. Disputes will begin among the workers. In matters of income and build-ings […] let there be a sort of deprivation. The participation of government and wealthy is harmful. The contributions of those who expect no fame from their gifts is a source of blessing. The honesty of such contributors is a source of stability.[56]

Many of the students at the school were also affiliated with Sufi orders, again a common tie (as above) with the Afghan descendants and inheritors of this system of schooling. The so-called 'mystical' side of Islam, Sufism focuses on the vertical relationship between the believer and God, seeking to personalise and individualise that connection through prayer, training and discipline.[57]

This basic principle is extremely common among rural Muslims in Afghan-istan, and its importance is attested to by the prevalence of *ziarat*s or shrines built over the graves of alleged 'holy men and women.' In the absence of non-traditional medicine or doctors, many villagers place their faith in a culture of miracles and signs instead.[58]

The school made a name for itself not in administrative changes, though, but through the quality and slant of its teaching:

In this one place, the school claimed, students would be trained in the specialties of the three great intellectual centers of North India: *manqulat*, the revealed studies of hadith or tradition and Qur'an associated with Delhi; and *ma'qulat*, the rational stud-ies of *fiqh* or law, logic and philosophy associated with the two Eastern cities of Luc-know and Khairabad. Basically, the school taught the *dars-i nizami*, the curriculum evolved at Farangi Mahall in the eighteenth century that spread throughout India. They made, however, important modifications, particularly in their emphasis on the two subjects of hadith and *fiqh*. […] They deemed hadith, the basis of correct practice and belief, the crowning subject. The most influential teacher was the *shaikh ul-had-ith* at the school; and only good students were encouraged to study the subject. More-over, the school de-emphasized the so-called rational sciences, logic and philosophy, that had been the chief distinction of the Nizami teaching.[59]

As becomes clear when looking at the precise nature of the educational syl-labus used by the Afghan religious students, the thrust of the education offered was not outward but inward. They sought to teach an interior, purified Islam that was self-moderating and self-generating:

Pursuit of these aims required reexamination and restatement of the proper sources of the law—the texts—and recovery of the proper modes of reasoning about them, enter-prises in which the Deobandis engaged in common with numerous other 'reformist'-tending groups of the time, and which led them, as others, to explore anew the limits of independent judgment and of acceptance of past exegetical authority, and to embody the results of this exploration in fatawa (legal opinions) and argument.[60]

There was relatively little desire for political involvement among the early pro-ponents and teachers at the Deobandi school—they didn't even speak out against the British, for the most part—and it was only in the final years of colonial rule (1947, to be precise) that a minority group detached itself from the Deobandis to set up the *Jami'at-i Ulema-ye Islam* to support the Muslim League and its demands for a separate Muslim state.[61] This was the starting position of a trend that would see a political and economic empowerment of many Deobandi-educated clerics in the twentieth century. Metcalf even goes so far as to deny a political stance for Deobandism: 'none of the Deobandi movements has a theo-retical stance in relation to political life. They either expediently embrace the polit-ical culture of their time and place, or withdraw from politics completely.'[62]

Deobandism lies at the root of the Taliban's religious identity. It is, in itself, relatively apolitical as a philosophy but external circumstances—particularly the 1980s anti-Soviet war—contributed to a shift in how it became instrumen-talised as an educational system.

Education

The school in Deoband attracted students from Pakistan and Afghanistan as well as India, but it was the export of the school's methods and scholastic focus to smaller madrassas in Afghanistan and Pakistan that would influence the Afghan religious students the most. The madrassas created by the Afghan gov-ernment in the 1930s and 1940s were sponsored and linked to the school at Deoband—this was intended to (and did) encourage enrolment—although relatively few Afghan students attended these institutions compared to those based in Afghanistan and Pakistan.[63]

Accurate and complete figures are hard to come by, but anecdotal evidence suggests that there was insufficient provision for the many would-be religious students from eastern, southern and south-eastern Afghanistan. It was normal for rural landowning families to send at least one of their children for religious education ('one is for the state and one is for God')[64] and many of these went to Pakistan.

Interviews with current and former Taliban members attest to the universal attendance of some kind of religious education.[65] A distinction is sometimes made between 'educated' or 'modern' and 'non-educated' Taliban who attended a better class of madrassa than others, but the difference seems marginal.

The main madrassas in Kandahar at the time were the Mohammadiyya and Ashrafiyya, but interviewees also stated these could not cater for all of the stu-dents and that the quality of tuition in Pakistan was always better.[66] In Uruzgan students could attend the Wano Pul madrassa (with Mullah Mohammad Shafiq as the head).

Matinuddin quotes Nangarhar's Hajji Qadir that 'there were around 2500 spiritual teachers and leaders enjoying a vital leadership role in the village and tribal society of Afghanistan before the failed attempt to introduce communist ideology in Afghanistan,' but Pakistan also had a large number of educated religious teachers.[67] This was even more true following Zia ul-Haq's military coup in July 1977, as he increased funding for a network of madrassas in Baluchistan and the North-Western Frontier Province (NWFP). Dorronsoro illustrates this trend:

From the 1960s both the number of *madrasas* in Pakistan and the number of students (*taliban*) had expanded dramatically. Between 1960 and 1983 the number of *taliban* increased tenfold, from 7,500 to 78,500, and of teachers from 321 to 2,217. There was no slackening in this increase, which was much more rapid than that of the population. In 1988 there were 1,320 *madrasas* in Punjab, but by 1997 there were 2,512 with 220,000 students. In Karachi there were twenty-nine *madrasas* which educated an average of 2,000 students each year.[68]

One important reason for the upsurge in enrolment in these religious schools (and the resultant Islamisation of society) was Zia ul-Haq's passing of a new law ensuring that religious students' graduation certificates would be accepted by secular colleges.[69]

These madrassas were not exclusively Deobandi—there were simultaneously Barelvi, *Ahl-e Hadith* and Shi'i tendencies in Pakistan—but Afghans tended to study at these Deobandi institutions because of their shared Hanafism.[70] The syllabus varied from school to school, but the broad lessons from their Indian parent-madrassa were followed.

Matinuddin outlines their basic course structure as follows:

The syllabi of these schools included the learning of the Holy Koran by heart; *tajweed* (correct pronunciation of the Koranic verses); *tafseer* (interpretation of the Holy scriptures); *fiqah* (Islamic jurisprudence); *shariah* (Islamic Laws); *ahadis* (life and decisions of the Holy Prophet [Peace Be Upon Him] on various issues brought before him by the faithful); *mantiq* (philosophy); *riazi* (mathematics) and *falakiat* (astronomy); *tabligh* (spreading the word of God) and a smattering of modern subjects. Shahabuddin claims that the subjects ranged from the *Baghdadi Quaida* to *Bokhari Sharif*.[71]

(Interviews in 2009 and 2010 of the nature of religious education during this time in southern Afghanistan confirmed the above list.)[72]

Many of the smaller madrassas in southern Afghanistan and in Pakistan would not have offered such a wide and comprehensive education. By all accounts, the standard of tuition was uneven and of a generally poor quality, often just amounting to a place for religious students to stay and attempt to learn the Arabic text of the *Qur'an* by rote (most times without understanding its meaning).

One Taliban member[73] recalled the education of most of the movement as follows:

Their education and thinking was very simple. They studied Islamic subjects like Hanafi *fiqh, tafseer, sarf* and *hadith*. They were thinking only about learning and then afterwards maybe teaching: to become a Mullah in a mosque. No more. In addition to this, these were not political people. They didn't know about politics and didn't care about politics. They even didn't listen to the news on the radio or tv. Their thinking was very simple in this respect.

Those who would later rise to leadership positions in the Taliban's government during the 1990s seem all to have received at least part of their education in Pakistan. The *Dar ul-Uloom Haqqaniya* madrassa seems to play an especially large role in this respect. Sources[74] state that the following senior Talibs were educated there:

- Mullah Mohammad Omar
- Mullah Mutawakil
- Jalaluddin Haqqani (for six years)[75]
- Amir Khan Muttaqi
- Mullah Khairullah Khairkhwa
- Arefullah Aref
- Mohammad Abbas
- Abdul Latif Mansour
- Mawlawi Qalamuddin
- Mawlawi Abdul Kabir
- Mawlawi Ahmad Jan
- Mullah Mohammad Hassan[76]

Attendance at the Haqqaniya madrassa is difficult to verify and sources are reluctant to provide corroboration as they stress the local, Afghan and nationalist inclinations of the Taliban movement. One source lists the names of 'at least 371 Afghan students [attending the Haqqaniya madrassa] between 1945–89.'[77]

The issue of whether Mullah Mohammad Omar attended this madrassa seems to be particularly sensitive. Interviewees for this book delivered a range of responses as to where the Taliban leader had received his education. The literature that addresses the subject seems to have devolved into a game of Chinese whispers: he appears to have been awarded an honorary degree[78] post-2001 by the Haqqaniya madrassa and its head, Sami ul-Haq, which many have simply taken to mean that Mullah Mohammad Omar himself studied there. It is by no means clear that he ever did study at that institution, or even in Pakistan at all.

* * *

It was not until the 1980s that *jihad* rose to become a prominent feature of the madrassa syllabi in Afghanistan and Pakistan, and instruction up to that point had kept the term relatively theoretical. Of course, there were numerous cases when *jihad* was declared and villagers had been mobilised; these instances had a cultural resonance in songs, poetry and oral history. But it was, even by the 1970s, a distant memory. It would take ten years of mobilisation during the 1980s (and the use of madrassas to stir students up for *jihad*) for this to become a much more potent force.

Across the border, there had been debates as to the role of *jihad* within the new Muslim state of Pakistan. Sayyed Abu al-A'ala Mawdudi, the founder of the *Jama'at al-Islami*, had issued a tract on the topic in 1927 which outlined his key innovation: justice as the core of a revolutionary movement to overthrow corrupt and oppressive governments.[79] But there was no active planning or scheming in Pakistan around the idea of Islam to bring about an 'Islamic revolution' or anything else at the time.

Zia ul-Haq's July 1977 coup ushered in a period of Islamisation of Pakistani society. His preferred allies were the *Jama'at al-Islami*, although since they too lacked any mass support Zia also included other sectarian and religious organisations.[80] He stated in his first televised speech that 'Pakistan, which was created in the name of Islam, will continue to survive only if it sticks to Islam. That is why I consider the introduction of [an] Islamic system as an essential prerequisite for the country.'[81] For religious education and the Taliban, this meant greater access to and the spread of madrassas in the tribal areas of Pakistan. The expansion by Pakistan also made external support come in faster, and Saudi funding for the provision of religious education increased during this period.[82]

For the early 1970s, though, the distinction between religion and politics still seemed to apply. As one Talib educated during that time remarked:

During the Zahir Khan and Da'ud Khan times religion was separate from politics. The government couldn't interfere in religious issues and the religious people like Mullahs couldn't interfere in the government.[83]

The religious students' attitude to religious authority was mostly one of respect. They held the knowledgeable and well-educated in great esteem and the Deobandi tradition was fundamentally conservative. This wasn't an education that taught students to find radical alternative solutions or ideas about religion and/or society. For the Deobandi madrassas in the tribal regions in Pakistan and Afghanistan, this was a scripture-centred and largely literalist reading of Islam that allowed very little freedom of interpretation.[84]

Another factor influenced the idea of religious authority. The Deobandi tradition—and Afghan society in general—included provision for the practice of *tasawwuf* or Sufism. The relationship between a Sufi elder (*pir*) and his follower (*murid*) is a key element that influences how someone will progress in his studies and Sufi practice. Many Afghan religious students—particularly those in the south—were affiliated with Sufi brotherhoods and/or had *pirs* whom they followed. This was another aspect of the conservative nature of the Taliban. The *pir-murid* relationship is lasting: teacher and follower form a bond.

The Taliban who passed through the madrassas during the 1980s (and, to some extent, rural Afghans in general) were imbued with a respect for those with religious knowledge; these religious students' often rudimentary understanding, however, and narrow curriculum meant that they were less able or willing to distinguish as to the usefulness of specific messages or directions that this religious knowledge suggested. The Taliban, along with the general public, regarded individuals from Saudi Arabia and the wider Arab world as somehow 'closer' to Islam due to their knowledge of the language of the *Qu'ran*, which gave visitors considerable respect and authority. This should be kept in mind when assessing the relationship between the Taliban and the Arab foreign fighters during the 1990s.

Aside from the isolated instances when religious students were mobilised around certain issues, relatively little group solidarity was manifested, either across southern Afghanistan or countrywide, that resulted from the education system or in any other organisational form.[85] The government's *Jami'at al-Ulemaa'* was supposed to fulfil this function and work as a bridge among the different religious students and clerics in the country, but this did not happen. Afghanistan was—and is—a place where local concerns almost always won out over those relating to the nation. The students at different madrassas in Kandahar (and, to some extent, Pakistan) knew of each other, and sometimes a well-known teacher would attain a certain prominence, but by and large these students were isolated. Some small gatherings, though, were part of the every-day life of a religious student or scholar in the Afghanistan and Pakistan of the 1970s (as today): turban-tying or *dastarbandi* ceremonies were occasions when students would meet, as were *Qur'anic* readings and meetings on Thursday evenings. These were times when students would gather, but these were not meetings for a political purpose.[86]

There were examples of Afghans coming together in the form of a very close-knit group dynamic: Hekmatyar's *Hizb-e Islami*—built around the structure of a political party with Islamism at the core—was one such organisation that was founded in 1975 in a break from a parent Muslim Brotherhood-style group.[87]

With hindsight, those individuals drawn towards the Taliban seem to have something akin to raw potential or the possibility to be shaped in the way they were educated. During the 1970s, though, they were not yet instrumentalised and thus their education had proceeded in a relatively isolated and limited way. Their hopes and goals were similarly limited: they had a specific role to play in society and there was little desire to induce social change.

Al-Qaeda's Ideological Forebears

Intellectual Heritage

Just as the Taliban come from a specific ideological, cultural and educational background, the Arabs who would later coalesce together under the banner of al-Qaeda were shaped and formed in an environment quite unlike the rural hinterland of Afghanistan and Pakistan.

Even discounting the different places in which they had grown up, those who would later be affiliated with al-Qaeda were essentially of a different generation from those who would form the Taliban. A comparison of the ages of key figures from both groups in 1970 illustrates this starkly:

Figure 1: Ages of al-Qaeda and Taliban Affiliates in 1970[88]

Taliban	Approx age	Al-Qaeda/Affiliates	Approx age
Mullah Mohammad Rabbani	15	Abu Hafs al-Masri	26
Mullah Obaidullah	9	Abu al-Walid al-Masri	25

Mullah Mohammad Omar	8	Ayman al-Zawahiri	19
Mullah Dadullah	3	Abu Mus'ab al-Suri	12
Mullah Fazl	3	Osama bin Laden	12
Mullah Abdul Razaq	2	Abu Qatada	10
Amir Khan Muttaqi	2	Khalid Sheikh Mohammad	6
Mullah Zaeef	2	Abu Mus'ab al-Zarqawi	4
Mullah Berader	2		

The Arabs were starting or in the middle of their education, while the Talibs were barely able to speak at this time. This is an important point to remember when evaluating their government post-1996—Mullah Mohammad Omar was only thirty-four years old then—as well as their interactions with the almost universally older Arabs. The significant age difference would also have a cultural dimension when it came to the interaction between the Arabs and the Taliban, in the context of social norms and customs, particularly in rural southern Afghanistan where respect for one's elders plays a significant role in social interaction.

As already outlined above, the socio-economic and socio-political context in which the later leaders of al-Qaeda spent their formative years was very different from that of rural southern Afghanistan. The failure of pan-Arab nationalism and the humiliating defeat of Arab military forces in the 1967 war with Israel fuelled the rise of Islamist movements (see above). Frustration at the weakness of the Arab nations—their military inadequacy, economic backwardness, and corrupt and failing administrations—found an outlet in the rising tide of Islamism, spearheaded by Egypt, with its long heritage of Islamist activism and Islamist movements opposed to the government.

In 1928 the Muslim Brotherhood (or *Ikhwaan al-Muslimoun*) was founded by Hassan al-Banna, one of the key figures of pan-Islamism.[89] Born into a poor family north of Cairo, Al-Banna was involved with the anti-colonial movement as well as Sufism, both influences that he would bring into the Muslim Brotherhood. During the 1930s he spoke in public around Cairo, seeking to mobilise Egyptians on behalf of the Brotherhood.[90]

Al-Banna's relationship with the Egyptian state was always in flux, even though it seems he was content to work within the state framework. He became more involved with politics and more demanding as the numbers of his Brotherhood grew. In the mid-1930s, al-Banna established *al-nizam al-khass*, 'the special section,' or *al-jihaz al-sirri*, 'the secret apparatus,' as it would become known outside the group, which amounted to the Brotherhood's clandestine armed wing. The very organisational structure of the Brotherhood's secret apparatus, formed by 'families' or individual cells of a few members, assured survival even when faced with government prosecution and was emulated by many militant Islamic groups.[91]

At his core, al-Banna seemed to have aimed to create a revolutionary movement that would, once it had reached critical mass, overthrow the current order. As Mitchell put it, 'it was a mistake to be candid, and that secrecy was necessary in the beginning of any movement to maintain its solvency and assure its survival.'[92]

Al-Banna's statements about secrecy and survival echo one of the Brotherhood's most famous members, Sayyed Qutb (1906–66). After attaining a degree from the same school as al-Banna, he worked at the Ministry of Education for years, doubling as a journalist and writer. In 1948, the Ministry sent him for training to the United States where he spent two years in several educational institutions around the country.[93]

Some commentators argue that Qutb's dispatch to the United States was an attempt to counter his increasingly radical Islamic tendencies,[94] but if so, his travels there had the opposite effect. He returned convinced of the moral bankruptcy of Western society and the need to reform Egypt. Only one year after his return, Qutb was elected to the leadership council of the Muslim Brotherhood.[95]

Two of the books that he wrote after returning to Egypt are essential to understanding the intellectual background of militant Islamist groups such as al-Qaeda: *Fii Zilal al-Qur'an* (*In the Shade of the Qur'an*) in 1965 and *Ma'alim fii al-Tariq* (*Milestones*) in 1964.[96] Key to Qutb's worldview are the dialectically opposed concepts of *jahiliyya*, or ignorance, and Islam, or the state of the *umma*. For Qutb, the entire world was in a state of *jahiliyya*, a condition that had befallen Egypt and the Muslim countries by following Western ideology and concepts. As he wrote in *Milestones*:

How is it possible to start the task of reviving Islam? It is necessary that there should be a vanguard which sets out with this determination and then keeps walking on the path, marching through the vast ocean of Jahiliyyah which has encompassed the entire.[97]

His concept of the 'vanguard' echoes that of Mawdudi, and, as Kepel notes, certain key concepts used by Qutb make it quite clear that he was familiar with Mawdudi's work.[98] For Qutb, the change is to be brought about by the vanguard through *jihad*. For him this does not constitute a defensive war, or the inner struggle against temptation, but rather an active military struggle to rid society of the rulers who perpetuate the state of *jahiliyya*.

The pronouncement of a turn to *jihad*, however, seemed to have been part of a general trend in Egypt at the time, notably expressed by Mohammad Abd al-Salam Faraj, to whom we will return below. Cooperation, he argued, was not an option and he even went so far as to classify the government as *kuffar* or infidels.

Central to this undertaking was the concept of *takfir*, reinvoked by Qutb. Takfirism is the process through which a Muslim is essentially excommunicated from the *umma* or Islamic community and deemed an enemy of the same.[99] While this concept itself has a long history dating back centuries—previously employed infrequently and very much as a last resort—applying it to an entire society and a government was Qutb's doing.[100]

Arguably, the treatment members of the Muslim Brotherhood suffered at the hands of the Egyptian security services helped Qutb's concept of *takfir* to find a wider following. He essentially brought *takfir* back into fashion through his application of it to the Egyptian government, establishing a precedent that was a key part of his legacy to the generations of militant Islamists that followed.

Part of his intellectual platform also sought to devolve the power to take decisions out of the hands of the traditional Islamic elites, the *Ulemaa'*, and transfer it to ordinary Muslims. Sayyed Qutb himself was not a trained religious scholar,[101] but held that passing judgement on the legitimacy of one's government, for example, was a matter to be decided by every individual rather than what he regarded as the co-opted religious clergy.[102]

Qutb distinguished between modernity and Westernisation; while he embraced modernity, he rejected Westernisation outright. He embraced the progress made in the physical sciences, while rejecting the philosophical discussions of the West.[103] This was in line with Mawdudi's position as well.[104]

Qutb's transformation from relatively benign teacher to Islamist activist and firebrand was not purely an internal intellectual struggle. In the aftermath of an assassination attempt against President Nasser in 1954, Qutb was arrested and sentenced to twenty-five years in prison.[105] He spent the next ten years in jail, mostly in the infirmary due to his weak constitution.[106] He is believed to have been subject to torture there, too, and his imprisonment shaped his views about the government.[107] He brought these to the public through his book, *Milestones*.

Qutb was released in 1964, rearrested in 1965, and eventually executed in 1966, an act which again spread and further disseminated his ideas.[108] He was and remains an indispensable influence on the subsequent generations of both Egyptian and international Islamists. In the words of Esposito:

It is almost impossible to exaggerate the direct and indirect impact and influence [of Mawdudi, Hasan al-Banna' and Qutb]. Their writings have been published and distributed throughout the Muslim world. Their ideas have been disseminated in short pamphlets and audiocassettes. The leadership of most major Islamic movements, mainstream and extremist, non-violent and violent alike, has been influenced by their ideas on Islam, Islamic revolution, *jihad* and modern Western Society.[109]

Indeed, his influence on the generation of Abdullah Azzam, Ayman al-Zawahiri and Osama bin Laden was profound.[110]

Mohammad Qutb, Sayyed Qutb's brother, was an associate of Abdullah Azzam, and had taught bin Laden in King Abd al-Aziz University in Jeddah, Saudi Arabia. Qutb's family, and with it his legacy, had further ties to events that would unfold in Afghanistan. Amina Qutb, Sayyed Qutb's sister, was married to Sheikh Kamal al-Sananiri, the first delegate sent by the Egyptian Muslim Brotherhood to Afghanistan in November 1980. Al-Sananiri in turn met Azzam in Mecca later the same year and convinced him to go to Pakistan to support the Afghan *jihad* against the Soviet Union.[111]

Qutb's ideas and those of the Brotherhood in Egypt were not being discussed outside the educated circles of Kabul and other universities in Afghanistan.[112] At the time, one cannot talk about a relationship between the Muslim Brotherhood and the madrassas in southern Afghanistan or the Pakistani borderland.

Interviews revealed that only two members out of the entire senior Taliban political and military leadership received their Islamic education in the Middle East. Mullah Mushr received his in Saudi Arabia and Mullah Mujahed—later the Taliban's unofficial representative to the United Nations—was educated in Egypt. Otherwise there was—this was universally remarked in interviews—very little appetite for an education in anything that wasn't a Deobandi or (at the very least) Hanafi institution. One Taliban member (an official during the 1990s government) based in Kandahar and Khost remarked:

'Nobody wanted to go to Al-Azhar or Medina or Mecca for education because they thought that if they went there they would get converted to Wahhabi ideas or education. Many of the Mullahs were very sensitive about these things, so people only liked to go to Deoband in India or to Pakistan.'[113]

Education

The 1970s was a decade of great ferment in the Arab world, as Kepel explains:

During the 1970s, the first generation to be born in the era of independence came of age in most of the Muslim world. These young people had no first-hand recollection of the anti-colonial tide of liberation that had legitimized the nationalist regimes under which they lived, and thus they were out of step with elites in government. Unlike their elders and parents, they had been born too late to benefit from the jobs and social advancement created by independence and from the sharing out of property abandoned by the departing settlers and colonists.

Between 1955 and 1970, population growth in the Muslim world approached 50%—a demographic change of spectacular proportions. By 1975, with urbanization and literacy advancing apace, the cohort under twenty four years old represented over 60% of the total population. The world of Islam, which had always been predominantly rural and governed by a small urban elite with exclusive access to reading and writing, now underwent a radical transformation with the arrival of this mass of literate young city dwellers.[114]

These demographic shifts meant that Qutb's ideas—particularly his combative attitude towards traditional sources of religious authority—fell on fertile soil. Universities were the main places of debate for young people at the time. In Egypt, the population explosion saw the number of students going to university in the 1970s double to half a million, while the facilities and postgraduate work opportunities were unchanged and could not cater to this massive increase.[115] This is where the Islamist groups stepped in:

Modern, secular values of instruction were called into question: the Gamaat denounced them as lies, incapable of reflecting social reality. Instead, the radicals offered their own vision of Islam as a system that was 'complete and total,' that could not only interpret the larger world but also transform it. On the level where students actually lived, the associations were masters at combining practical services with the inculcation of moral standards.[116]

Regardless of any Islamisation of the facilities, the lives of the Arabs attending university in Cairo, Baghdad and other cities of the Middle East were almost entirely different from those of Afghans in southern Afghanistan who would later come together as the Taliban movement in the 1990s. Nevertheless, the rising tide of ideology within the urban centres and universities, and the situation of graduates in Afghanistan, somewhat mirrored that of their Arab compatriots, as Edwards (2002) tells us. In his introduction to *Before Taliban*, he recounts a documentary called 'Naim and Jabar,' about two boys from the village attending school in the city and a meeting he had with a young government employee, Aqcha Poor, in Balkh in the 1970s. Edwards shows how Afghanistan had started to produce many more educated university graduates, who after having gained a degree faced few opportunities and meagre salaries working for the government but had gained significant insight into the rest of the world.

The growing number of educated Afghans, looking towards the Western world while still caught up in a culture of their own that seemed relatively conservative, together with the corrupt government and ongoing mismanagement, created an atmosphere that was unsustainable.[117] At the same time, it is important not to forget the deeply secular nature of much of city life in Egypt (and elsewhere) during the 1970s; the Islamists were increasing their influence, but they were by no means the leading power in society.

The educational backgrounds of a sample of prominent 'Afghan Arabs,' below, reveal that most of them received a wholly secular education. Any Islamisation or studies were received in addition to or outside their primary/state-provided education. This was different from Islamic studies as found in Afghanistan and Pakistan and happened at the same time as a shift away from traditional religious authorities; informal circles of individuals would discuss religious issues, formulate ideas and publish them on their own. This happened in Egypt and elsewhere in the Middle East. It also was a reflection of these individuals' relationship with Islamic religious authority: Qutb and others argued that the responsibility and authority to devise decisions as to the legitimacy of a government lay with each and every Muslim individual, thus bypassing the traditional religious authorities and 'clergy' who would usually have acted as a moderating influence in these matters.[118]

In order to bridge the gap between the educated Islamist leadership and the broad population—in particular in rural areas and also later for fundraising purposes—groups supplemented their often-ideological leadership with an al-Azhar-educated religious figure—as in the case of Omar Abdul Rahman and the *al-Gama'a al-Islamiyya* group—who would lend traditional religious credibility in the form of fatwas and sermons supporting their cause.

A more comprehensive survey of the educational background of al-Qaeda members and affiliates conducted by Marc Sageman also found that, out of a sample of 137, only 23 (17%) had an Islamic religious primary and secondary education.[119] The rest were educated in secular schools. When Sageman looked at the key individuals of what he terms the 'global Salafi jihad' he found that they were mostly well-educated—'88 percent had finished college and

Figure 2: Educational background of prominent 'Afghan Arabs'[120]

Name	Subject	Location/Institution
Abu Ubaida	(Police Academy)	Egypt
Mohammad Atef	Agricultural engineering	Unknown
Abu Yahya al-Libi	Chemistry	Sebha University, Libya
Mustafa Hamza	Computer science	University of Cairo, Egypt
Mohammad Abd al-Salam Faraj	Electrical engineering	University of Cairo, Egypt
Abu Hajer al-Iraqi	Electrical engineering	Iraq
Abdullah Azzam	Islamic studies	Damascus, Syria & Al-Azhar, Cairo, Egypt
Abdullah Anas	Islamic studies/army	Algeria
Osama bin Laden	Management	King Abdul Aziz University, Jeddah, Saudi Arabia
Abu al-Walid al-Masri	Mechanical engineering	University of Alexandria, Egypt
Abu Mus'ab al-Suri	Mechanical engineering	University of Aleppo, Syria
Ayman al-Zawahiri	Medicine	University of Cairo, Egypt
Sayyed Imam al-Sharif	Medicine	University of Cairo, Egypt
Abu Mus'ab al-Zarqawi	No secondary/religious education	

20 percent had doctorate degrees.'[121] A study by Diego Gambetta and Steffen Hertog has also demonstrated the overrepresentation of engineers among Islamist groups.[122]

Furthermore, many came from affluent or middle class families, with considerable exposure to higher education. Al-Zawahiri, for example, was born into an aristocratic Egyptian family.[123] His grandfather Abd al-Rahman Pasha Azzam was founder of the Arab League and deeply involved in Arab and Muslim politics before 1952.[124] He grew up in one of the most affluent neighbourhoods in Cairo and was an avid reader at a young age.[125]

Saudi Arabia, with its open door policy towards Islamists and a co-dependent relationship with its religious establishment, was one place where there was plenty of access to extra-curricular Islamic teaching and where Islamists like Mohammad Qutb, who faced prison or worse in his home country, congregated and spread their message freely. It wasn't until the 1990s, however, that significant numbers of Islamists started to speak out about the al-Saud family or the government of Saudi Arabia, since they were still concerned with their own home governments. Jamal Khalifa, one of bin Laden's childhood friends, relates one such memory:

In '76, '77 we used to read [Qutb's books] *Milestones* and *In the Shade of the Koran*. So Sayyid Qutb was concentrating on the meaning of Islam that it's the way of life. It influenced every Muslim in that period of time. Mohammed Qutb [Sayyid Qutb's brother who was a visiting professor at King Abdul Aziz University in the late 1970s] used to give [myself and bin Laden] lectures. He was giving us very good lessons about education—how to educate our children.[126]

Other key texts read by many during this time included Faraj's *Neglected Duty* and—at the very end of the 1970s—the writings of Juhayman al-Utaybi.

The concept of *jihad* as expressed and used by Islamists of the 1970s owed a lot to Sayyed Qutb but also to Mohammad Abd al-Salam Faraj (1952–82).[127] Faraj was the head of *Jama'at al-Jihad* and had written a manifesto entitled *Al-Farida al-Ghaiba* or 'The Neglected Duty,' a clear reference to *jihad*.[128] He argued that *jihad* be considered a prime duty of Muslims in Egypt—he saw it as a 'sixth pillar' of Islam, in fact—and criticised, as did Qutb, the quietist attitudes held by Islamist groups with regard to the government. For him, the government itself was corrupt and un-Islamic:

The present rulers have apostatised from Islaam. They have been brought up over colonial tables be they Christian, Communist or Zionist. What they carry of Islaam is nothing but names, even if they pray, fast and claim to be Muslims. [...] Indeed the scholars of the Muslims are agreed that if the rebellious group abstain from *mutawaatir* (clear) obligations of Islaam, fighting them becomes obligatory.[129]

This, he stated amid plentiful citations of precedents for his judgement, was justification for *jihad* to be declared and carried out against the government as the first point of call. Indeed, Faraj's lasting legacy to Islamists and jihadis (in Egypt, in particular) was to direct the focus of his struggle at the 'near enemy.' Interviews with Islamists at the time indicate that, while there was a clear recognition of the overbearing influence that foreign governments had on Muslim countries, the first step to addressing the problems (and elevating the status of Islam) would be to attack and remove the 'near' government in Egypt.[130]

In the Islamic countries, the enemy is at home; indeed, it is he who is in command. He is represented by those governments that have seized power over the Muslims, and that is why *jihad* is an imperative for every individual (*fard 'ayn*).[131]

Faraj's publication of his manifesto in 1981 was followed almost immediately by the assassination of al-Sadat. Faraj facilitated and sanctioned the plot against the Egyptian President and was arrested, along with many other Egyptian Islamists, quite early on. He was executed for his role in the attack in 1982.[132]

The powerful medley of ideas that Faraj synthēsised in *Al-Farida al-Ghaiba* brought together the ideas of *jahiliyyah*, *takfir* and *jihad* and laid out an operational plan of action. The manifesto was the key document for Egyptian jihadis (and those of other nationalities) at least until the early 1990s.[133]

Ayman al-Zawahiri, already a member of the *Jihad* group and who played a minor role in the al-Sadat assassination plot, was an associate of Faraj during the late 1970s. The principle that the 'near enemy' should be the primary focus of jihadi activities remained the key doctrine to which he adhered all the way until the late 1990s when, faced with the failure of his own organisation to topple the Egyptian government, he signed on to bin Laden's 'World Islamic Front' in 1998 with its goal as *jihad* against the 'far enemy', the supporter of their governments, namely the United States of America. Prior to that point, Zawahiri was well known, for example, for noting that 'the road to Jerusalem passes through Cairo.'[134]

The Islamist groups that formed in the 1970s in Egypt and other countries in the Muslim world under names like *al-Jihad*, *al-Gama'a al-Islamiyya* and others were a loose affiliation of several independent groups, mostly rallying around specific individuals that unified them. They would join together at times, but also frequently argued over ideology and strategy. Clusters of like-minded individuals emerged around some of the key figures of the time: Mohammad Abd al-Salam Faraj, Karam Zuhdi, Shukri Mustafa and Ayman al-Zawahiri. Each had a nominal 'group' that they represented, but accounts from that period indicate that there were many shifts of allegiance.[135] Egypt was very much a focal point for these developments, but other countries had their own home-grown Islamist activism.

Much non-Egyptian Islamism was initiated and exported elsewhere during the previous decades by Muslim Brotherhood affiliates and organisations. Iraq and Syria both had their own Muslim Brotherhood groups that in turn spawned and gave rise to a variety of other groups with differing levels of extremism and militancy. The group that Abu Mus'ab al-Suri joined in June 1980, for example, was an offshoot of the Syrian Muslim Brotherhood called 'The Combatant Vanguard' (*al-tali'a al-muqatila*).[136] The group 'considered themselves the 'real disciples' of the [Muslim Brotherhood], founded by Hasan al-Banna and Sayyid Qutb, and followers of their 'true path.'[137]

Aside from Saudi Arabia and the many Muslim Brotherhood members who found a safe haven there during the 1970s, it seems that the individual local

Islamist groups had no organised and co-ordinated relationship with each other. Instead, a loose network of associates and the changing nature of publishing media facilitated a wide reaching debate among the different groups.

Manifestations in the 1970s

Inside Afghanistan

Most of those who would later come to form the Taliban movement's leadership during the 1990s were still being educated in the 1970s, attending local madrassas in the villages and districts of southern Afghanistan and being taught by village mullahs and Deobandi *Ulemaa'*. Most were not even travelling to Pakistan during these early years. It was only later—with the Soviet invasion—that more links and possibilities for studying abroad would open up.

These young students were increasingly antagonised by the Afghan government, as were their teachers. Mullah Zaeef tells of his education during that time:

I was studying at a local madrassa in Sangisar and enrolled in a class led by Mullah Neamatullah. He had been one of my father's apprentices in Mushan and had great affection for me. The senior religious instructor at the school was Mawlawi Niaz Mohammad. He too had known my father, and bought clothes for me and the textbooks I needed to continue my education. Mawlawi Niaz Mohammad was a prominent provincial supporter of Noor Mohammad Taraki, a dominant figure of the Communist Khalq faction that had formed following a split from the Afghan People's Democratic Party in the late 1960s. When Taraki came to power in the spring of 1978, Niaz Mohammad switched allegiances and became a vocal supporter of the Communists. He even said that Taraki was an associate and envoy of the *Imam-e Mehdi* at that time. All his students left him soon after he started to support Taraki. Most of them went to Pakistan, others to different Mawlawis elsewhere in the region. I went to school in Kandahar City as my relatives thought it best that I receive a secular education while pursuing my religious studies at the madrassa.

I passed the examination for the fourth grade and enrolled in primary school, attending classes in Kandahar for a year. The city was alive at that time: the granary was full, water was plentiful throughout the province, and I remember people loved to play volleyball (we did not start playing football in Kandahar until much later).

One day I returned to Sangisar to see Mawlawi Niaz Mohammad. Mawlawi Saheb had changed. His support for Taraki had grown even stronger. As soon as we sat down and tea was served, he asked me: 'Son! Have you filled in the form or not?.'

After the coup, Taraki had moved fast, introducing legislation for land reform as one of his prized projects. He wanted to redistribute the land among the people. Everyone could apply and would receive up to ten jeribs per person. Mullah Neamatullah had talked about it in Kandahar. He had told us that we should take great care. It was un-Islamic, he said, to take the land and we should resist the temptation of wealth. So I answered: 'Mawlawi Saheb! Other authorities have told us that the land belongs to other people. And to take property from others is a sin. How can I take this land?.'

'This is the last share of the world's wealth, son,' he replied. 'Those who don't take part now will remain landless forever.' As I was young, he said that he would help me. 'You should most definitely do this!' he insisted. 'The King,' he said, 'is in charge. If he decides something then we should not doubt it. We must obey.' I stayed there overnight and left the next day for the city without saying goodbye to Mawlawi Saheb.

Mullah Neamatullah Akhund, my instructor, and all the other scholars had fled to Pakistan. No one I knew had stayed. Sayyeds, Khans, Maliks and Mullahs were all being persecuted by the government. Educated people living in the districts had advised the Communists that the best way to retain control of the countryside would be to imprison the local power holders. Many of them ended up in jail, but few were ever seen again.[138]

Mullah Mutawakil records similar, albeit brief, impressions in his account of the time, where the political impinged on his education only in so far as the things Zaeef describes affected everyone else in the country.[139] The education of the Taliban's future leadership figures began coming to an end in the late 1970s, and the only kind of *jihad* being promoted as part of their education or otherwise was the distinctly nationalist struggle against the Afghan Communist government and/or the Soviet troops that entered the country in late 1979. All the interviews conducted for this book confirmed this atmosphere at the close of the decade.

The Islamic landscape in southern Afghanistan was and remains very homogenous. Afghanistan is, broadly speaking, dominated by Sunni Muslims that adhere to the Hanafi school. Internal conflict between Muslim groups because of their ideological points of view[140] would have been seldom heard of in the countryside in southern Afghanistan. The most that one could find of this sort of conflict would be the occasional clash between two dominant sects, the Sunni and Shi'i, although this was mostly the product of ethnic tensions or land disputes rather than a specifically religious dispute. Conflict among Muslims on a tribal basis, however, was very common.[141]

Outside Afghanistan

The Islamist groups that emerged during the 1970s in the Middle East were focused on their own governments in their immediate countries of birth rather than on what Faraj and others regarded as the more distant enemy, Israel, the liberation of the Palestinian people and the al-Aqsa mosque in Jerusalem. In particular, the militant groups that emerged in Egypt during these formative years were very much focused on their home government.[142]

The actions carried out by the militant Islamists reveal a plan and strategy that specifically targeted the government or its institutions. These jihadis were attempting to Islamise the state from the top down rather than from the bottom up. As Gerges notes, there was 'no patience or faith in *al-da'wa* [inviting others to join Islam, an important part of most Islamist groups up to that point]'[143] and this was connected to their desire to focus on the 'near enemy.' They were about action rather than words. In Pakistan we can see an opposite trend in the *Tablighi Jamaat* (very much active during this period) who focus on preaching rather than preparing an uprising or violent regime change.

Qutb, Mawdudi and Faraj had all outlined broad strategies for how to move forward with the actual goal of 'bringing Islam to the people'—Faraj is notable for being the most specific in this respect—but the fledgling Islamist movements and groupings during the 1970s had to contend with multiple obstacles: the local state government apparatus and its security forces; traditionalist clerics from an older generation; and at least part of the local population who were not interested in a change to their lifestyle of the extent demanded by the Islamists.

Focusing on their home countries, the militant Islamists that congregated in Saudi Arabia (whose government readily offered refuge) were mostly engaged in the funding and support of their groups back home, and regrouping or engaging in propaganda efforts:

They staffed the offices of the Muslim World League, which opened in Mecca in 1962 to oppose Nasser's reform of Al Azhar University. They found jobs at the World Assembly of Muslim Youth, headquartered in Jeddah, which sought to federate Islamist youth organizations throughout the world, through internships, meetings and charity work in Africa that would rival the Christian NGOs. They cooperated with Muslim Brothers in Kuwait, who had established a political party, the Association for Social Reform (Jamaat al-Islah al-Ijtimai) and, more importantly, a weekly newspaper, *Al Mujtama* (Society), to serve as the movement's international mouthpiece. They joined the International Federation of Islamic Student Organizations, which translated texts into every language spoken throughout the *umma* and published the essential works of Sayyid

Qutb, Sayyid Abul Ala Mawdudi, and Hassan al-Banna—a homogeneous corpus of doctrine.[144]

Later, the Saudi government would encourage these Sunni Islamists as a bulwark against the increasingly confident Shi'i Islamists following the Iranian Revolution of 1979.

* * *

1979 saw three events occur that resonated throughout the Muslim world far beyond their immediate impact. The last of these—the Soviet invasion of Afghanistan—will be covered extensively in the next chapter, but the Iranian Revolution of January/February and the Siege of Mecca in November and December deserve a mention here.

The Iranian Revolution was a clear example of a bottom-up approach to changing society—as opposed to that advocated (and acted upon) by Mohammad Abd al-Salam Faraj in 1981—but Khomeini sought to make what had happened in Iran not just an important moment for the Shi'a, but something wider:[145]

Outside Shia contexts, Khomeini sought to downplay his Shia image. He posed as a champion of Islamic revival, and presented the Iranian revolution as the Islamic revolution that the Sunni thinkers of the Muslim Brotherhood and Jamaat-e Islami had been claiming was necessary if Islam's fortunes were to be restored. Iran, the bastion of Shiism, was also the vanguard of the global Islamic revolution.[146]

Sunni Islamists were not convinced, neither in Saudi Arabia nor in Afghanistan or Pakistan. In fact, the Saudi government were sufficiently worried that they increased their support and activities for a 're-Islamisation' of Saudi society.[147] Vali Nasr explains its limited impact abroad:

Sunni fundamentalism in Pakistan and much of the Arab world was far from politically revolutionary. It was rooted in conservative religious impulses and the bazaars, mixing mercantile interests with religious values. Its goal, as the French scholar of contemporary Islam Gilles Kepel puts it, was less to tear down the existing system than to give it a fresh, thick coat of 'Islamic green' paint. Khomeini's fundamentalism, by contrast, was 'red'—that is, genuinely revolutionary. Its goal was to shatter the existing state and replace it with something new. Khomeini's version of fundamentalism engaged the poor and spoke of class war. Its success in Iran suggested that for fundamentalism elsewhere to succeed, it too would have to go beyond concerns about personal morality in order to encompass social revolution. Although some Sunni fundamentalists were open to such a shift, most were not. Nor were their backers in bazaars and among the merchants exactly pining for a socioeconomic revolution that would redistribute wealth to the poor.[148]

By contrast, the siege of the Grand Mosque in Mecca carried out by Juhayman al-Utaybi and his followers was seen as far more potent a precedent for Sunni Islamists not involved at the time. The Saudi ruling elite were also worried since it was the clergy who had taken power only a few months earlier in Iran.

Al-Utaybi and his group were Sunni fundamentalists who believed that the Mehdi's return[149] was immediate. This took place on the first day of the New Year, 1400, by the Islamic calendar. While the siege is often regarded as unconnected with the wider world of Islamic movements or militant Islamists, many of al-Utaybi's central ideas would later be echoed by other militant groups.[150]

In a direct way, Khaled al-Islambouli, a prominent member of the Egyptian *al-Jihad* group who assassinated Anwar al-Sadat in 1981, is said to have closely followed the siege and was a keen reader of al-Utaybi's writings.[151] Abu Muhammad 'Asaam Maqdisi, the Jordanian religious writer and mentor to Iraqi al-Qaeda head Abu Mus'ab al-Zarqawi, also seems to have been tied to al-Utaybi's group through his brother-in-law, Abdul Latif Derbas, who was one of al-Utaybi's closest supporters and from whom he heard stories of detention in Saudi jails following the siege.[152]

While it is easy to overstate the Mecca siege's importance for Sunni Islamists of the time—Trofimov, for instance, sees it as a direct precedent that links all the way to the September 11 attacks—it was a dramatic event that underlined the extent to which Islamists were now prepared to take action in support of their beliefs.

Even though al-Utaybi's group were quite disassociated from the wider network of Islamists in the region and the intellectual discussion among its leadership, the siege nevertheless points towards the atmosphere and possibilities that had been opened up by the ideas of Mawdudi, Faraj and Qutb.

3

JIHAD (1979–1990)

Throughout my tours in Kandahar, I never saw one village whose people had not left it or in which one house had been spared from the bombing. I would even say that there was not one standing room in Kandahar.

Dr. Ayman Sabri Faraj, 'Afghan Arab'[1]

They are afraid of us. The West thinks we are all crazy Moslems—like Khomeini—who want to convert you or bury you. The West does not want to give us what we need to fight the Russians, because it thinks we will turn around and someday use these weapons on them. America remembers the Shah and what happened there. So it lets us bleed. After all, we are only crazy savages with turbans in Asia.

Gulbuddin Hekmatyar[2]

War unites men; it is peace which divides them. Man is an animal, a warrior, but man can also look at the stars; he can be a poet; that is God in him. He can kill and he can love, and he can love God and he can love women.

Mullah, Khost, 1983[3]

In the summer of 1979, US President Jimmy Carter signed a secret directive to support the nascent Afghan mujahedeen in their fight against the Soviet-backed Afghan government.[4] Starting in the north-east in 1978 followed by the west and the centre (the Dari-speaking parts of Afghanistan) and finally

41

in the south, a significant part of the Afghan population had mobilised against the government.[5] Soviet Foreign Minister Andrei Gromyko described the situation in a meeting held on 17 March 1979, saying that there were 'thousands, literally thousands' of insurgents. Nevertheless, he asserted that 'under no circumstances may we lose Afghanistan.'[6]

The decision to invade was formally taken on 12 December 1979, and was signed by all members of the Politburo except for the Chairman of the Council of Ministers who was ill. Soviet troops seemed to have been mobilising as early as 7 October,[7] and had begun to deploy to Bagram and other airbases in late November.[8]

The war that ensued would last ten years. The mujahedeen resistance was almost exclusively Afghan, albeit with small and by most accounts inconsequential pockets of foreigners mostly from the Arab world and Pakistan. The Afghans conducted a guerrilla-style campaign that would eventually cause the Red Army to withdraw. Millions of Afghans fled and sought refuge in Iran, Pakistan or further afield over the next decade as the war intensified.

Each region of Afghanistan, and each mujahedeen group, had individual characteristics, distinguishing the war in Panjshir, for example, from that of Kandahar. There was also comparatively little crossover among the different spheres—even from those that neighboured each other—in terms of commanders fighting in multiple areas. The *jihad* was, broadly speaking, a local affair.

Central to the effort undertaken in Afghanistan by the mujahedeen was the safe haven in Pakistan. The different mujahedeen parties had a common organisational structure; their leadership was mostly located in Peshawar and Quetta and concerned with logistics, funding, material support, training, and maintaining links to donors and their counterparts in Afghanistan carrying out the guerrilla campaign against the Soviet troops and the Afghan government. The split between the leadership and the fighting force, using Pakistan as a safe haven, became a dominant feature of how militant groups would operate in Afghanistan in the decades that followed.[9]

This book is primarily concerned with the east, south and south-east of Afghanistan—the border regions—and less with the other parts of the country. These were the primary areas in which Arabs and Afghans fought together and thus are of greater interest when examining these early points of contacts and the relationship that developed between the two. The individuals who would come together to form the Taliban in 1994 fought in the southern provinces of Loy Kandahar[10] for the most part.

Moreover, the war-without-end nature of the conflict was the forging crucible for both of the groups that this book examines: al-Qaeda and the Taliban both frequently refer back to the 1980s *jihad* as part of their founding narrative and as an explanation of their identity.[11] For this reason, if for no other, it is worth delving into this period in greater detail in order to understand the networks that would emerge from this period and their intersection.

Before analysing the interactions of the 'Afghan Arabs' and their Afghan counterparts during the *jihad* period, it is important first to identify and be specific about where these interactions were taking place. Errors of this order can lead to wild conclusions being drawn—the claim that Mullah Mohammad Omar fought in Nangarhar during the war, for example, might lead others to assume a possible meeting between the future Taliban leader and bin Laden.

Much primary-source and interview work needs to be done on this period, particularly for southern Afghanistan, and the analyses and information that follow are merely an outline that future researchers may build on.

The Taliban Fronts

The existence of so-called 'Taliban fronts' is usually given short shrift in English-language accounts of the 1980s *jihad*. This is mostly due to a lack of detailed information rather than any particular criticism of the idea. There is, however, a growing body of anecdotal and circumstantial evidence for this early history of groups that would go on to form the Taliban movement, both from interviews as well as Pashtu- and Arabic-language biographical accounts of the period. For this book, two regions of Afghanistan are particularly important:

1) Southern Afghanistan—most of the leadership of the 1990s Taliban movement had fought together in *Loy* or greater Kandahar[12] during the 1980s.
2) South-eastern Afghanistan—this was the stronghold of Jalaluddin Haqqani and Mawlawi Yunis Khalis, both key figures in the relationship between Arabs and Afghans, and also a region where the great majority of 'Afghan Arabs' fought.

Eastern Afghanistan was where Gulbuddin Hekmatyar and his *Hizb-e Islami* had a strong presence, as did a home-grown Salafist group, *Hizb ul-Da'wa wal Jihad*, based in Kunar and founded by Jamil ul-Rahman in 1985. The nature of these Afghan groups was different from that found in the south and south-east, and has relatively little bearing on the question of the relationship between the Taliban and al-Qaeda, and so this book will not examine these two groups or the area in any detail.

South

As stated above, the *jihad* was by and large a local affair with little crossover of fighters from one region to the next. The great majority of mujahedeen who fought in southern Afghanistan, therefore, originated from the south themselves, be it fighters who returned to the south from refugee camps across the border or people who had stayed.[13]

While we will assess the goals and motivations of the mujahedeen in later sections, it suffices for now to say that they could, broadly speaking, be characterised as a force of religious nationalists: communities—particularly those from rural areas—were motivated to participate in the *jihad* on the basis of religious fatwas sanctioning *jihad*, but also to protect their own land, their villages, traditions and customs. Many of the groups that were fighting in southern, eastern and southeastern Afghanistan developed along tribal lines, often presenting relative homogeneity; examples of these include the factions fighting under the leadership of Mullah Naqibullah in Arghandab who was heading the Alikozai tribe, with only small groupings of Barakzai and other Durrani tribal members.[14]

While groups were prone to switch allegiances among the seven major mujahedeen parties,[15] this had little impact on relationships on the ground beyond increasing or decreasing access to training, weapons and funding. The Taliban, in particular, were a young group (as was previously illustrated in figure 1), and most either had just finished their religious studies or had to interrupt their studies. In any case, the personalities that would become prominent in 1994 had little significance during the 1980s *jihad*; with a few exceptions, most were only minor commanders or fighters.[16] The initial fighters who took up arms were not yet subject to the religious fatwas that would be issued from early 1980 onwards in Afghanistan and neighbouring Baluchistan province, but were reacting to specific circumstances. As Dorronsoro notes:

In 1978–9 the people did not mobilise against the communist government in the name of an ideology: militants were rare among the rural population, and their rhetoric— including that of the Islamists—was incomprehensible to a population whose literacy was as undeveloped as its politicisation. The political parties had not made themselves known, or indeed were not established at all, until after the uprising, which they exploited but did not initiate.[17]

One commander related how, in mid-1979, a Tajik teacher named Abdul Mohammad from Mushan, a small village in Panjwayi district, was killed by a man called Hajji Akhtar Muhammad, and some five hundred local villagers took white flags and went to the central district authority to complain. Witnesses present that day tell how a white MiG plane flew overhead and fired on the demonstrators. Tanks were also dispatched from inside the district authority building and fired on the crowd. Some thirty people are said to have died. The next day, government forces were deployed in the area and arrested many people. Over one hundred villagers managed to escape that day to Pakistan, and twenty days later they started a guerrilla movement against the government, operating mainly from small bases in Registan, the desert area south of Kandahar City.[18] This is just one example of how local communities came to take up weapons and fight.

Another interviewee—who later worked as a Taliban government official in Kandahar and Khost—noted the primitive early days of the jihad:

When I was young my father was a Mullah and a commander of one *otaq* in Panjwayi district. My father called on people to do *jihad*, saying that *jihad* was *farz* [obligatory] for every single Muslim. We had all the *taliban* with us, of course, in the *otaq*, but also lots of ordinary people as well. Many people had swords, old guns, knives, wooden sticks and some iron bars. That's how we were fighting in the beginning.[19]

There were Talibs and religious clerics among the initial commanders that took up arms, most famous of whom was Mullah Mohammad Sadiq Akhund. In the early 1980s, most of the manpower for the Taliban fronts was supplied by Mawlawi Nabi Mohammadi's *Harakat-e Enqelab-e Islami*, a political party set up initially to encompass all the mujahedeen but (following squabbles among the senior mujahedeen leaders) later kept running[20] as a party representing the (mainly rural) religious clergy of southern and south-eastern Afghanistan.[21]

In greater Kandahar, there were literally hundreds of Taliban commanders[22] and dozens of Taliban fronts. Early incarnations saw the transformation of local madrassas into mujahedeen fronts, with the mullah leading his students or *taliban* as commander.[23] The Taliban sought to distinguish themselves from other mujahedeen groups by offering a more ostentatiously religious *jihad* to those who fought with them. The five daily prayers were observed and religious classes were offered for those not actively participating on the front lines. According to people who were part of the Taliban fronts[24] as well as members of other mujahedeen groups[25] operating in proximity of the Taliban fronts, the general atmosphere among the Taliban was different. The religious element was more pronounced, and they came across to other groups as more serious, more intense, or almost bookish.[26]

The Taliban fronts also distinguished themselves by the composition of their membership. As mentioned above, mujahedeen fronts in southern Afghanistan like in other regions tended to be structured along tribal and kinship lines; the Taliban, however, were connected by their common educational background and pursuit of religious studies. While commentators today often argue that the Taliban represent a confederation of Ghilzai Pashtun tribes due to the disproportionate presence of Ghilzai Pashtuns in the group—the argument runs that they therefore represent a group that evolved out of a long-standing conflict between the two major Pashtun tribal branches of southern Afghanistan and in essence therefore evolved out of tribal structures—the group itself has always and continues to describe itself publicly as having been formed on a religious basis. The disproportionate presence of Ghilzai Pashtuns among the Taliban can be better explained by socio-economic factors that caused more Ghilzai Pashtuns to seek religious education as well as increased numbers of certain tribal groups in certain areas. Within the context of rural southern Afghanistan, sending one's sons to a madrassa would lift the burden on a household to provide for them. Ghilzai Pashtuns throughout much of Afghanistan's modern history were dominated by Durrani Pashtuns, and were essentially poorer and therefore opted to send more children to madrassas.[27]

Certain areas were more saturated by Taliban fronts than others. In particular, what we now know as Panjwayi and Zheray[28] districts—and the fertile triangle in between the two branches of the River Arghandab—were dominated by Taliban fronts. These areas were chronically underdeveloped and neglected by the state; many families in Kandahar would send at least one family member to study at a madrassa, but the trend was exaggerated in these districts/areas.[29]

Throughout the *jihad*, the religious clergy also operated so-called mujahedeen courts that provided conflict mitigation and access to justice. Feuding mujahedeen groups would use the Taliban's court to settle disputes: prisoners, criminals, and most other instances where judgement was needed would be handled in this way. As such, it was an important service and the mujahedeen respected (for the most part) the court's judgement.[30] Contemporaries of the *jihad* would almost always relate stories of infighting between different mujahedeen groups and commanders and the role of the Islamic mujahedeen courts.

The main court in southern Afghanistan was located in Mahalajat,[31] initially run by Mawlawi Nazar Mohammad but then succeeded by Mawlawi Pasanai Saheb. For Kandahar, Mullah Samad Akhund had a court in Panjwayi, as did Mullah Naqib in Arghandab and Mullah Akhtar Jan in Spin Boldak. In Helmand, Mullah Naseem Akhundzada held the most-frequented court; Hafizullah Khan had a court for *Hizb-e Islami* and Mullah Atta Mohammad had a separate court in Sangin for those who did not wish to travel to that run by Mawlawi Pasanai Saheb in Kandahar.[32]

One former Taliban government official (who fought in Kandahar during the 1980s) explained how initially the courts were indistinguishable from the military clout of the *mullah*-commanders, but from around 1981–2 onwards these courts separated out as separate institutions.[33] Ayman Sabri Faraj, an Arab who fought in Kandahar during the late 1980s, described the courts as follows:

> ...the Islamic courts were very strict and would even sentence commanders or field leaders if they did something wrong. One time, a battle took place between two commanders so they went to court and asked for its ruling. The judge decided to arrest them both and beat them up before throwing them in jail. This judge and his court gained great respect in the Kandahar area because of that.[34]

There were two other locations where the Taliban operated courts: in Zangiabad and in Pashmol, two villages in Panjwayi district, although the latter was mobile for most of the time because of heavy bombing in the area.[35]

A number of prominent Taliban who came to play key roles in the 1994 movement joined ranks with *Hizb-e Islami*, most notably Mullah Mohammad Omar himself.[36] Jalaluddin Haqqani in the east, a Pashtun with strong tribal ties, managed to forge alliances with a number of *mullah*s from Kandahar, such as Mullah Malang and Mullah Obaidullah who later served as the Taliban's Defence Minister.[37] Most of the anecdotal evidence and personal accounts, such as the one of Faraj, place the small number of Arabs close to commanders like Mullah Malang.

The above illustration[38] maps out certain Taliban fronts in the Panjwayi/Zheray area during the 1980s. Black names are Taliban commanders, dark grey are Taliban fighters and light grey names are non-fighting religious clergy. Some squares mark the presence of a Taliban court in a particular place. Note the names in the centre of the map—seemingly untethered to a specific place. It was characteristic of the *jihad* in Kandahar province that mujahedeen would often not be based in a fixed location within a specific region. If a name is positioned inside a particular place name, then that individual is most closely associated with that place, but it does not mean that the fighter

Figure 3: Taliban fronts, commanders and fighters in Panjwayi/Zheray during the 1980s

remained in that area all of the time. Fighters remained in their wider geographical zones, though.

South-East

As in southern Afghanistan, there are not many first-hand written accounts of the 1980s *jihad* from the south-east. The few that do exist, though, support the thesis that resistance in the greater Paktya area had a predominance of 'mullah fronts' (to use Van Dyk's term). These are conceptually the same as the 'Taliban fronts' referred to above.

These were in part organised under Mawlawi Yunis Khalis' *Hizb-e Islami* party, which was noteworthy in that it represented the collision of a traditionalist clerical agenda with some of the modernising Islamist influences from Kabul. In south-east Afghanistan an important figure during the 1980s was Jalaluddin Haqqani, whose main base was located in the Shahi Kot mountains in Paktya province. Haqqani, much like Khalis, had a political Islamist outlook but relied almost exclusively on tribal backing.[39] Edwards describes one of the unique features of the Khalis/Haqqani fronts:

> [Khalis] was as much a man of the tribe as he was a party leader. [...] One of the marks of Khales's wing of Hizb-i Islami, conversely, was its ability to work with tribal leaders and to accommodate tribal customs, even if it meant contravening the formal dictates of Islamic law. I experienced this personally in the summer of 1984, when I visited mujahidin bases in Paktia Province that were run by Haqqani, Khales' chief deputy. Khales's local commanders worked closely with tribal leaders, sharing jurisdiction with them and allowing them to apply customary tribal law to resolve internal disputes. [This] helps to explain the considerable military and political success his groups enjoyed in the early 1980s in the areas under their jurisdiction.[40]

One Afghan working together with Khalis' *Hizb-e Islami* acknowledged the role of the mullahs in the south-eastern fronts: 'First we need the mullahs. They are good fighters. But ultimately they must return to the mosque. That is where they belong.'[41] And later on, in Quetta, in conversation with a tribal elder:

> It seemed most of the commanders [in Paktya] were mullahs. That is in Paktia, the most backward of provinces. The chief rules—not the mullah. Mullahs exist because they are good fighters.[42]

In the south-east, to a greater extent than the south, the old tribal Khans and Maliks were replaced by *mullah*s and *ulemaa*.[43] Haqqani and Khalis represent a merger of the tribal support headed by an Islamist-inspired leadership with the Mullahs.

Haqqani and the 'mullah fronts' of greater Paktya were part of a larger tradition. The extended and totalising nature of the 1980s *jihad* extended the pattern, but the use of mullahs as political tools was long-standing, particularly in south-eastern Afghanistan.[44]

Many such 'Taliban fronts' in the south-east were also associated with Nasrullah Mansour (and, in turn, with *Harakat-e Enqelab-e Islami*).[45] At one point many of the Taliban groups (largely from Zurmat and Andar) formed a group: *Tehrik-e-Tulaba* (Herakat). This sub-group was active in Paktya, Paktika and Ghazni during the 1980s. Moreover, the Nur ul-Madaris madrassa in Andar (associated with Mansour) was quite influential and produced many fighting mullahs and students. It has also been suggested that Mansour, through these means, contributed far more to the 1980s south-eastern Taliban fronts than Haqqani, who had a more mainstream mujahedeen membership.[46]

The 'Afghan Arabs' and Others

The outbreak of war in Afghanistan in 1979–80 was not initially met with a massive influx of Arab jihadist volunteers—as narrative accounts sometimes suggest—but rather with a slow trickle of a few important figures who worked to recruit others back in their home countries.[47]

First points of contacts were established through the Egyptian Muslim Brotherhood which sent an envoy in November 1980 in order to weigh up the situation in Afghanistan. Kamal al-Sananiri, who was the brother-in-law of Sayyid Qutb, had been dispatched by the supreme guide of the Egyptian Muslim Brotherhood and spent forty days in Pakistan assessing the Afghan *jihad*. While al-Sananiri never returned to Pakistan or Afghanistan, his trip would have a lasting impact on the trajectory of the Afghan Arabs. He returned to Egypt via Saudi Arabia where he met Abdullah Azzam and convinced him to support the Afghan *jihad*. Azzam would become a central figure of the Afghan Arabs and reshape much of the jihadist worldview through his writings and his role in the Afghan *jihad*. Nevertheless, the number of Arabs[48] who came to Pakistan in the early 1980s to support the Afghan *jihad* was small.[49] Certain nationalities had a stronger presence than others:

Al-Suri later estimated that the number of Syrians who went to Peshawar to the training camps or fought at the frontlines in Afghanistan in the period 1985–92 was in the range of tens, but less than one hundred. This was in sharp contrast to the much larger contingents from other Arab countries, such as Saudi Arabia, Yemen, Egypt and Algeria. [...] They were very few, perhaps numbering the same as the Tunisian contingency. [Abdullah] Anas estimates that the largest contingents were the Saudis, Algerians, the Yemenis, the Egyptians and Palestinians.[50]

Until the mid-1980s, there were relatively few Arabs in Afghanistan when Azzam and others initiated a debate among religious circles throughout the Middle East and beyond. The majority did not even play an active part in the fight inside Afghanistan, but volunteered for NGOs, working to bring aid and help the Afghan mujahedeen and refugees in and from Pakistan.[51] Their efforts were helped by the official stances of governments like Saudi Arabia and prominent religious scholars as well as much of the Western world. They regarded the war as a defensive war against an outside aggressor and from early on supported the Afghan mujahedeen through the ISI and increasingly through their own channels: 'they were perceived by the West as freedom fighters and by the Saudis as the vanguard of the Umma and the jihad.'[52]

In July 1980, Saudi Arabia agreed to match US funding of the Afghan mujahedeen, and its annual backing amounted to $300–500 million throughout the 1980s.[53] Funds for the Arab volunteers who wanted to join the jihad were scarce during the early years and many of the Arab jihadists who would later rise to prominent leadership roles in militant Islamist circles initially worked for Islamic charitable organisations or foundations or other NGOs.[54] Arabs initially sent to Afghanistan monitored the spending of funds raised and, as such, were affiliated with charitable institutions or worked in hospitals.[55] Mobilisation and recruitment from Arab countries increased exponentially in the second half of the 1980s, in part because governments—including in Egypt—realised that the *jihad* was a convenient way of disposing of their home-grown jihadis but also due to the effort of individuals like Azzam who published a number of widely read books and who toured the Middle East and beyond to fundraise and recruit for the Afghan cause.[56]

It is difficult to estimate how many Arabs went to Afghanistan (or at least Pakistan, where clearing-houses funnelled foreigners into Afghanistan);[57] estimates range between 8,000 and 25,000. Such numbers took time to arrive and most Arabs reached Afghanistan *after* the Soviet withdrawal.[58]

Abdullah Anas states that there were only twelve Arabs in Peshawar in 1983 when he arrived[59] and estimated later numbers as follows:

Up to '84 we were thirteen Arab mujahideen. By the end of '85, it was up to 90 or 100. So then the peak came between '87 and '89. We're not more than 3,000 to 5,000. The people who were inside Afghanistan active permanently, no more than 10 percent, 300, 400, 500 people. But 90 percent were teachers, cooks, accountants, doctors [over the border in Pakistan].[60]

Milton Bearden, the former Afghanistan CIA chief, has also stated that 'there were never more than 2,000 Arabs actually in Afghan territory at one time.'[61]

The Arabs who did come to fight were not distributed throughout Afghanistan in equal numbers. Anecdotal evidence, interviews, and an increasing number of biographical and narrative-historic accounts from Arabs and Afghans shows how most Arabs were embedded and involved with fronts allied to Sayyaf's *Ittehad-e Islami*, Khalis' *Hizb-e Islami* and Hekmatyar's *Hizb-e Islami*. Moreover, interviewees also explained how the Arabs did not even want to be associated with the three 'moderate' parties (Gailani's *Mahaz-i Milli*, Nabi Mohammadi's *Harakat-e Enqelab* or Mujadidi's *Jabha-ye Nejat*) or any of the Shi'i parties for ideological reasons.[62]

Azzam, the central figure around whom most Afghan Arabs tended to coalesce during the 1980s, was closely allied with Sayyaf, although he tried to deploy the Arabs among different groups around the country, notably sending a group of them (including Abdullah Anas) up to the Panjshir Valley to cooperate with Commander Massoud.[63]

Much of this imbalance can be explained by the earlier contacts of individuals with Islamic organisations—in particular the Muslim Brotherhood in Egypt prior to the jihad, during the late 1960s and 1970s. Contact networks, while not formal, extended from the urban elites and student body in Kabul out to the Arab world, and the Islamist groups that were formed at the university in Kabul built up on these initial contacts and firmed up ties. The relationship between the Afghan Arabs and the individual Afghan mujahedeen groups did not remain static throughout the *jihad*. In particular, Abdullah Azzam grew increasingly close to the Panjshiri commander, Ahmed Shah Massoud.[64]

From the perspective of the Arabs, al-Zawahiri explains how the *jihad* was a useful focal point for international Islamists:

In Afghanistan the picture was perfectly clear: A Muslim nation carrying out jihad under the banner of Islam, versus a foreign enemy that was an infidel aggressor backed by a corrupt, apostatic [sic] regime at home. In the case of this war, the application of theory to the facts was manifestly clear. This clarity was also beneficial in refuting the ambiguities raised by many people professing to carry out Islamist work but who escaped from the arena of jihad on the pretext that there was no arena in which the distinction between Muslims and their enemies was obvious.[65]

Al-Zawahiri's comments reflect his experiences in Egypt, where he saw little support at the time from the general population. His group's attempts to cause an uprising of the *umma* had failed, leading to his arrest, and after his release he had moved to Afghanistan to participate in the Afghan *jihad*.[66]

South

Due to the makeup of the mujahedeen fronts fighting in southern Afghanistan and their ambiguous relationship with the main mujahedeen parties and the Arab world, there appear to have been very few Arabs operating throughout the south.[67] As we saw above, some Arabs simply did not want to attach themselves to certain of the 'authorised' political parties, reflecting the bias between the two quite distinct groups of Afghan mujahedeen parties; one group was ideologically close to the Middle East while the other was far more influenced by the Hanafi school, Deobandism, and local concerns.

Exact numbers are, again, difficult to come by, and the best source on the Arab involvement in southern Afghanistan—Ayman Sabri Faraj's *Zikriyat Arabi Afghani*—is limited to the events and people that he saw with his own eyes. There is a little more that we can glean from Basil Mohammad's *Ansar al-Arab fii Afghanistan*,[68] and interviews with Afghan mujahedeen can give a few individual examples, but a comprehensive picture is impossible.

From what we do know, it seems that Arabs came in mostly through Sayyaf's *Ittehad-e Islami*.

Yes, we as Arabs completely trusted four parties (i.e. those of Sayyaf, Hekmatyar, Rabbani and Younis Khalis) believing that all the others were Sufi parties funded by America to compete with the enlightened Islamic parties. This may not be true at the level of the party leaders, but it is true at the level of the mujahedeen and the field leaders. After all, the Afghans were Afghans.[69]

The Afghan mujahedeen, however, seemed to see little use in Arab fighters on the ground.[70] Accounts like that written by Faraj tell of incidents where Arabs were not even allowed to fight in the most dangerous areas of the province. These injunctions and calls for restraint came from all sides: Abdullah Azzam, Sayyaf, and the Afghan mujahedeen commanders under whom they served. There was both a worry that the Arabs would be captured by the Russians (as did happen very occasionally) and that they would be killed.[71] This is not the same as saying that the Afghans disliked the Arabs or their presence. In fact, most interviewees had good memories of Arabs they knew during this time (as they do of the Arabs who lived in Kandahar post-1997).

The overall value of the Arab fighters as perceived by the Afghan mujahedeen differs widely. Some mujahedeen from southern Afghanistan point out that the Arabs for most of the 1980s did not know the lay of the land, did not speak the language, and had no feel for local customs.[72] They also often lacked fighting experience (in particular during the later years of the *jihad*), making them more of a liability than a help.[73] Other voices, such as a prominent mujahedeen commander in eastern Afghanistan—with an Arab front under his command—valued the Afghan Arabs highly and thought they made an impact.[74]

The data collated for this book reinforces these conclusions: the Arabs in southern Afghanistan were mainly concentrated in Mahalajat or areas close-by. Reports of Arabs fighting together with Taliban fronts in (greater) Panjwayi are extremely rare, and interviews with Talibs who fought at these posts have revealed no specific examples. Most recruits came (equally) from Egypt, Palestine or Saudi Arabia. From Faraj's account we know that most of these were ideologically driven; his book describes the period from 1987/8 to 1991, and there is scant other information about the early years of the *jihad*.[75] Nevertheless, the general trends observed in Peshawar indicate that there were even fewer Arabs between 1980–1986.

Aside from those who actually fought in Kandahar—like Faraj—the southern front lines have not embedded themselves as part of the 'Arab Afghan' mythology. That was forged east of Kandahar, in greater Paktya, where stories of fighters and battles fought continue to be traded on Islamist and jihadist websites to this day.[76]

Based on the evidence, there were some Arabs embedded or spending time together with Taliban fronts, yet—as the following 'Interactions' section will show—the relationship between Arabs and Afghans was far from straightforward, particularly on ideological grounds. The Taliban fronts that matter—i.e. those in Panjwayi, commanded by the Taliban's later leaders—reported no Arab fighters among them, and other circumstantial and anecdotal evidence supports this. Furthermore, none of the Arabs that are named in the various accounts played any significant role in the world of militant Islamic movements later on, in particular in al-Qaeda or the wider network around bin Laden and his inner circle. The 'Afghan Arabs' and individuals that would engage in a fight against the United States of America in the 1990s were yet to undergo their own ideological transformations, shifting away from many of the views they held during the 1980s.

South-East

The south-east of Afghanistan had the largest presence of Arab fighters and volunteers. The Saudis established direct links to Afghan mujahedeen leaders and organised gatherings in Saudi Arabia. This was helped by bin Laden, who had interacted with senior leaders in Saudi Arabia. In 1984, Azzam opened the first training base (Sada Camp) for Arab volunteers, with the permission of Sayyaf.[77] Azzam, bin Laden, Abu Hafs (aka Mohammad Atef), Abu Ubaida and many others locate the 'founding myth' of al-Qaeda to the mountains of greater Paktya.[78]

As in southern Afghanistan, the Arab presence was relatively insignificant until after 1986. That said, Jere van Dyk did meet several Arabs at Jalaluddin Haqqani's Shahi Kot base in the early 1980s.[79]

For bin Laden and the Arabs that followed him, in May 1986 a small group— bin Laden estimates that they numbered fifty[80]—of Arabs travelled into Afghanistan to link up with Sayyaf and Hekmatyar's fighters for an offensive, only to be turned back upon arrival. By the end of the year, though, bin Laden had decided to set up a permanent camp at Jaji (near to where they had first arrived) which would be manned by an all-Arab force. This was one of the first moments of friction between bin Laden and his erstwhile mentor Azzam, who regarded the role of the Arabs as a supportive one, under the leadership of Afghans.[81]

Bin Laden called his base *ma'sadat al-ansar*, or the Companion's Den,[82] and he was accompanied in these early days by a few Arabs, including Abu Hafs and Abu Ubaida.[83] They started digging tunnels, since the area was poorly situated and very exposed. There was relatively little fighting for the Arabs who were based in *Ma'sadat al-Ansar*, but on 17 April 1987 they managed to convince bin Laden to allow them to mount an attack against a nearby Soviet outpost in Khost.[84]

The attack was planned months in advance, but poorly executed by all accounts; as a result, the Pakistani government reportedly started closing down the Arab guesthouses in Peshawar.[85] May 1987 saw the Arabs carry out another attack, this time planned by Abu Ubaida, which was successful. Soviet forces mounted a heavy counter-assault on the Jaji camp and this fierce battle is the subject of many stories. Bin Laden cites the experience as being one of the key moments of the *jihad* for himself and the 'Arab Afghans.'[86] They held their position (eventually with Afghan help)[87] for three weeks, and this was enough to rehabilitate their reputation as courageous fighters after the fiascos of previous operations. The Peshawar guesthouses reopened.[88]

Fighting the *Jihad*

For Afghans and non-Afghans alike, the Afghan *jihad* was an experience without parallel. Even a cursory glance at the first-hand literature and accounts of the period from both groups confirms this: the long periods of boredom, the confusion and mistakes, the random timing of massively violent incidents and also the camaraderie of the trench.

The mujahedeen fronts were by and large places of deprivation, where one had to make do with limited resources and extremely restricted circumstances. The mujahedeen in southern Afghanistan, and indeed throughout most of the country, were organised into fronts and *otaq*s that had specific commanders associated with them, who would then be tied to a specific *amir* or chief, who would usually be fundraising across the border. The *amir*, in turn, would be affiliated with one of the seven mujahedeen parties officially sanctioned by the ISI, and could therefore gain access to funds, weapons and training.

Despite this apparent structure to the fighting groups, the boundaries and customs under which the Afghans operated often seemed confusing or nonsensical to the Arabs. Faraj relates one example from Kandahar:

The Afghans treated their prisoners so well that the Arabs were always mad at them. Indeed, they would eat with them, drink with them, wash their hands before the meals, clothe them and let them roam freely. What was even more amazing was that they put their names on the night guard shifts and slept while the detainees guarded them with weapons in their hands. More strangely, they would not hesitate to kill them after all that. Not everything in Afghanistan can be understood.[89]

Mullah Zaeef describes the time from the Taliban's perspective:

We fought on regardless of exhaustion, hunger and thirst, walking from Maiwand to Dand, from Shah Wali Kot and Arghandab to Panjwayi and other regions. We would even walk the hundred kilometres or so from Nelgham to Helmand or to Tirin Kot in Uruzgan. We would wear the same clothes for months at a time, surviving on just a loaf of bread or a few dates each day. Many were eager to fight, eager to die, especially young mujahedeen like myself.

We lived off the land and thanked those who donated food and money. People wanted to help just as we wanted to fight. If a commander left somebody out of an operation, that fighter would feel angry and disappointed. Just as normal people are eager to get married, we were desperate for martyrdom. At times you could hear mujahedeen cry out in the midst of battle, but not out of fear. Even though many of our friends were martyred, one after another, we weren't scared. We would have leapt at the first opportunity to run into open fire during battle, if only our commander hadn't reined us in. It is hard to believe, maybe, but we were happy. From time to time we danced the Atan, such was our elation. At other times we suffered grievously, but it was the true path: if one died, it was meant to be. What a happy life we led![90]

Rahimullah Yousufzai relates seeing an Arab Afghan camp under attack in Jalalabad. The Arabs had marked their tents out in white so that they would stand out. He asked them why. 'We want them to bomb us!' they replied. 'We want to die!'[91] This quote reflects the somewhat different motivations of the Arabs and the Afghans that took part in the Afghan *jihad*. Many of the accounts from Afghan Arabs as well as interviews conducted for this book echo the strong will to become a martyr. While this is sometimes echoed by the Afghan mujahedeen, it did not appear that the majority went to battle with the intent to die.[92]

There was also a considerable amount of infighting between the different mujahedeen commanders, both locally and nationally. Most mujahedeen from the south relate stories to this end, talking about different factions fighting with each other while being engaged in the war against the Red Army and Afghan government troops.[93] There is also a considerable amount of suspicion in southern Afghanistan to this day about the role of Northern Alliance commanders like Massoud who are blamed for letting Soviet supplies pass through to southern Afghanistan on account of his 'hatred' for the Pashtuns.[94]

Goals

Goals for Afghans

As with any conflict that sees the mobilisation of a significant proportion of the fighting population, there were many reasons to participate in the *jihad*, and many outcomes that people sought from it. Different parts of the population rose against the Kabul government at different times and for a variety of reasons. Some tribal uprisings, like the one that took place in the northeastern province of Nuristan, occurred due to the good relations of the tribes in Nuristan with the previous government and their tribal ties to a number of officials.[95] The Dari-speaking parts of Afghanistan rose up significantly earlier than the tribal south and south-east. Olivier Roy argues that this was, in large part, due to the ethnic composition of the government in Kabul that took power in 1978:

...from the beginning the new communist regime made great use of the social structure of the tribes ("Never trust anyone who is not a member of your own *qawm*") in order to maintain itself in power. Although in the early days this policy gained them the support of the Pashtun, it also meant that the non-Pashtun were automatically forced into opposition...[96]

Jihad, which in this case was a formally and religiously sanctioned war to defend the country and the land, was the most pronounced of these reasons.

The first *fatwa* sanctioning *jihad* came from Qazi Amin Hussein, *Hizb-e Islami*'s spiritual advisor, in 1975.[97] While this was distributed around the country and seems to have raised the status of *Hizb-e Islami*, it was not universally answered until local circumstances provoked each particular community. This lack of popular support was one of the reasons for the failure of the 1975 uprising led by Massoud and Hekmatyar, which, in any case, had found no supporters from Kandahar.

The *fatwa*s that were issued in Kandahar all came at the end of 1979 as people fled in large numbers to Pakistan.[98] In the Panjwayi area, where most of the Taliban fronts were located during the subsequent conflict, *fatwa*s were issued by:

- Mullah Khodaydad (from Taloqan)
- Mawlawi Salam Jan Agha (from Zangiabad; Sayyed by *qawm*)
- Mawlawi Shah Mohammad (a judge)
- Mawlawi Mohammad Ali (from Pashmol)[99]

This strong response from local clerics—*mullah*s and *mawlawi*s who originated mostly in the local communities—meant an immediate take-up of the cause among local religious students:

People in Kandahar respect their mullahs. We heard them telling us that this was *jihad*, and we followed their call. It wasn't such a big decision for us at the time. Fronts were formed out of the initial Talib fighters, and it was only later that the tribal elders came in and started up their own parties and wanted an influence on the fighting.[100]

The official call for *jihad* traditionally saw a shift in power towards the mullahs and religious clergy to the detriment of the Khans and other local leaders, whose power had already decreased after being targeted by the government. For the 1980s *jihad*, this was mostly true for the south and south-east.[101]

These religiously-motivated fighters, often very young, were not joining up for ulterior motives: they did so because they were told to. Also, by then, there was relatively little need for discussion as the Afghan Communist government's policies were almost universally disliked by the rural communities—and the vast majority of the population was living in the districts and not in the cities.

Attempts to implement land and social reforms across the country were met with resistance. Legal decrees sought to bring a profound change in the formal and informal organisation of Afghan life—infringing on local marriage customs, land ownership and the education of boys and, more crucially, girls—and, as such, were one step too far for the rural communities.[102]

The reforms decreed by the Taraki regime in late 1978 became symbolic grievances for rural communities, but people were more concerned with the aggressive suppression of local figures of authority. Khans, Maliks, Sayyeds and *mullah*s all started to disappear; in many cases these local leaders were imprisoned and executed. This policy was even more energetically implemented under Hafizullah Amin, Taraki's short-lived successor.[103]

Relatively early on, the idea of using the *jihad* to bring a 'proper' Islamic state to Afghanistan started to be voiced. This supplemented the proximate causes for the *jihad* with a socio-political programme for the post-war period—the country could be remodelled with an appropriate system. Even in the early 1980s, leaders of the mujahedeen parties were making statements to this end. Here is Hekmatyar, for example:

We are fighting *jihad* and we cannot lose. Our strength is our faith. [...] We are fighting the Communists, and we fight all vestiges of colonialism in our country. We will stop only when a pure Islamic state is established.[104]

Of course, Hekmatyar viewed the 1980s war from quite a different perspective than most, and this was one of the features of the Afghan conflict: different people wanted different things.[105] Many would pay lip service to the idea of creating an Islamic state—when one hears or reads interviews with ordinary fighters, one often has the feeling that these answers have been memorised by rote, so similar are they in content—but actions speak louder than words and the post-1990s civil war belied the main actors' pretensions.

There were other reasons to fight during the 1980s. For some it was purely about defending the land. Tribal disputes fed into this calculation: some mujahedeen were sent into Afghanistan to ensure their land was not being 'appropriated' by other tribes.[106] For others, these aforementioned reasons may have played a contributing role but much of the momentum can also be explained by the socio-political and socio-economic dynamics that had developed in the Afghan refugee camps, fostered by external support; a momentum had been established in certain areas whereby it was understood that many of the young men who reached a certain age would return to the country to fight.[107]

These additional motivations are mentioned here not because they fed so much into the calculations of the Taliban fighters of *Loy* Kandahar or the *'mullah* fronts' in *Loya* Paktya, but to demonstrate the variety of reasons as well as the underlying dynamics such as the regular infighting of the different mujahedeen groups.

The broad majority of those fighting—including those on the Taliban fronts—were doing so as a response to the Soviet invasion. This was not an ideological struggle for the broad majority of actors, and the little ideological input that played a role in motivating participants applied only to Afghanistan. There were few if any aspirations among the Afghan mujahedeen to move on to other countries or to Islamise foreign governments.[108] The *jihad* started as a reaction to the Afghan government's policies and the arrival of Soviet forces—ideology was definitely subordinate—but during the 1980s ideas of establishing an Islamic state increased, in part as a product of mobilisation propaganda and input from the outside world.

Goals for Arabs

For the Arabs, because the war in Afghanistan was invariably a separate and abstract event from their lives and those of their fellow countrymen back home, their reasons for coming to fight also varied. *Jihad* was the central motivation, and it was part of the summons that Azzam and others issued. Many of those who arrived at the end of the 1980s sought to answer this call. The key document was Azzam's *fatwa*, published in *Al-Mujtama* in Kuwait in 1983 and later expanded into book form as *The Defense of Muslim Territories*.[109]

If the infidels (kuffar) infringe upon a hand span of Muslim land, jihad becomes the greatest obligation (Fard 'ayn) for its people and for those near by. If they fail to repel the Kuffar due to lack of resources or due to indolence, then the obligatory duty (Fara'id) of jihad spreads to those behind, and carries on spreading in this process, until the jihad is Fard'ayn upon the whole earth from the East to the West.[110]

Azzam explained how the events taking place in Afghanistan represented an attack on 'a stretch of Muslim territory' and that there was an 'individual obligation' for Muslims to respond and defend their territory.[111] He distinguished between the *jihad* in Palestine and that in Afghanistan, finding a certain purity to the latter conflict—'the goal is clear,' and 'in Afghanistan, the cause is led by the mujahedeen, who refuse assistance from unbelieving states, whereas the Palestinian cause has been supported by the Soviet Union.'[112]

This original *fatwa* was later followed by a longer call to Muslims to come to Afghanistan for *jihad*, entitled 'Join the Caravan' and written in April 1987. Of the 'Justifications for Jihad' listed in this document,[113] one is particularly noteworthy, and is distinct from those reasons given by the Afghan mujahedeen:

TO ESTABLISH A SOLID BASE FOR THE EXPANSION OF ISLAM: Establishing a Muslim society on an area of land is as necessary for Muslims as water and air, and this territory will exist only through an organized Islamic movement that wages jihad, in actions and words, and makes of combat its goal and its defense. The Islamic movement will be able to establish an Islamic society only through a general popular jihad. Its movement will be a beating heart and a shining mind, similar to a small detonator that triggers a large explosion, by freeing the Muslim community's contained energy and releasing the sources of good that it contains deep down. [...] The popular jihadist movement, which has a long way to go, given the bitter suffering endured and the magnitude of the sacrifices and losses sustained, can purify souls and elevate them above reality. [...] Islamic society needs to be born, but birth takes place in pain and suffering.[114]

These were ideas that did not feature among the considerations of Taliban fronts in Kandahar. For Afghans, as explained above, *jihad* for the sake of God and for an Islamic state was a fairly ambiguous concept. For the Arabs—and Azzam was one of the key theorists of this group—*jihad* was central to their understanding of Islam and their worldview. Theorists before them had stated that *jihad* was of equivalent value and stature to the five pillars of Islam.[115] Indeed, Azzam later expanded on his idea of a 'solid base' (*qaeda sulba*) in an article for *Al-Jihad* magazine, published in April 1988. Referred to by many as the key theory behind bin Laden's al-Qaeda, Azzam outlined a 'vanguard' who would create 'an Islamic society':

[...] such a society cannot be founded without a movement that has been forged in the fire of trials, and unless its members have developed in the heat of conflict. This movement is the thunderbolt that causes the community's energy to burst forth, and triggers a long jihad in which its members take the role of leaders, pioneers, imams, and spiritual guides. [...] Today, America is attempting to seize the fruits of this marvellous jihad and to prevent legislation on the basis of God's book. The solid base is facing international pressure and global encouragement; but [its members] have refused to bow their heads before the storm, and have decided to carry on their exhausting march along a road of blood, sweat, and tears.[116]

The community Azzam refers to is the *umma*, that of believers, by which he means all Muslims. Azzam's idea is truly transnational. These were wildly different goals from those of the Afghan mujahedeen.

Even if we move from the Arab ideologues to individuals fighting on the ground, we find similar impulses. This, in autumn 1981, was the reason given by an Egyptian jihadi—he was a former major in the Egyptian Army—fighting in south-eastern Afghanistan:

I have come to fight *jihad*, to drive the Communists from Afghanistan, but now that Sadat is dead, I can return to Egypt; and we can drive all corrupt foreigners, like you Americans, away. *Insha'allah.*[117]

And here was the motivation offered by another Egyptian fighting in Kandahar:

We would receive news in Egypt on the Soviet invasion of Afghanistan and the stories of heroism of the mujahedeen. The latter were filmed in their dirty clothes, their long beards and their basic weapons. It was indeed a wonderful scene, and a very impressive one. This moved me a lot and I felt that I was unable to stand idle and watch these men sacrifice their lives and blood for my history and religion. I wanted to join them and take part in their glorious struggle. Besides, it was my duty as a Muslim to do something. I could not watch while other Muslims were being slaughtered and murdered. It was also my duty to help contribute in the creation of an Islamic state and society. I thus posted on my room's wall a picture of a newborn Afghan burned by napalm and screaming from pain and agony. Each and every morning I would take an oath and make a promise to this child that I will fight for him in Afghanistan.[118]

And also read here how one Algerian, Abdullah Anas, found and responded to Azzam's 1983 fatwa:

The new issue of the Kuwaiti magazine *Al-Mujtama'* came out that same day, and it contained a fatwa signed by a group of Muslim ulemaa' from the Arab Gulf, chiefly Imam Ibn Baaz (may Allah have mercy on him), along with Imams from Egypt and other countries. The fatwa declared Jihad in Afghanistan a duty for every Muslim. One of the signatories of the fatwa was Sheikh Abdullah Azzam. I was familiar with the name even before he had joined the Afghan mujahedeen, through his tapes and books, since I belonged to the Islamic Movement on the intellectual and not the organisational level. I was the founder of the Movement and one of its leaders in my region. I bought the magazine and headed to a coffee shop next to the library whose owner was famous for his espresso. After ordering a cup, I started reading the fatwa and its evidence. Amongst threats the fatwa warned against, was the danger of annexing Afghanistan to the republics of the Soviet Union and imposing atheism upon the Afghan people. Evidence made me convinced of the fatwa.[119]

One interviewee from Kandahar who was living in Quetta at the time told how Azzam and Sayyaf organised retreats to the woods for Afghans, bringing them together with Arabs to discuss politics in the Middle East and Islam:

I was invited. We went to the woods somewhere near Lahore. We stayed in tents; one Afghan together with Arabs. There would be discussions and we made posters together: these were against Sadat and Saddam Hussein and other people and they said they were not Muslims. Sheikh Azzam and Sayyaf came and talked. For us it was just a free trip and we got to see Lahore.[120]

Others among the Arabs saw Afghanistan as offering possibilities for training and preparations—away from the intrusive security services of their home countries—which would allow for the formation of a capable force who could then return to tackle their own governments. Afghanistan wasn't Afghanistan; it was a stepping-stone to a better-trained force. They also saw it as a place to regroup—to plan and to learn.[121]

One Arab who was closely involved in the training of Arabs (particularly at the end of the 1980s) was Mustafa bin Abd al-Qadir Setmariam Nasar, better known as Abu Mus'ab al-Suri. He had arrived in Peshawar in 1987 following a catastrophic experience back in Syria where the Islamist group that he was involved in had been dismantled by Syrian government forces.[122]

In his autobiographic accounts of his own life, he said that he and his companions 'left the Syrian cause because there existed no opportunity to revive it and we turned to the Afghan cause instead.'[123] He participated in some of the major battles, but seems to have spent a lot of his time back in Pakistan where he contributed to the military and ideology of the Arab mujahedeen. He also worked on a new framework from which to reconsider jihad and the various groups that were in Peshawar at the time.

[I] trained some of [al-Qaida's] first vanguards. I taught various military and organizational skills at its camps and also at the general camps for the Arab-Afghans, in particular in my fields of speciality, explosive engineering, special operations, and urban warfare. I had been highly trained in these disciplines in Egypt, Jordan and Iraq.[124]

Al-Zawahiri, the deputy head of al-Qaeda, listed the opportunities for training as one of the key benefits of the 1980s *jihad* in his autobiographical account, *Knights Under the Prophet's Banner*:

That jihad was a training course of the utmost importance to prepare Muslim mujahedeen to wage their awaited battle against the superpower that now has sole dominance over the globe, namely, the United States. It also gave young Muslim mujahedeen—Arabs, Pakistanis, Turks, and Muslims from Central and East Asia—a great opportunity to get acquainted with each other on the land of Afghan jihad through their comradeship-at-arms against the enemies of Islam. In this way the mujahedeen young men and the jihadist movements came to know each other closely, exchanged expertise, and learned to understand their brethren's problems.[125]

Azzam also saw the value in having a secure location where his 'solid base' could receive an 'education in jihad' (*tarbiyya jihadiyya*) and build up the military force necessary for a reconquest of Muslim territories.'[126] This contrasted with the Afghan mujahedeen, who sought to expel the Soviet forces from their country and then install an appropriate replacement government.

Others had arrived in an expression of Islamic solidarity, both with each other as well as with the Afghans. Particularly by the end of the 1980s, the Afghan *jihad* had taken on a symbolic value in the minds of many Arabs and other foreigners following an unprecedented public word-of-mouth campaign in the Muslim world. Azzam had also recrafted the *jihad* for Arabs as being primarily about the entire Muslim *umma* and not about individual nations:

In theory as in practice, Azzam promoted a form of Islamic internationalism that represented a marked change in relation to the rather nationalist orientation espoused by other radical Islamist groups before the 1980s. Azzam's obsession with Afghanistan was due to his great love not for the Afghan nation, but for the Muslim community: the *umma*. Azzam wanted Afghanistan to be the solid base from which to launch the reconquest of other Muslim territories. As he wrote: 'Palestine, Bukhara, Lebanon, Chad, Eritrea, Somalia, the Philippines, Burma, South Yemen, Tashkent, and Andalusia are still left.'[127]

Of course, many of those who arrived in Peshawar during the 1980s were likely to face severe repercussions if they were to try to return to their home countries. Al-Zawahiri is a good example of this. After the assassination of al-Sadat and the arrest of Egyptian Islamists, he was released in 1984 after having served a three-year sentence in Egypt. In the words of one of his friends from that time:

Zawahiri could not have stayed in Egypt after the authorities discovered his activities, as he relied mainly upon their remaining secret. [...] Another reason that Zawahiri did not return to Egypt is that, through the pain of torture, he was forced to confess against his friends, followers and disciples. He even tipped the police off about the whereabouts of one of his best friends Esam al-Qamari. Zawahiri might have thought that his leadership had lost its credibility in the eyes of his disciples because of this.[128]

A number of Arabs like al-Zawahiri could not return home, but with an ever growing propaganda machine in Pakistan that called for militant action abroad, more and more ex-jihadists faced problems in their home countries, even those who were not carrying out operations against their home governments. In an effort to curb the activities of small groups and cells, Arab governments would often themselves take radical measures, rounding up hundreds (at times thousands) of Islamists who often had nothing to do with the specific event but were merely part of the wider world of active political Islam.[129]

Functioning partly as a symbol of this new unencumbered and separate life, one of the first things 'Afghan Arabs' would receive upon arrival in Peshawar was a new name. It seems this was as much a question of security as it was a kind of spiritual re-birth—into a new life and world of *jihad*:

Sheikh Abdullah [Azzam] was the one to give me at that time the name 'Abdullah Anas.' I used to name myself, Anas, in Algeria because I liked it, despite my name being 'Bou Juma.' In Peshawar, Sheikh Abdullah started introducing me to mujahedeen saying: 'This is Anas. Abdullah Anas.' He turned to me and asked: 'Abdullah Anas?' I answered: 'It's fine, Abdullah Anas.'[130]

Maktab al-Khidmaat, or the Services Office, was founded by Azzam. Bin Laden and several others were part of it but arrived at different times. For Azzam, the issue of Palestine and Afghanistan both constituted *fard 'ayn*, a *jihad* that is the collective obligation incumbent upon all Muslims.[131] Azzam's concept and definition of the *jihad* were widely disputed and discussed, and he himself sought approval from the Saudi religious scholar, Abdul Aziz bin Baz.[132]

While bin Laden and Azzam were in agreement about the general idea of *jihad*, they differed in how they saw the duty of the Afghan Arabs and foreigners in general regarding the Afghan *jihad* and other struggles. This difference became apparent in the mid-1980s. Azzam's concept prevailed and the role he saw for himself and other foreign Muslims in Afghanistan shaped the Services Office under him. While Azzam helped Arabs and other foreign Muslims who wanted to join the *jihad*—providing training and dispatching them to different mujahedeen factions—he was concerned mainly with fundraising.[133] The latter became the largest part of the Services Office network, which included a sophisticated propaganda branch that produced magazines, books and tapes, held events and opened offices and recruited fundraisers and helpers worldwide. The Services Office also facilitated the visits of journalists.[134] Its flagship publication, *al-Jihad* magazine, was circulated throughout many countries.[135] While he supported the jihad against the Soviet Union, Azzam promoted the teachings of Islam and regarded the Afghan Arabs as having a support function. The non-Afghans who were sent into Afghanistan were concerned as much with teaching Islam and the *Qu'ran* as facilitating logistics, war materiel and fighting. Azzam not only tried to help the fight but was also concerned about the growing factionalism among the Afghan mujahedeen and envisioned the role of the Afghan Arabs as being to mediate between the different groups, to find common ground and later to broker peace.[136]

During the 1980s, Azzam went on numerous fundraising trips around the world and set up structures to disseminate his propaganda and channel funds back to the Services Office in Peshawar. In America, al-Khifa, a Muslim organisation, was set up with branches in Atlanta, Boston, Chicago, Pittsburgh and Tucson.[137] The Services Office's presence in America was informal but early on manifested itself in the formation of the al-Khifa and CARE International[138] organisations that promoted and raised funds for several groups around the world.[139] It had strong ties to the aid community and the wider world of Muslim organisations. Azzam had been a member of the Muslim Brotherhood in Syria and Jordan, and had frequently visited the family of Sayyed Qutb while studying at al-Azhar in Cairo. His strong ties to the Muslim Brotherhood would help the Services Office with contacts in Saudi Arabia. The Kingdom had become a safe haven for Muslim brothers who soon took significant positions within its newly founded charities and organisations, and who also supported Azzam's notion of *fard 'ayn* and *jihad*.[140]

The Services Office under Azzam in principle set up the funding structures that would later be inherited by bin Laden and other militant Islamic groups. The Services Office, like many of its affiliates, blurred the line between humanitarian support and active participation in the fight, which is a direct result of Azzam's interpretation of *jihad*. The affiliates of the Services Office, along with many other Islamic organisations, would hold fundraising events featuring mujahedeen speakers or presentations with videos and photos. They would also distribute magazines and leaflets outside mosques, collecting small donations and selling books in order to raise money. Not all donors even in the early 1980s would be aware that they were supporting armed militants. The blurred nature of activities of the organisations meant that funding that was intended for humanitarian ends could easily end up purchasing weapons and organising military training camps for volunteers.[141]

Ideological Progression

The war against the Soviet Union lasted ten years and was on many levels a fundamentally different experience for the different Afghan groups as opposed to the foreigners who took part in it. The war transformed society, destroying much of what was known and valued by Afghan communities. An entire generation grew up as refugees, or fighters, with hundreds of thousands of lives lost and their lands destroyed.[142]

For the foreigners who had followed the call of *jihad* to Afghanistan, the war was a catalyst for their ideas; this was particularly true for the core of jihadists who had long engaged in an intellectual discussion about the state and Islam and had fought against their home governments, often suffering long prison sentences and torture. As will be explored in this section, the transformation from a belief into a revolutionary approach, a decapitating strategy in the form of a coup and assassination of the leadership of their home countries, would give way to a new view, spurred by the idea of the unity of the *umma*; they would come to find a new enemy.

For Afghans, the destruction of their society would give prominence to the social ties forged during the *jihad*. These networks of friendship, based on the loyalty and the sacrifices that were made during the war, would form the new backbone of their communities, with their complicated tribal, religious and ideological mixture of identity.

The ideological differences and varying motivations amongst the Afghans were often reinforced by the experience of the *jihad* and directly translated into the collapse of the mujahedeen government and the disintegration of Afghanistan. The ideological war that had begun in the 1970s and earlier was reinforced by the alliances made and the support given by external actors.

For the Taliban

By the end of the 1980s, though, some of these shifts started to be foregrounded as the conflict started to wind down. For the Taliban, three things seem pertinent to mention.

They had spent many years together, not always in the same group but almost always in some form of close proximity or contact. They were young, and they had experienced fierce combat. Many of them were orphans—not because of the war, but more likely because of the very low life expectancy among Afghans then (and now)—and the war instilled an unshakeable bond among the mujahedeen alumni.

As students before the war, they may have studied the principles of Islam, faith, commitment to one's religion and so on, but the war gave them practical experience and tested them in all of these matters. They emerged from Panjwayi at the end of the 1980s as graduates of a programme of study that was not just theoretical but that had an emotional and practical resonance. Moreover, the experience of the 1980s *jihad* would inform their later decisions when they attempted to govern the country.

The *jihad* also gave them an idea of social transformation, that change was possible and that men could influence their own path. In the past, society was relatively static and the way to move forward was through exploiting the state to advance one's own position in the community.[143] The *jihad* showed that there were other ways, that men who came from nothing could become commanders, and that unity makes one strong.

The Islamic courts that operated throughout the south and whose judges, such as Mawlawi Pasanai, would come to play an important ideological role for the Taliban movement, symbolised the general shift: religious clergy, from the village *mullah* to the *'alim*, had increased in importance, a change that normally occurs in Afghanistan during times of *jihad* or war against an external enemy. Underlying this process is the unifying quality of Islam: while tribes and clans might fight against each other and feud for centuries, the common ground that can be found among them, particularly during times of great suffering, is their common belief.[144]

The Taliban's courts, too, were important in reinforcing the fact that they saw themselves as the custodians of Islamic justice—as their teachers had been before them—and the *jihad* enabled them to apply their interpretation of these precepts in a hitherto unprecedented manner given that the state had traditionally assumed some of these functions.

The transformative and traumatic impact of Afghanistan's *jihad*, in particular in southern Afghanistan, gave rise to new stronger networks forged throughout. The answer to Olivier Roy's question posed in an article published in 1995[145] (why did the Taliban suddenly become by far the most coordinated and mobilised distinct group?) is to be found on the battlefields of the Afghan *jihad*.

For the Arabs and Foreign Jihadists

These shifts were more pronounced for the Arabs at the time, and many started to think about their future. The next chapter will address the ideological shift and debates back in Peshawar, but since August 1988 saw the founding meeting[146] of what would eventually make up 'al-Qaeda,' it is worth briefly commenting here.

Azzam had started to outline an idea of how he envisioned the role of the Afghan Arabs once the anti-Soviet war was won. The foreign contingent had started to think about their future as far back as 1986, when it became clear that the Soviet Union was looking for a way to exit the conflict. His plan for a 'solid base' or *qaeda sulba*, for instance, contained an implicit criticism of the Egyptian jihadis, who always sought to focus on the 'near enemy.' Hegghammer notes that one of Azzam's central contributions was to foreground this change from the 'near enemy' to the 'far enemy.'[147]

Nevertheless, the Afghan Arabs, with few exceptions, were still predominantly concerned with their home governments and the fight they had left to join the Afghan *jihad* in this period. While it is difficult to verify, it seems clear, based on their actions in the early 1990s, that only a small number of the Afghan Arabs would have perceived themselves as a truly transnational vanguard fighting for the *umma*.

Interactions

The *jihad* transformed the relationship between Afghanistan and the rest of the world, in particular its relationship with the Arab world. Prior to the war it was largely the young men from the urban centres—Kabul University and a number of intellectuals—that had forged ties to institutions like al-Azhar, gained a Western education or spent extended amounts of time in the Middle East for study. The majority of the religious clergy—in particular the rural *mullahs*—looked almost exclusively towards India and the Deobandi madrassas for education and guidance.[148]

The *jihad* changed these relationships: the Afghan struggle took centre stage not only in the United States' Cold War with the Soviet Union, but also as a rallying point for many Islamists throughout the Muslim world.[149] As outlined before, these interactions were selective and mostly built upon the few ties that existed before the *jihad*. Afghan society, as is the case today, was deeply fragmented. Even though the population throughout Afghanistan joined the resistance, there were significant differences in their ties to foreign countries and the increasing number of Arab volunteers that flocked there and to Pakistan. More often than not, Afghans and Arabs clashed over ideological matters. While for the Arabs the *jihad* was a straightforward religious war, for the Afghans the motivations and underlying views on the struggle were often much more complicated, representing the intricate and complex nature of local identity.

69

Afghan interactions with foreign jihadists and influences during the 1980s were characterised by a mixture of respect and suspicion. While they welcomed the presence of the Arabs (who sometimes brought money and new technologies with them), their presence was not unquestioningly accepted. Once again, the south differed from the south-east or the east, and the broad majority of the Taliban fronts and fighters were not exposed to strong Arab influences—whether ideological, cultural or otherwise. Those who were fighting in the same area as the Arabs seem to have been more warily ambivalent than accepting.[150]

In particular, ideology seems to have been a bone of contention, even on occasion precipitating violence. Faraj explains how the idea of 'Wahhabism' as a secondary enemy took hold in Kandahar through radio broadcasts on the BBC and from Iranian channels:

If you were to ask any mujahed what he thought about the leader of the party to which he belonged, he would say without hesitation: he is a Wahhabi. Sometimes, he would even volunteer to tell us that the party leader is a Wahhabi without being asked. Whenever we inquired: 'So why are you fighting under his command?' he would say, 'We will get rid of the Russians and the communists first and then we will fight and eliminate the Wahhabis.' This was not only the opinion of the common people but also that of the majority of the young leaders. What was odd was that the party leaders facing accusations of Wahhabism in Afghanistan were the same ones facing accusations of Sufism in the Arab Peninsula which reveals there was a global conspiracy to fuel strife between the mujahedeen and those sympathising with them in the Arab countries and at the same time fuel strife between the commanders and their followers among the mujahedeen. This situation required patience and intelligence to deal with these conspiracies being weaved to generate dispute, to hijack ten years of jihad, the blood of a million and a half martyrs and a countless number of handicapped, widows and orphans.[151]

There seems to have been some wariness on the part of Afghans as to whether to allow the Arabs to assume all the risks that they did. It is possible this was an order directly from Sayyaf—who seems to have funnelled most of the Arabs who came to southern Afghanistan—but eventually the Arabs managed to persuade their Afghan hosts to relent.

As noted above, the Taliban on the fronts were both receptive to the Arabs as people and wary of their ideological stances. One interviewee noted that the Arabs often brought money and that this was enough to smooth over these disagreements.[152] There is perhaps a precedent here for the way bin Laden deceived the Taliban during the 1990s, whether with actual money or just the promise of future projects and donations.

At least one account by a prominent commander who fought alongside Haqqani in the 1980s holds that all Arabs fought under the command of Afghans. This would only change in the mid-1980s as bin Laden sought to establish independent Arab contingents in greater Paktya.[153] Others had no bad memories of the Arabs' presence in Kandahar together with the Taliban fronts. This is the recollection of one Taliban fighter who fought with Arabs in Arghandab in the 1980s:

They had habits like ours. Their prayer and worship was the same as ours. But sometimes they had different prayer habits—their movements and so on. But generally in Kandahar they were doing the same things as us: eating, drinking, swimming. Many of them wanted to learn and speak Pashtu, even.[154]

From the Arab perspective, Afghanistan is almost always referred to as a place where the religious beliefs of the local people leave a lot to be desired, but should be tolerated. Here is Azzam in 1987:

Afghans are like other human beings, with their ignorance and defects, and so we must not expect to find perfection in them. The difference between the Afghans and the others, however, is that the Afghans have refused to stand by and watch as their religion is dishonoured.

[...] The Afghan people are ignorant, educated in the Hanafi school alone. It has no rival in Afghanistan, which is why many Afghans believe that whatever is not mentioned in Hanafi jurisprudence does not exist in Islam. The absence of other schools in their country has bred in them a fierce attachment to Hanafism; whoever seeks to accomplish jihad with the Afghans, therefore, must respect the teachings and rulings of that school.[155]

Faraj also relates how Sayyaf and Abu Khabib (the well-known head of Sayyaf's *Ittehad-e Islami* offices in Quetta) both warned Arabs coming to southern Afghanistan to tread carefully over these ideological issues. Faraj and other Arabs even adopted the Hanafi prayer customs of their Afghan mujahedeen colleagues in an attempt to win favour.[156]

Here, for example, Abdullah Anas cautions Azzam on some of the problems that he faced on a trip to visit Afghan mujahedeen commanders in northern Afghanistan:

The Afghan people are fanatics for the Hanafi sect and do not know anything about other sects or confessions. Therefore, any Arab who wishes to enter Afghanistan must be aware of that. First: preachers to be recruited must be able to call for Islam [*da'wa*] wisely. They must be smart and polite enough, for not every preacher is good for the mission. They have to be able to deal with a complex and superficial society such as the Afghan one.[157]

The Arab presence in the early 1980s was quite different from that at the end of the decade. Bin Laden had by then set up independent contingents in the south-east where Arabs could visit and train with relatively little interaction with Afghans. The Arabs were, in any case, on a separate ideological path by that time and tried to stay aloof from the Afghan mujahedeen and their power struggle following the withdrawal of the Soviet Union.[158]

Outside Stimuli

Pakistan

The histories of Pakistan and Afghanistan have been intertwined since the founding of the two countries and the establishment of the Durand Line by the government of British Colonial India and Abdur Rahman Khan, Emir of Afghanistan, on 12 November 1893.[159] The shared border of 2,430 km that splits Pashtunistan down the middle of an otherwise culturally, linguistically and ethnically homogenous area has been a source of trouble and dispute ever since and features heavily in both countries' domestic and foreign policy decisions.

During the war against the Soviet Union the majority of refugees that fled from Afghanistan went to Pakistan, which ended up housing more than 3 million Afghan refugees along its borders.[160] Pakistan developed considerable leverage over the Afghan *mujahedeen* early on, not only by hosting them and providing the safe havens from which they could operate, but also by controlling most of the funding and war materiel. Pakistan played an important role in manipulating and organising Afghan mujahedeen political party alignments, for example.[161]

Pakistan was following a long-term strategy in its own interests, originally to prevent the Soviets from gaining a port on the Persian Gulf or Indian Ocean. Having fought several wars with India, Pakistan's goal was a government in Kabul that would be immune to Indian influence and close to Pakistan. It appeared to be in Islamabad's interest to back the more Islamist mujahedeen factions, such as Hekmatyar's *Hizb-e Islami*, Khalis's *Hizb-e Islami*, and Sayyaf's *Ittehad-e Islami*, all of which would find themselves close to Pakistan and would play a significant role in Afghanistan's future.[162]

We should, however, be wary of ascribing universal control or direction to 'Pakistani policy.' At the time, all accounts point to a clear shape to their interactions with the Afghan and Arab mujahedeen, yet there were factions within the government and security services that disagreed about the direction in which policy was taking them, and it is only with the benefit of hindsight that it is possible to talk about 'Pakistan' taking one policy line or another.[163] Furthermore, the issue of Pakistan having total control over the Afghan mujahedeen as well as the foreigners fighting alongside them is still a matter of dispute. This stems from the very nature of how the mujahedeen groups operated, as well as the oft-cited resistance of Afghan mujahedeen and others to being controlled by 'outside' influences.

For Pakistan's President, General Zia ul-Haq, the Soviet invasion of Afghanistan presented an opportunity on several levels. The United States was looking for a regional partner who could facilitate the implementation of what would become their biggest covert operation to date. Pakistan was not only the logical choice but almost the only option. General Zia saw all of this and made his demands to the United States. After initially rejecting an American offer for $400 million of support out of hand, he finally secured 'a package of economic and military assistance [...] worth $3.2 billion over a six-year period.'[164] The invasion and his provision of funding for the mujahedeen groups also served as a foil against domestic Islamist groups who had suggested that General Zia's purported Islamic agenda was 'lukewarm.'[165]

Pakistan received several billion dollars between 1979 and 1990, and conveyed this money to the Afghan mujahedeen groups in support of its agenda. Alongside its long-term objective, Pakistan forced the various Afghan mujahedeen fronts into the command of seven mujahedeen factions, channelling funds and training exclusively towards them.[166] As preferences and allegiances shifted over the course of the war, individual fronts in Afghanistan would switch alliances, in effect following the money and access to weapons and training.

Pakistan's relationship with Islamist groups has been dictated to a great extent by its own historical trajectory. It is home to a large Sunni majority as well as the second largest population of Shi'i Muslims in the world, and has faced almost constant conflict with India since its inception. Thus Pakistan has often reached out to Islamist networks that were regarded as readily available tools to be used clandestinely in the Kashmir conflict, or as reserve troops to be mobilised in times of crisis.[167] Consequently, while Pakistan had always supported groups like the *Jama'at-e Islami* and the *Tablighi Jamaat*, it was the

1980s that saw a core of specifically jihadi groups being founded with state sponsorship and funding.[168] Pakistan encouraged the formation of these groups not only to realise a Soviet defeat in Afghanistan, but also for deployment in its long-standing dispute with India over Kashmir.[169]

With the Partition of India in 1947 into the Union of India and the Dominion of Pakistan (of which Bangladesh was still a part initially until 1971), Kashmir remained independent; by and large a Muslim enclave, it was ruled by a Hindu ruler. Conflict arose almost instantly, with local tribes located in Pakistan and inhabitants of Kashmir rising up against the Hindu ruler who in turn reached out to India.[170]

All of the jihadi groups founded in Pakistan during the 1980s came with an active Kashmiri agenda. Following the withdrawal of Soviet troops in 1989, most of the Pakistani jihadis that had operated in Afghanistan were reassigned (or reassigned themselves) to focus on Kashmir.[171] The pre-eminent group in this respect was *Harakat ul-Jihad ul-Islami*, founded in either 1979 or 1980 by three Deobandi madrassa students: Qari Saifullah Akhtar, Ilyas Kashmiri and Mawlana Abdul Samad Sial. It was initially called *Jamiat Ansar ul-Afghaneen* ("Party of the Friends of the Afghan people"); it helped Afghan refugees during the jihad and also mobilised Deobandi religious students in Pakistan to fight in Afghanistan.[172] *Harakat ul-Mujahedeen* was a prominent offshoot, founded in 1984 following a dispute over the leadership of the group.[173] Kashmir was at the centre of their agenda, particularly during the 1990s.

Markaz Da'wa wal Irshad was founded in 1985 by Abdullah Azzam, Hafez Saeed, Dr Zafar Iqbal (Abu Hamza) and Hafiz Abdul Rahman Makki, a congeries of Pakistan and Arab interests which hinted at what was originally posited at a more internationalist Islamist stance than the other Pakistani jihadi groups of the time. Azzam's oft-cited involvement is interesting in this respect, although many suggest that he was most important as a conduit for funding.[174] By the late 1980s or early 1990s, *Lashkar-i Taiba* had also been established as a militant arm of *Markaz Da'wa wal Irshad*. Their agenda was simple: 'it intends to Islamise Kashmir and India, then embark on global conquest with the goal of restoring the Caliphate.'[175]

Another important Pakistani jihadi group, *Sipah-e Sahaba Pakistan* or SSP, was established in 1985. Although local factors—disputes over land and class— seem to have played an important role as a catalyst in its early days, the group's agenda soon took on heavily sectarian tones, and SSP became well-known for its attacks on Shi'i communities.[176] Another heavily militant sectarian group,

Lashkar-e Jhangvi, in turn sprang from the ranks of SSP. Many, if not most, of these groups were independently established but they all eventually came to be funded and sponsored by Pakistani state organisations. These groups formed a locus of expertise and support which went on to define the jihadi universe in Pakistan up to the present day (in various configurations, and allowing for the frequent splintering and name-changing that was so common).

The 1980s saw them establish their basic structures and build up a foundation of support. Members fought throughout Afghanistan,[177] shaping and mentoring a generation of young men who nowadays form the leadership cadre of the Pakistani jihadi movement. Some of the well-known key figures are in hiding or keeping a low profile, but there were many other lesser members of that generation who gained important combat experience in Afghanistan and who continue to play a role in Pakistan.[178]

These Pakistani groups were fighting all over Afghanistan, although regions bordering Pakistan saw more involvement. This was true of Mawlawi Jamil ur-Rahman[179] with his Salafist mini-state in Kunar province, as well as of the south-east greater Paktya region where Jalaluddin Haqqani held sway.[180] There was also a significant involvement of Pakistani fighters in southern Afghanistan, although the precise extent of this is difficult to determine.

As previously noted, the Pakistani groups seemed to absorb much of the ideological import of the Arab jihadis, although it is less clear how much the Pakistanis (aside from in specific cases) transferred to the Afghans, especially beyond the world of religious education where Pakistani influence was felt most keenly.

In southern Afghanistan, the few written accounts that exist attest to the presence of Pakistanis on the fronts, although not in any overwhelming numbers. Oral testimony from Kandahar also seems to play down the involvement of Pakistanis, although this is perhaps to be expected from former Afghan mujahedeen who are somewhat loath to share the glory of the Soviet defeat with other fighters. Interviewees did, however, identify certain Taliban from the south as having been directly linked to the ISI.[181] It is impossible to verify such claims, and linking people to the ISI or Pakistani funding is a common and easy enough slur in the present day for these claims, while not to be dismissed, to be viewed with a certain scepticism.

For the core group that would become 'the Taliban movement' in the mid-1990s, there seems to have been relatively little contact with Pakistanis— and certainly those of non-Pashtun descent.[182] This is an important point and distinction to make: the Pakistani mujahedeen that the Afghan Taliban came into contact with were fellow Pashtun Deobandis rather than Punjabi Salafists.[183]

In the east and south-east, groups affiliated with Sayyaf, Khalis and Hekmatyar played host to both Arab and Pakistani jihadis. This was also true for Haqqani, for although he was affiliated with Khalis he was de facto a key player on his own terms, which can be explained by the fact that his followers often were from his own tribe. There was thus significant interaction between the three Afghan factions and the Pakistani groups, most of whom cut their teeth on the fronts of greater Paktya.[184]

For the Afghan mujahedeen groups themselves, Pakistan was no less involved. The ISI administered the flow of money and arms from the (primarily) American and Saudi state donors to the political parties, dividing it up as and how they saw fit.

This meant that most of the funds and resources went to the Islamist groups—especially Hekmatyar's *Hizb-e Islami*—and more moderate or nationalist groups were sidelined and had to make do with far less—Gailani's *Mahaz-e Milli*, for example, with its agenda to restore Zahir Shah to the throne. This policy was condoned by the United States, who also saw the value in the more Islamist elements, believing that they made bigger gains on the battlefield and fought harder.[185]

One interviewee—a senior commander fighting with Haqqani in the southeast—explained his perception of where funds were going:

It was something like this: 22% of the funds went to Sayyaf, 18% went to Hekmatyar, 17–18% went to Rabbani, 14–15% to Yunis Khalis, 13–14% to Nabi Mohammadi, and the final 2–3% went to Gailani and Mujadidi's parties. The thing is that the Salafi ideology was very strong among the Arabs at this time and so they weren't very supportive of the *mullah* movements or the *pir* movements (Gailani and Mujadidi and so on). That's why the *mullah*s didn't get much money from the Arabs. ...they didn't trust them.[186]

Pakistani accounts of the funding of the Afghan mujahedeen during the 1980s deny this unequal distribution. The ISI head of the Afghan operation, Brigadier Muhammad Yousaf, for example, plays up Pakistan's role in working to achieve unity among the Afghan leaders and to find a way to support them equitably.[187]

Pakistan's most lasting contribution to the *jihad* was the education of a generation of mujahedeen in the refugee camps in Pakistan; this schooling in the makeshift ISI training camps was in military matters, but most enduringly it was the universalisation of *jihad* and the mobilisation of society for the war in

Afghanistan (mainly through madrassa education) that has lasted to the present in various forms.[188] This was not Pakistan's influence alone—significant Saudi funding and support also played its part—but overwhelming state resources were brought to bear on this sector, the after-effects of which we may observe in the present day.

For the southern Taliban fronts, Pakistani influence was felt as an indirect presence rather than an active shaping force. Many received training in Pakistan by the ISI[189] but this was often the extent of the relationship. It is well-known, for example, that Kandahar saw a massive shift in political-party allegiance around 1986—this was especially true for the Taliban—when mujahedeen fighting for *Harakat-e Enqelab-e Islami* shifted to support Sayyaf's *Ittehad-e Islami*. Sayyaf had just received a massive influx of funds and arms, and everyone shifted support to gain a piece of the pie. Allegiance was conditional, and the nationalist feelings of the southern mujahedeen were never far from the surface.[190]

Pakistan, and in particular the ISI, had a significant impact on the Afghan *jihad*. Its success in securing a position as sole liaison between foreign donors and the mujahedeen gave it considerable leverage over the mujahedeen factions. As outlined above, however, much of the relationship was uneasy. Pakistan pursued its own goals using this position. This was recognised by the Afghan mujahedeen, in particular the sections that received less support, and it also applied to much of the Taliban leadership. The ISI, furthermore, while having demonstrated significant continuity in its policies, is in itself not a homogenous or static organisation. Individuals and groups within the ISI played significant roles in the relationship with the Afghan mujahedeen.[191]

Saudi Arabia and the Arab States

The funding provided by Saudi Arabia and other Arab states was no less important than that given by the CIA. In fact, most accounts seem to suggest that the Saudis had even fewer safeguards against money falling into different hands than the ones they and the United States intended to reach. 'We don't do operations,' the former head of Saudi intelligence, Turki al-Faisal, once said. 'We don't know how. All we know how to do is write checks.'[192]

Saudi Arabia—and the other Gulf states—had many reasons to be interested in the Soviet invasion of Afghanistan. First of all, they didn't believe that Moscow had a strategic interest in Afghanistan itself, but rather in its possible use as a platform for further expansion south. If the Soviets managed to have a direct route into a warm-water port, it would pose a direct threat to Saudi political and trade influence in the Gulf.[193]

The Saudi ruling class were incensed about Soviet communist ideals expanding into their sphere of influence. In the wake of the Iranian Revolution, Saudi Arabia sought to stem the influence of Iran and Shi'i Islam, and they hoped to achieve this by funding and encouraging the Afghan Sunni mujahedeen as an Islamic bulwark in the region. The hinterland Arab states around Saudi Arabia were increasingly susceptible to communist influences and funding, which was seen as a threat.

Funding for the Afghan mujahedeen in turn was part of a Saudi plan to disseminate its own particular brand of Islam—Wahhabism—through a lavish, state-funded programme. In 1971, for example, the Saudi King had offered the head of Cairo's al-Azhar seminary $100 million to 'finance a new [such] campaign in the Muslim world.'[194]

Saudi Arabia's involvement in the Afghan jihad drew upon precedents that had begun decades before the Soviet invasion of Afghanistan. To counter Nasser's pan-Arab nationalism, King Faisal promoted his own model of pan-Islamism. In the 1960s he set up institutions that aimed to foster cooperation, mutual solidarity and religious awareness in the Muslim world: the Muslim World League (MWL) was founded in May 1972, followed by the Organisation of the Islamic Conference (OIC), in 1969. These were involved in an array of cultural, educational and humanitarian activities, and offered the meta-structures for smaller organisations to operate under.[195] Moreover, they were also heavily influenced by the Muslim Brotherhood. Many members of the Brotherhood had fled from Egypt and Syria and dominated the new structures, forming the underlying links to more militant networks.[196]

The OIC had the power to set up financial institutions, which became particularly significant after the 1973 oil crisis that gave OAPEC vast amounts of hard currency. These new groups brought a pronounced focus on the suffering of the *umma*, the unity of all Muslims, and a focus on humanitarian aid and disaster relief, as well as special attention to support for Palestine.[197]

The concept of the *umma* and Muslim solidarity became the justification for a whole range of different activities, including military support through weapons purchases; in 1948 Prince Faisal had set up the 'Committee for Aid to Palestine' that helped to arm the Palestinian struggle, while after 1967, the Kingdom started a number of initiatives to raise funds for Palestine.[198] Saudi Arabia would go on to stage major fundraising initiatives for events like the Israeli invasion of Lebanon in 1982, the intifada in 1987 and later on in support of different causes such as Afghanistan, Chechnya and Bosnia. The Saudi Arabian initiative increasingly took on a military dimension, supported by several OIC members in conflict with other non-Muslim states. This increase in support was an outcome of the media campaign by Saudi-funded institutions to make known Muslim suffering throughout the world.

Prince Faisal's early efforts to promote Pan-Islamism created a funding structure, as well as established support as a publicly acceptable and expected practice. The organisations, institutions and the network of fundraisers were put in place and directed their attention and financial resources to different crises and projects. From the very beginning, however, a significant subsection of individuals involved in Saudi Arabia's fundraising network had militant Islamist leanings and a contact network stemming back to their previous affiliations with the Muslim Brotherhood. These underlying structures and contact networks played a significant role in directing funds.

For Afghanistan, Saudi Arabia reached an agreement in July 1980 to match American contributions dollar-for-dollar,[199] and they honoured this commitment—by 1985 each state was paying $250 million per annum in support of the Afghan mujahedeen. Saudi contributions extended beyond this dollar-for-dollar agreement. This took the form of further state donations, pledges by charitable organisations as well as millions in popular donations collected outside mosques:

Imams at mosques were encouraged to deliver fiery sermons exhorting young men to join the fight. Large boxes were placed in mosque courtyards to collect donations from worshippers. I recall being at the mosque on Fridays when thousands were present, and seeing how eagerly they pressed around these boxes to deposit their offerings.[200]

Some have even claimed that official and direct state donations (from all international actors) made up as little as 25% of the total external financial input to the Afghan *jihad*.[201]

In many ways, it was not just the level of Saudi funding which became problematic in itself, but the lack of any real way of monitoring where this money ended up, as Saudi and American operatives involved in the covert funding operation have subsequently acknowledged.[202] The prominent Saudi Sheikh Abdul Aziz bin Baz was appointed to manage the charitable donations in Saudi Arabia, but there was little formal control over the process.

Sayyaf, the Afghan head of *Ittehad-e Islami*, became the main recipient of Saudi largesse, in part because of his fluency in Arabic. He even changed his name following a Saudi request that it conform to Wahhabi principles.[203] He was, to a large degree, a Saudi creation. Rubin has noted that Sayyaf had a marginal popular support base of his own apart from that attracted purely by the large sums of money to which he had access.[204]

There seems to have been relatively little ideological conditionality imposed alongside the official government funding; rather, it was the funding itself that was expected to offer ideological influence. If the objective of this Saudi funding was to encourage Afghans to switch from Hanafism to the Wahhabi strain of Hanbalism, however, this goal was left unrealised.

Many Afghan mujahedeen—barring some prominent, if isolated, instances—seem to have been incredibly conscious of these religious tensions, especially so in the south. Arab ideological influence was most keenly felt in the east and south-east, where it was the Afghan Arabs who seem to have gradually transferred ideas to certain local groups on both sides of the border. This process was deepened and accelerated post-September 11 in the tribal areas of Pakistan, as will be explored below.

Above all, though, it was the links and contacts made between Saudis—both state and non-state actors—during the 1980s that were the enduring influences in terms of the relationship between the Taliban and al-Qaeda. The Taliban fronts in southern Afghanistan were not in any way singled out (or probably even identified as such) during the *jihad*, but the contacts between the Saudi ruling family and Sayyaf, for example, were to pave the way for the return of bin Laden to Afghanistan in 1996.[205]

4

RETHINK (1990–1994)

Many of us. ...withdrew after Dr. Najib's defeat because we were not interested in the war booty. ...When we saw that things became worse day by day and factional fighting increased, our central commander Mullah Muhammad Omar Akhund started from Quetta to bring together the Taleban in order to establish peace in Afghanistan.

A Talib who fought during the 1980s[1]

They didn't think they would come into power. It wasn't even the vague glimmer of a dream for them.

Talib in Khost on the 'mullah fronts' of the 1980s[2]

Most if not all [jihadi] movements had a presence there. Peshawar and Afghanistan became a true university [...] This was a turning point in Muslim history. [...] It was a kind of birthplace. Much of what you see today is a result of this period.

Abu Mus'ab al-Suri on the late 1980s/early 1990s[3]

The United States and Western nations could not ignore the jihad against India in Kashmir so soon after supporting a similar struggle against the Soviets in Afghanistan. The Pakistanis reasoned that if the mujahideen in Afghanistan were recognized as free- dom fighters, the Kashmiri mujahideen, too, could gain similar recognition.

Hussein Haqqani on the post-Soviet period[4]

Many analysts and commentators assumed that the Afghan government would collapse within weeks of the Soviet Union's withdrawal,[5] yet President Najibullah managed to stay in power for the next three years. He would spend the last four years of his life as a refugee in a United Nations guesthouse in Kabul.[6] Najibullah's government relied heavily on the use of militias combined with the regular and costly provision of funding for mujahedeen commanders around the country.[7] His standing army saw a massive inflow of weapons and ammunition following the Soviet withdrawal. One report stated that, 'arms deliveries [...] in the six months following the withdrawal were worth US$1.4 billion.'[8] As cash payments increased, Najibullah simultaneously sought to consolidate the disparate mujahedeen and political forces around the country by appealing to a sense of nationalism; his efforts failed. Money was not enough to bind the mujahedeen together; only the existential threat of the *jihad* had managed (mostly) to keep intra-mujahedeen squabbles to a minimum, at least inside Afghanistan.

When outside funding from Saudi Arabia and the United States stopped, commanders looked for alternative resources to support themselves, their field-commanders and fighters.[9] While some elements continued fighting, other commanders grew complacent and decadent from the cash payments coming from Kabul. The effects were growing disunity—*Hizb-e Islami*'s carrying out of the Farkhar massacre[10] in July 1989 was one illustration of this, as was the poisoning of Hajji Latif in Kandahar.[11]

Much arm-twisting and deal-brokering among Afghan mujahedeen elites in Pakistan brought about mujahedeen rule. The Peshawar Accord (April 1992) set out the structure of a government, appointing specific figures to Afghanistan's new cabinet, but Hekmatyar was dissatisfied with the terms (as were others) and almost immediately began to spoil the agreement by rocketing Kabul, beginning a war against Massoud and Rabbani that would last for years.[12]

Mujaddidi, in a gesture to Arab countries, officially declared that he did not want the Afghan Arabs to stay in Afghanistan. In this way, he addressed the fear of Arab governments like Egypt and Algeria that Islamist groups would use Afghanistan as launch pad to conduct operations back home. Mujaddidi's announcement was echoed by Pakistan when its government expelled a number of Egyptian fundamentalists.[13]

The Islamabad Accords of March 1993 sought to bring Hekmatyar in from the cold; he was offered (and accepted) the post of Prime Minister, but these efforts ultimately came to nought.[14] The government was only nominally in control, and outside Kabul—where instability was the rule of the day—there were a variety of political actors who interacted and fought among each other without regard for the central government.

This chapter assesses this period first by analysing the goals of both Arabs and Afghans and showing where (if any) there were points of crossover or conjunction. Then the nature of the two groups is explored along with their movements and travels. Finally, the role played by external actors during this period is examined.

Goals

Afghans

The departure of the last Soviet troops from Afghanistan and the coming to power of the mujahedeen government in Kabul were victories that were rightly celebrated, although there was also great sorrow for those who died in the war. A tentative optimism was felt and those who had spent much of the last ten years fighting began to contemplate a life without war. This period witnessed a massive repatriation of refugees (primarily from Iran and Pakistan).[15] By 1992, some 1.4 million refugees had returned.[16] Social norms, however, had been destroyed, and 'everyone was a king' in the absence of any central power. Returnees found themselves in an even more desperate situation than when they lived in the camps in Pakistan and Iran.[17]

In February 1990, the aims of the Afghan mujahedeen seemed—on paper at least—both unchanged and unspecific:

The Muslim Afghan nation would continue its principled and armed jehad [sic] till the complete annihilation of atheism, infidelity [sic] and communism and their ruinous aftermaths, us [sic] long as the Islamic objectives are achieved and they are able to live once again in the revitalizing conditions of the Islamic system in a free and Islamic Afghanistan.[18]

In the areas of greatest destruction, people's concerns were, unsurprisingly, highly localised, and this local dimension was the perspective through which all aims and goals were projected. This was not a time in which the traditional religious clergy in southern or south-eastern Afghanistan sought to expand the *jihad* to other countries. It was a moment of consolidation, of rebuilding where possible, and of rest after the trauma and upheaval of the 1980s.

The Taliban who had fought against the Soviets saw themselves neither as the driving force of future political developments nor as the people who ought to implement the Islamic state for which they had fought. They waged a *jihad* as much *against* something as they did *for* something. Their *jihad* was a defensive one, not a revolutionary struggle fought in order to install a new government (although this is what eventually resulted). Many of the clergy already regarded Afghanistan as an Islamic state *prior* to the 1970s.[19]

We should remember also that while fighting for an Islamic state was a common rallying cry throughout the 1980s and later, there was arguably still very little idea of the exact nature of an Islamic state—and certainly much less agreement on what this would look like—among the different parties to the conflict. Interviews conducted with these rural Afghan actors revealed few if any details of what an Islamic state entails and how it would behave. The Taliban fronts, and arguably even the early Taliban movement, were reactionary forces who responded to the context of their surroundings and how they interpreted these circumstances.

Even for those fighting on the Taliban fronts, the end of the war did not bring about a specific desire to establish an Islamic state themselves:

Once the last Soviet soldier had left Kandahar in August 1988, we celebrated without a worry in the world. Mullah Marjan sang in joy using the top of an old stove as a drum while the rest of us danced the Atan. We still hoped that the mujahedeen would share the power among themselves and establish an Islamic government, so we could honour our dead, feed our orphans and support our widows. But the new government held on to power. [...] We no longer wished to fight, and most of us returned home to continue our studies. We contented ourselves with the fact that we had driven the Russians from Afghanistan.[20]

While the *Ulemaa'*, the *mawlawi*s and *'alim*s certainly saw themselves as people who should have a say in social policies, much of the Taliban did not, and nor did they regard themselves as being in this position; they were too young and too traditionalist. Indeed, beyond vague ideas of Islamic values and honour that in themselves were a mixture of traditional tribal cultural and particular interpretations of Islam, the Taliban had little concept of how the future Islamic state of Afghanistan would or should look. There simply was no real precedent for it.

Asked what kind of government the Taliban hoped to install in 1994 in Kabul, Mullah Mutawakil replied in an interview in March 1995:

How Islam and the population wishes. And all rights within it will be guaranteed. And we will first consult the Ulema, and the tribal elders and the population and then form an administration.[21]

As religious clerics, their opinions were sought to mediate disputes and to continue to administer 'Islamic *shari'a* justice' in and around Kandahar. One article written in February 1989 specified how some of these social policies would be implemented:

In an indication of what may unfold in Afghanistan, two elderly maulavi judges appointed by the mujaheddin have sent out edicts to rebel commanders urging them to exercise more control over civilians by curbing such excesses as 'the playing of tape-recorded music.' Music, like murder and theft, is 'un-Islamic.' One rebel commander in Helmand province seized more than 700 tape recorders and radios and destroyed them. But the rebel fighters love music and listen to their radios clandestinely. Some of the rebels are embarrassed by the decrees and hope things will become more moderate when the war ends. 'You must remember that this is a special time,' one explained.[22]

Indeed, these social policies were by no means limited to the religious clergy and students. A declaration of decisions taken at a 'joint council of seven mujaheddin [sic] organizations in Kandahar' issued on 16 June 1992 included the following two points:

1. Female education should be on Islamic principles.
2. Radio and Television programs [should] be changed and instead of music and other unbecoming programs, jehadic [sic] and Islamic programs be broadcast.[23]

The fact that these two points are stressed (out of a total of ten that are given) indicates the strength of these views at the time and helps explain how they would come to play a dominant role in the Taliban's social policies in the mid to late 1990s.

Hekmatyar's *Hizb-e Islami* held comparable views, broadcasting five principles to the population of Charasyab on 9 December 1994, of which:

1. Playing music in hotels, shops or cars is strictly forbidden.
2. The Population has to strictly abstain from the consumption of drugs such as hashish and other narcotic substances.
3. All Muslim sisters must wear Islamic clothing. Aimless walking and wandering are forbidden.[24]

Interviewees relate that these views were prominent among sections of the population, in particular among rural Afghans around the country (although particularly in the south and south-east).[25]

Even in Kabul, as one interview related, similar measures were implemented:

Discarding of Western dress for both sexes, growing of beards, the youth attending the mosques for daily prayers contrary to the past, clearing the city areas from anti-Islamic and communist slogans, observing veils for the fair sex, total ban on playing music in the hotels, and closing most of the cinemas.[26]

The well-known and much-feared court operated by Mawlawi Pasanai Saheb, however, faced funding problems following the departure of the Soviet troops, as one interviewee related:

The court of Mawlawi Pasanai Saheb, for example, had been getting some support from some people but in 1990 they stopped providing money and didn't have any support to be able to continue operating. For some time Sayyaf had given some money and later there was an ISI colonel who gave them money, but both stopped in the early 1990s. Pasanai Saheb was very weak and couldn't even gather together his court. After that the local people gave him some *zakat* and *ushr* so then he managed to restart his activities. Things picked up and it was an important place during the civil war for people to bring their disputes, but still there was no outside support.[27]

Their goals at the time were no more ambitious than this, while former members of the Taliban fronts seemed unwilling to take action to get their share of the spoils after the fall of Kandahar City to the mujahedeen on 20 April:

The most prominent commanders had all come together to discuss how to divide the city up among the Taliban and the other mujahedeen factions now that the Russians had abandoned it. At the very moment they were holding their meeting, though, other mujahedeen groups were speeding towards Kandahar. The commanders who now sided with Najib's government had decided that the Taliban should be excluded from the new administration. They had divided the city, and while the Taliban sat in the silo discussing what should happen next, commanders took positions throughout the city.[28]

Nor is it clear that they would have been able to secure some of this power for themselves without engaging in further violent conflict with other Afghans and former mujahedeen.[29] Mullah Zaeef describes how most of the Taliban and religious scholars who had fought together during the 1980s in the south simply went home or took up their studies again:[30]

The Taliban reduced their operations considerably once the Russians left Kandahar. Many others like myself focused more on their religious studies again, while maintaining security and conducting a few operations against the Communists in remote areas. I continued teaching villagers and religious students in Nelgham along with other mujahedeen, but we soon decided to settle somewhere else. [...] The Taliban didn't involve themselves in [the inter-party fighting in Kabul], and in any case most had returned home by now. Mullah Mohammad Omar turned our old mujahedeen base in Sangisar into a madrassa. I briefly considered staying there as well, but without any work it would be difficult. I decided to return to my wife and children.[31]

Some still remained in the city, and they offered their mediation services to locals out of a small office in western Kandahar (see below for more), but the old networks—while still present—were inactive for the moment.

Figure 3: Locations of prominent Taliban figures during 1990–4 period

Name	Location	Occupation
Amir Khan Muttaqi	Peshawar	Bodyguard to Nabi Mohammadi
Hafiz Abdul Majid		Village life
Mawlawi Abdul Rahman	Sangisar	Teaching/studying
Mawlawi Deobandi		Village life
Mawlawi Nuruddin Turabi	Kandahar	Nothing
Mullah Berader	Sangisar	Teaching/studying
Mullah Dadullah		Village life
Mullah Fazl		Village life
Mullah Ghazi	Sangisar	Teaching/studying
Mullah Khaksar	Quetta	Shopkeeper (shoes)
Mullah Mohammad Omar	Sangisar	Teaching/studying
Mullah Obaidullah		Village life
Mullah Rabbani	Arghestan	Village life
Mullah Yarana	Sangisar	Teaching/studying
Tayyeb Agha	Quetta	High-school student

The individuals who would come to form the Taliban in 1994 were largely passive in the years leading up to the formation of the movement and did not play a significant role in local power-games. In particular, the senior leadership of the Taliban, dominated by actual students who had not finished their religious education or those who were 'village mullahs,' went home or turned the *otaq*s back into madrassas in areas where they had fought during the 1980s.

The cessation of government funding from Saudi Arabia and Pakistan meant that many of the groups associated with the Taliban also had little or no financial and material support, having already received significantly less than other Afghan fighters during the peak of the *jihad*.[32] Here is one Taliban fighter (active on the movement's military fronts during the 1990s, as now) on the aspirations during the early 1990s:

There were some discussions about the civil war, I remember, but this was natural at the time. People asked what it was, why it had started and how it would come to an end, but even at this time there was nobody who was suggesting that they should start a movement called 'Taliban' or anything like that.[33]

Another former Taliban-in-government-era bureaucrat also found intent in the Taliban's apolitical stance. They were abstaining from involvement out of religious reasons, he said:

The period from 1990–4 was perceived to be a corrupt period so they went to the sidelines. For Hanafis whenever there are two Muslim factions fighting against each other they should not do anything (unless you think one of the sides is right and the other wrong). But the Taliban thought both were wrong, so they didn't take sides.[34]

Whatever the reason, there was very little political discussion at the time:

When the Soviets left, the Taliban were still in their otaqs and wanted to do *jihad* against the Najibullah communist regime but they were too weak. The Mullahs and Taliban did not participate in that fight. They were in their mosques studying religious books and reading these same books the whole time. Their discussions weren't about politics; they just spent their days and nights studying about Islam.[35]

There was, however, one set of fronts that did not cease fighting in the early 1990s: those connected to Mullah Nasim Akhundzada in Helmand. These were, by all accounts, quite different entities from the Taliban fronts that were found in Kandahar, Zabul and Uruzgan. An indication of this difference is given by the fact that the 1994 formal 'Taliban movement' went to war with Mullah Nasim and his fighters when they initially moved into Helmand. Former mujahedeen reminiscing about the 1980s *jihad* will almost always dismiss the war in Helmand as 'not serious' and comment that it much more resembled an intra-mujahedeen civil war than a *jihad* against the Soviets.[36] This is how one Kandahari veteran of the Taliban fronts described the early 1990s in Helmand:

Mullah Nasim wanted to capture all of Helmand, Kandahar, Zabul and Farah province and make a big empire in southern Afghanistan, but Sayyaf and HiG didn't let them. There was fighting all the time in this respect.[37]

In south-eastern Afghanistan, the mujahedeen around the pre-eminent local commander, Jalaluddin Haqqani, were more involved in efforts to rout the local pro-Najib government forces. They received direct help and support from foreign jihadis, notably Abu al-Walid al-Masri, who, with the support of al-Qaeda members and others, managed to force the closure of Khost airfield. However, the majority of foreign jihadis, and in particular bin Laden and the senior al-Qaeda leadership, were more committed to the east, as demonstrated in the disastrous battle of Jalalabad in March–July 1989. Furthermore, by 1991, too, bin Laden had begun to set his sights on the Middle East.[38]

The mujahedeen finally managed to retake the city of Khost on 31 March 1991.[39] This was one of the significant mujahedeen successes against the Najib regime, and the city's fall was arguably one of the first major signs that presaged the collapse of that government in Kabul. Haqqani was, therefore, busy with the implementation of the siege and, following Khost's fall, with ensuring that his successes were not snatched from his grasp by Hekmatyar's *Hizb-e Islami*, as well as with the follow-up operations in the greater Paktya area. The 'Khost Jihad Council,' for example, which was established in the wake of the government's fall in the area, saw many such disputes.[40]

One former field commander and later affiliate of the Taliban in the greater Paktya area explained how the '*mullah* fronts' dissolved into other entities following the Soviet withdrawal:

When the Soviets withdrew the scene changed. There were lots of changes—the amount and nature of the support changed substantially—and the policies changed to supporting a mere handful of commanders or leaders. ... In Paktika I was supported and in Khost Jalaluddin Haqqani was supported. They gave us weapons and logistics in a good way but this culture of the fronts faded away. The culture of having these fronts changed and Taliban dissolved into those entities that were still being supported.[41]

The Taliban referred to here were mostly the leadership of the 1980s as well as individuals that were affiliated with Haqqani during the jihad. Those figures who would form the core of the Taliban movement in the 1990s do not seem to have been involved. This also explains why none of the former Taliban leaders or important commanders was chosen to lead the new group in 1994.

1990 and 1991 saw another crisis erupting that most Afghan mujahedeen figures commented on at the time: Saddam Hussein's invasion of Kuwait and the dispatch of American troops to Saudi Arabia. Afghan newspapers from the first four months of 1991, for example, were filled with opinion pieces, commentary and interviews about 'what should be done about the Gulf Crisis,' often with strident and outspoken advice offered by Afghan mujahedeen commanders.

On 20 January, for example, here is Hekmatyar in *Shahadat*, reacting to the dispatch of Afghan mujahedeen to Saudi Arabia to defend the Holy Places:

We strongly condemn the US and allied aggression against Iraq and consider it a brutal step against a Muslim nation. It is not an action against a certain ruler but against an innocent nation. The Muslim ummah must not remain silent against such atrocities and must take steps to prevent further bloodshed. The stand taken by the USSR proves that atheist [sic] can never be friends of Muslims. They are supplying the Kabul regime with all kinds of arms to enable it kill the Afghans, but against an obvious aggression against Iraq they back the aggressors. Rulers who used to name the US as the great Satan, have either taken sides with them or have remained indifferent. It proves that they were not earnest in their slogans. Those who differentiate between Israels' [sic] aggression on Jordan and the US aggression on Iraq are either lacking common sense themselves or are under the impression that their people are ignorant. Israel has resumed the shape of a US gendarme in the region and acts as a drawn sword against the Arabs.[42]

Hekmatyar and Sayyaf were alone in condemning the deployment of American troops (and in implicitly supporting Saddam Hussein). The latter's argument was always framed in the context of an aggressive infidel nation (as part of a wider conspiracy involving Israel) trying to get a foothold on Muslim territory. Ironically, this could not have been further away from the thoughts or quotidian concerns of the Kandahari Taliban at the time, many of whom state that they were not even listening to the radio in those days, being content simply to continue their studies free from the distractions of the outside world.[43]

Even Jalaluddin Haqqani and his commanders would make statements containing such Islamist rhetoric, although it is not entirely clear at this point to what extent this was a serious belief or simply a token statement to ensure the continued financial support of those who shared these views in the Gulf. Here, for example, is Mawlana Mohammad Yaqub Shariatyar discussing the implications of the Khost victory:

...victory in Khost was the outcome of the mujaheddin's unity and solidarity which is painful to Zionism. Therefore the zionists are trying to weaken such victory by propagating false rumors of rift between mujaheddin commanders ...[44]

Here, though, is Haqqani outlining 'the obligation for jehad [sic] in Islam' in September 1991:

1) when an aggression is committed against him he is obliged to defend himself with resorting to arms;
2) when a Muslim finds out that his honor is in danger he should resort to arm and fight;
3) when the religion and faith of a Muslim and his religious rites are being abused and violated, jehad becomes obligatory on the Muslim and he should fight the aggressor;
4) When the land and property of a Muslim comes under aggression, the entire inhabitants of that country are obliged to resort to arms against the

aggressor. Where ever these four things are violated together there is no alternative for the Muslim than to resort to jehad and to arms.[45]

This is a far cry from an outright call for action and movement on the Central Asian states or elsewhere. Even with regards to the definition put forward by Azzam in the 1980s that called on all Muslims to fight if any member of the *umma* was under attack, Haqqani was outlining a relatively limited interpretation of *jihad* that is highly personal in nature and echoes much older definitions of the obligation.

Hekmatyar didn't limit himself to words. One account cites him 'recruiting Afghan mercenaries to fight in Azerbaijan against Armenia and its Russian allies [in summer 1993].'[46] Saudi funding had been withdrawn following Hekmatyar's statements of support for Saddam Hussein; this way, he could fundraise and export the jihad to other countries.[47]

Foreign Jihadists

Afghans who had fought on the Taliban fronts in the early 1990s may have gone home, but the foreign jihadists were in two minds about their next step following the Soviet exit. Intense discussions among Islamist circles in Peshawar and beyond were still raging with a number of prominent works in the jihadi canon being fiercely debated. The withdrawal of the Soviet forces and the changing environment in Afghanistan and Pakistan saw various experiments of individuals in their home countries and in other conflicts.

Several camps had been established for the 'Afghan Arabs' throughout the 1980s, particularly after 1986, and by the 1990s the legitimacy of the Afghan jihad was being called into question. For many, the removal of a physical Soviet military presence inside Afghanistan complicated the war in their minds: was this a *jihad*, or were they risking getting involved in local Afghan disputes which had nothing to do with *jihad*? The issue of fighting other Muslim soldiers was also problematic in their minds. Abdullah Anas recalls:

The clerics used to tell us that it was a duty to support our brothers in Afghanistan so we did. But the Russians had left and the communist regime had fallen. So I started reassessing the reasons for my presence there. I was no longer convinced about the need for staying.[48]

Mohammad Salah writes:

The Afghan war came to an end, and the Jihadi leaders turned against each other. Afghan Arabs found themselves forced to make a choice: either join the mujahedeen parties and join their fighting among themselves for power, or leave to other countries. The majority decided to leave. They chose Peshawar. However, things didn't turn out the way they wanted, as the Pakistani Government was concerned with their presence on its territories. This was especially true after the voices of officials were heard in many countries, especially Egypt, warning that Peshawar was turning into a terrorism management centre.[49]

Azzam himself cautioned the Arabs about getting involved in internal Afghan political disputes:

Sheikh Abdullah Azzam warned us many times not to get involved in Afghanistan's internal affairs. He used to tell us: 'We are orphans, the sons of a widow. Anyone who marries our mother is our father. We don't care who rules Afghanistan from among the seven leaders (Hekmatyar, Rabbani, Mujadidi, Nabi Mohammadi, Sayyaf...). We are not entitled to interfere in their affairs. If they agree on anyone of them and swear their allegiance to him, then we will recognise him. We do not interfere in their private affairs. If the mujahedeen enter Kabul and start fighting among each other then it is not right for us to take sides.' This was his message.[50]

The period that followed the withdrawal of Soviet troops paradoxically saw the largest numbers of 'Afghan Arabs' coming to Pakistan.[51] The infrastructure that was put in place in the late 1980s by Azzam and others was now being used to run recruitment networks. The role in these of Afghan jihadi alumni and the worldwide attention focusing on the Afghan *jihad* meant that even more young men flocked to the camps and guesthouses in Pakistan and Afghanistan.[52] However, the Afghan Arabs were far from united at the time. Instead, the individual national organisations, such as Egyptian Islamic Jihad, *al-Gama'a al-Islamiyya* and others, were competing with each other and often had outright disagreements about the future of the Afghan Arabs and their individual struggles. Central to the debate was the question of who the enemy was, and how to fight it.[53]

Chasms in the Arab Afghan community had developed in the late 1980s, in particular between 'Dr Fadl' and several Egyptian Islamic Jihad members on one side and Azzam and many of the Muslim Brotherhood's supporters on the other.[54] The jihadist milieu in Peshawar at that time could be characterised as fluid, buffeted by competing trends of thought and action. In the midst of this charged atmosphere arrived growing numbers of young recruits who were readily engaged by the older guard of the Afghan Arabs, namely those who were leading the debates and preparing for what would come after the Afghan *jihad*.[55]

Al-Suri has stated that Peshawar was an important founding crucible for the 'Afghan Arabs':

Peshawar and Afghanistan became a true university [...] This was a turning in Muslim history. People met, thoughts and perspectives met, and personalities met. Groups fought out their rivalries, and different thoughts and ideas competed. It was a kind of birthplace. Much of what you see today is a result of this period.[56]

A key catalyst and event for the debate among Arabs during this time was the assassination of Abdullah Azzam on 24 November 1989.[57] While the identity of the perpetrators of the bomb attack that killed him and two of his sons has never been conclusively proved, there are numerous theories about who was responsible. A number of commentators believe that bin Laden ordered the attack over differences regarding the future of the Afghan Arabs; others believe that it was Zawahiri and his circle of Islamic Jihad who killed Azzam over similar disagreements.[58] Another theory holds that Azzam was killed by Hekmatyar or maybe members of the Afghan KhAD;[59] towards the end of the 1980s, Azzam had grown increasingly close to Massoud, providing him with funding and support.[60]

Whoever was responsible, Azzam's death had a direct effect on the debates among the Afghan Arabs: Egyptian voices such as al-Zawahiri's gained considerable weight, not only among the wider jihadi community, but also with bin Laden. That being said, as al-Suri observed, in 1990 bin Laden 'was still very far from the Salafi-jihadi current represented by al-Zawahiri and the EIJ.'[61]

Abdullah Anas gives a sense of the confusion that these debates engendered:

After the mujahedeen entered Kabul, and signs started pointing to imminent strife among them, the Peshawar scene was witnessing a proliferation of oddities. It became a plagued scene in which the Arab volunteers splintered into many groups. The members of the Muslim Brotherhood regrouped under Abdul-Rasul Sayyaf. The Salafists gathered in Kunar under Sheikh Jamil al-Rahman, the founder of Salafism in Afghanistan. The Services Office did not remain aloof from these divisions as it also split into two. An alliance was forged between the Jihad group and Osama Bin Laden, which led to the formation of al-Qaeda. A Jordanian citizen set up a tent and started giving sermons on Fridays to some young men. He announced the formation of a group called 'Jaish Mohammad' (Muhammad's Army) then he disappeared suddenly to become a deputy minister in his country. Another Jordanian announced that he was the Caliph of all Muslims and that the groups and guest houses that did not recognize his status were blasphemers.[62]

There were still many 'Afghan Arabs' left in Afghanistan and Pakistan who had participated in the anti-Soviet *jihad*, among them a considerable number who played a role in the catastrophic attempt to take Jalalabad from the Afghan government in early 1989—including bin Laden and other prominent Arab jihadis.[63] The withdrawal of Soviet troops—effectively removing their *casus belli*—thus precipitated an existential crisis among the Arab contingent.[64] This prompted much discussion throughout the 1990s, and two opposing camps developed. Some, like Azzam, saw the Afghan *jihad* as a rallying-point for Muslims, a place where they could be trained and politically (or, as they would argue, religiously) mobilised, and a base from which the *umma* could respond to threats worldwide. This group disagreed over how fast the Arab 'contingent' would be ready to carry out operations globally; Azzam argued for patience, but some urged a faster mobilisation and the dispatch of recruits to other countries.

Others, especially those who gravitated towards the Egyptian Islamic Jihad head, al-Zawahiri, believed that the Afghan *jihad* had served its purpose as an external incubator for the political, religious and military mobilisation of the foreign contingent (particularly the youth), safe from the clutches of Arab security services, but that now was the moment to take this fight back home—to Egypt, Syria, and so on. These 'revolutionary jihadis' had increasingly started to think about the foreign sponsors of their local autocracies, but in the short-term focused on their home governments.[65]

The environment in Peshawar during the late 1980s and early 1990s thus had become dominated by those who sought to use the trained and mobilised Arab contingent for overseas action.[66] Much of the leadership present in Peshawar and the region in the early 1990s were still committed to revolutionary *jihad*—seeking to decapitate the state in a coup which would then rouse Muslim communities to topple the regime. The ideas of Azzam and others were also gaining traction.

The Iraqi invasion of Kuwait was followed by Operation Desert Storm in January 1991, but the Saudi government indirectly admitted its impotence by seeking American forces to protect its territories and oil fields from Iraqi aggression. This resulted in Operation Desert Shield in which American troops were deployed to Saudi Arabia from 1990–91. This foreign military deployment in the land of the two Holy Places was viewed by many as an invasion, not to protect Saudi Arabia but to take control of its oil and the wider region.[67]

It was, al-Suri says, like an 'earthquake' for the Arab jihadis:

One witnessed what might be described as an ideological and mental earthquake, particularly for the Arab-Afghan mujahidin, when the international allied forces under the leadership of America descended on the Arab peninsula under the cover of what was called 'the liberation of Kuwait.' It was abundantly clear that this was only a convenient curtain for the new vicious crusader campaigns, which America, Western Europe and the Jews launched towards the midst of Islam's homeland in the Levant, Iraq and the Arab peninsula. [...] There was no doubt whatsoever that the Islamic Nation, its holy places, and wealthy resources, especially its oil reserves were being targeted by a wave of direct Crusader-Jewish military occupation, an occupation which ultimately aimed at a complete liquidation of the civilizationary presence of Muslims. This earthquake was only months later, at the beginning of 1991, followed by another wave of seismic shocks with the self-proclamation of peace projects with the Jews to sell what remained of Palestine and Jerusalem.[68]

Bin Laden had already left Afghanistan and Pakistan, in late 1989, and was now spending time in Saudi Arabia, while increasingly focusing on Yemen. Several al-Qaeda members were with him then, including for a while al-Zawahiri. In Yemen, bin Laden supported Tariq al-Fadhali, who had become a close associate of his in Afghanistan between 1987–89 and had returned to Yemen and set up training camps in the north.[69]

As Turki al-Faisal stated in a television documentary almost two months after the September 11 attacks, the Saudi government, while appreciating his work in Afghanistan, had told bin Laden to 'leave things like that,' referring to his meddling in Yemen.[70]

The issue over bin Laden's support for radical groups in Yemen was the first serious point of conflict with the Saudi government. The decision to rely on American forces to defend Saudi Arabia would lead bin Laden to re-evaluate the house of Saud—to whom there had often remained a certain vestigial loyalty—and much of the religious establishment in his homeland.[71]

Prior to the start of Operation Desert Shield, bin Laden used his family connections to obtain an audience with Prince Sultan bin Abdulaziz al-Saud, the Saudi Defence Minister who had been outspoken about the dangers that Saddam Hussein posed towards Kuwait long before the fact.[72] He reportedly arrived with detailed plans telling the minister that Saudi Arabia did not need the American forces, and that no non-believer should be allowed in the land of the two Holy Places.[73]

Indeed, bin Laden stated that he, together with his Afghan Arabs, would defend the Kingdom. The details of the meeting are as much legend as fact, but bin Laden is said to have claimed that he could raise 100,000 men. Prince Sultan turned him down, and took up the offer of American Secretary of Defense, Dick Cheney; American troops were deployed to defend the Kingdom of Saudi Arabia.[74] As for many others in the jihadist circles, the deployment of almost 250,000 American troops by the early days of 1991 was regarded as part of an elaborate Western conspiracy against the Muslim nation.[75] For bin Laden it was proof of the 'infidel' nature of the house of Saud and he became an outspoken critic and increasingly clashed with the ruling family.[76]

In January 1991, Sheikh Abdelaziz bin Baz had issued a *fatwa* that authorised *jihad* against Saddam Hussein even if those carrying it out were nonbelievers,[77] which sanctioned the deployment of American forces to the Kingdom. Other well known members of the clergy in Saudi Arabia shared bin Laden's view—who at that time had little clout in Saudi Arabia—with only a small group of Afghan Arab followers. Dr. Safar al-Hawali was one of those speaking out openly against what they saw as violations of Islam, and sacrilegious acts. Dr. al-Hawali and others were arrested and imprisoned, which, as bin Laden would later claim, turned him against the Saudi government.[78] In sermons publicised through audiotapes bin Laden grew increasingly pronounced and militant, calling for action against *kufr* and regimes supported by *kufr*, the latter a reference to Saudi Arabia that was hard to miss.[79]

According to bin Laden's bodyguard, Abu Jandal, bin Laden was under quasi house arrest in Jeddah and received a one-time travel passport. The issue of his departure, the underlying reasons for it and why he received a passport at all remain unclear.[80]

The discussions during the founding meetings of al-Qaeda in the late 1980s offer a window into bin Laden's intentions. While the overall purpose was clear—creating a vanguard of the Muslim *umma* and the continuation of *jihad*—and all individuals involved wanted to harvest the fruits of the Afghan *jihad*, the exact nature of the strategy was still being debated. At this early stage, the group was more an idea than a reality as an organisation. Here is Abu Ubaida, a senior figure who drowned in 1996 in Lake Victoria, addressing one prospective recruit:

Now that the *jihad* has ended, we should not waste this. We should invest in these young men and we should mobilize them under [bin Laden's] umbrella. We should form an Islamic army for jihad that will be called al Qaeda. This army will be one of the fruits of what bin Laden has spent on the Afghan jihad. We should train these young men and equip them to be ready to uphold Islam and defend Muslims in any part of the world. The members of this army should be organized and highly trained.[81]

In early 1992, bin Laden was allowed to travel to Pakistan. He stayed for several months in Peshawar and according to some sources attempted to broker a deal between Hekmatyar and Massoud.[82] While in Saudi Arabia, concerned with Yemen and the threat of Iraq, he had maintained his contacts with

Hizb-e Islami and Sayyaf and had paid for members and leaders of each group to travel to Saudi Arabia.[83] At this time, it seems bin Laden's exact attitude and direction were—if not undecided—ambivalent. New developments in Saudi Arabia—and the events surrounding his engagement with Yemen and Operation Desert Storm and Shield—meant a definitive break with the house of Saud, who he regarded as enemies from then on. His attitude towards the religious clergy changed too: modes of Islamic thought that would allow him to challenge the status quo and reshape a vision of his own became more central to his understanding.[84]

An examination of his activities from 1990 to 1996 confirms this: first it seems as if he might remain in Saudi Arabia, but the arrival of American troops further invigorates bin Laden. He also contributes to the funding of militant groups in Yemen. When this provokes the displeasure of King Abdullah, he leaves Saudi Arabia for Sudan. There he seems to leave his options open, allowing for the presence and training of jihadi groups but at the same time spending much of his energy and resources on infrastructure development and construction works. It is only his expulsion from Sudan in 1996 that seems to crystallise and galvanise bin Laden into what amounted to his irrevocable stance against America.

Group Identities

As we have seen, the Taliban from 1990–94 essentially absented themselves from the clashes and horsetrading of the post-Soviet political landscape. Their solidarity networks remained intact and the shared experiences of the 1980s made it inevitable that they would come together and rely on and trust each other from this point on. Yet there was no sense of 'the Taliban' as an organised entity during this period, or at least not as they would become post-1994.

Dorronsoro writes of a group called *Jamiyat-i Taliban*,[85] but it neither played a significant role nor did it have many members. He is referring here to an office in western Kandahar which other residents of the time have confirmed as being 'the Taliban's office during the *topakiyaan* period.'[86] It was indeed manned by former mujahedeen of the Taliban fronts, but to call it an office is an exaggeration. Eyewitnesses recall that it functioned as a mediation centre or place where people could come to have their disputes resolved by Islamic scholars. It seems to have had no other purpose than this.[87]

To explore the foundations of the group that came together in 1994, one must look to the networks of individuals formed in earlier years that made up the backbone of trust and contacts. The networks of the 1980s were preserved through the associations and groupings of mullahs and religious elders into the 1990s, and their prevalence can be explained by the structure of the muja-hedeen fronts. The Taliban's military forces are constructed on the basis of the *andiwaal* system, which was the case in the 1980s *jihad*, in the 1990s, and throughout their rule and military campaigns up to 2001. It still holds true today. *Andiwaal* is the Dari/Pashtu word for friend. The smallest unit in the Taliban's force consists of a small group of some five to thirty members under the lead of a commander. This group is the building block of the *andiwaal* system. Ties between the commander and his troops are forged through long-standing relations built on family, clan, tribal affiliations and friendship. These groups are mostly local but at times—depending on the individual character-istics of group members and their commanders—can be moved, combined and called on for various activities and support.

Andiwaal groups are rarely restructured or formed but rather present a bottom-up model and need to be regarded as pre-existing networks or groups. They provide local expertise and in-depth knowledge of local communities and the surrounding terrain. Organisationally they are usually folded into larger units and have varying levels of a hierarchy of command above them. The latter is not necessarily a strictly organised pyramid, in a military sense, given the per-sonal nature of the relationship between individual commanders; in practice, different layers of command can have vertical and horizontal depth depend-ing on the ties between commanders.[88]

The *andiwaal* system is the underlying reason for the ongoing debate as to what extent the Taliban are structured around a strong central core with a top-down command structure or are a group of affiliates operating semi-indepen-dently. The system as it presents itself, while paradoxical, satisfies both extremes of the argument and combines independence with strong leadership that allows for flexible and rapid adjustment to local conditions, as well as to the chang-ing tactics of government and foreign forces. It takes into account conflicts with the local population and the movement's own long-term strategic plan-ning, along with vast and complex operations.

For the foreign jihadists, there was a far more tangible sense of mobilisation compared to what 'the Taliban' were doing at this time. The Afghan Arabs were quite fragmented by this point. The consolidation of the Arab veterans of the Afghan *jihad*—in particular the individuals that would rise to fame in the world of international jihadism—had begun during the 1980s, but would continue to evolve and play a role in conflicts and operations in a host of countries throughout the 1990s and early 2000s. During the early 1990s, for example, the dividing lines between the panoply of the different Arab Islamist groups were in many cases even more clearly drawn than before they came to Afghanistan and Pakistan.

It was the experience of returning home that for many reinforced the communal bond of the group. The alumni, often facing difficult situations at home, strongly identified with their experience of the Afghan *jihad* and regarded themselves as a mujahedeen elite. Many had survived close calls and intense combat in Afghanistan; this gave them a confidence that was unshakeable.

During this time, though, no concerted actions were carried out by the Afghan Arabs. Individuals were still very much divided into their national groups and many focused on preparing to renew the fight against their own governments. Afghanistan had given them training and expertise, but the key concepts of a revolutionary approach to change—the coup that would dispose the ruling elite at a very top-down level—was still the modus operandi for many.

The early 1990s was the ideological and operational morass from which the actions of the late 1990s would rise. Al-Qaeda, while formed in the late 1980s, was still not more than an idea, and many who later became leading figures, like al-Zawahiri, were pursuing their own campaigns. Even though members were recruited and trained in Afghanistan and bin Laden took an oath of loyalty from them, no clear plan had been formulated. This is as much a reflection of group dynamics as it is bin Laden's own indecision as to what to do with his jihadi acolytes.

Al-Qaeda was little more than a number of trained individuals who were sure that they wanted to continue the armed struggle and had access to financial resources, but were neither consolidated at the time and nor had they achieved any unity of purpose. As Jason Burke would later write about the group, it was shorthand for 'terrorist violence legitimised by a particular reading of Islam and conceived within a mythical religious narrative but rooted in a largely political project defined by local contingencies.'[89]

In the early 1990s, it appears, al-Qaeda was still consolidating its core contingent, knew it wanted to carry out a largely religiously-inspired political project, but was still very much subject to unfolding events around it, in particular the key leaders like bin Laden and al-Zawahiri.[90] It is interesting to note that none of these leaders seemed to be particularly interested in the conflicts raging in Bosnia and Tajikistan, at least not to the extent that they dispatched significant numbers of their followers or got personally involved.[91] Such passivity was symptomatic of this period; it was primarily about a search for purpose, goals and strategy, the assembly of the last pieces of the worldview that would later substantiate the rationale for much of al-Qaeda's narrative. Moreover, in the other countries where the 'Afghan Arabs' fought in this period—Bosnia and Tajikistan—people did not identify themselves as 'al-Qaeda,' but for the most part relied on the names of local outfits as their point of reference. As an organisation, al-Qaeda started out as a highly secretive group, its members having learnt hard lessons on the importance of secrecy in their home countries. Members of al-Qaeda often continued to be part of other groups, and al-Qaeda would issue statements after its attacks congratulating the perpetrators but would not claim responsibility.

A central misunderstanding commonly made when assessing al-Qaeda's strength and funding needs at this time concerns its membership and the solidity of its overall structure. Commentators and analysts often treat entities that take a name (like *Harakat ul-Mujahdeeen*, al-Qaeda or *Jaish-e Mohammad*) as organisational entities, categorising individuals by membership; the inside view appears to differ significantly. The practice of *bayat*, when it takes place and to what or whom allegiance is pledged, is key to deepening our understanding of this period. Various militant Islamic groups have a hierarchical, pyramid structure in which *bayat*—an oath or pledge of loyalty made to one's leader—is paid to the superior who in turn pays *bayat* to someone else. The compartmentalised form of *bayat* leads to a different organisational or network structure with different weaknesses from the *bayat* that is paid to leaders such as bin Laden or Mullah Mohammad Omar.

While the subject requires more systematic research, one can speculate that the core groups that pledge *bayat* to a leader form a group that displays greater flexibility, as well as greater willingness to evolve and change in accordance with a leadership decision compared with other militant movements. Compartmentalised *bayat* groups, on the other hand, or groups that do not rely on the *bayat* concept, are subject to frequent factionalism and are less stable entities.

Informed observers like Abu al-Walid al-Masri state that many of the individuals who came to be regarded as key leaders had not taken *bayat* before 11 September.[92] Abu Zubayda and Abu Khabab, the explosives specialists, were working independently in Afghanistan, running camps like Khaldan and Darunta.[93] These were, al-Masri suggests, more in competition with than part of the al-Qaeda group at the time.[94]

Those who became known as al-Qaeda affiliates or who ended up heading al-Qaeda satellite groups had often received training in Afghanistan in the 1980s or 1990s, but many of these joined only later on, and in the process had considerable disagreements with the al-Qaeda leadership and bin Laden. This should be taken into account, particularly in the period before the September 11 attacks. As Abu al-Walid al-Masri points out, many joined al-Qaeda only after those attacks and their individual circumstances and motivations are far from clear and should be reviewed on an individual basis.[95]

Movements

Many Arabs moved on from Afghanistan and Pakistan following the withdrawal of Soviet forces. Those who had arrived more or less by chance (while looking for work in Saudi Arabia, for example)[96] now sought to return home, and many did so without repercussions from the authorities. For those who had been involved in Islamist groups prior to their departure to Afghanistan, returning was more of a problem; they were forced into an itinerant life at this point. Many of those who wished to go back had plans to topple their home governments.

The 'Afghan Arab' diaspora was a global one but many had found their way back to the Arab world before Sudan became the international hub for jihadist organisations under its President Hassan al-Turabi. Yemen also seems to have exerted a gravitational pull[97] while other jihadists ventured to the Philippines, Indonesia and Malaysia as well as to Europe and America.[98] These men often set up organisations of their own—the Abu Sayyaf group in the Philippines, for example, came into being in 1991.[99] The nature of these networks can best be described as fluid between the various actors and groups. There was no central strategy, no central leadership, no central ideology, no unity of purpose, no common enemy and no common financial link that tied all the groups together.

One Haqqani affiliate from the 1980s explained the movement of Arabs following the Soviet withdrawal as follows:

When the Soviet Union collapsed and when the Central Asian states were liberated this saw a massive expansion of the Arab and external Islamic NGOs into Central Asia. They were supporting Abdullah Nuri in Tajikistan and Dudayev in Chechnya. Everyone was trying to get some influence in there since they were newly freed from the

Soviets. The Iranians wanted a foothold and even the Buddhists. So the Arabs were doing that too. This new wave of support happened, and I think the fighters followed not long after.[100]

Nevertheless, the individuals who would soon achieve fame in the jihadist community (as well as among international governments and their counter-terrorism units) were interconnected, had personal relationships, had fought together and had been discussing their plans for years if not decades. The core of the Afghan Arabs had forged a network that far more than hitherto had the potential to connect the various small groups and their financial supporters throughout the Middle East and beyond.

The plots and attacks that were carried out in the mid-1990s—the World Trade Center bombing of 1993, for example—reveal the nature of the early threat: unorganised and lacking unity, but nevertheless able, via some key individuals, to rely on support and draw together resources and backing from the wider community of jihadists and former Afghan Arabs.

Ramzi Yousuf, the nephew of Khalid Sheikh Mohammed, had conceived of the idea of the World Trade Center bombing in 1991 and assembled various helpers, assistants and funders along the way. Prior to his journey and successful attack on the World Trade Center, Yousuf was in Pakistan for much of 1991 and 1992, training Arabs in Peshawar in the electrical-engineering skills involved in bomb-making.[101] He made a short trip to the Philippines with the founder of the Abu Sayyaf group in 1992.[102]

Yousuf found his accomplice for the World Trade Center bombing in the Khaldan training camp in Afghanistan, and both flew to New York in August 1992. Further assistance in funding and constructing the truck-bomb was found once Yousuf was in New York, where he got in touch with individuals at the Islamic Center, *al-Khifa*, in Brooklyn that had already served as the main hub for Azzam's Services Office in the 1980s and had ties to Pakistan and Afghanistan. His accomplice was held up at border control after an airport search revealed bomb-making literature in his luggage.[103]

This, the best known operation carried out by those associated with the 'Afghan Arabs,' was a relatively isolated plot, and certainly not part of any top-down strategic effort on the part of bin Laden. This is more than apparent in accounts of the first meeting between Khalid Sheikh Mohammad and bin Laden, in 1996. At least one source claims that his audience with bin Laden took place on account of his nephew's fame in attacking the United States.[104]

After his brief stay in Peshawar in 1992, bin Laden relocated to Sudan. Close associates of his who had taken the oath of loyalty had already been on a scouting mission and had made arrangements with the Sudanese government headed by Hassan al-Turabi and Omar al-Bashir.[105] His relationship with the Saudi government continued to deteriorate, and several members of his family came to Sudan in order to convince him to return to Saudi Arabia and the family. Bin Laden refused.[106] On 5 March 1994, the Saudi government stripped him of his citizenship.[107]

Meanwhile, many of the Egyptian Arabs close to al-Zawahiri and his Egyptian Islamic Jihad first relocated to Yemen, which was regarded as an ideal place to continue operations for their purposes.[108] Sudan, in addition to being the choice of bin Laden, offered an amenable government that cooperated with the Islamists. Al-Zawahiri himself made trips to the United States during this period—including a fundraising drive to California in 1993—but Egypt remained his main focus.[109] He regarded Islamic Jihad as offering the best chance to overthrow Mubarak's government and had still not formally committed himself to bin Laden and al-Qaeda and their increasingly vocal calls to strike at the 'far enemy' rather than the 'near enemy.'[110]

The Taliban who had fought together during the 1980s stayed firmly put during this time. This is not surprising, given their very localised concerns and goals following the withdrawal of Soviet forces.[111] At most, they sought involvement and had a role to play in local Afghan politics—this was more true of later affiliates of the Taliban like the Haqqanis than it was for the core Kandaharis themselves—but on the whole these mujahedeen went home or perhaps travelled to Pakistan for education or for business.[112]

Jalaluddin Haqqani remained almost entirely in *Loya* or 'greater' Paktya during this period, mostly confining his movements to the area around Khost Airport following the siege of Khost in March 1991.[113] Training camps for foreign jihadis were operating in territory under his control during the early 1990s but Haqqani does not seem to have played an active role in shaping the agenda or activities of such camps, instead functioning as a de facto 'sponsor', albeit not in a financial sense. Yunis Khalis was also still Haqqani's *amir* and as such Haqqani is believed to have been less politically active during this period. Hekmatyar was active in Afghanistan's national politics—securing for himself as much of the spoils as possible—and also operated training camps of his own.[114] This included Darunta camp east of Jalalabad that later became known for specialised courses in explosives and chemical engineering.[115]

Hekmatyar was also travelling extensively during this time; he is known to have made trips to Japan, Bangladesh, Malaysia, Singapore, Indonesia, Brunei, Australia, China and the United States.[116]

The picture that emerges from the various activities and movements of future or current members of al-Qaeda during this period presents an organisation that was still in the throes of consolidation. Key figures like al-Zawahiri were consumed with independent operations; individuals were reconnecting to their home fronts or establishing links to new groups that were forming. Some former Afghan Arabs ventured to new *jihadi* fault lines; others left Pakistan and Afghanistan to fight in Central Asia, or on other fronts.[117]

Interactions

Arabs who remained in Peshawar in the early 1990s retained connections to Afghans they had known in the 1980s, although relatively few were returning to Afghanistan aside from trips to training camps in the east and south-east. Mohammad Salah contends that those who remained behind in Afghanistan and Pakistan in the early 1990s could be divided into three groups:

The first is a small group that stayed with Massoud/Rabbani in Kabul. The second joined Hekmatyar's camps and fought alongside his forces against Rabbani. Most of those left him in protest when the communists and Shiites entered an alliance with him, and a tiny number stayed with him after his confrontations with the Taliban. The third part formed the majority of those who stayed. They were neutral, some working, and the others residing in camps. The campaigns against those residing in Peshawar forced a number of them to return to Afghanistan for stability and security reasons. Those were the nucleus of the Arabic community in Afghanistan, and some of them assisted Tajik and Kashmiri mujahedeen.[118]

In 1995, following various incidents where 'Afghan Arabs' had been involved in criminal activities or attacks, the Pakistani government attempted a head count of the Arabs on their soil:

...they gathered more than 5,000 names, including 1,142 Egyptians, 981 Saudis, 946 Algerians, 771 Jordanians, 326 Iraqis, 292 Syrians, 234 Sudanese, 199 Libyans, 117 Tunisians and 102 Moroccans.[119]

Some of these had married into Pakistani or Afghan families during or following the 1980s *jihad* and were there without ulterior motive, but many were based in Peshawar and Islamabad to take advantage of the Islamic education and jihadi training being offered by the old Services Office infrastructure established by Azzam and bin Laden.[120]

The numerous camps along the Afghan-Pakistan border were administrated by several different individuals. While they cooperated with leaders such as bin Laden or al-Zawahiri, they were nevertheless fairly autonomous regarding trainees and the camps themselves. The camp infrastructure, very much like the alumni network, was unstructured. It had multiple funding streams and contained a number of highly idiosyncratic individuals who were affiliated with, cooperated in and regarded themselves as part of the same community, working for the same overarching goals. But they lacked any formal consolidated structure or operational coordination.

The camps remained open and individuals such as Abu Khabab continued to administer training, but aside from a generalised instruction regimen and ideological syllabus there was no overarching plan as to what these various foreign jihadis were being trained for.[121] The Services Office centres remained open in Peshawar, and an 'office of information' even opened in Jalalabad in 1992.[122] There were several guesthouses also open to Arabs: '*beit al-shuhada* (house of martyrs), *beit al-salaam* (house of peace) and *beit al-mu'mineen* (house of the faithful) and a fourth guesthouse in Hayatabad.'[123]

The Arab presence inside Afghanistan was nominal during this period. The number of fighters still involved with the Afghan mujahedeen was in the low hundreds, and most of these were in the east and south-east. Even the large Khost siege of 1991 apparently saw the participation of only around 250 Arabs.[124] In southern Afghanistan, mujahedeen interviewees say that the few Arabs that they had seen during the late 1980s had almost completely disappeared by the 1990s, with the last big mujahedeen offensive featuring Arab fighters being the operation to take Zabul province in March 1990.[125]

There was a temporary increase in the numbers of foreigners coming into Afghanistan from 1992–93 onwards following a stern warning from the United States to Pakistan that they were considering placing the latter on its list of state sponsors of terrorism. Pakistan thus shifted all training that was previously taking place across the border into Afghanistan—this brought the Pakistani Kashmiri jihadis physically together and in close proximity with the Arabs and their internationalist agendas.[126]

Clarity as to who was in charge of the training camps during this period is hard to come by. Sayyaf, Hekmatyar, Khalis and Haqqani are all frequently listed as having been 'in charge' of the various camps in and around the Jalalabad area during this time, and one source even suggests that the ISI bought off the Jalalabad *shura* to allow their blessing for the expansion of the foreign camps in their sector.[127] It is likely that there was no single figure in control of the administration of these camps or who monitored those who came in and out of Afghanistan. Pakistan's army and security services were content to have somewhere to train their jihadis for Kashmir, and—for the moment—less concerned about the possible future repercussions.[128]

The numbers of Afghans travelling abroad during this time were relatively small—especially in any sense that impacts or relates to the subjects under scrutiny in this book. The Taliban who had fought together during the 1980s remained in Afghanistan or Pakistan, either studying or engaging in small business. In the south-east of the country, Haqqani remained in the *Loya* Paktya area, but the influx of foreign jihadis meant that he didn't have to leave the country to come into contact with these men.

External Actors

Pakistan

Pakistani policies towards Afghanistan saw broad continuity from 1990–1994, despite passing through three separate civilian administrations during the period and a similar rate of change in the military/intelligence sector. Pakistan's military saw the withdrawal of Soviet troops in 1989 as the opportune moment to cash in its investment of the past decade in support to the Afghan mujahedeen. In pursuit of their goal of a Pakistan-friendly government that would be inimical to India, they sought a Pashtun government in Kabul with Hekmatyar as its face.[129]

This desire ran contrary to Pakistan's new and idealistic prime-minister, Benazir Bhutto, who sought a coalition government for Afghanistan brought about through a political process (albeit one sponsored by Pakistan).[130] Her demand for a mujahedeen takeover of a major city[131] was one of the main reasons for the rushed push to take Jalalabad in 1989, which became an operational disaster in which all its principal planners have sought to minimise perceptions of their involvement.[132]

Ultimately, Pakistan served as midwife to a negotiated government made up of the various mujahedeen parties, but it fell apart almost as soon as these various groups moved into Kabul. Hekmatyar acted as spoiler *par excellence*, shelling the capital and preventing the interim mujahedeen administration from consolidating its ranks—although it is likely that this would have happened anyway (regardless of Hekmatyar's personal and idiosyncratic role).[133]

Pakistan had concerns of its own during this period, and Afghanistan descended into civil war without any major intervention or palpable concern manifested on the part of the Pakistani military or intelligence establishment.

A plan had been drafted in 1984 for a renewed offensive in Kashmir under Zia ul-Haq,[134] but Indian actions in the Valley and an increasingly vocal domestic lobby within Pakistan forced the ISI's hand on the matter: they had to advance their plan faster and earlier than originally expected. The early 1990s thus saw a significant increase in covert military and political support for jihadi groups to train for and conduct activities in Kashmir. Relations between India and Pakistan during this time were, in any case, 'the worst since the 1971 war.'[135]

The ISI sought to exercise control over the jihadis, however, and this meant supporting Pakistani groups rather than indigenous Kashmiris, who were seen as being less malleable. There also seems to have been some support for or toleration of an active campaign whereby Pakistani jihadis would target and eliminate their Kashmiri counterparts in an attempt to gain such dominance.[136]

Some groups were backed heavily—Pakistan attempted to retain some control over its creations—but others were soon more or less abandoned.[137] Pakistan was the base from which all the foreign mujahedeen operated, and this explains why there was a significant amount of contact between the Arabs and the Pakistani mujahedeen. Contact extended down to the lower ranks of fighters and occurred not only among leadership circles (as in the case of Abdullah Azzam and *Markaz Da'wa wal Irshad*).

The ideological[138] influences of the Arab mujahedeen and, by the late 1980s, the participation of Pakistani mujahedeen in the debates over long-term strategy in Peshawar and other places, meant that the 1990s saw Pakistani jihadi involvement in various international conflicts, including in Bosnia, Tajikistan, Burma, the Mindanao conflict in the Philippines, Uzbekistan, Chechnya and Kashmir, as well as Afghanistan.[139] All the while the Pakistani military and security services sought to walk a narrow tightrope with the United States. Initially, in the wake of the Soviet withdrawal, Washington turned a blind eye to both Pakistan's support for Kashmiri jihadis and its nuclear programme, which were implicitly tolerated. Pakistan was occasionally able to pull the proverbial rabbit from the hat, as exemplified by their help in locating and detaining the World Trade Center bombing suspect, Ramzi Yousuf, in February 1995.[140]

The targeting of American citizens in 1995 (by a small jihadi group that kidnapped six Western tourists in Kashmir) ended this arrangement and George H.W. Bush's government told Prime Minister Nawaz Sharif in May 1992 that the support for 'militants' would have to stop.[141] As Pakistani authorities discussed how to respond, they argued almost universally that the United States was not particularly interested in this matter beyond its obvious desire to avoid being embarrassed by an ally, and decided to continue supporting groups fighting in Kashmir but in a more covert manner.[142]

The Afghan political landscape in the aftermath of the collapse of the Najib government, with the unstructured disassembling of his security apparatus and the disintegration of the fragile alignment of the mujahedeen commanders, proved to be difficult terrain in which to manoeuvre, even for the ISI and the Pakistani government.[143] Actors like Hekmatyar—who had forged close ties with them and who had received most of the material support during the *jihad*—showed how little control the ISI exerted over them. Nevertheless, Pakistan continued to pursue policies dictated by its ultimate goal of an anti-Indian, pro-Pakistani government in Kabul. Pakistan continued to focus on its long-term allies; there is little conclusive evidence that the Taliban were in contact with Pakistan at this time, while the Afghan Arabs saw their previously good relationship with the Pakistani security apparatus deteriorate, making it increasingly difficult for them to continue operating.

Saudi Arabia/Arab States

The Saudis and the Arab Gulf states heaved a sigh of relief when the Soviets left Afghanistan: the threat to their strategic and economic interests had passed. They became less interested in Afghanistan as a strategic asset and—like the United States—rapidly drew down their funding of the mujahedeen. They were content to follow Pakistan's policy regarding the post-war outcome; they wanted to consolidate their interests by seeing a pro-Saudi (the same as a pro-Pakistani) government in Kabul, and assumed that the way to force Najib out would be through a military campaign.[144]

Saudi Arabia also sought to reinforce the ideological interests that they had supported throughout the war—i.e., support for the Wahhabi brand of Islam and antipathy to Shi'ism and Iranian support for the *jihad*—and it was not afraid to be blunt about this. Here, for example, is a statement issued by a prominent Saudi *ulemaa'* and published in *Shahadat* on 24 May 1992:

Please do not assign any role to the heretic Shias and be aware that they cannot tolerate a Sunni government in Afghanistan. Once again we draw your attention to these dangers and to the fact that if you join hands with the enemies in a conspiracy [...] there would be no justification for it in the light of the Islamic Code. There is no harm in your having a difference of opinion with them. But it is not permissible to join hands

RETHINK (1990–1994)

with the enemies. Your enemies would be happy over the weakening of [*Hizb-e Islami*] because the true mujaheddin will have lesser influence in the government.[145]

Sayyaf and Hekmatyar's stance in favour[146] of Saddam Hussein in the Gulf War of 1990–91 led to Saudi Arabia cutting its funding. From 1992 onwards, and in the wake of new deals made among the mujahedeen to come together as an interim coalition government, Saudi Arabia encouraged Hekmatyar's spoiling influence and resumed funding of *Hizb-e Islami*.[147] While exact data on Saudi funding of the Afghan mujahedeen parties is difficult to come by, *The Middle East* magazine claimed in June 1993 that Saudi funding for the two years prior had amounted to $2 billion.[148]

'Afghan Arabs' who sought to return to their home countries had different experiences. In the United Arab Emirates, for example, one interviewee stated that Sheikh Zayed instituted a particularly generous package of rewards for returnees in the early 1990s: the hundreds of Emirati nationals—mostly from the poorer, northern emirates such as Ra's al-Khaimah and Fujairah—'were given stipends to help them get back on their feet, and their children received particularly generous scholarships etc.'[149] But in Egypt and elsewhere in North Africa there was far more suspicion of the returning 'Afghan Arabs.' For Zakaria Ahmed Bashir, for example, Egypt posed particular problems:

So, I sent my wife back to Egypt. I was planning to perform Hajj in Saudi Arabia and to look for a job there. I attempted to obtain a Hajj visa, but the Saudi embassy in Pakistan asked for the approval of the Egyptian ambassador. However, the Egyptian embassy refused, and I realised that going to Egypt would mean my arrest, because I heard that all those returning from Afghanistan were being arrested. We read that the laws against terrorism punished anyone fighting for a second country. I started to think of going to another country to work.[150]

An internal Saudi government report from 1995 stated that 12,000 Saudis had reportedly travelled to Afghanistan in the 1980s and early 1990s.[151] The Saudi authorities were extremely concerned as to what these jihadis would do upon their return, particularly after a large bomb attack in November 1995.[152]

5

CLOSER AND FARTHER
(1994–1998)

The Taliban advised [bin Laden] that he should not misuse Afghan soil and that he should control himself; it would make Mullah Mohammad Omar upset. [...] But he'd go ahead and do it anyway and then come and promise not to do it again. But then it would happen another time. Keeping bin Laden was, for the Taliban, like tending to a fire.

Senior political Talib[1]

The truth was that we didn't know where the Taliban would go. We didn't begin it with the idea of taking over the country.

Mullah Khaksar[2]

The Soviet Army had installed and funded local militia groups in its wake so as to stall a speedy collapse of Najibullah's government and his control of the country. At the same time, they massively increased payments (via the local provincial administrations) of bribes that decreased meaningful violence[3] against the government. The surfeit of money saturated the local commanders in southern Afghanistan; they would still carry out occasional attacks, but for the most part busied themselves with local and internal power struggles

111

and with consolidating their positions and hold over the tribes through land purchases.[4]

The Soviet strategy was effective and allowed for an orderly withdrawal from Afghanistan. By 1992 domestic problems within the (by then former) Soviet Union prompted a cutoff of funding to its Afghan allies, and local militia commanders were forced to find other avenues of funding in order to hold together their groups of fighters.[5] This was especially true in southern Afghanistan, where the primary objective was to take Kandahar City, divide it among the various tribes and commanders, and preside over a massive looting and auctioning off of the city's and province's assets. Tanks were cut up for scrap and sold in Pakistan. Electrical and telephone wires met a similar fate, while one band of Noorzai tribesmen spent several days breaking into Kandahar City's bank vault.[6] The opium economy that had been fostered in southern Afghanistan during the anti-Soviet *jihad* was another source of income for the warring parties, and was highly contested, particularly in Helmand.[7]

The central leadership in Kabul increasingly lost control of individual units or sub-commanders who, when not paid by their superior, would act unilaterally to find other resources, often turning to crime. In the south-east there were many similar instances:

For those two months of Mujaddidi there weren't many issues. We didn't have this problem with the *topakiyaan* [men with guns] really. But in the meantime new figures emerged in this scene. The main reason was the unplanned collapse of Najib's regime with lots of reserves and caches. There were still remnants from the Najib regime in some provinces like Lowgar, Ghazni, Paktya and those areas and the north, where there were many weapons reserves and cash. Those opportunistic remnants of the Communist regime were just looking for these opportunities [to make money of their own].[8]

Many of the remaining militias and remnants of the Najib government played an important role in the civil war that followed. As with tribal militias in the south, armed groups, individuals and parts of the army seized weapons across the country.[9]

Initially, much of the Afghan population had high hopes for the new mujahedeen government in Kabul. This, people said, was the government that they had fought for. Now the *jihad* would bear fruit, an Islamic system would be implemented and people could go about their daily lives.[10] Unfortunately the alignments and temporary deals soon unravelled, and Hekmatyar, Massoud and others fought each other on the streets of Kabul.[11] In these squabbles, the fate of Kandahar was forgotten, and local mujahedeen soon started to prey on the people.

The checkpoint became an everyday feature of life in the south. Different commanders controlled different sections of the roads and each would extract a toll from passing vehicles and passengers. Interviews attest to how people were being killed or raped as they passed through these checkpoints; the rule of law was absent.[12] Within Kandahar City itself, the main commanders would fight among themselves, at times even deploying tanks. These ongoing conflicts caused an ever-deteriorating situation for civilians throughout the late 1980s and early 1990s.[13]

This chapter and the next cover the entire period of the Taliban's government, from the time when they were just another local group to their rise and eventual control over much of Afghanistan's territory. It assesses the key events and trends that impacted their susceptibility to the influence of al-Qaeda and bin Laden, who were using Afghanistan as an operational base.

A particularly important theme is that of foreign influence (i.e., international actors' policy towards al-Qaeda and the Taliban) and the way this shaped the relationship between the two groups—albeit often unintentionally. The late summer of 1998 seems in many ways to have been the tipping point: bin Laden's group carried out the American embassy bombings in East Africa, the Taliban were caught unawares by the retaliatory cruise missile strikes, and conspiracy theories about the implacable hostility of the international community to the 'Islamic Emirate' were rife.

1994–1996: Independent Action

The Taliban

By early 1994 security conditions had further deteriorated in southern Afghanistan, particularly in Kandahar province. Commanders who had previously drawn funds from foreign donors or from state assets had started, absent other sources, to turn on people in their areas as well as traders passing through to substitute their income. The loose networks that constituted the Afghan *jihad* against the Soviet Union, which were artificially brought under the thumb of the seven ISI-sanctioned mujahedeen fronts by Pakistan, had started to unravel. The decline in funding revealed the true nature of the alliance, where commanders would switch from one mujahedeen party to the next in order to gain access to money, resources and training. Now, however, they were ignoring the main leaders, and small groups and commanders acted unilaterally.[14]

'It was a time when everyone was a king,' many inhabitants of Kandahar recall, and there was no end in sight to the increasingly hazardous chaos.[15] It was in this period—in late 1993 and in 1994—that the mujahedeen who had formerly fought on the Taliban fronts in the 1980s came together and debated what might be done about the problems in their area.[16] As Olivier Roy notes, there was nothing new about Taliban groups themselves: their phenomenal success was due to their coordination. As early as 1995, Roy hypothesises, the Taliban movement 'developed on the basis of the network of these fortified madrassas.'[17]

Most of these former mujahedeen were at home, studying or teaching, but a series of discussions—initially private but then formalised with several semi-public gatherings—led eventually to the decision to take action.[18] Mullah Zaeef tells of the final meeting:

Mullah Mohammad Omar took an oath from everyone present. Each man swore on the Qur'an to stand by him, and to fight against corruption and the criminals. No written articles of association, no logo and no name for the movement was agreed on or established during the meeting.

The shari'a would be our guiding law and would be implemented by us. We would prosecute vice and foster virtue, and would stop those who were bleeding the land. Soon after the meeting, we established our own checkpoint at Hawz-e Mudat along the Herat-Kandahar highway, and we immediately began to implement the shari'a in the surrounding area.[19]

When Mullah Zaeef went to visit Mullah Mohammed Omar to ask whether he wanted to become the senior commander for the movement, for example, he was told that these discussions had already been taking place in Sangisar, independently from what Zaeef and his friends had been working on.[20]

In spring 1994, Mullah Mohammad Omar took action close to where he was based: in Sangisar just off the main highway between Kandahar City and Herat. This is the well-known founding myth of the movement, a story that is retold in every account of the early days.[21] A hagiographical account of Mullah Mohammad Omar's biography written by an Arab *jihadi* author offers the transcript of a radio broadcast[22] made by Mullah Mohammad Omar where he recollects those early days:

He [...] began pursuing some thieves that stole a convoy from some travellers and abducted some women near Qandahar [sic]. Then the students, and at their head was Mulla Mohammad Umar, captured the thieves' weapons and found some of the women killed. Then the thieves fled from them away from Qandahar. [...] And this is the story of the beginning which [Mullah Mohammad Omar] narrated [on the radio]. He said:

'I used to study in a school in the city of [Sangisar] in Qandahar with about 20 other of my fellow students. Then corruption took over the land, murder, looting and robbery reached alarming proportions, and control was in the hands of the corrupt and wicked ones, and no one imagined that it was possible to change this condition and rectify this situation. And if I too thought that and told myself "Allah burdens not a person beyond his scope."'[23] [...]

The beginning of the movement was that I folded my books in the school in [Sangisar], and I took another individual with me and we walked by foot to the area of [Zangiabad]. And from there I borrowed a motorcycle from a person named Surur, then we went to [Taloqan]. This was the beginning of the movement, and remove any other thoughts from your minds.

We began visiting the students in the schools and the study circles in the morning of that day, and we went to a study circle in which approximately 14 individuals were studying, then I gathered them in a circle around me and said to them, 'The Religion of Allah is being stepped on, the people are openly displaying evil, the People of Religion are hiding their Religion, and the evil ones have taken control of the whole area; they steal the people's money, they attack their honour on the main street, they kill people and put them against the rocks on the side of the road, and the cars pass by and see the dead body on the side of the road, and no one dares to bury him in the earth.'

I said to them, 'It is not possible to continue studying in these situations, and those problems will not be solved by slogans that are not backed up. We, the students, want to stand up against this corruption. If you want to truly work for the Religion of Allah, then we must leave the studies. And I will be honest with you, no one has promised to help us even with one Rupi, so that you will not assume that we will provide food for you, rather we will request food and help from the people.'

I said, 'This is not the work of a day, nor a week, nor a month, nor a year, rather it will take a long time. Are you able to perform that or not?'

And I used to encourage them and say to them, 'This evil one who is sitting in his centre like a black cauldron due to the extreme heat—and those days in the summer season were very hot—is openly waging war against the Religion of Allah, and we claim that we are from the People of the Religion of Allah, and we are not able to perform any action to support to His [Shari'a].'

I said to them, 'If we conquer an area, we will defend it, then do not complain that there is no studying or a lack of money and weapons, so are you able to perform this action or not?' [...]

Then no one from those fourteen accepted to perform this action, and they said, 'We might be able to perform some of the duties on Fridays.' So I said to them, 'Who will perform them the rest of the days?'

This movement was the result of a pure trust (in Allah) because if I had gauged the rest of the schools and (study) circles according to this (study) circle, I would have returned to my school. But I fulfilled the oath I had taken upon myself for (the sake of) Allah, [...] and he treated me with what you have seen. Then I went on to another study circle in which there was about seven students, so I presented the matter to them just like I presented it to the students of the first study circle, then all of them got ready for action.

All of those ones were one nation, there were no differences between them from being young men and old men, or children and young men, or male and female, but this work was based upon Wisdom from Allah, [...] so he placed me in a test since the beginning of it. Then we travelled on this motorcycle to the schools and study groups until 'Asr prayer, until fifty-three People of the True Trust (in Allah) were ready. Then I returned to my school and said to them, 'Come tomorrow morning,' but they arrived at one in the night to [Sangisar], so this was the beginning.

The work started before (even) twenty-four hours had passed on the idea. And one of my friends led the people in prayer, so when he lead them in the Fajr prayer, one of the followers said, 'This night while I was sleeping, I saw the Angels entering [Sangisar], and their hands were soft, so I asked them to wipe me with their hands for blessings.'

And the next morning at ten o'clock, we asked for two cars from [Hajji Bashar], one of the businessmen of the area, so he gave us two cars; a small car, and a large cargo truck, then we moved those students to the area of [Keshkinakhud], and others joined us. And when the numbers became many, we borrowed weapons from the people, so this was the beginning of this movement, until it continued.[24]

Following this early success, some local funding was obtained. Multiple accounts confirm the early support of the chief of nearby Keshkinakhud, Hajji Bashar,[25] an instrumental figure in the early days of the movement. The rest of that spring and summer was devoted to dismantling the checkpoints of local commanders in western Kandahar who stood up to the Taliban.

Some have claimed that Rabbani (and Massoud) in Kabul chose to support the Taliban at this point, giving as much as $1 million in cash to the fledgling movement during the summer.[26] While numerous anecdotal and incidental accounts[27] seem to confirm the broad outlines of support (at least of an implicit or passive kind), the evidence for the early provision of so much money is unsubstantiated.

In mid-October 1994, the Taliban took Spin Boldak, after which they captured a former *Hizb-e Islami* arms dump in Pashai Ghund in Spin Boldak close to the border with Pakistan.[28] This huge cache—according to the ISI director at the time—consisted of 17 tunnels worth of ammunition and weapons, enough to supply three divisions,[29] and was an important moment for the movement which from that point onward had few problems arming itself.[30]

By 5 November Taliban fighters had taken Kandahar City. Neither the Taliban's early discussions nor their actions appear to have been based on long-term strategic goals. Their activities, as was the case with the Taliban front lines in the anti-Soviet *jihad*, appear to have been reactionary in nature.

Mullah Zaeef's account of the Taliban's early motivations at the point when they had taken Kandahar is worth quoting at some length:

'The objectives of the Taliban, when they first started their activities, were simple. Based on the complaints of the people, the Taliban set out to clean the roads from the commanders that had established checkpoints along them, charging security fees and taxes, robbing travellers and threatening the lives and property of those who passed by or lived in the area. In this way, the Taliban were only focusing on a small area, mainly Highway One, the road that connects Herat and Kandahar and that passes through Helmand and Kandahar province. In accordance with the founding principles of Islam, the Taliban tried to avoid fighting where possible, always sending delegations to negotiate first, asking people so cease their illegal activities and abandon their checkpoints. Only when the Taliban's demands were not met, would they move on their opponents using violent means.

'The Taliban sought to give security back to the community, not only by removing rogue commanders and criminal bands from the roads, but by installing an actual legal system, enforced by them and based on the *shari'a*. In the absence of any government and given the ongoing fighting, the people had become helpless. There was no one to turn to, no one who held people accountable; the power of the gun was the only thing governing in most of southern Afghanistan and in other parts of the country. The Taliban established courts, settling local conflicts and complaints, holding people accountable.

'Many people longed for the *shari'a* and Islam to bring peace and an end to the chaos; they wanted to finally reap the fruits of the long *jihad* against the Soviet Union and the Communist regime.

Most people wanted these things, and the impatient demands of other provinces, districts and cities expanded the zone of our operations and our objectives.'[31]

Mullah Mutawakil was also involved in the movement from the early days and his account lists three priorities: the prevention of crime and insecurity through the implementation of Islamic law; 'ending the chaotic situation'; and the fact that 'Afghans wanted to live in peace under the blessings of security under Islamic law.'[32] Another interviewee who was present during that time confirmed the limited nature of the movement:

When the movement first started they published some letters. They stated the following: 'we want to remove the chains [checkpoints], thieves and robbery. We do not seek to rule Afghanistan nor are we doing this for money. We don't even ask for *zakat* or *ushr* from you. We don't want to pressure people to fight for us. If people want to join with us we will be happy to welcome you. If people want to give us *zakat* and *ushr*,[33] we will be happy.' After that, many traders from Kandahar offered their help and support to the Taliban because the traders were unhappy with the situation. They supported the Taliban against the *topakiyaan* [men with the guns] and robbers.[34]

The movement had coalesced around a limited agenda, and as its actions gathered momentum it found itself engaged in a larger endeavour. The input of Pakistan at this point—and the extent of its involvement is still not entirely clear[35]—neither invalidates nor disproves this initial limited set of goals. The Taliban emerged in 1994 as a reaction to local circumstances.[36]

The movement that came together, formed by largely unknown madrassa students who had fought as minor commanders during the 1980s *jihad*, was forged on the basis of their understanding of Islam. These men regarded the *qur'an* and their interpretation of *shari'a* as their guiding principles, representing a mixture of local customs and a literalist reading of religious texts. Their sense of self-identity was that of a bulwark against corruption, both moral and civil, that opposed them to local mujahedeen groups and their supporters. From the beginning, therefore, they were initially wary of allowing their group to be hijacked politically or watered down by anyone else.[37]

Mullah Mohammad Omar still remained an enigmatic figure at this point. Along the lines of the old Soviet model, he had an *amir* of his own,[38] responsible for political decisions and the direction of the movement, but as he played a more and more central role—and after the linking-up of some other separate 'Taliban' fronts which had sprung up in the southern region and their swearing of allegiance to Mullah Mohammad Omar and not the *amir*—he soon became the *de facto* leader[39] of the movement.

He was, however, a classic Talib of the older generation[40]—educated in the Deobandi curriculum and deeply influenced by the 1980s experience that saw the emergence of a fiercely nationalist and Afghan understanding of *jihad*. Raised in rural southern Afghanistan, Mullah Mohammad Omar very much represented and strongly supported rural Pashtun cultural practices that were (and in parts still are) the norm for rural Pashtuns in the south.[41] He held a deep respect for religion and religious custom, and many interviewees have attested to his constant desire to 'make sure we do this properly and Islamically.'[42] This was a commonly stated motivation and desire at the time.[43] The initial impetus was for a movement of values.[44] Qualification for membership (at least initially) was determined by whether a particular person conformed (or was willing to conform from that moment on) to the Taliban's standards, values and beliefs.[45]

Mullah Mohammad Omar seemed to acknowledge that he was not necessarily the one with the knowledge or wisdom to implement the 'perfect Islamic system,' and he was known (at least at the beginning) for deferring to others.[46] It was his understanding of religion and its cultural background that would prove to be an exploitable vulnerability for those who had their own agendas in the country—notably bin Laden. At the same time, it was his own inflexibility (given this understanding and background) that determined many of the movement's decisions.[47]

The Taliban movement was by and large welcomed in the south and east of Afghanistan by the local population, but it was not only they who offered support in the early months: internationally, too, the Taliban were initially welcomed. Hamid Karzai, Afghanistan's current President, was an early supporter. He told Richard Smith, the US Consul General in Peshawar at the time, to support them.[48] In Washington, acting State Department spokesman Glyn Davies said that the United States could see 'nothing objectionable' about this development. Two months later, Assistant Secretary of State for South Asian Affairs, Robin L. Raphel, stated that the Taliban had to be 'acknowledged' as an 'indigenous' movement that had 'demonstrated staying power':

They control more than two-thirds of the country, they are Afghan, they are indigenous, and they have demonstrated staying power. [...] The real source of their success has been the willingness of many Afghans, particularly Pashtuns, to tacitly trade unending fighting and chaos for a measure of peace and security, even with several social restrictions. It is not in the interest of Afghanistan or any of us here that the Taliban be isolated.[49]

High degrees of local support for the Taliban were manifested. Local people genuinely sought to take part in the movement at this time as it moved through a country that was plagued by lawlessness and conflict. It was only later that issues such as the Taliban's forced conscription to the armed forces and increasingly alien decrees became contentious in the south.[50]

The Taliban were to change the nature of their rhetoric as they widened their grip on the country. Early on they had proclaimed relatively limited goals: the provision of security and the implementation of the *shari'a* and a return to true Islam, with no or limited political ambitions or programme. However, they experienced their first defeat and setback after more or less six months of successive victories and deals in March 1995, while trying to take Kabul.[51] This reverse was followed by indiscriminate shelling of the capital, the same tactics the mujahedeen had applied before in their claim for sole power in Kabul.[52]

It is worth taking a moment to consider the role that Pakistan played in the formation and evolution of the movement.[53] The group that emerged locally in the spring of 1994 to operate against the plethora of commanders that dotted the roads in western Kandahar had done so indigenously and without external support. Even Pakistani accounts of the early days of the Taliban admit this, and the point of the debate nowadays mainly focuses on the extent of support, influence or control.[54] As Nawaz explains: 'The ISI did not have a great deal of leverage over the Taliban once the latter established themselves, but they did have key contacts and used them effectively.'[55] Aside from the emergence of the Taliban as a viable 'third way' fighting force in 1994, the 1994–96 period demonstrated a high degree of continuity with that which preceded it. Hekmatyar, admittedly, was starting to look like a lost cause and seemed not to be the answer to the Pakistani military and intelligence services' desire to install a friendly Pashtun government in Kabul.[56] Moreover, business interests—many of which were intricately linked back into the state and to the armed forces—and trucking companies in Pakistan were keen at that point to see an opening up of trade routes through Afghanistan up to Central Asia, via Kabul.[57] The Salang Pass and the crossing of the northern border at the town of Hairatan into Uzbekistan were unfeasible due to heavy fighting and Pakistan had hopes for the southern route; this would see goods transported via Quetta through Kandahar and onwards via the western city of Herat into Turkmenistan.[58]

In autumn 1994, a delegation headed by General Nasirullah Babar, the minister of the interior in Benazir Bhutto's government, went to Chaman, on the border between the two countries.[59] The security arrangements were made by Sultan Amir Tarar, better known as 'Colonel Imam,' who had coordinated much of Pakistan's activities throughout the 1980s Afghan *jihad*. At the time, the southern provinces were in a state of disarray, with multiple commanders feuding, and he would prove a useful guide through the chaos. When Babar returned, he dispatched a convoy with goods along the southern route, organised by the Army's National Logistics Cell.[60] The situation, however, had changed: the thirty military trucks were captured by a local commander. The Taliban had by then taken the city of Kandahar[61] and were able to 'rescue' the convoy.[62]

The sending of a military convoy at a time when the Taliban were ascendant was interpreted as support for the movement. The erroneous belief that emerged was that the Taliban were a Pakistan-created entity.[63]

In fact, so much trade passed through Afghanistan during the initial months following the Taliban's assumption of power that food prices in Pakistan plummeted.[64]

Much of the current perception about the early beginnings of the Taliban as a consolidated movement has to do with its sudden and unpredicted rise and success. Articles written at the time, and indeed many accounts from the present day, marvel at the sudden appearance of the movement. It is worth noting that in March 1995, former General Mirza Aslam Beg accused the United States of having created the Taliban in order to stop the growing influence of Iran and other Islamist influences.[65] There was considerable confusion on all sides regarding the emergence of the Taliban.

The early success of the movement rested on a number of factors. The Taliban transcended tribal divisions as a group.[66] Islam was at the core of their proclaimed identity, albeit tied to a form of Afghan nationalism. Their proclaimed values resonated with the population. Furthermore, the power vacuum and the various non-unified commanders and groups offered room for manoeuvre. It was the failure of the mujahedeen commanders and groups to provide security and prevent chaos that gave the Taliban its broad public support in southern Afghanistan and beyond in the early days.[67]

There is some credible evidence that the Taliban received financial support from Pakistan in 1995 and 1996.[68] Initially this seems not to have been the pattern. Weapons and counsel were the common currency, and they were not necessarily delivered in a direct fashion. In this way—as with the seizure of the Pasha arms dump following the fall of Spin Boldak—the path was indicated.[69] Indeed, witnesses report seeing Taliban fighters with brand new Kalashnikov rifles as well as some trucks containing new munitions still with the plastic covers wrapped around them.[70] There were enough weapons dumps and supplies within Afghanistan for there not to have been a major problem of logistics for the time being.[71]

While Pakistani support was forthcoming from an early stage of the Taliban movement's existence, the connection was fragile and statements from both the Pakistani ISI as well as the Taliban early on demonstrated the uneasy nature of the relationship. The ISI and Pakistan aimed to exert control, while the Taliban leadership manoeuvred between keeping its independence and sustaining support.[72] By the time the Taliban had moved up northeast towards Kabul, analysts were reporting a new 'mobile' style of fighting which their new 4x4 vehicles allowed them to conduct.[73] The vehicles need not have been given to them directly by Pakistan—indeed, there were numerous other donors or traders during this period who could have facilitated such a supply—but their use in battle may have been suggested by Pakistani advisors (some of whom were seen within Afghanistan during this time) and at the very least they had to arrive via Pakistan.[74]

Despite all this evidence, how important were Pakistani contributions and to what extent did this imply control? A partial answer will emerge later in this book, but as stated above this early period seemed not to be a case of the Taliban following orders from Pakistan. It was a conflicted relationship, with Pakistan aiming to gain increasing control of the movement.

Supporters flocked into Afghanistan from madrassas in Pakistan.[75] In March 1995, reports talk of hundreds of students from Peshawar being transported to Kandahar.[76] The Taliban showed an unerring ability to mobilise significant numbers of fighters and members in a short time. Reports of madrassa students being sent from Pakistan include remarks that young Uzbeks and Tajiks from northern Afghanistan were also joining and travelling to Kandahar, which played a key role in the Taliban's rapid growth and success.[77] The joining up of madrassa students and support lent by the *Imams* and *Ulemaa'* from the border region do not necessarily mean state-sanctioned support. The ties between the Pakistani *ulemaa'* and the Afghans among the Taliban were strong and went back many years,[78] which would have been enough for the fledgling Taliban movement to call on support from across the border.

The Taliban movement had two principal supporters in Pakistan: General Naseerullah Babar, who continued to seek influence in Afghanistan and aimed to open up trade routes to Central Asia, and *Jami'at-i Ulema-ye Islam* (that part under the leadership of Mawlana Fazlur Rahman). The group represented Deobandism and aimed to counter the influence of the *Jama'at-e Islami* and growing Wahhabism.[79]

Business interest in the Taliban was strong at the time. As the movement gathered momentum, and once it had demonstrably taken large swathes of southern and south-eastern Afghanistan, this was seen as a positive development by many, not just in regional terms. A small group of officials at the US State Department began to consider the possibility that the Taliban might achieve their objective of improving security in a manner that would help their plan for an oil pipeline, circumventing Iran and connecting the Central Asian oil and gas fields to a sea port.[80]

At this point the relationship between Pakistan and the Taliban did not concern the foreign jihadists or their wider ambitions. They played no role in the Taliban, and only a fraction of the real leadership (along with fighters) were still to be found in Pakistan and Afghanistan. At the time there was little indication that they would be moving back to Afghanistan in any significant numbers, having been building up other operational locations.[81] Pakistan did continue to send Pakistanis training for Kashmir into Afghanistan and the camps being run in the east and south-east of the country.[82] This did not change after the Taliban 'took over' these areas, mainly because—in the case of *Loya Paktya*—the Taliban's manner of gaining control was more a case of striking a deal with the local strongmen like Jalaluddin Haqqani.[83]

When the Taliban moved into south-eastern Afghanistan in February 1995, they did so following consultation with the local commanders and tribal elders.[84] The areas now corresponding to Paktya and Paktika reportedly posed few problems, but Khost was more challenging:

There were checkpoints along the roads, commanders were fighting, and the population was suffering. The mujahedeen commanders there were divided about the Taliban. Most of those who opposed us did so out of greed and personal interest, not wanting to give up the power they had. Hekmatyar was also doing his best to provoke commanders to oppose and fight the Taliban; his efforts yielded little fruit. Jalaluddin Haqqani and Mawlawi Mohammad Nabi Mohammadi were the two most influential mujahedeen commanders in Khost.[85]

Their eventual acquiescence tipped the scales in favour of the Taliban and the bulk of greater Paktya came under their control.[86] The initial friction between the tribal and military elites of the area and the Taliban has continued until the present day, albeit at a different degree and for the most part beyond the public eye.[87]

When the success of the Taliban in moving beyond greater Kandahar became manifest, there was no longer any pretence in Pakistan that Hekmatyar was the solution. Instead, Pakistani resources were aligned with the Taliban movement in the hope that they would fulfil their ambitions for a pliable, Pakistan-friendly government in Kabul.[88]

In its first two years the Taliban generated an immense sense of momentum. The founders sought support and funding from sources they considered respectable and Islamic so they approached Saudi Arabia and other Arab states. Adnan Basha, the secretary general of the International Islamic Relief Organisation, stated that his group gave $60 million to the Taliban.[89] While the Taliban may have sought funds from the Arab world in their early days, it was only the formal establishment of a government in Kabul and the granting of diplomatic recognition by Saudi Arabia in 1996[90] that seemed to open doors for significant official state funding.[91] In the early years support was more indirect and less systematic. The Taliban played host to Saudi and Emirati princes in January and February 1995 as they hunted bustard in the deserts south of Kandahar City.[92] The Arabs left behind many off-road vehicles and other sundry items which the Taliban then appropriated.[93] Private donations were also reportedly high, especially from Saudi Arabia, during this period, but there are no useful estimates to gauge exactly how much this amounted to.[94] The land route through Pakistan also opened up opportunities for the smuggling of goods to and from the United Arab Emirates. There was, Matinuddin argues, made 'enough money available [for] the Taliban to buy their weapons from those willing to sell them.'[95]

And as for the foreign jihadis who had remained in Afghanistan following the end of the 1980s, the Taliban simply inherited them, much as they would eventually 'inherit' bin Laden. They were, for the most part, neither a concern nor a priority for the movement at this time.

As outlined in previous chapters, most interactions between international jihadist and Afghan mujahedeen groups took place in the east and south-east of the country. *Hizb-e Islami* under Hekmatyar, Sayyaf, and a number of other groups continued to play host to the internationals. All of the Afghan groups mentioned were opposed to the Taliban; they represented competing ideologies deriving from the Muslim Brotherhood, Wahhabism or the Hanbali school of Islamic jurisprudence. Even later members such as Haqqani were opposed to the Taliban at the time.[96] While *Hizb-e Islami* fighters regarded the Taliban as potential allies, Hekmatyar was fiercely opposed to them, as were prominent Arabs who ran training camps in Afghanistan.[97]

Al-Qaeda and the Arabs

1994–96 saw a growing pattern among the various international groups that were involved in the 1980s *jihad*. Many of the foreign jihadists were travelling in search of new bases and causes. A number of national groups returned to their fight at home and picked up the trajectory they had been on before the Afghan *jihad*, while others, in particular al-Qaeda, started to strategise and consolidate. These developments were spurred on by the increasing scrutiny of Pakistan, which by early 1995 was less amiable to the continued presence of foreign fighters along its border.[98]

'The international brigade of jihad veterans, being outside the control of any state, was suddenly available to serve radical Islamist causes anywhere in the world. Since they were no longer bound by local political contingencies, they had no responsibilities to any social group either. [...] They became free electrons of jihad, professional Islamists trained to fight and to train others to do likewise.'[99]

In 1994, there were relatively few Arabs left in Pakistan and fewer still remaining in Afghanistan, most of them being found at the training camps that operated in the south-east.[100] The mid-1990s were a period that Abu Mus'ab al-Suri called 'the phase of diaspora and temporary safe havens'[101] and this characterised the wide dispersion of the Arab veterans of the Afghan *jihad*. He summarises the most important havens for Afghan Arabs during the mid-1990s as follows:

• 'Europe, especially Britain, and Scandinavia, but also Canada and Australia;
• Sudan, where the EIJ leadership, the JI leadership, the al-Qaida leadership, a large bloc of LIFG members, and also a number of other jihadi groups gathered;
• Other Muslim countries that had no security restrictions on wanted jihadi fugitives, especially Yemen, where a number of Egyptian jihadis sought refuge in the early 1990s. Turkey and Syria also served as safe havens, in particular for North African and Libyan youths. A smaller number of Arab-Afghan veterans emigrated as far as the Philippines, Indonesia, Thailand, and Latin America or to the African continent.
• Chechnya and Bosnia, both of which became new arenas for the jihadi movements, especially the latter, which attracted several thousand mujahidin fighters, including many Arab-Afghan veterans.'[102]

Mohammad Salah explains further:

'Some of them managed to secure themselves in European countries thanks to the asylum they were able to obtain, while the majority wandered in other countries. However they were always looking for countries with unsteadiness and interior troubles, so they could use the interior situation and the deteriorating security procedures to access the country and reside there. Meanwhile, others managed to reach countries that sympathised with their situation. With time passing by, Afghan Arabs spread in Bosnia, Chechnya, and Somalia, in addition to Egypt and Yemen of course. However, Egyptian efforts to convince countries to stop protecting Egyptian fundamentalists and turn them in for trial aroused fear among Islamists themselves. But those residing in European countries were convinced that it was impossible to pressure European governments to surrender the Islamic leaders residing in Europe.'[103]

By 1994, Algeria was one of the key active locations of Arab Afghans seeking to recapture the atmosphere of the 1980s *jihad* as a communal Arab activity. Al-Suri described its importance as follows:

From the beginning of 1994 the hopes of all jihadis were linked to the Algerian cause and that it would be the second step for the Arab-Afghans towards the Arab world after the Afghanistan period. Osama bin Laden sent some of his assistants to reconnoitre the situation, and he attempted to offer assistance in terms of money and weapons. Doctor Ayman al-Zawahiri, Emir of the Egyptian Jihad Group, corresponded with 'Amin,' the emir of the GIA. [...] Al-Zawahiri supported the jihad and reminded 'Amin' of the importance of unifying the efforts of the jihadis there. The Libyan [Islamic] Fighting Group sent tens of its best mujahidin to participate in the field in the Algerian jihad. Many of the Moroccan jihadis worked in rear logistical services, transporting weapons and fighters to Algeria. Similarly, some of the Tunisians contributed with jihadi efforts. Hence, this cause constituted the main axis of interest for the jihadis in that period.[104]

Indeed, al-Suri later stated that the Algerian *jihad* was 'among the most important experience[s] for the jihadi movement in the second half of the twentieth century.'[105] Bin Laden does not seem to have been as active in support of the Algerian *jihad*; Hegghammer confirms that he did not send recruits to Algeria from Sudan.[106] Initially it was a relatively easy decision to take to travel to Algeria for this purpose (or to help with the media and fundraising efforts in support of that *jihad*), but with the rise of the *Groupe Islamique Armé* (GIA) and their increasingly brutal tactics, fewer people wanted to become involved.[107]

Bin Laden had moved to Sudan in 1992, although many Arabs had preceded him there.[108] Khartoum was seen as a good base on account of the favourable reception given by the country's two key figures, Omar al-Bashir and Hassan al-Turabi. A plethora of jihadi groups—including many who had fought in Afghanistan in the 1980s—flocked to Sudan, although this became so blatant that in 1993 the United States placed Sudan on its list of state sponsors of terrorism.[109]

Mohammad Salah suggests that bin Laden played a key role in the spread of these Afghan Arabs around the world:

Bin Laden had returned to Afghanistan following the Gulf war where he played a major role in arranging the departure of groups of Afghan Arabs to other countries using his connections, relations, money, and authority. He also hired some of them to work in the companies he owned in Asian and African countries. That's why it wasn't weird to hear information about the presence of Egyptian Afghan fundamentalists in countries like Indonesia, Philippine, Thailand, Ecuador, Argentina, and Paraguay.[110]

The various Arab factions who had debated their goals so vigorously during the early 1990s were now trying to realise them. 1992 saw the beginning of a five-year campaign in Egypt, largely motivated and reinvigorated by the return of Afghan Arabs. Many returnees were arrested—they had attempted to pass undetected back into the country through desert routes in the south—but enough made their way back.[111] The assassination of Farag Foda, a secular Egyptian intellectual, on 8 June 1992, was the opening shot in this campaign.[112] They later targeted Egypt's tourist industry—the November 1997 massacre in Luxor was the culmination of that strategy—through direct attacks and bombings.[113]

Egypt during this period fell prey to dozens of such attacks—as well as an attempt to set up an Islamic 'state' in Embaba[114]—but an assassination attempt against the President, Hosni Mubarak, in Addis Ababa in June 1995 proved a tipping point for the Egyptian security services who responded swiftly and severely.[115] It was a severe mis-calculation—as was the murder of two children recruited to spy on al-Zawahiri's group in Sudan in mid-1995—that earned al-Zawahiri's Islamic Jihad group the ire of Sudan's Hassan al-Turabi; members of Islamic Jihad were expelled from Sudan and ended up in Afghanistan, Jordan and Syria.[116] The group faced a significant public backlash within Egypt when, in an attempt on the life of the country's Prime Minister, a young schoolgirl was killed (and twenty-one injured). The death of Shayma Abdel-Halim stirred up Cairo residents to chant against 'terrorism' as they bore her coffin through the streets.[117]

In particular, the activities of al-Zawahiri and Egyptian Islamic Jihad demonstrate how groups, while associated with others and cooperating on various levels, still pursued their own struggles and goals that were quite distinct from what al-Qaeda would come to follow as part of its long-term strategy. Nevertheless, they did display certain features that would later become the hallmark of al-Qaeda's operations—like the targeted killings of civilians.

In the early 1990s Sudan had become a haven for Islamists after Hassan al-Turabi proclaimed his solidarity with oppressed Muslims from around the world and members of Hamas, Hizbullah, Egyptian Islamic Jihad and the GIA flocked to Khartoum.[118] Bin Laden—following a falling out with the house of Saud and a brief stay in Peshawar during which he reportedly was asked to negotiate a settlement between Hekmatyar and Massoud[119]—had dispatched a delegation to assess the possibility of relocating his operations to Sudan, and he moved to Khartoum in 1992.[120]

Sudan's economy lay in shambles and bin Laden brought hard currency and began to invest heavily in the country. He bought several farms, opened a number of businesses and began infrastructure projects. He invested dozens of millions.[121] He also provided the Sudanese government with urgently needed hard currency loans for food.[122]

Reports about his attitude and activities there are contradictory. Some sources claim that at first bin Laden was somewhat disengaged from the militant side of operations and focused on his business interests and enjoying his new found freedom and peace.[123] Sudan would be a turning point for al-Qaeda, and the organisation saw immense changes while based there. Hegghammer argues that, 'in Sudan, al-Qaida became a relatively structured enterprise with a central leadership, functionally differentiated committees and a salary system.'[124] In its role as a new hub for militant groups, Sudan was where bin Laden and al-Qaeda's core reached out to multiple groups throughout North Africa and the Middle East, establishing links and offering support.[125] At a White House meeting in 1995, a CIA analyst reportedly characterised bin Laden's activities in Khartoum as resembling a 'Ford Foundation' of Sunni 'Islamic terrorism.' In this way, al-Qaeda was approached with ideas and plans, and could then choose to sanction them and help with finance, planning and strategy afterwards.[126]

Al-Qaeda was still far from becoming the franchise brand into which it evolved in the early twenty-first century, and even those closely associated with bin Laden's group ran their individual groups and operations without consulting him. It should also not be forgotten that al-Qaeda at this point was little known, while individuals associated with bin Laden had a larger public profile. These included Abu Hajer al-Iraqi, Omar 'Abd al-Rahman, and al-Zawahiri.[127] While in Sudan, bin Laden maintained contact with individuals in Afghanistan and continued to finance guesthouses and activities there and in Pakistan.[128] In 1993, the United States government concluded that Sudan's government was sponsoring terrorism and imposed sanctions. Bin Laden was regarded as the focal point of much of the activities and groups that were congregating in Sudan, and international pressure mounted to expel him.[129]

In May 1996, bin Laden left Sudan after being told to do so by Turabi.[130] Opinions about the exact nature of his departure and the disengagement with Turabi and the Sudanese government are disputed, as is the success of his business ventures in Sudan. The predominant view is that they had largely failed to make any profits and that bin Laden had lost significant amounts of money. Furthermore, Turabi and the Sudanese government unceremoniously kicked him out, buying his properties and businesses at knockdown prices and leaving him with relatively few funds.[131]

The options for waging a *jihad* against America were heatedly debated during this period. It was clear that al-Qaeda was at a crossroads. Two new *fatwas* from Abu Hajer, the head of al-Qaeda's *fatwa* committee, seemed to push bin Laden in one direction:

A new vision of al-Qaeda was born. Abu Hajer's two fatwas, the first authorizing the attacks on American troops and the second, the murder of innocents, turned al-Qaeda into a global terrorist organization. Al-Qaeda would not concentrate on fighting armies but on killing civilians. The former conception of al-Qaeda as a mobile army of mujahideen that would defend Muslim lands wherever they were threatened was now cast aside in favor of a policy of permanent subversion of the West. The Soviet Union was dead and communism no longer menaced the margins of the Islamic world. America was the only power capable of blocking the restoration of the ancient Islamic caliphate, and it would have to be confronted and defeated.[132]

As Bonney states, bin Laden regularly refers to Ibn Taymiyah in his statements: 'As early as August 1996 he had praised him for "arousing the ummah of Islam against its enemies."'[133] Whether or not bin Laden's citing of Ibn Taymiyah is justified or taken out of context is another discussion to be had. In terms of bin Laden and al-Qaeda's world view, however, their activities (as argued by members) are sanctioned as part of a defensive *jihad*. Bonney goes on to explain how bin Laden regarded 'the rulers of the Arab states as having betrayed Allah, the Prophet and the "nation."'[134] This was a clear sanction for violence for bin Laden, who constructed a narrative that saw the rulers of the Arab states as being a function of the United States' interference.

Even during this period, however, bin Laden still seemed unable to decide how to proceed with his group. Many of those around him had solid ideas and actionable plans, but he seemed to vacillate during these years. He had retained an ingrained sense of loyalty to the Saudi royal family through his family ties, but his being stripped of his citizenship in 1994[135] together with the arrests of the Saudi clerics Salman al-Awdah and Safar al-Hawali had eroded his position.[136]

Robert Fisk, a British journalist, interviewed him during this period in Sudan, noting that bin Laden seemed almost at home there. They had a brief discussion about the 1980s *jihad*—bin Laden stressed the formative nature of the experience—but there was less of the Islamist and jihadist rhetoric that dominated subsequent interviews.[137] Abdel Bari Atwan, who also visited him, has written that he 'consolidated his presence in Sudan and sought to establish a safe haven for young men in search of *jihad* as well as the many Arab mujahedeen who had been refused the right to return to their homelands after the Afghan war.'[138] Bin Laden's life, however, was increasingly difficult on a purely practical level; he was often confronted with tough decisions as to where to move next and what to do there.

The foreign jihadis were relatively unconcerned with events back in Afghanistan. Most had moved on, whether to Sudan or to other *jihad*s, and Afghanistan seemed to have fallen into a state of chaotic decay—one which didn't deserve to be called a *jihad*, they thought.[139] Arguably it was the circumstance they found themselves in that forced Afghanistan back to the forefront of their minds. Training camps continued to function in Afghanistan at this time (1994–96) but they were, relatively speaking, islands removed from the Afghanistan around them; the camps and their logistical supply networks were only in touch with certain elements of the surrounding population and were by and large isolated from others.

Al-Zawahiri had moved from Sudan[140] to Yemen to plot his revenge against the Egyptian government. Again, he would miscalculate. On 19 November 1995, his operatives attacked the Egyptian Embassy in Islamabad; sixteen people were killed (excluding two suicide bombers) and over 60 wounded.[141] The operation provoked an immediate reaction from the Pakistani security services who rounded up some two hundred Arabs in Peshawar.[142] Egypt pressured other countries to extradite Egyptian Islamists and members of what Cairo classified as 'terrorist' organisations. Al-Zawahiri's operations contributed to this effort and bin Laden was forced to start looking for a new sanctuary. The bombing was also provocation enough for the Pakistanis to pursue any Arab jihadis still remaining. Around two hundred were reportedly flown out by bin Laden in planes that he specifically chartered for the purpose.[143]

For the foreign jihadis, 1994–96 was a period without a clear unified objective, characterised by stagnation, consolidation and exploration dependent on individual actors. Circumstance would force them to move from place to place, but their activities encompassed a mixture of action and inaction. The senior jihadi figures (both ideologues and people like bin Laden) were still consolidating their plans and justifications for those plans, and if their activities seem disjointed this was a reflection of their seeming uncertainty of purpose.

April 1996–July 1998: Getting to Know Each Other

1996 was the year the Taliban themselves attempted some consolidation of power. They had moved east and west out of Kandahar—taking Herat and most of the territory south and south-west of Kabul.[144] The capture of Kabul would give the Taliban a moment to reassess their movement and its goals as well as reinforce the desire of the political Talibs for international recognition.

Becoming Amir ul-Mu'mineen

The proclamation of Mullah Mohammad Omar as *Amir ul-Mu'mineen* in April 1996 was an important moment for the Taliban both within Afghanistan as well as for how they were seen by the outside world. Taliban forces were seemingly stuck outside Kabul, unable to breach front lines in Lowgar, and resorted to indiscriminate rocket attacks on the city.[145] Around 1,500 scholars from across Afghanistan (and some from Pakistan) came to Kandahar to discuss the Taliban movement's future.[146]

There seems to have been some confusion as to the purposes of the meeting. One Mullah—Mullah Khudaidad—from eastern Khost said that 'we all wondered what Mullah Omar wanted from us. We hadn't been told much except to come to Kandahar.'[147] On the third day, the discussion shifted and it was proposed that Mullah Mohammad Omar accept the title of *Amir ul-Mu'mineen*.

This title had previously been applied to Caliphs (like Abu Bakr, Omar ibn al-Khattab, Osman, Ali and Omar bin Abdul Aziz), but many argued that to accept the title would not imply laying claim to authority over the Muslim world as a whole, but rather to finalise and firm up the authority of Mullah Mohammad Omar and his movement, and to settle a simmering internal debate.[148]

Interviewees confirmed that the purpose of the title was to reinforce Mullah Mohammad Omar's claim to authority and to boost his Islamic credentials among foreign observers. One former mujahed who had fought on the Taliban fronts and was present at the discussions characterised their intention as follows:

The Ulemaa wanted to make the territory strong and the leadership strong; nothing else. They wanted to sanction the Rabbani government as illegal and to give the power to the Taliban government and make it legal. They wanted to give the Taliban government Islamic sanction as well as an Islamic name.[149]

Another echoed this with a different interpretation, suggesting that a settlement of the leadership issue was more important for local people than the national perspective:

And the common people were happy because this was a sign of security and stability for the future. When the [leadership] conflicts finished it meant the chance of fighting and instability was also over.[150]

131

Image, it seems, was the central concern, both for locals as well as internationals looking in. Another Talib present for the deliberations stressed the impact it would have on the wider Muslim community:

Those 1500 mullahs gathered to give the title to Mullah Mohammad Omar in order to show the world that only he could make an Islamic government for his country and no one else. He also wanted to show the ordinary Muslims of the world that they could also join up forces with *Amir ul-Mu'mineen* and bring changes in their countries as well.[151]

The opinions of Taliban associated with the movement then and now differ as to the reason for the change of title. One member close to the leadership said that:

The people only wanted peace in that time, and the Taliban brought it. Mullah Mohammad Omar needed to be president, though, or to be given some sort of title. We chose *Amir ul-Mu'mineen* because it was not just for the Afghan people but for all Muslims. [...] We sought to show to the world that Mullah Mohammad Omar was the correct person for the establishment of an Islamic government—not anybody else—and we also wanted to show to the ordinary Muslims of the world that they could join up with [him] and bring changes in their own countries as well.[152]

Another Taliban official stated that the title was given simply to clear up challenges to Mullah Mohammad Omar's leadership and to smooth out internal conflict:

A decision was taken to hold this meeting and gather together the Mullahs in order to prevent conflicts among the Taliban over the leadership. There had been some in the past, so we gathered together the *Ulemaa'* to make a final decision over the leadership and to prevent these conflicts for the future. [...] In the end, things worked out because we didn't have any such problems or internal conflicts over this matter in the future.[153]

The Taliban failed to anticipate a negative reaction from the Islamic world. Many countries responded negatively to the April declaration, and particularly among staunchly Sunni Arab states the announcement was seen as presumptuous by the leaders.[154]

Mullah Khaksar, a former Taliban intelligence chief, has argued[155] that the meeting was engineered and hijacked by Pakistani actors and interests. They sought, he claimed, to isolate the Taliban's leadership from the rest of the Islamic world and to preserve their own control and prioritise access to the Taliban's leader. The title, moreover, would ensure that the Taliban would remain under Mullah Mohammad Omar's leadership as long as he remained fit to rule and alive:

It was an unfair thing to do to Mullah Omar. It was Pakistan that wanted this. They were not trying to help him and to help Afghanistan. They wanted to turn the world against us. They wanted to keep Mullah Omar alone and to make the rest of the world, even the Muslim world, against him. It was a betrayal of Mullah Omar. When it was announced that he was Amir-ul Momineen, it meant that he was Amir of Muslims all over the world, and of course the Muslim world complained. How could one man say he is Amir of all Muslims? What gave him the right?

'When Mullah Omar said he was Amir-ul Momineen, it was as if we had put a big wall between us and other Muslims. I knew that among these ulema, religious leaders, were mullahs who were working for Pakistan, who were intentionally trying to create problems for Mullah Omar, with other Islamic countries and with the rest of the world. Mullah Omar didn't understand that they wanted the world against him. They wanted Afghanistan to be alone in the world because then they would be in control. Mullah Omar just couldn't see this.'[156]

Mullah Mohammad Omar's appointment as *Amir al-Mu'mineen*, as with many other episodes that would follow, reveal several things about the Taliban leadership and the inner dynamics of the movement, as well as their outlook and understanding of their actions on their international relations. In particular, since the first setbacks of the movement—the defeat at the gates of Kabul in 1995—the growing numbers of followers and foreign interests had led to internal strife. A 'second wave of recruits,' one senior political Talib noted, had joined the movement to fill the bureaucratic void in the administration as they took over more areas.[157]

The appointment was mostly designed to solve internal rivalries and clearly demonstrate to the followers not only the indisputable leadership of Mullah Mohammed Omar, but also the universal nature of the movement that transcended Afghanistan's tribal and ethnic divisions. The appointment propagated this very message by making clear that the legitimacy of the movement and its leadership were derived from Islam and stood in the tradition of the caliphates that had ruled over a great many people and countries. It is also likely that instead of regarding his appointment as a claim to rule over each and every Muslim, as represented by the *umma*, the aim was rather to rally support from Muslim nations to clearly show the Islamic nature of the movement, and its centrality within Islamic history, in an attempt to broaden its appeal.[158]

While internal disputes continued under the surface, Mullah Mohammad Omar remained the leader of the Taliban and his appointment as *Amir al-Mu'mineen* consolidated it under his leadership. Much of the Muslim world considered the appointment as the act of a megalomanic, idiosyncratic leader of a fanatical group that had few formal religious credentials upon which to claim its pre-eminent position or to rule the *umma* and the imagined caliphate.[159]

The majority of the leadership in general and Mullah Mohammad Omar in particular simply failed to envisage the backlash and quite open hostility that the announcement precipitated, a pattern that appears to be characteristic of much of the Taliban leadership's understanding of foreign relations—as regards individuals, countries, or to the wider religious community. As one former US State Department official observed after taking part in talks with the Taliban during this period: 'They were very naive. They knew little about the world and had little idea about foreign policy.'[160] There were sections of the leadership, though, who were concerned that the Taliban's policies were increasingly isolating them from the rest of the world. In the years to come, most Taliban political figures who shared these concerns were sidelined and saw their influence and access to the senior council and Mullah Mohammad Omar steadily diminish until they were completely isolated from decision-making processes.[161]

Indeed, one of the starkest conclusions that can be drawn from this episode—as from many others during this period—is the seeming naiveté of Mullah Mohammad Omar. Not all of his retinue seemed oblivious to the effect of such events and public statements, but the combination of the growing reliance on Mullah Mohammad Omar as *the* Taliban authority and official voice, coupled with the sidelining of competent and useful counsel, would change the movement significantly.

The titling of the Taliban head as *Amir ul-Mu'mineen* was also an indication that the Taliban intended to complete their military assault on Kabul and probably the north as well. The name of the country also changed as a result. An *amir* needed an *emaraat*, and accordingly Afghanistan became officially known to the Taliban as the 'Islamic Emirate of Afghanistan.'[162]

Inheriting Osama

Bin Laden left Sudan clandestinely in early May 1996 with a small number of family members and associates.[163] The chartered plane took off from Khartoum's international airport—built only a few years earlier by Bin Laden Construction Company[164]—landed briefly in Sharjah for refuelling and then continued its journey on to Jalalabad, Afghanistan.[165] Vahid Mojdeh has claimed that a party of mujahedeen representing Khalis' *Hizb-e Islami*, Hekmatyar's *Hizb-e Islami* and Sayyaf's *Ittehad-e Islami* had visited Sudan earlier in the year and made arrangements for the arrival of bin Laden.[166]

[I was told that they said:] We talked to Osama and asked him to come to Afghanistan to broker a deal between the mujahedeen and the Taliban, but Osama replied that 'your leaders are bad people and they don't keep their promises.' But this problem was cleared up for us by Abu Mus'ab al-Suri.[167]

Sources differ as to who exactly was present at the airfield on the day. Abu Jandal, bin Laden's bodyguard, says that Engineer Mahmud, a well-known *Hizb-e Islami* commander and member of the ruling Jalalabad *shura*, met the retinue,[168] while Mojdeh suggests that Mawlawi Khalis himself and three of his commanders were present.[169] Abu al-Walid al-Masri has written that four people met the plane: Doctor Amin, who had served as a medic during the battle of Jalalabad years before; Abd al-Haq; (Engineer) Mahmud, from Khalis's *Hizb-e Islami*; and 'Saznour,' from Sayyaf's *Ittehad-e Islami*.[170] The various accounts all list individuals associated with factions and groups that at the time were strongly opposed to the Taliban and often were clashing with their forces advancing on the eastern region.

Abu Mus'ab al-Suri has also written an account of bin Laden's arrival and Khalis' response:

I heard something incredible from Yunis Khalis ... during a meeting. [...] He said to Abu Abdallah [bin Laden], in his thickly accented but proficient Arabic, 'I have nothing but myself, and it is very dear to me. However, you are more precious to me, and your well-being is more important than my own. You are our guest, and no one can get to you. If anything happens with the Taleban, tell me. Though there is little I can do after they reach you, I will do all I can.'[171]

The reasons the individuals involved themselves in facilitating Osama's return to Afghanistan are murky. Several analysts and interviewees claim that Massoud and Rabbani had personally sanctioned his return, believing that bin Laden could help to negotiate with the advancing Taliban, and would also bring development in the form of infrastructure projects, much along the same lines as he had done in Sudan.[172]

Rabbani thought that Osama bin Laden had a lot of money. If he [bin Laden] came to Afghanistan, he [Rabbani] thought, then he will change the balance of power to my favour; lots of Arabs and Afghans will come over from Gulbuddin's side because of that money. So he invited Osama to Afghanistan, but when bin Laden arrived he evaluated the situation and found that the balance of power was such that the Taliban were the best choice: they were actually in power in many places. He left Rabbani, because naturally you don't want to stay with someone weak.[173]

Mojdeh's account gains credibility from the fact that Rabbani was actively trying to reach out to the Taliban to hold peace discussions; as early as December 1995, he had formed a special team to engage in talks.[174] Caution should be applied to analysis of the motivations of Rabbani and Massoud at the time, however. Much can also be explained as political manoeuvring on their part, since their statements and actions often did not appear to be pursuing the same objectives.

The Taliban were preoccupied with their renewed attempt to take Kabul, which had got bogged down, and were unaware of Osama's arrival or activities during this time.[175] Mullah Zaeef notes in his forthcoming history of the movement that bin Laden and his associates 'stayed under the radar while Osama established and strengthened his good relations with local commanders and government officials, often assisting them financially.'[176] The Arabs were initially placed in a guesthouse associated with Sayyaf, but then found a place of their own outside the city near the Tora Bora mountains. This was familiar territory for bin Laden, but the sparse settings and facilities did not appeal to his family or jihadi associates.[177]

Bin Laden was initially reticent, reluctant to get involved in the squabbles of the Afghan civil war. One, probably speculative, suggestion was that he mediated between Hekmatyar and Sayyaf prior to their reconciliation that resulted in Hekmatyar's famous arrival in Kabul.[178] Abu al-Walid al-Masri's account of the period contends that the decision was taken by Rabbani's government and a credible threat of arrest (in the form of a warrant) of bin Laden was what pushed him towards the Taliban.[179] He had not yet met them, nor had the movement taken the area in which he was living, but Rabbani's attempts to curry favour with international opinion at this point—coupled with the pervasive political influence of Massoud—make this an intriguing suggestion. This is repeated by Mullah Zaeef:

There were also rumours of a threat that Rabbani had delivered to Osama: if he didn't pay money to support the defence of Jalalabad, Rabbani said, then he would be handed over to Saudi Arabia or the United States. Osama had told Rabbani that he did not have the sum of money he had asked for, but pledged that he would try to find it.[180]

Zaeef's account, in particular the claim that bin Laden stated that he did not have the funds demanded, gain credibility in the light of his likely financial situation after the departure from Sudan.[181]

The Taliban moved into the Jalalabad/Nangarhar area on 11 September, 1996, and it was at this point that the movement 'inherited Osama.'[182] It is worth taking a moment to assess just how much the Taliban and bin Laden knew of each other at this point.

From the Taliban's perspective, they were familiar with the Arabs from the 1980s—this would have been repeatedly stressed by their reported interlocutor at initial points of contact, Jalaluddin Haqqani, the south-eastern commander who had also joined up with the Taliban movement—but none of their recent history was known. Interviews with senior Taliban officials even today indicate a significant level of misunderstanding as to the specific details and motivations of the Arabs.[183]

Abdel Bari Atwan suggested in an interview (as did another Taliban interviewee in Kabul) that the Taliban were initially well disposed towards bin Laden:

Bin Laden said to me, 'I was the instrument, or the mediator between the Taliban and Jalaluddin Haqqani.' He was the commander of Afghani forces under the Rabbani government. [...] So he said to me, 'I did the Taliban a very big favour when I introduced Haqqani—who is a close friend of bin Laden—to defect and leave the Rabbani government, and join the Taliban.' And because of that, the Taliban managed to actually conquer Kabul. Why? Because Haqqani is a professional general, a professional military man. And the Taliban lacked their professionalism[184]

Regardless of the truth of that claim, the Taliban had heard that the Arabs were rich, and stories of bin Laden's spending during the 1980s only encouraged expectations that he would embark on a construction and development funding spree within Afghanistan. Vahid Mojdeh sums up the situation at the time:

Contrary to Mujahideen leaders, the Taliban leaders had no experience in working with Arabs. Osama and his loyalists were of course well aware of how to influence the Taliban, relying on their previous experiences with Mujahideen leaders. The purchase of expensive automobiles for Mullah Omar and his loyalists was the first step in that direction. Financial support in the war against the Taliban's opposition, in particular buying off the opposing commanders proved to be an effective instrument in the Taliban's advancement. Osama thus established himself among the Taliban in a position far above that of a mere guest.[185]

The oft-repeated assertion that the Taliban's first encounter with bin Laden on the eve of its attempt at taking Kabul also saw a cash payment of up to $3 million is both unproven and unlikely given his probable financial situation.[186] Several interviews conducted for this book suggest that bin Laden played a role in the deal brokered between Haqqani and the Taliban.[187] Haqqani at the time was opposed to the Taliban, but due to their popularity among the population in the greater Paktya area and among his fighters he saw himself pushed towards an alliance.[188]

The Taliban did not initially regard bin Laden as a particularly problematic figure. Mullah Mohammad Omar was unaware of who bin Laden was and what his followers and wider network's objectives were.[189] Furthermore, Mullah Mohammed Omar seemed even more oblivious of developments in the wider Arab world, and of the various jihadi groups, organisations and their discussions.[190] But the Taliban soon came to understand, and scrambled to interpret the implications of the international allegations that had followed the Saudi fugitive:

In contrast to America and the rest of the world, the Taliban never considered Osama to be a serious problem or issue, and never conceived of him as such. The issue soon spiralled out of the control, however. An explosion near a commercial centre that killed 30 people in Saudi Arabia and the attack on the USS Cole in Yemen that killed 17 American soldiers led to a further deterioration of the situation. Saudi Arabia increasingly involved itself, asking the US government to pressure the Taliban to hand over Osama or to drive him out of Afghanistan.[191]

Abu al-Walid al-Masri relates how Saudi pressure on the Taliban movement was exerted almost immediately after Kabul fell under their control:

...the Saudi ambassador was already asking that bin Laden be handed over to the United States. The ambassador and the request were transferred to Kandahar since the matter fell under the prerogative of Mullah Omar. [...] The ambassador assured the Prince [i.e. Mullah Mohammad Omar] that he was demanding bin Laden's surrender to the United States. [Mullah Mohammad Omar] understood from what he said that bin Laden was no longer a Saudi citizen after he was divested of his Saudi nationality and that he was not accused of any specific crimes against the United States. He thus failed to conceal his disdain toward Mr. Ambassador and began hating him on a personal level from that moment, because as [Mullah Mohammad Omar] said, he was working as America's ambassador instead of as Saudi Arabia's. He even told him with the blunt Kandahari honesty: 'I will not surrender a Muslim to an atheist!' There is no doubt that this sentence decisively defined the fate of the relations between the United States and the Taliban movement.[192]

Nevertheless, at least according to one account, bin Laden's first meeting with officials from the Taliban took place soon after their capture of Jalalabad, in the house of Mawlawi Yunis Khalis, in which Mullah Ehsanullah Ehsan assured bin Laden that he would not be handed over to the United States even if it would mean sacrificing the Taliban. The reason why this early assurance was given was the fundamental principle that the Taliban would never hand over a fellow Muslim to non-Muslims, let alone a *mujahed* who had fought against the Soviet forces, along with general precepts of politeness and custom.[193] Abu Mus'ab al-Suri has also written an account of this first meeting:

And I personally witnessed a meeting [between the Taliban and Arab mujahedin]. I was a guest visiting Shaykh Abu Abdallah, 'Usama,' when some high-level Taleban figures came in, including a minister and officials. One said 'you are the Muhajarin [the early followers of the Prophet Muhammad] and we are the Ansar [those who sheltered Muhammad and his followers],' causing the eyes to well up with tears. At the very end of the meeting, the minister said, 'You are not just our guests and we your servants, rather we serve the very ground you walk on.'[194]

At such an early point in the movement's trajectory, few would have been able to imagine how much damage this would cause the Taliban, or that sheltering bin Laden would become an issue at all.

Bin Laden and Arab jihadi affiliates' knowledge of the Taliban seems to have been just as poor. Abu al-Walid al-Masri has written that 'Al-Qaeda did not have a clear idea about the Taliban Movement, and in general, they were not ready to trust any Afghan party,'[195] and one other account by an Arab who joined up with bin Laden from the north graphically illustrates this lack of understanding:

Actually, many of the inhabitants of northern Afghanistan were misleading us. They warned us against the Taliban and said they were communists. At the time, we did not know exactly the identity of [them]. Suddenly, we heard reports of battles and that the Taliban had stormed into Jalalabad [...] We did not know at the time that Taliban was an Islamic and a religious movement, and we were very afraid that we would be handed over to those communists, that is, to the Taliban. We began to send brothers individually to Kunduz province through a group of Sheikh Abdul Rasoul Sayyaf. I was the last to move with them, because of my dark complexion, because I was afraid they would discover my Arab identity.

'I moved with a military convoy that belonged to the forces of Ahmad Shah Massoud. Its commander spoke Arabic fluently because he had studied in Riyadh. He took me to the front between the Taliban forces and the former government forces led by Ahmad Shah Massoud. He said to me: These are my borders, and those are the Taliban forces. May God be with you. I took him aside and asked him about the identity of the Taliban and told him: I ask you to tell me the truth. What is your view of Taliban? He replied: They are good. I said to him: Why do the Afghan radio stations in Kabul and Kunduz say they are communists? He told me those radio stations were government radio stations that sought to mislead the people in order to gain their loyalty.

'After that, I moved toward the Taliban front across a road [...] When I reached the side under Taliban control—and I was in a state of panic, in view of what I heard about them and because I feared they would arrest me—I was surprised by them. They were young men who were applying the sunnah by growing their beards and through their clothes, including some who wore turbans, and their eyes were darkened with kohl.

Some of them were sitting on armoured cars and reading the Koran. One of them looked at me and asked: Are you an Arab? I answered him: Yes, I am an Arab. He shouted toward the commander: An Arab, an Arab, an Arab. Then many people gathered around me and insisted that I have tea with them.

'I told them about my destination, and they put me in a car under guard and told me: You are safe until you get to Jalalabad—although the distance was very far and the road, to my knowledge, was full of bandits and highwaymen. However, the situation had changed. The road was really safe, and there was no sign of bandits or highwaymen. The country was truly safe.[196]

The confusion about the Taliban, the lack of information about their leadership and the unprecedented success of their military campaign, are reflected in the numerous articles written about the movement by commentators, journalists and international experts at the time. This extended into Afghanistan itself, where other groups had just as little grasp of the movement in the early years.[197] Physical points of contact between the two groups also were initially few. The Taliban in Jalalabad seem to have left bin Laden alone for the most part[198] but even when the Arabs moved down to Kandahar in early 1997 (see below), they kept mostly to themselves. According to interviewees present in Kandahar and other locations, Arabs were responsible for guard duties, and Afghans were technically forbidden from entering the Arab compounds.[199]

The first meeting between bin Laden and Mullah Mohammad Omar took place in the 'winter of 1996.'[200] The Taliban leader took bin Laden to task over his media campaign—bin Laden had been busy in Jalalabad, issuing statements calling for a *jihad* against the United States in August 1996[201]—and warning him about the dangers of drawing too close to figures and groups within Pakistani jihadi circles. Bin Laden's pronounced media campaign and increasing engagement with the international media can partially be explained by his need to raise his profile in order to mobilise funding networks and encourage recruits to flock to Afghanistan. Al-Qaeda was coming into its own.

A third point was allegedly discussed: that of the presence of 'Americans and Jews' in Saudi Arabia. Al-Masri says that bin Laden made a strong case for the importance of expelling these people, but Mullah Mohammad Omar called for patience. The Taliban, he said, were busy with work within Afghanistan:

'You and I are both Muslim mujahedeen. We are not cowards. After all, we fought the Soviets and sacrificed many martyrs until we defeated them and we will be with you in the battle to liberate the holy sites. That is our duty.' But Mullah Omar added that the current situation did not allow the Taliban to join that fight yet since it firstly needed to establish itself in Afghanistan and to end the civil war in the country. He added, saying: 'When we are well in place, we will be in the front lines with you in order to liberate our holy lands. You will see.'[202]

It is important to interpret many of the statements made by individual senior Taliban—in particular, reports from conversations that were not intended for public consumption—in the context of local customs and traditions that dictate conversational etiquette. The nature of conversations, particularly in southern Afghanistan, and the information and the sensitivity of statements, should be analysed alongside the backdrop of these caveats. Local custom dictates much of what is being said in conversation. In particular, official or semi-official meetings between people who are not well acquainted pose a special problem. This is even more true when one of the sides is foreign and therefore a guest on Afghan soil. Each statement, therefore, should be evaluated individually and not taken at face value, since much of what is being said can simply be a reflection of politeness rather than of conviction.[203] In the above case, Mullah Mohammed Omar could easily have promised things and made assurances without fully committing to carrying them out or seeing them through. Furthermore, while he may have shared the sentiments expressed, this does not necessarily translate into shared views as to how to bring about the desired state of affairs.

Bin Laden was unused to having to play a subservient role, and tried once more to win the Taliban leader over to his ideas. After all, he had few other options for a country in which to find refuge:

In that historic meeting between those two giants—or between the Qahtani[204] and his victim, Mullah Omar—the first tried to get support for his private actions especially in regard to his media activities. He was very upset over the continuous pressure exerted on him by many officials in the Islamic Emirate to stop talking to the media, but Mullah Omar rejected his appeal firmly but politely. Bin Laden asked that the *Amir* give him the chance to talk to the media in order to explain why the Islamic Emirate in Afghanistan was legitimate and by doing so, call on Muslim merchants to invest in it. The meeting lasted two hours after which the *Amir* asked his guest to abide by the decision taken by the Taliban officials and not to talk to the media. In the last seconds of the meeting and while bidding his guest farewell, Mullah Omar said: 'Do not be sad, you are a *mujahed* and this is your country. You are most welcome here and you can do whatever you like.' Bin Laden used that last sentence to act as if he had received a *carte blanche* from Mullah Omar to do whatever he wanted. In other words, he considered that he had received the approval to talk to the Western media, convincing himself and those around him that this was true.[205]

The description of this conversation further elaborates on the cultural need for both sides to be aware of social norms. Bin Laden, in this specific case, exploited what he regarded as a loophole. Mullah Khaksar says that bin Laden even penned a special poem for the occasion:

'There is no lion in the world, only Mawlawi Khalis, because you gave me shelter. There is no better place in the world than Kandahar because, Mullah Omar, you have announced Sharia and you are the hero of Islam.'[206]

The picture that emerges from this first meeting of the two leaders is typical of some of their future encounters. Bin Laden would appeal to Mullah Mohammad Omar's need to be perceived as a strong Muslim leader transcending his Afghan upbringing and the nationalist tendencies that fuelled the Taliban in their early days. While Mullah Mohammad Omar is and was a highly reclusive leader, it appears that public opinion—in particular the judgements of religious authorities and his adherence to what he regarded as the central doctrine of Islam—dictated many of his decisions. This often came at great cost to the Taliban and Afghanistan as a whole. The naiveté of the Taliban's senior leadership—and the reluctance of its second-tier leaders repeatedly and directly to challenge Mullah Mohammad Omar on these issues—combined with bin Laden's motivation (given his lack of alternative locations where he could consolidate his network) gave him significant room to argue, and exert pressure. These characteristics were coupled with their inflexibility regarding their relations with the outside world. The Taliban's reliance on the *qur'an* and the *sunna* for their policies meant that they had little room to change decisions once they had been made.

By August 1996, bin Laden had formed some of his central doctrines regarding the future of al-Qaeda and the militant Islamic struggle. His *fatwa*, entitled 'Declaration of War against the Americans Occupying the Land of the Two Holy Places,' was published in *Al-Quds Al-Arabi*, a London-based newspaper with which bin Laden held contacts via his media office and representative in London, Khalid al-Fawwaz. This was published on 23 August 1996.[207] In the *fatwa*, bin Laden outlined a narrative that drew heavily on frequently-cited verses from the *qur'an* and doctrine developed by Ibn Taymiyya, weaving them into a world view that framed history as a continuum of the Christian-Muslim wars, with the occupation of the Arabian Peninsula by American forces as a further attack on the Muslim *umma*.

Several key points can be drawn from this *fatwa*, some of which had earlier featured as themes in sermons and other small publications. He identifies the House of Saud, in the person of King Abdul Aziz, as having betrayed the early mujahedeen in the struggle for Palestine and causing the loss of the first *qibla*.

For bin Laden, this extended to his son, King Fahd, who he said was again trying to deceive the *umma* and who looked as though he would lose the last two holy sites by hosting American forces in Saudi Arabia. This was a direct attack on the House of Saud: he equated it with being '*kufr*' and receiving the support of the 'big *kufr*,' the United States.

Bin Laden also justifies al-Qaeda's central doctrine of conducting indiscriminate mass casualty attacks against civilian and government facilities by drawing on several events he regards as proof that the United States, even though a superpower, could be easily defeated by a spectacular blow that would shake its foundations. To this end, he cites the 1983 bombing in Beirut that killed 241 Americans[208] or the death of 19 soldiers in Mogadishu in 1993.[209] He states:

> Utmost effort should be made to prepare and instigate the Umma against the enemy, the American-Israeli alliance-occupying the country of the two Holy Places and the route of the Apostle (Allah's Blessings and Salutations may be on him) to the Furthest Mosque (Al-Aqsa Mosque).[210]

By mid-1996, Khalid Sheikh Mohammad, a veteran global jihadist, had arranged to meet with bin Laden through his contacts with al-Qaeda's military chief, Mohammad Atef (also known as Abu Hafs).[211] He had worked as a secretary for Sayyaf during the 1980s as well as together with Azzam. It was at this meeting that he presented the al-Qaeda head with a number of potential plots and operations against American and other interests, including the first outlines of what would come to be known as the September 11 attacks, which were referred to as 'the planes operation' by the handful of people who knew of it. Bin Laden at this point, however, did not sanction any of the suggested projects; it would take another two years before he offered his support.[212] In fact, bin Laden reacted quite coldly to the plan, mainly because he considered it too grandiose an idea, but the discussion signified bin Laden's early resolve to attack American targets. With the declaration of the formation of the World Islamic Front for Jihad against Jews and Crusaders in February 1998, he left little doubt about his intentions. The statement that narrates his by-then-solidified world view and the conclusion of the same with an all-out attack of the United States (as the new Crusaders attacking the Muslim *umma*) includes a *fatwa* that calls on all Muslims to follow the duty of *jihad* (*fard 'ayn*):

> Killing the Americans and their allies—civilians and military—is a duty for every Muslim who can carry it out in any country where it proves possible, in order to liberate Al-Aqsa Mosque and the holy sanctuary [Mecca] from their grip, and to the point that their armies leave all Muslim territory, defeated and unable to threaten any Muslim.[213]

The signatories to this declaration represented a number of militant Islamic groups from Pakistan, Egypt (including al-Zawahiri) and bin Laden himself.[214]

Until the Taliban had taken Jalalabad and Kabul, they had no Arabs fighting alongside or with them.[215] This would change, though, when bin Laden sought to form stronger links with his new hosts. The Taliban's stance was still ambivalent; they gave unambiguous public statements saying that bin Laden was a guest and that they would never hand him over, but in private there was far more room for discussion.

The Taliban Take Kabul

The Taliban movement took the Afghan capital on 26 September 1996.[216] Massoud's forces were outnumbered three to one and the swift rise of the Taliban deeply affected troop morale. Furthermore, the Taliban, in keeping with much of the strategy of their campaign up to this point, managed to turn a number of Rabbani's commanders, thus exposing one of the flanks of Kabul's defences.[217] The Taliban did not move effortlessly into Kabul, though. Anthony Davis explains the Kandaharis' miscalculations:

Taliban field commanders, Mullahs Rabbani, Borjan and Ghaus, evidently had very little understanding of the military and political situation in the city. Unsophisticated men with little or no formal education beyond Koranic studies, they appear to have made the mistake of transposing their experiences in Kandahar and the south to the altogether different climate of Kabul. Many believed the popular disgust with the Mujahideen and support for their moral authority that they had encountered in Kandahar would be mirrored in the capital.[218]

Almost immediately, the social policies which had been implemented in the rural south were applied to the comparatively more liberal urban residents in Kabul. Mullah Mohammad Omar, when asked a year or two later why the Taliban had done this, responded:

True, we did not intend to take power. Our goal is not simply to rule, and this is how we did it in the beginning. But when we managed to end corruption, we had a large ulama gathering. Their decision after shura was that we should take power to implement God's laws and Sharia on earth.[219]

By May 1997, a Taliban official handout listing the objectives of the Taliban read as follows:

– restoration of peace

– collection of weapons
– implementation of the shari'a[220]

One interviewee stated that at this time the Taliban regarded the geographical integrity of Afghanistan as a central objective of their movement, another
indication of their nationalist leanings.[221] Many of the dynamics that developed between the Taliban leadership and the expanding region—and with the
population under its control—would come under close scrutiny from the outside world. The policies implemented by the Taliban, even though turning
increasingly radical, offered few surprises and found precedent in those of other
organisations like Hekmatyar's *Hizb-e Islami.*[222] Much of the dynamic is often
framed through the lens of the Afghan urban-rural divide. This had played
itself out throughout Afghanistan's history and intensified in the 1970s and
1980s, with the urban elites trying to bring reforms to the rural countryside,
which then in turn lashed out in reaction. Much of the *mullah* networks, for
example, have often shown an almost unchanging opposition to the central
government, no matter its orientation.[223] The Taliban's capture of Kabul lends
itself well to the characterisation as a 'rural revolution':

The aim of the Taliban's assault on Kabul was to turn it into a City of God. All signs of
Westernization, such as 'British and American hairstyles,' had to be erased. Women
were banned from work and hidden from public view. The religious police decreed that
'women going outside with fashionable, ornamental, tight and charming clothes to
show themselves ... will be cursed by the Islamic *Sharia* and should never expect to go
to Heaven.' Music was banned, and so were television, kite flying, chess, and soccer.
Adultery would be punished by stoning, and drinking alcohol by whipping. The only
law was *Sharia*, or religious law. And Kabul would be governed by a six-man *Shura*, not
one of whom was from Kabul. Not one of them had ever even lived in a city before.[224]

The measures implemented by the *Amr bil Maroof wa Nahi 'an al-Munkar*,
the Ministry for the Promotion of Virtue and Suppression of Vice, headed by
Mawlawi Qalamuddin, included the severe restriction and de facto end of
women's participation in society, ranging from banning them from workplaces
and education, to preventing them from leaving home without being accompanied by a male member of their family.[225]

Kabul was a milestone for the Taliban. It meant more responsibility and
implicitly contained (so they thought) the promise of international recognition, but it also meant more people to administer and execute the functions
of government, to which the Taliban at least sought to pay lip-service. These
bureaucrats were often the same as those who had been working before the

Taliban's arrival, albeit minus department and ministry heads as appointees from the movement.[226] The Taliban's ideals—initially somewhat simpler and undiluted—were now mixed in with the aspirations to power of members as well as some of the more common by-products of conflict (revenge, corruption and so on).

Beginnings of an Internal Taliban Debate

Some have argued that the Taliban grew wise to the problems associated with bin Laden and his al-Qaeda retinue only much later in the Taliban's rule in Afghanistan, but this ignores the increasingly fractured nature of the movement and its leadership starting almost as soon as Kabul fell.

The Taliban gave bin Laden a house in Kabul, in the Kart-e Parwan area, and he reportedly spent his time travelling between various places in the east, and Kabul and the south.[227] Bin Laden and his family were encouraged to move down to Kandahar in March 1997 following a reported threat on bin Laden's life[228] and even a perennially suspicious observer such as Abu al-Walid al-Masri is inclined to believe this.[229] This was after Mullah Mohammad Omar and bin Laden had met, but there is no evidence for a subsequent meeting aside from one or two exchanges conducted through intermediaries.[230]

The Taliban's representatives had come under international pressure—particularly from Saudi patrons who were concerned about bin Laden's activities and open calls for struggle against the Saudi government. This followed a particularly busy time for the al-Qaeda *amir*: he had given interviews to Channel 4 (UK) in late 1996, CNN (US) in March 1997 and issued fifteen statements in 1996 and 1997.[231] Saudi pressure was intense from the outset:

Saudi Arabia and the United States, they were trying to woo the Taliban. They were putting a condition: 'If you kick out Osama bin Laden, you will have the recognition of the international community. You will have the seat of Afghanistan in the United Nations. You will have the seat of Afghanistan in the Islamic Conference Organisation in Jeddah, Saudi Arabia.'[232]

Wakil Ahmad Mutawakil, the Taliban's former foreign minister, has written that, 'since Saudi Arabia insisted on the monitoring of his activities, so bin Laden and his comrades were resettled in Kandahar.'[233] A subsequent interview confirmed this:

The Taliban transferred them to Kandahar: firstly, to have much more control over them than Jalalabad, and secondly so that they could be out of the sight of the media.[234]

A later chapter heading from Mutawakil's book characterises the problem from the Taliban's perspective: 'Problems for the Host from the Conduct of the Guests.'[235] On a very local level, interviewees reported varying degrees of cordial relations between the Arab guests and Afghans living in Kandahar. One Talib said that the Arabs had little interaction with Afghans because they didn't speak Pashtu, for the most part.[236] Another noted the Arabs' generosity; at times they would hand out gifts of 'rice, wheat, ghee, beans and other things for winter like blankets, gasoline.'[237] This does not chime with accounts from Arabs as to their living conditions and access to funds at the time; deprivation seems closer as a characterisation of how they lived in those first months following their arrival in Kandahar.[238]

The first two years of bin Laden's presence in the country hardly challenged the Taliban's ability to defend and argue against international interlocutors who demanded he be handed over, since up to this point there had been no significant international actions undertaken by al-Qaeda. That would all change with the 1998 bombing of two US embassies in Africa,[239] but for the moment the Arabs were still seen as relatively benign by the Taliban leadership.[240] For Mullah Mohammad Omar, the Arabs had even proven helpful to the movement: the collapse of Taliban defences and their catastrophic defeat stage-managed by Massoud with the major counterattack launched in July and August 1997, recapturing Bagram air base and shelling Kabul airport, threatened the Taliban's control of Kabul. Heavy fighting caused thousands of civilian casualties and 50,000 people fled their homes. This pushed the Taliban to mobilise whatever forces were available. Accounts tell of forced conscription in mosques in Kabul and madrassas being closed in Pakistan to send more Taliban in order to reinforce the defence lines around the capital city.[241] Mullah Zaeef claims a sudden surge in Taliban troops managed to hold off the advance of the northerners:

At the same time, reinforcements from the surrounding provinces came flooding into the capital, rushing to strengthen the Taliban's defensive positions in Shakardara, Guldara, Bagram and Sarak-e Jadid. People crowded the streets to see the Taliban with their black and white turbans, passing through towards the front line.[242]

But the confident, accomplished and experinced Arab mujahedeen sent to help by bin Laden also played an important role at this time. Abu al-Walid narrates:

The *Amir al-Mu'mineen* [i.e. Mullah Mohammad Omar] was highly tense and the lack of trust forced him to violate the red line and send a special envoy i.e. his first political advisor Mullah Jalil, to see Bin Laden in the New Arabkhel village on the edges of the Kandahar airport, asking him to mobilise all the Arab troops under his command to defend Kabul. This was a historic opportunity whose importance was realised by Bin Laden who immediately set his mind on the extent to which he wished to push the situation to serve his plan through the sudden need for his services. He thus imagined that from then on, the Emirate would never dare control his activities and that his great rise in Afghanistan would start from Jabal Seraj. However, the developments on the battle ground did not go as Bin Laden had expected, since he imagined he was leading an Arab invasion of the Jabal Seraj village while what happened on the field was close to a total collapse of the Taliban troops and the crushing progress of Massoud's forces towards Kabul. A number of men from Bin Laden's group partaking in the battle were killed, others kidnapped while others went missing in action. When Massoud's army was at a stone's throw away from the capital, what deterred it or the main reason behind this deterrence was a young man from Upper Egypt who was passing through that area by coincidence.

The man was one of the 'returnees to Afghanistan' from the Egyptian *al-Gama'a al-Islamiyya*. At the time, they amounted to five people at the most. During this crisis, no changes worth mentioning had affected the number of Arabs who had joined Bin Laden. However, the summer season brought a limited number of 'jihadist tourists' from Yemen and Saudi Arabia, attracted to Afghanistan by Bin Laden's strong statements and the lights shone on him by the international media. Moreover, men from several jihadist organisations returned to Afghanistan on account of international pursuit. As for the Pakistani group, it had several thousand fighters in Afghanistan, dozens of whom joined Bin Laden in his project on the Northern front of Kabul. Nonetheless, this cooperation did not entail any practical results for administrative, logistic and even physiological reasons. One day after the delivery of the mobilisation call, a group of Al-Qaeda's cadres headed by Abu Hafs the Egyptian, the organisation's defence minister, arrived in Kabul to study the situation and see what could be done. The delegation included a number of those who closely watched the developments of the previous war on the thresholds of Kabul against Dostum's forces. They had closely seen the organised technical work led by Haqqani, through which he was able to deter the hostile campaign and take all its equipment with the least number of human losses and a limited consumption of ammunition. The performance was extremely professional. It was thus easy for these Arab observers to detect the differences between the two campaigns and quickly and accurately point to the flaws, thus predicting within hours while touring the military posts that the situation was on the brink of catastrophe. They therefore rang the alarm bells everywhere before Al-Qaeda's delegation had defined the role it could play with its limited capacities, tried to push toward reform and avoided the disaster before it occurred. Thousands of men arrived to Kabul from Jalalabad carrying all the heavy equipment they were able to bring along, from heavy artillery to tanks and BM-41 missile launchers equipped with rockets reaching as far as thirty kilometres. The military bases were extremely crowded and the chaos was indescribable. However, when they decided to use their heavy artillery, the scene was deplorable. To the viewers who loved Taliban the image was devastating, while to those who hated it, it was hilarious.[243]

On the other hand, one interviewee who met with bin Laden around this time cast some doubt on the military efficacy of the Arabs:

When the Taliban took over, Osama bin Laden told me personally that he sent Arab mujahideen, al-Qaeda men, about 300 of them, to go and fight with the Taliban against Dostum on the north, near the border of Tajikistan. And he told me personally that a great number of them died, because of snowstorms, because of cold weather. And they are Arabs. They're coming from Arabia. They don't know about this weather, harsh weather. So they died even before they reached their destination to fight with the Taliban against Dostum and against the others. [...] Even at that time, the Taliban did not need al-Qaeda as a military force to help them. Because how many members of al-Qaeda in that time? A thousand? It's not really a lot. Two thousand? It's not really much. Most of them were foot soldiers; they were not really commanders. They didn't need, for example, suicide bombers. They didn't need guerrilla warfare at that time. As I said, he sent 300, and they died in the snow, in the icy weathers there. So I don't think the military side was that important. Later on, maybe, but not at that time.[244]

In the end, Haqqani was brought in and managed to hold off Massoud's advance, albeit with massive casualties and desertions.[245] Many expected he would be appointed Defence Minister at this point, but instead—al-Masri argues that this was because of jealousy on the part of the southerners—was given the Ministry of Border Affairs.[246]

Despite this and other occasional grand gestures from bin Laden and the Arabs, some figures among the Taliban movement became increasingly vocal about the problems that he was causing for their very legitimacy. Three figures in particular dissented from the outset:[247] Mullah Mutawakil, Mullah Mohammad Khaksar and Mullah Mohammad Rabbani.[248]

Mullah Mohammad Khaksar had met bin Laden in 1996, just after the al-Qaeda head had arrived in Afghanistan. Khaksar was deputy interior minister at this time, and encountered bin Laden together with Mullah Mohammad Rabbani:

I told bin Laden 'It is time for you people to leave our country. Of course there are some differences among Afghans, but it's our internal issue and in the course of time we will solve these problems.' This meeting caused tension between me and Osama, and we were not to see each other again. At that time, Mullah Rabbani told me to leave the session. I never met bin Laden again. [...] No one wants a guest to hurt the honour of the house. From time to time I was telling Mullah Omar, 'Look, Mullah Sahib, there is no need for Osama to stay in Afghanistan. It will hurt our country.' My position about bin Laden is why the Taliban leaders had lots of problems with me.[249]

This group later coalesced around Mullah Mohammad Rabbani, but during the last months of 1996 and the first few of 1997 the key figure seemed to be Mullah Mohammad Hassan. Bin Laden was, he argued, 'directing' Taliban foreign policy with his media speeches and remarks and this was doing the movement no favours.[250] Abu al-Walid reports that hostility towards bin Laden and his entourage was rife during this period. One rumour apparently went round the Taliban ranks that bin Laden had given an American envoy the opportunity to scout for targets and to examine the possibility of striking at the Taliban movement.[251] Reports like this seem irrelevant for some, but they represent the general mood and perspective of a sizeable amount of people at the time, much like today's rumours and conspiracy theories reflect deep-seated feelings towards the Afghan government and the foreign forces in Afghanistan.

Bin Laden's move down to Kandahar and occupation of several derelict and shoddy compounds in March 1997 led to a growing bond between him and Mullah Mohammad Omar. The important Islamic holidays, for example, were occasions when bin Laden would visit Mullah Mohammad Omar to congratulate him.[252] The two didn't meet regularly at all, but each meeting is tinged with a larger-than-life significance in the retelling; this is almost certainly the tint of the retrospective view, in which every action is heavy with meaning.

But Mullah Mohammad Omar was grateful for the Arabs' help in defending the north of Kabul, and there seemed to be a natural respect granted to bin Laden. He could still play on the myth of his exploits during the Afghan *jihad*. His very presence in Afghanistan, having travelled from Saudi Arabia and left behind a life of luxury to dedicate his life to *jihad* and Islam, made a big impression on the Taliban leader, no matter how much his vision and interpretations may have differed from those of the Taliban in general.[253]

Mullah Mohammad Omar's visits to bin Laden's residence in early 1997 seem to have been aimed primarily at encouraging the Arabs to start construction work and knowledge transfer within the country. Indeed, many within the Taliban movement had at least some hope that the Arabs would bring money and expertise with them which would help in the reconstruction of Afghanistan.[254] Bin Laden, though, had neither the money nor the focus to start rebuilding Afghanistan. Al-Masri explained:

Bin Laden, who understood Mullah Omar's offer, rejected it in a polite way since he considered that he was—according to the international media—more important and more powerful than the 'Prince of the Believers,' Mullah Omar. In fact, in all his actions, in his general behaviour and even in his tone, Bin Laden considered that he should be the Prince of the Believers. True, he always praised Mullah Omar but he never linked those praises with obedience to the latter. In his private meetings and discussions he even said: 'Our brothers and friends in the Taliban movement, may Allah protect them, do not know the Muslims' interests in Afghanistan and in the world. We are more capable than they are in grasping those interests.'[255]

A central feature of the developing relationship was the fundamentally different concerns of bin Laden and al-Qaeda and those of the Taliban leadership.

They [...] had one thing in common. That's actually that their enemy was the Soviet Union in that time. And they were both Sunni fundamentalists. Both of them are salafists, but they differed at that time—not now—when it comes to the United States and the West. Maybe they hate the West because it is Christian. For them, it is not Islam. So maybe both sides don't agree with the West, [...] but in that time, I don't believe the Taliban considered the West and the Americans as enemies. Maybe they are not friends, but not enemies. Al-Qaeda considered the United States and Europe as enemies because they sent troops to Saudi Arabia[...]. And Osama bin Laden told me that he considered the American and European troops in the Arabian Peninsula as an occupation, exactly like the Soviet occupation of Afghanistan. But the Taliban did not see it the same way, or at least they never mentioned this. Maybe deep down they are not with it, but they never considered it as their issue, their story, as their priority. They never looked at the American business in Saudi Arabia as a priority, to get rid of them as a priority. They liberated their country, and this was enough for them.[256]

Bin Laden, while trying to consolidate his influence over the training camps, recruitment processes and organisational structures, was looking to launch his international campaign against what he regarded as the main enemy, namely the United States and the governments of the Arab world. Much of bin Laden's and al-Qaeda's operations and franchising appeared to rely on opportunities that presented themselves; again, the comparison to the Ford Foundation seems to hold true.

The ongoing conflicts within Afghanistan had an impact on his wider focus: establishing firm relationships and aiding his hosts would allow him to pursue his international goals. The training camps, not only for tactical and military training but for ideological instruction and recruitment, were central to al-Qaeda's success.[257] His real focus was not to help the Taliban, who found themselves in an increasingly severe war with a consolidating force around Ahmed Shah Massoud in Afghanistan's north. The Taliban sought to expand the territory under their control, moving up to the north, and to establish an Islamic *sharia*-compatible government in Kabul and the other areas under their control. These fundamentally different focuses would add to the growing friction between the two movements.

In May 1998, matters came to a head for the Taliban and bin Laden. The latter had publicly announced the formation of a 'World Islamic Front Urging Jihad Against Jews and Crusaders'[258] and this widely-publicised media event—he had invited thirteen Pakistani (and one Chinese) journalists[259]—angered the Taliban considerably. Mullah Mohammad Omar and his senior political advisors had hoped he would keep to his promise of making no statements as long as he remained a guest of the Taliban:

'It also angered the Taliban Movement and especially the anti-Bin Laden wing, resulting in a feud between Kabul and Kandahar. Mullah Omar found himself alone with no one supporting him, since he was perceived by the Taliban Shura members as being weak and unable to impose his authority on Bin Laden. A question was even raised regarding who truly ruled Afghanistan: Bin Laden or Mullah Omar?'[260]

One Taliban member present in Khost at the time also felt it was a bad decision to hold the conference:

'The Khost conference was a big event. I was there in Khost when it happened, together with Khairullah Khairkhwa, the Taliban minister of the interior, and we were quite unhappy because we (and the other Talibs) thought that Osama was trying to bring all the world's enmity onto the Afghans. They even distributed books against the Saudi government on the eve of the conference. This tells us that the coalition of the Taliban and Osama did not actually exist.'[261]

Mullah Mohammad Omar was reportedly apoplectic. 'How can he hold a press conference without my permission? There is only one ruler. Is it me or Osama?' Rahimullah Yousufzai recalls Mullah Mohammad Omar saying in a phone call after he learnt what had happened.[262] The Taliban leader closed down Khaldan camp at this point as well as the ones operated by Pakistani groups.[263] Bin Laden had held his press conference at Jihadwal camp, in defiance of the Taliban's constant denials that such camps even existed.[264]

Abu Mus'ab al-Suri wrote an email to his aide, Abu Khalid al-Suri, explaining the situation at this time:

The results of this crisis can be felt even here in Kabul and other places. Talk about closing down the camps has spread. Discontent with the Arabs has become clear. Whispers between the Taliban with some of our non-Arab brothers has become customary. In short, our brother [Bin Laden's] latest troublemaking with the Taliban and the

Leader of the Faithful jeopardizes the Arabs, and the Arab presence, today in all of Afghanistan, for no good reason.[265]

Interestingly, al-Suri suggests that bin Laden's confrontational attitude towards the Taliban and their leader was a result of his experiences in Sudan, where he had followed all the restrictions placed upon him by the government only to find himself expelled and swindled. He was determined that this should not happen a second time.[266] As al-Masri notes, it had given the anti-bin Laden camp a legitimate complaint around which to rally, and it seems that this period between May and July 1998 saw serious Taliban efforts to try to draw a line under the bin Laden question. 'The anti-bin Laden wing had become the silent majority within the movement's leadership,' he wrote.[267]

In June 1998, Prince Turki al-Faisal arrived in Afghanistan for a discussion with Mullah Mohammad Omar over what to do with bin Laden. He reportedly received a pledge that 'enough is enough' and was asked that a joint Islamic commission be set up to legitimise the expulsion.[268] In July, Mullah Mutawakil travelled to Saudi Arabia to confirm the deal. A *Wall Street Journal* article has since commented that 'the Taliban replaced bin Laden's team of Arab bodyguards with Afghans loyal to Mullah Omar.'[269]

There was also conflict and mistrust from the foreign jihadis towards the Taliban. One account, based on the experience of two training camps within Afghanistan from 1995–96, Omar Nasiri's *Inside the Jihad*, explained the reasons for the antipathy as well as why they were unable to act on these opinions:

No one at the camp liked the Taliban. We didn't talk about it openly, because we were discouraged from talking about the politics of our host country. But there were whispers, of course, and off-hand remarks. The trainers and the other brothers said many of the same things I had heard from Amin and Yasin already: the Taliban were overreaching in their application of sharia; they were too strict; they were innovators.[270]

I hated the Taliban. When I was in Belgium, I had read about them and seen them on TV. They were vicious, completely uncivilized. I was disgusted by the public executions and decapitations, and the way they held the country in fear. And I also hated the Taliban because they were the enemies of Massoud. He was still my hero, a noble mujahid who had earned the respect even of his enemies.

I never spoke about any of this, of course. None of us did. The Taliban had taken over huge swaths of Afghanistan, and we needed Afghanistan, the land of jihad. We needed to stay and train.[271]

A more religiously-intoned Arab set of voices against the Taliban would later emerge, but for the moment there were just whispers of dissent.

The picture that emerges is one of al-Qaeda and bin Laden manoeuvring to facilitate their actual goals and aims while not compromising their safe haven to the degree that would see them expelled. Any relocation would have been difficult at the time. Many of the other options, like Somalia and Yemen, had been explored in the early 1990s, and in particular the assessment of Somalia ruled out the possibility of establishing operations among the warring tribes and amid its raging civil war.[272] Yemen had been a port of call for many of the Egyptian jihadists during the early 1990s, but it appeared to offer little hope for establishing an amiable relationship with the government. Ali Abdullah Saleh was looking towards the West and Middle Eastern leaders for support and cooperation.[273]

The Taliban and International Recognition

The capture of Kabul in 1996 may have been a milestone for the Taliban movement, but they remained internationally isolated. The changing tactics, in particular the indiscriminate rocketing of Kabul combined with statements that called for the sole power to be handed to the movement, gave the Rabbani government more justification in the eyes of the international community.[274]

This changed with the capture of Mazar-e Sharif in May 1997.[275] Pakistan, Saudi Arabia and the United Arab Emirates all officially recognised the Taliban government. Other countries did not follow suit, and this was clearly perplexing and frustrating for the Taliban's leadership. One senior political Talib characterised their perception as follows:

The problem was that one party was ready and present, but the other party was absent. The Americans were absent. We tried, and sometimes we would joke with the Americans who visited us—'why are you looking at us through your satellite?'...why don't you come and visit us on the ground and see us? Your embassy is empty.' But there were no bilateral relations.[276]

A meeting between Taliban and United States representatives in December 1997, for example, laid bare this frustration.[277] The Taliban repeatedly expressed their desire for better relations with the United States, 'urging them,' for example, to reopen the Kabul embassy. The main point of disagreement in the entire encounter seems to have been over the movement's social policies. Karl Inderfurth, heading the meeting, repeatedly brought this point up, stressing that '[the US] attitude toward the Taliban would be influenced by its behaviour relating to medical care, education, and opportunities made available to women.'[278] The Taliban do not, at this point, seem to have hardened into an instinctually defensive stance on these issues, nor do they seem to have completely adopted the narrative of bin Laden and al-Qaeda and its underlying world view against the USA, but there are moments in the meeting where the Taliban delegates express clear confusion over what they see as double standards. Why, they ask, was there so little international condemnation following the massacre of Taliban fighters in the north earlier in the year? Inderfurth points to a Voice of America op-ed article which laid the blame on 'both sides,' but this did not satisfy the Talibs.[279]

One senior Taliban political member involved to a high level at this time described the character of these meetings:

Several times I was invited by the [US government] in Peshawar who wanted ideas from us. I told them the same story: the Taliban are not Muslim Brotherhood types, nor do they have any links with Wahhabi people. Please don't force them, they are totally traditional people, not revolutionary. They are totally empty-minded politically speaking, with no links to the whole world and no links to the Islamic world even, and especially no links with the western world. They are pure nationalists. [...] They came to solve the problems of the people of Afghanistan. [...] They have no political agenda, no political mind, no political experience, no economic experience, no managerial experience, no educational capacity and so on given their limited madrassa education: none of this gave them the capacity to run a country as bureaucrats and politicians. There was a total lack of experience.

Everything was distorted at the time; the economy was destroyed, people had no income or resources. I told all these diplomats about these things. I told them that the Taliban's Islamic government would not be any more than what was to be found in Saudi. The Saudi one, in fact, was more radical because they are salafis. [...] Afghanistan is ruled by Islamic and traditional rules and Afghan culture combined with that. We didn't know French laws, Italian, British or American or any others. I told them, 'don't force them. Please support them.' Do you know why? Support is support. If there is financial, military, political and diplomatic support then this will influence the policy of any society. Their policies will be affected by this support. Unfortunately, none of the western countries supported them.[280]

The political drivers of the movement—the kind of people who had attended these meetings—were searching for any means to achieve international recognition for the movement at this point. On 5 November 1997, for example, Mullah Mohammad Omar called for a deployment of UN monitors at all Afghan airfields. 'The deployment is necessary to stop arms supplies into the country from outside,' he was quoted as saying.[281]

The Taliban established a three-stage plan to deal with the cultivation and use of narcotics and aimed to complete this programme in 2000.[282] They had already once undertaken an attempt to ban cultivation early on, but had aban-doned the project due to local opposition.[283] Narcotics were a central issue of concern and criticism from the United States and other countries, and the Tal-iban seemed to regard this new policy as a possible first step to improve the strained relations, one that also happened to be sanctioned by the Taliban's leadership in accordance with their interpretation of *shari'a* law.

Yet they failed to appreciate just how much their social policies—particu-larly those that affected women and girls' schooling—were harming their attempts to gain international recognition. Their argument—pointing to a lack of resources to allow for separate girls' schools and facilities for women as well as their still being engaged in an internal civil war with commanders from the north—then, as now, lacked credibility and was certainly not enough to appease the by-now vocal women's rights lobby in the United States and Europe. Here, for example, is one such position:

The Taliban regarded women as a part of the community: under Islam they were granted certain rights, honour and dignity. The rules that were enforced did not dishonour women, but were rather designed to safeguard them and restore their dignity. The Tal-iban believed that the current times are ones in which women are exploited (particu-larly in the West) for commerce and business. Newspapers and magazines use the beautiful glances of women, showing them nude to boost their commercial interest. TV channels and the film industry defame and dishonour women for their own profit, disguising it as human and women rights. [...] In order to reverse this trend—one that the Taliban thought was exploitative and dishonourable—they banned all women from working in the government, ordering them to stay at home. Opinions were divided but the Taliban stated that the ban was only a temporary measure and that the women would receive their salaries while staying at home. They also provisionally prevented girls from going to school or attending university. They repeatedly stated, though, that they were not opposed to girl's education in general. 'Education is the right of both men and women and is an obligation,' they said. 'Presently, however, we don't have the facil-ities for women's education. Women should go to school wearing veils, should have spe-cial transport services, their own school and madrassa buildings and so on. We are unable to provide this yet, especially since this should be made available for all Afghans.'[284]

In May 1997, Amnesty International published a report entitled 'Women in Afghanistan: The Violations Continue';[285] in September Emma Bonino was briefly detained by the Taliban on a visit to Kabul as representative of the Euro-pean Union[286] and in November, Madeleine Albright visited an Afghan refu-gee camp in Pakistan and called the Taliban's treatment of women 'despicable,' saying that, 'it is impossible to modernise a nation if half or more of the pop-ulation is left behind.'[287] From then on it was a prominent issue in the United

States, especially with celebrities (the wife of talk show host Jay Leno, Mavis Leno, was especially vocal) supporting the cause.[288]

Those Talibs that were engaged with the internationals on these issues often seemed to dig their heels in more firmly when these issues were discussed. Much of the Taliban's political manoeuvring was reactionary in nature and lacked political finesse. Here, for example, is Mullah Mohammad Omar, in December 1997:

We do not accept something which somebody imposes on us under the name of human rights which is contrary to the holy Koranic law. [The holy Qur'an] cannot adjust itself to other people's requirements; people should adjust themselves to the requirements of the holy Koran.[289]

The realities of the Taliban's policies are one thing, but the discussions with international actors over changing them seemed (from the Taliban perspective) calculated to affront and patronise them.[290] If the international engagement with the Taliban over social issues was troubled, the international community's dealings with the senior leadership over bin Laden would be equally, if not more, conflicted.

6

A BONE IN THE THROAT
(1998–2001)

Osama bin Laden told me that he considered the American and European troops in Arabian Peninsula as occupation, exactly like the Soviet occupation of Afghanistan.

But the Taliban did not see it the same way, or at least they never mentioned this. Maybe deep down they are not with it, but they never considered it as their issue, their story, as their priority. They never looked at the American business in Saudi Arabia as a priority, to get rid of them as a priority. They liberated their country, and this is enough for them.

Abdel Bari Atwan, January 2010[1]

The Taliban and al Qaeda are one enterprise and we see Pakistan as backing that enterprise. [...] Bush is very serious and could declare the Taliban a terrorist group in which case Pakistan would be directly held responsible for backing terrorism.

Senior US diplomat, July 2001[2]

August 1998–December 1999

In early August 1998, the Taliban were unaware of bin Laden's plans. The government that had formed in Kabul and Kandahar faced growing internal difficulties with a seemingly uncontrolled influx of personnel staffing ministries

159

and official positions. The different commanders who had joined the movement, moreover, expected recompense and feuded among each other for influence within the administration. Problems were mounting, exacerbated by the
lack of expertise and competence of much of the Taliban leadership, as well as
by dwindling financial resources. They had little or no experience in running
an administration and yearned to break with the old structures.[3]

Their military campaign had stalled in the north. The Taliban had shown
themselves to be ruthless strategists: they had closed off all access points to
central Afghanistan, which precipitated a severe famine among the local, predominantly Hazara, population whom they were seeking to subdue. Furthermore, the northern front line saw widespread atrocities and war crimes carried
out by both sides.[4]

Moreover, each new stretch of territory acquired also meant the acquisition
of a fragile network of brokered deals and conflicts within local communities,
exacerbated by the Taliban's rigid application of social policies, much of which
was derived from their understanding of southern rural communities. These
fast-changing internal dynamics significantly overextended the limited abilities of the Taliban's bureaucracy.

Interviews with former officials from that time concur that there were two
key priorities then: the ongoing '*jihad*' (i.e. bringing the rest of the country
under their control) and—for some—starting to make Afghanistan under the
Islamic Emirate function as a real country.[5]

Even though international pressure was mounting, bin Laden was not a high
priority at that time, and the worries of a select group within the movement
had not yet gained traction. They were still eagerly seeking international recognition, so they could not afford to ignore the issue completely, but there was
still some room for discussion. The movement had not hardened its stance
against the international community, nor was there a unanimity of opinion;
dissent on a variety of issues was found beneath the public veneer. The Taliban's priorities as of early 1998 were set out as follows:

A. Restoration of Full Security of the Citizens
B. Pursuance of Honest and Sincere Negotiation
C. Support for the UN and OIC Peace Efforts
D. Respect for UN Rules and Principles
E. Search for Mutual Respect and Friendly Relations Towards all Countries
F. Establishment of a Credible and Accountable Islamic Regime
G. Protection of Human Rights and Liberties

you launch rockets without knowing where he would be. Generally it was a secret policy, people thought. The US policy was not clear. We didn't understand what they wanted for Afghanistan or the region. It was very confusing for us.[19]

Another Talib explained what they thought the reason for the attack was:

Some Talibs said that the USA is attacking Afghanistan because we have a good Islamic government and don't like democracy or care about US demands. They want to fake a reason in order to destroy our Islamic government.[20]

Unfortunately, bin Laden also seemed to have an argument with which to convince the Taliban leader. He once again appealed to Mullah Mohammad Omar's weakness and tendency to regard matters as black or white: the need to appear to be Islamic and not to be dictated to by non-Muslims. The exact chain of events that saw bin Laden apologise to Mullah Mohammad Omar and pledge his obedience is unclear. There are various accounts of what transpired in the meeting,[21] but the most detailed is to be found in a recent autobiography by bin Laden's son Omar, who claims to have been present.

Osama tried to seem contrite, putting on a large feast for the visiting Taliban leader—apparently 'the first time that Mullah Omar had left his home to pay my father a visit'[22]—but this approach failed. Mullah Mohammad Omar sat at the opposite end of the garden, far away from bin Laden, and addressed him in Pashtu:

The Taliban leader was displeased at my father's militant activities. Concerned only with the internal affairs of Afghanistan, Mullah Omar had no desire to attract interference from the outside world. [...] 'The political situation is heated,' Mullah Omar concluded. 'It is best if you and your men leave Afghanistan.'[23]

This was clearly the last thing that bin Laden wanted to be hearing at this point, and he made an impassioned plea for clemency to Mullah Mohammad Omar, citing the various times he had come to the Taliban's assistance, ending with this appeal:

Sheikh, if you give in to the pressure of infidel governments, your decision will be against Islam.[24]

To which Mullah Mohammad Omar responded

Sheikh Osama, I will fulfill your request. I will give you the same courtesy as did the Sudanese government. You have my invitation for another year and then a half a year. During that year and another half year, make arrangements for your move. Do find another country for your family.[25]

Bin Laden had won another reprieve, and more time with which to win over the Taliban leader.[26] He would be helped by the increasingly confrontational international diplomacy of the United States. Negotiations over bin Laden, in particular, seemed to go round in circles, and many discussions were characterised by a lack of understanding of each side regarding the nature and conduct of diplomacy.[27] While Washington appeared to have addressed this issue head on, it failed to account for the limitations of the Taliban leadership, particularly regarding its underlying interpretation of Islamic doctrine and Afghan cultural customs. Thus talks between the United States and the Taliban had an adverse effect: the inflexibility of American demands, combined with the implications for the Taliban leadership of submitting to them, determined the outcome in advance. This, in a way, reinforced the Taliban movement's stubbornness—despite all the internal debates concerning the continued presence of foreign jihadis—and failed to let the movement save face.

This was borne out when Mullah Mohammad Omar called the US State Department two days after the African Embassy bombings. He lectured the person who took the call in Washington, saying that he had seen no evidence that bin Laden was behind the attacks.[28] The conversation seems otherwise to have been a mundane one—aside from the very fact that it took place—but it opened up a channel for communication. There were other matters to bring up, but bin Laden was the main priority for the United States—and 1998 and 1999 saw a growing number of meetings between American representatives and members of the Taliban.[29]

In late August 1998, Mullah Mohammad Omar was reported to have called on bin Laden to refrain from his 'threatening statements' against Americans:

I sent a message to Bin Laden yesterday making it clear to him not to make military and political statements against anyone from our soil. [...] I am angry because Osama is making anti-American statements from our soil and I stressed on him not to do so. [...] He has broken his promise of not using our soil for making such statements because he had been stopped from doing so in the past as well.[30]

August 1998 was also a turning moment for the Taliban leader. The Saudi Prince, Turki al-Faisal, had visited Mullah Mohammad Omar in June and had a reportedly productive and frank conversation about bin Laden.[31] Mullah Mohammad Omar was frustrated by his guest, but needed some sort of face-saving mechanism that would allow him to defend himself against accusations of being 'un-Islamic.' The outlines of an agreement were reached, and Saudi Arabia reportedly sent 400 four-wheel-drive pickup cars and cash to fund the

Taliban's upcoming northern offensive as a de facto down-payment to confirm the agreement.[32]

Prince Turki returned in August (after the bombings and the cruise missile strikes), reportedly to collect bin Laden and bring him back to Saudi Arabia. Taliban representative Mullah Mutawakil had visited Saudi Arabia in July to confirm the outlines of the agreement and to ensure that the Saudi offer of a religious panel which would condemn bin Laden and his activities was serious. In the August meeting, also attended by ISI chief General Naseem Rana, Mullah Mohammad Omar reneged on his promise.[33]

Mullah Mohammad Omar reportedly replied that the Taliban had no intention of turning bin Laden over to Saudi Arabia. He further stated that the Saudi government was 'illegitimate' because it had allowed American troops to remain in Saudi Arabia. He even claimed that the Saudi government was planning to allow the United States to occupy the two holy sites of Mecca and Medina. They had no business interfering in Afghan matters and the *umma* would rise against it, he said.[34] In the words of one Taliban attendee at the meeting:

Mullah Mohammad Omar started his own comments. He started with Saddam Hussein, saying that, 'your family are afraid of Saddam Hussein! Saddam was a communist and he was not a good person. His presence in Iraq caused the presence of America in the region and it is because of the American presence in the region that we have all these problems now. But your father and his father were not like you...they were *sahib* and they expanded Islam all over. But you are not doing the same thing.' Mullah Omar wanted to give him his own ideas, but Turki could not tolerate this and he left the meeting.[35]

Prince Turki was angry about this reversal; the Saudi government announced on 22 September that it was recalling its *charge d'affaires* in Kabul and expelled the Taliban representative, Shahabuddin Dilawar, from Saudi Arabia. A final pressure point seems to have been deployed: the Saudi government threatened to withdraw permission for Afghans to make the *Hajj* pilgrimage.[36]

The fallout with Saudi Arabia seemed to have caused a wider split within the Taliban. Mullah Mohammad Rabbani, who was known to have close ties to Saudi Arabia, was angered over Mullah Mohammad Omar's treatment of Prince Turki, and rumours about a possible coup against Mullah Mohammad Omar were heard in Kabul at the time.[37]

The Taliban leadership then reached out to its other allies, the United Arab Emirates and Pakistan. Mullah Mutawakil travelled to Abu Dhabi in an effort to ensure that relations would not be further downgraded.[38] It was around this time that Pakistani officials also made independent enquiries with Mullah Mohammad Omar about the possibility of finding a solution to the bin Laden problem:

Ziauddin recalls going to meet Omar and asking him to send away his dangerous guest. [...] He found Omar reluctant at first but found some give in his position later on. 'He is like a bone stuck in my throat, I can't swallow it nor can I get it out!' explained Omar. When Ziauddin asked Omar whether it was the money that Bin Laden gave the Taliban that made Omar 'beholden' to him, suggesting that, if that was the case, alternative sources of financing could perhaps be found, Omar responded in Pashto: *Da mata ywa rupay na rakarray de!* ('He hasn't given me even one rupee!' [...]). 'My people will lynch me if I hand him over. He is a hero!'[39]

Mullah Mohammad Omar's stance on bin Laden[40] seemed, however, to be unchanged, in particular with regards to his rhetoric that the Saudi government was opposed to the *umma*, a view that was eschewed by other senior Taliban leaders. During their years in power, the Taliban had a broadly positive attitude towards the Saudi government and *ulemaa'*, incidents like the one above notwithstanding.

There seems to have been a reaction on Mullah Mohammad Omar's part, though, to the claim that the Taliban could not control bin Laden, that led to clear restrictions being applied at this point; a group of ten Taliban guards were appointed to stay close to the al-Qaeda leader and watch over him at all times, and (in February 1999) his communications equipment was confiscated. The Taliban had communicated an unambiguously stern warning that bin Laden was to maintain a low profile from this point on.[41]

As often, the actions and the statements of the Taliban were at odds. Placing bin Laden under closer restrictions seemed to be a direct concession to Saudi Arabia, while an apology for Mullah Mohammad Omar's treatment of Prince Turki seemed to be out of the question. One possible explanation is that the restrictions—much like other policies applied to the issue of bin Laden—were an effort to appease the Taliban's internal factions, arguing in effect that delivering him would not be Islamic, while demonstrating that he would be controlled and forced to respect the sovereignty of the movement's leadership.

Mullah Mohammad Omar and Osama bin Laden

The relationship between Mullah Mohammad Omar and bin Laden has been much discussed yet hard, first-hand evidence regarding it is limited. This fact therefore casts doubt on the veracity of the accepted accounts and observations, making it difficult to arrive at any firm conclusion. Little is known about Mullah Mohammad Omar, and even the basic facts of his life are disputed. The Taliban leader is shrouded under a veil of secrecy that he encouraged. Moreover, his personality is such—he is not given to grand gestures or press conferences—that we understand far less about his motivations and desires than we need to in order to come to grasp his reasoning and motivation.

The few first-hand accounts that have been written—both about the Taliban and the relationship between Omar and bin Laden—invariably reflect a strong line in defence or criticism of one or the other, and there appear to have been very few neutral witnesses on a topic that is so frequently analysed. A number of books have been published that contain fragments of interactions with Mullah Mohammad Omar as well as interview transcripts.[42] Some material collected during interviews with the Taliban leader from 1994–2001 has subsequently been published in full, and various signed orders and notices that bear his signature have surfaced since 2001, but these only offer the barest outlines of the man. There are many figures who knew Mullah Mohammad Omar personally, but they are naturally reticent to discuss him for the time being.

From these different (albeit relatively few) accounts, some common themes emerge. The two leaders did not meet often.[43] Specific issues (as we have seen above) occasionally meant a face-to-face discussion, but bin Laden mostly travelled to Mullah Mohammad Omar's office for those. Bin Laden would also visit Omar as well as a whole host of Taliban officials for *eid* and other prominent Islamic holidays, as is the custom, but these were largely perfunctory encounters.[44] Indeed, the oft-stated image of bin Laden sitting at Mullah Mohammad Omar's side, whispering conspiracies into his ear, playing Iago to Omar's Othello, seems to lack substance. For one thing, multiple interviewees stated that bin Laden had no more than a basic smattering of Pashtu and that he always used Arab translators to communicate with the Taliban leader.[45]

We do know—and this has been widely reported both from Arab sources as well as from the Taliban's inner circle—that the two grew closer together during the final three years of the movement's rule in Afghanistan.[46] Something had changed, although it was probably not—as many allege—simply a matter of bin Laden's facility with words. Rather, it seems that the combined pressures of an increasingly combative and inflexible international lobby and diplomatic campaign, as well as the growing isolation of the Taliban, meant that bin Laden, in a similar situation, was able to communicate in a way that resonated with Mullah Mohammad Omar; he believed that bin Laden was at least one ally in this struggle. Statements made by Mullah Mohammad Omar as early as 1998 show him commenting about issues of governance in the Islamic world and in Saudi Arabia in particular.[47]

This one-sidedness is another prominent feature of the relationship, although the contours are only apparent with the benefit of hindsight. Bin Laden came to Afghanistan without any obstruction from Rabbani's government, who had hoped that he would facilitate development and usher in a shift in support from the Arab world.[48] Upon his arrival, bin Laden and his entourage soon realised the growing strength of the Taliban and sought to engage with Mullah Mohammad Omar; bin Laden had an agenda and he was sufficiently convinced of the importance of his cause as to have few qualms about manipulating or co-operating with the Taliban or their leadership, or indeed any other group that would facilitate an operational base.

At the same time, though, bin Laden was also a supporter of the idea of an Islamic government in Afghanistan and the creation of an Islamic state. This wasn't purely about manipulating the Taliban; he wanted to support them.[49] To this end, the issue of whether bin Laden actually took an oath of allegiance, or *bayat*, to Mullah Mohammad Omar is an important one. A report by Vahid Brown[50] draws on an account by Abu al-Walid al-Masri to shed considerable doubt on the variety of circumstantial evidence that suggested in the past that this did take place. If al-Masri's account is to be believed—and the broad outlines of the argument do make sense in context—then bin Laden sent al-Masri on his behalf to deliver the *bayat* to the Taliban leader, a gesture that cannot have failed to make an impression on Mullah Mohammad Omar for it was an undeniable slight. This delivery of the *bayat* at one remove was confirmed by two Taliban interviewees.[51]

The final two years of the Taliban's rule in Afghanistan, though, were characterised by the growing isolation of Mullah Mohammad Omar from Taliban internal dissent on the issue of bin Laden. His close advisors, who held alternative opinions on bin Laden, found themselves shut out of the inner circle based in Kandahar and were sent to work in Kabul or overseas.[52]

One of the most important 'sweeteners' between the two leaders, though, seems to have been money. The promise of Arab cash and hopes for a massive reconstruction programme had initially convinced Mullah Mohammad Omar to suspend his judgement on the Arabs, but from 1998/99 onward it seems bin Laden was able to command funds that he directed towards the Taliban.[53] The Taliban in 1999 would have been particularly susceptible to bin Laden's offerings, as they were in need of materiel and finances.[54] The money bin Laden directed towards the Taliban did not necessarily come from his personal funds—about which relatively more is known[55]—but rather from a network of funding organisations and interests that could transfer and mobilise funds that were at his disposal. Since his return to Afghanistan, bin Laden had raised his media profile and mobilised support networks that doubtless helped in channelling funds to him and his organisation.

Interviews with Taliban members confirmed this ('money and weapons were key to the agreement between the two')[56] although most claimed there was relatively little contact or meetings ('maybe once every two months')[57] in Kandahar. In particular, two Talibs noted that bin Laden could not speak Pashtu—a small but important fact that so far has been missing from the literature. One anecdote told by Mullah Mohammad Omar's driver[58] gives some colour:

During the Taliban's rule, Pakistan was trying to impose itself on the Taliban, but this influence could not be felt on the relationship between Mullah Mohammad Omar and Osama. When Zarqawi came from Pakistan unofficially, he met with Mullah Mohammad Omar and asked him whether it would be possible to set up a camp to start training people for fighting. Mullah Mohammad Omar shared this request with Osama, but Osama wasn't happy with the idea and didn't want him to make these plans, so Zarqawi went to Herat and was quite ineffective there.[59]

Accounts like this suggest that bin Laden functioned as a sort of elder or senior figure for the Arabs and foreign militants within Afghanistan, and that Mullah Mohammad Omar at least at times consulted him on issues concerning the foreigners in Afghanistan. Bin Laden also provided men and advice for the Taliban's ongoing campaigns up north. Indeed, one of the reasons journalists' access to these northern fronts and other parts of the country was restricted from 1999 onwards by the Taliban was on account of the presence of Arabs. Multiple sources have stated that Arab units were engaged in combat on the northern front, even though they did not fight alongside the Taliban but rather in their own units.[60]

One aspect of the relationship that is often brought up is the rumoured marriage of bin Laden's daughter to Mullah Mohammad Omar (and vice-versa). These rumours gained currency in the chaos and misinformation of the days following the initiation of the US campaign against the Taliban and al-Qaeda in 2001.[61] They have no basis in truth, however; yet, interestingly, both the Taliban and al-Qaeda have generated their own explanations surrounding this myth. Mullah Mohammad Omar's driver, in an interview for this book, stated that bin Laden had originally proposed that the Taliban leader marry one of bin Laden's daughters. This reportedly prompted Mullah Mohammad Omar to go by car to Maiwand where he took a fourth wife to prevent this possibility.[62]

From the Arab side, al-Masri has claimed that Omar proposed that bin Laden marry off his daughters to Taliban members (and that Omar might possibly retain one for himself). Bin Laden did not take well to this suggestion, apparently, and 1999 saw all of his daughters married off to thwart this possibility.[63]

A number of sources have stated that the relationship between the two never developed to the point of close cooperation, partly due to the very character of Mullah Mohammad Omar, a reclusive man of few words, but also due to ideological differences. Omar, like other Afghans, was suspicious of Islamist ideology rooted in Muslim Brotherhood or 'ikhwani' thought. He not only associated this with avrious factions with which he found himself in conflict (such as Sayyaf, Hekmatyar and Rabbani), but also found this difficult to reconcile with his own education and background, grounded as he was in the Deobandi madrassa curriculum and the Hanafi school along with a strong undercurrent of Sufism. In particular, anecdotes of his views on dreams and their applicability to real life are often ridiculed by observers.[64]

Neither of the men seemed to be willing to make that extra commitment: from the material that exists on the issue, it appears clear that both realised that they were different. They were from different worlds, with different beliefs, different customs, different agendas and—until the September 11 attacks— different paths for the future. More importantly, it seems that the relationship between the groups never differed from that between their respective leaders. Even this core interaction was plagued with problems (as we have seen above), and the evidence by no means shows a joint agenda or any interest on bin Laden's part in sharing operational details with the Taliban.

The Taliban and International Recognition

Despite and alongside all of these internal machinations at the highest levels of the Taliban and al-Qaeda leadership, many within the Taliban movement continued to seek international recognition. In particular, political Taliban officials who joined the movement after Kabul had fallen point to the inexperience of the political apparatus in their continued effort to engage the international community. They were trying to convince governments, in particular the United States, not to isolate the Taliban but to engage them and establish formal working relations that would help shape the future of the government.[65] If only, they argued, more countries would offer official diplomatic recognition then the movement would finally be able to deal with the very many social and political problems within the country.[66]

Bin Laden was not the only issue that confronted the Taliban's government at the time. The movement's harsh social policies—most of all, their attitudes to girls and women—had attracted international attention and there were several lobby groups devoted to bringing this to the attention of policy-makers in Washington. US Secretary of State Madeleine Albright was particularly vocal on this point, saying in 19 November 1997, that 'we are opposed to the Taliban because of their opposition to human rights and their despicable treatment of women and children and great lack of respect for human dignity.'[67]

In March 1998, Mavis Leno testified on the treatment of women in Afghanistan before Senator Diane Feinstein of the US Senate Foreign Relations Committee.[68] During the same month, British Secretary of State for International Development, Clare Short and European Commissioner Emma Bonino called for the international community to mark International Women's Day by taking a stand against 'gender apartheid' in Afghanistan.[69] In May 1998, the French fashion magazine *Elle* announced it would be priced at one franc higher than the usual retail price in order to help raise money for the women of Afghanistan.[70] In July 1998 the European Union froze funding of humanitarian aid projects in Kabul because of the Taliban's adverse treatment of women. The suspension of aid covered about $4 million, or 40 percent of all aid the European Union had earmarked for Afghanistan over the next twelve months.[71] There were many more such interventions over the Taliban's treatment of women during this period.

Bin Laden's American Embassy attacks of August 1998 had made the Taliban movement more of a liability for international business partners—for US oil company UNOCAL, for example—and, in addition, the movement's inability to take the north made it difficult for its oil pipeline project to move forward. UNOCAL had been involved in preparing a project that would see the installation of an oil pipeline bringing oil deposits from Central Asia (the Caspian Sea area) via Afghanistan and Pakistan to the Indian Ocean.[72] These efforts had begun in the early 1990s, when a new oil boom erupted in Central Asia; exploration rights to Yashlar in eastern Turkmenistan were asssigned to Bridas[73] in January 1992 and Keimir in February 1993.[74] UNOCAL was founded in 1890, and had operated in the United States for the most part until the 1930s when it began drilling for oil in Australia.[75] The company brought a mix of high-reaching political connections, large investment capital and the knowledge that their agenda matched a larger national agenda of the United States government.[76]

By late 1999, too, the first signs of domestic opposition within Taliban-controlled areas had begun to be felt around the country. Herat demonstrated against the Taliban in April and May—reportedly resulting in the deaths of 100 civilians[77]—and other provinces like Khost saw similar surges of opposition.[78] By now, Taliban members and leaders who had some contact with foreign representatives and the world outside Afghanistan had developed a sense of how badly the 'Emirate' was perceived and where the damage was being inflicted. Unsurprisingly, most placed the blame at the door of the international community.

Inside the country, there was very little consideration of the damage being done (particularly by the Taliban's social policies) which led to an increase in conspiracy theories as to why the international community had failed to bestow diplomatic recognition and why the United Nations seemed to be stuck in a rut of confrontation with the Taliban government. Many blamed America, which they believed was actively involved in preventing countries from officially recognising the Islamic Emirate of Afghanistan.[79] Domestic problems, in turn, began to be blamed on foreigners; if the international community came on board and provided humanitarian and other urgent support to the Taliban, the argument ran, then they would finally be able to start improving the lives of the people and to provide schooling for girls and find a way to normalise and legislate the presence of women in the workplace.[80]

It was a similar story with counter-narcotics efforts: the Taliban felt that they had, at least by 2000, delivered on their promises to tackle the problem of opium cultivation but that they were then offered no support by the international community.[81] Of course, those involved in the opium trade—and there were links with the Taliban's leadership—benefited from the ban of 2000 since prices rocketed; many of those involved were reported to have stockpiled supplies prior to the ban's full implementation.[82]

In September 1999, Mullah Mohammad Omar wrote to the American President, Bill Clinton. The letter was couched in language so undiplomatic that the Taliban's envoy did not want to pass it on to the State Department, but it stated clearly that the Islamic Emirate of Afghanistan had no intention of meddling in other countries' affairs and wanted good relations with the United States of America.[83]

Ours and your Almighty God has obliged us to serve our religion. We are not mad nor are we in love with power. We are in the service of God and that is why we are strict on our position. If you have any objection to anything we do, you should look at our deeds in the light of Islam (whether they are according to Islamic principles) and if they are in accordance with Islam—you should know that that is why we have to follow this path, how indeed could we change it? Please be a little fair.

Much is going on in the world. And it is possible that your strict position regarding us might be flawed. So let me bring another point to your attention and it is this: if we were overthrown, there would be major chaos and confusion in the country and everyone including every single oppressed individual would blame you for it.[84]

It seems that even at this point the Taliban wanted to find a way to interact usefully with the United States and their other international interlocutors, especially over the issue of bin Laden. Many of the Taliban's decisions, however, seemed to be guided by their need to maintain what they saw as their good standing in the Muslim world. This was the case with the Saudis as well as with the United States. The Taliban saw themselves as cornered by international policy, which in turn reinforced their stubbornness and alienated potential allies.[85]

The undercurrent to these dynamics are difficult to dissect given the absence of a clear strategy by the Taliban leadership. It appears that they regarded their Arab guests as a gateway to the Arab world and particularly to the Muslim communities which they regarded as natural allies. Many had begun to think that this was their only option given the increasingly strained relationship with the international community.[86]

Taliban Opposition to bin Laden

The group within the Taliban that opposed the presence of bin Laden and his acolytes grew closer together during this period, partly as a result of being increasingly shunned by the Kandahar core leadership and Mullah Mohammad Omar himself. Their objections were not simply a pragmatic response to international pressure—although pragmatism formed a central core of their calculations—but a considered response to his statements and actions. Bin Laden was not in Afghanistan because he wanted to help the Taliban, they believed, but to pursue his own objectives. This was clearly demonstrated to them in the years leading up to the September 11 attacks, not just in the aftermath.[87]

By 1998, Mullah Mohammad Rabbani—the head of the Kabul *shura*—was the leading figure among this group. They have often been characterised as 'moderates' within the movement, but this name is less accurate as a label in itself—the individuals who belonged to this group cannot really be described as holding 'moderate' views—than in relative terms on the issue of bin Laden in comparison with others in the movement. The 'moderate' label was applied by people in the international community more as a reflection of their hopes that such a faction within the Taliban existed and could be engaged. In fact, even the so-called 'irreconcilable' Taliban wanted to engage with the internationals at this point—albeit with certain caveats.[88]

Mullah Mohammad Rabbani was more forceful in stating his opposition to bin Laden in 1998, and in November—following a series of arrests in Jalalabad a month earlier—he was summoned to Kandahar to explain himself; his loyalty was in question.[89] By 1998, Rabbani was already making regular visits to Saudi Arabia—he was reportedly 'the favourite' of Prince Turki al-Faisal—to treat the cancer that would eventually kill him.[90] The final two years of his life were full of conflict with Mullah Mohammad Omar, and in August 2000 he was seated on the far side of the stage at a military parade, which commentators claim was an indication of his having been sidelined.[91]

In April 1999, Mullah Khaksar travelled in secret to Pakistan to meet with American representatives in order to try to broker some sort of agreement over bin Laden.[92] These interlocutors explored the possible ways of dealing with the problem of bin Laden. Khaksar wanted to build up a strong front from within the Taliban movement which could take care of the problem internally, but a later message turning down his offer suggested that the Americans merely wanted to get bin Laden direcly. They offered $5 million as possible compensation. This was not a serious offer, Khaksar reasoned, since there would undoubtedly be reprisals against the individuals involved, and against their families. Without some kind of support following any capture or assassination of bin Laden, the mission would likely not have had a definitive effect.[93]

Late 1999 also saw the Taliban's then foreign minister, Mullah Mutawakil, sidelined from the Kandahari core leadership. Prior to this point he had been a familiar face at meetings and functioned as a personal aide to Mullah Mohammad Omar, but after his appointment in Kabul to the Foreign Ministry, he was reportedly cold-shouldered in Kandahar.[94]

There were a multitude of logistical difficulties in mounting a successful bid to oppose bin Laden, but the Taliban were confronted with several constraints that prevented them from taking action. The need to avoid *fitna*, or conflict, among the Taliban's leadership core was apparently very strong[95] and enough of a reason on its own for some members to keep their opposition to themselves. Past experience had taught them that this was an issue over which Mullah Mohammad Omar could become curt or angry, and many learned not to bring it up.[96] They were restrained also by the internationals' failure on the issue of bin Laden to offer them a face-saving mechanism to present to the Taliban leader. Mullah Zaeef has told of the various suggestions that he offered on behalf of the movement as possible ways of dealing with bin Laden—international courts, legal proceedings and so on—but all of these were rejected.[97]

The final straw for this group came with the United Nations-led sanctions that were adopted in United Nations Security Council Resolution 1267 on

15 October 1999. The resolution put sanctions on individuals who were associated with bin Laden, al-Qaeda and/or the Taliban.[98] The group and their internal opposition efforts were effectively silenced; they lost their leverage over the Taliban leader, who by this point was convinced of an international Judeo-Christian conspiracy against his 'Emirate' and who felt surrounded by 'enemies.'[99]

Arab Relations with the Taliban

Bin Laden was not the only Arab actor with something to say about the Taliban and the relationship of host and guest. 'Al-Qaeda' was still more a conglomerate of separate actors than a homogenous organisation, and not all groups were supportive of either bin Laden or the Taliban. Much of what would come to be considered the core leadership of al-Qaeda—those who would set up international affiliate franchise operations—had not yet taken an oath to bin Laden or al-Qaeda. Many other groups co-existed, trained and were organised within the network of camps spread out over southern and eastern Afghanistan.[100]

Support: Abu Mus'ab al-Suri

Abu Mus'ab al-Suri was a Syrian veteran of the 1980s *jihad* against the Soviets, and one of the most outspoken strategic thinkers among the Arab jihadis who—during the 1990s—sought to outline a way forward for the next phases of *jihad*. After spending several years involved in the jihadi debates in Europe, as well as playing an important role in discussions over activities in Algeria, al-Suri returned to Afghanistan with his family. He had followed bin Laden's activities and the discussions surrounding his announcement of the 'World Islamic Front' in 1998. This was and could become a new stage in the *jihad*, al-Suri believed, and Afghanistan was a good base from which to prepare—albeit one that had the potential for being mishandled.

Al-Suri arrived in Kandahar in August 1997 but later moved with his family to Kabul.[101] He was a firm supporter of the Taliban and believed they—as hosts—had to be properly treated. This brought him into inevitable conflict with bin Laden, particularly following the August 1998 bombings in Africa. Al-Suri not only had apparently already warned bin Laden of the problems of overly-centralised organisations[102] but saw these attacks as damaging to the Taliban government. A dispute in Jihad Wal camp between the two earlier in the spring seemed symptomatic of this: al-Suri had argued that 'bin Laden had

175

acted as if he were Afghanistan's ruler,'[103] and this was the beginning of a long chill in their relationship.

From that point on, al-Suri was independent of bin Laden, working together with the Taliban as a 'media advisor' and also busy with his own writing. He produced a report entitled 'Afghanistan, the Taliban, and the Battle of Islam Today' in October 1998—he had published another shorter report in 1996—which outlined his position of support towards the Taliban.

Many had argued—as in the case from Peshawar, examined below—that the Taliban were ideologically not a match for the Arab jihadis and that this was a serious problem. Al-Suri was far more pragmatic over the matter, writing that:

the Taleban must be considered 'a legitimate Islamic Emirate in Afghanistan,' despite some shortcomings in their implementation of Islamic law (*shari'ah*). [...] He had met many senior Taleban officials, and he was particularly struck with their modesty and aversion to modern luxury. [...] In his opinion, the Taleban commanders were far better leaders than the previous mujahidin commanders and warlords.[104]

Together with his defence of the movement, al-Suri also sought to warn against sabotaging the opportunity offered by Afghanistan and the Taliban's hospitality. This, in particular, was directed at bin Laden, who, he said:

[...] will help our enemies reach their goal free of charge! [...] The strangest thing I have heard so far is [bin Laden's] saying that he wouldn't listen to [Mullah Mohammad Omar] when he asked him to stop giving interviews [...] I think our brother [bin Laden] has caught the disease of screens, flashes, fans, and applause [...][105]

The Taliban did, therefore, have Arab allies who understood the harm that bin Laden was causing, and who sought to encourage a different attitude towards their hosts.

Al-Suri's case demonstrates one position held among the jihadist groups within Afghanistan and Pakistan regarding the Taliban (as well as their ideological differences). The members of foreign jihadist groups did not form a homogenous entity and did not necessarily share a common ideology. They often differed significantly among themselves on issues: from religion, strategy, goals and overall leadership to organisational structures.[106] They were, however, unable to sway the leaders of their groups and had little clout despite their forcefully expressed opinions.

Opposition: Peshawar Group

Others were less happy about the Arab presence in Afghanistan, especially when it led (they said) to bin Laden formally making a pledge of loyalty to

Mullah Mohammad Omar (see above). The root ideological clashes between the Arabs and the Afghans—as we saw during the 1990s, as well as in 1995—were still alive and well. In particular, a group of Arabs in Peshawar were especially irate.

The Taliban were most frequently challenged on their Islamic credentials. The basic differences between the Hanbali and Hanafi legal schools were always present, but the Afghans' preference for graveyard shrines, for example, and other local traditions were subject to attack. 'We differ with our people here about the Taliban regime,' one said. 'They see them as God's righteous saints, while we view them as heretics and apostates.'[107] Many of these debates stemmed from the opinions which continued to be held by many Arab mujahedeen, more associated with the ideology of the Muslim Brotherhood, who had fought alongside the Afghan groups in the 1980s.[108]

These were sufficiently common accusations that both al-Suri and Sheikh Yusuf al-Uyayri were forced to address them openly in two position papers which they wrote on the Taliban in 1998 and 2000 respectively.[109] Indeed, the report begins by acknowledging these claims: 'Those who have diseases in their hearts, the munafiqun and ruwaybidhah, have recently started to call Amir al-Mu'minin al-Mulla Muhammad 'Umar and the Taliban with vile names.'[110] The report then mentions five points of dissent—specific matters of doctrine—and examines each one in turn.[111]

Another key focus of criticism was the Taliban's seeming desire to gain a seat at the United Nations. Al-Suri states that he had discussed this with the movement's leadership and that the Taliban would not be pursuing the matter.[112] A letter from al-Suri to one 'Abu Mohammad' also outlined these points of criticism following a meeting he had had in Peshawar—with Abu Mus'ab al-Zarqawi, no less—during this period, even noting that the Taliban are characterised as 'extremists of the Sufi sect and straying from the right path.'[113]

In a report sent from the Arab circles in late 1998, the claims again revolve around the idea the Taliban's perceived religious illegitimacy disqualified them from taking the key role in Afghanistan. Just as during the 1980s, the Taliban are seen as promoting 'tomb-worship' and even that this warrants '*takfir*'[114] being applied to the Taliban.[115]

Within Afghanistan, the ideological differences were minimised in a deliberate isolation[116] of foreign jihadists from the Afghan population and the Taliban. From the battlefield, where the foreigners formed their own units, to the training camps, the Arabs set themselves apart while the leaders aimed to reduce vocal confrontations about the subject. This policy was applied due to the realisation of the importance of having Afghanistan as a base for operations and organisation for their own goals that lay far beyond the borders of the Islamic Emirate of Afghanistan.

* * *

The pace of international isolation of the Taliban increased exponentially after August 1998, but so did the extent of interactions between the Taliban and foreign jihadis based within Afghanistan. As more foreigners arrived in Afghanistan, the Taliban movement took further steps to systematise their presence with restrictions and rules.[117] The Arab and other foreign jihadi groups were mostly located around Kabul and Kandahar during this period, and the Taliban tried to ensure that these camps were isolated from local Afghan communities.[118] Meetings between Arabs and Afghans in Kandahar, for example, were brief and often accidental. There was no attempt at or encouragement of interaction between the foreign guests and the local population. In fact, it was prohibited by the Taliban.[119]

Numerous accounts from all parties testify to military cooperation on the northern fronts between the Taliban and the foreign jihadis. In some cases this was on account of the actual location of training camps, but it was also part of a calculated strategy. The foreigners wanted combat experience and the Taliban could use the support on their front lines. Interviews conducted with Taliban members for this book as well as the written accounts by Arab jihadis present in Afghanistan all attest to the segregation of these front lines, however.[120]

The Arabs were living in different places not mixed with the Taliban. For instance, the Arabs were on the front line of the northern fronts and then came the Taliban fronts. The Arabs bought weapons themselves, not getting them from the Taliban, and the same went for their vehicles, food, blankets and other things. The Taliban, on the other hand, got these things from the Taliban government's Ministry of Defence.[121]

Another interviewee who fought on the fronts in the north explained that the two groups initially fought together but later separated 'when the Arabs saw the indiscipline of the Taliban units.'[122] Despite the segregation, the number of foreign fighters operating on the front lines continued to rise. In the final two years of Taliban rule, for example, there were 1,500–2,000 fighting on the front lines in the north against Massoud.[123]

In general, the foreign jihadis were keen on keeping their affairs out of the sight of the Taliban. For this reason, they were happy to comply with Taliban demands to restrict access to their facilities. The Taliban, for their part, believed that they had a good idea of what was going on inside the camps. Here is one senior Taliban political figure commenting on the camps and how much the movement knew about what was going on there:

They had to live somewhere, so they had these remote places which were isolated from the rest of the population—we did not want them to get mixed with the rest of the population—and they were living with their families. They had their families and kids there, so that's why the camps were somewhat separate.

They were not totally invisible from us. We knew where all their camps were. There were people around, shepherds etc, regular Afghans. Neither from these people, nor from the intelligence side or the satellites that the CIA had etc, were there any strange activities that we had no idea about.

Of course there were inevitably some tunnels—that I think we have to assume. But it was pretty transparent what was going on there. We had a good idea of what was going on there. And the security was done by the Afghan Taliban—the barrier gates and the surrounding checkpoints—all of this was done by the Afghan Taliban.[124]

For the Taliban and Mullah Mohammad Omar—the final arbiter on the presence of the Arab and other foreign jihadis—the calculation seems to have been not the encouragement of training of recruits for a conflict with other countries or for terrorist acts as the international community supposed, but rather a realisation that, for the moment, the foreign fighters were useful for the Taliban's campaign in the north and were actually some of the few allies that the movement had at this time.[125]

Bin Laden, as far as we know, interacted with the Taliban's sub-leadership relatively little, although meetings with Mullah Mohammad Omar continued on an irregular basis. This was clearly bin Laden's strongest link to the movement, and the structure of the Taliban command hierarchy meant that it was an important connection for him to cultivate. Mullah Mohammad Omar's driver stated that the two would often drive around in Kandahar together and discuss plans for the reconstruction of Afghanistan in the back of the car, but other interviews suggest that this was an infrequent fixture.[126] Whatever the exact number of times the two leaders met each month, this period saw the beginning of an increasingly segregated relationship between the organisations of the Taliban and al-Qaeda, both as a function of the Taliban's increasingly conflicted attitude to the foreign jihadis and also because the foreign guests sought a level of secrecy for their activities.

2000–2001

Taliban Goals: Had They Changed?

By 2000, following the Indian Airlines hijacking (see chapter 7, pp.195), the Taliban seemed to be at a point of no return with regards to international recognition.[127] None of the gestures that the Taliban was prepared to offer were met with any serious discussion, it seemed to them, and so it was in the second week of January that the Taliban hosted a delegation from Chechnya.[128] The Chechens had apparently been baying at the doors of the Taliban government for several years, but it was only in January that they finally received an invitation and participated in a series of meetings in Kabul. Their earlier visit had apparently failed because of the Taliban's sensitivity to the international community:

During a cabinet session, the members agreed that the Chechen Republic should be recognised. This was communicated to Kandahar. Kandahar in return ordered the Chechen delegation to take the next morning's Ariana flight to Kandahar. They did so and met in Kandahar with Mullah Omar. But we were soon informed that since there is a lot of tension between the Taliban and the international community, the recognition would have to be postponed to a later date. Disappointed, the Chechen delegation returned home.[129]

In January 2000, though, official recognition was extended to the Chechen government and diplomatic representatives would be dispatched to both Kabul and Grozny.[130]

The final two years of Mullah Mohammad Omar's rule in Afghanistan also offer the intriguing case of a couple of statements made by him that endorse a more international *jihad*.[131] In December 2000, for example, one newspaper reported that he 'has called on Muslims throughout the world to stage *jihad* against "the atheists in the United States and the Security Council" in retaliation for new international sanctions and a deadline to extradite the Saudi oppositionist [sic] Usamah Bin-Ladin to the United States to stand trial there.'[132]

Statements like this may seem to suggest that, by this point, Mullah Mohammad Omar had completely absorbed bin Laden's internationalist agenda and sought to expand the Taliban's 'Islamic rule' outside Afghanistan, beginning in particular with the countries of neighbouring Central Asia.[133] While evidence suggests that the Taliban leader was drifting in with bin Laden's crowd during the final year of his government, there is little to indicate that Mullah Mohammad Omar planned to act on any of this new rhetoric.[134]

Interviews with Taliban figures close to Mullah Mohammad Omar during this time, though, suggest a more probable explanation for their leader's *volte face*: he was increasingly concerned with how other Muslim countries saw him. Just as bin Laden had exploited this weak spot in order to get Omar's acquiescence for his continued stay in Afghanistan, there seemed to be a desire on the part of Mullah Mohammad Omar himself to remain publicly committed to his interpretation of Islam.

Time spent together with bin Laden had apparently convinced him of the validity of a variety of causes outside Afghanistan—most prominent of which was the need to expel American troops from Saudi Arabia—and thus these statements were made.[135] The Taliban movement at this time remained heavily isolated from the international community, and Mullah Mohammad Omar was convinced—as were many others within the Taliban—that there was an international conspiracy against the Taliban on account of their being Muslim. One interviewee also stated that Mullah Mohammad Omar was not particularly concerned about these international Islamic causes but was persuaded to make these statements in order to ensure a continuing stream of funds from donors in the Gulf states.[136]

This was made clear to two foreign journalists in June 2001 while they were in Afghanistan for an interview with the Taliban leader:

'Afghanistan, according to Mullah Omar's entourage, has suggested to the United States (via the U.S. Embassy in Islamabad, Pakistan) and to the United Nations that international "monitors" keep bin Laden under observation pending a resolution of the case, "but so far we have received no reply." Aides said they had also informed the United States they were putting bin Laden on trial for his alleged crimes and requested that evidence be presented. The court allegedly sat for 30 days without evidence being presented against bin Laden. It extended its hearing for another 10 days, according to the same aides, to give the U.S. side time to act. "But nothing materialized," said the aides.'[137]

If there was one incident which seems to characterise this period—the relations between the Taliban and the outside world, as well as the isolation of Mullah Mohammad Omar—it is the destruction of the Bamiyan Buddhas in March 2001.[138] Mullah Mohammad Omar issued a decree in early February stating that 'all statues and non-Islamic shrines located [in Afghanistan] must be destroyed.' This was immediately followed by the destruction and vandalism of various artefacts in the Kabul Museum, the work of two senior Taliban officials.[139] But in March the Taliban would spend two weeks destroying the Buddha statues in Bamiyan—supervised by Mullah Dadullah—even after major international attempts to save the relics.[140]

A great body of officials within the Taliban movement—including Mullahs Mohammad Rabbani, Mutawakil, and Zaeef—thought that this was a bad policy decision and took every opportunity in private to caution the Taliban leader against issuing an order for the destruction of the statues.[141] In public, they remained loyal to the government and defended the decision, albeit with reluctance.[142] Mullah Mohammad Omar had originally ordered the protection of the Buddhas when the Taliban first conquered Bamiyan in 1998. Gutman quotes the Pakistani journalist, Hamid Mir, who recalled an interview with al-Zawahiri during which he claimed that he was able to manipulate the Taliban and its leadership over this issue.[143] The incident neatly illustrates Mullah Mohammad Omar's isolation from those within his government who understood the outside pressure that was being brought to bear on the Taliban and who were trying to find some traction internationally for what they would consider as a reasonable discussion over issues.[144]

By this point, most discussions about bin Laden seemed—to the Taliban's diplomatic corps—somewhat staged and well-rehearsed. On 2 August 2001, for example, US Assistant Secretary of State, Christina Rocca, met with Mullah Zaeef in Islamabad and broached the issue, but neither Rocca nor Zaeef emerged from the meeting with any sense that the other had responded. Zaeef later wrote that 'she flouted every diplomatic principle, and every single word she uttered was a threat, hidden or open,' but she suggested in a statement that Zaeef had not listened to her arguments.[145]

But was the decision to destroy the Buddha statues an indication of a shift in Taliban goals? The timing and broad rejection of international mediators and advocates for the Buddhas—including a delegation of Arab scholars who were also poorly received[146]—seemed to be a calculated shot at the Taliban's critics. Moreover, it seems to have been another case of Mullah Mohammad Omar being sensitive to the image of the Taliban and his rule that he had built around himself. Indeed, he reportedly cited posterity as one of the important reasons for carrying out the destruction, most famously observing, 'I am not the sculpture seller, I am the sculpture destroyer [*"bot shakan"*].'[147]

Many Taliban figures, both political and military, seem to remember those words; they have taken on a life of their own.[148] The influence of foreign Arab advisors on Mullah Mohammad Omar is frequently cited as a reason for his change of mind,[149] but it appears more likely that Pakistani clerics were responsible.[150] Interviews conducted for this book unanimously cited this influence, sometimes also naming figures within the ISI who accompanied the Pakistani clerics on their trips to meet with the Taliban leader.[151] The destruction was, however, positively received by Islamist circles and the jihadist community, and reportedly led to an increase of Arab recruits.[152] This, after all, was proof for those who had defended the Taliban among Arab critics that they were serious about following the *shari'a* and eliminating *bid'a*. Even abroad, Islamist scholars wrote texts justifying Mullah Mohammad Omar's decision.[153]

The Taliban lost most of the few people who were still advocating for a political solution and engagement with the group prior to the destruction of the Buddhas. In the end, though, this was more a continuation of the situation that had already existed since at least 1998, whereby the Taliban movement's political corps felt that they were being intentionally isolated. Here, for example, is Mullah Zaeef following the Buddha destruction: 'The Afghan government is not afraid of international isolation resulting from the destruction of the Buddha statues, because Afghanistan is already isolated.'[154]

Taliban Domestic Policies

Even four years into their rule, the Taliban had not managed to provide an interim solution to the country's internal problems. The United Nations had nominally taken on the responsibility for the provision of emergency food aid—unwilling simply to pull out of Afghanistan—and the second year of a drought had further devastated conditions for many Afghans around the country.[155] There were 1.15 million people internally displaced by mid-2001[156] on account of drought and ongoing conflict, and international assistance organisations had slowly been isolated and restricted throughout 2000 and 2001 by the Taliban government.[157]

While observers often refer to the growing radicalisation of the Taliban and their social policies during this period, many of their ideas and interpretations of the ideal Islamic society remained very much the same throughout their time in power. The rules they imposed on the local population from Kandahar to Mazar-e Sharif throughout their time in power often differed little. Much of the belief that the Taliban grew more 'radical' is a reflection of how these policies affected the greatly varied types of communites in different regions of the country and in urban vs. rural areas within Afghan society at the time, and which are differences that can still be found around the country today.

Policies that interfered little in communities in rural southern Afghanistan (which have always been more conservative and traditional as a rule), in particular those impacting the status and role of women within society, entailed a radical shift for the urban society of Kabul, and the Uzbek, Tajik, Hazara and other communities in central and northern Afghanistan. Different parts of

Afghanistan were also differently affected by the war; the level of chaos and insecurity that made much of the population support the Taliban in southern Afghanistan was not found throughout the country. Furthermore, with the growing consolidation of their power, the Taliban had more time and opportunity to enforce their programme throughout the country.

The edicts issued by the Taliban leadership and to a great extent by Mullah Mohammad Omar himself, surrounded by a council of *'ulemaa*, were the outcome of a lack of political vision. The call for an Islamic state that takes the *shari'a* as its basis and the *Qu'ran* as its central point of reference—a caliphate or emirate—and which was a pronounced goal for many groups from Egypt to Indonesia, falls short in envisioning the actual shape, structures and administrative tools of such an entity. The Taliban seemed to pick and choose as they pleased. There was, for example, no precedent for a six-man council in the capital city while the official leader of the group lived somewhere else in the country, wielding all the power.

The Taliban, like many others, had few concrete ideas of what an Islamic state entailed. As senior members of the Taliban government observed, much of what was still being implemented by Taliban cadres in influential positions such as the major cities like Kabul was a direct continuation of socialist policies that were simply taken from what had been pursued in earlier decades.[158]

Setting out to create an Islamic state, the Taliban leadership seemed deeply concerned about how they were viewed by those they regarded as their religious peers. Many of their edicts—those addressing issues like music, beards, the banning of women from the workplace, education, the flying of kites and various other activities—were taken from what they believed to be the model of the early *umma* surrounding Prophet Mohammad. These aimed to transform society as a whole, echoing the ideas of the *tablighi* movement and the principle of *da'wa*, social reform from the bottom-up. Every individual was seen as a cornerstone of the *umma*.

Here is the account, for example, of the *Amr bil Marouf* by one such senior political Talib:

The Ministry was responsible for ensuring that the people and government personnel were compliant and was therefore monitoring the different government institutions.

The Ministry would make sure that the people prayed the five obligatory daily prayers, that they fasted during the month of Ramadan, that they follow the Sunna of the Prophet Mohammad (PBUH) so that Islamic values were being actively followed, and that the Prophet's example was followed in manner and appearance. Any actions in conflict with Islam would be avoided by all government departments.

The Ministry made sure that the people obeyed the religious orders and did not commit any sinful actions. The Ministry was responsible for men and women alike, since both have their place and responsibilities in society. In this way, women had to observe the *hejab*; avoid strolling, idle chatting or talking with men who did not belong to their family; and they had to be accompanied by a male family member or *mahram* while traveling and so forth. The Ministry also took care of issues like narcotics, harmful drugs, cigarettes, alcohol, hashish, opium and heroin; all these were banned. Gambling, bribery, music and adultery were also forbidden.[159]

Their pursuit of an ideal Islamic state, the growing number of edicts and restrictions, together with brutal enforcements and severe punishments for misconduct, disrupted the fragile balance between local traditions and Islam. This attempt at total control ('for the good of the people') resembled that of a totalitarian state.

Moreover, open opposition—in areas nominally under 'Taliban control'— had started to erupt around the country (see above). These sporadic incidences were a reaction both to the harsh style of the Taliban's rule and also to an aggressive army recruitment strategy that had—by this time—led to widespread resentment. Even in southern Afghanistan, where, superficially at least, little evidence of this resentment was visible, people were weary of having to supply their men to fight the Taliban's seemingly endless battles in the north. This was, in fact, one of the biggest sources of opposition to the movement from the local population.[160]

On 24 August 1999, a massive truck-bomb exploded outside Mullah Mohammad Omar's residence in Kandahar in which several people were killed and dozens injured.[161] While it remains unclear who was responsible, the attack does not seem to have been the work of local popular opponents, but rather of the Northern Alliance, of foreign actors or of the Afghan Arabs themselves.

Another deeply unpopular measure taken at this time was the continuation of the Taliban's three-stage strategy to eliminate the cultivation of opium. On 1 August 2000, Mullah Mohammad Omar issued a decree formally banning the cultivation of poppy, and the movement set about enforcing this ban. In the end, they were broadly successful, but their intended audience for this measure—the international community—was unconvinced. The Taliban had already undertaken a previous effort to ban opium in Helmand province, soon after they had captured it in 1995. The importance of the opium economy for the general population as well as for the networks of traders and smugglers, caused them to retract their earlier efforts when they faced local resistance to a policy that at this early stage of the movement's evolution proved to be too damaging to pursue.[162]

By this time, international opposition had solidified and even as dramatic a measure as the opium eradication activities of the Taliban were insufficient to overturn this scepticism. There were very few supportive gestures that would allow the Taliban to mitigate some of the resultant farmers' problems. The limited resources and possible neglect by the Taliban leadership in perceiving the devastating impact of the eradication once again caused widespread resentment. No measures were taken to find a substitute for the opium economy that fuelled much of the rural communities' livelihoods, alternative crops for people to cultivate never arrived, and there was no sense that this gesture had been noticed by the internationals.

It was another blow to those within the Taliban who had been arguing—publicly and in private—that the movement needed to reach out to the international community, to meet them halfway. The lack of reaction seemed to offer clear evidence to Mullah Mohammad Omar that the internationals were no longer interested in engaging with the Taliban, and that he alone would have to defend the honour of the movement.

Al-Qaeda-Taliban Relations

The segregation and distance which characterised the relationship between the Taliban and al-Qaeda in previous years was reinforced between 2000 and 2001. The Arabs remained isolated and removed—for the most part—from contact with Afghans or even with the Taliban. There were a few Arabs who moved between the two poles, but this was by no means the norm.

By 2000–2001 the foreigners in Afghanistan still defied characterisation as a homogenous unit or group. There were still hundreds of independent actors within Afghanistan, notably Abu Mus'ab al-Zarqawi, who was based in Herat during this period.[163] Many of these had a strained relationship with al-Qaeda and bin Laden, turning down invitations to join with the organisation and formally make a pledge or *bayat* to bin Laden.[164] For the Taliban, too, bin Laden was hardly their primary concern, although he was the one causing the most problems for the movement's desire for normalisation of relations with the outside world.

The well-known Saudi religious cleric Sheikh Yusuf al-Uyayri visited Afghanistan and met with the Taliban leadership in July 2000. He seems to have been invited by Abu Mus'ab al-Suri and other defenders of the Taliban in order to offer yet another positive report of the Afghan 'Islamic Emirate' to present and win over the Arabs who remained unconvinced as to their religious legitimacy.

His report legitimised the Emirate by refuting most of its detractors' claims. Al-Uyayri and al-Suri both seem to have found it difficult to move on from allegations that the Taliban were 'Sufi' and 'Deobandi,' though, even going so far as to suggest that Mullah Mohammad Omar imprisoned two 'Naqshbandi-yya Sufis' and 'warned them from repeating what they had done.'[165] Indeed, late 2000 saw the Saudi clerics of the Shu'aybi school begin to issue 'fatwas on the need to support the Taliban.'[166]

Within the Taliban, the little continued resistance to the presence and activities of the foreign jihadists that had expressed faltered with the death of Mullah Mohammad Rabbani on 16 April 2001. Their group was left without much of a voice, having been already sidelined and moved away from the centre of power in Kandahar.[167]

Arabs based in south-eastern Afghanistan acted upon their religious qualms with Afghan practices in 2000 and early 2001 when they smashed a number of Afghan graveyards and shrines in what they saw as a legitimate attack on 'innovative' practices far from the truth of 'true Islam.'[168] The Taliban intervened in the local altercation between the Arabs and the Afghan population surrounding the destruction of graveyards and shrines, settling the issue, while senior Arab leaders instructed their followers to abstain from any such actions in the future.[169] Jalaluddin Haqqani himself even stepped in to calm both sides down, counselling the Arabs against carrying out these kinds of actions and trying to minimise the Kandahari Taliban (and local) backlash against the Arabs in turn.[170]

It was yet another indication of the highly tenuous state of relations between the Arab jihadis and their Afghan hosts. Far from being synonymous groups by this time—as some have alleged—with similar goals and overlapping structures, the disparate Arab and Afghan actors seem rather to have been more disengaged and conflicted than ever.

Differing Agendas

Bin Laden had already set in motion the September 11 plot by this time; the Hamburg 'cell' had already made his acquaintance in Kandahar and had been dispatched back to Europe and on to the United States.[171] The al-Qaeda head was firmly on a course for confrontation with the United States. January 2000 saw a failed attempt to bomb the USS *The Sullivans* and a successful attempt in October against the USS *Cole*, both in Yemen.[172]

All of this was happening independently of Mullah Mohammad Omar and the Taliban movement. Bin Laden's agenda differed from that of the Taliban, who were still making a last ditch effort to garner legitimacy and support from the international community.[173] Bin Laden's interests in Afghanistan were pragmatic: he needed a base from which to conduct his operations, and thought that Afghanistan would be a good location in which to ensnare the United States when it finally reacted to his provocations.[174] Al-Qaeda also made considerable progress in its media campaign, issuing its first recruitment video celebrating the USS *Cole* attack, and in general having a larger media presence that allowed them to multiply the propaganda effect of the attacks.[175]

The relationship between the two leaders continued to grow close, especially when—after the almost-successful Yemen attacks—bin Laden's finances were arguably in better shape given his greater exposure; if this was the case, he could afford to contribute to the Taliban's coffers again. Tension did, however, still remain between the two. A 'stormy' meeting that reportedly took place in August 2000 saw the two clash over their respective agendas:

[Mullah Mohammad Omar] was willing to accept Bin-Ladin in Afghanistan just as a refugee who performs no political or propaganda activities, while Bin-Ladin said that he would not end his declared war against the United States. [...] Mola [sic] Omar used sharp words when he was addressing Bin-Ladin.[176]

There were other signs of conflict between the two groups during this period. Murshed claims that Mullah Mohammad Omar started a process to try to deal with bin Laden during mid-2000 (see above) but this was also at a time when the Taliban closed down several of the jihadi training camps: the Taliban 'ordered its training camps to be brought under the control of the Afghan Defence Ministry, which subsequently amalgamated six camps into three, and then announced that it was temporarily closing all of them.'[177] Two weeks later, however, the Taliban reopened some of them again.[178]

An interview with Mullah Mohammad Omar conducted in June 2001 by an American journalist included comments as to bin Laden's lack of the appropriate religious credentials necessary to issue Islamic *fatwas* or religious edicts. Mullah Mohammad Omar was hard on bin Laden, saying that his *fatwas* were, in fact, 'null and void':

Bin Laden is not entitled to issue fatwas as he did not complete the mandatory twelve years of Koranic studies to qualify for the position of mufti.[179]

7

SEPTEMBER 11, 2001

'Hafeezullah pointed out that during World War II, when Afghanistan came under
pressure from the Allies to hand over several hundred Germans living in the country,
the request was denied. "These were not even Muslims," he said, "and we did not hand
them over."'

Peter Bergen, Holy War Inc.[1]

'"I will not surrender a Muslim to an atheist!" [said Mullah Mohammad Omar.] There
is no doubt that this sentence decisively defined the fate of the relations between the
United States and the Taliban movement. This was even the sentence based on which
it was decided that war was inevitable and that America will not relinquish the toppling of the Taliban rule even if this necessitated its direct intervention. At the time,
certain Arab hard-liners cautioned the Taliban command, saying: "By doing so, you
have declared war on the United States." [...] The Taliban officials did not grasp most
of these philosophies and shrugged their shoulders saying: "We rely on Allah and we
will implement Islam whether America accepts it or fights it."'

Abu al-Walid al-Masri, writing about a meeting in 1996[2]

On 11 September 2001, three hijacked planes crashed into the Pentagon and
the two towers of the World Trade Center, and a fourth crashed into a field in
Pennsylvania. Almost 3,000 people were killed in the attacks. The planning,
training and execution of the September 11 attacks took little more than two

and a half years and cost somewhere between $400,000 and $500,000, involving nineteen attackers and a small number of trainers and logistics operatives.[3]

The attacks were informed by al-Qaeda's world view that had identified the United States as its enemy. Bin Laden had been putting forward a narrative outlining why this was a retaliation for America's involvement in the wider Middle East and Muslim world, framed as the continuation of a religious war reaching back to the Crusades.[4]

The attacks demonstrated that al-Qaeda regards civilians as legitimate targets.[5] There had been attacks on American government installations and attempts to target civilians in the past, but these had taken place in distant countries. Even though they were by and large unsuccessful, bin Laden regarded them as the first volley in a war supporting his central goal: a withdrawal of US forces from the Muslim world and an end of American support for Middle Eastern governments.

The attacks that took place in the United States on 11 September 2001 had a profound impact on US and international foreign policy. They helped form the rationale for the dispatch of international forces to Afghanistan under the leadership of the US military. On 12 September 2001, Article Five was invoked for the first time in the history of the North Atlantic Treaty Organisation (NATO), declaring the attack on the United States an attack on all nineteen members of the alliance.[6]

As we have seen in previous chapters, bin Laden—the man who was identified at the centre of the plots—was not unknown to the intelligence community around the world. Both the United States and Saudi Arabia had exerted pressure on the Taliban government in Afghanistan, who were hosting bin Laden and his entourage; they had sought his extradition for years, to no avail.

The Taliban's political leadership had not shifted on their position regarding bin Laden; they constructed reasons why they could not meet the demands of the United States—the lack of bilateral agreements to extradite individuals or recognition of their government. Negotiations were at a stalemate, with both sides demonstrating no visible signs of diverting from their stances. Mullah Mohammad Omar strongly believed that it would be a violation of Islamic law to hand over a Muslim to a non-Muslim country, one which would also reflect badly on perceptions of local Afghan customs.[7]

The September 11 attacks, coupled with the unrelenting nature of the Taliban's negotiation style in the years beforehand, were taken by international media outlets as evidence of strong links between the two groups, if not cooperation at the highest levels.[8] The Taliban, after all, had sheltered bin Laden and al-Qaeda for the past five years, allowing them to train on Afghan soil along with dozens of other militant Islamic groups and individuals. This was reflected in senior US policy discussions, too.[9]

This issue remains at the centre of a debate that has still not reached a unified conclusion among commentators, policy-makers and analysts. The attack is the reason for the current international presence inside Afghanistan, just as the Bush doctrine outlined—'We will make no distinction between those who planned these acts and those who harbour them.'[10] The attacks play a key role in the fears of the current American administration and its allies when considering a withdrawal and Afghanistan's possible future.[11] Many of those who advocate a close relationship between the two groups often place the attacks (and the possibility of a repeat) as a centrepiece of their argument.[12]

This chapter temporarily departs from the chronological framework that previous chapters have followed, because earlier operations are often cited as having set a precedent for the September 11 attacks and should be assessed and analysed together, as they are below in this chapter.

For most people, this traumatic event appeared to come out of nowhere. A closer look into the individuals involved, their biographies and the conditions they found themselves surrounded by, in conjunction with the ideological debates they led—often reaching back decades—offer considerable insights into how a small group of individuals came to launch an offensive salvo against the United States and the Western world. As mentioned above, the individuals who conceived and executed the plot had been engaged in an ongoing discussion that led them to construct a narrative of history that came to focus on the United States, or the 'far enemy,' as their prime target (see chapter 4).

The Taliban, as we have also seen in earlier chapters, played little or no role in this debate, and in all likelihood only became aware of many of the issues relating to the al-Qaeda leadership when they captured Kabul. This is important to remember when looking at the September 11 attacks: the Taliban represented a different world to the global jihadists, not only in terms of their background, education and goals but also in their general social behaviour, decision-making processes and convictions.

In essence, bin Laden and al-Qaeda abused the Taliban's hospitality (although many of the foreign jihadists were unhappy with this unilateral decision taken by bin Laden). Even if records of conversations between the al-Qaeda head and Mullah Mohammad Omar regarding possible attacks on the United States are dubious, these accounts do acknowledge that Mullah Mohammad Omar was opposed to attacking the United States.[13] Furthermore, while Mullah

Mohammad Omar appears to have taken unilateral decisions on multiple occasions that were enforced and accepted by the Taliban at large, the political leadership of the movement was far from united over how to deal with bin Laden. Their relationship to Mullah Mohammad Omar was often strained for this reason. Many regarded his continued provision of a safe haven as a strategic error and voiced their concerns to the Taliban leader.[14]

The Bojinka Plot

The Bojinka plot was an ambitious plan that aimed to see twelve[15] commercial airplanes explode midway en route to the United States.[16] It is believed to have evolved out of Abdul Hakim Murad's and Ramzi Yosuf's idea of loading a light aircraft with explosives and crashing it into a high-profile building in the United States. The pair allegedly developed the idea in 1994.[17] The plot was made possible by Yosuf's key innovation of an explosive device that could pass undetected through airport security.[18]

Yosuf and Murad had both travelled to Manila with the help of Yosuf's uncle, Khalid Sheikh Mohammad, and Ridwan Isamuddin (aka Hambali), the leader and founder of the *Jamiat Islamiyya*.[19] This was a militant group set up in southeast Asia which had quite a distinct organisational structure and more professional cadre. It did, however, still belong to the universe of militant Islamic movements and retained strong links back to Afghanistan.[20]

Khalid Sheikh Mohammad, a Kuwaiti of Baluch descent, began his career within political Islam when he was sixteen years old by joining the Muslim Brotherhood. He attended Brotherhood desert camps, attained a degree in mechanical engineering in North Carolina, and spent most of his time as a free agent of global *jihad*.[21] He went to Afghanistan in the 1980s, and from then on moved in militant Islamist circles.[22] Until the mid-1990s and even after, Mohammad remained an independent agent with his own extensive contact network. Long before cooperating with bin Laden and al-Qaeda, Mohammad was planning and executing attacks on the United States and other targets, forming and organising groups in various countries.[23]

Mohammad and his network of contacts exemplify much of the professional global jihadist scene and its means of operation. As the 9/11 Commission's report states:

There were also rootless but experienced operatives, such as Ramzi Yousef and Khalid Sheikh Mohammed, who—though not necessarily formal members of someone else's organization—were traveling around the world and joining in projects that were sup-ported by or linked to Bin Ladin, the Blind Sheikh, or their associates.[24]

In Manila, Mohammad's group also sought to assassinate the Pope.[25] Other sources claim that the Abu Sayyaf Group[26] was involved or played a support-ive role in Yosuf's plot by facilitating access to safe houses, logistics and material.[27]

On 11 December 1994, Yosuf conducted a trial run of his plan, purchasing a flight ticket under the name Armaldo Forlani. He boarded a Philippines Air-lines flight in Manila flying to Tokyo via Cebu.[28] He concealed the explosive charge in his shoe, extracted it on the plane and used a Casio watch as timer, hiding the bomb under his seat. Haruki Ikegami took his place in Cebu, where the plane landed (and Mohammad exited) before heading towards its final des-tination. The explosion occurred mid-air, killing Ikegami and ripping a hole in the plane's fuselage but the pilot managed to make an emergency landing.[29]

On 6 January 1995, while preparing chemicals for another bomb, an acci-dent produced thick smoke which led police to an apartment in Manila. Murad was arrested and Yosuf's computer was seized, revealing the outline of the Bojinka plot.[30] The one-room bachelor pad also contained street maps of the city showing the motorcade route of the Pope's forthcoming visit, documents pointing towards plans of attack, and a number of bomb-making materials, along with a bomb which was home-made and undetectable by airport secu-rity. Dozens of passports were also found, leading to the identification of Ahmed Saeed as Abdul Hakim Murad. Yosuf, however, slipped away unnoticed.[31]

A statement found in the flat outlined the broad objectives of the group:

All people who support the US government are our targets in our future plans and that is because all those people are responsible for their government's actions and they sup-port the US foreign policy and are satisfied with it. We will hit all US nuclear targets. If the US government keeps supporting Israel, then we will continue to carry out oper-ations inside and outside the United States.[32]

Just like statements associated with Yosuf from the World Trade Center bombing in 1993, the text lacked any reference to early Islamic history or any other significant reference to Islam.[33]

The various links that were discovered between individuals revealed that many had biographies tracing back to the Afghan *jihad*. They spread out in the early 1990s around the Muslim world, even though they weren't part of one organisation. This is the backdrop in which al-Qaeda would come to foster its plans and projects and consolidate individuals into a wider network of associates with shared goals and varying degrees of cooperation.[34]

Bojinka offers a clear precedent for the September 11 attacks. The involvement of Khalid Sheikh Mohammad and the use of airplanes as weapons were two features that would continue to be developed. Furthermore, the central aim of causing mass civilian casualties as a means to engage the United States demonstrates the similarity of goals between the two operations.

Yosuf and Khalid Sheikh Mohammad had both perceived airplanes as weapons for some time and both were independent actors who moved within worldwide militant Islamist circles. This had allowed them to pull together the resources, gain support and implement the plot.[35] The near-secular nature of the attackers' demands would change for the September 11 attacks. The expertise for such attacks would be merged with bin Laden's now extensive—if not entirely consistent—commentary on the reasons for attacking the United States and the 'far enemy.'

Bojinka was a visible operational success for Mohammad, one that at least gave him the credibility of having almost carried out his plan. Matched with bin Laden's resources and a broader structure of support for funding and planning, the original kernel of an idea would bear fruit.

The discovery of a large amount of data relating to the plot and the plot's perpetrators undoubtedly was a lesson that the plot's architects took into account, namely that of operational security. For the September 11 attacks, therefore, there was a very tight compartmentalisation of information (even among the attackers) and a very limited desire to expose anyone outside a small group to the workings of the plan. When the final arrangements had been made, bin Laden started to make references to the plot, but this policy of secrecy suggests again that the Taliban would not have been privy to such information. Even after the attacks, bin Laden and al-Qaeda refused to claim responsibility for it until autumn 2004.[36]

While Bojinka was a first step on a path that led towards the September 11 attacks, it is perhaps too easy to draw a line between the two. The actors were different, it was carried out on the latter's own initiative (and not subcontracted), and the goals were different from those of the September 11 plot. Again, however, there was no Taliban involvement. The important lessons learnt for Mohammad related to operational security, the possibility of using planes as both targets and instruments for attacks, and the need for a secure base of operations and funding to carry out a larger-scale plot. Afghanistan would fit all these requirements.

The Indian Airlines Hijacking

The Indian Airlines plane that was hijacked in 1999—and ended up in Kandahar—is cited by some commentators as a precursor of the September 11 attacks.[37] These accounts often also point to the involvement of the Taliban and at times link the hijacking to bin Laden and al-Qaeda. The following section looks at the hijacking, the response of the Taliban, and the individual actors involved.

On 24 December 1999, Indian Airlines flight 814 took off from Tribhuvan International Airport at Kathmandu, Nepal, flying to Indira Gandhi Airport in Delhi. After the plane entered Indian airspace, five men hijacked the plane and forced the pilot to divert from its planned course.[38] The hijacking lasted for eight days and ended on 31 December with the handover of three prisoners from the custody of the Indian government. 192 people survived, one person was killed and another wounded. The five perpetrators and the three men who were released escaped.

After taking control, the hijackers forced the pilot to change course and landed in Amritsar (India), Lahore (Pakistan) and Dubai (UAE), after which the hijackers directed the airplane to Kandahar, Afghanistan. The hijackers forced Captain Sharan to take off from Amritsar without refuelling, fearing an Indian commando attempt to retake the plane. Prior to touching down in Amritsar the hijackers had attempted to land in Lahore but had not received permission to do so and the pilot himself was worried about landing in Pakistan.[39]

On approaching Lahore, the authorities shut down the air traffic control services and all airport lighting in an attempt to prevent the aircraft from landing. A severe shortage of fuel forced the pilot to attempt a landing nonetheless, believing he could make out the airstrip (which turned out to be a main highway), and only at the last minute were the airport lights switched back on, allowing the plane to land.[40] A National Geographic documentary on the hijacking described Pakistani hostility to the plane landing on their soil: the Pakistani government threatened to shoot down the aircraft as it approached Lahore, denied permission to offload hostages or injured passengers, and less than three hours later (after refuelling) the plane was in the air again.[41]

From Lahore, the plane flew to the United Arab Emirates, where twenty-seven passengers were released.[42] Rupin Katyal, a 25-year-old Indian, was the only fatality of the hijacking; he had been stabbed multiple times by one of the hijackers and died on the plane.[43] The plane then landed in Kandahar on the morning of 25 December.[44]

The negotiations in Kandahar lasted for seven days. As a result of the talks, the Indian government released Mawlana Massoud Azhar, Ahmed Omar Saeed Sheikh and Mushtaq Ahmad Zargar. India's Foreign Minister, Jaswant Singh, flew to Kandahar with the prisoners, where the three men were exchanged for the remaining 154 people on board the plane.[45] The five hijackers and three freed prisoners then left Afghanistan, most likely driving over the border and into Pakistan via the Chaman border crossing, a claim denied by the Pakistani government.[46] There have been claims that bin Laden hosted the hijackers and freed prisoners on that first night, but interviews for this book uncovered no evidence to either confirm or repudiate this story.[47]

Back Story

Mawlana Massoud Azhar was born in 1968 and graduated in the 1980s from Binori Town's Deobandi madrassa in Karachi. By his own account, he was recruited by *Harakat ul-Mujahedeen* some time after his graduation while teaching in Karachi. His relationship with bin Laden and al-Qaeda in the early years of the 1990s is disputed. By 1993, however, he had risen within *Harakat ul-Mujahedeen* and played a prominent role in the merger of *Harakat ul-Mujahedeen* and *Harakat ul-Jihad ul-Islami* to form *Harakat ul-Ansar*. He was involved in the jihadist universe, linked to developments in Somalia, Chechnya and Central Asia. *Harakat ul-Ansar*'s focus, however, was Kashmir. Azhar travelled to Srinagar in Kashmir in 1994, reportedly to help settle growing tension between *Harakat ul-Mujahedeen* and *Harakat ul-Jihad ul-Islami* factions, and was arrested by India along with Sajjad Afghani. Azhar remained imprisoned until his release on 31 December 1999.[48]

The hijacking of flight 814 was not the first attempt by *Harakat ul-Mujahedeen* to free Azhar. In 1994, Ahmed Omar Saeed Sheikh was dispatched to India where he met up with other operatives and was instructed to kidnap five foreigners in order to exchange them for *Harakat ul-Mujahedeen* prisoners, primarily Azhar.[49] The Indian security services managed to locate one of the hostages and arrest Saeed Sheikh and others after a gun battle. Saeed Sheikh was one of the three people who were exchanged on 31 December 1999.

Planning

The five-man team which boarded the Indian aircraft in Kathmandu was led by Mohammad Ibrahim Athar Alvi, the younger brother of Mawlana Massoud

Azhar, and was referred to as 'chief' on board the aircraft. The other men, all Pakistani nationals, were Akhtar Sayyed from Karachi, Sunny Ahmed Qazi from Karachi, Mistri Zahoor Ibrahim from Karachi and Shair Sukkur from Sukkur.[50]

According to an investigation subsequently carried out by the Indian government, the hijackers and their associates, who were based in Mumbai, made a number of trips in autumn 1999 between India and Kathmandu.[51] They also relied on help from several individuals in India.[52] Ibrahim Athar obtained a visa for Nepal under the name Farooq Siddiqi. Following the kidnappings, security personnel at Tribhuvan International Airport were suspended and security controls were improved at the airport.[53] It remains unclear how the hijackers managed to bring the weapons—one pistol,[54] a hand grenade and several knives—on board the plane.[55] The Indian government maintains that the Inter Services Intelligence (ISI) agency in Pakistan played a role in the hijacking and its preparation, aiding the hijackers.[56] For example, they stated that the landing in Afghanistan was an indicator of the involvement of Pakistan's ISI.[57]

From the progression of the plot it appears that the initial hijacking was well-prepared and executed. Airport security at Kathmandu had been scouted before, and it is likely that it was chosen for its lax security procedures.[58] The plane's odyssey from airport to airport with rejection of landing permission at multiple stages, however, indicates a lack of alternative plans or contingencies, which saw the hijackers improvising. While the ultimate destination that the hijackers intended for the plane cannot be determined, it appears clear that Pakistan or Afghanistan both suited them well. The long-standing relationship of the Taliban to *Harakat ul-Mujahedeen* might have influenced the decision.[59]

According to one news report that cites 'intelligence sources,' the hijacking was 'remote controlled' and merely executed by the hijackers.[60] The subsequent arrest of known associates in Mumbai makes it clear that the hijackers had a support network that facilitated various parts of the plot.[61] The extent of outside control of the hijackers during the negotiations remains unclear. Decisions taken during the journey from Kathmandu until arrival in Kandahar, as well as various parts of the negotiations, appear to have been led by Ibrahim Athar.

Taliban Reaction

The Taliban's stance and involvement in the hijacking seem to have undergone several stages. From the various statements made by senior Taliban figures and others, it seems clear that the Taliban did not play any role in the planning or execution of the hijacking itself. Indeed, at first the Taliban refused to grant landing rights. Although they eventually conceded this,[62] they stated that they did not want to be involved in negotiations and tried to force the hijackers to leave Afghan soil.[63] The initial stance of the Taliban was one of non-involvement.[64] The Taliban leadership first denied landing rights to its airport in Kabul[65] and called for a negotiation role for the United Nations and a team from India to solve the crisis.[66] A Taliban official interviewed on the runway in Kandahar just after the plane's arrival stated, 'we are expecting that the Indians will come soon and take this situation seriously, but they are playing it very cool.'[67]

The hijackers reportedly then requested that the plane be refuelled and flown out of Kandahar to a new destination. The Indian pilots refused on the grounds that it would be unsafe to fly the plane out without a thorough engineering inspection.[68] It was at this point that the hijackers went down into the hold of the plane and brought up bags filled with weapons.[69]

Abdul Hai Mutma'in's[70] statement—'we [the Taliban] don't want to be blamed for anything'[71]—should be taken seriously. At the time, the Taliban faced severe international pressure over the issue of bin Laden, the treatment of women, human rights abuses, and the tactics used in their ongoing war with Massoud and his allies. A significant part of the leadership was keen to gain international recognition and establish relationships with foreign governments. These people understood the possible repercussions of being involved in a hijacking crisis and tried to mitigate the possible fallout.

This understanding informed their subsequent considerable involvement in the events that unfolded, and in which they found themselves hosting the various international actors on the ground in Kandahar—most notably, the Indian negotiation team. The Taliban played an increasingly involved role in the talks, even forcing some of the hijackers' demands off the table.[72] They denied the request for political asylum made by the hijackers, for example, along with their demand for the body of Sajjad Afghani on the grounds that both were un-Islamic. It is likely that many of the decisions that the Taliban made regarding the hijacking were driven by the view that the outcome and their behaviour during the crisis could end up leading to another potential foreign policy disaster for the movement. Therefore they pursued a fast settlement and hoped to avoid bloodshed.[73]

The Taliban played a significant role in the negotiations, including limiting India's options in how to deal with the crisis by denying them the possibility of military action, not merely by stating their opposition but by positioning forces around the aircraft.[74] Furthermore, from the beginning of the crisis they put pressure on India to fulfil the demands of the hijackers and speed up the negotiations.[75] The information that is publicly available does not allow for a definitive assessment, but the position of the Taliban appears to have been neutral or ambivalent at best, and actively supportive of or sympathetic to the hijackers at worst.

The Taliban did have a real and significant prior relationship with *Harakat ul-Mujahedeen*. The latter operated jihadi training camps in south-eastern Afghanistan during the 1990s, and they retained strong ties to both Haqqani and the southern leadership. Pakistani fighters affiliated with the group are widely reported to have taken part in the Taliban's attack on Mazar-e Sharif in August 1998.[76]

The primary interest of the Taliban leadership, though, was to end the crisis without any casualties and without committing to either side, in the hope that they would in this way avoid any collateral damage to themselves. One passenger related how there was mistrust between the hijackers and the Taliban. Afghans, sent into the plane to clean the toilets on 28 December, were searched:

> The Afghan workers came to clean the toilets. But soon after they finished the hijackers became suspicious. They were lined up and thoroughly searched. Apparently the hijackers thought the Afghan government had sent a team of commandos to rescue the passengers.[77]

This observation is confirmed by statements made by the Taliban leadership on 27 December that it would storm the plane if the hijackers started killing hostages.[78]

Aftermath

While many commentators and international governments at first praised the Taliban for their handling of the crisis[79]—some even approved of the Taliban's stopping India from taking military action and thereby possibly preventing a bloodbath—the movement's leadership soon began to face growing criticism.[80] In particular, the issue of the destination and free passage of the hijackers following the conclusion of the crisis was controversial.[81] Members of the Taliban claim they upheld the agreement that was reached by all parties, while others regarded this stance as manifesting support for the hijackers.[82] The Taliban's handling of the situation and the firing of an airport employee due to his repeated unauthorised public statements to journalists helps shed a little light onto the issue.[83] The Taliban regarded the hijacking as a chance to improve their foreign relations as much as they saw it as a danger for the same reasons.

Neither the hijackers nor the freed prisoners were brought to justice for the hijackings. Ahmed Omar Saeed Sheikh was later arrested and convicted for the murder of Daniel Pearl.[84] Mawlana Massoud Azhar announced the formation of *Jaish-e Mohammad* a few weeks after his release; this group was soon joined by many members of other Pakistani jihadi organisations. Note, also, that Azhar returned to Afghanistan to visit Mullah Mohammad Omar in either February or March 2000.[85] Azhar was arrested and released by Pakistani forces in both February and April 2000 and has since maintained a low profile. He remains a key point of interaction between al-Qaeda affiliates and Pakistani jihadis.[86]

Taliban and Pakistani Jihadi Groups

In the context of the Taliban's unintended involvement in and their subsequent handling of the Indian Airlines hijacking, it is worth examining the relationship between Pakistani jihadi groups and the Taliban. This relationship had a long history. They shared an educational background, subscribing to the same Islamic school of thought, the Hanafi tradition, and thus were broadly speaking ideologically aligned. This shared religious and cultural heritage was the most important point of reference in their interaction and it facilitated the relationship between them and smoothed over initial encounters.

The Taliban did not have relations with [the jihadi parties like those that were fighting in Kashmir] and so on. Some of the ulema, though, were coming to Kabul and other Afghan cities because they had the same Deobandi background, and because they were pro-Sharia and supportive of the agenda of the Taliban. There wasn't any kind of agreement or contract between the two sets of actors, however.[87]

The participation of many Pakistani Deobandi madrassa students in the 1980s *jihad* against the Soviet Union meant that they also had shared experiences. Most of the Pakistanis who would later come to prominence in jihadist groups like *Harakat ul-Mujahedeen*, *Jaish-e Mohammad* and *Lashkar-e Taiba* had fought in the south-east of the country.[88] None of the prominent figures seem to have been combatants in the south, with the Kandahari Taliban fronts, or if they did, they made little name for themselves. The participation of Pakistani fighters (and they had their own groups by the mid-1980s) is well remembered in south-east Afghanistan.[89]

As we saw in chapter two, many of the Afghan Taliban were schooled in Pakistani Deobandi madrassas. This shared educational experience—they had teachers and religious elders in common from this time—was important later on for the facilitation of initial connections between the two. The Taliban's connections to other groups and figures seems at first glance to have been relatively informal, but it was this referral system from their alma maters which formalised the connections and served as a kind of initial screening process for whom they could and couldn't trust.

All the Pakistani *ulemaa'* would come to Afghanistan to see Mullah Mohammad Omar because of their similarities and shared agenda and because there were relations between the Taliban and the political parties and their *ulemaa'.*[90]

Despite these similarities, there were points of difference and conflict. The Taliban's agenda during the 1990s was limited in both aspiration and reality as they were focused on Afghanistan. This could lead to problems when Pakistani groups either sought to encourage the Taliban to support actions outside the country (in Kashmir, for example) or when they caused problems for the Taliban government's international relations. The Indian Airlines hijacking is a clear case in point: the Taliban wanted to distance themselves from it but were forced by circumstance to play a more central role as it unfolded.

Their close relationship with Pakistani jihadi groups and foreign policy of trying to establish and maintain good relations with everyone often meant that the Taliban ended up in the midst of conflicts. Mullah Zaeef describes in his book how he was invited to functions and meetings organised by many different groups and organisations, some of which were in open conflict with the Pakistani government.[91] The Afghans, moreover, were very sensitive to any Pakistani attempts to manipulate their movement's agenda. This was undoubtedly compounded by the general feelings of superiority on the part of the Afghans; there was a sense that Pakistani jihadi groups had less of a legitimate opinion on *jihad* than the Afghans. Here, one interviewee described Mullah Mohammad Omar's attitude to external advisors:

Mullah Mohammad Omar was a very independent person. *Very* independent. Even sometimes to Pakistan. People always say that the Taliban were controlled by Pakistan, but I myself sat in on meetings together with Pakistanis and Mullah Mohammad Omar when he spoke very straightforwardly and directly to them, let alone al-Qaeda as a small group in their role as guests.[92]

The training camps (located around the country, but mostly in the east and south-east) were a specific point of conflict between the Taliban and the Pakistani groups that used them. International pressure was such that the Taliban even denied the existence of the camps for much of their rule.[93]

Mullah Mohammad Omar himself met with large numbers of Pakistani jihadi leaders and group members, but this at least partially needs to be understood as a function of his position and was also mediated through his alumni ties to the Pakistani *ulemaa*.[94] The fact that he sat down with many Pakistani jihadis does not necessarily indicate anything other than sympathy with their general world view and an expectation that the Taliban would continue to be supplied with fighters if and when the situation required. As we have also seen above, the Taliban leader was extremely deferential to the religiously learned— he was not even a *mawlawi* when he took on the leadership of the movement— with the result that he was sensitive to any charges of not being serious or willing to follow what he believed (or was told) were the exact strictures of Islamic *shari'a* law.[95] Based on press statements and interview testimony, Mullah Mohammad Omar appears to have acted at times independently, and at times on advice of the *ulemaa*. For al-Qaeda, all this simply meant that there would always be a link between the Pakistani and Afghan Deobandis as well as the possibility of external support from the Pakistanis (with whom bin Laden and the foreign jihadis had far better ties) if the relationship with the Afghans soured. The Pakistani groups also gave al-Qaeda a viable option for retreat.

Conclusion

The Indian Airlines hijacking again continues the airplane theme that we saw from the Bojinka plot, albeit with a different set of actors. It does not, however, fit well into the characterisation of India's foreign minister, who said that it was very much the 'dress rehearsal' for the September 11 attacks since many of the actors involved were the same.[96] This seems to misrepresent both the actors—he must, for example, have been including the Taliban in his analysis as having been involved in the negotiations and, by extension of the metaphor, in the September 11 attacks—as well as the extent to which the Indian Airlines hijacking fits into the al-Qaeda model.

The instrumentalised hijacking of airplanes for the release of hostages was not a novel tactic; groups in the Middle East had used them since the 1960s and 1970s as a tactic, and the Indian Airlines case fits neatly into this pattern.[97] Al-Qaeda's operations, on the other hand, aimed at high casualty numbers and large propaganda value, something that was not the case for the 1999 hijacking.[98]

The 9/11 Report quotes from an intelligence report regarding a suspected study conducted by Mohammed Atef during his time in Sudan; he had concluded that ordinary hijackings (as was the case with the 1999 flight 814) were not desirable for al-Qaeda and that mass casualties, resulting from mid-air explosions, were more in line with al-Qaeda's objectives.[99] An official statement from al-Qaeda also distanced itself from the hijacking.[100]

On the other hand, the different positions that Taliban spokesmen and key actors took with regards to addressing and publicly explaining the situation are a clear indication of their ambivalence: they were improvising policy on the hoof. Moreover, they tried too hard to be all things to all people. They sought to mitigate the negative effects of the hijacking on their public image; they also sought not to appear weak, from an Islamic perspective, in the face of a very vocal diplomatic and press corps (as mobilised by India).

Thus, for the Taliban, the Indian Airlines hijacking is a useful precedent for examining how they responded to such incidents—used by another group and caught by surprise, only to have to justify it and find itself at the centre of international attention for someone else's actions. Furthermore, the lack of any credible account of Taliban operations outside Afghanistan, their pre-occupation with their internal struggle and the lack of a strong motive to support the hijacking are further indicators that shed doubt on the claim that the Taliban played a part in the event. The hijacking was a precursor of the September 11 attacks only insofar as it forecast how the Taliban would become irrelevant in the plans and actions of others; bin Laden seems to have had little regard or regret for the problems the attacks precipitated for his hosts.

The incident also neatly spotlights the Taliban's conflicted agenda. A variety of imperatives motivated the various Taliban actors,[101] and this divergence was reflective of internal dynamics within the movement at the time. Above all, Mullah Mohammad Omar was conscious of his image as a Muslim for other Muslims around the world. There also was clearly some attempt to prevent the hijacking from reflecting badly on the Taliban's diplomatic and political relations with other countries (both regionally and those further afield) and to salvage their media image (regardless of diplomatic or political considerations).[102] Then came their relationship with the plethora of Pakistani jihadi actors; Mullah Mohammad Omar was under pressure from these groups as well as from figures from within the Pakistani ISI throughout the crisis.[103] Finally, although this was almost an irrelevance for the Taliban's leadership, there was some consideration for the movement's internal and domestic image among ordinary Afghans.[104]

These conflicting imperatives for the Taliban highlight how the movement tried—as happened after the September 11 attacks—to be all things to all people, all too often lacking the understanding or the will to see the organisations and individuals involved for what they were. Central to the Taliban's policy here is the internal conflict over the differences within Islamic groups and its undifferentiated understanding of religion.

The Assassination
of Ahmed Shah Massoud

In early September 2001, Ahmed Shah Massoud sent an intelligence report to the CIA about two Arab television journalists who had crossed into Afghanistan.[105] The two men carried Belgian passports and claimed that they were originally from Morocco. They brought with them a letter of introduction from the Islamic Observation Centre in London and were introduced to the mujahedeen party leader Sayyaf by an Afghan Arab who had fought alongside Sayyaf in the 1980s against the Soviet Union in Afghanistan.[106]

The two men had camera equipment with them and asked to interview Massoud for a television report about Afghanistan. Sayyaf contacted the Panjshiri commander, informing him about the two journalists and their intentions. Massoud was at that time unhappy with how he was perceived in the Islamic world: he had suffered military setbacks and was in need of assistance.[107] Meeting the two Belgian journalists offered an opportunity to correct his image in the Arab world[108] and they pointed out that they themselves aimed to portray Massoud in a favourable light.[109] Massoud sent a helicopter to pick them up and he brought the journalists to Khwaja Bahauddin, his retreat just inside the Afghan border with Tajikistan. He was, however, in no hurry to meet them straight away. The two men waited there along with other journalists in Massoud's guesthouse, shooting footage around the camp while growing increasingly impatient. They pressed to see Massoud; otherwise, they said, they would have to leave again.[110]

On 9 September 2001, Massoud prepared to leave to inspect his forward positions when he was informed that the interview would take place in the office of Engineer Atif, his intelligence aide. The two journalists came in while Massoud settled down in the concrete room.[111] One went over a few questions, including: 'How will you deal with the Osama bin Laden issue when you are in power, and what do you see as the solution to this issue?', one of a set of questions later found on a computer used by al-Qaeda.[112] The other began to set up the tripod and the camera. Massoud said he was ready when the cameraman triggered the bomb hidden in the camera. The explosion killed the cameraman and sent shrapnel flying into Massoud's chest, who collapsed immediately. Several other people were killed and injured. The second journalist, however, was not hurt and tried to escape but was caught and detained. Massoud's aides evacuated the leader immediately—the helicopter pad was close by and they could reach a hospital within twenty minutes. But Massoud died of his injuries on the way.[113] The second journalist managed to escape from the room in which he had been detained, squeezing through a window, but was shot dead while attempting to flee.[114]

The al-Qaeda Link

El-Sattar and el-Ouaer both moved in radical circles in Belgium and Western Europe with strong links to militant Islamic groups such as the GIA and to individuals associated with al-Qaeda in Afghanistan.[115] They were part of a wider network of several individuals who had contacts with al-Qaeda and its associates reaching back to the 1980s. Operating mostly autonomously, many members of the group received training in Afghanistan and travelled to the country several times in the second half of the 1990s.[116]

Principally involved were recruiters and facilitators, as well as the broad structures of al-Qaeda and militant Islamist groups. One should be careful of viewing these groupings as being too structured, however. Individual contacts and networks did, though, link groups closely to al-Qaeda. Operatives in Europe seemed to be highly self-motivated and often had previous involvement in militant groups in other countries such as Tunisia and Algeria.[117] While al-Qaeda at the time had already developed the skills in-house to prepare and execute operations such as the Massoud assassination, it is worth noticing that almost all of the planning and preparation for Massoud's assassination took place in Europe; forged documents were provided and produced in Europe by associates later convicted.[118] What is very clear, too, is the importance of the training camps in establishing the contacts with the central leadership and in recruiting operatives for al-Qaeda's ends.[119] These links, to no one's surprise, were still there from the 1980s war against the Soviet Union.

In a discussion with Muttaqi about the tension within the Taliban leadership, in particular regarding the Taliban's Foreign Minister Mullah Muttawakil, bin Laden is reported to have said, 'Very well. I will solve your internal problems. I will get rid of your internal enemies so you don't tell me I'm nothing but trouble for you.'[120]

The conversation, recorded in Mojdeh's memoir, outlines the differences between the Taliban and bin Laden and al-Qaeda. Bin Laden then said:

The Taliban have wasted four years of my life. They have created obstacles in the way of our jihad even though at this time jihad is our religious duty. I have given allegiance to Mullah Omar, who is a symbol for the Imams, but when a follower follows a leader, the leader cannot ban him from doing so.[121]

Many have drawn a link between Massoud's assassination and the September 11 attacks; this seems to have been, in part, a result of their close proximity in time. It seems clear from how both plots developed that the only decision that could have been made is that they wanted the assassination to happen before the September 11 attacks, but even this seems speculative, given that both events' timelines had been subject to change and external factors. For instance, the two assassins did not reach Massoud until later than planned, having had little control over the exact point in time or day on which they would meet him. The September 11 plot, at least according to Khalid Sheikh Mohammad, was pushed back several times.[122]

Did the Taliban Know?

The evidence suggesting that the Taliban knew that Massoud would be killed is both limited and speculative. The 9/11 Commission's report includes a statement—albeit one extracted under duress from Khalid Sheikh Mohammad—implying that Mullah Mohammad Omar was privy to the plan to assassinate Massoud, possibly to the extent that he or the Taliban played some role in moving this plan forward:

As they deliberated earlier in the year, Bin Ladin and Atef would likely have remembered that Mullah Omar was dependent on them for the Massoud assassination and for vital support in the Taliban military operations. KSM[123] remembers Atef telling him that al Qaeda had an agreement with the Taliban to eliminate Massoud, after which the Taliban would begin an offensive to take over Afghanistan. Atef hoped Massoud's death would also appease the Taliban when the 9/11 attacks happened. There are also some scant indications that Omar may have been reconciled to the 9/11 attacks by the time they occurred.[124]

Contradicting this account, Laurence Wright wrote that it was two Saudi members of al-Qaeda who first informed Mullah Khaksar, the deputy Interior

Minister, that Massoud had died, at a time when the Northern Alliance was still claiming that he had only been injured in the attack.

They boasted that bin Laden had given the order to kill Massoud. Now the Northern Alliance was leaderless, the last obstacle to the Taliban's total control of the country removed by this significant favor.[125]

Then there is a claim that the attack was immediately followed by a Taliban offensive on Massoud's positions in the Panjshir Valley. This attack, advocates of this position argue, was planned beforehand and the Taliban were waiting for Massoud to die before launching a new attempt on the last part of Afghanistan not under their control.[126] Neither of these claims is particularly credible, and nor are they supported by the evidence of Taliban testimony and news sources from 10 and 11 September, 2001.[127] The manner of the attack was also foreign to how the Taliban would have planned such an operation—suicide operations were not a tactic that the Taliban used or even condoned at the time. Even the more widespread use of suicide bombers by the Taliban movement post-2004 generated considerable internal conflict and debate among the leadership tier (see below).

It was also a complex operation—the planning involved a variety of actors (both witting and unwitting, as seems the case with Sayyaf, under whose imprimatur the two Belgians were able to reach Massoud) as well as a level of subterfuge in which the Taliban had not shown any special previous proficiency.

The Taliban and the Arabs were at odds by this point—although the Taliban's political circle had lost their figurehead following the death of Mullah Mohammad Rabbani in April that year—and the personal connection between Mullah Mohammad Omar and bin Laden was the main remaining point of contact. The two were close, but there is no indication from former members that the Taliban leader was ever informed about the Massoud operation.[128] In fact, there were even some discussions taking place between the Taliban and Massoud during the last two years of their government.[129] The Taliban reaction at the time, moreover, is another indication that they were taken by surprise (elated surprise, granted, but still surprise) by Massoud's death.[130] For several days, too, those close to Massoud and the leadership in the Panjshir Valley sought to give the impression that Massoud was not yet dead, and the Taliban's statement reflects this general state of confusion.[131]

Nor did a special Taliban offensive materialise, aside from an opportunistic set of attacks launched on 10 September.[132] In fact, news reports from 9 September report an offensive by anti-Taliban forces intended to besiege Taliban troops in Taloqan.[133]

The Taliban claim that they were not involved in the plot to kill Massoud. And many of them, as with other al-Qaeda plots, doubt even the involvement of or the reasoning for bin Laden to have carried out the attack. As Mullah Zaeef points out:

> The Taliban denied being involved in the killing at the same time as trying not to crit-icise him. Indeed, the Taliban were not involved in his killing, as otherwise they would proudly take responsibility. War is not a thing of fun and games! If al-Qa'ida had done this, what would the reason for it have been? And why would they have neglected to mention such a major plan to the Taliban? There are many unanswered questions. God knows better![134]

These statements are echoed by a number of other former Taliban members, who all claim that they had been unaware of the assassination plot, that they would have publicly endorsed and justified it had they been involved, and over-all fail to imagine a reason why al-Qaeda would have killed Massoud.[135] One senior former Taliban political member even suggested that bin Laden was not behind the attacks, proposing Russia instead as his strongest suspect.[136]

Conclusion

It is highly unlikely that the plot to assassinate Massoud was known among the Taliban. The Taliban were aware of the fact that they were close to defeat-ing Massoud and the Northern Alliance, having captured all but 5–10% of the country.

As was explored earlier, there was considerable strife within the Taliban's leadership over the issue of bin Laden. Bin Laden might have regarded the assassination of Massoud as a way to better his relationship with the Taliban leadership and prove his worth to them. While this is speculative, he could have regarded it as a strategy not with regards to the Taliban and their posi-tion on his presence, but as a way to demonstrate the union of the two entities to the outside world just days before the September 11 attacks.

Bin Laden, however, also regarded Massoud as his own natural enemy. It was well known, for example, that Massoud was running sophisticated intel-ligence operations throughout Afghanistan and that the CIA had tasked him with gathering information about bin Laden and his activities, as well as the activities of Arabs and other foreigners in Afghanistan.[137] As interviewees have pointed out, if the Taliban had been responsible and had been involved, they would not only have claimed responsibility but would have justified it.[138]

It is important—with the assassination of Massoud—to distinguish between Taliban and al-Qaeda intentionality in the operation. This was an al-Qaeda planned operation, one that had meaning beyond how the Taliban benefited from his death; for in the war that bin Laden envisioned unfolding in Afghanistan following the September 11 attacks, Massoud would have been a major obstacle.

Al-Qaeda's senior operatives also did not trust the Taliban. There is no credible evidence, even anecdotal, of the kind of relationship that would have been required them to share operational details on a regular basis.

September 11 Attacks

The Plot

On 11 September 2001, 19 people boarded four planes in the United States. The planes were hijacked shortly after takeoff. Two were piloted into the World Trade Center in New York City, causing two twin towers to collapse, killing thousands. American Airlines Flight 77 crashed into the Pentagon, ripping a hole into the side of the building. United Airlines Flight 93 crashed into a field near Shanksville, Pennsylvania.[139] The 'planes operation,' as it was referred to by those involved, was planned thousands of miles away in Afghanistan. The idea was the brainchild of Khalid Sheikh Mohammad, who suggested the plot to bin Laden in mid-1996.[140]

The assembly of the team of attackers took a significant amount of time, and much seemed to have relied on chance.[141] Al-Qaeda at the time was under close scrutiny already, and had put far more checks and vetting into place for people who wanted to come and train in the camps in Afghanistan and join bin Laden.[142] The group that is today known as the Hamburg cell, and which consisted of not only the operational leader Mohammad Atta but also of two of the other three pilots who would navigate the planes into the targets, came to join al-Qaeda (as well as many other operatives) through a desire to be part of the wider cause of *jihad*. Through recruiters and the jihadist network in Europe (discussed above), they came to train in southern Afghanistan. They took an oath to follow bin Laden and volunteered for the suicide mission almost immediately after it was offered to them.[143]

Much of the operational planning was carried out by the individuals themselves, albeit with the financial support and guidance of the central leadership,

Khalid Sheikh Mohammad and bin Laden. Bin Laden seems to have been involved only in the grand design, however, discussing targets, the timeline and the scope of the operation. Mohammad seemed at times to function as a screen between bin Laden and the would-be hijackers when bin Laden sought to move the date of the attack forward.[144]

As we have seen above, Mohammad and others in his extensive network—including his nephew, Ramzi Yosuf—had perceived of airplanes as possible targets and weapons for several years. Mohammad reportedly first met bin Laden in 1987 when they fought together in Afghanistan[145] but did not establish any close links to him. Mohammad claimed to be close to Azzam, even though other eyewitnesses like Abdullah Anas do not recall encountering him.[146] He did, however, fight under Sayyaf in Afghanistan during this period.[147]

The second meeting between Mohammad and bin Laden took place in mid-1996.[148] Mohammad is believed to have partially relied on the fame of his nephew Yosuf, and arranged the meeting via Mohammed Atef, bin Laden's head of military operations.[149] During the meeting, Mohammad presented a number of plans. One of them involved hijacking ten planes in the United States, piloting nine into buildings, while he himself would be on the tenth, first killing all male passengers before disembarking at an airport in America and giving a statement.[150] Bin Laden reacted coldly to this plan, and it would take two years before his opinion would change.[151]

During the second half of the 1990s, Mohammad was living with his family in Karachi, but he continued to travel back and forth to Afghanistan, building up his relationship with bin Laden and his deputies, Mohammad Atef and Saif al-Adl.[152] Mohammed was alleged to have joined al-Qaeda formally in 1998–99, around the same time that bin Laden gave his blessing for the planes operation, albeit in a limited version of the original plan.[153] It would be planned and coordinated by Mohammad, who by that time had relocated his family to Kandahar.[154] The operation went through several development phases. At times, Mohammad considered incorporating a southeast Asian element in the plan; and he dispatched people and contacted Ridwan Isamuddin (aka Hambali), but this part of the operation was dropped.[155] It appears that the date for the operation also changed. Originally it seems likely or possible that it would have been part of the so-called 'millennium plots.'[156] Later, 9 September was chosen by Mohammed Atta.[157] Bin Laden had been pressing him to start the operation for several months.[158]

The September 11 plot demonstrates one of al-Qaeda's most distinct characteristics, the ability and indeed preference for long-term planning, and its durability. While many of the group's operations failed—often due to bad planning or incompetent operatives—the leadership's will to carry on never subsided. According to one intelligence report, it is likely that Mohammad Atef had contemplated operations involving planes, using them as weapons or orchestrating mid-air explosions to cause mass casualties, in 1996 while still in Sudan.[159]

In the spring of 1999, bin Laden, Mohammad Atef and Khalid Sheikh Mohammad held discussions in Kandahar about the planes operation.[160] An initial target list was compiled that allegedly included the White House, the US Capitol, the Pentagon and the World Trade Center.[161] According to Khalid Sheikh Mohammad, no one else was present at these discussions.[162] In the first serious planning meeting with Mohammad, bin Laden suggested Khalid al-Mihdhar, Nawaf al-Hazmi, Walid Mohammed bin Attash (also known as Khallad), and Abu Bara al-Yemeni for the operation.[163] Al-Hazmi and al-Mihdhar were both suggested as pilots; they were both from Saudi Arabia, and along with the others were experienced mujahedeen. Khallad failed to attain a visa and was arrested in Yemen. Only Al-Hazmi and al-Mihdhar would take part in the actual operation, but would prove to be inept in attaining a pilot's licence. The Yemeni nationals in general faced severe obstacles when trying to attain a visa for the United States, and were frequently flagged as possible economic immigrants.[164]

With hindsight, it was pure chance that Mohammad Atta, along with the other three students from Hamburg, came to Afghanistan to train and fight there. Like many other would-be jihadis, they originally wanted to join the fight in Chechnya. They travelled separately to Pakistan and onwards to Afghanistan in the late autumn of 1999.[165] The group had carried on discussions for years about *jihad*, martyrdom and the plight of the Muslim people.[166]

While the members of what came to be known as the 'Hamburg cell' showed distinct characteristics and the group faced several obstacles and difficulties over the next two years, much of its early sign-up to a suicide mission and endurance can be explained by what Sageman dubbed as 'love for the in-group.' He points out that most of those who were involved acted not out of hatred for someone or something but rather out of love for the group. This is seemingly paradoxical, but the various statements and the trajectory of the individuals involved support Sageman's analysis. Sageman outlines the development of groups that would come to join militant Islamic groups or form their own groups. In his sample he shows that group dynamics played and continue to play a significant role in the radicalisation process.[167] The general nature of recruits joining al-Qaeda often saw small groups join, rather than single individuals. Individuals were related, or shared a common upbringing.

The group received training in Afghanistan. Another element that should not be underestimated when it comes to operational security, group cohesion and acculturation, as well as in keeping defection rates low, is the importance of the training camps. Their value was not primarily for training in weapons and special tactics, but rather the routine, the group-building and the preaching. Much of the camps' routine seemed to copy military training camps, albeit with fewer facilities. Recruits who graduated from the course would not only possess (depending on the exact courses they took) a wide skill set but, at least as important, would feel part of a group. Through the adoption of a new name and the training, the camps would transform individuals and give them a greater sense of community that went beyond nationality and the society they were used to and grew up in. The camps, when functioning at their best, would take individuals already predisposed to various parts of their curriculum and truly transform them.[168]

The hijackers are commonly categorised into two groups: the first group around Mohammad Atta, the pilots; and the second group known as the 'muscle hijackers' that would be responsible for controlling the passengers and taking charge of the cabin.[169] According to McDermott, the original plans might not have involved pilots at all, but perhaps had aimed for different means to bring the plane under control.[170]

The pilots had been in the United States for at least a year before the attack commenced, while the muscle hijackers only arrived a few weeks or months before. McDermott, author of a history of the plot, claims that the majority of the muscle hijackers were part of a group that had come to Pakistan believing they were on a *tablighi* trip, but found themselves being shuttled off to a remote camp in Baluchistan where Khalid Sheikh Mohammad gave lectures every day for over a month.[171]

Some commentators have speculated regarding how much previous knowledge the individuals had about the mission they were sent on, with some arguing that the majority or all of the muscle hijackers were unaware that they were going on a suicide mission. Leaflets written by Ramzi bin al-Shibh, which were found among their belongings later on, seem to prove that they had all been aware of the nature of the mission.[172] A question that remains unclear, however, concerns the extent to which the muscle hijackers knew precise details of the mission. Some accounts state that their training was designed to include all sorts of operations in an effort to hide the exact nature of the one they would be involved in so as to increase operational security.[173]

Bin Laden's treatment of information on previous attacks makes it likely that he dropped hints or made remarks in speeches and conversations that would have revealed that he was planning something spectacular, possibly even that it involved planes at times.[174] Just months before the attacks against the US embassies in Tanzania and Kenya, for example, bin Laden gave an interview to John Miller of ABC News to the backdrop of a world map centred around Africa.[175]

Khalid Sheikh Mohammad's previous involvement with plots that were somehow similar, and his wide-ranging contact network among jihadist groups, also suggests that his teaming up with bin Laden in Afghanistan did not go unnoticed and likely sparked rumours among the international jihadist community and the immediate circle of Afghan Arabs in Afghanistan. The number of individuals who knew about the specifics of the plot before the attacks were carried out is highly disputed. The 9/11 Report has a section entitled 'Dissent within the al-Qaeda leadership.'[176] The few pages of this section outline a disagreement over an alleged ruling by Mullah Mohammed Omar, who it is said was opposed to attacks against the United States.[177] Mullah Mohammad Omar's ruling in this case, as the report states, caused a rift within the al-Qaeda leadership over how to proceed. The 9/11 Report at this point fails to distinguish between the specific versus the general. The language and discussion is as vague as the sourcing of the information appears to be. The footnote relating to Mullah Mohammad Omar's ruling is sourced to an interview of a detainee who said that 'when bin Ladin returned after the general alert during July, he spoke to his confidants about Omar's unwillingness to allow an attack against the United States.'[178] The section jumps from a general and unspecific discussion—always using the indefinite articles 'a' and 'an'—to talking about specific discussions about the September 11 plot amongst the al-Qaeda leaders. This seems to imply a connection between the two where there likely was no such link.

It should also be noted that at no point is it indicated that Mullah Mohammad Omar was talking about a specific plan here. Furthermore, a ruling, which would have been made in general terms opposing any and all such attacks, is very much in line with the Taliban's statements in general that highlighted the nationalist nature of the movement's ambitions. The Taliban leadership—both Mullah Mohammad Omar and the faction close to Mullah Mohammad Rabbani—had two conditions for providing hospitality to bin Laden and the al-Qaeda leadership: bin Laden was not to communicate with the media without consulting the Taliban, nor were they to move against the United States or antagonise it.[179] The September 11 plot would have violated both of these conditions.

While it remains highly questionable that bin Laden or Mullah Mohammad Omar would have had discussions regarding global *jihad*, given their complicated relationship, even if such discussions would have occurred it is doubtful that bin Laden would have discussed specific operations, in particular the September 11 plot. The strained relationship with the Taliban leadership had only recently shown small signs of improving.

Mullah Mohammed Omar's purported ruling on attacks against the United States should be considered as one of a general nature. He and the Taliban at large did not want bin Laden and the al-Qaeda leadership attacking foreign countries in any fashion as long as they resided on Afghan soil.[180] Fazul Abdullah Muhammad, an al-Qaeda operative active in the 1990s, stated in his memoirs that only bin Laden, Abu Hafs al-Masri and Khalid Sheikh Mohammad knew about the plot before the fact.[181] His statements are echoed by Abdul Walid al-Masri's writings that state:

...preparation for the attack of September 2001, about which no one knew any details save for three individuals, one of which was [bin Laden] himself [...] Nobody outside the first or second inner circle had any idea of what was going on. Of course, Mullah Omar topped the list of those kept in the dark...[182]

Khalid Sheikh Mohammad also said that only bin Laden, Mohammad Atef, Abu Turab al-Urduni, Ramzi bin al-Shibh and a few of the senior hijackers knew the specific targets, timing and operatives. He even claims that al-Zawahiri learnt about the plan only in mid-summer when he became bin Laden's deputy.[183]

Besides the possibility of general chatter and veiled hints of bin Laden to trainees and fellow jihadists, the organisational structure of the plot was compartmentalised to the degree that, outside the inner cell of the pilots, few of the details (which, as detailed above, were in flux until close to the actual day of the attacks) would have been known to even the 'muscle hijackers.' Information was communicated on a need-to-know basis.

The Hamburg cell and the fourth pilot did not know the specific targets. Only Mohammad Atta received a pre-selection list.[184] Most of the specifics of the plot only came together months or weeks before it took place, and it is unlikely that the leadership, even bin Laden, would have known the exact planes that were to be hijacked.

Facilitators like Khalid Sheikh Mohammad's nephew Ali Abdul Aziz Ali, while being aware of the parts of the operation such as the involvement of planes and pilot training, would have had to speculate about the timing or the place of the attacks and the format, given the place and targets of previous plane operations.[185]

From the various warnings received by the United States from a number of intelligence services and reports about surveyed conversations mentioning attacks in a variety of details, it seems clear that the basic facts about the attacks were known among at least some al-Qaeda operatives and members prior to the operation taking place.[186] Many within that community were aware that a suicide attack involving planes on American soil would take place in 2001. Several statements were made by senior al-Qaeda figures close to the date and key members were ordered back to Afghanistan or left their homes in anticipation of American retaliation.[187] Several al-Qaeda cells seem to have been aware, including associates in London and Milan in mid-2000.[188]

Mohammad Atta, the principal agent coordinating, planning and leading much of the operation, was in continuous contact with the leadership in Afghanistan. This contact included face-to-face meetings with facilitators; one such meeting occurred in Spain in July 2001.[189]

The network responsible for logistics and money transfer as well as the transmission of messages appears to have been mainly managed by Khalid Sheikh Mohammad, who worked with his nephew Ali Abdul Aziz Ali in the United Arab Emirates along with individuals in Europe (mainly Germany).[190] While much of the communications seemed to rely on fairly conventional technology—phone and email—certain sensitive issues were only discussed in person. The leadership of al-Qaeda were aware that they were being closely watched by a number of intelligence agencies and that their communications were being monitored. By the end of the 1990s, most of them had years of experience in avoiding capture, working clandestinely, using multiple identities and circumventing security checks.[191]

Did the Taliban Know?

The evidence in support of the claims that members of the Taliban had foreknowledge of the September 11 attacks is not extensive, nor are the claims indefensible. The 9/11 Report, as we saw above, claims that bin Laden had a discussion with Mullah Mohammad Omar as to the legitimacy of carrying out attacks on the United States—of which the Taliban leader disapproved—but does not suggest that this was in reference to a specific attack.[192]

A story for the *Independent* newspaper stated that the Taliban Foreign Minister, Mullah Mutawakil, had received a warning that attacks in America would take place from the head of the Islamic Movement of Uzbekistan, Tahir Yuldash.[193] The authors of this book also heard from a former BBC journalist the claim that a Taliban member called a friend in the United States weeks before the attacks to warn him to stay away from New York and planes on

September 11.[194] The Taliban member in question—unidentified by the source—was reportedly a senior military figure within the Taliban government. There is no corroborating evidence to confirm this anecdote, however, since Taliban and other Afghan sources who were in Kabul, Kandahar and Pakistan at the time testify to no pre-knowledge of the attacks.

An extended series of articles written by Camille Tawil on the basis of interviews conducted with former jihadist Noman Benotman also offer the following claims:

Noman Benotman stresses with regards to this that the Taliban, like many of the Arabs in Afghanistan, were certainly aware that al-Qaeda was preparing to deliver a blow to the United States and that they warned the United States in advance of an impending strike against it. However, they were unable to specify the exact date or target.

Benotman alleges that an important Taliban leader, Mullah Jalil, was a key party in the warning made to the Americans. If this is true, it would confirm that the movement's leadership—and therefore not just one of its members—had wanted to notify America. [...]

According to Benotman: 'about a week before the 9/11 operations, Mullah Jalil issued an order to one of those responsible for the Taliban's representation in New York asking him to inform the U.S. administration that al-Qaeda was planning to attack the United States. The Americans were told that there were unusual goings-on (in terms of debates and movements) on the part of al-Qaeda in Afghanistan, that the Arab fighters had withdrawn outside Kabul and that some of the fighters were leaving their positions and were heading towards Tora Bora. In their warning message, the Taliban stated that al-Qaeda seemed to be on the verge of implementing an operation, but that they were ignorant of the date and target.'

It is unclear why the Taliban wanted to alert the Americans as to the impending strike against them, and whether this was to clear itself of all responsibility and thus avoid a U.S. blow in retaliation for al-Qaeda's attack. However, it is now certain that the Americans were in possession of enough information which would have allowed them to conclude that an al-Qaeda attack was imminent. But, of course, like the other warnings which reached the Americans, the Taliban's warning was not specific enough.[195]

Bruce Riedel has written the most recent claim of Taliban involvement in the attacks:

Bin Laden personally handled other essential elements of the [September 11] plot as well, bringing on board the Taliban [...] and its leader, Mullah Omar. In his interrogation, KSM suggests the Taliban were uninformed about the Manhattan raid until the last moment and even pressed bin Laden not to attack American targets. However, other evidence strongly suggests Mullah Omar was well inside the loop much earlier and a partner in the overall plan, if not the details.[196]

Riedel makes the claim that the relationship with Mullah Mohammad Omar and the Taliban was a crucial element of the September 11 plot. He offers evidence from Khalid Sheikh Mohammad's interrogation (and does so later) to suggest that the Taliban found out at the last moment. Parts of Mohammad's interrogation, however, have been shown to have been conducted using techniques such as water-boarding, and statements such as the one above should be handled with extreme caution. The 'other evidence' to which Riedel refers is not cited or given and therefore cannot be assessed. The research conducted for this book has not brought to light any evidence to support his claim.

These claims of Benotman and Riedel should be set against the testimony of senior al-Qaeda and Taliban figures. Abu al-Walid al-Masri has written an account indicating that the Taliban were taken by surprise by the attacks.[197] Within the Taliban, almost the entire senior political leadership has made statements to the effect that they had no prior knowledge of the attacks and several have indicated that they would have taken measures to try to prevent them had they known.[198] Of course, this is what the Taliban would be expected to argue, but the consistency of these claims over such a long time (coupled with eyewitness testimony from Kabul, Kandahar and Pakistan as to the Taliban's reactions upon hearing of the attacks) is noteworthy.[199]

There are various other reasons why Taliban members would not have been told. The relationship between the Taliban government and the Arabs/al-Qaeda was already strained, and the al-Qaeda leadership did not trust the Taliban.[200] The few Arabs who knew details of the attacks were not going to tell the Taliban when they could not be trusted not to spread this information further. The same was true for Mullah Mohammad Omar and bin Laden. The closest bin Laden seems to have been to telling the Taliban was in the anecdote related by Mojdeh and reproduced above in which bin Laden makes a suggestion that an attack was on the way.

It is also important to question what the value would have been to al-Qaeda of confiding in members of the Taliban. They must have had a strong suspicion that the Taliban would not have been supportive of their plans—one reason not to tell them beforehand—and they couldn't have afforded any such risks. The senior al-Qaeda operational chiefs were savvy enough to avoid such amateur mistakes.

The Taliban reaction to the attacks—both public and private—is another indication of their surprise. Interviewees for this book stated that there was a mixture of happiness upon hearing the news—more out of a sense that this was America's comeuppance rather than anything else—and ignorance that anything had happened at all.[201] Some also made sure to distinguish between ordinary people within the movement, and those among the political cadre, who, everyone agreed, were concerned about the implications of the attacks.

A general sense that bin Laden was not the real culprit was stated even by non-Taliban figures. Burhanuddin Rabbani, for example, made the following point in an interview published in Russia's *Izvestia* in April 2002:

I personally don't understand it that such a complex, thoroughly planned and techni-cally well organized operation, which the US September 11 attacks were, could have been organized and carried out by a small bunch of bandits located in the lifeless Afghan mountains—however, anything is possible. But none of the people who knew him has told me that Bin Laden is a great man. On the contrary, everyone who knew him speaks of him as an ordinary warlord, a totally ordinary man. Bin Laden spent a long time in the mountains. You don't rule the world from there. Other people were and probably are behind Bin Laden, and I would like to know who they are.[202]

Mullah Mutawakil, in Kabul at the time, recalled contacting the Taliban leader upon hearing the news:

At the time when that story [9–11] happened, I was in Kabul. I contacted Mullah Mohammad Omar in Kandahar immediately asking what should we do. He told me, 'condemn it. Condemn this action as harshly and strongly as you can.' And I think the Taliban government was one of the first governments who condemned this action, and besides condemning it they also denied their involvement and they said that the kill-ing of innocents wherever they are is not allowed (*haram*). Al-Qaeda at that time never said 'we did it.' If they did say something, then they said something like 'whoever did that thing, we think it's a good thing.' They appreciated it. That's a big difference, that one side [the Taliban] condemned it, but the other side, al-Qaeda, appreciated it.[203]

In Islamabad, Mullah Zaeef received similar instructions, and dispatched a copy of the press release to the US Embassy.

Bismillah ar-Rahman ar-Rahim. We strongly condemn the events that happened in the United States at the World Trade Center and the Pentagon. We share the grief of all those who have lost their nearest and dearest in these incidents. All those responsi-ble must be brought to justice. We want them to be brought to justice, and we want America to be patient and careful in their actions.[204]

Note that the Taliban's later position—refusing to hand over bin Laden— does not negate this early response (or the later internal reaction) to the attacks. The movement put on a brave face and took refuge in what they saw as a prin-cipled stand in line with their previous policy on bin Laden following attacks— call for proof and an independent court to assess claims, and refuse to hand him over to the United States, all the while couching the claims as adhering to Islamic *shari'a*.

8

COLLAPSE (2001–2003)

Rest assured, my true Muslim people, that the Taliban [are] filled with the spirit of jehad and martyrdom and [would] turn the earth red with the blood of the invaders and make them spend sleepless nights. Every day, the foreign aggressors are suffering losses of men and material due to the murderous assaults by our proud and brave Taliban. [...] So-called democracy has been gifted to our mujahid nation in the form of killings, bombings, demolition of houses and promotion of un-Islamic practices and obscenity.

Mullah Mohammad Omar, November 2003[1]

Unlike other wars, Afghan wars become serious only when they are over.

Olaf Caroe[2]

The military response of the United States and its allies to the September 11 attacks directly affected the relationship between the Afghan Taliban and al-Qaeda. After years of fruitless negotiations between the Afghan Taliban, the United States and Saudi Arabia over the issue of bin Laden and foreign jihadist groups operating on Afghan soil, the United States under the leadership of President Bush declared that both terrorists and those who harbour them would be treated in the same way. The Taliban's leadership found themselves pursued just as bin Laden and al-Qaeda did; at this point they shared the same fate.

219

Moreover, much of the conventional wisdom about the relationship between al-Qaeda and the Taliban was formed in the wake of the September 11 attacks.

Commonly-cited claims of the Taliban and al-Qaeda relationship for the post-2001 period fall into five broad categories. Military support is most commonly alleged, particularly with reference to the Haqqanis operating from south-east Afghanistan.[3] Logistical and training support is also frequently claimed by analysts and foreign military forces.[4] The lucrative opium trade and other illicit smuggling enterprises are also often seen as evidence of Taliban and al-Qaeda cooperation and interaction on funding issues.[5] The Taliban are seen as having bought into (or as having always subscribed to) a global jihadist ideology since 2001, and external input into the Taliban's political vision and agenda is also increasingly stated as being a reality of the post-September 11 environment.[6]

September 11–6 October 2001

This section explores the months between the September 11 attacks and the commencement of Operation Infinite Justice, later renamed Enduring Freedom.[7] It explores the political stances of the principal actors, their interactions and their preparations.

* * *

On 11 September 2001, around 3.30pm, George Tenet, the head of the CIA, reported in the first meeting of the National Security Council that it was almost certain that bin Laden was behind the attacks. The CIA had identified three known al-Qaeda operatives on the flight manifest of American Airlines Flight 77 that had been piloted into the Pentagon, among them Khalid al-Midhar.[8] Al-Qaeda and bin Laden had been high up on the alert list, and Tenet had sent multiple security reports regarding the issue to President George W. Bush from when he had taken up office earlier in January 2001. Even before that, Tenet had stated that al-Qaeda was among the most serious national security threats to the United States.[9]

The United States government moved rapidly in the aftermath of the attacks. Bin Laden and al-Qaeda had been identified within hours of the attack as perpetrators, and the Taliban in Afghanistan were harbouring them. Tenet told a security meeting that it was essential to deny al-Qaeda sanctuary, that they were finished with the Taliban: 'The Taliban and Al-Qaeda [are] really the same.'[10] On 12 September, Bush held a discussion with Colin Powell, Secretary of State, and his cabinet. Powell stated that he was ready to send a message that 'you're either with us or you're not' to Pakistan and the Taliban. President Bush concurred, adding that, 'handing over bin Laden is not enough.'[11]

CENTCOM, the US military command centre that covered Afghanistan, had no pre-made plans for an invasion of Afghanistan,[12] and Tenet moved quickly, presenting suggestions on 15 September to the President, securing a lead role for the CIA in the attack on Afghanistan. CIA agents together with Special Forces teams would lead Northern Alliance troops and other Afghan allies against the Taliban under the cover of heavy air support.[13] President Bush, lacking any alternative (knowing that a conventional mobilisation of the military would take a long time) signed an order on 17 September granting the CIA 'enormous power.'[14] On the same day, Bush also approved the CIA's rendition programme, whereby prisoners captured abroad could be transferred to allied countries to be interrogated.[15] On 20 September, President Bush addressed a joint session of Congress and issued several demands to the Taliban:

By aiding and abetting murder, the Taliban regime is committing murder. And tonight the United States of America makes the following demands on the Taliban:

Deliver to United States authorities all of the leaders of Al-Qaeda who hide in your land. Release all foreign nationals, including American citizens, you have unjustly imprisoned. Protect foreign journalists, diplomats and aid workers in your country. Close immediately and permanently every terrorist training camp in Afghanistan. And hand over every terrorist and every person and their support structure to appropriate authorities. Give the United States full access to terrorist training camps, so we can make sure they are no longer operating.

These demands are not open to negotiation or discussion. The Taliban must act and act immediately. They will hand over the terrorists or they will share in their fate. [...] And we will pursue nations that provide aid or safe haven to terrorism. Every nation in every region now has a decision to make: Either you are with us or you are with the terrorists.[16]

Pakistan was already aware of what was coming. General Mahmood Ahmed, head of Pakistan's ISI, happened to be on Capitol Hill for some meetings when the attacks took place. On 12 September, he was summoned by the Deputy Secretary of State, Richard Armitage, who informed him that President Bush had a simple message to the world: 'Either you are with us or you are with the terrorists.'[17]

In Pakistan, President Pervez Musharraf held a meeting with his generals and some civilian cabinet members on 12 September.[18] He made it clear that Pakistan was on the verge of being declared a terrorist state which would result in its international marginalisation and bring about close cooperation between the United States and India in the military operation in Afghanistan. 'In that situation,' Musharraf explained, 'what would [happen] with the Kashmir cause?'[19] The outcome of the meeting was agreed upon by all: Pakistan would accept the American demands, trying to buy itself some room for manoeuvre later on.[20] On 19 September, Musharraf made a speech on Pakistani television:

I have done everything for Afghanistan and the Taliban when the whole world was against them. We are trying our best to come out of this critical situation without any damage to them.[21]

On 13 September, Armitage presented Ahmed with a list of seven demands:

Stop al-Qaida operatives at your border, intercept arms shipments through Pakistan and end all logistical support for bin Ladin;

Provide the U.S. with blanket overflight and landing rights to conduct all necessary military and intelligence operations;

Provide as needed territorial access to U.S. and allied military intelligence, and other personnel to conduct all necessary operations against the perpetrators of terrorism or those that harbor them, including use of Pakistan's naval ports, airbases and strategic locations on borders;

Provide the U.S. immediately with intelligence, [EXCISED]

Continue to publicly condemn the terrorist acts of 11 September and any other terrorist acts against the U.S. or its friends and allies [EXCISED]

Cut off all shipments of fuel to the Taliban and any other items and recruits, including volunteers en route to Afghanistan that can be used in a military offensive capacity or to abet the terrorist threat;

Should the evidence strongly implicate Usama bin Ladin and the al-Qaida network in Afghanistan and should Afghanistan and the Taliban continue to harbor him and this network, Pakistan will break diplomatic relations with the Taliban government, end support for the Taliban and assist us in the formentioned [sic] ways to destroy Usama bin Ladin.[22]

Many nations, such as the United Kingdom and others, pledged support early on to the United States; others were persuaded through various incentives. In this way, the United States prepared for war in less than a month.[23] The mobilisation moved on several levels, aiming not only to build a coalition against the Taliban but also to isolate them from the few nations that had established formal relations with the Islamic Emirate of Afghanistan. The United Arab Emirates severed its ties on 22 September, followed by Saudi Arabia three days later.[24] Aircraft carriers moved into position in the Indian Ocean and Uzbekistan granted the United States the right to use the Karshi-Khanabad airbase that saw the arrival of American troops on 5 October.[25]

While President Bush was approving the war plans for Afghanistan and putting the CIA in the lead, General Mahmood Ahmed visited Mullah Mohammad Omar in Kandahar together with six others.[26] This was followed by a second visit[27] on 28 September, when Ahmed led a delegation that included his chief of intelligence and a number of influential clerics in a purported attempt to convince the Taliban leader to hand over bin Laden. They were unsuccessful.[28] The exact nature of the meeting and what transpired in it are subject to some debate. Ahmed claims to have urged Mullah Mohammad Omar to give up bin Laden in the face of impending war,[29] while others (senior Taliban members) later stated that he had, in fact, urged Omar to resist American pressure. Another account recounts him as being passive while the clerics praised Mullah Mohammad Omar.[30]

Numerous interviewees, however, recount how a great number of people—among them senior Taliban military commanders—travelled to Kandahar to demand that bin Laden be expelled from the country. Mutawakil recounts in his book a gathering of the religious clergy in Kabul that came to the same conclusion, and states that the Afghan people did not understand why the leadership were not following the decision of the *ulema*.[31]

Omar had first summoned bin Laden to Kandahar to explain himself, but it is unclear whether bin Laden ever attended this meeting. In any case, it is known that there was some communication between the two leaders subsequent to the September 11 attacks.[32] One source—in Kandahar among Taliban leadership circles at the time—stated that bin Laden told Omar that:

I didn't do anything against the US government. They are only talking about investigation as a way to capture me and then to finish Islamic movements and governments all over the world.[33]

Another letter from bin Laden to Omar—part of an exchange between the two—explained the rationale that should inform his decisions from this point on:

If the Americans enter Afghanistan they will be defeated. If they don't attack Afghanistan then this will be evidence of their fear. In both those cases we have won.[34]

The conference of Islamic clergy took place at the Presidential Palace in Kabul on 19–20 September and was attended by around 1000 Afghans and Pakistanis.[35] It was initially meant to take just one day, but extended into a second when delegates failed to reach a conclusion by the end of the first. Mullah Mohammad Omar had called the *ulemaa'* together to take the decision, by which he said he would abide. At the beginning of the session on the first day, a letter that he had written in Kandahar was read out:

Osama has denied his involvement. It is unfortunate that America does not listen to us and levels all sorts of charges and threatens military action. [...] We have held talks in ... the past with US governments several times, and we are ready for more talks. [... If America] still wants to attack us ... and to destroy the Islamic government of Afghanistan, [it is up to] our respected religious scholars [to deliver a fatwa whether Muslims in Afghanistan and other countries should declare a holy war against the US.][36]

The letter carried an implied verdict. Mullah Mohammad Omar had made his own decision already and the sense of an international conspiracy against the Taliban during the preceding two years seemed to have been confirmed by the American statements that had followed the September 11 attacks. By 20 September, however, the *ulemaa'* council had decided that bin Laden should leave the country and that they would no longer offer him sanctuary:

To avoid the current tumult, and also to allay future suspicions, the Supreme Council of the Islamic Clergy recommends to the Islamic Emirate of Afghanistan to persuade Osama bin Laden to leave Afghanistan whenever possible. [...] The ulema [...] voice their sadness over American deaths and hope America does not attack Afghanistan. [...] If infidels invade an Islamic country and that country does not have the ability to defend itself, it becomes the binding obligation of all the world's Muslims to declare a holy war.[37]

Muttaqi, talking to journalists after the announcement, made clear that bin Laden would be given some time to leave:

It will take time. You know that Osama bin Laden has a lot of opponents. It can't be that he goes out on the street and catches a taxi to go to another roundabout.[38]

This was announced in Kabul as well as in Pakistan through the Taliban's ambassador, Mullah Zaeef. Zaeef stated that Mullah Mohammad Omar had also approved the decision of the *ulemaa'* council and would abide by it. He added that bin Laden was missing and they had not been able to notify him of the decision in person.[39] At first sight this seems to be merely a Taliban gesture to stall for time, yet a closer examination reveals yet another manifestation of divisions within the movement itself. The council's meeting was intended simply to rubber-stamp Omar's opinion, but once they had announced their decision contrary to that opinion, Mullah Mohammad Omar could not renege on his promise.

One interviewee stated that Omar was defiant in the face of other political Talibs who tried to get him to change his mind in order to save their government:

Some Taliban ministers came to Mullah Mohammad Omar to speak about an issue. They told him, 'we need to think about keeping our movement and need to find a solution for Osama or to send him to another country.' Mullah Mohammad Omar became very angry and told his ministers, 'you just care about your posts and your money, your ministries, but I don't care about mine. My position is bigger than yours but I don't care about it. Stop talking to me about these things. I am not prepared to give up my brother-in-religion to non-Muslims. I am ready to lose my leadership, but not to hand over Osama to the Americans or send him to another country.'[40]

The council was unable to enforce its decision, and the divisions within the movement—bin Laden had certain allies within the Taliban—meant that the discussion came to nought. In any case, the Taliban were not even in a position to hand over bin Laden, given that they had genuinely lost track of his precise whereabouts.[41] Even if they knew his location, Mullah Mohammad Omar would have spurned any offensive action by the Taliban against the foreign jihadists and their leader in the face of what he believed to be an international conspiracy against his government. The contents of a letter, addressed to Muslims around the world, sent by the Taliban leader in October 2001 seems to confirm this:

O Muslims. Know that the Sunnah of Allah, Ta'ala, in the Universe is that if Truth and falsehood meet in a destined, inevitable encounter, then Allah, 'Azza Wa Jall, will give victory to his soldiers and Awliya.' And Allah gave victory to His Prophet Musa, and his oppressed nation over Fir'awn, the tyrant. And He gave victory to Muhammad, over the disbelievers of Quraysh in the great Battle of Badr, and in the Battle of Al-Ahzab. And He gave victory to the truthful Muslims under the leadership of Al-Mudhaffar Qutuz over the tyrannical Tatar. And here we are today, in our destined encounter with the superpower of the entire world—the disbelievers of them and the hypocrites of them. We are living in decisive days that will give rise to a manifest victory for Islam and its people, if Allah wills. And surely, we announce to the entire world that, if Allah wills, we will not submit nor become lenient. And we will remain steadfast with the Permission of Allah, the Maker, until we attain one of the two good ends: victory or martyrdom. So rejoice, O People of Islam, and know that the full moon of victory has appeared in the horizon, and with the intensification of matters comes relief and a great victory from the Mighty, the Most Strong. So Allah, Allah, O Muslims, by assisting us, and with supplication for us, and with money.[42]

Mullah Zaeef met with Mullah Mohammad Omar along with several other military commanders before the start of the US bombing campaign. They questioned the Taliban leader as to whether he had taken the right decision, stating that they, as Afghans, had been used by bin Laden and that they should not tolerate this. Omar replied as follows:

I summoned Osama and asked him that question. He swore that he didn't do it. I couldn't pressure him beyond that. If you have proof of his involvement, then show it to me. But I haven't seen any proof and even the American government hasn't shown us any proof.[43]

Rumours have surfaced about whether or not the United States intended regime change when it planned Operation Enduring Freedom.[44] It remains unclear to what extent the US had predetermined the exact outcome of the war or whether things simply turned out that way.[45]

Many members of the Taliban—and not just Mullah Mohammad Omar— had come to believe that the United States had already decided[46] that they wanted to go to war against their government:

The leadership thought that once the attack was planned for Afghanistan that nothing could change this. Handing over Osama, killing him or whatever wouldn't have changed anything. It was like the issue of Saddam. It was decided beforehand and it was useless to try anything.[47]

The driver of the Taliban leader also related some observations from this time:

A list arrived for Mullah Omar containing more than seventy articles to be accepted by the Taliban. Mullah Omar told his friends that, 'America says one thing yet does another; it has two faces.' He said that maybe the Taliban government would fall, but that handing over Osama to the non-Muslims would 'bring great shame upon me.' He told his friends that, 'all Muslims—like Chechens, Arabs or others—within Afghanistan are our brothers and we will protect them from the non-Muslims.' 'Even if we hand them all over,' he said, 'then America will start talking about human rights or women's rights and will find another pretence with which to accuse us. Then the next day they will say we shouldn't have executions, and then the next day they will tell us to bring all of our women into the cities.' Yes, it is true, there were some disagreements within the Taliban about handing over Osama.[48]

In any case, the first team of CIA operatives arrived in Afghanistan on 26 September 2001.[49] CIA officer Gary Schroen led Operation Jawbreaker, and the team of ten operatives would remain the sole American presence on Afghan soil until 19 October,[50] when American Special Forces arrived in larger numbers. On 7 October, coinciding with the beginning of US bombardment, Musharraf replaced Mahmood Ahmed on account of pressure from the United States, who knew of his double-dealings with the Taliban.[51]

Al-Qaeda and the Taliban

The Taliban relayed a message to the United States in the immediate aftermath of the September 11 attacks. Initial statements condemned the attack while expressing reservation and disbelief that it really was the work of bin Laden:

What happened in the United States was not a job of ordinary people. It could have been the work of governments. Osama bin Laden cannot do this work, neither us. [...] We are not supporting terrorism. Osama does not have the capability. We condemn this. [...] This could have been the act of either internal enemies of the United States or its major rivals. Osama cannot do this work.[52]

Mullah Mohammad Omar himself echoed this argument in a statement on 14 September:

We regret the incident of terrorism in America but Osama's involvement in it was not possible since he was practically not capable of undertaking such a sophisticated operation... The US has neither made any contact with us nor has asked for extradition of Osama. If the US is interested in extradition of Osama bin Laden, it must provide us concrete proof of his involvement in the incidents of terrorism.[53]

This was restated by Mullah Mohammad Omar in a letter issued the next day:

Despite the clarity and candidness on the position of the Islamic Emirate of Afghanistan with regard to the explosions that took place lately in America, some American quarters continue to accuse Osama bin Laden of those explosions, regardless of the fact that Osama was not capable of carrying out those explosions, and he does not have the means necessary for the training of the pilots and carrying out explosions of such magnitude from the East in the West.

America has started to gather the world nations to join her aggression against Afghanistan. We take this opportunity to stress to all the states and especially the Muslim states, that allowing the American forces to use their land and airspace will entail many risks:

1. If these forces are let in they will stay forever, and the governments of these states will not be able to make them leave, and the evidence of that is in existence. These forces will be a source of instability in the region.

2. Any state allowing the American forces to attack from or across its territory will be considered as having declared war against Afghanistan, and an aggression against its independence and sovereignty.

And hence the mujahidoun will attack these forces of aggression in these states. Those states alone will bear that responsibility.[54]

The Taliban position and reaction to the September 11 attacks may have been initially cautious and stressed their disapproval, but the tone quickly became defensive as they reacted to international pressure on them to hand over bin Laden (along with a revival of all the old criticisms of the Taliban government over its treatment of women and human rights abuses). As pressure and demands on them increased from outside actors, the Taliban responses became more belligerent. Their understanding of US intentions for Afghanistan, too, seems to have been informed by the old conspiracy theories that had gained currency in the aftermath of the 1998 cruise missile attacks. On 19 September, for example, Mullah Mohammad Omar said:

Islam is a true way of life and our enemies and those against our religion believe that we are their enemies. [...] They are trying to finish us on various pretexts. One of their pretexts is Osama bin Laden's presence in Afghanistan.[55]

And by 25 September he repeats himself:

... What they want in Afghanistan is that they want to end [the] Islamic system in Afghanistan, create chaos and install a pro-American government here. [...] Any US attack will put the whole region in danger...[56]

Bin Laden and his followers had not claimed responsibility for the attack, and while al-Qaeda retreated, the Taliban were left to explain an attack about which they had not known and in which they had not taken part. The diplomatic staff of the Taliban's embassy in Islamabad found themselves at the centre of this attention.[57]

In stark contrast to the Taliban, al-Qaeda was prepared for what would unfold in the aftermath of the attacks. Multiple intelligence services had picked up on a steady increase of 'chatter' in the weeks prior to 11 September.[58] Several key operatives involved in operational logistics and other individuals disappeared in the run up to the operation, leaving Western Europe for Pakistan, Afghanistan and other destinations.[59] Within Afghanistan, al-Qaeda moved many of its personnel out of the training camps in the south-east and transferred them to Kabul and Kandahar, anticipating airstrikes in retaliation.[60]

While nations throughout the world publicly stated their support for the United States and their grief over what had unfolded on 11 September in America,[61] the situation in Pakistan was different. There was considerable public support for the Taliban, particularly in the border areas, and madrassa students and others travelled into Afghanistan against what was being popularly held as an invasion of non-Muslims.[62] Bin Laden also issued a 'call to arms' which roused many Pakistanis to come to Afghanistan.[63] Sufi Mohammad was reported to have crossed the border in the last week of October with 10,000 volunteers.[64] *Tehrik-e Nifaz-e Shariat-e Muhammadi* claimed 30,000 would-be fighters had travelled into Afghanistan through Dir and Bajaur.[65]

Even among Pakistani officials, there was a public and a private line. Visits by senior ISI officials to Mullah Mohammad Omar prior to the beginning of US airstrikes were—on the surface—last-minute attempts to convince the Taliban leader to change his mind. But in reality, the ISI officials seem to have been encouraging him to hold out and they used the visits to pass information to him about the future attack plans.[66]

While the United States found willing allies in northern and central Afghanistan under the umbrella of the Northern Alliance—they recruited and supported these individually—there was no significant Pashtun resistance in the south and the east of the country. In the absence of any information, the CIA turned to the British Secret Intelligence Service (MI6) for support. MI6 mobilised a number of Pashtun leaders, supplying them with large amounts of cash and weapons in order to persuade them to move into Afghanistan.[67] Much of the group was hastily put together out of old 1980s and 1990s *mujahedeen* or militia commanders, many of whom had old scores to settle.[68]

Bin Laden and his affiliates had gone to ground following the attacks: not even the Taliban's leadership had a real handle on where he was or stayed in regular contact with him.[69] Al-Qaeda's leadership had believed that America would respond with a conventional attack with thousands of ground troops and thought the Taliban would keep them bogged down in a Soviet-style rerun of the 1980s.[70] Jalaluddin Haqqani, possibly echoing rhetoric that the Arabs were using at the time, stated: 'We will retreat to the mountains and begin a long guerrilla war to reclaim our pure land from the infidels and free our country again like we did against the Soviets.'[71] Al-Qaeda's main priorities for the first few months were to survive and to ensure that periodic messages and statements could continue to be passed to the media. For this, though, they had little or no need for the Taliban.

Al-Qaeda was prepared. Rashid writes that bin Laden had a prearranged plan to send his top managers out of Afghanistan and he also left Kandahar prior to 11 September, only leaving a small group of fighters behind.[72] Bin

Laden had informed the al-Qaeda leadership council about the imminent attack against the United States. There appears to have been considerable disagreement about the attacks, in particular regarding the fallout and effect on Afghanistan and al-Qaeda's and other organisations' relationship with the Taliban, but the attack went ahead. Bin Laden and his key lieutenants had taken a unilateral decision.[73] Noman Benotman revealed in a letter to bin Laden that even Abu Muhammad al-Zayyat, head of al-Qaeda's security committee, had objected to the operation that would be carried out on 11 September.[74]

Much like President Bush's announcement, which sent a clear message to the nations of the world to choose sides in the aftermath of the attacks, bin Laden managed to seal the fate of militant Islamic groups around the world: they found themselves isolated from former state sponsors and allies, which compelled them to form a more cohesive front in the face of the new threat.

The United States' reaction to the September 11 attacks effectively forced the conditions that would lead to the square-off of the US and its allies against militant Islamic movements around the world which up until then had been only a loose network of individuals and organisations with considerable internal conflicts and differences.[75] The War on Terror, launched by the United States, was not targeted exclusively against al-Qaeda, but against what was perceived as a wider network of organisations and support structures. There appears to have been little differentiation between groups, making the United States the enemy of a host of different organisations and groups who found themselves targeted in the aftermath of the attacks. No matter what impact bin Laden and those among al-Qaeda's leadership might have hoped for, the operation—coupled with the United States' reaction to it—created a new dichotomy, forcing the hand of a number of actors who had been operating independently from al-Qaeda prior to the events.

By 2001, al-Qaeda had been at war with America for several years. In statements made since 1996, bin Laden and others like al-Zawahiri had identified the United States as their principal enemy. The United States in turn had a dedicated investigation team solely concerned with bin Laden and his activities since January 1996.[76] While it originally only had one member, it nevertheless marked the first time that so much attention was devoted to a single person by the CIA. The United States government had reacted to previous attacks by al-Qaeda by putting pressure on known associates and host governments as well as through direct retaliation against what were regarded as al-Qaeda's interests.

It is difficult to reconstruct bin Laden's and al-Qaeda's assessment of the possible ramifications of the September 11 attacks. They sought to prompt the *umma* to rise up; this was in line with al-Qaeda's strategic objectives and their expectation of how the United States would react. Muslims around the world, in bin Laden's assessment, would rush to the Taliban's and al-Qaeda's aid. Bin Laden stated in an interview in October 2001 that, 'our goal is for our nation to unite in the face of the Christian Crusade'.[77] The war that would unfold in Afghanistan, he believed, was another battle in the ongoing conflict between Christianity and Islam, from King Louis VII of France to King Richard the Lion Heart and Holy Roman Emperor Frederick I of Germany.[78] The passages above are taken from bin Laden's statement aired on the Qatari TV station *al-Jazeera* on 7 October, 2001, aimed at rallying Muslims around the world.[79]

Bin Laden would have expected a heavy footprint for their attack that included ground forces, especially since Massoud was dead and there were few viable partners for the US to work with. As with previous attacks, neither bin Laden nor his group claimed responsibility for the attacks, but waited several years, releasing a statement to that end only in October 2004.[80]

There had been several internal discussions about the September 11 plot within al-Qaeda. Many regarded the attacks as a mistake, and said they would further jeopardise their relationship with the Taliban. The likely fallout could not only cause the Taliban's government to collapse but could pose a real threat to al-Qaeda itself.[81]

The Taliban by this point had a new set of priorities of their own: survival and damage-control were highest in the minds of the political leadership; for the military, a credible defence of their country had to be mounted; and for the public leadership and spokesmen it seemed that a view to posterity and their fellow Islamic countries meant that keeping the movement's Islamic reputation clean was the highest priority.[82] The Taliban, much like other Islamist and jihadist groups, found themselves forced to take a decision in the increasingly bipolar world of post-September 11. There were few options and little leeway.

International Response

Initial reactions to the attacks in the Western media and officialdom drew an immediate (if implicit) line connecting the Taliban to al-Qaeda. In many ways, the parameters of 'TalQaeda' were drawn in the aftermath of the September 11 attacks. Even though the Taliban were not explicitly indicted for their involvement in the actual plot, the rhetoric of commentators in the run up to Operation Enduring Freedom and in the months of war that followed convinced many that there was little to distinguish between the Taliban and al-Qaeda.[83] Much of this perception was helped along by the limited understanding of Islam among a considerable part of the general public.

As outlined above, the United States issued many demands to the Taliban and set about preparing to attack the Islamic Emirate of Afghanistan. While Pakistan continued to communicate with the Taliban, the US government seemed set on the path to war, and Tenet presented a narrative that allowed for little if any distinction to be made between the Taliban and al-Qaeda.[84]

Condoleezza Rice initially questioned whether the Taliban had to be defeated, but Tenet stated that leaving the Taliban in place would offer a 'rallying point for terrorist elements.'[85] As to what might be achieved by the winter of 2001, Tenet envisioned that the north would be taken, resupplied through Uzbekistan; Kabul would be under control and a safe passage would be established into the south via Paktika from Pakistan.[86] The Taliban's intransigence was regarded as a clear sign of their de facto union with al-Qaeda. The differences between the two groups and individuals that formed them were lost on most in those early months.

The reasoning that informed the United States' actions and plans in the days after the September 11 attacks was based on a number of key ideas. The most important of these was the Bush doctrine that already saw the Taliban as deserving of the same treatment as al-Qaeda.[87]

America—while busy building a coalition to secure overflight rights, logistical support and sharing of information—had no desire that the decisions lay ahead to be subject to approval by an international committee or council. Furthermore, Bush and his administration made clear that America would not concern itself with nation-building, an undertaking considered expensive and having a doubtful outcome.[88]

On 12 September,[89] NATO released a press statement declaring that Article Five of its treaty[90] would be invoked if the perpetrators of the September 11 attacks resided outside the United States. Bush and his US government, however, were not interested in NATO playing any part at that time in what would unfold in Afghanistan, and moved forward on their own by building a coalition of bilateral allies.[91]

The official reactions of the Taliban to this international reaction and diplomatic pressure did not help. Official responses were often combative, and at times responses that might have been accepted in any other circumstances were seen here as uncooperative. While the Taliban were among the first to issue a message of concern and support to America, their subsequent line was that evidence was needed to indict bin Laden and that they would not be dictated to by any other country. The Taliban thereby closely echoed their behaviour in the aftermath of the 1998 African embassy bombings when they pursued much the same line. And just as the Taliban stuck to their previous approach, the United States seemed as rigid in its stance. A different development of the conflict at this point is imaginable. Neither the United States nor the Taliban displayed the political will or insight to make that happen.

The Taliban

There were numerous external factors influencing the Taliban in the three months that followed the September 11 attacks. Most of these seemed to work against them and pushed them to an intransigent position, albeit one that they were well-disposed to favour; in addition, now it was possible for the fighters of al-Qaeda to claim in meetings with the Taliban that they had warned them that this was an international plot to invade Muslim countries.[92]

There was some level of debate about bin Laden and his actions among the political Taliban, but by this point it was relatively pragmatic—the most important goal was to ensure the survival of the Taliban government and to preserve its reputation. The impending and then unfolding war also helped to polarise the Taliban: talk of negotiation with America or of trying to find a compromise that would allow the movement to survive was seen as capitulation.[93] This did not stop members of the Taliban approaching Mullah Mohammad Omar and asking him to consider handing over bin Laden. The Taliban leader's driver recalled a story told to him by friends:

I didn't see this myself, but friends told me that when the Taliban movement was ending, Mullah Mohammad Omar and Wakil Ahmed [Mutawakil] were speaking about Osama. Mullah Mohammad Omar kicked Wakil Ahmad and pushed him out of his office and then later shouted at him over the radio. All of this was because Wakil Ahmad told Mullah Mohammad Omar to hand over Osama to the Americans.[94]

There was also a very real fear of division and internal conflict during this period.[95] The international media were constantly reporting about internal coups and new fronts being set up by the 'moderate Taliban,' and while this was mostly little more than speculation it served as a warning to the Taliban's political leadership.[96] Policies of 'divide and rule' were well-known by the Taliban—the British had been particularly enthusiastic about these a century before—and the increasingly belligerent rhetoric of America and the United Nations served mostly to draw the movement together. Defection and integrity had been of concern to the Taliban since the movement's founding; in the early 1990s they had emerged taking up arms against a plethora of armed groups and had formed fragile alliances while taking control of more and more districts and provinces.

The Taliban held that they would be willing to assess any evidence against bin Laden. If their court found him guilty, they said, then they could hand him over or transfer him to another Islamic country. They made this offer repeatedly throughout the weeks prior to the beginning of the bombing in October.[97] This seems to have been more rhetoric and principle than a serious offer, but it was grounded in the position in which the Taliban found themselves: they sought above all else to preserve the reputation that they believed they had in the Islamic world. We have seen how this helped motivate Mullah Mohammad Omar in the debate over the Bamiyan Buddha statues, and it remained a priority in the post-September 11 environment. Pakistan continued to assure the Taliban of its support, contributing to the Taliban's firm stance in the face of international calls to hand over bin Laden.[98]

Within days of the September 11 attacks, Pakistan received the above-quoted list of demands from the United States that was accepted almost immediately by Musharraf. In parallel with what amounted to a Janus-faced Pakistani government policy,[99] the Pakistani *ulemaa'*, religious clergy and much of the population were supportive of the Taliban, and tens of thousands of would-be fighters and volunteers crossed into Afghanistan at the beginning of the US airstrikes to join Taliban forces on the ground.[100] Pakistan supported America's efforts to hunt al-Qaeda and foreign fighters but had little interest in targeting its home-grown Kashmiri jihadist organisations or their allies in Afghanistan.[101]

Only in the last few days before the United States attacked did the Taliban prepare its defences:[102] Mullah Dadullah, Mullah Fazl and others would resist the Northern Alliance and the American forces in the north. Even then Mullah Mohammad Omar did not believe the United States would launch a full-scale attack.[103] Mullah Zaeef has even written that Mullah Mohammad Omar did not believe that the US would go to war with Afghanistan and the Taliban at all:

In Mullah Mohammad Omar's mind there was less than a 10 per cent chance that America would resort to anything beyond threats, and so an attack was unlikely.[104]

The Taliban's position on al-Qaeda and the sacrifice Mullah Mohammad Omar made for not handing over bin Laden is difficult to rationalise for foreign commentators. As this book has tried to show, the Taliban's world view and their underlying fear of alienating the Muslim *umma* formed the basis for their decisions and was of particular importance to Mullah Mohammad Omar. It is also important to take into account the increasingly problematic relationship between the Taliban and parts of the Afghan population that had formerly supported them.[105]

The decision not to hand over bin Laden appears to have been neither 'radical' nor irrational. The protection of guests was both a religious as well as a cultural duty, but bin Laden, in the eyes of Mullah Mohammad Omar and other Taliban and Afghans, held unique significance. The latter was almost forty years old at that time and as *amir ul-mu'mineen* had found himself increasingly confronted by international politics, interest groups and regional power dynamics. He had become more independent, while recognising the need of international support. In his mind, bin Laden had come to represent the wider Muslim *umma*.

As Abu al-Walid al-Masri points out in his book, the Taliban had gained respect for hosting bin Laden in the past.[106] In the face of the growing isolation and mounting international pressure, Mullah Mohammad Omar saw bin Laden as a bridge to millions of Muslims he would potentially alienate by surrendering him.[107] In an interview with Voice of America radio, he stated:

We cannot [give bin Laden up]. If we did, it means we are not Muslims; that Islam is finished. If we were afraid of attack, we could have surrendered him the last time we were threatened and attacked. So America can hit us again.[108]

And in conversation with Rahimullah Yousufzai:

I know I can't fight the Americans, but if God helps me I will survive. I don't want to go down in history as someone who betrayed his guest. I am willing to give my life, my regime; since we have given him refuge, I cannot throw him out now.[109]

Much of the reasoning that informs decision-making in other societies cannot easily be applied to southern Afghanistan. In a place where there are no institutions that fulfil the basic needs of individuals, social standing—governed by cultural and religious conventions—is of central importance for one's own survival as well as that of one's family. What might be perceived by foreign observers as irrational choices can often be more easily explained when seen through the local context.

Decisions were made on moral grounds, for personal and group reasons, and arguments were constructed on the basis of an emotional attachment to their interpretation of Islam. We have already shown how this had a history of its own and was at least partially handed down to the group of young men who, by the time they took action, had spent half of their lives fighting. Omar said as much when he stated:

I am thinking of two promises; the Promise of Allah and the promise of Bush. With regard to Allah's Promise, it is vaster and more protective than any threat in the world. As for the promise of Bush, then it is transient no matter how long the consequences of it not being carried.[110]

October 7–December 7, 2001

The Military Campaign

On 7 October 2001, President Bush announced that the United States had launched Operation Enduring Freedom in Afghanistan.[111] Prime Minister Tony Blair confirmed later the same day that British air assets were also engaged in the bombardment of targets in Afghanistan.[112] Several cruise missiles were launched in an attempt to kill Mullah Mohammad Omar and bin Laden, hitting Kandahar and eastern Afghanistan.[113] The United States and the United Kingdom were bombing targets all over Afghanistan, many previously identified by the team that made up 'Jawbreaker' (see above). On the same day, al-Jazeera aired a statement by bin Laden who saw his world view confirmed with the commencement of the US attacks:

I say to you that these events have divided the entire world into two separate camps—one of faith, where there is no hypocrisy, and one of infidelity.[114]

Over the next few weeks, 'Jawbreaker' would successfully lead the Northern Alliance force towards Kabul, coordinating close air support that facilitated much of the rapid advance.[115] Throughout October the rhetoric of the United States seemed to change from declarations made early in September 2001 regarding its objectives in Afghanistan. While al-Qaeda and bin Laden had been at the forefront of earlier statements, the senior US leadership, particularly in the military, slowly began to see the war effort directed as much against the Taliban as against al-Qaeda.[116]

Gul Agha Shirzai, the son of Haji Latif, was among those the CIA recruited to retake the south and capture Kandahar. As Sarah Chayes relates in her book, 'the Americans have promised more than a million dollars for this job. They told me that when we get to the border, every vehicle but ours will be bombed. Only we will be able to move.' Shirzai is reported to have said this in the run up to his entry into Afghanistan.[117] According to an unnamed State Department official, Shirzai had been introduced by the ISI to the Americans.[118] Given the lack of available opposition commanders in the south, he would have been the natural choice given his ability to raise men and his willingness to go into Afghanistan.[119] He formed a militia of some 650–800 men in October.[120] The group moved into Afghanistan on 12 November, escorted by Pakistani forces. They were supplied with weapons and met up with Special Forces team ODA 583,[121] which would facilitate air support. After little fighting the group captured Kandahar within a month.[122]

Tenet's strategy of relying on small Special Forces teams that would coordinate air support and a battle of land forces absent any significant American ground troops was without precedent. Neither the Taliban, nor al-Qaeda nor even American officials in the US embassy in Pakistan[123] expected a campaign like this. US air assets flew continuously over Afghanistan; warplanes would linger in the sky waiting for targets to be identified.[124] In a few days the United States ran out of these strategic targets. Afghanistan, after twenty years of war, had little infrastructure and the Taliban only possessed limited heavy equipment that could be destroyed to any effect. The military and the CIA were pressed to find targets worth bombing.[125]

On the northern front, ordnance (including two 15,000 pound BLU-82 'Daisy Cutter' bombs)[126] were dropped on Taliban positions and fortifications for days before the ground forces moved in. The sheer firepower the CIA and Special Forces soldiers commanded outgunned the Taliban and their abilities. As Gary Schroen would later state, Kabul could have fallen in October if the Special Forces had come in earlier and supported his operation.[127]

The lack of Taliban preparation was undoubtedly an important reason why a defeat of their government and military forces was so swiftly accomplished. Although Pakistani officers had apparently been advising Mullah Mohammad Omar's office on the Americans' war plans for Afghanistan, this does not seem to have translated into much action besides the initiatives of individual commanders and heads of sections of the Taliban military forces.[128] It is possible that Mullah Mohammad Omar was so wedded to his delusions by the start of the US bombing campaign that to have started preparing for the end of the Islamic Emirate might have felt premature.[129]

Taliban commanders started to return to the south from the collapsing front lines around the country with a view to focusing on Kandahar and perhaps mounting more durable defences, yet by the time they arrived the leadership was preparing its departure.[130] Regional commanders around the country complained about the lack of direction coming from the central command hub in

Kandahar.[131] Orders came late or not at all, and often seemed to be impractical and removed from ground realities.

The foreign jihadist forces inside Afghanistan were under a separate command and were never centrally directed by the Taliban leadership.[132] Even among the foreign fighters themselves, different groups and command structures existed. They were under the overall command of Juma Namangani (as per an order issued by Mullah Mohammad Omar), but there was no overall coordination and individual groups acted independently and pursued different tactics at the time.[133]

International forces in Afghanistan were under two distinct commands and operating towards separate objectives from 2002 onwards: the International Security Assistance Force (ISAF) was initially put in place under a UN mandate to secure and protect Kabul, while the American-led Operation Enduring Freedom pursued the 'War on Terror,' tracking down members of al-Qaeda and the Taliban along with a number of other individuals designated as terrorists, predominantly in the southeast.[134] With President Bush's pronounced stance against nation-building, his commitment to a 'War on Terror' and early attempts to shift the focus onto Iraq, the two missions soon started to diverge. The allocation of priorities soon proved detrimental to developments in Afghanistan.[135] International NGOs commented that the allocation of priorities was wrong: in hindsight, the ISAF force should have been the priority rather than the mission to capture bin Laden or the Taliban.[136]

The Taliban Defence

One source has estimated that the Taliban gathered a force of 100,000 men, volunteers and 'regular forces' including some 13,000 foreign fighters from different neighbouring countries for the defence of Afghanistan.[137] The early days of the war saw an influx of tens of thousands of Pakistani madrassa students and others who joined the Afghan Taliban.[138] The latter were mixed with the Afghan Taliban everywhere, while the Arabs, foreign fighters—among whom al-Qaeda could be found—made sure to keep themselves apart. According to a number of interviewees for this book, al-Qaeda and the Arabs did not share their plans with the Taliban, and fought in separate locations and from their own bases. One interviewee stated that they would not even allow Taliban on their bases because 'they did not trust the Taliban.'[139]

'I remember after 9/11 when Americans invaded Afghanistan, many Arabs came to Kandahar and divided themselves into three areas. Most of them went to KAF [Kandahar Air Field] and some were in Kandahar city and a few were in Panjwayi district centre. They changed their places round every day. They didn't want to mix with the Taliban forces, or even to show their locations to the Taliban or ordinary people.'[140]

Much of this was particularly evident in the final days of the military campaign in Kandahar, which saw fierce resistance and fighting until the death of Arab pockets in the city, in Panjwayi and at airport, while the Taliban had melted away or given up the fight.[141]

In November, Taliban defences in northern and central Afghanistan collapsed. On the 9th it was Mazar-e Sharif and on the 10th there were a series of Northern Alliance attacks on cities and towns in northern and central Afghanistan, including Khwaja Ghar, Ishkamesh, Baghlan, Pul-e Khumri, Nahrin, Aibak and Bamiyan. All fell, as did Hairatan. On 11 November, Maimana fell, on 12 November Herat fell and the Northern Alliance started to move in on Kabul, and on 13 November the Taliban fled Kabul and the Northern Alliance entered. On 14 November, Jalalabad fell. On 26 November, Kunduz was captured following heavy aerial bombardment.[142]

In fewer than 2 months, the [Northern Alliance], supported by US [Special Forces] and air power, decisively defeated the Taliban and al-Qaeda forces in northern Afghanistan and liberated 6 provinces, 3 key cities, and nearly 50 additional smaller towns and villages in the region. [Northern Alliance] forces killed nearly 10,000 enemy soldiers and took several thousand more prisoners.[143]

In the north, Mullah Dadullah managed to escape through the enemy lines that now surrounded the Taliban in Kunduz and in other locations, allegedly through a large cash payment.[144] Other senior Taliban commanders—like Mullah Mohammad Fazl—handed themselves over to Dostum's forces; they had not heard from their senior leaders in Kandahar, despite efforts from the Taliban's embassy in Islamabad to negotiate a possible release, and they were hoping to be treated according to their stature within the movement.

Mullah Mohammad Omar had appointed Jalaluddin Haqqani as overall military commander of Taliban forces on 6 October in the run-up to the commencement of Operation Enduring Freedom.[145] Haqqani's appointment signifies a realisation of the seriousness of their situation; with his appointment, Mullah Mohammad Omar handed over a key senior position within the movement to a non-Kandahari, access that had been long denied to Haqqani. The latter delivered fiery speeches about resistance, but seemed to do little on the ground to organise the same. Possibly with input from the ISI, which regarded him as a strategic asset, he did not mobilise and instead retreated across the border into Waziristan.[146]

Mullah Mohammad Omar, a day before the commencement of the bombing campaign against the Taliban's forces, reportedly made a speech:

[He] emphasizes that the Taliban are confronting the most powerful of enemies and sets the stage for the long run: eventually the forces of Islam will be victorious, he says, but do expect death and defeat to begin with. In an inspired piece of rhetoric, he considers his own likely demise in the imminent conflict. Mullah Omar admits he is scared, for himself and his family, and he makes a clean breast of his own weak human nature. Accordingly, he questions the sincerity of his thoughts. 'It is very strange that I am not greedy,' he says, and he clearly knows already that he will likely lose everything in this battle, 'for I know my power; my position; my wealth; and my family are in danger.' But, Omar continues, there is something worse than losing power, family and wealth, and that is becoming a friend of non-Muslims. 'However, I am ready to sacrifice myself and I do not want to became [sic] a friend of non-Muslims, for non-Muslims are against all my beliefs and my religion.' 'My family, my power, and my privileges,' he concludes, 'are all in danger, but still I am insisting on sacrificing myself, and you should do likewise.'[147]

The swift collapse and withdrawal of Taliban resistance seems not to have been anticipated by Mullah Mohammad Omar. Reports of his state of mind during the final days while negotiating the fall of Kandahar,[148] his final broadcast to his troops, and the general atmosphere among his commanders all imply that this was not a scenario that he had imagined would come so soon. Taliban commanders on the front lines were particularly incensed with both the leadership and the United States alike, as they saw their men struck down by foreign air forces.

The bombs cut down our men like a reaper harvesting wheat. Bodies were dismembered. Dazed fighters were bleeding from the ears and nose from the bombs' concussions. We couldn't bury the dead. Our reinforcements died in their trenches. I couldn't bring myself to surrender, so I retreated with a few of my men in the confusion. Everything was against us. The highway south to Kabul through the Salang Tunnel was blocked. We walked four days in the deep snow without food or water. Kids started shooting at us from the hilltops, hunting us like wild animals.[149]

The behaviour of Mullah Mohammad Omar provoked much indignation among the military and civilian leaders of the Taliban. One report of his state of mind during the final days of the movement in Kandahar show him 'distraught [...] at times on the verge of weeping.'[150] A final appeal made to fighters to 'completely obey your commanders and not to go hither and thither,' and to 'regroup, resist and fight,' on 13 November was apparently received ambivalently among members of the movement still fighting.[151] He had earlier said that, 'a small piece of land suffices us in continuing to defend ourselves, in refusing to surrender and in fighting to the last breath,' but now seemed himself to break down as he organised the exit of his family from Afghanistan to Pakistan.[152] One report also suggested that as the final negotiations for the surrender of Kandahar proceeded apace, Mullah Mohammad Omar grew more anxious; assuaging these worries even forced a new clause into the Bonn agreement.[153]

A last-minute initiative was taken by Taliban commanders that reportedly accepted Hamid Karzai as interim leader (as selected at the Bonn Conference) and 'acknowledged that the Islamic Emirate (the official name of the Taliban government) had no chance of surviving.' This effort was spearheaded by senior Taliban leaders at a meeting in Kandahar which included 'Tayeb Agha, at one point Mullah Omar's top aide, Mullah Beradar, a former governor and key military commander, Sayed Muhammad Haqqani, the former ambassador to Pakistan, Mullah Obaidullah, the Defense Minister, Mullah Abdul Razzak, the Interior Minster, and many others.'[154]

Al-Qaeda's Role in the 2001 War

It is difficult to construct a coherent picture of the role that al-Qaeda played in the months following the deployment of the CIA's 'Jawbreaker' team and during the heavy air campaign against the Taliban. Based on interviews and written witness testimony published since, it seems clear that there was a significant involvement of foreigners—Arabs and others—in the Taliban's resistance.[155] Foreign fighters, however, according to almost all sources, operated separately from the Taliban, were not under their direct command and did not coordinate on the ground. Al-Qaeda members had long regarded the Taliban military as incompetent and lacking the willingness to sacrifice themselves. Arabs and other foreign fighters put up stiff resistance throughout the country, their forces being located in small pockets in the north, Kabul and the south.[156] Bin Laden himself was reported to have 3,000 Arab fighters with him, most of whom managed to escape into Pakistan.[157]

There were many foreign groups operating in Afghanistan at the time; al-Qaeda was only one group among many.[158] It seems clear that the great majority of al-Qaeda operatives left early for Tora Bora (near Jalalabad), where they took up positions and resisted the bombardment and ground forces for several weeks before fleeing across the border into Pakistan.[159] Nevertheless, al-Qaeda did not expect the tactics applied by the United States. The Taliban

241

regime's swift collapse and, possibly also, the perception that large sections of the Afghan population actively supported the United States, were both unwelcome surprises for al-Qaeda's leadership.

One interviewee claimed that bin Laden was in Wardak for most of the month that followed the September 11 attacks, staying at the house of a certain Mullah Hafizullah:

He had many weapons with him and he had even brought honey with him to keep for food. But when the attacks on Afghanistan began he ran away. We don't know where he went.[160]

Abu al-Walid al-Masri reports that many of the foreign fighters arriving in Afghanistan after September 11 were directed straight to the northern provinces. In fact, Mullah Mohammad Omar appointed an outsider, Juma Namangani (non-al-Qaeda and non-Arab), as head of the foreign forces in northern Afghanistan:[161]

We return to Mullah Omar's decision to appoint [Juma Namangani] as Commander in Chief of the foreign volunteers and we say that it was considered a serious blow to al-Qaeda that was received by many of its leaders with severe resentment, unlike bin Laden, who met it with a sporting spirit. He ordered all of al-Qaeda's capabilities be put towards the defence line at Kabul under the disposal of the new leader. He refused a suggestion from angry cadres to withdraw al-Qaeda's equipment from the defence lines as a means of retaliation. [Namangani] responded with an intelligent initiative by appointing a smart commander of al-Qaeda as his deputy. He was an excellent young Iraqi man. He also took the initiative of sending five al Qaeda cadres to northern Afghanistan to help [Namangani] organize the new Arabs. Anyway, everyone there was killed.[162]

During the 2001–2002 clashes with foreign troops different elements were involved. Senior Taliban military commanders and the political echelons would make occasional trips to the battlefield after the initial bombing campaign had lessened, but their role was minimal.[163] Of course, there are examples of senior al-Qaeda and foreign military commanders being caught up in the American bombing. Both Mohammad Atef and Juma Namangani lost their lives in this way.[164] The mid-level foreign fighters—usually with a political bent—took the opportunity to flee into Pakistan or elsewhere.[165] The fighting on the ground—around the country—was carried out by a relatively small number (relative to the number that were originally inside Afghanistan), and even fewer that had decided on their death/martyrdom.[166] During the final days, a report also surfaced that the Taliban had granted Afghan citizenship to five Arabs: bin Laden, al-Zawahiri, Sheikh Asim Abdur Rahman, Saif ul-Adl and Mohammad Atef.[167]

The battle of Tora Bora took place between 12 and 17 December in a mountainous area southeast of Kabul. Multiple witnesses have attested to the presence of both bin Laden and al-Zawahiri during this period.[168] Initially there were several days of massive airstrikes against cave complexes in which the Arab and foreign jihadists were located, but after that international special forces (mainly American and British) moved in on locations where they believed bin Laden to be.[169] Their progress was halted by news of a surrender bid and cease-fire that the Special Forces' Afghan allies were conducting.[170] It is likely that it was about this time that bin Laden and the senior al-Qaeda leadership fled across the border to Waziristan, leaving behind some fighters to resist so as to slow down the pursuit.[171]

By the end of fighting, approximately 200 foreign fighters had been killed. The battle of Tora Bora was not the final set piece of the foreign fighters' effort inside Afghanistan, but for bin Laden and al-Qaeda it probably was. Bin Laden had reportedly been in Tora Bora since November.[172] Tora Bora was not so much a battle (in that there was very little that the foreign jihadists could do to defend themselves against incessant air strikes against their cave hideouts) as the moment of final departure for some of the senior leadership (including probably bin Laden). The accounts of Arabs who survived the battle (and were captured and transported to Guantánamo) as well as memoirs penned by American soldiers and intelligence officers on the ground at the time indicate that there was no significant Taliban or Afghan presence at this battle.[173] This was al-Qaeda's moment.

External Factors

Pakistan's Musharraf had agreed to support the United States in the fight against al-Qaeda but had fallen short on publicly condemning the Taliban. He had explained to his commanders that not complying with the United States' demands at the current moment would mean that Pakistan might be declared a terrorist state, and that India would become a stronger US ally in the war and in the region.[174] Public opinion in Pakistan, however, meant a public declaration could potentially cause a considerable backlash.

Musharraf managed what the Taliban had not: as Pakistan would continue to do, it became all things to all people. While officially supporting the United States, Musharraf explained to its new-found allies that public support was low and that the government needed clear signs of commitment.[175] In return for its cooperation, sanctions on Pakistan were lifted and the country received almost $1 billion in military aid for granting overflight rights and the transport of goods into Afghanistan.[176] Meanwhile, groups within the ISI had not stopped supporting the Afghan Taliban.[177] Public support for the latter in Pakistan was high.[178] Various sources allege that the ISI was directly supporting the Taliban at least until October 2001, with advisers and war materiel.[179]

Furthermore, during the siege of Kunduz, in late November 2001, Pakistan airlifted thousands of Pakistani and other nationals out of Kunduz in night airlifts that took place over several days. Some sources allege that as many as 5000 individuals were flown out of Kunduz into Pakistan. Musharraf, according to Hersh, had explained the possibly fatal fallout that the discovery of dead Pakistani nationals would have for the United States.[180]

December 2001–2003

The first two years following the fall of the Taliban government were a time of post-traumatic shock and recuperation for the movement's leadership. They had no real structures or hierarchies with which to regroup and revive, nor was there even a firm position on whether to start an insurgency or to try to have a voice in the new political realities within Afghanistan. The Taliban had crumbled.

The senior Talibs were mostly in Pakistan by early 2002; some had been captured or killed during Operation Enduring Freedom, but the vast majority had survived. This first 12–18 months, interviewees recall, were a time of stasis and reflection. There had been no plan for this eventuality, and groups of Taliban found themselves hiding, without lines of communication to each other, in Pakistan.[181] A number of high-profile figures, like Jalaluddin Haqqani, the overall commander of the Taliban forces, did very little during the first 18–24 months. Individuals and groups weighed their options, sought out information, and at times tried to get in touch with the new Afghan government that was being formed in Kabul.[182]

There do not seem to have been significant efforts at mobilisation. In the immediate aftermath of the Taliban's ouster, the Afghan population at large was content and looking towards the future while listening to the various promises being made by world leaders.[183] There was no desire from the population nor from the decision-makers to include elements of the Taliban, who appeared to have been obliterated, in decision-making. A new political paradigm was in play and it excluded the Taliban.

Much of this mood had evolved in the months prior to the launch of Operation Enduring Freedom; the increasingly restrictive and oppressive rules, in particular the ban on opium in the absence of any comprehensive programmes to counter the fallout for the local farmers and day labourers, had turned sizeable parts of the population in the south and east against the Taliban.[184] Many among the old Taliban leadership even seemed to accept this new reality. Some went home and others even signed off on the new politics and sought to play a role.[185]

While the mood among the general population was one of relief, the United States was preoccupied and found its attention diverted: the war on terror and hunting down al-Qaeda members along the border and within Afghanistan remained important, but preparations started to be made for what would unfold in Iraq.[186]

The international presence in Afghanistan was small, an outcome of the light footprint of foreign troops during the October–December campaign. The small International Security Assistance Force (ISAF) in September 2003 had only 5000 troops stationed in Afghanistan, with the US military numbered 9,800.[187] The United Nations Assistance Mission to Afghanistan (UNAMA) and the international security forces would only expand out to the provinces years after the Taliban were ousted. Little attention was paid by anyone to local political developments.[188]

Even the Afghan commanders who had returned under the cover of and with the financial backing of the United States initially expected that their patron would take charge and oversee a wide-reaching disarmament process.[189] Nothing materialised. A number of commanders were used by the US military to pursue the 'War on Terror' while others who had returned to their former strongholds had the freedom to consolidate their networks and were eagerly incorporated into the fragile government structure by Hamid Karzai with the assistance of the international community. These commanders used their access to the government to further strengthen their hold over their own power bases. Northern Alliance commanders carved up the north,[190] while Ismael Khan held sway once again in Herat.[191] Kandahar was under the control of Gul Agha Shirzai, Mullah Naqibullah and Ahmed Wali Karzai.

On 5 December 2001, the Bonn Agreement was signed, and Afghan President Hamid Karzai was sworn in on 22 December as head of the interim government consisting of thirty members.[192] The groups that attended the conference were approved by the United Nations,[193] but left much to be desired. The composition of the interim government and the people who attended the Bonn conference already set a bleak outlook for the possibility of a wider political settlement. By December 2001, the Northern Alliance commanders were in control of more than half of the country. This presented new ground realities and allowed them to gain key ministries and positions within the new administration.[194] Furthermore, the individuals at the conference table were largely from the Northern Alliance or the former King's office.[195]

Karzai attempted to navigate the evolving political landscape by forming broad alliances and offering government positions to individuals in exchange for support.[196] In the years that followed, he sought to switch individuals around, removing them from their traditional power bases, or exiling them as ambassadors. These figures, however, have largely maintained their power bases, in particular in the light of an increasingly unpopular Afghan government and a failing administration.[197]

For the first two years, the International Security Assistance Force, under the mandate of the United Nations Security Council, was confined to Kabul. Only after NATO was asked to take over the leadership of ISAF operations on 11 August 2003 was the mission expanded to include other urban centres around the country, and the six-month national rotation of command came to an end.[198]

Taliban Goals

For the first years following the brisk American success in ousting the Taliban, it was far from certain that the Taliban movement would start a military campaign against the new government in Kabul and foreign forces, Mullah Mohammad Omar's periodic statements notwithstanding. The attitude of senior Taliban figures as well as those of the general population attest to this.[199] In the absence of a plan, the Taliban's overall organisational structure had collapsed. The Taliban, just like the mujahedeen fronts in the 1980s, owe much of their perseverance to their underlying structures; these are inherent to militant organisations across Afghanistan and are found in different forms, among tribal militias, for example.

The Taliban's military force was and is constructed on the basis of the *andiwaal* system. This was the case during the 1980s during the *jihad*, in the 1990s and throughout their rule and military campaigns up to 2001. It still holds true today. The smallest unit in the Taliban's force consists of a small group holding some 5 to 30 members under the lead of a commander. This is the building block of the *andiwaal* system. Ties between the commander and his troops are forged through long-standing relations built on family, clan, tribal affiliations and friendship. *Andiwaal* is the Dari word[200] for friend. These groups are mostly local, but at times—depending on the individual characteristics of group members and their commanders—can be moved, combined and called on for various activities and support.[201]

The *andiwaal* system is the underlying reason for the ongoing debate as to whether the Taliban are structured around a strong central command with a top-down command structure or are a group of affiliates operating semi-independently. The system as it presents itself, while paradoxical, satisfies both extremes of the argument and combines independence with strong leadership that allows flexible and rapid adjustment to local conditions, as well as to the changing tactics of Afghan government and foreign forces.[202] Commanders are responsible for recruiting their own forces, and prestige as well as importance rises with the number of sub-commanders and men under one's control. In the years following the initial collapse of the Taliban, the heterogeneous nature of the movement—different from region to region—could also be seen in the way individual sub-commanders reacted to the new status quo.

The underlying structure also becomes apparent when looking at early attacks on the foreign forces and the Afghan government. These operations were sporadic, uncoordinated and lacked overall structure or strategy. The insurgent network is a heterogeneous group of actors who, as explored earlier, fight for a variety of reasons and motivations. The Taliban, with its various branches and organisational structure, is constantly managing the various actors, trying to enforce its command over the insurgency.

During these first years there was very little that might be described as a unified or cohesive political programme on either side. There seems to have been little desire by the United States and their Northern Alliance allies to reconcile or integrate Taliban members or their leadership into the new political process.[203] Even the political Taliban who sought to communicate were subject to incarceration and harassment.

There were individual attempts by certain figures to reconcile with the new administration—dominated by former members of the Northern Alliance[204]—and its leader, Hamid Karzai, but this was by no means systematic and was plagued by the absence of a coherent foreign attitude to the returning Talibs (by and large from the political cohorts of the movement): some were accepted without much fanfare, while others were sent to Guantánamo or other detention facilities.

Mullah Zaeef, for example, was handed over to the United States in January 2002 and was subjected to interrogation in a variety of facilities inside and outside Afghanistan, before being transferred to the new prison at Guantá-namo Bay. The manner of his detention and the fact of his being imprisoned without charge for over four years has influenced how he views the United States and other foreign governments.[205]

Mullah Mutawakil, another political Talib, chose to hand himself over voluntarily to US troops in February 2002.[206] This, he argued, was in order to remain within the political process:

At the beginning I went to Quetta. At that time, everything was hot. The United States were angry, and their local allies were angry. I tried to save myself from those things for a few days, but in Quetta there wasn't really anything going on. So I went back to Afghanistan. My professional and personal experiences in Afghanistan meant that I wanted to return and maybe start up a madrassa. I said, 'if someone has a problem with me then we should talk.' I ended up being in prison for two years. But the main thing is that I didn't go to the mountains. I am a political person and you can't do politics if you're in the mountains. Things like peace initiatives you can't do from the mountains or if you're in hiding, so that's why I came back.[207]

The senior Taliban who found themselves in Pakistan were disunited over what they should do. While some seemed to be eager to fight, others preferred political solutions, and a third group was no longer interested in participating in any grand projects. Circumstances had clearly changed.

The top leadership occasionally made statements referring to the calamity of the past year, but it was usually couched in threats. In May 2002, for example, Mullah Mohammad Omar was interviewed by the London-based Arabic daily *al-Sharq al-Awsat* newspaper.[208] Asked about the September 11 attacks, he remarked that, 'There were reasons behind these great deeds. America should seek to remove these reasons—and it knows them well—so that such accidents do not recur.'[209] One month later he reportedly gave another interview, denying that the Taliban had suffered defeat: 'we have suffered minimum losses and are still ready to fight. A holy war is only beginning. The fire of this war [will] reach America and burn down its capital, which started this campaign of infidels against the Muslims.'[210] As with the occasional statements issued after 2000, this statement should be viewed in the context of the time and the situation in which it was made, as well as with hindsight of current Taliban communications. Mullah Mohammad Omar's statements should not be regarded as evidence of the Taliban leader taking the movement down a new path, but rather as rhetorical threats more than anything else. By September 2002, a message released just before the first anniversary of the September 11 attacks stated that *jihad* was being carried out against 'the invaders' and that victory would soon come.[211]

It seems that there was a considerable amount of anger among the broad mass of mid-level Taliban commanders directed at al-Qaeda and its leadership.[212] One Talib, interviewed in Pakistan during this time, remarked that:

We sacrificed our pure Islamic government for the sake of one unimportant man: Osama bin Laden. [...] Osama should have left the country when he saw that America's sword was hanging over our heads. Thousands of Afghan lives were sacrificed for his safety.[213]

While another looked forward:

We don't need the help of Osama his Qaeda or any other foreigners. We will not allow these outsiders to steal our Islamic movement again.[214]

The Taliban and al-Qaeda were not in regular contact since their respective leaderships had crossed the border, and mostly they were not staying in the same areas, but both groups understood the new dynamics. They watched from the outside in Pakistan as foreigners arrived only to see a parcelling out of power and patronage to many of the strongmen whom the Taliban had exerted their efforts to remove during the mid-1990s.[215] Another reason for the lack of a solid political programme was the fact that many of the movement's political minds were now being held in Guantánamo or in Afghan jails. This did not entirely rule out certain initiatives being made. In November 2002, senior Taliban figures gathered in Pakistan and considered making an offer to the Afghan government to work together.

I was there at the meeting. Mullah Mohammad Omar wasn't there, but everyone else was, all the high-ranking ministers and cabinet members of the Taliban. We discussed whether to join the political process in Afghanistan or not and we took a decision that, yes, we should go and join the process. But later some other hands entered into the mix and sabotaged our decision on this matter. Some other Talibs—small Talibs—who were outside the inner circle started to turn people against us and also propaganda started to come into play. They would say things like: 'these are not real Talibs! They are just *Harakat-e Enqelab-e Islami* people trying to join up in the political process. Make sure not to join up in the political process with them.' It was sabotage. So it came to nothing, but the fact of us all having come to a decision was an important moment, even though it fell apart.[216]

One interlocutor asked to engage with this group at the time has since stated that this was an important moment for the Taliban leadership; if they had been given some assurance that they would not be arrested upon returning to Afghanistan, he said, they would have come, but neither the Afghan government nor their international sponsors saw any reason to engage with the Taliban at that point in time—they were a spent force.[217]

In the first eighteen months after being ousted from power, the Taliban movement disintegrated into its natural components, and parts of the movement attempted to fill the void by creating alternative groupings. In early 2002, a group led by Mawlawi Nabi Mohammedi's son broke away from the main movement and revived a group called *Jamiat-i Khudam ul-Qur'an*,[218] but they were later absorbed again. This offshoot was set up as a 'moderate' alternative to the Taliban movement itself. They were reportedly supported by Pakistan, but by 2004 there was little enthusiasm for the group.[219]

Another group, *Jaish ul-Muslimeen*, broke from the Taliban over the progression of the insurgency in September 2003. This group was actually led by a Kandahari commander, Sayyed Akbar Agha, who had managed to attract some other prominent figures following his dispute over the speed at which the insurgency was being stepped up. Akbar Agha himself was arrested by Pakistani forces in Pakistan in December 2004, and the group was in any case losing support by then. As with *Khudam ul-Qur'an*, the group was later reabsorbed into the main Taliban structure. In retrospect, this group had little to do with a political vision for the Taliban; they were mainly engaged in criminal activities.[220]

This, however, was not a moment at which the Taliban leadership decided to join up with al-Qaeda and the other foreign jihadis on the run in Pakistan. There was little or no political activity during this time except from 2003 on, when several local communities in Afghanistan started to reach out to former Taliban commanders and the political leadership. Even among sections of the senior commanders, there was initially little support for the idea to reignite an insurgency; it would be the actions of the foreign military forces and the Afghan government that would push a significant part of them in that direction as the years passed.[221]

The last years of the Taliban's rule—the increasingly idiosyncratic and conservative edicts they issued together with the opium ban and forced conscription—had seen their support base erode and had given them little space to reemerge from within local communities, in particular in their former strongholds where society was polarised by their rule.[222] People were happy so see the back of them, especially as the new government promised positive changes in their lives. It was only as the realities of the new regime and the behaviour of its foreign accomplices became clear—the entrenched corruption within the Afghan government and its 'favouritism,'[223] along with night raids and discrimination—that individuals and certain groups started to lose faith in Karzai's new order.[224]

The United States' lack of political vision—Bush clearly stated that he had no interest in nation-building[225]—ran in concert with that of their chosen allies like Shirzai, who even after the ousting of the Taliban still seemed instrumental for the 'War on Terror,' but who used his considerable room for manoeuvre to capture the local state apparatus. Individuals, warlords, and semi-warlords fought about shares in the state and monopolised access to the government, foreign forces and resources. These dynamics continue to shape Afghanistan's political landscape today and played an important role in facilitating conditions for the return of the Taliban.[226]

In Kandahar, Shirzai and his contemporaries consolidated their power and settled old and new scores.[227] The United States unknowingly became their instrument, at times being used to act on false intelligence provided by these Afghan partners. Entire tribes—the Eshaqzai in Maiwand, a district west of Kandahar City, for example—were systematically targeted and denounced as Taliban members, leading to their arrest.[228] Family, *qawm* and tribal members of senior Taliban were harassed and deprived of access to the government, thereby marginalising them. The Noorzai tribe, members of which had previously held government positions during the Taliban's Emirate in Spin Boldak, were extensively sidelined by the Achekzai with the help of Shirzai.[229] Local power struggles continued as the years went by. Shirzai was fighting with one of his own commanders, Khalid Pashtun, over the distribution of power while other tribal leaders consolidated their hold over villages and districts.

The vacuum that followed the ejection of the Taliban left ample space in which old and new conflicts might erupt. Bandits and rogue commanders seized the opportunity to resume their trade, while family members of Taliban and tribal elders fell victim to abuses by individuals associated with the new interim government and were further alienated.[230] Individuals and communities who saw themselves marginalised, or who seemingly by default became the opposition to the new government, actively reached out to the Taliban leadership that was regrouping across the border from Kandahar, in Quetta, Pakistan. This gave the fledgling resurgent movement a contact network and footholds into local communities throughout 2002.[231]

Similar processes are still continuing today: local communities regard the government as corrupt and unjust; often actively targeted and excluded, they side with the Taliban in a mixture of ways (from tacit non-objection to offering direct support), and more out of pragmatism than from ideological motives.

The Taliban, meanwhile, have employed a mixture of tactics: from intimidation to exploitation of local conflicts in order to coerce and reward local communities into cooperating with them.[232]

From the outset the insurgency projected, based on its religious tenets, the same core message as it did in the early 1990s: security and justice. It is as much the failure of a non-functional government on a local level as it is due to the Taliban's propaganda campaign that much of the population in southern and eastern Afghanistan later bought into this point of view; then as now, perception was all.[233]

Militarily, the Taliban leadership was still consolidating its hold over the various groups that had begun fighting. As outlined earlier, its leadership and command structure is a meta-organisation that aims to lead and enforce its will over the multitude of groups that see themselves in opposition to the Afghan government and foreign forces. As we will see, from 2003 onwards the leadership has been much concerned with group cohesion and strengthening its chain of command and hold over individual commanders. There were some early high profile attacks against foreign forces and the new government, but the movement had not mobilised itself formally and politically in a centralised manner.

This early period of 2002 saw some attacks, but these were—for the most part—small guerrilla operations with only a few men and often mounted from Pakistan. These took place either in the south-east or around Kabul, and there seemed to be no wider logic to how they were being carried out.[234] By the end of the year and in early 2003, the Taliban were issuing threats to teachers in some areas of southern Afghanistan, and during the summer they assaulted Afghan soldiers and outposts that involved groups of up to fifty insurgents.[235] On 27 January 2003, for example, a large group of Taliban fighters were surprised near Spin Boldak (Kandahar province) when they encountered an international military patrol, one of the first prominent indications of their early resurgence.[236]

In June 2003, four German ISAF soldiers were killed in a suicide attack in Kabul, most likely facilitated by al-Qaeda affiliates or Hekmatyar's *Hizb-e Islami*.[237] The Taliban's assassination campaign against local elders and government affiliates really began in spring 2003.[238] Training camps (as many as seven) were reported to be operating in Pakistan for Taliban fighters.[239] The most significant development in 2003, though, was the establishment and focus on Dai Chopan district of Zabul province as a sanctuary for Afghan Taliban fighters.[240]

Outside the areas that the Taliban had decided to focus on in 2003, smaller groups, initially operating on their own, had started to coordinate, and it was this initial core nucleus that the Taliban's political leadership-in-hiding committed to supporting and encouraging in the years that followed.[241] Early on, the groups that emerged used communication as one of their key weapons, issuing night letters to individuals who cooperated with the new interim government or the foreign forces; they often were able to address entire villages and communities by posting the letter near the local mosque. Many local mullahs also sided with the insurgency and facilitated communication with the population.[242] The so-called mullah networks were important for the dispersal and gathering of information. The mullahs had also been marginalised after the Taliban's fall, even in traditional strongholds like Kandahar, and a revival in 2003 saw them looking to regain some of that influence.[243]

From Pakistan, the Taliban's leadership had erected a formal structure to lead the insurgency and consolidate its power. In early June 2003, the formation of the *rahbari* or leadership *shura* was announced.[244] This group was made up of ten members and was responsible for the Taliban's political and military strategy. It was led by Mullah Mohammad Omar, but included most of the older generation of Taliban leaders—those who had fought together during the 1980s—remaining from their rule a few years earlier. Most were Kandaharis, but space was made for Jalaluddin Haqqani, for example.[245]

Around the time the *shura* was formed, recruitment began in a serious manner.[246] Mullah Dadullah was dispatched by Mullah Mohammad Omar to the madrassas of Baluchistan and Karachi, reportedly accompanied by Pakistani authorities.[247] Mullah Obaidullah was also reportedly involved in recruitment efforts in early 2003:

The Taliban's defense minister, Mullah Obaidullah, came to see me—the first senior Taliban leader I had seen since our collapse. He was traveling around Pakistan to rally our dispersed forces. Half the Taliban leadership was back in touch with each other, he said, and they were determined to start a resistance movement to expel the Americans. I didn't think it was possible, but he assured me I could help. He said to meet him again in two weeks, and gave me an address. I was surprised at the number and rank of the people I found at the meeting. There were former senior ministers and military commanders, all sitting together, all eager to resist the Americans. Obaidullah told me: 'We don't need you as a deputy minister or bureaucrat. We want you to bring as many fighters as you can into the field.'[248]

This early period following the fall of the Taliban movement does not reveal an evolving political and military strategy, but rather offers examples of its leadership reacting to circumstances. It was, however, the developments within Afghanistan—the failure of the new government to capitalise on the political will and support of the people, and the strategic mistake of handing over the government to former strongmen and warlords—that aided the Taliban's return.

This was particularly true in the south and east of the country, but, as we shall see later, in the north as well, built on the conflict lines between communities, local leaders and the individuals who took power in the new Afghan government.

Al-Qaeda's Goals

Al-Qaeda and the foreign jihadis were in a very different position from that of the Taliban in 2001–2003. The sudden collapse of the Taliban brought about a fundamental change in the environment in which al-Qaeda had to operate, a change that would mean shifts in its operational structure and indeed in its role in the jihadi universe. Al-Qaeda could no longer tap into readily available fighters in training camps and recruit the most promising and able candidates for its cause. While it had already been highly sensitive to its operational security, the new environment and circumstances meant a far greater compartmentalisation of the organisation.[249]

Nevertheless, the retreat option that doubtlessly was discussed and prepared for was North Waziristan. Bin Laden had long-standing ties with the local communities there reaching back into the 1980s, and had maintained multiple guesthouses there throughout the years.[250] A sizeable number of foreign mujahedeen had settled among the tribes of the mountainous borderlands.[251] Bin Laden and his fighters seem to have initially found refuge among the same communities.[252]

A first wave of foreign fighters crossed over into Pakistan in mid-December 2001, while a second followed in March 2002 after suffering defeat at Shahi Kot.[253] One witness to the arrival recalled:

I watched as wounded, disabled, and defeated Taliban fighters straggled into Wana and the surrounding villages, along with Arabs, Chechens, and Uzbeks. Every morning as I went to school I could see them wandering around town, almost like homeless beggars. Little by little, the tribal people started helping them, giving them food. Some people even took them into their houses; at first these once proud jihadis survived, thanks to the people's charity. The Arabs were disappointed the Taliban hadn't stood and fought. They told me they had wanted to fight to the death. They were clearly not as distressed as the Afghans. That was understandable. The Arabs felt they had lost a battle. But the Afghans were much more devastated—they had lost their country.[254]

Bin Laden issued belligerent statements during this period, all the while taking care not to claim personal responsibility for the September 11 attacks. In October he was urging 'every Muslim' to 'rise and defend his religion' and that 'America will not live in peace before peace reigns in Palestine, and before all the army of infidels depart the land of Mohammad.'[255] In November, a statement was issued hitting out at the United Nations' involvement in the conflict in Afghanistan and criticising 'the West' for supporting the 'oppressive campaign' against the Taliban.[256] In December he continued to make his case for a defensive *jihad*:

The events of 22nd Jumada al-Thani, or Aylul [September 11] are merely a response to the continuous injustice inflicted upon our sons in Palestine, Iraq, Somalia, southern Sudan, and other places, like Kashmir. The matter concerns the entire *umma*. People need to wake up from their sleep and try to find a solution to this catastrophe that is threatening all of humanity. Those who condemn these operations [9/11] have viewed the event in isolation and have failed to connect it to previous events or to the reasons behind it. Their view is blinkered and lacks either a legitimate or a rational basis.[257]

There were numerous cases of international Islamist plots and attacks from 2001–2003. They included an airline plot and attacks in Singapore and Tunisia in 2001. In 2002–2003 there were attacks in Yemen, Kenya, Saudi Arabia as well as in Indonesia and Turkey.[258]

The fall of the Taliban government in December 2001 had come too soon for bin Laden, who was hoping for a far greater defence to be mounted. In fact, a situation more akin to a rerun of the 1980s war was closer to bin Laden's initial vision that he thought would materialise immediately. In a letter written to Mullah Mohammad Omar dated 3 October 2001, he explained:

A U.S. campaign against Afghanistan will cause great long-term economic burdens [on the United States] which will force America to resort to the former Soviet Union's only option: withdrawal from Afghanistan, disintegration, and contraction.[259]

Three key principles defined his strategic calculus during the early years while in hiding. Survival was the foremost priority. Bin Laden was a symbol of al-Qaeda by this time, and he needed to ensure that he was not killed or captured. At the same time, though, visibility was also a priority; al-Qaeda needed to continue to demonstrate operational capacity (although many of the attacks carried out in the first years following September 11 were to some extent preplanned by the leadership). It also had to continue functioning as a catalyst for other groups; this was all the more important as their own scope for activity was limited. Thus, Al-Qaeda set out to consolidate and enlist other groups to act on its behalf.

Once the foreign jihadists had arrived across the border into Pakistan, they then moved elsewhere: Arabs to North and South Waziristan and Bajaur,[260] Uzbeks to Wana in South Waziristan where they found support among Ahmadzai Wazir tribesmen,[261] and others back to the Gulf or Arab countries.[262] The foreigners had brought money with them to exchange for hospitality.[263] Some of the senior al-Qaeda and affiliated members went to the urban centres in Pakistan; they were often hosted by Pakistani jihadi groups.[264]

The al-Qaeda leadership also aimed to capitalise on the September 11 attacks; they had not only caused a rift between the West and many Islamic movements, but had also somewhat polarised the Muslim world, with support for bin Laden spiking initially.[265] For their relationship with the Taliban, this continued sense of purpose (albeit in different circumstances) initially meant very little; al-Qaeda was trying to mobilise outside support, drive forward plots outside Pakistan and Afghanistan, and consolidate its ranks with other groups, while the leadership tried to stay alive. Moreover, many Talibs were angry at the foreign jihadis for having taken unilateral action that had such catastrophic results for their movement.[266]

Initially, there were attempts by foreign jihadists to provoke and stir up the senior Taliban leadership to mobilise an uprising within Afghanistan, but this fell on deaf ears.[267] There is likely to have been some contact between the two groups—they now faced the same enemy and similar circumstances in Pakistan—but certainly this was limited to discussion about Afghanistan; it was not a moment when the Taliban decided on the validity of waging a global *jihad*.

In the face of overwhelming international pressure, Musharraf made a speech on national television on 12 January 2002, in which he banned several Pakistani-based jihadi groups, including *Jaish-e Mohammad, Sipah-e Sahaba Pakistan, Lashkar-e Jhangvi, Sipah-e Mohammad, Lashkar-e Taiba, Harakat ul-Mujahedeen*,[268] but this pronouncement was mostly a smokescreen for a widespread renaming and reforging of jihadist parent groups.[269] At the time of the speech, there were reportedly twenty-four different Pakistani jihadist groups, although the lines between them were undoubtedly highly blurred.[270]

Soon after the invasion of Afghanistan, bin Laden took a strategic decision to open up a battlefront in Saudi Arabia that saw the return of several hundred Saudi jihadis from Afghanistan in spring 2002. Preparations were made under the leadership of Sheikh Yusuf al-Uyayri that would culminate in the establishment of its first branch, al-Qaeda on the Arabian Peninsula (AQAP).[271]

While the central leadership was sending out forces to Saudi Arabia, the impact of the United States' reaction to the September 11 attacks and the launch of Operation Enduring Freedom meant an increase of leading jihadist figures signing up to join al-Qaeda. While al-Qaeda's campaign in Saudi Arabia came to little, 2003 saw a number of suicide bombings and attacks in the Kingdom.[272]

The Haqqanis Turn Away from the State

Jalaluddin Haqqani had remained rather passive after being appointed by Mullah Mohammad Omar as overall military commander of the Afghan Taliban.[273] It appears that he was more concerned with his own situation at the time, moving to North Waziristan and not sacrificing capital or lives in the defence of the Taliban government. One source claims that Pakistan's ISI chief warned him not to hand over al-Qaeda members just days before the air assault of October 2001 commenced.[274]

While Jalaluddin and his family retreated to Waziristan, the Bonn Conference commenced, appointing the transitional government. The Border Affairs post went to Amanullah Zadran, the brother of Jalaluddin's archenemy, Padshah Khan Zadran.[275] Jalaluddin made overtures to the government in the early years, sending his brother Ibrahim to Kabul in 2002, only to have him be humiliated, beaten up and sent back.[276] Given this environment and the threat to his business interests, Jalaluddin decided to join the insurgency and pick up the fight. His enemies had gained a strong foothold in the government, and his political advances were rebuffed. Even though he had opposed the Taliban in the 1990s and only joined them later, he decided once again to fight under its banner. As one analyst explained, this decision was probably informed by the fact that alone he would have lost credibility and would simply have been one of many warlords fighting against the government. The Islamic Emirate conferred a sense of legitimacy on his actions.[277]

Jalaluddin's group is still recognised as an autonomous entity within the Taliban, though, a network set apart from the rest of the Afghan Taliban insurgency. The group's leadership is primarily bound together by tribal lineage and family membership, and his son Serajuddin has already taken over much of the day-to-day operational concerns. The relationship between the Haqqanis and al-Qaeda will be explored in greater detail in subsequent chapters.

Interactions

The relationship between the Taliban and al-Qaeda during this period was governed by circumstance. Although the senior leadership of both groups hid in Pakistan, their respective situations differed significantly: the Taliban leadership found itself destroyed, disorganised and without a plan, while al-Qaeda had more experience and durability in a situation like this. Given the lack of organisation and formal structures among the Taliban leadership, interactions between the two groups relied on personal ties and links rather than any kind of formal contact. There was considerable physical distance between the two, however, since the tribal areas of North and South Waziristan in which many al-Qaeda members took refuge were far away from Quetta and Baluchistan where the Afghan Taliban had far stronger roots and connections. Those who retreated into Pakistan aligned themselves along old ties and friendships.[278]

On an abstract level, this early period saw the gap between the Taliban and al-Qaeda closing on account of the American presence within Afghanistan (in terms of how they were defined publicly in the world at large) as well as on account of their actions. The aftermath of the 2001 war in Afghanistan saw a significant influx of a large number of international jihadists. Bin Laden and others like the Shu'aybis in Saudi Arabia had called on Muslims to join the Taliban even before the September 11 attacks, and these calls led to an influx of non-Afghans wanting to fight the American presence in Afghanistan, and the movement had to deal with these new entrants.[279] The Taliban were, moreover, no longer a state and began an insurgent campaign against the foreign presence. The first attacks were uncoordinated; small groups in Afghanistan took up arms for a variety of reasons.

The Taliban's increasingly sophisticated media campaign is often given as evidence for the group's links with al-Qaeda. There is, however, little that connects the two in terms of direct media cooperation, and the expertise and knowledge that informed the Taliban's media department could easily have been facilitated by Pakistani groups or actors.

Al-Qaeda's media outreach was much more developed and comprehensive than that employed by the Taliban (at least initially), but Pakistani support for a Taliban propaganda campaign is much more likely to have been the decisive factor in taking it from zero to the current level of speed and sophistication. There is relatively little data on the exact nodes of interaction regarding the media programme, however.[280]

From around summer 2003, there are some accounts of foreign jihadists training Afghan Taliban fighters in Pakistan along the border in small groups of between five to eight trainees.[281] Here is one Afghan Taliban member, Qari Younas, describing these early years:

At first I didn't hear the Afghans talking about going back to fight. But the Arabs did, and they encouraged the Afghans and the local tribal people not to give up. Nothing much happened for the first year or so, but then the Arabs started organizing some training camps. The first one I heard about was at Shin Warsak village, near Wana. When I had some time off from school, I decided to visit. I was really impressed. There was more than one camp. One was run by Arabs, and another by Chechens and Uzbeks.[282]

Some crossover through host Pakistani groups and jihadis between the two groups seems much more likely than direct contact—these sometimes functioned as and offered sites for interaction, although this is more applicable to al-Qaeda than it is for the Afghan Taliban. The Afghan Taliban, after all, had places to go themselves, among the Afghan communities in Pakistan; they were far less 'foreign' a presence in Pakistan than the al-Qaeda members and affiliates. While there was a somewhat continuous foreign militant presence from the 1980s onwards in the tribal areas of Pakistan, the numbers involved never reached those following the 2001 war. Except for the very senior leadership, where there are anecdotes and indications of some time spent together during the early days,[283] this seems rather a point of disconnect between the two.

Al-Qaeda members continued to spread and propagate their ideology and world view amongst local groups and populations in the tribal areas as they had done during the 1980s. The Afghan Taliban were much less involved in this, as they do not seem to have seen this as their role; if at all, the Taliban would have been asking for support for the fight against the foreign forces, quite a different thing from that which the foreign fighters were seeking. Interviewees state that there were some individual contacts over strategic matters (i.e., broad long-term considerations) in these early years, but this was more than the Taliban were interested at that time as they had not yet conclusively decided on their stance and plan.[284]

While the Afghan Taliban leadership was still discussing possible steps, a number of al-Qaeda affiliates and Taliban associates in Gardez staged what perhaps was the largest set-piece military engagement with international and Afghan-government-affiliated fighters: the battle of Shahi Kot, also known as Operation Anaconda. Between 100 and 5000 fighters[285] (mostly foreign, but there were Afghans present) had gathered in the Shahi Kot area and fought for several days against a concerted attempt to expel them.[286] It took place between 1–19 March, 2002.[287] If Tora Bora in December 2001 had not offered the final battle for al-Qaeda and the foreign militants, Shahi Kot in March 2002 was the corrective to that. There do not seem to have been senior al-Qaeda or foreign political figures present, but rather mid-level militants who had spent some time digging in and preparing themselves for an assault on their positions.[288]

9

REDUX (2003–2009)

When the Taliban governed we were not happy. They were too harsh and they oppressed people. When the Americans came we thought they would bring prosperity and be good for the country. But after they started injuring and killing and oppressing people we realised that the Americans were not here to help, but to help themselves and impose their will on us. Right now we don't have a problem with the Taliban. It is clear what the US and the Karzai government are doing. What reservations we have with the Taliban are overshadowed. We will sort them out when we have kicked out the Americans.

Mullah Qudratullah, July 2006[1]

What we want are posts in Karzai's government. As soon as we are part of the government and as soon as all foreigners leave, we will stop fighting.

Taliban field commander, Panjwayi district (Kandahar), 2006[2]

2003–2005

2003–2005 saw the Taliban consolidating and setting up structures to mobilise support in order to expand and popularise an insurgency throughout Afghanistan. The Afghan state was itself attaining more of the architecture of power—through the *loya jirga* of 2003 and Afghanistan's new constitution in

261

January 2004—and was slowly putting in place a highly centralised political system with considerable presidential powers.

Local perceptions had started to shift in late 2003. While the majority of the population had been supportive early on, by 2003 communities in southern and eastern Afghanistan had found themselves sidelined and at times openly targeted by the new authorities. In a replay of processes last seen in 1994 in southern Afghanistan, parts of the communities started reaching out to the Taliban who at the same time started to actively reach out to former allies and commanders. The failure of the Taliban's meeting in late 2002, the opening of the detention camp at Guantánamo Bay in the same year, and the experiences of individuals such as Mullah Zaeef and Mullah Mutawakil, were all visible and active representations of US policy towards Afghan Taliban members and the local populations out of which they had grown. The developments were further helped along by America's invasion of Iraq, which saw the United States shift its focus to the new war in the Middle East.

This period covers the initial attempts of the Taliban to field an insurgency around the country up until the time when it started to gain momentum and bring significant areas under its control. It also precedes the arrival of NATO troops and the expansion of a foreign military presence in southern and, to a lesser extent, eastern Afghanistan.

Taliban Goals

In Kabul, 2002 was the time at which a series of political milestones administered by the United Nations began: a *loya jirga* in 2002, another constitutional *loya jirga* in 2003, the ratification of the constitution in January 2004, and by October the same year Karzai was being voted in as President of Afghanistan.[3]

By 2003, however, the senior Taliban leadership based in Pakistan had either been themselves targeted inside Afghanistan (and then fled) or had received calls for support from communities in the country; there was a sense of affront. This slow aggravation of the movement's members' grievances in 2002–2003 was helped along by the Afghan government as well as by the foreign military forces.[4] For example, in Ghazni:

The Americans and their Afghan allies made mistake after mistake, killing and arresting innocent people. There was one village in Dayak district near Ghazni City where the people had communist backgrounds, from the days of the Russians, and had never supported us. But the police raided the village, beat the elders at a mosque and arrested them, accusing them of being Taliban. They were freed after heavy bribes were paid.

After that incident the whole village sent us a message asking forgiveness for the abuses of the communist era.[5]

The Taliban's priorities were relatively simple at this stage. Politically, Mullah Mohammad Omar had rhetorically committed to a fight against the 'imperialist invader' already in 2001, stating clearly in an interview with the BBC that, 'we will not accept a government of wrong-doers. We prefer death than to be a part of an evil government.'[6] The stance he took in 2001 was less ideological than that being promoted by al-Qaeda; Mullah Mohammad Omar drew a historical line connecting the Taliban's struggle post-2001 with the wars against the British over a century ago.[7]

The initial attempts to mobilise the insurgency had been put together along predominantly tribal lines, albeit not for specifically tribal reasons from the Taliban's perspective. The Afghan local government represented a small part of the Pashtun areas' tribal diversity, and whole groups that were left out were eager to find an outlet for their discontent and to defend themselves. At first, the insurgency was slow to pick up, in part because dissatisfaction with the Afghan government and the foreign reconstruction presence had yet to bubble over into discontent.

Militarily, plans were made for a series of operations to take place in the summer of 2003. Mullah Dadullah led a successful attempt to take Dai Chopan district of Zabul and much of Paktika province was also captured during this time.[8] 2004 saw activity in Uruzgan and Kandahar provinces, and 2005–2006 saw Helmand come into focus for the Taliban along with Ghazni, Paktya, Khost, Lowgar and Farah.[9] Suicide operations, moreover, had grown as a prominent tactic in mid-to-late 2005 in the south and south-east. The high point of this initial strategy was the Taliban's battle for Pashmol in September 2006 (see below).

The operations mounted by the Taliban in the summer of 2003 were relatively small, and targeted in purpose. The attack in Ghazni against a vehicle carrying Afghan Red Crescent staff in August 2003[10] is such an example, as is the kidnap of a Turkish engineer in Zabul.[11] The winter before had been spent planning and organising the logistics, although there were no special tactics or training needed at this stage. Weapons and manpower were the first priority, but both appear to have been available in ample supply.[12]

Al-Qaeda's Goals

Support from al-Qaeda and their affiliates for the Taliban during this period was sporadic and borne out of shared circumstance. There is very little evidence

263

or reason to suggest that al-Qaeda was heavily involved in working together with the Taliban; strategically, the Taliban followed the path they had decided upon in late 2002/2003, albeit with some tactical adjustments along the way. In fact, incidents attributed to al-Qaeda or their affiliates began to stack up during the 2003–2005 period: attacks in Casablanca in May 2003; multiple suicide bombings in March 2004; similar attacks in London in July 2005; bombings in Sharm al-Sheikh, Egypt, in July 2005; and further bombings in Delhi, India, in October and Amman, Jordan, in November of the same year.[13]

A report of an al-Qaeda strategic meeting that took place in 2004 (one week before General Khattak's offensive)[14] tells of senior leaders (including Abu Faraj al-Libi) discussing future plans; at the top of the agenda were plans to carry out attacks in the UK and USA.[15]

In Pakistan, where many of them were based during this time, there were a series of events which al-Qaeda and other foreign militants had to react to and engage with. April 2004 saw the Pakistani Army (led by General Khattak) mount a military operation to hunt al-Qaeda fighters; it was the largest since September 11.[16] Nek Mohammad was killed in June 2004; he had been the leader of local militants sheltering al-Qaeda fighters in the area between Wana and Azam Warzak.[17] In mid-2004 there was a wave of arrests of al-Qaeda figures: Ahmed Khalfan Ghailani was captured in Gujrat in July 2005; Abu Faraj al-Libi was captured in Mardan; Abu Hamza Rabia was killed in December 2005 in North Waziristan (he was the chief of al-Qaeda operations in Pakistan following al-Libi's arrest).[18]

In statements made by bin Laden and al-Zawahiri during this time, Iraq was the central focus.[19] Pakistan was the core hub from which the central al-Qaeda leadership could function, but Iraq was their main concern during this period. A number of attacks carried out in Turkey, Indonesia, Iraq, Saudi Arabia and Pakistan were attributed to and at times claimed by al-Qaeda. At least some operations appear to have been organised by independent cells or affiliated groups. 2003 also saw much activity by al-Qaeda in the Arabian Peninsula with several attacks carried out in the Kingdom of Saudi Arabia.[20] Indeed, al-Qaeda statements during the period did the following things:

1) showed that the central leadership remained alive
2) incited and commented on events
3) claimed responsibility for certain attacks
4) influenced international politics—as bin Laden attempted with his statement a few days prior to the November 2004 US presidential election

Even if the Taliban had been interested in some sort of cooperation with al-Qaeda, at this point it is difficult to see what interaction there could have been aside from strategic advice; al-Qaeda were in no position to support the Taliban in any other way.

The Iraq War

The American invasion of Iraq was the key event during this period. The United States had already started to shift its focus away from Afghanistan soon after the fall of the Taliban, buoyed by a sense of expectation and possibility brought about by the success of its light-footed military engagement in Afghanistan. Special Forces teams and assorted military planning units found themselves reassigned to Iraq in late 2002 and early 2003 amid a sense that the Taliban was no longer a serious threat.[21] Even as early as 12 September 2001, US Secretary of Defense Donald Rumsfeld suggested Iraq as a possible target as part of the 'War on Terror.'[22]

Beginning in March 2003, but with a long lead period that fuelled discussion in Afghanistan and Pakistan, at least 15,000 Iraqis died in the immediate military invasion, and by 2007 there were 4.7 million refugees who had fled their homes or were living outside Iraq.[23] American and British unilateralism in the run-up to the commencement of military operations squandered considerable amounts of international political capital; this was only compounded in the aftermath of the collapse of Saddam Hussein's government and military, when so-called 'weapons of mass destruction' were not found, and as violence spiralled in the years that followed.

For the Taliban, the war further nourished the by-then common perception that America and allied foreign countries were involved in a conspiracy or 'crusade' against Muslim peoples (as it did around the Muslim world). The Taliban were, accordingly, outraged and the invasion and its later mismanagement played to their sense of affront as Muslims.[24] It had a massive effect in Pakistan, too, where the scenes reported from Iraq on Pakistani television provoked an intense and angry reaction.[25] The Afghan Taliban's public condemnation of the Iraq War was much more muted than might have been expected. Their communication channels were not as well-oiled as those of the non-Taliban groups. Indeed, one of the first statements[26] of public condemnation only came in September 2003, and the speaker, Mullah Hedayatullah, didn't spend long singling Iraq out:

'We urge you to resist the foreign occupation of the lands of Palestine, Chechnya, Afghanistan and Iraq,' he said. 'One could wonder what Iraq has done wrong,' he went on. 'They have not been able to find any weapons of mass destruction, and there is no Bin Ladin in Iraq, so why is it occupied?'[27]

In later years the Taliban took up the theme of Iraq and Afghanistan 'under occupation' much more often, but in the early days there was little Taliban commentary. Even Mullah Mohammad Omar's *eid* statement (issued at the beginning of the last week of November 2003) made little of the events happening in Iraq aside from an oblique reference to 'Islamic countries':

So-called democracy has been gifted to our mujahid nation in the form of killings, bombings, demolition of houses and promotion of un-Islamic practices and obscenity. [...] Our enemies want to weaken Islam by attacking the morals of Muslims, they are keen to tackle jihad under the pretext of fighting terrorism, and their goal to take control of the assets of Islamic countries.[28]

The Iraq War offered another example for the Taliban—in their statements—of a foreign power entering another country without any regard for its sovereignty. These statements often noted the 'imperialist' intentions of the foreigners. See, for instance, the interview with Mullah Berader in June 2009:

The war started by the Americans and their imperialist allies has clear materialistic and non-materialistic purposes which are not hidden from anyone. The drama of [the so-called threat of] terrorism is that it is a deceiving slogan used by the enemies to hide their imperialist objectives from the eyes of the world.[29]

For this reason, individual groups of Afghans going to train in Iraq (see below) or even to fight probably didn't do so out of any sense of Islamic internationalism, but rather went to the country for similar reasons that had led mujahedeen commanders to send Afghans to Saudi Arabia in 1990 (see chapter 4). This, again, is another instance where the Taliban's far more orthodox understanding of *jihad* is highlighted.

The diversion of American resources and attention to Iraq also meant that southern and south-eastern parts of Afghanistan were neglected for several years. The Taliban used this time to regroup and recruit; the Iraq War, of course, was a useful discussion point and rallying call for recruiters. Asked how the Middle East and Iraq helped the Taliban, Mansour Dadullah noted that:

It has a positive influence rather than a negative one. The war in Iraq and in Palestine keeps us supplied with soldiers and weapons.[30]

The implication there was that Iraq and Palestine functioned as reasons for people in Afghanistan to want to fight against their own 'Americans.'

For al-Qaeda and the foreign fighters based in Pakistan, the Iraq invasion was an opportunity, one that meshed with bin Laden's hopes for what would happen to the United States: American troops were now tied down on two separate fronts, far from home, and busy fighting the occasional attacks around the world by affiliates, franchise groups or branches of al-Qaeda. The invasion mobilised and rallied a large number of recruits directly into their hands, both in Iraq itself as well as in Western countries. The 7/7 bombings in London in 2005, for example, can trace their roots back to the Iraq invasion.[31]

In Iraq itself, direct al-Qaeda involvement was minimal. Al-Zarqawi, who pledged allegiance to al-Qaeda in October 2004,[32] had travelled into Iraq through the north and forged ties to a local group, *Ansar ul-Islam*, which was effective in stirring up local resentments. The top-tier leadership and heads of affiliate groups, however, did not travel to Iraq but remained for the most part in Pakistan. Some travelled to Saudi Arabia for the new front there.[33]

The Sinjar records, a catalogue of foreign fighters who passed through Iraq after 2006, show that many came from Saudi Arabia and Libya (as well as North Africa) rather than from Afghanistan. These fighters were mostly fighting out of a sense of grievance at a perceived foreign aggression against Islam, rather than out of any loyalty or pledge to al-Qaeda.[34]

As a tactic, suicide bombings were used often. Al-Zarqawi sought to provoke a chaotic civil war, but his brutality provoked terse messages from bin Laden and al-Zawahiri, who were wary of granting official franchise status to al-Zarqawi as he seemed to be alienating people rather than winning them over.[35] A pledge was eventually made in October 2004, but not without misgivings.[36] Al-Zarqawi had targeted Iraqis working with the new government in the police and armed forces, civilian contractors and NGO workers as well as Shi'ites.[37]

The Iraq war did not precipitate significant changes for the Taliban or al-Qaeda, although the propaganda and recruitment opportunity was not lost on either. The Taliban continued with their own strategy, and now they had some breathing space in which to incrementally take areas and win groups over while American attention was diverted. For al-Qaeda, Iraq offered an opportunity for intense involvement, but the top leadership were not involved in circumstances on the ground, offering management and commentary from time to time, from afar. The group continued their encouragement of internationalist groups as well as their old goal of striking at Saudi Arabia. The Madrid Bombings are a good example of an attack where the senior al-Qaeda leadership did not even have to engage in the plot—a Spanish investigation 'found no evidence that al-Qa'ida helped plan, finance or carry out the bombings, or even knew about them in advance'[38]—since 'inspiration' from propaganda videos and statements had a similar effect.[39]

Al-Qaeda Training the Taliban

Published in September 2005, an article in *Newsweek* carried a full report based on interviews with two Taliban commanders who had reportedly travelled and trained in Iraq.[40] The interviews described small teams travelling to Iraq via Iran at the instigation of bin Laden himself. Teams seemed to be drawn from the south-east (Lowgar and Khost were the two provinces cited in the article) and Afghans travelled together with Arabs and some Central Asians. They were taught IED techniques—particularly that of the 'shaped charge'—but were not allowed to fight themselves.[41] Interviews conducted for this book (and others), though, indicate that the number of Afghans travelling to Iraq was extremely small, and that if there was any significant training it took place in Pakistan in the border regions.[42] One account published in a later article in *Newsweek* ran as follows:

Arab and Iraqi mujahedin began visiting us, transferring the latest IED technology and suicide-bomber tactics they had learned in the Iraqi resistance during combat with U.S. forces. The American invasion of Iraq was very positive for us. It distracted the United States from Afghanistan. Until 2004 or so, we were using traditional means of fighting like we used against the Soviets—AK-47s and RPGs. But then our resistance became more lethal, with new weapons and techniques: bigger and better IEDs for roadside bombings, and suicide attacks.[43]

The massive increase in the use of IEDs in the wake of the Iraq war is often directly attributed to training or exchanges of information such as those described in the *Newsweek* article. Interviews conducted for this book, however, relate that these training trips were far from common. The Iraq war revealed the conventional military's weakness when exposed to the use of IEDs,[44] but this wasn't a new tactic for Afghanistan. Afghan fighters had used types of IEDs during the *jihad* against the Soviet Union.[45] Even today, serving American soldiers have testified that compared to the complex, advanced charges that they often found in Iraq, those in Afghanistan have posed fewer problems[46] since the Taliban prefer to rely on the size of explosive material used rather than a complex setup.

Taliban Structures

The organisational and command structure of the Taliban movement closely mirrors their key objective. While much has changed since the 1990s when the Taliban first rose to power, their priorities have not. They continue to focus on security and justice. With these two priorities, the movement reinvented itself to fight as an insurgency that focused on the population from the out-set. While their military organisation borrows much of its operational structure from the mujahedeen fronts that fought against the Soviets in the 1980s, as well as the movement's own operational culture from the 1990s, the organisational structure has evolved over time to cope with the challenges the Taliban faced. Parallel to their military operations, the Taliban have fielded a shadow government, giving areas under their control or influence an administrative oversight that allows the local population to engage with them; they provide 'security and justice' through mobile, and in some cases static, courts addressing local grievances. Control is exerted not through military dominance but through the local population: the Taliban exploit local conflict and use their sophisticated propaganda machine to separate local people from the government and foreign forces, much as the foreign forces have long aimed to distance them from the local population.[47]

The structure of the Taliban-led insurgency in Afghanistan is somewhat paradoxical. While the core leadership has formed solid administrative structures under the leadership of Mullah Mohammad Omar, the exact composition and details of operational processes remain unclear. Official Taliban media outlets and independent research offer an outline of the Taliban's administrative structure, one that has evolved out of the initial leadership council formed in 2003, which remains the central organ among the administrative apparatus.

The central organ originally formed in Quetta (often referred to as the Quetta *shura*) is the *rahbari* or leadership *shura*. This was expanded on several occasions, beginning with a membership of eleven, but is currently believed to number up to thirty-three. Today the *rahbari shura* in Quetta has a parallel structure in Peshawar.[48] While the overall leadership lies with Mullah Mohammad Omar, day-to-day operations and decisions are made by the head of the *shura*, who can be regarded as the overall commander guiding the Taliban in its operations. The *nizami shura* is the Taliban's military council, sub-divided into four individual councils in Quetta, Miram Shah, Peshawar and Girdi Jangal. The Taliban have a dedicated apparatus of individuals who are responsible for the assassination campaign that they have been implementing since 2003; it is likely that the individuals involved in the campaign are part of the Taliban's secret police.[49] Many of the administrative functions of the Taliban are fulfilled by committees under the control of the provincial *shura*. Committees include the Group of Directors, Provincial Commissions, Administrative, Cultural, Political, Military, Complaints, Recruitment, Prisoner and

Martyrs' Families Affairs as well as, in all likelihood by now, a mediation and appeals commission.[50]

The relationship between the various elements of the leadership based in Pakistan and the commanders in Afghanistan is more complex. As we outlined earlier, the command structure as well as the components that form the insurgency on the ground are less organised and rely on a mixture of personal contacts and local conflict drivers. The Taliban have tried to account for the nature of the insurgency by introducing administrative processes that allow for considerable independence and decision-making on the ground, while making sure that the central leadership remains in command. Section six of the most recent Taliban rule book lays out, in over 400 words, how the leadership envisions local governance structures behaving and evolving.[51]

While the administrative structure—with its various organs and institutions—suggests a clear hierarchy, the ground realities of the insurgency reveal an amorphous network of groups and individuals. None of the organs mentioned in press communiqués or interviews have listed a dedicated logistics department or central procurement office, another sign of the semi-independent nature of the field commanders.

Military Command and Operations

As described earlier, the military forces of the Taliban are constructed on the basis of the *andiwaal* system. Strategic operations are normally controlled, planned and sanctioned by the Taliban's top leadership in Quetta (often including its military commanders) and handed down to regional and local *shura*s and commanders. Independent initiatives, depending on scale and type, often need approval by the relevant regional *shura*; this does not always hold true, though, as the nature of small units in the *andiwaal* system almost guarantees at least some level of independence of action and thought. Almost all operations seem to at least pass through a higher level of oversight (whether that is a commander's immediate superior within a specific district or a *Mawlawi* or some such senior cleric based in Quetta).

Higher levels of command are directly appointed by the Quetta *shura* and dispatched or sent to lead *andiwaal* groups in an area or region.[52] This direct control has been demonstrated several times in southern Afghanistan, for example, when the Quetta *shura* ordered a reshuffling of commanders, switching the midlevel commanders from one province to the next, pairing them with local deputy commanders who provide the local expertise.[53] In order to ensure compliance and to exert more control as well as to strengthen communication with the individual cells and commanders, the Quetta *shura* has a long established group of messengers who travel back and forth between the central command in Pakistan and the regional commanders; this includes networks of women.[54]

In Kandahar, for example, there are usually two or three senior commanders for the more important districts (Maiwand, Zheray and Panjwayi). Subcommanders below them function as facilitators—especially if their superior is not originally from Kandahar.[55] A rotation system is also in place that takes commanders away from the field for a few months each year and brings them to Quetta where they are familiarised with the system and hierarchy above them; this is similar to Taliban practices during the late 1990s, when governors and commanders were often switched around to prevent the emergence of strongmen. The Taliban leadership is aware of the dangers of individuals achieving financial independence within their organisation, a pitfall that has often led to the splintering of other insurgent groups who gain access to financial resources that allow them to ignore the leadership and pursue their own goals and objectives.

In late 2003, when Mullah Mutawakil was released from US detention in Bagram, there seems to have been some enforcing of the central Taliban line.[56] His brother was killed in Quetta in an attack that seemed designed to send a warning signal to possible independent figures within the movement.[57] In 2006, Mullah Khaksar was also killed; his was a far more straightforward case (at least on the surface) in that he had surrendered to the Northern Alliance on their capture of Kabul, but his assassination was again seen as a warning.[58] Even for the Haqqani network, Serajuddin Haqqani often takes considerable pains to communicate that they see themselves as subjects and mere followers of the leadership in Quetta; the reality is, of course, considerably more complicated, and the Haqqani network has considerable independence. Here is one example:

'The Haqqani Group or the Haqqani Network Group is not an official name or a name we chose. This name is used by the enemies in order to divide the Mujahideen. We are under the highly capable Emirate of the Amir of the Faithful Mullah Umar, may Allah protect him, and we wage Jihad in the path of Allah. The name of Islamic Emirate is the official name for us and all the Mujahideen in Afghanistan.'[59]

This trend has been reinforced nowadays (see below).

The Shadow Government

The Taliban have established a shadow government that mirrors their old governance structures and the current structures of Kabul, thus perpetuating the idea that they are still being the legitimate government of Afghanistan. The Quetta *shura* appoints governors and district chiefs mostly from the local population. By now, almost every province and district throughout Afghanistan has a Taliban governor and district chiefs.[60] Most districts in provinces with a sizeable Taliban presence have district chiefs; this conforms to the system as outlined in the latest version of the Taliban's *layeha* or rule book.[61] The Taliban, however, have their own administrative division of some provinces not entirely conforming to Afghan governmental cartographical orthodoxy. For this reason, the Taliban have more official district chiefs than the government. It should be noted, though, that locally the districts recognised by the Taliban are also recognised by the local population and to an extent by the local government, even though they are not formally established and do not appear on official government maps or reports.

As with the official government structure, district chiefs and governors often play a greater role in governing due to the lack of other institutions and, in many cases, surpass their mandate, fulfilling a myriad of government functions. They are the official representatives and therefore are the link to the local population: they address local grievances and arbitrate conflict.

On the back of their shadow government the Taliban first dispatched mobile courts that heard cases involving local conflict, often cases that were not handled by the official government. Justice is applied through the *shari'a* and cases are handled swiftly, making Taliban courts the first port of call for many. The government's own judicial system is highly corrupt and has a great backlog of cases.[62] In Kandahar, for example, there are two fully-operating static Taliban courts and several mobile versions.[63]

2005–2008

The 2005–2008 period saw the insurgency come into its own and achieve significant territorial and propaganda successes against the Afghan government and foreign forces. Mullah Dadullah was in part responsible for this (from a military perspective) and the arrival of NATO's 'phase three' troops[64] in southern Afghanistan in 2006 appears to have helped motivate many to side with the insurgency at the time. In many parts of the country—nowhere more than in Helmand which was officially under the lead of British forces—individuals joined up as a reaction to what was perceived by many as a 'settling of scores' dating back to the Anglo-Afghan wars, and the Taliban capitalised on a feeling of disappointment and disenfranchisement of the general population.[65]

They were, of course, also helped by the Afghan government's own inadequacies, particularly since concerns about the legitimacy and intentions of local representatives had started to be voiced by this point. Internationally, the 'war on terror' rhetoric had lessened, but fears of another September 11 were still present and were frequently cited by the Bush administration as a reason for being engaged in Afghanistan.[66] For the new NATO deployment, the line that, 'we are in Afghanistan to secure our own countries back home' was repeated many times as politicians sought to justify the deployment to their own constituencies. In August 2009, for example, UK Prime Minister Gordon Brown stated that:

'The work of our troops—providing security, through operations like Panther's Claw [in Helmand], building up the Afghan army and police, and allowing politics and economic development to take root—is vital to preventing al Qaeda once again using Afghanistan as a base for terrorist attacks against Britain and other countries.'[67]

Taliban Goals

By the summer of 2006, the Taliban had developed their military and political strategy. They had a very ambitious idea of what could be achieved in the summer of 2006 and how much of Afghanistan could be brought under their control: this extended to the belief that they could take the south of the country.[68] Even individual Taliban commanders in the field seemed to have a strong sense of what they were hoping to achieve:

What we want are posts in Karzai's government. As soon as we are part of the government and as soon as all foreigners leave, we will stop fighting.[69]

Taliban fighters around the country attempted to fight the foreign military forces in conditions similar to those that they had experienced during the 1980s. Mullah Dadullah outlined his views on taking entire cities as part of the Taliban's military campaign in July 2005:

Taking cities is not part of our present tactics. Our tactics now are hit and run; we attack certain locations, kill the enemies of Allah there, and retreat to safe bases in the mountains to preserve our mujahidin. This tactic disrupts and weakens the enemies of

Allah and in the same time allows us to be on the offensive. We decide the time and place of our attacks; in this way the enemy is always guessing. We have attacked and occupied certain locations for a short period of time. This was done only to achieve the objectives of the operation. But we will always retreat to our safe bases.[70]

Despite this realism in his sense of what was possible or wise for the Taliban to aim at, there was a serious attempt to force the international community and their military forces to rethink its involvement in Afghanistan by ramping up attacks. The south saw the main thrust of the Taliban's push with a combination of tactics: frontal assaults on foreign military positions (mostly unsuccessful), a massive increase in the number of suicide bomb attacks, an increase in the use of non-suicide IEDs, a campaign to kidnap foreigners (whether associated with the foreign military presence or not) as well as an aggressive public relations strategy.[71]

Politically, there was some 'talk about talk' in terms of a dialogue between Karzai and the Taliban spokesman, Zabiullah Mujahed, but no serious efforts were made nor did the idea receive genuine support.[72] An examination of Mullah Mohammad Omar's *eid* statements (issued twice a year during the period with a few exceptions) shows that 2006 was a period when a more coherent political strategy emerged—before then it seemed mainly reactionary.[73] Foreign forces launched operations throughout 2006 to counter the growing insurgency. This began with Operation Mountain Thrust in May 2006, mostly in eastern Afghanistan, but also in Uruzgan and northern Helmand and Kandahar, followed by Operation Medusa in September.[74]

Taliban forces had gathered in and around Pashmol, expanding the natural trench system of the vineyards and the pre-existing network of trenches left from the 1980s in an attempt to hold the ground and establish a stronghold from which to operate. With the advance of foreign forces, a fierce battle ensued. The Taliban had gathered hundreds of fighters who attempted to engage the Afghan and foreign military in a ground battle leading to massive losses among the Taliban and their ultimate defeat.[75] As a model for this engagement, they sought to replicate the success of previous similar battles during the 1980s against Soviet incursions.[76] The battle of Pashmol is an exception in the insurgency war which the Taliban had been carrying out, although there were some comparable examples of ground battles from other provinces (although perhaps not in size). It was, however, an uncommon occurrence. It is difficult to see the rationale behind the shift in tactics. Speculation ranges from the fact that the Taliban did not believe the foreign troops would engage them on the ground, to the belief that Pashmol would be impossible to capture and clear.[77]

Operation Medusa proved a learning experience for the Taliban, who soon after abandoned large gatherings and conventional engagements with foreign forces.[78] They renewed their focus on IED attacks, suicide bombs and ambushes. They also shifted targets, and stepped up their assassination campaign against mid-level government representatives. Attacks on schools and other soft targets had been on the rise for the past several years, more than doubling between 2004 and 2005 throughout Afghanistan.[79] Even though Pashmol was a resounding failure for the Taliban, there were still occasional attempts frontally to assault a foreign base or position in the provinces *en masse*. These still continue, although they are uncommon.[80]

2006 was Mullah Dadullah's year of action and the spring and summer of 2007 were also planned to be equally busy, but for his death in May 2007.[81] The momentum generated for the 2007 campaign was in no small sense built up by Dadullah himself, and his death marked the end of a significant expansion plan of that kind. The Taliban's efforts from 2008 onwards took the movement in a different direction: expanding new fronts in the north and west, as well as more aggressively pursuing their trial and assassination programme against figures who might have been able to offer credible resistance to their expansion.[82] They also sought to protect their hold over territory already de facto under their control.

The Dadullah Effect

Mullah Dadullah was a key figure in the revival and remodelling of the Taliban as an insurgent group from their previous government functions in the time from 1994 to 2001. He is an important part of the story of the Taliban during this period because he introduced new tactics and ways for the Taliban to expand their operations around the country.

Born in 1966 or 1967, Dadullah is part of the old generation of Taliban, but one who defies the usual mould of this group. He was Kakar by tribe, born in Munara Kalay (Chahar Chino district) in Uruzgan, but his family moved to Deh Rawud shortly after.[83] He fought on the Taliban fronts in Panjwayi district of Kandahar during the 1980s *jihad* along with the others who would later form the core Taliban leadership. The official Taliban biography published in *al-Somood* magazine after his death[84] states that he joined the *jihad* in 1983 (he interrupted his studies in Pakistan), fighting in Arghandab district under Mawlawi Akhtar Mohammad for his first battle.[85]

He then fought in Helmand from 1989–1992 under Mullah Naseem Akhundzada, at which point (the fall of the Najib government) he returned to Kandahar and then Quetta, where he resumed his studies. From 1994 onwards, he joined up with the Taliban as they took territory in southern Afghanistan, participating in all of the military offensives in southern and south-western Afghanistan during this period. He lost his leg fighting against Ismael Khan's troops in either Farah or Herat in 1995, when he stepped on a land mine.[86] By 1996, he had recovered and was appointed as a commander of a unit based in Kabul but with responsibilities for pushing the Taliban northwards.[87] He played a key role in defending the Taliban's island of influence in Kunduz between 1999 and 2001, and also fought to take Mazar-e Sharif in 1997. In 1999, he took part in the movement's campaign in Bamiyan and central Afghanistan. He was temporarily relieved of his command by Mullah Mohammad Omar in early 2000 following his strong-armed tactics[88] that other members of the Taliban spoke out against, but this seems to have only been a brief reprimand; he was needed in the north. In January 2001, around 300 unarmed men and some women and children were killed by Taliban forces in Yakawlang (Bamiyan province). Dadullah has since been tied to this massacre in a supervisory role.[89] In March 2001, he is also alleged to have 'supervised' the destruction of the Bamiyan Buddha statues.[90]

Following the September 11 attacks, Dadullah was tasked with commanding the Taliban's northern forces (along with Mullah Fazl and others). He escaped capture in Kunduz,[91] passing through Kandahar and made his way to South Waziristan.[92] The Newsline article cited in the Jamestown Foundation report states that Dadullah received donations there: a land cruiser and a pledge of shelter from fellow Kakar tribesmen. In 2002 he is reported to have met with seventy 'trusted' Taliban members and outlined the new hierarchies and strategy for the rebirth of the movement as an insurgent organisation.[93] In June 2003, Mullah Mohammad Omar formed a ten-man leadership council or *rahbari shura*, of which Dadullah was a member.[94] In the years that followed, he took a prominent role, particularly in military operations. In 2003, he was in charge of the Taliban fighters who took Day Chopan district (Zabul province), the first district to 'fall' to the resurgent movement.[95]

Dadullah gave an interview to the Arabic-language broadcaster *Al-Jazeera* in 2004,[96] and in July 2005 stated that the Taliban were receiving assistance from fighters in Iraq.[97] 2006 saw the expansion of ISAF's role in Afghanistan and NATO troops arrived in southern Afghanistan. Dadullah had stepped up his fund-raising and alliances in advance, travelling to the United Arab Emirates in early 2006[98] and announcing ties to bin Laden in February of that year.[99]

2006 was Dadullah's year. He gave several interviews to the *al-Jazeera* TV station, establishing his public reputation in a way that other Taliban commanders were not wont to do, and during the summer he carried out operations in Kandahar, Zabul and Helmand. Attacks were up compared to the year before, and NATO troops arriving in the south found themselves entrenched in many places far sooner than they had expected. Dadullah also travelled to Pakistan's tribal agencies that summer, ordered by Mullah Mohammad Omar to reach out to Pakistani jihadis and tribal fighters to encourage them to fight in Afghanistan rather than against Pakistani state actors.[100]

It was around this time that Dadullah started to make increasingly strident statements of support for a global *jihad*, one in which attacks in Europe and the United States were not to be ruled out.[101] Dadullah was, in contrast to most other Talibs of his generation, a 'true believer' in this rhetoric. Some commentators have suggested this is pathological,[102] but a possible explanation can be found in the time he spent with foreign jihadis both on the northern fronts during the 1990s as well as post-2001, when he was in South Waziristan. He was frequently used as a go-between for the Taliban in Pakistan and retained ties to the foreign al-Qaeda affiliates as well. Moreover, the use of suicide attackers— not traditionally a Taliban tactic—was spearheaded and bound into the insurgency strategy of the Taliban from 2004 onwards; Dadullah and his brother, Mansour, were among its strongest advocates within the Quetta *shura*.[103]

The death of Dadullah on 12 May 2007 was perhaps inevitable for someone who seemed so blasé about his own security (appearing in person for so many interviews with *al-Jazeera*, or spending so much time inside Afghanistan directing operations from the front lines), but it dealt a temporary blow to the Taliban's military operations in certain respects: one analyst reported that suicide bombings were down when compared against the same period the year before,[104] and morale was certainly affected.[105] This was reinforced by the belief among many within the movement (as well as among some commentators) that Dadullah may have been betrayed from within the movement, even by someone close to Mullah Mohammad Omar, but these remain unconfirmed rumours.[106]

Dadullah's operations and prominence between 2005–2007 have distorted perceptions of the Taliban's broader agenda. Articles noting the Taliban's internationalist ambitions often refer directly to Dadullah's statements or those made by Mansour in the wake of his brother's death.[107] These statements and the figure of Mullah Dadullah seem to have been the exception rather than the rule for the Taliban, however. The leadership has otherwise been far more cautious about commanders with personality cults as well as those who made statements showing support for al-Qaeda and non-Afghan Taliban groups.

Dadullah was well-known in part because of his operations, but also for his promotional savvy. At times he even had his own press spokesman independently of the official Taliban spokesmen.[108] He was becoming more independent, almost like a brand, and this was something which the central leadership was concerned about. The *layeha* or rule book published in 2006 is in some ways clearly an attempt to push back against this trend.[109]

Dadullah was happy to associate with al-Qaeda and affiliated Pakistani groups because he in turn subscribed to many of their beliefs. In an interview with al-Jazeera in July 2005, he explained:

Cooperation between us and Al Qaeda is very strong. Many of our Arab mujahideen brothers are fighting alongside of us to establish the religion of Allah. We will accompany Al Qaeda anywhere to fight the enemies of Allah.[110]

He was, however, aware that the Afghan Taliban leadership at large did not support this wider association with al-Qaeda and its affiliates—as long as it did not affect the war effort—but in any case, he threw himself into the task of aggressively mounting operations within Afghanistan as much as possible. This was the first priority. After his death, though, his brother, Mansour, took up the mantle as leader of the Taliban forces in southern Afghanistan—he was appointed in July 2007—and he made several outspoken messages in support of an expansive global *jihad*.[111] For example, asked about the relationship between the Taliban and al-Qaeda, he replied that, 'We enjoy warm and friendly relations. We share their main aims.' When asked about *jihad*, he stated:

Jihad is a duty for every upstanding Muslim. Jihad must not be restricted to Afghanistan or Iraq. Ours is a global struggle, and I have promised Allah that I will spread it across the world until the end of my days.[112]

It was this kind of rhetoric, the proclamations of links between the Afghan Taliban and al-Qaeda, as well as the growing sense that Mansour was another loose cannon, that led Mullah Mohammad Omar to sack him in December 2007.[113] As if setting the record straight, the Taliban leader stated in an interview with Pakistan's *Dawn* newspaper that, 'we have never felt the need for a permanent relationship [with al-Qaeda].'[114]

Suicide Tactics

Mullah Dadullah oversaw much of the transition into the use of suicide bombers within Afghanistan—from cultivating the links with those in Pakistan who initially supplied people, to forging a place for such attacks within the propaganda apparatus[115]—and was personally involved at the head of those who would promote its use within the Afghan battlefield.

The Taliban's effectiveness at inflicting casualties on international ISAF/NATO troops from 2004/2005 onwards was not the result of replaying the old 1980s tactics as employed against Soviet troops, but was rather to a large degree stimulated by two new and improved tactics: the increased use of IEDs and of suicide bombings, although the Taliban have shown much less facility with the latter.[116] The rise in instances of both of these from 2004 onwards is frequently attributed to information flows from Iraq, where the insurgency employed both of these to great effect; the directly causal nature of this relationship, however, is less than certain.

Prior to the assassination of Massoud in 2001, there were no prominent instances of the use of suicide bombings within Afghanistan as part of a concerted military campaign (or even at all). In Pakistan, the 1995 bombing of the Egyptian Embassy in Islamabad (orchestrated by al-Zawahiri) stands out more as the exception that proves the rule.[117] 2004 saw a tentative use of the tactic, most likely primarily directly inspired by what people were seeing in Iraq combined with the fact that such operations did not need special training that wasn't already available in Pakistan. In Pakistan, there were around 20 suicide bombings between March 2002 and May 2004, killing over 200 people.[118] In 2004 in Afghanistan, however, there were only 3 suicide bombings. By 2005, there were 17 attacks and in 2006 there were 123 attacks.[119] In 2007 there were 137 attacks (causing over 1730 casualties), and in 2008 the number increased again.[120] Figures in Pakistan were lower for the same period, but there was still a significant increase post-2004.[121]

Initially, many of these suicide attackers seemed to come from Pakistan—they were either Pakistanis or Afghans who had been brought up in Pakistan[122]—but from 2007 onwards the proportion of Afghans carrying out suicide attacks increased until the present day, when Afghans living inside Afghanistan are almost always the attackers (although this generalisation is less true for Kabul).[123] Suicide bombers inspired fear and a greater projection of the movement's capacity than was actually the case, but—as Iraq helped show—the extensive use of this tactic can produce a backlash among the local population when civilians start being injured or killed in large numbers.[124]

The Taliban have retained an ambivalent attitude to the tactic, reflected in a debate in Quetta as to the legitimacy within Islam of suicide bombings, along with the realisation that too many civilians were being caught up in the attacks, and that this was alienating the general population.[125] Of course, there are pragmatists or those with fewer compunctions within the movement who believe that the use of suicide bombings, in combination with an effective propaganda campaign that places the blame for civilian casualties strictly on foreign forces, can be an effective way around this.[126]

In public interviews and statements this initial ambivalence was reflected in an unwillingness to go into too much detail as to the justifications for and specific uses in which suicide bombings were legitimate, but this seems to have eased off to the point where, in 2009 and 2010, in two separate editions of the Taliban's rule book, four conditions are specified that need to be fulfilled when using the tactic; the emphasis is placed on avoiding civilian casualties, and on the special nature of suicide attacks (i.e., that they not be wastefully employed).[127]

Ordinary fighters from southern Afghanistan interviewed in 2007 by a researcher for *The Globe and Mail* said very little to detract from the use of suicide bombing as a tactic.[128] It is likely that these responses did not necessarily reflect the true opinion of the fighters, and rather reflected the movement's propaganda 'line,'[129] since suicide bombings were by then being used frequently by the Taliban in southern Afghanistan. An interview with a Taliban commander from Takhar in 2006 included the following remark:

They have proven very useful. Very effective. You know, the *shari'a* allows this. Any method that kills the enemy is acceptable. This allows us to spend money, for example, fight face to face or from a distance, or even fight with the pen. Anything, in order to win the war. And if I am killed, I will go to paradise.[130]

There was, regardless, a major debate that broke out in Quetta among the leadership of the Afghan Taliban as to the validity of it as a tactic, particularly when the numbers grew so large, and when the Afghan public started to question its use on an Islamic basis. Later that year, letters reportedly from the Taliban's military council were published in a local newspaper in Kandahar stating that suicide bombings were not legitimate tactics and that they were the work of 'foreign fighters.'[131]

IEDs had more of a history in Afghanistan, dating back to the 1980s war, where mines (whether anti-personnel or anti-vehicle) were commonly used in both improvised (i.e., homemade) and manufactured varieties.[132] As a concerted tactic, 2004 was again the year where both the 'prevalence and effectiveness' of IEDs began to increase.[133] In Kandahar, for example, there were at least 14 instances of use in 2004, but 2005 saw 47, 2006 saw 124, 2007 saw 138, and 2008 saw 180.[134] Claims have, again, been made for the influence of the 'Iraq effect,' whereby expertise and motivation has come to Afghanistan as a result of the Iraq war.[135] There are, however, several components to this 'Iraq effect' which the Afghan parallel does not fulfil. For example, different IED techniques 'predated or conflicted' with those being used in Iraq—instead finding more influence from Kashmiri jihadists—and there are several IED types that were common in Iraq which have not filtered back to Afghanistan.[136] The practice of recording video testimonials by suicide bombers was never widely adopted in Afghanistan, either, where the practice is much less common and tends to be limited to missions that amount to suicide attacks.[137] Even in the case of training, we know that some Taliban members received training in the construction and use of radio-controlled IEDs (RCIEDs),[138] but even after Iraqi jihadis abandoned this type of IED—on account of the increased international forces' use of jammers—the Taliban continue to use them.[139]

Al-Qaeda in Pakistan and the Rise of Tehrik-e Taliban Pakistan

Pakistan was going through its own turmoil during this period, with uncertainty over Musharraf's future and with the return of Benazir Bhutto.[140] The presence of al-Qaeda, the Pakistani Taliban and their affiliates in the tribal areas of Pakistan was an internal jihadi problem for the Pakistani state. The October 2005 Kashmir earthquake had given Pakistani jihadists opportunity for social involvement in the relief effort.[141] This meshed well with the fact that many of the jihadist groups had reinvented themselves as social welfare organisations following Musharraf's ban in 2002.[142] This was their chance to demonstrate that and exploit the situation for recruitment.

On 13 January 2006, missiles from a CIA drone strike hit a village called Damadola in Pakistan, killing at least 18 civilians.[143] This, followed by another on 29 October that killed 83 madrassa students in Chenagai, was an important trigger for Pakistanis to join militant groups, some of whom were then used as suicide bombers in Afghanistan and Pakistan.[144]

2007 saw the (re-)formation of Tehrik-e Taliban Pakistan. It had originally been founded in 1998 in Orakzai agency by Mohammad Rahim; at the time, he denied any links to the Afghan Taliban across the border and said that he was setting up the group to 'cleanse the society of crime.'[145] The 2007 revival saw the forces of four prominent militant leaders come together under one umbrella: Beitullah Mehsud from South Waziristan, Mullah Nazir from South Waziristan, Mullah Faqir from Bajaur, and *Tehrik-e Nifaz-e Shariat-e Muhammadi* in Swat.[146]

The internal Pakistani jihadi problem was amply demonstrated by the Lal Masjid siege in June 2007, where several hundred Pakistani militants were holed up in a mosque in central Islamabad, inspired to action by Mawlana Abdul Aziz and his brother Abdur Rasheed Ghazi. Ghazi was killed during the operation to retake the mosque along with more than a dozen Pakistani soldiers and officers.[147] The weeks that followed, moreover, saw a dramatic increase in suicide attacks against the Pakistani state. Of the 56 attacks in 2007, at least 36 came after the July operation.[148]

Al-Qaeda and the Afghan Taliban did not take this moment to merge their efforts through the Pakistani crucible, however. Rather, these events seem to have placed another wedge between the two groups. There were some opportunities for links between the two—and some Taliban allies made use of these—but the core Kandahari leadership were very worried about the consequences of fighting on two separate fronts and in any case were not interested in carrying out operations in Pakistan itself.[149]

Mullah Dadullah, for example, travelled frequently to Waziristan, often to mediate between different groups or to forge alliances of his own. In December 2008 and January 2009, Mullah Mohammad Omar reportedly also sent a team of six Talibs to Waziristan to ask Pakistani groups to 'settle their internal differences, scale down their activities in Pakistan and help counter the planned increase of American forces in Afghanistan.'[150] The Haqqanis, closely allied to various groups within the Pakistani establishment, even issued a letter in June 2006 stating that Pakistan was not their priority:

'[Attacking Pakistan] is not our policy. Those who agree with us are our friends and those who do not agree and [continue to wage] an undeclared war against Pakistan are neither our friends nor shall we allow them in our ranks.' Sirajuddin Haqqani has gone further, explaining in an interview that he opposed 'any attempt by Muslims to launch attacks in non-Muslim countries.' In May 2009, he argued to two French journalists: 'It is a mistake to think that al-Qaeda and the Taliban are pursuing the same aim. Al-Qaeda is trying to spread its influence throughout the world. This does not interest us. The Taliban's aim is to liberate Afghanistan from foreign troops.'[151]

Indeed, the Haqqanis participated in the deal between militants and the Pakistani government in early September 2006. That deal was suspended in May 2007, but then revived again in February 2008, again supported by the Haqqanis.[152]

2008–2009

The 2008–2009 period was overshadowed by the presidential election in America. Obama's campaign slogans—'change we can believe in' and 'yes we can'—

resounded far beyond America's borders. There was a widespread discussion surrounding Obama's campaign promises in Afghanistan, not only in the cities but also in the districts and villages.[153] Obama was often tied to the claim that Afghanistan was the 'good' war—even though he seems never to have actually used that phrase in public addresses—and that it was under-resourced, but it was unclear what to expect.[154]

After taking office on 20 January 2009, the new US administration seemed to sideline President Karzai and change course in its relationship with him. The US ambassador to Kabul had met with other presidential candidates and there was a clear and growing distance between the US administration and the Afghan President.[155] Karzai, however, used the United States' behaviour to paint himself as a nationalist champion, setting himself up on a platform of opposition to the foreign forces and continuing his statements about mounting civilian casualties.[156]

The White House started to angle itself away from the Afghan government only to find itself forced to continue to work with it.[157] Afghans around the country witnessed the public spat between the two allies and it occasionally bubbled over into discontent against foreign troops and foreign organisations. It fell to US General Stanley McChrystal to counterbalance this doubtlessly damaging episode by ramping up public appearances with the Afghan President as a clear display of unity.[158]

Obama, once in office, chose to embark on an ambitious multiple-level review programme that refocused attention back onto Afghanistan from Iraq, which was calmer than in previous years.[159] A key policy speech made by Obama in March 2009 stated that the United States sought to 'to disrupt, dismantle, and defeat al-Qaeda in Pakistan and Afghanistan, and to prevent their return to either country in the future.'[160]

In the aftermath of the full scale standoffs and attacks against foreign forces in Afghanistan in 2006 that had failed (with heavy casualties), the Taliban realised that a violent environment in the rural areas of the south and southeast could only help in their continued propaganda strategy, demonstrating for many that neither the Afghan government nor the foreign forces could protect the local people.

While violence increased throughout 2008–2009, local Taliban commanders, in what seems to have been a central directive from the leadership *shura*, changed how they engaged with parts of the population. On the surface, the Taliban appeared to try a softer line in attempting to win over local communities and tribes. This included more emphasis on services and accountability among the Taliban's own ranks,[161] and was coupled with increased threats and assassinations against those who continued to work in collaboration with the Afghan government or foreign military forces or NGOs in the country, and was intended to further polarise local society and deepen the split with the local government.

Towards the end of this period, as well, the calculation had started to change in terms of the relationship between the Afghan Taliban and al-Qaeda, since the rhetoric of foreign failure had started to seep into ongoing military and political discussions, a factor that was only emphasised more strongly after the US presidential election in November 2008.[162] Negotiations started to be mentioned with an increasing frequency while security deteriorated throughout the country, and the Taliban began to realign themselves to meet this new reality.

Taliban Goals: Rethinking al-Qaeda

The last three years (2007–2010) have seen the Taliban take considerable care in their public statements as to the relationship between themselves and al-Qaeda. Particularly in 2009, even the issue itself seemed to be toxic for all but the most senior political members, who refused to speak frankly about the topic on the record. Even non-active Taliban members like Mullah Zaeef have remained relatively silent over the issue; his book, *My Life With the Taliban*, published in 2010, contained very little that substantively dealt with the relationship between the Taliban and al-Qaeda.

Serajuddin Haqqani, asked in January 2010 about his relationship to bin Laden and al-Qaeda, responded:

Osama is an international jihadi figure who fights infidels all over the world. We neither have any linkage and relation to Osama nor do we get any assistance and help from him. If he had any relationship with the Afghan Mujahidin, that relationship was subjected to the Islamic Emirates laws and regulations.[163]

Signals had been passed—the Taliban had long ago realised the importance of the issue to the internationals and, in hedging their bets given the increased talk of a possible negotiated settlement, seemed to concede this public commentary. This is not to say that there was no interaction between the Taliban and al-Qaeda during this time. One report from June 2008 states that TTP[164] fighters were killed in Helmand and that efforts were made from Pakistan to return the bodies of the eighteen fighters to Makeen village in Waziristan.[165] Similarly, in March 2008 Mawlawi Iqbal (associates of Mullah Nazir in Wana) and several fighters were reported killed in Paktika.[166]

The Afghan Taliban pushed further to extend their control over the country during this period. It was apparent that, without the foreign troops, the Karzai government would fall. By 2008, the problems of the Afghan government were manifold and easy to observe. The institutions and figures in place were predatory—not least in the active sense of much of the Afghan National Police forces employed around the country—and were viewed by Afghans as acting in their own self-interest. The dysfunction of Karzai's government, and its attempt to grasp power and financial structures around the country, were obvious, and the fraud and blatant manipulation of the 2008 presidential election were merely the final confirmation of what many had known and experienced in their daily lives prior to that point: that the Karzai government was more concerned with holding on to power more than it was focused on any idea of how to govern properly.[167] The government was, by 2008, still too far removed from the provinces, both in distance and in thought; while many living in the districts far from Kabul had limited expectations of what that central government could or should be expected to provide, the few times they interacted was to be subject to either military operations or corruption.[168] The blurred lines, moreover, between senior government figures and the narcotics trafficking industry (as well as the farming of opium) was clear for all to see among the Afghan population, and harmed the foreigners who fought in public and within Afghan political circles for the government's presence, status and existence.[169] The association of the Afghan government with the foreigners—particularly the widespread idea that without them, the Karzai government wouldn't last a week—was toxic.

The Taliban had brought their own version of services and accountability into the districts and they did a better job than the Afghan government or foreign military forces, at least in the perception of many Afghans in southern and eastern Afghanistan.[170] The Taliban have engaged in a campaign to win over rural Afghans since 2005–2006, but it was only in 2008–2009 that the provision of services and accountability became more widespread. This took different forms. A system of courts had been operational since 2001, albeit in a highly reduced form, but from 2007 onwards these court sessions spread to different locations and met more regularly.[171] This happened parallel to the rolling out of a more responsive complaints system whereby inhabitants of rural areas could request investigations into corrupt Taliban commanders or members or other actions where they felt they had been wronged. Many of these complaints seem to have been addressed in a systematic manner—with high-level investigations and figures coming from Pakistan—and, most importantly, to the satisfaction of locals.[172] The *layeha* was a public expression of this seemingly newfound devotion to public accountability. Contained within was a full outline of this drive for accountability as well as how redress could be sought. Of course, only a tiny percentage of ordinary Afghans inhabiting the districts will have seen or read this document, but its value was more symbolic (i.e., that it had been issued at all) than real in terms of judges using it as a legal reference.

2009, therefore, saw a definite shift in the Taliban's political stance: Afghanistan was the focus and they fashioned a relatively clear political agenda. Mullah Dadullah was dead and politics within the Taliban was now conducted by committee and through consultation. 2008–2009 was a period when the Taliban's leadership felt they were close to gaining serious and wider political control over the southern regions of the country. This reinforced their sense of grievance that had been so effective at motivating them in the early years post-2001, as did the impression that in many places the Taliban were actively governing.

For most political figures across Afghanistan—not just for the Taliban—this period was characterised by a long wait to see how the new US President would choose to act in terms of the ongoing war. Obama's election campaign became strongly associated with the idea that Afghanistan was the 'good war' and it was clear that there would be some sort of change—if only a reinvigoration—of the US engagement there. Until that moment came, however,—in December 2009, with the dispatch of 30,000 extra troops on the advice of his senior military commanders—political groupings within Afghanistan played a waiting game. This was apparent from both the Taliban as well as from the Afghan government. The Taliban issued statements voicing their doubts about Obama's intentions and plans, and Karzai avoided the issue of his government's being criticised by the US administration.[173]

Nevertheless, the decision to send extra troops came as a disappointment for some senior Taliban political figures who had hoped that Obama might offer a different tangent to US policy in Afghanistan.[174] A new US administration could potentially have offered a stronger political leadership role and found a way to initiate discussions about the Taliban's future role in Afghan society and politics.

The news of extra American troops was met with messages promising a military escalation by the Taliban. Two statements were released in the week that followed, one simply entitled 'On Obama's New Strategy,' and the next entitled 'Obama, Following Bush's Steps.'[175] There was a sense among the Taliban leadership that this was a time for pushing through.[176] The day of the Afghan presidential election in 2009 is a good example of the reach that they had by then. Attacks all over the country—around 400 of them—were coordinated and carried out. This is an indicator that the movement in 2009 was implementing, on some level, a national strategy.[177]

The Layeha and Rebranding

The *layeha* published some time in 2006 was the Taliban's first post-2001 attempt to codify the practices and standards by which commanders and fighters should seek to abide. It was in part an exercise in rebranding the movement publicly as a group that could both manage its own affairs and be accountable to the Afghan public it claimed to be representing.

The collection of regulations issued by the Taliban's central *shura* in 2006 are quite unstructured, especially when compared to the later editions of this document.[178] Many of the rules are aimed at consolidating authority—either from those claiming to be Taliban and acting without official sanction or in terms of maintaining a central controlling role over important financial and political transactions. Some of the guidelines refer queries to a senior authority—using phrases like 'except without permission of their commander' and so on—and others are simply attempts to outlaw looting (rule number 17) or the selling of 'jihadi equipment' by Taliban members (rule number 11). There is very little in the rule book of 2006 as to the motivations for *jihad* or the more spiritual or larger political aspects of their fight. It was a response to a list of problems which the Taliban experienced at the time and the rule book was an attempt to place some centralising control over members as the insurgency expanded. Sentencing for transgressions is also always deferred to a later decision by *shura*; there are no irrevocable positions as to obligatory punishments.

One interview with a Taliban commander in Kandahar at that time stated some matter-of-fact considerations which dictated how the rules were compiled:

According to our rules, we have no prisons. We simply cannot. Instead we have judges who we appoint to pass sentencing. Those who are spies we kill. If it is a case of a simple foot soldier, we will release that person.[179]

The second iteration of the Taliban code of conduct is considerably revised and structured when compared to that issued in 2006. This is more than double the size of the old version—67 rules compared to 30, and with much fuller explanations. Considerable thought and time had been invested. A set of instructions on the back of the book is clearly calculated for media impact, but the full collection has less of a feeling of a calculated media exercise than a serious attempt to codify and legislate for some of the problems that the movement had faced. There is less of the paranoia and concern that characterised the first version and much more a sense that the movement has an idea of what it stands for and how its bureaucracy functions and that it can adapt to the task at hand. This was not the case in 2006. Entirely new issues are also addressed here, including prisoners, suicide-bombing and the exact ways and means by which people can join with the Taliban. Similarly, there is a whole section devoted to the identification and interrogation of spies; interestingly, the rules categorically specify that evidence obtained through torture or coercion is invalid and that the filming of executions of spies is forbidden.[180] An administrative section (number six) entitled 'Mujahedeen Organisation' deals with the exact composition of the Taliban's provincial and district representation, albeit with the sense that the suggestions are more the ideal than necessarily a definite prescription, and certainly that is how these injunctions are being taken in the field.[181] The later rules and restrictions are the ones that have been more prominently featured in media reports—the prohibition of cutting off noses and the injunction 'to keep people and their property safe'—but, taken in the context of the whole document, these are peripheral regulations and the bulk of these prescriptions and proscriptions are once again concerned with reinforcing the authority of the central command, and providing a framework for addressing internal conflict.

The different versions of the *layeha* are useful in offering us a changing picture of what the Taliban leadership worries about, how they address these problems, and in general how the movement has grown and adapted. We know from elsewhere (and through interviews in the field) that the Taliban have developed a massive internal bureaucracy to deal with this change and centralisation of authority. All official night letters or other written communications from the Taliban are logged and copies are retained; this is just one example of the paperwork that the movement is currently generating.[182]

This reinvigoration of the Taliban's bureaucracy, even at a time of military overreach and high levels of activity, was an indication of their making the first preparatory attempts to be taken seriously as a political force, one that was ready to assume responsibilities. Accordingly, the old bureaucracy was reactivated as part of the movement's new accountability drive, especially now that there were large sums of money and taxes passing through the Taliban's commanders and representatives; there was a need to show that money was really being processed properly where possible, even though there seems to have been some tolerance of commanders pocketing war profits.[183]

The movement's central administration seems to have been concerned about an epidemic of false night letters written in the name of the 'Islamic Emirate' but used as threats by competitors or rivals, for example. There was a need to tighten up control of these and to verify (via a central processing authority) that letters were actually from the 'Islamic Emirate.' This was one instance where concerns over decentralisation were acted upon. Their solution involved registering each letter sent out—most of which include a high level of detail as to the addressee's particular charges and not merely mass mailings to large numbers of people—with a numbering system that is kept both locally, at the provincial level, as well as (this is the ideal) at the zonal administration level.[184] There are also various stamps employed, although these are easier to forge than the numbering system. This system is then advertised on the letters, stating, for instance, that if participants wish to object or check the specific charges laid against them, then they can call a central number which will be able to confirm those details.[185]

The propaganda value of releasing the rule book in a form that they know will be made public and noted by media outlets is obviously important—otherwise they would retain it for internal circulation only, as doubtless they have with other iterations—but more has been made in the media of this than is actually in the documents. This is *not* the Taliban's 'counter-counter-insurgency' doctrine.[186] Rather, it represents the Taliban's attempt to shift the movement from being personality-driven to something that persists regardless of individuals.[187]

There are, moreover, several different ways in which the Taliban have been seen by locals to 'soften' their stance despite continuing to apply coercive and violent measures: over communications technology/mobile phones, television and radio, popular festivals like the egg festival in the south-east, female education and female employment, music at weddings (on a case by case basis) and encouraging a limit to wedding dowries (which has been extremely popular wherever enforced).[188] There are other examples of where the Taliban have made compromises to their public stance on cooperating with internationals: the polio vaccination campaign, the UN 'Peace Day,' provision of access to prisoners and engaging in dialogue with the International Committee of the Red Cross.[189]

10

THE FORGE (2010)

The extraordinary capacity of Islam to generate a language of justice also helps explain its great value to people seeking to resist governments that are plainly unjust.

Noah Feldman, *The Fall and Rise of the Islamic State*[1]

The lesson of the sad, repeated failure of the moderates, or a 'third force', to compete against opposing extremes is one of constant relevance to the contemporary scene; whether it be in Northern Ireland, Southern Africa or Latin America. As in 1793 or 1917, in modern revolutions it is the Montagne that triumphs over the Gironde.

Alastair Horne, *A Savage War of Peace*[2]

The next 9/11 will come from FATA.

General David Petraeus[3]

The takeover of the US and NATO mission in Afghanistan by General Stanley McChrystal in summer 2009 meant that US forces and NATO were for the first time under a single command.[4] After conducting a strategic review of the situation in Afghanistan, McChrystal recommended the implementation of a population-centric counterinsurgency strategy (COIN) with a troop surge of 35,000 soldiers.[5]

This chapter examines the situation of the insurgency in Afghanistan in 2010 and the impact of the strategy originally outlined by General McChrystal, later implemented by General Petraeus.[6] It will try to outline trends resulting from the strategy pursued by the foreign forces in the country, ending with a brief look into what this has meant for the relationship between the Afghan Taliban and al-Qaeda.

The period following the Afghan presidential election of August 2009 saw significant changes, and security conditions have deteriorated all over the country.[7] In the south and south-east, attacks rose to all-time highs, as did numbers of casualties among both Afghan and foreign forces. The east witnessed a similar pattern. In the west, instances of criminal and insurgent activity both increased, although not to a level comparable to the south or east. The north saw greater Taliban infiltration and influence, some of which were initiatives organised from outside that region while others were local reactions to local conditions.[8]

A Pentagon report to the US Congress estimated that 48 of 92 districts assessed were supportive of the Taliban in March 2010, a 16% increase compared to December 2009.[9] Amrullah Saleh, the former NDS chief, estimated that in early 2010 the Taliban leadership numbered around 200 people, with approximately 1700 field commanders that led anywhere between 10,000 and 30,000 fighters.[10] In August 2010 ISAF recorded 4,919 'kinetic events,' a 49% increase over August 2009, a month that had already been exceptionally violent on account of the Afghan presidential elections.[11] The Afghan NGO Safety Office (ANSO) recorded 1,353 insurgent attacks for the same month.[12] Insurgents increasingly rely on Improvised Explosive Devices (IEDs). These roadside bombs wounded or killed 6,200 foreign and Afghan military forces in 2009, an increase of 63% compared to the previous year, with trends already indicating that there will be another jump in 2011.[13] There has been a noticeable increase in coordinated suicide attacks, with groups of insurgents executing well-planned and often prolonged engagements targeting high-value targets in urban areas across Afghanistan,[14] or focusing on purely civilian targets that are frequented by foreign civilian contractors and NGO staff, as was seen at the attack on Kabul's Finest Supermarket.[15]

The troubled relationship of internationals with President Karzai was tested in the aftermath of the August 2009 elections, and the subsequent year saw various different approaches attempted or discussed regarding how to work together with him.[16] International ideas and debate on how to move forward positively in Afghanistan were also wildly inconsistent during this period, wavering from pledges of long-term assistance and commitment, to highly public debates over the advantages of a swift withdrawal.[17] This ongoing and highly public policy debate continues to create uncertainty among the Afghan population, in particular in the volatile south since its people are the focus of much of the discussion.[18]

After his appointment, McChrystal conducted a strategic review which saw the restatement of a population-centric counterinsurgency campaign.[19] Soon after his arrival—with Brigadier-General Ménard leading the Canadian forces in Kandahar and Major General Nick Carter commanding NATO's southern headquarters—the military accelerated its capture-or-kill campaign targeting insurgent commanders.[20] Both Generals McChrystal and Ménard had formally commanded Special Forces teams, and Carter[21] had worked closely with US forces in Iraq and Afghanistan.

After the publication of a controversial article in *Rolling Stone* magazine,[22] General McChrystal was relieved of his command, and General Petraeus stepped down from his position as head of CENTCOM to take the lead in Afghanistan, continuing to implement what McChrystal had started.[23]

The various leaders of the insurgency continued to hide and operate from across the border in Pakistan, outside the reach of United States' ground forces. With the leadership of al-Qaeda in hiding on Pakistani territory, the United States had to rely almost exclusively on drone strikes against al-Qaeda and jihadist groups in Pakistan.[24] Also, as was revealed in Woodward's *Obama's Wars*, the United States trained a paramilitary force of around 3,000 Afghans to pursue insurgents retreating across the border.[25] In Pakistan, the drone campaign has arguably brought only limited success (see below), and—given the spate of jihadist plots against the United States over the 2009–10 winter[26]—should be reassessed in terms of its long-term viability.

Two international conferences—in London in January 2010 and in Kabul in July—were held in 2010, albeit to a somewhat disparaging reception by international analysts and the Afghan general public.[27] The London conference marked a shift within the discussion about the goals and strategy pursued in Afghanistan, with reconciliation for the first time taking centre stage as a possible political solution. Financial pledges were made in support of the Afghan government's reconciliation and reintegration programme, and the conference in Kabul was seen as a firm international endorsement.[28] While a number of commentators continue to call for a more widespread set of talks or negotiations to be conducted on a higher level, the military leadership engaged in the conflict (particularly that of the United States) appeared to regard these programmes as a part of their military campaigns; accordingly, they seem to be trying to create ground realities that would force at least segments of the insurgency to accept the pre-set conditions for reconciliation. While the conventional wisdom of negotiating from position of power has since been challenged,[29] it is still employed among policy-makers today.[30]

In the autumn of 2010, the possibility of a US troop withdrawal in July 2011 loomed over all discussions about strategy and politics in Afghanistan and the wider region. President Obama had appeared in public to reaffirm the notion that 'the deadline' was not really a deadline but a point where a decision as to the efficacy of the current strategy would have to be assessed.[31] The announcement of the withdrawal, coupled with the ongoing debate and confusion about its actual meaning, helped fuel conspiracy theories (believed by many Afghans) as to the true intentions of the US government.[32] The Lisbon Conference in November 2010, however, stated firmly that 2014 was the date toward which NATO forces were working toward, and emphasis on this point was increased in the months that followed.

The Pakistani security establishment made a series of arrests in early 2010 that targeted old-generation Taliban figures based in Quetta and Karachi.[33] Although the full story behind these arrests has yet to emerge, it seems likely that they were an attempt to (re-)assert Pakistani control over the unfolding possibility of a political settlement with the insurgency.

The developments of 2010 and early 2011 show that whether reconciliation or negotiations are pursued, most interest groups—from Pakistan to Iran to women's rights activists and commanders or community leaders—have an opinion on how these will be conducted and seek to influence this process as much as possible. This means the environment in which political and military action[34] is being conducted will be changing continually throughout.[35]

TalQaeda Across the Border?

In analysing militant Islamic groups found in the border regions of Afghanistan and Pakistan (as well as individual groups within the Afghan Taliban) and the relationships between them, much of their current dynamics should be seen as the outcome of structural causes that limit the options of the individuals and groups involved. The idea of *burgfrieden* in the face of a common enemy, not by choice but in reaction to a perceived threat, has given rise to a greater commonality among otherwise discrete entities. This development has been assisted by their being lumped together as one homogenous group by outside forces.

The Afghan Taliban's leadership face a government dominated by former foes and are entrenched in a battle with the United States and NATO. They rely on their safe haven in Pakistan, with whose administration and government the old guard of the Taliban have an uneasy relationship. The other jihadist groups in Pakistan have been subject to the same processes.[36] Now, nine years after the launch of Operation Enduring Freedom, and with a renewed effort by the United States, the insurgents believe they are making significant progress.[37] The current environment makes a public announcement distancing themselves from other militant Islamic groups problematic, however. Differences are often very clear; while the relationship of the Afghan Taliban to Saudi Arabia might be fraught, it is still regarded as a legitimate facilitator for talks by large sections of the leadership, a position diametrically opposed to that of al-Qaeda, which regards the government of Saudi Arabia as a prime enemy. Al-Qaeda has also announced, through its franchise group, al-Qaeda in the Arabian Peninsula (AQAP), that it aims to revive its efforts to topple the house of Saud.[38]

The individuals and groups that make up the insurgency in Afghanistan have various motivations and incentives to participate. Defining their relationship to each other as well as to other groups outside Afghanistan is a difficult undertaking. The authors of the 9/11 Commission's *Monograph on Terrorist Financing* noted the following:

Understanding the difficulties in disrupting terrorist financing, both in the United States and abroad, requires understanding the difference between seeing 'links' to terrorists and proving the funding of terrorists. In many cases, we can plainly see that certain nongovernmental organizations (NGOs) or individuals who raise money for Islamic causes espouse an extremist ideology and are 'linked' to terrorists through common acquaintances, group affiliations, historic relationships, phone communications, or other such contacts. Although sufficient to whet the appetite for action, these suspicious links do not demonstrate that the NGO or individual actually funds terrorists and thus provide frail support for disruptive action, either in the United States or abroad.[39]

The same caution should be applied when looking at the relationship of al-Qaeda and the Taliban today. 'Common acquaintances, group affiliations, historic relationships, phone communications or other such contacts' do not automatically lead to a union of purpose regarding all goals, beliefs, tactics and ideology.

The core al-Qaeda membership is and has always been a small group of individuals numbering in the low hundreds at most.[40] A more differentiated view of the relationship between the Taliban and al-Qaeda should recognise the complexity of the multiple layers of that relationship, from individual contacts and common goals, to structural reasons for seemingly displaying a unified front at times while keeping silent or noncommittal at others.

Aspirations

The rhetoric and self-image of the senior al-Qaeda leadership has remained consistent at its core, while having evolved over time. They continue to issue threats and carry out plots against the governments and people they have long identified as their enemy. While consolidating other groups into the wider al-Qaeda network,[41] much of al-Qaeda's effort has been and remains the propaganda machine it operates. Much like a growing number of Afghan Taliban operations, attacks are informed by their strategic communication value. Al-Qaeda has consistently worked to maintain the central message throughout its affiliates and branches. Maintaining cohesion among its ranks in the wider network has seen multiple challenges throughout the years. Nevertheless, al-Qaeda appears to be able to continue to play a significant role within the wider network, one that exceeds the pure propaganda campaign and messaging; Farrall has stated that al-Qaeda continues to hold considerable operational control over certain strategic areas.[42]

From the return of bin Laden and al-Qaeda to Afghanistan in 1996 until the present day, al-Qaeda's relationship with the Afghan Taliban and other Islamic groups in the region has been unequal. A subtle but nevertheless telling fact is al-Qaeda's continuous pronouncement of its subservient relations to the *amir ul-mu'mineen*, Mullah Mohammad Omar, while the Afghan Taliban only infrequently comment publicly on their relationship with al-Qaeda.[43]

There is considerable disagreement among subject specialists and analysts over the nature of al-Qaeda and the threat it poses to the United States and other Western countries.[44] It seems increasingly to be developing along the model outlined by Abu Mus'ab al-Suri and others, with individual, self-motivated and self-trained groups taking unilateral action or having brief communications with some al-Qaeda-associated figures. Al-Qaeda operations are increasingly a bottom-up effort, with decreasing strategic input by key leaders.[45]

Those opposing this argument hold that the senior leadership do play and have played an important role in plots planned from Pakistan, and that the original impetus for operations since September 11 has generally been from the top level down. The alleged plot against targets in Europe, for example, revealed in September 2010 and supposedly still active, was reportedly ordered directly by the late bin Laden himself.[46]

Regardless of who is initiating attacks from Pakistan, al-Qaeda sees people already holding European and US passports as their best means of carrying out an attack on their enemies' home soil.[47] The plots that have been attempted in recent years have followed this pattern. There has, however, been no documented substantial involvement or recruitment of Afghans or Afghan Taliban for this purpose.[48]

One of the few incidents known of an Afghan national to have confessed to playing a part in a terrorist plot connected to al-Qaeda outside Afghanistan was Najibullah Zazi. Zazi was born in Paktya province in 1985, moving to Peshawar when he was seven years old and to the United States when he was fourteen, where he later attained permanent residence. He stated during his court case that he travelled to Pakistan in spring-summer 2008 in order to join the [Afghan] Taliban and fight against US troops in Afghanistan. Upon his arrival he was recruited by al-Qaeda and received training in Waziristan before agreeing to carry out a suicide mission back in the United States. Around the anniversary of 11 September 2009, Zazi planned to kill himself and others in a suicide operation on the New York subway.[49] According to the prosecution, the plan was instigated by Saleh al-Somali, allegedly head of al-Qaeda's external operations, and Rashid Rauf, a member of *Jaish-e Mohammad* reportedly killed by a US drone strike in North Waziristan in November 2008.[50]

Zazi's story follows a familiar pattern of al-Qaeda recruitment. Individuals who want to join the *jihad* in a specific country—as with the Hamburg Cell in the 1990s (see chapter 7)—found themselves being recruited by al-Qaeda for different tasks. Zazi explained in his statement that he hoped to join the Afghan Taliban, reasoning that he wanted to fight against the US troops because of their behaviour in Afghanistan.[51] Zazi is, of course, the exception among Afghans, because he neither represents the Afghan Taliban nor is he really representative of the Afghans living in rural areas inside Afghanistan. While Zazi's case offers little evidence for an operational cooperation of the Afghan Taliban in an international al-Qaeda-planned plot, the events should pose questions as to the potential for 'radicalisation' among the Afghan expatriate community around the world; an ideological shift within the Afghan Taliban inside Afghanistan and in Pakistan could see a mobilisation of those who live overseas.

Links and Facilitation

While the nature of the jihadist training camps and the number of volunteers have dramatically changed—those coming to Pakistan to join the *jihad* or militant groups are now in the hundreds rather than in the thousands—the majority of all individuals involved in terrorist plots can still be traced back to the mountainous regions of North and South Waziristan.[52] Local society there is deeply tribal and has resisted outside influence from governments for several hundred years.[53] The region played a pivotal role as the staging and training ground for Afghan, Pakistani and foreign fighters during the 1980s *jihad* in Afghanistan, and local communities have strong ties to a number of different Islamist and jihadist organisations.[54] The pro-jihadist and pro-Islamist rhetoric amounts to quasi hero-worship in some communities.[55] Waziristan has also continuously housed foreign jihadists, many of whom settled here during the late 1980s. Some of al-Qaeda's senior leadership are rumoured to be based there, as are the Islamic Movement of Uzbekistan and members of Pakistani jihadist groups and the Haqqanis.[56] In the words of the jailer of one Western journalist who described the jihadist universe in the border areas of Pakistan: 'There are all kinds of animals in the jungle.'[57]

Support by elements of the Pakistani government and security apparatus for the Afghan Taliban and the many other militant groups is still forthcoming, although the distance between the establishment and the jihadist world has grown considerably, not only because of the open conflict between the Pakistani government and the *Tehrik-e Taliban Pakistan* but also because of American actions:

While old contacts with organizations such as Hezbul Mujahedeen, Harkatul Mujahedeen and Lashkar-e-Taiba may be intact, the microscopic surveillance by the CIA and FBI, through an elaborate chain of contacts, restricts the ISI from conducting business the way it did until 2004.[58]

The links are often personal and seem to extend to financial, intelligence and logistical support. It has been frequently claimed, for example, that the Haqqanis receive warning prior to raids on their compounds and facilities, giving them time to leave and take sensitive materials with them.[59] Pakistan's interests in the jihadi groups[60] led to the creation of many of them during the 1990s. Recent developments, however, have given rise to concern among parts of Pakistan's establishment regarding the trajectory of the groups and a possible growing threat to the state.

The Pakistani establishment[61] would benefit from settling the current conflict in Afghanistan, capitalising on its policies towards the Afghan Taliban and being able to focus on the militant Pakistani groups under less scrutiny from the international community. The relationship between these groups and the Pakistani establishment is thus characterised more by influence than by control. It is a strategic calculation on Pakistan's part, informed by what it regards as its vital national interest.

Al-Qaeda-affiliated groups like *Lashkar-e Taiba* have, according to some commentators, become more independent and increased their presence in Afghanistan, fighting a proxy war against Indian government officials and workers there.[62] While some reports of *Lashkar-e Taiba* members carrying membership cards when crossing into Afghanistan seem far-fetched given the nature of the organisation, Pakistani jihadi groups have expanded their operations significantly in the past few years. Often based in Waziristan, these groups have long-standing links with individual Afghan Taliban members and/or commanders reaching back to the 1990s, predominantly through the clergy and the madrassas.

While not the precise subject of this book, Pakistani groups have an interest in perpetuating the conflict in Afghanistan, and, particularly in Waziristan, they have operational links with groups mainly concerned with Afghanistan, such as the Haqqanis. The Afghan Taliban, while having opened up communication to all groups during the 1990s, take pains not to appear connected directly in any significant way with groups like *Lashkar-e Taiba*. There have, however, been reports of emissaries being sent to Pakistani jihadist groups from the Afghan Taliban leadership urging them to step up their fight in Afghanistan against the foreign forces instead of fighting against the Pakistani government.

The main battlefront for most Pakistani jihadi groups remains Kashmir and India, and they are in no way under the command or control of Mullah Mohammad Omar. They remain allies of convenience and necessity. On the other hand, *Lashkar-e Taiba* is believed to be allied with the TTP and associated with al-Qaeda.[63]

Claims of a close or symbiotic relationship between the Afghan Taliban and al-Qaeda and their affiliates are frequently made in the media by journalists and military spokesmen alike.[64] In the past, as was explored in Chapters 8 and 9, claims of links are mostly routed back to statements of Mullah Dadullah and his brother Mansur.[65]

Al-Qaeda themselves are sometimes cited as having played a role in the Afghan Taliban's operations. The suicide bomber who attacked Bagram airbase while Dick Cheney, US Vice President, was visiting in February 2007, for example, was claimed by Mullah Dadullah in an interview with *Al-Jazeera* in April 2007 as an operation that was personally planned by bin Laden.[66] The video footage of the interview with Mullah Dadullah shows no known al-Qaeda members and al-Qaeda did not claim responsibility subsequently for the attack. This, together with the spontaneous nature of Dick Cheney's visit which would have allowed little time for planning and communication with bin Laden, casts doubt on Mullah Dadullah's claim.[67] Similarly, with the attack on a United Nations' guesthouse in October 2009, the attackers, believed to be part of the Haqqani network, are alleged to have been 'trained by al-Qaeda.'[68] The claim of al-Qaeda's involvement in that event is sourced to the former Afghan intelligence chief Amrullah Saleh, who said in a press conference that the operation was led by the Haqqanis and an al-Qaeda operative called Ajmal.[69] His claims remain uncorroborated, with no joint statements issued by al-Qaeda or the Taliban. The attack's significance, as Anand Gopal explained, is that it was carried out by the Haqqanis unilaterally, exposing a rift between them and the Quetta *shura*.[70] The suicide attack on the CIA officers in Khost in December 2009 is a clear and more straightforward instance of collaboration between al-Qaeda, the Pakistani Taliban and possibly the Haqqanis. Khalil Abu Mulal al-Balawi, the attacker, was later revealed in a video together with Hakimullah Mehsud, the leader of the *Tehrik-e Taliban Pakistan*.[71]

Instances of joint attacks either planned or supported by foreign militants are the exception rather than the rule, and direct al-Qaeda involvement in southern Afghanistan remains minimal.[72] An intelligence officer for the international military forces stated that they had identified only seven foreign voices in 13,000 intercepted conversations in the south in April 2010.[73] Another indicator is the small number of foreign prisoners in Bagram air base. Out of the 950 prisoners, only 50 are foreign and three-quarters of those are from Pakistan. 'This is a very local fight,' the US commander of the detention facility has stated.[74]

More importantly, aside from small interventions like that of al-Balawi—which was reportedly provoked by the killing of Beitullah Mehsud[75]—fighting a drawn-out insurgency is not the modus operandi of al-Qaeda, which lacks manpower. They are interested in perpetuating the conflict and sabotaging a political process of any kind, and increasingly they are attempting to gradually build a base of ideological support within the Afghan Taliban's up-and-coming younger generation. It has also been claimed that Jalaluddin Haqqani has a seat on the al-Qaeda consultative council,[76] but no evidence is provided for this, nor does it fit with statements made by Jalaluddin Haqqani or his son Serajuddin.[77] Furthermore, the pattern of al-Qaeda since 2001 has been to be quite compartmentalised as a group—and they were before 2001—to retain an organisational structure separate from that of the Afghan Taliban.

Rumours of shared memberships on councils are common: several insurgents interviewed for a study examining the relationship between the ISI and the Afghan Taliban claimed that the ISI had 'participants/observers' on the Afghan Taliban's Quetta *shura*.[78] Statements of this kind should be treated with great care in the context of the structure of the Taliban insurgency, in particular from field-level commanders, who in increasing numbers have little direct contact with the senior leadership in Quetta. While it is highly likely that elements of the ISI maintain close relations with members of the Quetta *shura*, the nature of the relationship with regards to control, leverage and influence remains disputed.

Moreover, there are no al-Qaeda representatives on the Quetta *shura*. This is admittedly a bold statement. In the context of the current conflict, the Afghan Taliban have remained until now exactly that—Afghan. While a few foreigners fight alongside the Afghan Taliban, the leadership and commanders have always been Afghan, there has been no equivalent of Khattab to date.

Interviews conducted for this book yielded no specific claims of cooperation between the Taliban and al-Qaeda aside from the general observation that it is in al-Qaeda's interest that the Taliban continue to fight within Afghanistan and thus abstain from negotiations—and that there is some support being given to the Taliban.[79] Another interviewee stated that, 'the Taliban have many problems amongst themselves, and it is only the American pressure which gives [al-Qaeda and the Taliban] something to be united about.'[80]

The 'Afghanistan War' Wikileaks documents (released in July 2010) cover the period 2004–10 and contain a number of unconfirmed claims as to the relationship between the Afghan Taliban and al-Qaeda. These often seem to amount to no more than rumour. In December 2005, for instance, a report was issued claiming that Hekmatyar and 'Bin Ladin's financial advisor,' a certain Dr Amin, flew to North Korea from Iran, returning to Helmand. They reportedly made a deal there to purchase 'remote-controlled rockets for use against American and Coalition aircraft.'[81] In August 2006, another report was made claiming that monthly face-to-face meetings were taking place between Mullah Mohammad Omar, bin Laden, and Mullahs Dadullah and Berader in Quetta in order to plan suicide attack operations for Afghanistan. Huge amounts of money were then allegedly allocated as compensation for the bombers' families, and meetings even reportedly discussed specific targets for individual operations. The allegations are uncorroborated, and have been met with wide scepticism by the analyst and research community. Indeed, they appear so far removed from the realms of possibility that their inclusion and very presence within the Wikileaks data should cast doubt over other reports.[82] There is also a strong motive for the Afghan NDS and other Afghan informants to feed this kind of misinformation.

Similarly, in August 2008, a report came in stating that the Taliban were attempting to use chemical weapons against international military forces as well as trying to acquire uranium for use in a bomb against a military facility in Kabul.[83] While the veracity of this claim cannot be assessed, it is another claim of interaction between foreign jihadists and the Afghan Taliban that remains unconfirmed and seems dubious in the context of the modus operandi of the groups that make up the Afghan Taliban.

Outside Pressure

If it wishes, Pakistan can apply considerable pressure on the Afghan Taliban and act as the ultimate spoiler; Mullah Mohammad Omar seems to be tightly under lock and key; the arrests of 2010 offer an implicit threat to sub-senior leaders; the Haqqanis are positioning themselves as actors with more to say in any possible deal to be made with the insurgency, despite their relatively small constituent base of support; and the leading figures of the insurgency fighting in Afghanistan are probably almost all in Pakistan.[84] These factors give Pakistan a de facto veto on any attempt at unified political action for a settlement within Afghanistan.

Pakistan officially denies the United States and NATO forces the possibility of following insurgents across the border into Pakistan, hence the United States has been relying heavily on drone strikes. The number of attacks per year have increased from just one a year in 2004 and 2005 to 34 in 2008, 53 in 2009 and 79[85] in 2010. A study by Peter Bergen and Katherine Tiedemann estimated the number of deaths from these drone strikes as 301 in 2008, 502 in 2009, and 130 (as of 24 February 2010).[86] The numbers are the average of the highest and lowest reported figures available, but when compared against the numbers of 'militants' allegedly killed, 32% of casualties were civilian.

The drone attacks do seem to have had an effect in that both insurgents and inhabitants of the areas where drone strikes have happened often report considerable fear and unease about the silent threat in the sky.[87] They were, according to an American journalist kidnapped and held in the tribal areas, a 'terrifying presence' that dictated much of what the jihadis would do in the open.[88] A survey conducted in Pakistan's tribal areas from June to July 2010 showed that three-quarters of local people in the FATA were opposed to the drone strikes.[89]

While drone attacks have disrupted militant operations operating or based in the FATA, their long-term effects may prove counter-productive. Drone strikes have limited the possibility for training outside, forcing training camps to be moved underground and meaning sessions to be held in small groups inside houses. Planning and coordination, due to the severe threat against leadership figures, has also suffered significantly. The drone campaign, therefore, may fulfil the short-term objectives of denying freedom of movement and disrupting operations while failing to address the long-term issues.[90]

Afghan Taliban

Taliban Aspirations and Goals

Eight years after the beginning of Operation Enduring Freedom Mullah Mohammad Omar issued a statement in 2009 claiming that the Taliban 'did not have any agenda to harm other countries, including Europe, nor do we have such an agenda today.'[91] In January 2010, while the Afghanistan conference was being held in London, another communiqué was issued by the central office: '[t]he Islamic Emirate want[s] to have good and positive relations with the neighbouring countries in an atmosphere of mutual respect and take far-reaching steps for bilateral cooperation, economic development and prosperous future.'[92]

While often in direct violation of international human rights norms, in particular with regards to women and girls but also towards men, the Afghan Taliban leadership, and especially its founding and early members, represent a movement imbued with values based on their interpretation of Islam and socio-economic heritage. These values are frequently cited in Taliban press releases, in interviews and in their video propaganda materials. These values still represent a mixture of local customs and religious norms that resonate in a number of Afghan communities, particularly among the rural Pashtun south and east.[93] These offer, too, a broad-brush political vision, albeit one lacking specifics of how their broad goals are to be implemented or even how they would alter the precedents set when they ruled Afghanistan in the 1990s. An *eid* letter writ-

303

ten by Mullah Mohammad Omar (issued on 8 September 2010) comes as close
to an outline of their domestic policies as we have:

The victory of our Islamic nation over the invading infidels is now imminent and the
driving force behind this is the belief in the help of Allah (SwT) and unity among ourselves. In the time to come, we will try to establish an Islamic, independent, perfect
and strong system on the basis of these principles—a system with economic, security,
legal, educational and judicial aspects being based on the injunctions of Islam and conducted through a consultative body joined by persons with experience, knowledge and
expertise. All God-fearing, experienced and professional cadres of the Afghan society
will be part and parcel of this system without any political, racial and lingual [sic]
discriminations.

Administrative responsibilities will be devolved on them according to their talent and
honesty. We will respect the Islamic rights of all people of the country including women;
will implement Sharia rules in the light of the injunctions of the sacred religion of Islam
in order to efficiently maintain internal security and eradicate immorality, injustice,
indecency and other vices; will strictly observe the law of punishment and reward and
auditing in order to bring about administrative transparency in all government departments. The violators will be dealt with according to the Sharia rules.[94]

While still focusing on their key message of security and justice, Taliban
actions on the ground are often ad hoc and reactive. Much of this can be
explained by the internal structure of the Taliban insurgency: the governance
structures to which the Taliban leadership itself aspire grants significant auton-
omy to district- and province-level Taliban *shuras* and commanders.[95] There
are also strategic considerations that affect regional policy: for example, there
is an encouragement of franchise groups operating in the north—groups that
bear the Taliban's name but may never have had significant interactions with
the Taliban's leadership in Pakistan or any past associations with the movement.[96] This loose association is encouraged because a strong and resurgent
northern 'front' is sought, but in the long term there will almost certainly be
some attempt to consolidate and solidify these groups and bring them in under
the Taliban's hierarchy in order to enforce its rules. Section six of the most
recent *layeha* deals specifically with some of the rules and restrictions for these
franchise operations.

While the leadership apparatus works to retain unity, the overall Taliban
group—a diverse set of actors—manifests considerable internal strife. In response,
the leadership conducts damage control in the public media and attempts to
implement checks and balances to enforce its command and increase group cohesion. This may take the form of official denials of attacks in which large numbers

of civilians die or are injured,[97] or greater local engagement with communities. The appointment of individuals and organs that deal with mediation and public complaints demonstrates awareness of these increasing problems.[98]

By 2010, it appeared that much of the public opinion in southern and eastern Afghanistan broadly reflected the narrative of the Taliban's information war. Much of what is perceived as successful Taliban propaganda concerning the Afghan government and the foreign forces today is in fact made up of narratives that reflect beliefs broadly held by increasing numbers of Afghans, particularly those living in rural areas of the country; this applies both to individuals that are pro-Afghan government and against the Taliban, as well as to those supporting the insurgency.[99] There is a widespread belief in a host of conspiracy theories, often perpetuated by Taliban propaganda, which flourishes and makes an impact without being dependent on official messaging by the insurgency. For example, large public suicide attacks, or IEDs that cause large numbers of civilian casualties, are often believed to actually have been conducted by foreigners. In the aftermath of a vehicle-borne IED explosion in central Kandahar City that destroyed dozens of shops and killed and injured over a hundred people, numerous individuals interviewed in its aftermath independently stated that they had seen the 'foreign' or 'American' helicopter or jet that dropped a bomb or fired a missile.[100]

The claim that Pashtuns are xenophobic and that foreigners are unwelcome is not innate to Pashtun communities—as some commentators have claimed[101]—but it has slowly taken root since 2001. The Helmand River Valley Authority Project, launched with US assistance in the late 1940s to attend to solve irrigation problems in southern Afghanistan, is a useful corrective to this widely-held belief: the project was not subject to attack, 'mullah rebellions' or significant public disapproval, nor were the American staff who worked on it.[102]

When the Taliban's successful propaganda campaign merges with conspiracy theories that are now widely accepted in local communities, an incendiary combination obtains. There has been a noticeable shift in the perceptions of the local population in Afghanistan's southern and south-eastern provinces. Statements made by President Karzai claiming that foreign helicopters transferred Taliban fighters from the south to the north[103] echo a now-common perception regarding the American presence. While many used to doubt such conspiracy theories—for instance, those claiming that the United States is not in Afghanistan to defeat the Taliban, but rather chooses to prolong the conflict for reasons ranging from regional power politics to US dominance of Central Asia and the natural resources to be found there—today, most southern

Afghans seem convinced.[104] This shift in Afghans' perception of the United States is arguably more worrying, with increasing numbers of people believing that it[105] is no longer interested in defeating the Taliban.[106] Many hold that the United States is actively supporting the Taliban.[107] If they weren't, the argument runs, how is it that the world's greatest military power—with all its 'satellites, spies and money'—cannot defeat a few thousand individuals in southern Afghanistan with 'old Kalashnikovs' from the 1980s.[108] This perceptual shift amid an insurgency ultimately undermines the efforts of the United States and other international actors.

The Taliban have used a host of different coercive tactics and incentives to entice the population and separate it from the government, while individuals who have actively joined the Taliban or tacitly supported them have a host of motivations to do so. The grievances of the Afghan population that drive much of the insurgency today have stemmed from the environment that has emerged, often with the help of the United States and its allies, in the aftermath of their arrival in 2001. This seemingly causal relationship is not lost on the Afghan population.

The Afghan Taliban have a host of conditional allies—many of whom fall under the characterisation of a 'marriage of convenience.' The relationships vary among the different parts that make up the Afghan Taliban and the many other groups located along the border region in Pakistan and that operate in Afghanistan.

These relationships often amount to little more than sporadic personal contacts and a distant tacit acceptance based on the commonality of being Muslim and having a current common enemy. At other times, close proximity in Pakistan, together with shared locations and support networks, have resulted in the rise of closer cooperation, as is the case with the Haqqani network in North Waziristan. Many groups engaged in Afghanistan's conflict and based along the border rely partially on the same logistics and support networks. These are more or less service providers, whose motivations rank from ideological to financial; they include smugglers, traders, money-changers and *hawala* agents.[109]

The importance of the safe haven is paramount to the Afghan Taliban's leadership who have therefore avoided conducting operations on Pakistan's soil. The frequent attacks on NATO convoys inside Pakistan seem to be exclusively carried out by other groups, albeit supported by the insurgency in Afghanistan. Nevertheless, the relationships among the individual groups are complicated; as the Afghan Taliban have taken care not to anger the ISI, they have stayed neutral and withheld comment on their relationships to other groups based in the FATA since the death of Mullah Dadullah. The Afghan Taliban face the world's most sophisticated army; antagonising other groups or perpetuating other conflicts is not in their interest.

While at times differing on ideological, strategical strategic and tactical issues, the Taliban share long-standing tribal, cultural and social ties with a number of the groups located along the border stemming back to the late 1970s and 1980s when many were studying together in Pakistani institutions and madrassas.[110]

The Taliban's declared intentions and goals for Afghanistan have been relatively consistent, and are reflected in public statements by both the leadership based in Quetta and the political Talibs based in Kabul, the second of whom do not speak officially for the movement but may be seen as unofficial advocates for a political solution. While there can be speculation about the Taliban's long-term goals, today or in their incarnation in the 1990s, the movement as such (as explored in chapters 5–10) has been subject to continuous change and has been strongly influenced by policy decisions by the international community and neighbouring states, which makes predictions about its trajectory highly speculative.

As a movement, the Afghan Taliban remain concerned primarily with Afghanistan. Individual voices as well as official statements have repeatedly stated that they seek good relations with the world and do not intend to interfere in other countries' affairs or attack them. Statements calling for a 'global *jihad*' or in support of such actions taken by other groups are not to be found in recent years from the Afghan Taliban, and there are implicit indications that they are systematically trying to emphasise this point. See, for example, the section of Mullah Mohammad Omar's 2010 *Eid* message relating to international relations:

Our upcoming system will be based on mutual interactions with neighbouring, Islamic and non-Islamic countries. We want to frame our foreign policy on the principle that we will not harm others nor allow others to harm us. Our upcoming system of government will participate in all regional and global efforts aimed at establishing peace and stability, human prosperity and economic advancement on the basis of the Islamic laws and will cooperate with regional countries in all common problems of the region like (finding solution to) narcotics, environment pollution, commercial and economic problem.[111]

A question mark hangs over whether the Taliban seek to take over the country again, or simply participate and influence politics in a manner conducive to their views on the implementation of *shari'a* law. On the one hand, they consistently refer to themselves as 'the Islamic Emirate of Afghanistan' in statements, continuing to present themselves as a government in absentia. On the other hand, the content of their statements, and of conversations with the authors of this book as well as interlocutors with Talibs or Taliban-affiliates, suggest that the movement and its leadership doesn't seriously believe it can take the principal role in government again—borne out of an assessment of their failure to provide for the country during the 1990s—but that as long as they have a say and representation politically, culturally and socially, then they would settle for that.[112]

The new generation of insurgents, a younger group with no recollection of an Afghanistan that was not at war, are less inclined to reach a political settlement. While data on this younger generation is scarce, individual voices suggest that they seek a return of the Emirate, capturing the entire state. While older Talibs often reflect carefully and at length in interviews as to their exact demands and goals, compared to the somewhat uncompromising official statements being put forward by the movement at large, the younger generation appears to seek the most strict and rigid application of the official line. In short, the older generation appears more pragmatic and aware of the function of propaganda, while the younger generation is not.[113]

Layeha 2010

The third (known) version of the Taliban's rule book was published in May 2010.[114] It offers some useful examples of how the group has been developing as an organisation, and gives a clear indication of the central concerns which the leadership has and how they seek to address them. Contrasting the different versions of the *layeha* shows how the leadership, and with it the insurgency at large, has changed over the years. The third edition is considerably longer than its two predecessors, and some sections relating to the movement's bureaucracy verge on being impractical in their suggestions since they don't reflect realities inside Afghanistan.

Older versions included relatively little about the motivations for fighting or joining the Taliban, but version three has an introduction which attempts this.[115] The main focus of the *layeha*, according to its introduction, is to ensure that the targets of attacks be made clearer, more specific and more justified. Much of the rule book is concerned with the command structure, and seems to aim to reassert the central leadership's command. In 2006 the list of rules was almost a collection of individual complaints, but by 2009 it manifested more thorough organisation. Greater attention was paid to the overall style and composition of the document and better methods of enforcing the rules throughout the entire group were specified. The latest version reads almost like an ideal version of reality, outlining processes and procedures the leadership does not have the ability to control on the ground.

There are only a few new major substantive features: rule 26 categorically states that contractors providing labourers to 'the enemy' should be killed;[116] similarly, there is a new rule on the prerequisites for carrying out large-scale attacks on 'enemy bases' (56).[117]

Where are the Taliban Heading?

The addition of over 30,000 foreign troops—the last of whom arrived in September 2010[118]—to the field in Afghanistan has had different effects on the ground. The Afghan Taliban believe that they can outlast the foreign presence; in this, they are comforted by media reports of the indecisiveness and frustration of the US administration with the rate of progress in the country.[119] This is true even now that they have come under increased pressure and suffered increasing losses. Nevertheless, the Afghan Taliban's own campaign continues to be effective, of which assassinations, IEDs and a propaganda machine functioning almost autonomously are prominent features.

The date and nature of the drawdown of troops has undergone several adjustments since its first announcement by President Obama and continues to sow widespread confusion in Afghanistan and elsewhere. US Secretary of State Hillary Clinton announced the beginning of a troop withdrawal in July 2011, handing over security responsibility to Afghan security forces and envisioning an end to combat operations by 2014. US Secretary of Defense Robert Gates, in a comment made on a visit to Afghanistan in early 2011, said that American forces might stay beyond the announced date.[120] Already, in the aftermath of President Obama's speech of December 2009 and amid an ever-deteriorating security situation, Afghans who were more mobile and had the option to go started to move away from the south, freeing up assets and relocating their families.[121] With the international effort focusing on Afghanistan's south, the climate has grown increasingly polarised, in particular in Kandahar, and the international forces as well as the insurgency have stepped up their campaign. The Afghan population finds itself between the two. While a definitive answer as to the effect of the surge strategy has yet to materialise, there is reason to be cautious in calling the strategy a success.

Current trends seem to indicate at the very least a continuation of the conflict, with comparably high levels of violence, for some time to come. An escalation of force has seen the conflict intensify, particularly throughout the south and east. The argument often advanced by the military—that levels of violence have increased because they have been taking the fight to the enemy—seems to hold true; a surge of NATO force has seen a surge of effort among the insurgents. The long-term viability of the surge as a strategy that sets Afghanistan on the road towards peace remains doubtful.

Taliban in the North

The Taliban's increasing focus on northern Afghanistan was one of the notable trends of 2010 in that the Quetta-directed attempts gained some traction after at least two years of being relatively unsuccessful. Most provinces in the north—in particular Kunduz, Baghlan, Badghis and Faryab—now have active Taliban or Taliban-affiliated groups operating. The issue of exactly which groups are fighting there is indicative of how the Taliban are trying different methods of expanding their influence. Thus, there are Talibs sent from southern and eastern Afghanistan up to the north to rally members of the local Pashtun communities; there are reports of members of the Islamic Movement of Uzbekistan (IMU) and the Islamic Jihad Union (IJU) operating in various provinces in the north, although estimates seem to suggest that there aren't more than a couple of hundred at most;[122] there are some Haqqani-affiliated groups of Uzbeks and other Central Asian foreigners operating in the north, mainly in Kunduz;[123] and there are even disaffected former *Jamiat* and *Junbesh* commanders who have now allied themselves with the insurgency.[124] The structure and nature of the insurgency in northern Afghanistan reflects the significantly different environment in the north, with its diverse ethnic population and different power structures.

An identifiable pattern of how the Taliban seek to expand into new districts and provinces has now emerged. It is usefully summed up as follows:

The Taleban seem to have perfected their insurgency 'template,' which consists of a number of phases of recruitment as well as the selection of appropriate strongholds from which to operate in relative safety. These phases of recruitment can be observed all over the north: the infiltration of political agents to re-establish contact with old supporters or to identify new ones; the arrival of preachers who invite locals to join jihad; the establishment of small groups of armed men (a mix of returning locals and outsiders) to conduct armed propaganda and the intimidation of hostile elements; and finally, extensive local recruitment and military escalation.[125]

The decision to focus on the north was reportedly taken in 2007, but there were sporadic attacks and attempts to kindle more movement in 2005–2006.[126] In Kunduz, for example, proper efforts began in early 2007 that culminated in a suicide attack on a German military convoy in May. As a result, the German military cut down on patrols and the Taliban had some space and freedom to continue building up their forces. By 2008/2009, Chardara district was under their control, and by late spring 2009 there were extensive shadow governmental structures in place there.[127] Explanations for the Taliban's success in expanding its influence into the north are often the same as for their revival in the south: grievances with the local government structures, the actions of foreign troops, and a lack of access to justice, in particular with regards to local land disputes; all these factors have played a role. The ethnic factor in the north is another major reason, along with the anti-Pashtun reprisals post-2001. The Taliban envoys sent as representatives of the Islamic Emirate were adept, moreover, at exploiting local rivalries (whether ethnic disputes or more straightforward struggles for power) and they were helped by widespread sympathy among local clergy dating back to the 1990s.[128] There are reports that there has been some tolerance of these insurgent groups by the Karzai government, supposedly with a view to retaining a strong Pashtun influence in and over the north.[129]

For the Taliban, a move into the north helps to show that the movement is not merely a southern phenomenon and that they could claim to represent other ethnic groups and regions other than just rural Pashtun communities. They have had considerable difficulties in winning over non-Pashtun communities, but in 2009 there were at least three non-Pashtun Taliban shadow governors in the north, and local Taliban had made significant inroads into Uzbek and Tajik communities.[130]

Creating a second front in the north has also forced significant redeployment of international troops.[131] The near-simultaneous appearance of unconnected groups in different provinces across the north in 2007–2008 should be regarded as evidence that this is a centrally-directed campaign. The increasing success of the traditionally Pashtun-dominated Taliban to recruit from other ethnic groups is a worrying development, and is likely to lead to a further deterioration of the security situation in the northern provinces. Voices from Quetta suggest that the Taliban aim to commit more resources to the north in 2011.[132]

US Policy to Fracture the Insurgency

A new strategy outlined by General Stanley McChrystal and endorsed by President Barack Obama in November 2009 advocated a temporary troop 'surge' in Afghanistan and a use of counterinsurgency tactics to reverse the momentum that the insurgency had generated over the prior few years that saw them gaining ground around the country, and to train and mentor Afghan security forces so that these could take over security operations when the American and other foreign troop withdrawals commenced.

While analysts have pointed out that Afghanistan is in the midst of a political conflict that needs a political solution, and international conferences have highlighted the need for a political strategy, there still seem to be considerable differences in how this strategy is articulated.[133] As General Petraeus stated,

You don't end an industrial-strength insurgency by killing or capturing all the bad guys. You have to kill, capture—or turn—the bad guys. And that means reintegration and reconciliation.[134]

The US military regards much of the political strategy as part of its war effort to win the military conflict. The counterinsurgency campaign, focusing on southern Afghanistan, is meant to exert pressure on the Taliban and force them to the negotiation table on terms favourable to international and Afghan government forces. It is held as vital to negotiate from a position of strength.[135]

Kandahar is at the centre of these efforts; it is the birthplace of the Taliban and several districts of the province can be understood as their traditional support base. The plan to focus on Kandahar City was announced at the beginning of 2011, just as a separate military offensive in neighbouring Helmand province was drawing to a close. In Helmand's Marja, the aim was to drive the Taliban out and to replace it with something that offered local people some basic services, the so-called 'government-in-a-box.'[136] Reports written since the official conclusion of that operation suggest that the installation of legitimate Afghan government representation in the far-off hinterlands is proving difficult. The Taliban have stepped up their campaign of intimidation and fear through threats and assassination.[137] Reports of the operations in Helmand province vary widely in their assessment of the current situation and the effect of the efforts undertaken by the US military.[138] The areas that have been the focus of the recent and current operations, such as Marja, Naw Zad, Garmsir and Sangin, all appear to see a continuation of the conflict; some areas even claim a resurgence in fighting.[139]

For Kandahar in summer 2010, the goal seemed to be equally simple: reverse the trends of previous years which saw the Taliban gain strength and popularity in the face of the Afghan government's descent into illegitimacy and corruption. There were, thus, two targets of the campaign. The US military (with the Afghan army in tow) would carry out a focused campaign against the Taliban in the areas they currently dominate; this would—the argument ran—demonstrate to ordinary Kandaharis that a new force has come to the south, one that means to stay.[140]

As a second front, efforts would be taken to reform and reintroduce the Afghan government to the people of Kandahar. This would mean closer supervision of and attention to local representatives, ranging from the police to the judiciary to the provincial council. The end goal, as publicly stated, was for the people of southern Afghanistan to shift their support from the Taliban to the institutions and figures that represent the Afghan government.[141]

It is the policy of the United States military to attempt to fracture and divide the insurgency.[142] It seeks to do this through financial, military, moral and logistical pressure:

'Actual reconciliation, or bringing members of the Taliban into the government, isn't likely until after they see the prospect of defeat,' Petraeus said, referring to a position often expressed by Gates. 'That's not to say there shouldn't be an effort to achieve national consensus on reconciliation, should the opportunity present itself,' Petraeus said.[143]

Arrests and an aggressive capture-or-kill campaign being conducted in both Afghanistan and Pakistan by foreign military forces has meant that the older generation of Taliban leadership is struggling to maintain its hold over the insurgency.[144] It is close to impossible to determine exact numbers of Taliban commanders that have been killed or captured in the past year; statistics vary widely or are not available. In July 2010, the *New York Times* quoted NATO military statistics as showing that, in the prior six months, 130 important insurgency figures had been captured or killed in Afghanistan.[145] In the same month, Amrullah Saleh, the former NDS chief, said that under General McChrystal, 700 Taliban commanders were captured or killed.[146] In October 2010, ISAF announced that it had conducted 3,279 special operations in the three previous months, resulting in 293 insurgent leaders killed/captured and 2,169 insurgents captured.[147] The figures released in early spring 2011 covered the period 24 April 2010 to 15 April 2011, during which, ISAF claimed, there had been 11,500 Special Forces operations, 3,200 'insurgent fighters' killed, 1,500 'insurgent leaders' killed or captured and 800 'insurgent fighters' captured.[148]

This, when taken together with the arrest of a number of members of the Afghan Taliban's leadership council in Pakistan in early 2010,[149] indicates how the insurgency has seen a turnover from its highest executive council to the regional and local levels, down to the district-level commanders. While there seems to be ample manpower to fill these positions, a point well reflected in the still-increasing number of insurgent attacks per month in comparison to 2009,[150] the switchover of entire command networks has weakened the chain of command, threatening the overall integrity of the leadership's hold over the insurgency. Younger Taliban members have moved into the command structures and leadership positions. There have also been errors in the targeting of insurgency leadership figures.[151]

Members of the older generation that are still active have seen their authority and ability to speak for the movement wane rapidly over the past twelve months. This applies not only to the leader, Mullah Mohammad Omar, but also to those one level below him: Mullah Obaidullah and Mullah Berader are but two of the most well-known examples.

The campaign to target the mid- and high-ranking leadership appears to be a key part of the foreign engagement with the Taliban as of summer 2011 and its impact has undeniably been felt.[152] As the older generation's numbers diminish, the vacant positions and power vacuum are filled by two younger generations: the clerics and bureaucrats involved in the Taliban's government during the 1990s, and an even more youthful set of commanders. This latter generation is potentially a more serious and different threat. With little memory of Afghan society prior to the Soviet war in the 1980s, this disparate set of commanders is more ideologically motivated and less nationalistic than the older generations, and are therefore less pragmatic. They are not interested in any negotiations or compromise with foreigners. They do not remember nor were they present during the Taliban's government of the 1990s; as such, they have little incentive or desire to compromise. They have never lived in an Afghanistan that was at peace.

What makes this development potentially dangerous is the shift in ideology that seems to follow together with the fact that al-Qaeda operatives and other groups have been known to seek direct contact with Taliban field commanders inside Afghanistan.[153] This new generation, as outlined above, increasingly frames the conflict in ideological terms. Where the veterans would talk of a fight against foreign invaders, the new generation is resisting infidel crusaders. With al-Qaeda making tentative advances, their world view is increasingly infiltrating the younger generation of the Afghan Taliban. This appears not to be widespread yet, but it is a noticeable trend.

The Western aim appears to be that its aggressive targeting of the insurgency will weaken its structures and leave it more open to reconciling its various fragmented branches with the government, rather than dealing with the group en masse.

This will, the argument runs, lead to military victory and the demise of the movement at large.[154] The more likely outcome, however, is potentially very different.

Contrary to what might be expected, the current processes fragmenting the insurgency are unlikely to lead to its demise. The insurgency's structure in itself is deeply fragmented, with the Taliban leadership trying to enforce its command over all its discrete elements—its fighters and subcommand—and has proven considerably more durable than expected. Furthermore, much of the support structure is provided by a separate network of groups. Weapons, ammunition and other supplies are provided by a diverse network of traders and smugglers, some affiliated with the Afghan government and security forces.[155]

The weakening of the chain of command within the Afghan Taliban is further fuelled by the increasing financial independence of local Taliban field commanders who are mostly responsible for their own weapons and logistics supplies, which they fund from their activities.[156] The Taliban leadership are continuously working on maintaining the cohesion of the overall insurgency but only manage to control parts and sections. While the overall strength of the insurgency is unlikely to be diminished by these processes, the deeper fragmentation gives room for groups like al-Qaeda to infiltrate and manipulate Afghan Taliban groups, fostering an ideological shift away from national concerns and towards the international conflict in which al-Qaeda and other such groups conceive themselves to be involved.

While the targeted campaign against the Taliban leadership and command structures has been active for over a year now, there has been no significant downturn in violence or insurgent attacks. The side effects of the capture-or-kill campaign, however, have been significant. Much of the information that forms the basis for arrests and night raids to extract individuals appears to be plagued by faulty intelligence.[157] While civilian deaths at the hands of foreign troops have decreased, anecdotal evidence suggests that night raids and the imprisonment of innocent individuals who find themselves handed over to corrupt Afghan security services and the Afghan justice system have increased. More often than not, this has severe repercussions for the United States and foreign troops' relationships with entire communities.[158]

Increased Decentralisation

Commanders in the south and south-east have gained significant financial independence from the central leadership, having gained enough control and

315

access to most of the business activity in their areas to be able to extract taxes.[159] Individual Taliban commanders also often profit directly from foreign aid projects by providing security or receiving payoffs from local implementing partners in exchange for security.[160] New commanders that replace those who have been killed or captured inherit the local financial network, one whose volume has increased significantly with the increase of foreign aid and investment. The younger generation is less tied into the wider insurgency structure and the command network of the central leadership, and financial independence gives them considerable room to continue the fight and ignore senior commanders or the leadership in Quetta, which with each turnover has to re-establish and enforce its command.

This financial independence and the challenge of coherence among the ranks of commanders is seen as a problem by the central leadership, and this is evidenced by remarks in all three iterations of the Taliban rule book that have been released since 2006. The problem has increased alongside the increase in foreign assistance—whether in the form of security contracting or simply for construction projects.[161] Even 'official' Taliban district governors and judges affiliated with the central leadership in Quetta occasionally have found that commanders in their areas of responsibility have taken unilateral action. This was the case in July 2010 when night letters warning tribal elders were distributed in certain villages of Panjwayi.[162] The elders, who had good relations with the Taliban authorities in their district, allowing them to remain there, queried the new warning letters and were told that they had been issued by someone over whom the movement had no control. The elders were assured that the Taliban's central administration would carry out a full investigation.[163]

The incorporation of new commanders and groups into the insurgency is a difficult undertaking that demands continuous effort and oversight. The Taliban try to micro-manage their relations with individual communities and aim to control the behaviour of individual commanders so as not to alienate those on whose support they rely, but they are increasingly losing control.

Fractures Within the Taliban

Challenges to Mullah Mohammad Omar

One symptom of this increased radicalisation is the waning influence of Mullah Mohammad Omar.[164] This is perhaps inevitable given that he hasn't appeared among members of the movement for several years now and seems to function more as a symbolic or strategic figurehead rather than as an actively involved leader.

It is only recently, though, that lower ranks and their commanders have started to air their dissatisfaction with Mullah Mohammad Omar.[165] In early summer 2010, for example, there was considerable confusion and discussion surrounding a Taliban figure who claimed to be the successor to Mullah Berader following his capture. Mullah Gul Akhund, originally from Kandahar and very close to Mullah Mohammad Omar, reportedly had a letter signed by the Taliban's head stating that he was the leader, while other figures refused to believe this claim.[166] Beyond Mullah Mohammad Omar's core southern constituency, there were always lines of dissent—the attitude of the Haqqanis towards the southerners more or less from the point that they signed up with the movement in 1995 is an example of this—but the fact that such remarks are made these days is noteworthy.

Mullah Mohammad Omar has not been credibly sighted for several years. In 2003 he reportedly visited a mosque in Quetta and spoke to some Afghans,[167] and in 2006 he was again seen there, but since then the only contact between the Taliban leader and the public has been the twice-yearly dispatches put out on *eid ul-fitr* and *eid ul-adha*. These have not always been regular and it is clear that the authority of Mullah Mohammad Omar is weakening the longer he continues to live under presumed house-arrest in Pakistan.[168]

It is now easy to issue letters or statements under his name without challenge. The most recent example—much publicised by ISAF media spokesmen—was an order to assassinate government members.[169] The Taliban's website, aside from offering a channel through which to issue statements to the internationals in Afghanistan, exists in large part simply to preserve some semblance of Taliban orthodoxy given this problem. When a statement is published on the website it can be safely assumed that this reflects the position of the older-generation Pakistan-based Afghan Taliban leadership. The decision to sack Mansour Dadullah was announced on the website for exactly this reason.[170]

Mullah Mohammad Omar's position, however, is unlikely to be openly challenged; as *amir ul-mu'mineen* his position holds a religious status. An open challenge would be understood by many as drawing close to *fitna*, or 'disorder,' among the *umma*. Yet twenty-four fighters—more than half of the mid-ranking Taliban commanders interviewed for Graeme Smith's *Talking to the Taliban*—'were willing to say that [Mullah Mohammad Omar] was not necessarily required for their war, nor necessarily the best leader for Afghanistan.'[171]

The Afghan Taliban are evolving as a group; if current trends are not fundamentally altered, the movement will be increasingly less subject to hierarchies and restraints on the part of its senior leadership. The most significant challenge to the leadership of Mullah Mohammad Omar currently can be found in the younger generation of commanders who are more and more independent, both financially and ideologically, from the old-school Kandahari Taliban leadership based in Quetta. Internal threats to the credibility of the senior leadership are not, however, threatening their integrity and ability to implement decisions for the moment. Loyalty seems to be relatively robust. Of course, field commanders will often be the first to speak out against their senior leadership,[172] but this is normal in every military organisation and not necessarily particularly unique to the Taliban.

Mullah Mohammad Omar, moreover, has managed to keep his moral authority relatively intact in the eyes of many in the movement. That said, learning the lessons of the September 11 attacks must have required a rethink of the role and suitability of Mullah Mohammad Omar as the leadership figure within the movement. It is entirely possible—although this is speculative—that the penultimate tier of Taliban leaders (those visible on the ground and taking decisions as to the future direction of the movement on a daily basis) are not entirely dissatisfied with Mullah Mohammad Omar's currently limited presence and influence.

Negotiations or Reintegration?

The prospect of reconciliation and a reintegration programme backed by hundreds of millions of dollars is of concern for the senior leadership in Quetta, as illustrated by statements issued on their website.[173] The Taliban has run a targeted counter-campaign since the idea started to be discussed in mid-2009 in which an increasing number of interlocutors is active, individuals who move back and forth between Afghanistan, the commanders and representatives on the ground as well as among the leadership in Pakistan.[174] Afghan government reintegration programmes that were being implemented in Helmand in summer 2010 are indicative of the procedures adopted. Individuals who wanted to take part needed a sponsor who would guarantee them and have various Afghan government officials to sign off on their reintegration, while agreeing to the following conditions:

I renounce the actions and objective of the Taliban and other groups that seek to undermine GIRoA or harm either the Afghan National Security Forces (ANSF) or the International Security Assistance Forces (ISAF).

I pledge to provide no support to the enemies of GIRoA and will inform GIRoA, ANSF, or ISAF officials any time I have information concerning Taliban or criminal activities.

I agree never again to raise arms against my Government and will work towards building a peaceful community.

I understand that my final reintegration requires the approval of GIRoA officials and my solemn commitment to this pledge.

I voluntarily submit my biometric data with the understanding that it can be used to identify and prosecute me if I break solemn pledge.

I make this pledge on my honor and also that of my sponsor.[175]

The Afghan government's programme states that reintegrated Talibs must accept the Afghan constitution, put down their weapons and renounce al-Qaeda. Since the Afghan government started this reintegration programme at the same time as the capture-or-kill campaign conducted by foreign military forces in Afghanistan and across the border in Pakistan, the Afghan Taliban, like the senior military leadership of the United States, regard this programme as part of the overall military campaign that seeks to divide the insurgency.[176]

The programme itself seems riddled with problems even though it isn't the first time reconciliation has been attempted. The lessons from previous programmes do not seem to have been learnt.[177] A central problem with the current reconciliation programme is the lack of protection the government can extend to individuals who choose to take part. Entire groups, large enough to protect themselves, would have to be reconciled, or individuals relocated and put under permanent protection in order to ensure their safety.[178]

Data published by the *New York Times* have shown that the hopes for reintegration as a major solution in Taliban-dominated areas—as the London Conference seemed to suggest—have come to nought.[179] Only 100 fighters had joined the government side between April and early September 2010, and a senior official at the Peace and Reconciliation Commission stated that '[the programme's] almost dead.' Even enlistments into the Afghan National Army have lagged. In August 2010, just 66 of 3,708 recruits from southern Afghanistan were Pashtuns, and this was after a concerted effort to recruit southerners through appeals to tribes and provincial councils.[180]

Quetta versus Waziristan

The insurgency in Afghanistan is made up of a multitude of different groups.[181] The Taliban are the largest and arguably leading faction, but they themselves are made up of a number of distinct larger groupings. The most influential and indeed oldest of these is the group surrounding Jalaluddin Haqqani and his family, in particular his son Serajuddin who has taken over what is commonly referred to as 'the Haqqani network.'

As elaborated in chapters 3, 5 and 6, Haqqani rose to prominence during the 1980s *jihad*, and joined with the Taliban in February 1995. Since 2003, Haqqani has played an increasingly important role within the insurgency, heading the Miram Shah *shura* and having a seat on the Taliban's leadership *shura* in Quetta as established in 2003. Haqqani, with his long-standing ties to the Arab world and Pakistan's ISI, has gained significant influence and power among the Afghan Taliban. The strict isolation of Mullah Mohammad Omar and the arrest of a significant number of members of the leadership *shura* means that Haqqani and his group have gained in importance. They operate as a semi-independent network; commanders forge personal ties to him and his influence extends to groups throughout Afghanistan far beyond his original peer group of the Zadran tribe in greater Paktya.

The arrests of senior Afghan Taliban figures by Pakistan in early 2010 was a sign of the group's inability to balance its relationship to the ISI with its own agenda. It indicated the significant pressure the Afghan Taliban leadership circles are under, and caused the Haqqanis' status to rise further. With longer and better ties to the ISI and a greater flexibility and freedom of manoeuvre, the Haqqanis increasingly appear to be appropriating power within the insurgency. Their role and independence has long been recognised and the US State Department and members of the Afghan government have reportedly communicated between each other via messengers.[182] Jalaluddin and his son, however, have stated on several occasions in interviews and other communications that they regard themselves as mere military commanders under the leadership of Mullah Mohammad Omar, and that political negotiations will have to be conducted with the *Amir ul-Mu'mineen*. As with other commanders, the idea of *fitna* and the quasi-religious institution of Mullah Mohammad Omar are not to be subverted openly.

There is considerable speculation about the ideological and political orientation of the Haqqanis; in particular, this extends to Jalaluddin's son Serajuddin, a man in his early thirties who grew up among some of the world's most renowned international jihadists and whose world view has been shaped almost exclusively by war. While there has been some doubt about Seraj's standing among the Haqqani commanders, it appears that he is well-respected and followed.[183] His statements regarding the Quetta *shura* and Mullah Mohammad Omar show the lines he is not willing to publicly infringe.

I am a soldier of the Amir of the Faithful Mullah Muhammad Umar, may Allah protect him and deliver him from all harm. What is said about the lack of an oath of allegiance is slander. Indeed there are not different armies. There is one Amir, and he is the Amir of the Faithful: Mullah Muhammad Umar, may Allah protect him. There will not be an internal war after the triumph—Allah willing—and whatever messages emerging from the media to this effect are an attempt at heresy, to split the ranks of the Mujahideen. They will not succeed, Allah willing.[184]

Serajuddin clearly articulates a difference between the Afghan Taliban and al-Qaeda as well *vis-à-vis* the Pakistani Taliban. On the relationship with al-Qaeda, he states:

In our faith in Islam, we are one. In the countries that we want to capture, our geographical location, our organizational structure and our fighting tactics, we are different.[185]

And for the relationship to the Pakistani Taliban he says:

They are in Pakistan and they operate there. We are fighting in Afghanistan. According to the Islamic Emirate's rules and regulations we are not allowed to interfere in other countries' domestic affairs. So we don't have any relation to them.

The final verdict in the balance of power between Quetta and Waziristan is likely to be decided in the course of any future negotiations; this is a good enough reason for the Haqqanis' deciding tentatively to participate, albeit in a limited manner so far.

11

CONCLUSION

We have seen no evidence that they are truly interested in reconciliation, where they would surrender their arms, where they would denounce Al-Qaeda, where they would really try to become part of that society.

Leon Panetta, CIA Director, July 2010[1]

[The United States is] not going to talk to the really bad guys because the really bad guys are not ever going to renounce Al Qaeda and renounce violence and agree to re-enter society. That is not going to happen with people like Mullah Omar and the like.

Hillary Clinton, Secretary of State, January 2010[2]

You can't do politics if you're in the mountains.

Senior former Taliban member[3]

The previous chapters sought to broaden the discussion on the relationship of the Taliban and al-Qaeda. This book began by looking into the educational background and socio-economic environment of the individuals who would play pivotal roles in the Taliban or al-Qaeda. The core leaderships of the Taliban and al-Qaeda, respectively, came from different ideological, social, and cultural backgrounds and were of different nationalities and generations. The trajectories of the lives of al-Qaeda's leaders, none of them Afghans, can be traced back to political developments in the Middle East and North Africa.

More often than not they engaged for decades in militant campaigns against their home governments. Their movement responded to regional events, mainly in the Arab world, and was based on the militant Islamism formulated by Arab ideologues like Sayyid Qutb in the 1960s and before.

Most of those who would come to form the Taliban, on the other hand, were too young even to attend school at that time. They grew up in rural southern Afghanistan, isolated from both global political events and the developments in political Islam to which the Arabs were exposed.

The 1980s *jihad* against the Soviet Union's intervention in Afghanistan was a turning point for both groups, however. That war broke open the closed world of rural Afghanistan and swept it into global politics. Militant Islamists and jihadists came to Pakistan and Afghanistan to support the Afghan *jihad* from throughout the Middle East, Africa and beyond; some of these would sign up with and co-found al-Qaeda. A number of Afghan mujahedeen groups, in particular in south-eastern Afghanistan, interacted and cooperated with the foreign mujahedeen, but those who later became the core Taliban leadership had little contact with them.

The war against the Soviet Union in Afghanistan transformed the international jihadist landscape.[4] The experiences of the 1980s reshaped the Afghan Arabs' understanding of *jihad*.[5] The Palestinian cleric and former Muslim Brotherhood member Abdullah Azzam, who led the Services Bureau that coordinated the foreign jihadis in Peshawar, led the way with his book, *Join the Caravan*. Azzam's teachings connected the battles the militants had previously fought in their home countries to the Afghan *jihad*, turning some of them into a new transnational network of committed and battle-hardened jihadists.

In contrast, most of those who would later rise to prominence in the Taliban were too young to play more than minor roles in the war against the Soviet Union. They participated as members of the fronts composed of madrassa students (taliban) that made up a significant number of the fighters of the two madrassa-based parties of the Afghan resistance.[6] Their conception of *jihad* remained almost apolitical—an individual duty of resistance to invasion by non-Muslims—and the majority returned to their religious studies after the withdrawal of the Soviet forces in 1989. That Soviet withdrawal provoked crises within both groups. The Afghan mujahedeen disintegrated into factions, and some fell into war with each other. The foreign jihadis faced their own internal debate in the light both of the failure of the Afghan mujahedeen to form an Islamic government in Afghanistan and of events in the Middle East, especially the First Gulf War.

While Afghanistan descended into civil war, the loosely-connected foreign jihadists split into various groupings. Some stayed on to fight in Afghanistan; some settled in the border region in Pakistan; others started an itinerant life, fighting in Bosnia, Tajikistan, and Chechnya or seeking to establish new bases of operations in Yemen or Sudan. The top leadership left the region.

Security in southern Afghanistan deteriorated as commanders feuded over control, and international interest subsided after the Soviet withdrawal. In 1994, a group of religious students mobilized against criminal gangs west of Kandahar City. This early Taliban movement was a local group concerned with the situation in their area; they represented a blend of local culture and literalist interpretation of Islam, a reactionary force trying to impose order on a chaotic situation. They were not a movement concerned with anything beyond local circumstances.

As the movement gathered momentum, it advanced from Kandahar province to Zabul, on to Helmand and Uruzgan, capturing Herat in September 1995 and Jalalabad and Kabul in September 1996. The five years that followed saw the Taliban struggle to conquer central and northern Afghanistan and to consolidate their hold over the country and its diverse population while imposing highly conservative social policies. The Taliban's unprecedented rise was in part enabled by external support by the government and security apparatus of Pakistan and by the arrival of madrassa students from across the border. The wars to take more territory saw some of the older-generation commanders killed, however, and this meant the identity and goals of the movement started to change.

Osama bin Laden and his followers had returned to Afghanistan after being expelled from Sudan in May 1996. They flew to Jalalabad, where they were hosted by commanders and allies from the region whom bin Laden knew from the 1980s war. Bin Laden did not fly to any of the areas under Taliban or Northern Alliance control, as neither group included his main Afghan associates. En route to capture Kabul in September 1996, the Taliban took Jalalabad, thus inheriting custody of bin Laden and the group around him.

The relationship between al-Qaeda and the Taliban during the second half of the 1990s was complicated, and there was often tension. The two groups knew little about each other; bin Laden pursued an independent agenda, often to the detriment of the Taliban. Nonetheless, Mullah Mohammad Omar and bin Laden grew close—although the extent and details of this remain somewhat unclear—during these years, particularly so from 2000 to 2001.

Bin Laden's activities caused a rift within the Taliban leadership. While Mullah Mohammad Omar regarded him as an important link to the wider Muslim world, a group of leaders around Mullah Mohammad Rabbani, the chair of the leadership *shura*, was concerned that bin Laden's international enterprise and media presence were the principal obstacles to the Taliban gaining the international recognition they sought. This group, however, was sidelined and lost traction from 1999 onwards. While publicly proclaiming his support for Mullah Mohammad Omar, bin Laden continued his activities, often in direct violation of Mullah Mohammad Omar's specific directives. Mullah Mohammad Rabbani died in April 2001, effectively sidelining and silencing the Taliban's internal opposition.

When the US launched Operation Enduring Freedom on 7 October, 2001, the Taliban's organisation disintegrated under the pressure of the military campaign. Many Taliban returned to their villages and waited to see what would happen. Soon they found themselves targeted by US Special Forces and the new foreign-backed Afghan elites. These actions were dictated by President Bush's policy of making no distinction between the Taliban, whose regime had harbored al-Qaeda, and al-Qaeda itself. Those who escaped death or capture and detention in Guantánamo or Bagram fled to Pakistan.

Isolated and in hiding across the Durand Line, the leaders discussed the possibility of joining the political process in Kabul—notably at meetings in 2002 and 2004—but these discussions came to little. A combination of factors caused the leadership to begin an insurgency. Internal factions, in particular a younger generation, opposed a political process. Arguably more important, however, was the lack of real options. The policy choices of the Afghan government and its foreign allies, and the strong interests of neighboring countries such as Pakistan and Iran, helped steer the leadership towards taking up arms once again. By 2003, they had regrouped and put command structures in place, connecting to local groups inside Afghanistan to begin an insurgency.

Al-Qaeda, while surprised by the swift demise of the Taliban resistance, was better prepared to pursue its own agenda during these years, organising and administering a series of attacks around the world. The September 11 attacks polarized the Islamic world and reshuffled the jihadist universe. An undifferentiated response by the United States—as expressed in the Bush doctrine where one was 'with us or against us' and in which no distinction was made between hosts and 'terrorists'—led to a creeping consolidation of groups previously at odds with one other. This cooperation promoted a growing perception that the Taliban and al-Qaeda were in some respects becoming integrated.

In reality, however, the relationship was strained and generally extended no further than individual contacts. The supposedly unbreakable link between the Taliban and al-Qaeda is the principal strategic blunder of the war in

Afghanistan: a major intelligence failure that continues to cloud the response to Afghanistan and Pakistan. Al-Qaeda and the Afghan Taliban remain two distinct entities, with different memberships, ideologies and objectives. The interaction and contacts that do exist between the two groups are found in three main forms: personal/individual ties, the commonality of a shared religious belief, and their circumstances (a shared location and enemy). The core Kandahari leadership of the Taliban, however, recognises the damaging impact of the foreign jihadists and treads a cautious path to demonstrate their independence and difference, while avoiding friction or tension. The al-Qaeda leadership relied and coordinated closely with Jalaluddin Haqqani, a former commander of *Hizb-e Islami* (Khalis) and his son, Serajuddin.

Arrests by Pakistan in early 2010 of a significant number of members of the Taliban leadership council, together with the military campaign targeting insurgent leaders within Afghanistan, has weakened the overall command structure and the ability of the central leadership to enforce decisions. A reshuffling of the leadership, along with all layers of ranks of commanders, has seen the rise of a younger and more radical generation. This in turn has caused the decline of Mullah Mohammad Omar's influence; he is now more of a symbolic religious figure than an authoritative commander.

The new and younger generation of Afghan Taliban are more susceptible to approaches by foreign jihadist groups, including al-Qaeda, causing an increasing ideological shift in the conflict. This development, paired with an overall increase in suspicion among the Afghan population as to the United States and its 'real intentions,' bodes ill for the future. Current policies pursued by domestic and international actors—spearheaded by the United States—are a key factor driving the Afghan Taliban and al-Qaeda together; this is effectively changing the Afghan insurgency while not diminishing its operational capacity.

The Taliban

Taliban Objectives and Strategy

It is difficult to talk of a single Taliban strategy or set of goals given the heterogeneous nature of the movement combined with the increased fragmentation of the different groups and the power struggle taking place on Pakistani soil over the Afghan Taliban's future. Even within the leadership council there appear to be significant differences of opinion regarding the Taliban's political and military future.

Not all of the groups fighting against the Afghan government and the foreign presence in the country would agree over a vision for the political future of the country. While this book does not deal with the relationship of Hekmatyar's *Hizb-e Islami* to the Taliban and the foreign fighters, it should be noted that *Hizb-e Islami* is a distinct group that not only has clashed with the Taliban in the past, which spearheads much of the opposition to the current Afghan government and foreign forces in certain areas outside Kabul and in the north-east. Withal, it is known to be pursuing discussions with the Afghan government and other parties.[7]

An examination of the Taliban communiqués issued since 2001 shows that there are certain issues and questions which the leadership regularly fails to address. Do the Taliban desire power in the same form as in the mid-late 1990s? This is not often subjected to much scrutiny—it is assumed that the Taliban desire control over the whole country in order to implement the *shari'a* and a caliphate to boot—but the outside powers should also consider whether the Taliban in their 2011 manifestation are different from those who ruled the country in the 1990s. In short, can they be expected to behave any differently if they were to play a political role in the country as part of a wider settlement?

In terms of their rhetoric, lessons from the 1990s seem to have been learnt, at least by the older generation of Taliban leadership. While many of their on-the-ground tactics employ physical threats, assassinations and intimidation of Afghan civilians and government employees, their statements and the interviews conducted as part of this book suggest that there is an awareness among Taliban veterans as to the importance of human rights to the international community and the need to prevent attacks against other countries from being launched from areas under their control.[8] While this assessment seems to try to combine mutually exclusive points—the tactics on the ground and the acceptance of the importance of issues at hand—it should be regarded as the natural divide between the fighting vanguard of the movement and its political base. There seem to be few public calls for the Taliban flag to be flying over the presidential palace in Kabul again, for example, which suggests perhaps an element of 'knowing one's own limits.'

Taliban statements as to their goals and objectives are often vague. For example:

The Islamic Emirate has curtains [sic] goals to achieve. They are:

1. Complete independence of the country.

2. Establishment of an Islamic system representing the wants and aspiration of the Afghan people.
3. Progress and prosperity of the country and people.

Our first priority is to achieve these goals through talks and negotiation. But if the invading powers in Afghanistan are not ready to give the Afghans their natural rights which is the right of independence and establishment of a government based on their aspirations and wants, then the Mujahideen of the Islamic Emirate are determined to carry on the fight until the realization of the said goals.[9]

While the Taliban clearly see themselves as being responsible for bringing about these changes and goals, there is little in this that allows for an assessment of their exact involvement. In this statement from November 2009 about the group's 'aims,' it is again unclear who is being referred to and to what extent the Taliban regard their views as a majority view of the Afghan people and therefore representative of all Afghans:

... the Mujahideen's objectives are clear. They want to establish an Islamic system based on justice and equality and gain independence of the country where the Afghans will be owners of their own country and fate. Education, spiritual and material uplift and reconstructions are other aims of the Islamic Emirate. It has declared time and again that it will implement these goals upon gaining independence.[10]

In a statement issued in March 2011, the Taliban state the following on the possibility of peace:

We think, if the Contact Group, the Islamic Conference and other circles really want to bring the current war in Afghanistan to an end, then the solution is very clear and feasible—they should withdraw 150,000 foreign forces from Afghanistan unconditionally and pave the way for establishment of an Islamic System on the basis of the Islamic and national aspirations of the Afghans.[11]

There is certainly a discussion to be had on the extent to which different parts of Afghan society have national aspirations and how much of a consensus there is on what an 'Islamic' system of government would look like, especially given the rural-urban divide.

The basic message of the Taliban today still relies on the same promises and goals that the movement had in the 1990s, even though the circumstances are not the same. Much of their message incorporates legitimate complaints of the population against the foreign forces and the Afghan government. There is in particular a critical breakdown regarding these grievances on the local and provincial government levels.

The core goals of the movement are justice and a role in the political future of the country. International commentators often voice concern about the revisionist nature of analyses of the Taliban, pointing towards the countless human rights abuses the movement committed while in power and since their ousting in 2001.[12] These correctly point out that the movement are far from being 'modern Robin Hoods' who simply defend their own rights or those of the people; it is nevertheless informative to examine the underlying developments. Local shifts in perception reflect at least a partial reality: corruption and the poor performance of the Afghan government in conjunction with oft-voiced promises and pledges have eroded the credibility of the government in Kabul and the international actors. There is an obvious disconnect between the message and the deed. The Taliban, on the other hand, while employing terror tactics, appear to be consistent in message and in deed, and if not in reality then at least in the perceptions of many.[13] These developments have translated in some parts of Afghanistan into a greater support of the local population for the Taliban; they are regarded as the more predictable and lasting option. The considerations seem pragmatic for the most part rather than an explicit subscription to the Taliban's goals and narrative.

For the short-term, however, the Taliban's list of priorities is more practically-oriented. They will continue with their military activities (including the heavy reliance on IED strikes against foreign and Afghan government vehicles) in response to the foreign military surge. Operations in Kandahar and Helmand over the winter of 2010–11 saw significant numbers of local Taliban fighters relocating to Pakistan, with IED groups left behind to coordinate bombings in the city and beyond. There are indications as of early 2011 that the leadership will continue to drive and foster new fronts in the north, incorporating more groups as part of a loose network of affiliates.[14] A series of complex attacks that resulted in dozens of civilian casualties seem to reflect new tactical calculations among the Taliban.[15]

In the south and parts of the east, the leadership is aware of the need to strengthen its hold over the various field-level operations, an undertaking that will be difficult in light of the increasingly centrifugal nature of insurgent groups' relations with one other. For the immediate short-term, however, the senior leadership in Quetta realise that Kandahar must be visibly seen to fail as the centrepiece of the US strategy in 2011–12.[16]

Given the impact of current military strategy and the internal evolution of the Taliban, it appears likely that the veteran leadership of the old guard Taliban will be increasingly marginalised. This is likely to translate into an ideological shift of the wider Afghan Taliban movement with elements of it drifting towards more radical ideas, and closer to groups like al-Qaeda.

Will the Taliban Break With al-Qaeda?

There are a number of ground realities that this book has tried to outline regarding the history of the relationship as well as several elements regarding the nature of the groups assessed. Much of the discussion seems to be riddled with assumptions, even extending to something as basic as the size of al-Qaeda, whose central membership is estimated to be in the low hundreds.[17]

The actions and statements of individuals and groups involved in the current conflict need to be seen in the context of their individual situations. Informed to a large degree by a deep-seated lack of trust on all sides, the Afghan Taliban find themselves in an environment with limited options for action from their perspective. Current US strategy is perceived, arguably correctly, as being driven by the military; any change that will come, they believe, will only be in the realm of incremental tactical adjustments. The present situation offers few incentives for the Taliban to publicly position themselves against any militant Islamic group, be it al-Qaeda or any other. With state supporters coming under increased pressure, the number of potential or current allies is limited; an open position contrary to al-Qaeda or other Islamist groups could have considerable consequences for the Taliban leadership, and their leadership based in Pakistan would likely face a backlash.

The lack of trust in the Afghan government, by the general population as well as by the Taliban, together with the significant interference of neighbouring countries and a confusing and unconsolidated international strategy, leave little room to move forward. Excepting a tectonic shift in the political environment—among the Afghan government, regarding the international stance on negotiations, and regarding the demands of the Taliban—there is no room for the Afghan Taliban publicly to differentiate itself from other militant Islamic groups in the region, including al-Qaeda.[18]

The current dynamics within the Afghan Taliban also appear to decrease the chance of negotiations as time passes. There are still possible interlocutors and options for discussions at the moment, but the veteran Taliban's leverage over the chain of command is becoming increasingly limited, to a degree that significantly hampers their influence over all parts of the movement currently fighting, rendering the chance of forging a lasting peace more and more unlikely.[19] The insurgency is changing; this change sees new forces consolidating power while the overall coherence of the organisational structures, as well as the reach of the Taliban leadership to influence individual field commanders, appears to be waning. While the exact effects of these developments are disputed, the likely impact will make high-level talks with a centralised leadership—one that represents at least a significant part of the insurgency—increasingly unlikely as time passes.

A discussion of the Taliban's position on al-Qaeda must be—at least on the surface—exactly that: a discussion. A firm and imposed pre-condition prior to the start of a dialogue—as Saudi Arabia has publicly demanded[20]—is highly unlikely to yield positive results. Red lines are helpful as internal yardsticks, but should remain internal, and options should be explored that recognise the constraints of all actors involved. The current trajectory of war—a hybrid counter-terrorism and counter-insurgency strategy—is always available.

The environment and settings chosen for high-level discussions will have a profound impact on their success, and even on their possibility.[21] It is not enough for either the Taliban or their international counterparts to hold this discussion through a public exchange of documents and statements, nor will this yield any serious results.[22] Much will depend on the framing of concepts and the approach to talks;[23] international actors will have to work towards their goals while recognising the Taliban's situation and unique predicaments.

Members of the (Afghan) Taliban's senior political echelons do not appear to be at odds with international actors over the issue of al-Qaeda—as part of a wider political settlement, having learned from the September 11 attacks. This is an indication that there is space for discussion of the issue, and foreign interlocutors would do well to allow for the possibility of useful dialogue here.[24]

To Taliban leaders, the issue of the movement's relation to al-Qaeda appears to be one that is founded more in how they regard Islam and fellow Muslims—as seems to have been partly the case with Mullah Mohammad Omar—combined with fears about the integrity of the movement. Given the strong public stance taken by Mullah Mohammad Omar regarding bin Laden in the past, at least until the latter's death, a change of position of the leadership or individuals could have further threatened the integrity of the movement.

As of mid-2011 there are some positive signs that the parameters of the current relationship appear mostly circumstantial; a change in these could potentially provide the space needed for the Taliban to alter their position. An examination of the Taliban's public statements—particularly those from the past two years—shows the care being taken over any reference to al-Qaeda and affiliates; there are no congratulatory postings in response to the actions of foreign international jihadist groups, but rather a sense that the leaders are acutely conscious of the problem that their relationship—both the realities and the perception—has caused and is causing them.

The issue of al-Qaeda is, at least superficially, at the heart of international goals in Afghanistan and Pakistan, is the one thing on which the international community would like to see results. This is not the case for the Taliban. The al-Qaeda issue is much lower down on their list of priorities,[25] and any discussion must take this into account. The Taliban agenda focuses on a whole different set of local political concerns and of goals of individuals within the leadership. If progress is to be made on the issues concerning international terrorism, the Taliban will be hoping to advance their own agenda.

Are the Haqqanis Reconcilable?

The vast unanimity of analysis and commentary emphatically rejects the possibility of reconciliation of the Haqqanis with the mainstream Afghan political establishment. An essay by Jeffrey Dressler entitled 'the Irreconcilables' underscores the point,[26] as do the efforts by General Petraeus to officially designate the Haqqanis as 'terrorists.'[27] Moreover, two recent and richly-textured accounts by Americans who were held captive for long periods by the Haqqanis and others having a similar ideological persuasion to them confirm this basic position.[28]

We should, however, be aware and conscious of the dangers of self-fulfilling prophecies. Not everything that seems to be the case, is the case, especially in Afghanistan. Focusing too much on the present realities could be obscuring our better understanding of why certain actions were carried out in the first place, or our responses to these immediate realities could be closing off the possibility for any change.

The argument that the Haqqanis are irreconcilable rests mostly on the perception that they are implacably ideologically aligned with al-Qaeda, and that this literalist reliance on fierce Islamist tenets—coupled with a specific world view that identifies the West and/or the United States as an enemy—rules out any possibility of discussion or political compromise. When assessing the Haqqanis, one should incorporate both cultural and actual precedents for what can be described as pragmatic decision-making among this very same group. The Haqqanis' decision to join up with the then-nascent Taliban movement in early 1995 was one such instance. Moreover, there have been occasions in the post-2001 period where the Haqqanis have sought some kind of political accommodation. In 2002, for instance, Jalaluddin Haqqani's brother Ibrahim came to Kabul to meet with American and Afghan government officials to enquire about this very possibility. He was detained, held in prison and allegedly harshly tortured.[29]

It is probably the case that the Haqqanis are not prime candidates for inclusion in some kind of political process within Afghanistan in the short term, especially given the context of the military surge, Pakistani policy and manipulation, the targeted capture-or-kill campaign conducted with drone strikes, as well as the increasingly shrill public denouncements of the group issued by American politicians and government officials. This does not mean, though, that the possibility should be completely discounted, at least while Jalaluddin is still alive and has a say. There is, however, a generational shift currently affecting the Haqqanis; Jalaluddin's leadership is different from that of Serajuddin.

Do the Afghan Taliban Pose an International Threat?

A central motivation and key goal of the foreign intervention in Afghanistan has been the denial of safe haven to designated international terrorist groups like al-Qaeda.[30] Much of the current efforts continues to be informed by this underlying imperative. A stable, democratic Afghanistan that has sovereignty and effective governance over its territory and that is part of the international community, will deny to groups such as al-Qaeda sanctuary as well as the space to plan and execute attacks on foreign targets. Any fundamental change in the political paradigm in Afghanistan—the inclusion of the Afghan Taliban into the political process, for example—will have to address this central concern that directly impinges on the national security of several countries.

Afghans have not been involved in any significant way in international terrorism, nor have the Afghan Taliban (barring some specific anomalous cases) absorbed the internationalist jihadi rhetoric adopted by affiliates of al-Qaeda or as currently espoused by members of the Pakistani Taliban. None of the September 11 hijackers was Afghan, and the only prominent reported case of an Afghan involved in an act of international terrorism is the case of Najibullah Zazi in Denver who had lived in the United States since the age of fourteen.[31] There has even been a vigorous debate among the Afghan Taliban as to the legitimacy of al-Qaeda's preferred tactic of suicide bombers. Several people interviewed for this book were keen to point out that the Afghan Taliban have not carried out any attacks outside Afghanistan.

Conversations with senior members of the Afghan Taliban reveal almost uniform acknowledgement and understanding of the damage done by the September 11 attacks and the movement's association with bin Laden/al-Qaeda.

In many ways, the years since September 11 have been a difficult crash course for the political leadership of the Taliban in the realities of international relations and the tolerance thresholds of foreign governments.[32] There is no evidence that the leadership of the Afghan Taliban (as currently found) are seeking to conduct attacks abroad. This status quo, however, could change. The international community should appreciate that its policies have a direct impact on the trajectory of the ideological development of the movement and its relationships to other militant Islamic groups that represent a significantly different world view and international threat. The United States and its international partners should move away from regarding the Afghan Taliban as a static actor that did not and will not change. One senior Taliban political strategist envisioned joint counter-terrorism patrols of Taliban and international foreign forces within Afghanistan's borders. While the current situation and the trajectory of the conflict seem to belie ideas like this, they are nevertheless interesting and offer perhaps significant different perspectives from inside the active Taliban.

A policy that fails to imagine different futures will probably not generate much that is different from the default trajectory of the current conflict. The importance of actionable and observable signs of cooperation—confidence-building measures, to all extents and purposes—as opposed to symbolic statements of rejection, should not be underestimated.

Significantly, political elements from within the senior Taliban do not see the issue of al-Qaeda as being one of the major issues which might cause serious problems for the possibility of a political solution. They assume that a solution can be found which all parties will find amenable. This suggests that—within the context of a wider set of discussions over the political future of Afghanistan—the issue of international terrorism from within Afghanistan's borders may not necessarily be as big a potential problem as is currently believed. Grappling with Pakistan is a separate issue, of course.

Political Solutions

Who Has an Interest in Talking Now?

The US engagement in Afghanistan, its longest war to date, has come under increasing criticism in the light of mounting Afghan civilian as well as US and international military casualties. With the US government under significant economic pressure, the prolonged commitment of substantial financial resources, as well as the sacrifice of life, have caused the war's US domestic approval rates to decline, and have opened up the discussion as to the sustainability and future of the international engagement.[33]

There has been increasing talk about a political solution, one that potentially holds the promise of stopping the current downward spiral, and which could perhaps not only prepare the ground for the withdrawal of foreign troops, but perhaps even achieve a much-desired stability in Afghanistan that prevents the country from becoming a terrorist haven once again. If they are left as they are, there is considerable doubt that the current government in Kabul will remain viable and that the Afghan security forces will have the ability to control and counter the growing insurgency. Riddled with corruption and stripped of legitimacy by endemic election fraud, much of the central state seems to be riven with internal conflict and is currently held together only by foreign actors. On the other hand, a potential political process that would see a change in the balance of power within the central state as well as on the local level will be met with considerable resistance from the incumbent elite.

Pakistan has long defined Afghanistan as a vital national security interest. With much of the insurgency's leadership residing in the FATA and Baluchistan, Pakistan is able to veto any political process between the Afghan Taliban and the Afghan government. While not opposed to a political settlement, it has given clear indications that it has the ability to sabotage any such attempts if it is left out of the discussion. Pakistani considerations are heavily influenced by its long-standing conflict with India over Kashmir, which has caused three wars and multiple border skirmishes since the founding of the Pakistani state. While Pakistan seeks 'strategic depth,' India aims to counterbalance its influence in Afghanistan.[34]

Analysts often suggest that the issue of Kashmir must first be addressed (or start being addressed) before there will ever be progress on the Indian and Pakistani positions as played out in Afghanistan. But the reasons for Pakistan's behaviour might be more complex and the causalities not necessarily as straightforward as this argument suggests.[35]

As the previous chapters outlined, the insurgency at large should not be regarded as a unified body that has a clear goal-driven policy. The Afghan Taliban's senior leadership is a distinct group that has thus far managed to structure and control much of the insurgency in Afghanistan.

For the Taliban's leadership, there are a mixed set of factors at play. In contrast to what the US military might see as the overall demise of the insurgency, the senior Taliban leadership is aware that the current capture-or-kill campaign has had a significant impact on its ability to lead and is beginning to marginalise it as a group. The overall insurgency will continue regardless, albeit with different leaders and potentially a different ideological position. While the current leadership is opposed to the Afghan government and the foreign presence in the country, it is aware of the devastating possibility of another civil war that looms if no political solution is found.[36] The new generation of Taliban leaders who are currently moving into the lower ranks, however, are less likely to engage in any political process, a fact which is also recognised by the older generation and by the political voices in the Taliban. Moreover, the core Kandahari leadership of the movement is certainly subject to battle fatigue, having grown into older men with families, arguably less subject to the fiercely uncompromising stances of youth.

While there might be incentives to find a political solution, there are also factions within both the insurgency and the Afghan government that are opposed to a settlement, or a substantial inclusion of the insurgency into the current political paradigm. President Karzai has stressed that he seeks reconciliation, but there are significant voices within the current administration that are not interested in any such process. While the ongoing capture-or-kill campaign is removing credible negotiation partners among the Taliban, the current Afghan government also lacks credibility. Time, however, is of the essence.

Moreover, the perception among the Taliban at large is that they are—in a broad sense—'winning'.[37] General Petraeus has announced that the insurgency's momentum has been reversed, but this does not reflect the perception of much of the general public—in particular in Afghanistan's south and east but increasingly in the north of the country as well.[38] The withdrawal from the Pech Valley in Kunar, for example, was seen as an admission of defeat by many among the Taliban.[39]

The underlying assumption of the surge, that negotiations need to be held from a position of strength, and that the Taliban should be *forced* to the negotiation table by military pressure, offers a bleak prospect for peace. A key incentive in the other direction can be found in the realisation that the present conditions are a precursor for civil war. This prospect of a return to civil war—similar to that of the 1990s—offers an incentive for all participants in Afghanistan to begin working on a political settlement that could prevent this from becoming a reality.

The question of whether Mullah Mohammad Omar will be a part of the political process and/or settlement is important. As outlined above, the Taliban leader's role within the insurgency is somewhat contradictory; he is increasingly sidelined and Taliban voices within Afghanistan seem more critical, yet at the same time he represents an institution that gives considerable cohesion to the movement at large. His participation and role within the insurgency and in a political settlement therefore depends heavily on how he is approached by the international actors involved. A US State Department press spokesman has remarked:

From our view, Mullah Omar has been attached at the hip to bin Laden for some time. So, based on everything that we know about him today, in fact he will not meet the criteria that we have laid out. [...] So you know, there's nothing that we see that indicates that Mullah Omar will, in fact, change his stripes. As a result, we don't see that he qualifies to play a constructive role in Afghanistan's future.[40]

There will, no doubt, be more statements in this vein if any negotiated political process is launched. Mullah Mohammad Omar brings a certain cohesion (albeit symbolic) to the Taliban movement; he is a link to the past and to the dysfunction of the Taliban's previous interactions with the international community, but circumstances have now changed and any negotiated process would likely not see him ascend to the head of the Afghan government or to any role that gives him more than symbolic value. In the course of discussions, there might be ways to promote the role of those in the tier underneath him—providing this level of the command structure are not killed in the meantime—without removing him completely, and thus avoid a possible backlash.

His exclusion from the political process outright or against his will would likely have severely negative consequences for any negotiations or reconciliation. His title represents a de facto religious institution. Mullah Mohammad Omar retains ample power to act as a spoiler in any negotiations, so he would have to voluntarily agree to any sidelining or retirement from the leadership.[41]

Regardless of the future role of Mullah Mohammad Omar, the various differing statements made by the US government and its military as to the nature of the July 2011 withdrawal, the 2014 deadline, and possible US involvement during and after this time period, have created much confusion as to the United States' intent. The somewhat arbitrary timeline put forward by the United States has been regarded by large parts of the Taliban as a sign of its waning commitment, a sentiment also often heard from the general public and voices from within the Afghan government.[42]

The effect of a drawdown of US forces—even if cosmetic—on the fragile Afghan state is far from clear. Analysts have warned that the Afghan National Security Forces are unlikely to be able to provide security nationwide in the timeframe currently proposed for the turnover of security operations by international forces.[43] The composition of Afghan security forces as well as various other actors and their networks—which should be regarded as interest groups—shed doubt on the current strategy because it seems to fail to account for the fractured nature of the Afghan government at large. Many of these groups' interests do not match international or even broadly national interests.

The latest incarnation of the local militia programme, currently referred to as 'Local Defence Initiatives'—being implemented around the country in order to fill the security vacuum to facilitate the withdrawal of foreign forces and boost the size of governmental security forces—is advocated as a speedy solution to the deteriorating security situation. Past experience, however, has shown that an incorporation of such forces into the formal security apparatus of the Afghan government is problematic. Those militant groups who supposedly have been woven into the Afghan government's security forces since 2001 have neither withered away nor seen their powers transferred to the government. Individuals formerly associated with the Northern Alliance and others have used the past decade to strengthen and reinforce their own self-interested positions. Of special concern are voices from within the Afghan National Army suggesting that its coherence and integrity are fragile.[44] The lack of unity among Afghan actors, based on their particular ethnic and regional orientations, should be taken into account when assessing the possible effects of deadlines and troop withdrawals.

The insurgents, particularly the Afghan Taliban element, are a swiftly changing group; they have various voices and opinions regarding possible negotiations and settlements. An additional complication is that the senior political class of the Afghan Taliban truly believe in the justness and righteousness of their cause, which is a strong theme in both their public and private discourse, and this belief has become only more acute as the Afghan government has itself become increasingly corrupt.[45] The true ideological fighters of the Afghan Taliban—of whom there are relatively few—are also opposed to doing a deal with international actors because they see them as an illegitimate occupying presence, one that is in cahoots with an Afghan government that is itself regarded as corrupt and illegitimate. So the obstacles and pitfalls on the way to a political process that would address not only the current conflict but its underlying causes are manifold.

After Osama

Bin Laden's death may be a watershed moment for al-Qaeda, but for the war in Afghanistan and for the Taliban it changes little. This is not to understate the importance (however symbolic) of the US raid, since the circumstances have called the US relationship with Pakistan into question along with the fundamental rationale for an extended foreign troop presence inside Afghanistan. Bin Laden himself does not seem to have played a key operational role in the day-to-day running of his organisation in recent times—much as he might have liked to do so—but rather his value came in offering some level of ideological cohesion to various disparate groups, along with the propaganda value of his continuing to evade capture.

For the Afghan Taliban's leadership, his death comes at an opportune moment when the United States and other governments are reconsidering their stance on negotiations, allowing for the possibility of an adjustment of their relationship with other militant organisations based in Pakistan. In addition, it comes at a time when senior political cadres within the Afghan Taliban are increasingly offering various signs of distance from or ambivalence regarding the foreign fighters of al-Qaeda and their affiliates. In the United States and Europe, the mood for some kind of political reconciliation involving the Quetta-based Taliban leadership also has grown more propitious.

Initial reactions from Taliban fighters following the death of bin Laden were relatively consistent with each other. These three samples give an indication of the position they expressed. All are active fighters based inside Afghanistan at the mid-level of the insurgency in the southern region:

I think they don't want to leave completely. Only some soldiers will leave, but they want to make permanent bases and continue their illegitimate actions in Afghanistan. But we will try to push them completely from Afghanistan. They have very bad aims and goals to stay in Afghanistan and continue their bad plans. Insha'allah we will continue our *jihad* to finish all their dreams of staying in Afghanistan and push their black faces (like the Russians and British) out. I also want to mention that Osama and the al-Qaeda fighters in Afghanistan are only a pretend excuse for them; they want to finish Islam in the region. That's why they attacked Iraq, now Libya and why they have struggles against other Islamic countries and want to fight in other places as well. On the one hand they support Pakistan but on the other they are against Pakistan and want to start fighting there as well. In the end, their fight is one against Islam not one against terrorism.

and

This fight is a fight between Muslims and infidels because when Americans entered Afghanistan their goal was to target Muslims in general, not Osama or Mullah Mohammad Omar. They wanted to kill Muslims. They have done so and now continue in the killing of many Muslims. When they attacked Iraq there was no Osama but they still attacked and killed many Muslims. If they are in a war against terrorism, then they should go there and start fighting with the Israelis, but no, they support Israel who are the real terrorists. Our jihad will continue against the invaders—not against ordinary non-Muslims. To be clear, a non-Muslim who doesn't seek to harm any Muslim is someone who we must keep safe (whether they are inside or outside Afghanistan), but for invaders the *jihad* is *farz* until the day of judgement.

and

'This war will continue as long as American forces remain in Afghanistan. If they leave Afghanistan and finish their interference in Afghanistan this will end the fighting. But if they continue their interference in Afghanistan they will continue to cut their hands on Afghanistan. Unfortunately, the Americans want to have a fight between Muslims and non-Muslims just as Mr Bush said when he was in power ('this is a crusade,' he said). But according to Islamic rules, we Muslims don't have permission to fight against non-Muslims who don't want to fight against Muslims.'

The Taliban have, as of early June 2011, put out three written official statements relating to the death of bin Laden.[46] None of these address the major substantive issues raised in the wake of his death, focusing instead on redirecting attention back to the war in Afghanistan.

A very short initial statement was released on 3 May. In light of the lack of confirmation from those close to bin Laden, Zabiullah Mujahed noted, and given the lack of evidence provided by the United States, it would be 'premature' to release an official statement.[47]

A second, longer statement was issued on 7 May, almost a full week after bin Laden's death, and this was signed by 'the leadership council.'[48] Part of the delay seems to have resulted from problems in getting a consensus view from the various council members—communications were restricted and phones turned off in the days that followed bin Laden's death. This statement includes the expected pro-forma Qur'anic quotations. The council called bin Laden a 'great martyr' and a 'caller to Islamic jihad against the invading infidels.' A small potted biography notes that he took part in the jihad against the Soviets, 'fought shoulder to shoulder with the Afghans,' 'offered sacrifices' and was an 'ardent advocate for occupied Palestine' and that he fought against 'Christian and Jewish aggressions in the Islamic world.'

All of this is framed in rhetoric that emphasises Islam and a shared sense of purpose. The council talks back against the idea that bin Laden's death will sadden people in Afghanistan because 'the sapling of jihad has always grown, spruced and reached fructification through irrigation by pure blood.' This abstracts the discussion away from bin Laden's actions, refocusing attention on the war inside Afghanistan. In a similar vein, they continue to say that the raid was 'a strike by colonialism' which in turn 'breed[s] sympathy and produces an urge to strike back.' This is all redirected back to the Afghan situation: 'But the ground realities have it that the use of force brings in opposite consequences here. This popular movement can be bracketed with a spring which, when you pressurize [sic], bounces back with the same intensity.' To conclude, they predict that it will give 'new impetus' to the *jihad*.

The statement in its entirety did little to address basic questions about the Afghan Taliban's view on al-Qaeda, and is more an acknowledgement that is meant to take the two audiences it addresses into account: other militant Islamists who stood and support bin Laden, and the West spearheaded by the United States. It tries to bring attention back onto the war in Afghanistan—a 'war against colonialism' or 'war against invaders'—but is interesting more for what isn't said than what is. There is, for example, no mention of the September 11 attacks, no mention of Pakistan, and no mention of the claims of Taliban-al-Qaeda links.

A third statement was issued as an op-ed opinion piece on 11 May.[49] It was accordingly unsigned and with less weight than the second 7 May statement, while still reflecting the orthodox position of the movement. Again, bin Laden is referred to throughout as a 'martyr.' His death is part of the 'crusade against the Islamic Ummah for the past decade' and he was a 'skyscraper of bravery, a dedicated supporter of the Islamic Ummah.' He spent a big part of his life 'striving to deliver the Muslims lands from the claws of the infidels and gain freedom' (with specific mention of 'occupied' lands) and as such helped out in 'the task of rearing, training, enlightenering [sic] and equipping Mujahideen.'

The statement then broadens out to say that the *jihad* will continue as long as the 'invading infidels' are 'continuing their colonialist ambitions against the Islamic Ummah.' All of this, the writer says, is part of getting rid of the 'occupation' and then the ushering in of an 'Islamic reign.'

A central point is the world view that the Taliban statement seems to support, that of an ongoing crusade against the *umma*, which has been propagated by bin Laden and al-Qaeda since the mid-1990s. In this context, it is essential to understand the Afghan Taliban's understanding of the concept and duty of *jihad*—i.e., to what extent do the Taliban today subscribe to the doctrine put forward by Abdullah Azzam in the mid-1980s that frames *jihad* as the individual duty of all Muslims wherever Muslim lands are under attack?[50]

The Afghan Taliban's record over the past ten years shows an exclusive and unwavering focus on Afghanistan, encouraging others to join 'their jihad' in a rerun of the 1980s *jihad* against the Soviet Union but not espousing world-wide *jihad* against other nations or peoples. While matters of doctrine are not static—as is apparent in the evolution of the Taliban throughout the 1990s and since 2001—the stance the Taliban might take once they took control over the whole country or following any kind of settlement is open to speculation given the reactionary nature of the Taliban.

None of these statements address the really key issues that are raised by the death of bin Laden, but it is often the case that the Taliban take their time in responding to major incidents like this.

In terms of the ongoing field operations of the Taliban's commanders and fighters, the death of bin Laden has few implications. The Taliban have independent funding, training and logistical hubs and it is hard to see what the short term effect might have been. It even seems unlikely that Afghan Taliban figures were meeting with bin Laden, despite the claims of at least one figure from within the movement.[51]

Taliban commanders, fighters and others affiliated with the movement with whom we have spoken all made similar basic points—that they had not been fighting for bin Laden in the first place, and that he and the fighters of al-Qaeda had offered minimal or no input into day-to-day operations inside Afghanistan. The evidence that we have to date backs this up: al-Qaeda's involvement in the day-to-day fighting is minimal and limited to certain areas and certain Taliban sub-groups. Since bin Laden's death the Taliban have continued their spring offensive announced on 30 April and named Badr after the battle fought in 624 by the Prophet Mohammad. The so-called spring offensive and the numerous operations the Taliban have carried out since its launch have seen a shift in focus and demonstrated their ability to conduct complex attacks and operations.

The death of bin Laden could potentially have direct implications for political calculations being made with regards to the long-mooted possible political settlement between all parties to the conflict in Afghanistan.

We have already seen what the Taliban said in public in reaction to bin Laden's death—i.e., very little—and while the discussion within senior circles was vigorous in the initial weeks, it changes very little for them in terms of their strategic vision. They are concerned with the conflict inside Afghanistan which they term a defensive jihad against 'occupiers' and 'invaders.'

Operationally, as we have already discussed, there is little that the Taliban need to change, and so therefore they also do not need any strategic shifts in how they currently engage in the war.

The only potential effect of significance is that a public political shift in the future on the Taliban's position regarding al-Qaeda is more possible now—that the personal relationship between Mullah Mohammad Omar and bin Laden is no more. But this is speculative, and in any case changes in the Taliban's overall political positioning had started to happen already anyway, independently of considerations regarding al-Qaeda and bin Laden.

The personal tie that Mullah Mohammad Omar had with bin Laden was the last close personal link that he had with the non-Pakistani foreign jihadists. In and of itself, this is important. A lot of what happened pre-2001 while the Taliban were in power was bound up in this personal relationship. Without it, it would have been somewhat easier for Mullah Mohammad Omar to chart a different course. But it is impossible to assess the likely effect bin Laden's death has had on the Taliban leader, on his view of the conflict, and on long-term considerations as to his and the Taliban's relationship with the United States.

We can probably expect some commentary on the matter in at least one of the 'Eid letters' this year, although it is unlikely that there will be strong or sharply divergent sentiments expressed. There will also need to be a good deal of reading between the lines, as is always the case with his statements.

There have been discussions between senior Taliban figures and international representatives since bin Laden's death, so clearly it doesn't seem to have affected the possibility of talks in general. Some parts of those discussions are completely independent of the issue of foreign fighters—i.e., internal Afghan political matters—so this is perhaps understandable—but other parts are completely tangled up over the issue of al-Qaeda. One of the most important unresolved issues remaining is the presence of al-Qaeda members inside Pakistan and Afghanistan following a potential peace deal being made. What happens to them? Nobody has an answer to this yet.

Support for reintegration and reconciliation both rhetorically and in terms of funding seems to indicate that international actors have eased their previous positions on the possibility of a political solution and now see it as the forefront of any strategy. Nevertheless, contradictory messages continue to be transmitted, as evidenced when a US Treasury Department statement blacklisted three alleged Taliban and Haqqani 'financiers.'[52] The three men, Mullah Gul Agha, Amir Abdullah, and Nasir Haqqani, had all recently been engaged in discussions with the Karzai government—in April, early spring, and in June respectively of 2010.[53] While there could be other reasons for their blacklisting, this move was seen by the Taliban's leadership as a direct US attempt to control the start of any negotiation process and prevent these groups from reaching out independently of American influence. General Petraeus himself is believed to be the source of this interference.[54]

There are complex issues which still need to be dealt with if plans for integration are to be successfully pursued. Many of these, with red lines and preconditions, perceive reintegration as another tactic being employed in the ongoing conflict to divide the insurgency so as to weaken it. This perception obviously handicaps elements within the Taliban who are seeking a political solution. However, reintegration does seem to have the full public support of international actors. While it doesn't rule out the possibility of other simultaneous discussions, it might complicate more credible suggestions and processes.[55]

Pakistan is also positioning itself for a negotiated settlement together with the Afghan government and is applying uneven pressure on different parts of the Afghan Taliban. Its actions suggest that Pakistan is using its hold over parts of the insurgency as leverage over the Afghan government and its international partners. Pakistan is likely to involve itself in any significant round of discussions (barring very local meetings within Afghanistan) involving the Taliban and/or the political future of Afghanistan.

Gulf States, particularly Saudi Arabia, the United Arab Emirates and Qatar, have also initiated some negotiation efforts, albeit with different motivations and goals. Saudi Arabia—involved in Afghan affairs already for decades, even prior to the Soviet invasion—supported the Taliban government during the 1990s and seems[56] to support the idea of a Taliban role in a new coalition-style government post-negotiations, but so far its efforts have been ad hoc and unsystematic, taking advantage of the presence of Talibs in Saudi Arabia for *Hajj* or *umra*, for example, but not putting together a more coherent initiative. Qatar and the United Arab Emirates are smaller players in this arena, but they retain ties to the Taliban from the 1990s, and their rulers seek involvement in an international political deal. So far, however, none of these efforts has led to any significant progress, and unfolding events in the Middle East are likely to affect the role that the governments of those countries will play in Afghanistan.

A small but dedicated group of international would-be mediators is also involved, and those parties are each positioning themselves. Much of their activity has focused on understanding the various positions of the different parties to the conflict in Afghanistan. There is, however, no framework in which these activities take place, so they have mostly taken the form of preliminary explorations outside any real context or setting for discussion. While various actors have recently expressed sincere interest in negotiations and several initiatives have been suggested in the past, there is still a lack of coherence among international actors and within the Afghan government; there is no clear framework with articulated goals and a leadership.

In general, initiatives to date appear to have been preliminary and insignificant. Trust from and of all parties is lacking, and the decision to push for a military surge—informed by the underlying reasoning of forcing the insurgents to the negotiation table—has raised suspicions among the insurgency that international encouragement of talks might just be a trap. There continues to be a lack of a political vision and a clear roadmap with regards to a political settlement; the military remains in the lead, pursuing its capture-or-kill campaign at the same time it is trying to fight a counterinsurgency campaign. This two-pronged approach appears to rely on concepts developed in the context of Iraq and is likely to be counterproductive if a political settlement is actually sought.

The developments of 2009–2010 demonstrate the deteriorating impact of the current policies, which not only create a much more difficult environment for negotiations, but also open up opportunities for more radical ideologists to shift the discussion within the insurgency, as well as its goals.

The repeated assertion among international politicians that troops are in Afghanistan to prevent terrorism 'back home' seems to imply that the Afghan Taliban are the threat.[57] The failure to investigate this idea and distinguish between the various elements within the insurgency mean that it is hard for foreign (especially Western) politicians to present serious negotiations as a plan that is in the interest of their own country and their domestic constituencies, as well as for the region at large.

The realisation among many parties that the present conditions are a precursor to civil war rather than to peace or victory by either side is one reason why there is considerable room to start a discussion now. The prospect of a return to internal fratricide—similar to that of the 1990s—offers an incentive for all participants in Afghanistan to begin working on a political settlement that could prevent this from becoming a reality. Similarly, the old-generation Taliban leadership have an interest in finding a way to consolidate and retain their authority over the movement, something that negotiations might allow them to do. As of early 2011, this group still represents much of the insurgency and could be engaged in negotiations. That situation, however, could change swiftly over time, after which this group might not be said to 'represent' the movement anymore.

Could the older generation leadership be relied upon to keep Afghanistan free of international terrorists? There can, of course, be no answer to this except after the fact. Yet, the reaction of the insurgency depends in part on how we choose to engage them. A break with al-Qaeda is something for which there would be support within the senior leadership, but how this is processed and instrumentalised will demonstrate how likely a possibility it would be.

For political negotiations to address the significant core grievances and political inequalities that help the insurgency by alienating the Afghan people from the Afghan government and from foreigners, these negotiations must occur on multiple levels, nearly simultaneously. The conducting of these multiple negotiations is important to reinforce the message—and the reality—that discussions about Afghanistan's political future must include all parties and not just be a quick-fix deal with insurgents.

There is perhaps some cause for concern in what is said publicly by American and European governments as to the goals and processes of negotiations. 'Talks with the Taliban' is not a silver bullet to end the conflict, nor will a swiftly assembled 'peace deal' among elites solve the root causes of the insurgency. There is a lot about the current proposals and activities to offer cause for concern; a negotiated settlement must not simply be seen as a short-cut route.

There is no exclusivity between fighting and negotiating; these can and will happen in parallel. The way the conflict is conducted—what kinds of strategies are being pursued—is important here. If a political settlement is indeed being sought, there would be little sense in trying to destroy the organisations with which one is simultaneously trying to hold talks.

Even if circumstances might seem to belie the expectation of responsible Afghan political action (particularly at the higher levels), there is nothing to suggest that such responsible action is impossible, nor that others (including foreigners and regional players) do not have a role to play in creating expectations as to just how responsible they should be.

Unfortunately, past experience, the proven track records of regional actors and insurgents, the Afghan government and current US policy all combine to suggest that a wide-ranging set of talks of this kind is ultimately unrealistic as a possibility for the near-term Afghan political calendar. In that case, the international community would do well to begin preparing for possible scenarios that would involve the displacement of large numbers of Afghans outside and inside the country as refugees, as well as escalated levels of conflict that will increasingly resemble the violent civil war of the 1990s.

London, May 2011

NOTES

1. INTRODUCING TALQAEDA

1. Gray (2003), 103.
2. Packer (2007), 37.
3. Fergusson (2010), 135.
4. See Gutman (2008) and Riedel (2008).
5. See http://www.pollingreport.com/afghan2.htm (accessed 25 July 2010).
6. Ibid.
7. See Bergen (2009) and Rohde (2009).
8. See chapter 2 for more on Deobandism.
9. Felicia Sonmez and Matt DeLong, 'Panetta: 50–100 al-Qaeda remain in Afghanistan,' *The Washington Post*, http://voices.washingtonpost.com/44/2010/06/panetta-50–100-al-qaeda-remain.html (accessed 29 July 2010).
10. See al Bahri (2004), al-Masri (2004), Al-Zayyat (2004), Anas (2002), Bergen (2006), Faraj (2002), Nasiri (2008), and Salah (2001) to sample some of these.
11. Currently available accounts include: Mojdeh (2008), Mustas'ad (2006), Mutawakil (2007), Zaeef (2010) and Zaeef (2011). A manuscript written by Amir Khan Muttaqi, the Taliban's former head of the Culture and Information Committee, exists, although the authors have not seen a copy.
12. For example: Tolo-ye Afghan, Shariat, Khelafat, Kandahar, Anis, Hewaad, Erada, Herat, Faryab, Sangar, Kamkino, and Misak-i Khun.
13. For example, see the reports issued by BBC Monitoring or the Open Source Center.
14. Translations of some of these books were provided by Mideastwire.com. This was made possible with funds provided by New York University's Center on International Cooperation. References to where citations are made within a text will be provided where possible, but where difficult these will refer to chapter or section numbers.

349

2. FOREBEARS (1970–1979)

1. Metcalf (2002), 1.
2. Nasiri (2008), 150.
3. Dupree (1980), 559.
4. Ibid., 531–3.
5. Al-Azhar University in Cairo, Egypt, is a religious institute that was founded in 970–972 and remains the most prestigious of all Sunni religious institutes around the world.
6. Ibid., 531.
7. Ibid., 532.
8. Roy (1990), 4.
9. Ibid., 532.
10. Olesen (1995), 239.
11. Dupree (1980), 565; Vogelsang (2008), 295.
12. Edwards (2002), 48.
13. Maley (2002), 21.
14. Ahmad (2004), 11.
15. The advisors of Da'ud Khan had already been trained at al-Azhar and a number of university professors had close ties to Egypt and the Muslim Brotherhood. Dupree (1980), 531.
16. Kepel (2005), 23.
17. Roy (1990), 69–74.
18. Wiebe (1978), 79.
19. Wiebe (1978), 205.
20. Firman or 'edict' no. 8 of 2 December 1978 set out the framework of the land reform. The idea was that small 'peasant' farmers would be more inclined to support the regime, coupled with the more general centrality of land reform to the communist ideal. The edict defined seven different categories of land (separated by distinctions of quality). Any one family could henceforth not own more than six hectares of land of the highest category. Redistribution would be carried out primarily in favour of day labourers. Agrarian reform was abolished by Karmal in March 1981 in the hope of winning over ordinary Afghans. Other policies enacted included 'the establishment of an official clergy, the policy of nationalities, the recruitment of notables and the establishment of militias' (Dorronsoro (2005), 179).
21. Note that Da'ud was borrowing money in order to make the project happen; it was not a gift.
22. They were nonetheless of significant size.
23. Dupree (1980), 514–22.
24. Roy (1990), 74; Vogelsang (2008), 301; Olesen (1995), 221–22.

25. A faction of the Communist Party in Afghanistan.
26. Vogelsang (2008), 300.
27. Olesen (1995), 222; interviews, Kandahar, 2006–10.
28. Interviews, Kandahar, 2008–10.
29. Haqqani (2005), 131–157.
30. Interview, Kandahar, May 2010. The interviewee outlined how he fled in the late 1970s to Quetta, Pakistan, with his family. He described the continual arrivals, and how many officials of the Najibullah administration came after the fall of that government in the early 1990s and again how the Taliban came in 2001.
31. Dawisha (2003), Kindle Electronic Edition: Location 29–33.
32. Kepel (2005), 132.
33. Al-Zayyat (2004), 23.
34. Hegghammer (2010), Kindle Electronic Edition: Location 274–77; Kepel (2006), 69.
35. Coll (2008), 175.
36. See Olesen (1995) and Roy (1990) for a more detailed account of this transformation.
37. Olesen (1995), 108.
38. See below for a more detailed discussion and definition of this term.
39. Ibid., 131–133.
40. Nawid (1999).
41. Roy (1990), 54–68.
42. The Mujaddidi family was one of the prominent religious families of Afghanistan; Olesen (1995), 185.
43. Olesen (1995), 193–4.
44. Ibid., 192.
45. Olesen (1995), 196–7.
46. Unveiled women were attacked with acid. Unlike in the 1920s when protests had stopped reforms from being passed, or 1959 when the issue of unveiling caused a riot in Kandahar, here the sympathy lay with the women who were attacked.
47. Olesen (1995), 212–5; Edwards (2002), 39.
48. Olesen (1995), 216.
49. See Edwards (2002), 177–278, for a richly-textured account of this period.
50. Pakistan also continued to refuse to allow aid to reach the traditionalist and royalist groups.
51. Roy (1990), 20ff.
52. Muslims in Afghanistan may be divided by sect as follows: approximately 80% Sunni, 19% Shi'i and 1% other. Most Sunnis follow the Hanafi legal school and most Shi'i follow the Ja'afari. The 1% 'other' is made up by a significant minority of Ismailis, many of whom live in Badakhshan. (CIA World Factbook (2010 edition), https://www.cia.gov/library/publications/the-world-factbook/print/tex-

tversion.html (accessed 30 June 2010)). Note that these statistics, like many applied to Afghanistan, are only loose approximations on account of the absence of baseline data like census materials, etc.

53. Roy (1990), 57; Metcalf (2002); Roy (1995b), 8–10.
54. A revivalist scholar, Shah Waliullah combined a devoted attention to scripturalist Islam while engaging in local politics and what he saw as encroaching British influence.
55. Metcalf (1978), 112.
56. Ibid., 115.
57. Schimmel (2003), 3–22.
58. Authors' observation in southern and south-eastern Afghanistan, 2005–2011.
59. Ibid., 117–118.
60. Robinson (1984), 337–345.
61. Metcalf (2002), 12; Nasr (1994), 111–5.
62. Ibid., 14.
63. Of course, Pakistan did not exist at that point as a country.
64. Interview, Kandahar City, August 2009.
65. Interviews, Kabul, Kandahar and Quetta, 2010.
66. Prominent religious clerics during the 1970s in Kandahar were (according to interviewees): Mawlawi Mohammad Noor Saheb; Jinab Mawlawi Saheb; Hazratul Mawlawi Saheb; Mawlawi Sadozai (Tayyeb Agha's father); Abdul Rab Akhundzada; Mawlawi Abdul Ghaffar Barialai (Mutawakil's father) and Mawlawi Abdul Ali Deobandi (who had actually studied at Deoband in India).
67. Matinuddin (1999), 13.
68. Dorronsoro (2005), 276.
69. Haqqani (2005), Kindle Electronic Edition: Location 2790–2.
70. One of the four main Islamic schools of legal thought, it is predominant in Afghanistan (and also is the largest globally in terms of adherents). Named after the legal scholar Abu Hanifa (d. 767), it advocates a more liberal approach to the Islamic law or shari'a.
71. Matinuddin (1999), 15.
72. Zaeef (2010), 5–9, and Mutawakil (2007), 4–9, for full accounts. Also, interviews, Kandahar, October 2009 and January 2010.
73. Interview, Kabul, June 2010. This interviewee worked in the National Directorate of Security with the Taliban during the 1990s.
74. Note that many of these names were taken from Rashid (2001a). All interviewees, for example, disputed that Mullah Mohammad Omar was educated outside Afghanistan and held that he only left the country for medical treatment during the jihad in the 1980s. The authors of this book found no specific evidence that he had ever been educated there. See below for a further discussion of this point.
75. Ruttig (2009a), 64; Elias (2002), 10–11.

76. He also is alleged to have spent time studying at Farooqia madrassa in Karachi but cut his studies short in order to fight in the jihad.
77. Haroon (2007), 199.
78. 'Mullah Omar never graduated, our guide explained, "but we gave him an honorary degree anyway, because he left to do jihad and to create a pristine Islamic government."' (Friedman (2001)); 'Earlier this decade, the school even granted an honorary degree to Afghan Taliban leader Mullah Omar. It is the only honorary degree ever bestowed by Darul Uloom Haqqania, but Sami ul-Haq says it was nothing more than the recognition of a person with special qualities—exactly as is done in all cultures. "We honored Mullah Omar for his contribution to peace, just like your universities did with Mother Teresa," he says.' (Mayr (2008)).
79. Bonney (2004), 200–11.
80. 'Collaboration with Zia ul-Haq's military regime strained some religious parties internally.' (Haqqani (2005), 137.)
81. Quoted in Talbot (1999), 251.
82. See comments made by Vali Nasr and Richard Holbrooke to PBS (http://www.pbs.org/wgbh/pages/frontline/shows/saudi/analyses/madrassas.html (accessed 20 February 2011)).
83. Interview, Kabul, July 2010.
84. Note, however, that Zaman (2002) argues that there has actually been considerable change and evolution of Deobandist scholarship and philosophy over the past century in response to outside change.
85. Interviews, Kabul and Kandahar, 2010.
86. Ibid.
87. Edwards (2002), 153–4.
88. Note that Abu al-Walid al-Masri was not formally affiliated with or pledged to al-Qaeda.
89. Kepel (2006), 27–30.
90. Mitchell (1969), 10–12.
91. Mitchell (1969), 32.
92. Ibid., 31.
93. Kepel (2005), 38–9. Calvert (2010), 139.
94. Kepel (2005), 39.
95. Ibid.
96. 'We might distinguish three different kinds of justice that are intertwined in this usage: social justice, political justice, and legal justice. The first of these terms has an important legacy in Islamist thought, dating to the publication of Qutb's 1949 classic Social Justice in Islam. Although the book of Qutb's that has received most Western attention recently is "Milestones"—a key text in the emergence of radically violent jihadism—the earlier work is a more important text for mainstream Islamism and its political-constitutional platform.' (Feldman (2008), Kindle Electronic Edition: Location 1110–13.)

97. Qutb (1964), 4.
98. Kepel (2005), 49.
99. Kepel (2005), 52–59.
100. Coll (2005), Kindle Electronic Edition: Location 2306–8.
101. Mawdudi was a fully-qualified and educated Deobandi *'alim*, although he didn't publicise the fact in later years (Nasr (1996), 9–18.).
102. Kepel (2006), 26 and 31.
103. Mamdani (2004), Kindle Electronic Edition: Location 802–4.
104. Mandaville (2007), 62–8.
105. Wright (2006), Kindle Electronic Edition: Location 524–26.
106. Calvert (2010), chapters 6 and 7.
107. Ibid., chapter 6.
108. Wright (2006), Kindle Electronic Edition: Location 563–66 and 575.
109. Quoted in Bonney (2004), 223.
110. Gerges (2005), Kindle Electronic Edition: Location 206–16.
111. Hegghammer (2010), Kindle Electronic Edition: Location 3690–91 and 508–11.
112. Burhanuddin Rabbani, for instance, translated at least one of Sayyed Qutb's works into Dari (Burke (2004), 66–7).
113. Interview, July 2010.
114. Kepel (2006), 65–66.
115. Ibid., 82.
116. Ibid., 82.
117. Edwards (2002), 11–14.
118. See Roy (1990), 6.
119. Sageman (2004), 74–5.
120. Various sources, including interviews.
121. Ibid., 75.
122. Hertog and Gambetta (2009), 201–230.
123. Burke (2004), 113.
124. Al-Zayyat (2004), 8.
125. Ibid., 16.
126. Bergen (2006), Kindle Electronic Edition: Location 695–700.
127. Read Jansen (1986) and Jansen (1997) for more.
128. Note the title of this book has also been translated as 'The Absent Obligation,' 'The Neglected Obligation' and 'The Forgotten Obligation.'
129. Faraj (2000), 24 and 32.
130. Gerges (2005), 296n7.
131. Faraj quoted in Kepel (2005), 209.
132. Al-Zayyat (2004), 21.
133. Gerges (2005), 44–45.

134. Ibid., 11.
135. Kepel (2005).
136. Lia (2009), 35–40.
137. Ibid., 38.
138. Zaeef (2010), 8–9.
139. Mutawakil (2007), 4–5.
140. Within Islam. Of course, the 1980s *jihad* was, in part and on one level, a dispute between Islam and communism.
141. Interviews, Kandahar and Khost, 2007–2010.
142. Kepel (2005), 73–104.
143. Gerges (2005), Kindle Electronic Edition: Location 1163–70.
144. Kepel (2004), 172–3.
145. Nasr (2007), 137–8.
146. Ibid., 137.
147. Kepel (2004), 179–181.
148. Nasr (2007), 148–9.
149. The *Mahdi* is a religious figure commonly portrayed in messianic and eschatological tones. Although not mentioned in the *Qur'an*, the idea is that the *Mahdi* will deliver the world from corruption and bring justice. The *Mahdi* is, however, mentioned in the *hadith* record.
150. Trofimov (2007), chapter 31.
151. Ibid., Kindle Electronic Edition: Location 3715–19.
152. Ibid., Location 3731–35.

3. *JIHAD* (1979–1990)

1. Faraj (2002).
2. Van Dyk (2002), 129.
3. Ibid, 149.
4. Cooley (2002), 13.
5. Roy (1990), 98ff and 102.
6. Maley (2002), 30–31.
7. This is exactly, to the day, twenty-two years before the commencement of Operation Enduring Freedom.
8. Ibid, 34.
9. Interviews, Kandahar, 2009–10; see chapter 2.
10. 'Loy Kandahar' (literally 'Greater Kandahar') refers to the provinces of Helmand, Kandahar, Uruzgan and Zabul. When people refer to 'Kandahar' in ordinary conversation, they are often referring to this larger grouping.
11. Interviews, Kandahar, 2008–10; Also see Zaeef (2010) and Kepel (2008a).
12. Loy or 'greater' Kandahar refers to today's provinces of Uruzgan, Helmand, Kandahar, and Zabul.

13. Interviews, Kandahar, 2008–10.
14. See Gumnam (1986) and Gumnam (1996).
15. Zaeef (2010), 33.
16. Interviews, Kabul and Kandahar, 2009–2010.
17. Dorronsoro (2005), 105.
18. Interview, Kandahar, June 2009.
19. Interview, Kabul, June 2010.
20. At the behest of Mawlana Fazulur Rahman.
21. Edwards (2002), 244–7.
22. A 'commander' in terms of the mujahedeen fronts was anyone with men serving underneath them. It does not necessarily imply a large or important position.
23. Roy (1995b), 8–10.
24. Interview, Kabul City, April 2009.
25. Interview, Kandahar City, (mujahed who fought in Mahalajat and Kandahar city) May 2010; Interview with Talib who fought in Panjwayi and Kandahar City, May 2009.
26. Interviews, Kandahar, summer 2008 and 2009.
27. Interviews, southern Afghanistan, 2008–11.
28. Zheray district was formed only recently (i.e. since 2001) and people generally refer to Panjwayi to mean both districts.
29. Interviews, southern Afghanistan, 2008–10.
30. Interviews, southern Afghanistan, 2006–10.
31. Mahalajat is a suburb of Kandahar City that lies to its south. The two are extremely close, and during the 1980s it was a de facto mujahedeen-controlled area from which they would mount attacks.
32. Interviews, Kandahar, 2009–2010.
33. Interview, Kabul, July 2010.
34. Faraj (2002).
35. Interviews, Kandahar, 2008–2010 and Kabul, July 2010.
36. Rashid (2001a), 19.
37. Roy (1990), 128.
38. This is a partial screenshot of a map developed by the authors using Tinderbox software and covering the 1980s Taliban fronts across Afghanistan (but with a special focus on the south).
39. Coghlan (2009), 65; Roy (1990), 128.
40. Edwards (2002), 251–2.
41. Van Dyk (2002), 161.
42. Ibid, 170.
43. Roy (1995b): 8–10.
44. For the history of this tradition in the past century, see Haroon (2007).
45. Roy (1990), 113–4 and 124.

46. Email exchange, Anand Gopal, December 2010 and January 2011.

47. Interviews, London, autumn and winter 2010; interview, Kabul, July 2010; conversation, Thomas Hegghammer, Boston, 23 February 2010; interviews, former 'Afghan Arabs,' London, spring 2011.

48. Note that our term 'Arabs' here can also apply to other non-Afghans, although it was the case that those who came to Pakistan for the sake of jihad in Afghanistan were mostly actual Arabs. This applies for the rest of the book when we refer to 'Arabs.'

49. Hegghammer (2010), Kindle Electronic Edition: Location 3690–91 and 507–511.

50. Lia (2009), 73–4.

51. Interview, Kabul, July 2010; also see Wright (2008).

52. Kepel (2006), 141.

53. Wright (2006), Kindle Electronic Edition: Location 1901–7.

54. Wright (2008).

55. Kepel (2006), 144.

56. Kepel (2008a), 94–5; Salah (2001).

57. Which is to say that not all of the Arabs who came to Pakistan to fight in the jihad actually made it into Afghanistan; only a small proportion did.

58. Interview, Thomas Hegghammer, Boston, February 2010.

59. Anas (2002).

60. Bergen (2006), Kindle Electronic Edition: Location 1110–13.

61. Cited in Kepel (2006), 397n37.

62. Interviews, Kabul and Kandahar, 2008–2010.

63. For more on this last group, see Anas (2002).

64. Roy (1990), 69ff.

65. Al-Zawahiri (2001).

66. Wright (2008).

67. Mullah Khahsar, for example, states: 'Mullah Omar didn't know Osama during the jihad. During the holy war [against the Soviet Union] Osama never came to Kandahar. There were some Arabs who were in Kandahar during the jihad, but it was less than in other places. Maybe thirty Arabs would be there at any one time. They fought in different bunkers with different groups. They would come and go. Sometimes they would stay for a little while and other times they would just come for an operation and then go.' (Gannon (2006), 32).

68. This is an account of the Arabs who passed through Afghanistan during the 1980s jihad.

69. Faraj (2002).

70. Coll (2008), Kindle Electronic Edition: Location 3926–33. Interview, Kandahar, July 2010.

71. Faraj (2002).

72. Kathy Gannon wrote that, 'when the mujahedeen in Kandahar spoke of Arab fighters they did it with derision, always ready to take their money but never counting them as friends.' (Gannon (2006), 32).
73. Interview with former mujahed, Kandahar, July 2009; Faraj (2002).
74. Interview, Kabul, July 2010.
75. Faraj (2002).
76. *Loya* Paktya is the present-day provinces of Paktya, Paktika, Khost (and North and South Waziristan in Pakistan).
77. See Coll (2008), 248, and Al-Masri (2004), chapter 1.
78. Kepel (2008a).
79. These meetings are detailed in the first half of Van Dyk (2002). Also, interview, Kabul, July 2010.
80. Kepel (2008a), 42.
81. Interview with an Arab Afghan close to Azzam, London, February 2010.
82. Often called 'the Lion's Den.' In fact the translation 'Companion's Den' is more accurate. See Kepel (2008a), 273n10, for more.
83. See ibid., 41–6, for an account of this period written by bin Laden.
84. Wright (2006), Kindle Electronic Edition: Location 2130.
85. Ibid, Location 2142–7.
86. Bergen (2006), Kindle Electronic Edition: Location 1365–72.
87. Wright (2006), Kindle Electronic Edition: Location 2210.
88. Wright (2006), 120.
89. Faraj (2002).
90. Zaeef (2010), 26.
91. Wright (2006), Kindle Electronic Edition: Location 1978.
92. Bergen (2006), Kindle Electronic Edition: Location 1256–63.
93. Series of interviews with former-mujahedeen commanders, Kandahar and Kabul, 2008–10.
94. Interviews, Kandahar, 2008–2010.
95. Edwards (2002).
96. Roy (1990), 99ff.
97. Edwards (2002), 241, and Roy (1990), 74.
98. 'By August 1980, 90,000 Afghans were reported to be entering Pakistan each month.' (Quoted in Haroon (2007), 202).
99. Interviews, Kandahar, August 2008.
100. Interview, Kandahar City, August 2008.
101. Roy (1990), 61.
102. Olesen (1995), 256–7; Zaeef (2010), 8–10.
103. Interviews, Kandahar, 2009–10.
104. Van Dyk (2002), 61.
105. Interviewees from among fighters on the Taliban fronts during the 1980s all noted that there were two strands to the call for jihad: one was the more tradi-

tional nationalist version and the other ("that of the *ikhwaanis*") was more international in aspiration.

106. Interview, Kandahar City, June 2009.
107. Interviews, southern Afghanistan, 2008–10.
108. Interviews, southern Afghanistan, 2008–10; conversation, Gilles Dorronsoro, Washington DC, February 2010.
109. Kepel (2008a), 92.
110. Bonney (2004), 357.
111. Kepel (2008a), 106.
112. Ibid, 108.
113. See Ibid, 110–125, for a translation of excerpts of this document.
114. Ibid., 118–9.
115. Kepel (2008a), 151.
116. Ibid., 141–3.
117. Van Dyk (2002), 99.
118. Faraj (2002).
119. Anas (2002).
120. Interview, Kandahar, June 2010.
121. Interviews, London, spring and autumn 2010.
122. Lia (2009), 35–50.
123. Ibid., 74.
124. Quoted in ibid., 81.
125. Al-Zawahiri (2001).
126. Kepel (2008a), 100.
127. Ibid., 100.
128. Al-Zayyat (2004), 49.
129. Ibid., 55.
130. Anas (2002).
131. Aboul-Enein (2008), 3.
132. Hegghammer (2010), Kindle Electronic Edition: Locations 390–1 and 541–2; Aboul-Enein (2008), 3–4.
133. Tawil (2010b), chapter 2.
134. Ibid., 583.
135. Bergen (2006), Kindle Electronic Edition: Locations 906–927.
136. Anas (2002).
137. Kean and Hamilton (2004), Kindle Electronic Edition: Location 58.
138. Note that this is a separate organisation from the other, larger international humanitarian that goes by the same name.
139. National Commission on Terrorist Attacks Upon the United States (2004).
140. *Al-Jihad* magazine praised the support of seven charities in its December 1986 issue; these included the Red Crescent of Saudi Arabia and the Muslim World

League, the large Mecca-based charity. Coll (2008), Kindle Electronic Edition: Location 4524–6.

141. Hegghammer (2010), Kindle Electronic Edition: Location 560ff.
142. Maley (2002), 154–5.
143. Roy (1995b): 8–10.
144. Roy (1990).
145. Roy (1995b): 8–10.
146. See chapter 4 of Bergen (2006) for more details.
147. Kepel (2008a), 99.
148. Interviews, Kandahar and Kabul, 2010.
149. Woodward (1987).
150. Interviews, Kandahar and Kabul, 2010.
151. Faraj (2002).
152. Interview, Kandahar City, July 2010.
153. Interview, Kabul, July 2010.
154. Interview, Kandahar City, July 2010.
155. Kepel (2008a), 123–124.
156. Note that the prayers (portions of the Qur'an, certain prayers, blessings, etc.) said within the prayer (*namaz, salat*) are identical. What is slightly different are some of the outward motions and postures. Hanbalis raise their hands each time they bow (*ruku'*), stand up from bowing (*qiyam*), and go down to prostrate (*sajda*). Also, in congregational prayer (*salatu l-jama'a*) when the Imam (prayer-leader) finishes *suratu l-fatiha* (the opening sura of the Qur'an), Hanafis praying behind say '*amin*' silently, while Hanbalis say it audibly.
157. Anas (2002).
158. Interviews with former 'Arab Afghans,' London, autumn and winter 2010.
159. http://www.khyber.org/pashtohistory/treaties/durandagreement.shtml (accessed 2 August 2010).
160. Schöch (2008).
161. See Edwards (2002).
162. Coll (2005), Kindle Electronic Edition: Location 2643–2654.
163. Haqqani (2005).
164. Maley (2002), 70.
165. Haqqani (2005), chapter 5.
166. Maley (2002), 62–4 and 74–6.
167. Rashid (2008), 111–20.
168. Ibid.
169. Ibid.
170. Gayer and Jaffrelot (2009), 136.
171. Haqqani (2005), 261–309.
172. Jamal (2010a).

pp. [74–80]

173. Rana (2004), 244–5.
174. Tawil (2010b), chapter 2.
175. Abou Zahab and Roy (2004), 35.
176. Gayer and Jaffrelot (2009), 160–2.
177. These Pakistanis were mostly assigned to the same political parties as were the Arabs, but there were far more smaller groups or individuals fighting together with the whole range of small mujahedeen fronts in southern and south-eastern Afghanistan.
178. See Gul (2010) and Hussain (2008).
179. He was Afghan.
180. See Dorronsoro (2005), 230–2; Abou Zahab and Roy (2004), 38 and 48; and Hegghammer (2009), 251.
181. Interview, Kandahar, July 2010.
182. Interview, Kabul, July 2010.
183. Interviews, Kandahar, 2008–10.
184. Wright (2006), chapters 5 and 6.
185. Coll (2005), Kindle Electronic Edition: Location 2643–2654.
186. Interview, Kabul, July 2010. Fisher (2011): 'analytically, the best fighters—the best organized fighters—were the fundamentalists.'
187. Yousaf and Adken (1992), 37–43.
188. Borchgrevink (2010).
189. See Zaeef (2010), 31–5, and Yousaf and Adken (1992), 113–127, for accounts of this from both Afghan and ISI perspectives.
190. Interviews, southern Afghanistan, 2008–10.
191. See Yousaf and Adken (1992) for more on this relationship from the ISI perspective.
192. Coll (2005), 72.
193. Blanchard (2010), 8n11; Rubenstein (1983).
194. Burke (2004), 55.
195. Hegghammer (2010), 270.
196. Kepel (2006), 70–80.
197. Ibid., 280.
198. Ibid., 287.
199. Coll (2005), Kindle Electronic Edition: Location 1981.
200. Atwan (2006), 36.
201. Burke (2004), 57.
202. Coll (2005), 84.
203. Ibid, 83.
204. Rubin (2002), 221.
205. See chapter 5.

4. RETHINK (1990–1994)

1. Quoted in Ruttig (2010), 11.
2. Interview, Kabul, July 2010.
3. Lia (2009), 89–90.
4. Haqqani (2005), 289.
5. Robert Gates was reportedly a strong advocate of this scenario within the CIA. (Interview, Washington DC, June 2010).
6. Murshed (2006), 36.
7. Giustozzi (2009), 53–80.
8. Cited in Maley (2002), 170.
9. Interview, Kabul, July 2010.
10. Thirty of Massoud's commanders were murdered by one of Hekmatyar's commanders in Takhar, Sayyed Jamal.
11. Hajji Latif, one of the best-known mujahedeen commanders in Kandahar, was poisoned in Arghestan district on 7 August 1989; 'Hajji Abdul Latif: Obituary,' The Times, 11 August 1989.
12. Maley (2002),197–99.
13. Like Mohammad Abd al-Rahim al-Sharqawi who had formed the first clandestine cell in Egypt together with al-Zawahiri in 1968. (Al-Zayyat (2004), 55.)
14. Maley (2002), 199–200.
15. 'The largest and fastest spontaneous repatriation of refugees in modern history.' (Maley (2002), 195.)
16. Ibid.
17. Interviews, Kandahar, 2009–10.
18. Afghan Mujahedeen, 'AIG's Communique on Anniversary of Russian Invasion of Afghanistan,' Afghan Jehad, 27 December 1989.
19. Interview, Kabul, July 2010.
20. Zaeef (2010), 49–50.
21. Press conference, Kandahar, March 1995 in Mahfel (March 1995). (Translated from Pashtu into German into English.)
22. Anderson (1989).
23. Afghan Mujahedeen, 'Decisions held at the joint council of seven Mujaheddin organizations in Kandahar,' Afghan Jehad, August 1992, 35–6.
24. Pashtu radio broadcast, Mahfel (March 1995). (Translated from Pashtu to German to English.)
25. Interviews, Kandahar/Khost, 2006–10.
26. Interview with Waliullah Salim, Afghan Jehad, August 1992, 180.
27. Interview, Kandahar, July 2010.
28. Zaeef (2010), 50.
29. Interviews, non-Taliban commanders and fighters, Kandahar, summer 2008.

30. One Afghan cleric who fought as a commander in Paktya described how the withdrawal of the Soviet troops caused a 'massive change' in that the 'culture and daily life of jihad faded away, along with the fighters.' He stated that 'the religious students just dissolved away, some into other groups, and others just went back to their homes.' (Interview, Kabul, July 2010.)
31. Ibid., 49–52.
32. Interview, Kabul, July 2010.
33. Interview, Kandahar, June 2010.
34. Interview, Kabul, July 2010.
35. Interview, Kabul, July 2010.
36. Interviews, Kandahar and Helmand, 2008–10.
37. Interview, Kabul, June 2010.
38. Al-Masri (1990).
39. See Afghan Jehad magazine for this period.
40. Ibid.
41. Interview, Kabul, July 2010.
42. 'Untitled,' Afghan Jehad, 4, no. 2 (1991): 229–230.
43. Interview, Kabul, July 2010. Interviews, Kandahar, summer 2008.
44. 'Untitled,' Afghan Jehad, 4, no. 3 (1991): 226.
45. 'Untitled,' Afghan Jehad, 4, no. 4 (1991): 153.
46. Cooley (2002), 150.
47. Weinbaum (1994), 121.
48. Anas (2002).
49. Salah (2001).
50. Anas (2002).
51. Thanks to Thomas Hegghammer for this observation. Conversation, Boston, February 2010.
52. Ibid.
53. Interview with former 'Afghan Arab,' London, March 2010.
54. Lia (2009), 91. 'Dr Fadl' was, at this time, the de facto amir or head of Egyptian Islamic Jihad group. (See Wright (2008)).
55. Interview with former 'Afghan Arab,' London, March 2010.
56. Ibid., 90.
57. Kepel (2008a), 96.
58. Baker (2009); interviews, London and Boston, 2010.
59. KhAD is an abbreviation of Khedamat-e Ittla'aat-e Dawlati, or 'State Security Service.' Its name was changed to WAD by President Najibullah, but it is still commonly used to refer to the internal state security apparatus.
60. Anas (2002); interviews, London, 2010.
61. Quoted in Kepel (2008a), 94.
62. Anas (2002).

63. Gutman (2008), 28.
64. Randal (2005), 99.
65. Gerges (2005), chapter 3.
66. Lia (2009), 88–108.
67. Lia (2009), 94.
68. Quoted in ibid., 95.
69. Bin Laden and Lawrence (2005), 32n4; Burke (2004), 141.
70. Randal (2005), 102.
71. Randal (2005), 99; Kepel (2008a), 21–22; Gutman (2008), 35.
72. Gutman (2008), 35.
73. Wright (2006), chapter 7.
74. Randal (2005), 105.
75. Sigler (2009).
76. Bergen (2006), Kindle Electronic Edition: Location 2935–2953.
77. Bin Laden and Lawrence (2005), 3.
78. Bin Laden and Lawrence (ed.) (2005), 49–50.
79. Burke (2004), 138–139.
80. Coll (2008), chapter 27; Bergen (2006), Kindle Electronic Edition: Location 2307; Bergen (2001), Kindle Electronic Edition: Location 1637.
81. Bergen (2006), Kindle Electronic Edition: Location 1805–1812.
82. Randal (2005), 112; Gutman (2008), 36.
83. Burke (2004), 137; Gutman (2008), 37.
84. Coll (2008), chapter 27.
85. 'The Taliban had their origin in the Jamiyat-i Taliban (Society of Taliban), a subsidiary of Harakat-i Enqelab, which came into being officially around 1990 but had earlier existed informally.' (Dorronsoro (2005), 245).
86. Interview, Kandahar, June 2010.
87. Interview, Kabul, July 2010.
88. Interviews, Kandahar, 2008–10; Gopal (2010b); Afsar, Samples and Wood (2008).
89. Burke (2004), 23.
90. Bin Laden's time (and that of the other Islamist groups) in Sudan is, however, in need of closer examination on account of the lack of detailed information on and analysis of both the evolution of his thought as well as the nature of ties between the myriad number of individuals there during the 1990s.
91. Kohlmann (2004); Schindler (2007); Hegghammer (2010), Kindle Electronic Edition: Location 690–702; Kepel (2006), 237–253.
92. Al-Masri (2004).
93. Nasiri (2008).
94. Al-Masri (2004); see also Kean and Hamilton (2004), 500n5, for further context.
95. Al-Masri (2004).
96. See Salah (2001).

97. Al-Zayyat (2004), 56.
98. Salah (2001); Lia (2009), 143–4.
99. McDermott (2005), 2264–70.
100. Interview, Kabul, July 2010.
101. Burke (2004), 98–99.
102. Reeve (1999), 71–4.
103. Kean and Hamilton (2004), 58.
104. Ibid, 149.
105. Wright (2006), 163–5.
106. Coll (2008), Kindle Electronic Edition: Location 6101–6122.
107. Randal (2005), 113.
108. Al-Zayyat (2004), 56–58.
109. Wright (2006), 179 and 183.
110. Gerges (2005).
111. Their age was also a significant factor here.
112. See above.
113. Interview and email exchange, Anand Gopal, Kabul, July 2010; al-Masri (1990).
114. Cooley (2002), 213–4.
115. Nasiri (2008), 218, 296, 328.
116. Ahmad (2004), 37.
117. Salah (2001); Tawil (2010b); Reeve (1999); Kepel (2006).
118. Salah (2001).
119. Cited in Burke (2004), 115.
120. Faraj (2002).
121. Nasiri (2008); Abou Zahab and Roy (2004); Tawil (2010b); Gutman (2008).
122. Ibid., 95.
123. Ibid., 95.
124. Ibid., 95.
125. BBC Monitoring (1990); Faraj (2002).
126. Gul (2010).
127. Rashid (2001a), Kindle Electronic Edition: Location 4045–49.
128. Haqqani (2005), 272–5.
129. Ibid., 214; Lieven (2011), 406.
130. Haqqani (2005), 213.
131. Ibid., 214.
132. Al-Masri (2004); Gutman (2008), 28–9.
133. Maley (2002), 198–9.
134. Haqqani (2005), 273.
135. Lawrence Ziring, quoted in ibid., 212–3.
136. Ibid., 277–9.
137. Gul (2010), 249–59; Lieven (2011), 185–197.

138. The close physical proximity and shared living arrangements meant that ideas that the Arabs held strongly were passed on to Pakistanis. The ground, of course, was already fertile and responsive to these ideas in the wake of the 1980s *jihad*.

139. Reeve (1999); Burns (1995).

140. This arrest came in good time, just before an April 1995 visit of Bhutto to Washington on her second official visit (ibid., 230).

141. Haqqani (2005), 236, 294–5.

142. Ibid., 242.

143. Maley (2002), 189–201.

144. Ahady (1998), 121.

145. Assorted Saudi Ulemaa,' 'Verdict of distinguished Saudi Arabian ulama regarding the situation in Afghanistan,' *Afghan Jehad*, 5, no. 3 (1992): 36–37.

146. It was in fact more a stance directed *against* the United States' presence in Saudi Arabia than support *for* Hussein.

147. Ahady (1998), 123.

148. Cited in Ahady (1998), 123.

149. Email correspondence, Dr. Christopher Davidson, July 2010.

150. As related in Salah (2001).

151. Hegghammer (2010), Kindle Electronic Edition: Location 599.

152. http://www.cnn.com/WORLD/9511/saudi_blast/11am/ (accessed 2 August 2010).

5. CLOSER AND FARTHER (1994–1998)

1. Interview, Kabul, July 2010.

2. Gannon (2006), 30.

3. Mujahedeen groups would stage attacks against government positions; there would be an agreement that gunfire would not directly target assets or personnel on either side. (Interviews, Kandahar, 2009–11.)

4. Interviews, Kandahar, 2006–10.

5. Ibid.

6. Interviews, Kandahar, Summer 2008.

7. Feldab-Brown (2010), 114–9.

8. Interview, Kabul, July 2010.

9. Interviews, southern Afghanistan, 2008–9.

10. Zaeef (2010), 49–50; Saikal (1998), 29.

11. Isby (2010), Kindle Electronic Edition: Location 1942.

12. Interviews, Kandahar, 2008–10; Fergusson (2010), 10–13.

13. On 10 April 1993, for example, the ICRC reported that two hundred people had been killed in Kandahar City as the result of inter-group clashes.

14. Rashid (2001a), 21.

15. Interview, Kandahar, April 2010

16. Murshed (2006), 42; Zaeef (2010), 65.

17. Roy (1995a), 9; Roy (1995b), 9.

18. Interviews, Kandahar and Kabul, 2008–10.

19. Zaeef (2010), 65.

20. Ibid., 63–4.

21. See, for example, Murshed (2006), 43; and 'Taliban schon seit 1985/86?' in Mahfel 45 (March–April 1995), 6; Rashid (2001a), 25; Nawaz (2008), 478.

22. This source is interesting for being one of the longest (and only) contiguous narrations by Mullah Mohammad Omar as to the early days of the Taliban in 1994.

23. Taken from the Qur'an, surat al-baqarah, 286.

24. Ibn Mahmud (date unknown), 16–18.

25. Hajji Bashar is a senior Noorzai tribal actor from Kandahar who played a significant role in both the 1980s and 1990s; he supported the Taliban's rule in the mid-1990s and was convicted of drug trafficking charges in the United States in 2008. See Gutman (2008), 63; and Zaeef (2010), 69–70; 'Taliban schon seit 1985/86?' in Mahfel 45 (March–April 1995), 6.

26. Gutman (2008), 63 and 277n3. This was in part an attempt to undermine Hekmatyar.

27. Interview, Kabul, July 2010. This interviewee (working with the Rabbani government at the time) claimed air support was also part of their backing for the Taliban.

28. Ibid., 65; Rashid (2001a), 27; Matinuddin (1999), 60–2.

29. Gutman (2008), 65; Nawaz (2008), 479. (Nawaz states that the seventeen tunnels had enough supplies to equip an army corps.)

30. Analysts have subsequently claimed that this arms dump seizure offers a convenient excuse (or a 'thick smoke-screen') for the Taliban to deny support from Pakistan in subsequent years (since from then on they had all the weapons they needed). See Davis (1998), 46.

31. Zaeef (2011), chapter 3; and 'Taliban schon seit 1985/86?' in Mahfel 45 (March–April 1995), 6.

32. Mutawakil (2007).

33. One of the five 'pillars' of Islam, the practice of almsgiving or zakat is widespread and encouraged in southern Afghanistan. It is also—to a certain extent—systematised in such a way that it is in many instances a highly formalised type of charitable donation, whereby those with financial means must donate 2.5% of their annual earnings and liquid assets for the needy. Apart from a nominal sum given to them by the government, the religious clergy—particularly in rural areas of the south—often have to rely on zakat and other donations from their fellow villagers. In Afghanistan this exists alongside the tradition of Ushr, whereby 10 per cent of profits are shared out to fellow villagers.

34. Interview, Kabul, July 2010.

35. The exact relationship and input of the ISI and Pakistan in the early days of the Taliban movement remains contested. While early support from Pakistan was forthcoming, opinions differ among analysts and commentators: some state that Pakistan was fundamentally involved in the Taliban's rise to the extent that they controlled the movement, while others maintain that the influence over the Taliban and the relationship was more diluted and did not constitute control over decisions and/or strategy. See Nawaz (2008), 479; Rashid (2001a), 29; Zaeef (2010), chapters 7 and 8; Hussain (2008), 28–30; Sinno (2008), chapter 8.

36. 'Another factor in explaining the Taliban's success is that they consistently downplayed tribal or regional identities in favour of what might be called "village identity." [...] In identifying purist culture and tradition with the Islam of the village, the Taliban were indirectly condemning the Islam of the parties since most of the party leaders were products of Kabul University or had worked for state-sponsored institutions. They were also putting themselves on a par with the people whose support they had to enlist if their movement was going to be successful.' (Edwards (2002), 294).

37. Interviews, Kabul, spring and summer 2010.

38. This was Mawlawi Abdul Samad. See Zaeef (2010), 65.

39. Talibs involved during this period state that one of the important reasons for choosing Mullah Mohammad Omar as head was the relatively limited role he played during the 1980s jihad in comparison to other more prominent figures (which would have made them more biased, the argument ran). Interviews, Kabul and Kandahar, 2009–10. Also see ibid., 63–4. Interviewees also echo the statement made by Ahmed Rashid: 'Some Taliban say Omar was chosen as their leader not for his political or military ability, but for his piety and his unswearing belief in Islam.' (Rashid (2001a), 23.)

40. Note that the term 'older generation' is a retrospective one.

41. There is an inherent tension between aspects of 'Pashtunwali' in the ideal form and Islamic shari'a in its ideal form. It is not clear, though, to what extent this conflict was perceived as such in the minds of the Taliban's leadership; in general, there was more of an attempt to try to shift the emphasis in the Taliban's rule to something approaching 'pure shari'a,' but this tension was never fully resolved.

42. Interviews, Kabul and Kandahar, 2010.

43. Interviews, Kabul and Kandahar, 2008–10.

44. The initial euphoria seemed to sour within 12–18 months. In 1995, here was what one man had to say: '[The Taliban] have grown in darkness amidst death. They are angry and ignorant, and hate all things that bring joy to life.' (Quoted in Mamdani (2004), 161.)

45. Interviews, Kabul and Kandahar, 2010; Zaeef (2010), chapter 7 and 8.

46. Interviews, Kandahar and Kabul, June and July 2010.

47. Interviews, Kandahar and Kabul, June and July 2010.
48. Gutman (2008), 61.
49. Fergusson (2010), 80.
50. Interviews, Kandahar, June–July 2010. Note, too, that the local population were initially much more willing to accept whatever restrictions the Taliban imposed because the Taliban also brought security. This acceptance started to fade as the years passed.
51. Rashid (2001a), chapters 1–3.
52. Ruttig (2010), 3; Ruttig (1995), 1–2.
53. Sinno has commented on the extent of Pakistani support for the Taliban: 'Pakistani support for the Taliban might have been substantial, but it couldn't possibly compare in scale with Soviet support for the PDPA/Watan or even the resources later poured by Western and other donors in support of the Karzai regime. And, while Pakistan supported the Taliban, its rivals were actively backed by Iran, Russia, and India—the situation was hardly lopsided.' (Sinno (2008), 233.)
54. Murshed (2006), 42; see also Gutman (2008), 62 and 67: General Qazi stated that, 'the movement was not engineered from outside or trained from outside. If someone had had to plan and launch the Taliban, I would have had to do it. I certainly did not do it.'
55. Nawaz (2008), 534.
56. Gutman (2008), 65; Rashid (1998), 74.
57. Rashid (2001a), 22; Rashid (1998), 76–ff.
58. Gutman (2008), 62; Rashid (2001a), 26.
59. Rashid states he just went to Chaman (ibid., 27)
60. Rashid (2001a), 28. The National Logistics Cell was responsible for logistical support of the Afghan mujahedeen during the 1980s *jihad* against the Soviet Union. It provided weapons and other material to the mujahedeen and was implicated in drug trafficking at the time. Also see Nawaz (2008), 361.
61. Key to the Taliban's success in taking Kandahar City was Mullah Naqibullah's decision to cooperate with them. Gutman states that Naqibullah had been instructed to 'welcome' the Taliban by Rabbani and Massoud (Gutman (2008), 68). It seems unlikely that Rabbani or Massoud would have had the power over Mullah Naqibullah at the time to order him to step down, especially since Rabbani had little money (Matinuddin (1999), 24). Rashid also relays a rumour that Mullah Naqibullah accepted a large bribe from the ISI (Rashid (2001a), 28).
62. Murshed (2006) and Berman (2009) state that the convoy was bringing aid and medical supplies to be distributed along the way to hospitals and left Pakistan on 31 October 1994. Gutman, on the other hand, says the convoy was filled with goods (including medicine) meant for trade in Turkmenistan and left on 29 October 1994 (Gutman (2008), 65). Griffin adds the possibility that the convoy transported Pakistani regular troops disguised as Taliban (Griffin (2001), 34.)

63. Murshed (2006), 45.
64. Berman (2009), Kindle Electronic Edition: Location 433–4.
65. Beg (1995), 4.
66. Ruttig (2010), 3.
67. Roy (1995a), 8.
68. Gutman (2008), 62; Coll (2005), Kindle Electronic Edition: Location 5762.
69. Nawaz (2008), 479.
70. Davis (1998), 50.
71. Interview, Kandahar, December 2009.
72. Rashid (2001a), 29; and also see Coll (2005), Kindle Electronic Edition: Location 5762: 'The ISI brigadiers complained to Bhutto that the Taliban's leaders were stubborn, that they would not follow the military and political advice Pakistan offered.' Nawaz (2008), 534.
73. See comments, for example, made by Ken Guest at a Frontline Club event (http://frontlineclub.com/events/2010/02/understanding-the-taliban.html).
74. Davis (1998), 55.
75. 'Between 1994 and 1999, an estimated 80,000 to 100,000 Pakistanis trained and fought in Afghanistan.' (Rashid (1999)).
76. Jan (1995), 12.
77. Ibid. The article mentions that out of the approximately 240 Taliban that left Peshawar for Kandahar on 3 March 1995, 110 were Uzbek and 80 Tajik. Rashid states that by December 1994, 12,000 Afghan and Pakistani students had joined the movement (Rashid (2001a), 29).
78. See chapter 2.
79. Roy (1995b), 10.
80. Rashid (2001a), 177–8.
81. At this time they (or their affiliates) were based in the African subcontinent, southeast Asia and the wider Middle East.
82. Hussain (2008), 52–3.
83. Interviews, Kabul, July 2010.
84. Zaeef (2011).
85. Interview, Kabul, July 2010; and ibid.
86. Ruttig (2009a), 65.
87. 'The policy of the Taliban at this point was not to give a prominent role to people like Haqqani, and they [Haqqani etc] knew it but they still continued to cooperate and work together.' (Interview, Kabul, July 2010).
88. Rashid (1998), 74.
89. Ehrenfeld (2003), 39 and 215n28; originally sourced from Ottaway and Morgan (2001).
90. Maley (2002), 244.
91. Rashid (2001a), 20; Ahady (1998), 127.

92. Ibid., 76.
93. Rashid (2001a), 201; 'On one such "hunting trip," the UAE Defence Minister Sheikh Mohammed al-Maktoum flew in from Dubai with a hundred brand-new Toyota Land Cruisers all fitted with field radios' (Fergusson (2010), 95).
94. Interviews, Kabul and Kandahar, 2009–10.
95. Matinuddin (1999), 57.
96. Interview, Kabul, July 2010.
97. Nasiri (2008), Kindle Electronic Edition: Location 3347.
98. Ibid., Kindle Electronic Edition: Location 1930.
99. Kepel (2006), 219.
100. Interview, Kabul, June 2010.
101. Quoted in Lia (2009), 106–7.
102. Quoted in ibid., 107; Hegghammer (2010), Kindle Electronic Edition: Location 668; Sharaf-al-Din (1999).
103. Salah (2001).
104. Lia (2009), 127–8.
105. Ibid, 112.
106. 'One of the very few Saudi jihadists to have gone to Algeria was Abd al-Aziz al-Muqrin, who went there for about a month in 1994 or 1995 after coming into contact with Algerians in Bosnia.' (Hegghammer (2010), Kindle Electronic Edition: Location 679.)
107. See Lia (2009), 111–125; Nasiri (2008); and Evans and Phillips (2007), 143–214.
108. Bergen (2006), 106; Burke quotes London-based newspaper al-Quds al-Arabi stating that bin Laden arrived in Sudan in 1992 (Burke (2004), 142.) Cooley states that bin Laden moved to Sudan in 1991 (Cooley (2000), 121).
109. http://www.state.gov/s/ct/c14151.htm (accessed 4 August 2010); Al-Zayyat (2004), 58.
110. Salah (2001).
111. Ibid.
112. Kepel (2006), 276 and 287.
113. Ibid., 277.
114. Hafiz (1992); for more on the district of Embaba, see Abdo (2000).
115. Wright (2006), 213–5.
116. Ibid., chapter 12.
117. Ibid., chapter 9.
118. Coll (2005), 267; Burke (2004), 146.
119. Coll (2005), Kindle Electronic Edition: Location 4655–57. A later attempt to reconcile Mullah Mohammad Omar to Sayyaf and Hekmatyar is mentioned in Scheuer's biography of bin Laden (Scheuer (2011), Kindle Electronic Edition: Location 2353 and 5044).

120. Gutman (2008), 36–37.

121. Coll (2005), 268; Burke (2004), 145.

122. Coll (2005), 267 and Kindle Location 5271 and 5276; Farah (2004), Kindle Electronic Edition: Location 1807; Coll (2008), Kindle Electronic Edition: Location 6174; Salah (2001); Napoleoni (2005), Kindle Electronic Edition: Location 2368.

123. Wright (2006), Kindle Electronic Edition: Locations 3493 and 3092; Fisk (2005), 4–6 and 8–9.

124. Hegghammer (2010), Kindle Electronic Edition: Location 1223.

125. Wright (2006), chapter 10 and 12.

126. Coll (2005), Kindle Electronic Edition: Location 5334.

127. Reeve (1999), chapter 3.

128. Interview, London, January 2010.

129. Reeve (1999), 183–7.

130. Coll (2008), Kindle Electronic Edition: Location 7034.

131. See *Ibid*, Location 7034 and 6295; and Hegghammer (2010), Kindle Electronic Edition: Location 1526; Wright (2006), Kindle Electronic Edition: Locations 9262, 3572, 3584 and 4052; see also Kean and Hamilton (2004), Kindle Electronic Edition: Location 1342.

132. Wright (2006), Kindle Electronic Edition: Location 3219–3224.

133. Bonney (2007), 123.

134. Ibid.

135. Hegghammer (2010), Kindle Electronic Edition: Location 1526.

136. Bergen (2006), 149.

137. From Fisk (2005), chapter 1.

138. Atwan (2006), 40–41.

139. See chapter 4.

140. Al-Zayyat (2004), 58.

141. Wright (2006), Kindle Electronic Edition: Location 3960.

142. Ibid., Location 3970.

143. Wright (2006), 218.

144. One prominent former mujahedeen commander interviewed in Kandahar stated that the Taliban were simply implementing an old Kandahari mujahedeen plan dating back to 1992 in which the area from Herat to Kabul would come under their control. (Interview, Kandahar, August 2008.)

145. Ruttig (1995), 1–2; Murshed (2006), 49.

146. Interviews, Kandahar and Kabul, June and July 2010.

147. Gannon (2006), Kindle Electronic Edition: Location 553.

148. Note, they had not yet changed the name of the movement to the 'Islamic Emirate of Afghanistan.' That would happen on 26 October 1997, albeit as a consequence of Mullah Mohammad Omar's new title.

149. Interview, Kabul, July 2010.
150. Interview, Kandahar, July 2010.
151. Interview, Kandahar, July 2010.
152. Interview, Kabul, July 2010
153. Interview, Kabul, July 2010.
154. Rashid (2001a), 42–3.
155. See Gannon (2006), chapter three.
156. Ibid., 560–67.
157. Interview, Kabul, July 2010.
158. Two interviewees stated that the title was only applicable to Afghanistan, and was not about assuming the leadership of the entire Muslim community or *umma*. (Interviews, Kabul and Kandahar, July 2010.)
159. Gannon (2006), Kindle Electronic Edition: Location 562–70.
160. Interview, Washington, March 2010.
161. Interviews, Kabul, 2009 and July 2010.
162. Murshed (2006), 48–9; AFP, (1997a).
163. Bergen (2006), 162.
164. The airport construction project was granted to Bin Laden Construction Company, and was supervised by Osama's brother, Omar bin Laden. While there has been some speculation about Osama's involvement (at least peripherally) it appears that the project was an entirely separate affair that had no connection to Osama. It should also be noted that by the time Osama relocated permanently to Sudan the project was already well on the way (Coll (2008), Kindle Electronic Edition: Location 6039.)
165. There are conflicting accounts about the exact events surrounding bin Laden's departure from Sudan: how many planes, who arranged for the plane/s, and who initiated the contacts, etc. (see above).
166. Mojdeh (2003); this is partially confirmed by an interview with Burhanuddin Rabbani aired on al-Jazeera in May 2011 (see http://www.youtube.com/watch?v=lm4DMg1vQ7s (accessed 12 June 2011)) and an interview conducted in London in May 2011 with a former 'Afghan Arab' in touch with Rabbani at the time.
167. Interview, Kabul, July 2010.
168. Al-Bahri (2004).
169. Mojdeh (2003).
170. Al-Masri (2004), chapter 2.
171. Scheuer (2011), Kindle Location number 2008.
172. Interviews, Kabul, December 2009 and July 2010.
173. Interview, Kabul, July 2010.
174. Matinuddin (1999), 110.
175. One Taliban commander at the time claimed in an interview that the Taliban had initially clashed with Arabs near to the area around 'Warishmeen Tangi' but

later sorted out their dispute and reconciled at a meeting in Jalalabad. (Interview, Kandahar, July 2010).

176. Zaeef (2011).
177. Al-Masri (2004), chapter 2. See also bin Laden, bin Laden and Sasson (2009).
178. Gutman (2008), 36–37.
179. Al-Masri (2004).
180. Zaeef (2011); also from interview, Kabul, July 2010, during which the source suggested that the amount of money demanded was sizeable and amounted to tens of millions of dollars.
181. Coll (2008), 461–2.
182. Zaeef (2011). Atwan (2006), 75.
183. Interviews, Kabul and Kandahar, June and July 2010.
184. Interview, London, January 2010.
185. Mojdeh (2003).
186. See LeVine (2007) for more details; also see the introduction to this study.
187. Interviews, Kabul and Kandahar, June and July 2010.
188. Interview, Anand Gopal, Kabul, July 2010.
189. Interview, Kabul, July 2010; Interview, Kandahar, August 2009.
190. Interview, Kabul, July 2010; Rashid (2001a), 60.
191. Zaeef (2011).
192. Al-Masri (2004).
193. Interview, Kabul, July 2010. See also bin Laden, bin Laden and Sasson (2009).
194. Quoted in Scheuer (2011), Kindle Location number 2011.
195. Al-Masri (2004), chapter 2.
196. Al-Bahri (2004).
197. Interview, Kabul, July 2010; Beg (1995), 4; National Security Archive (1994).
198. This is also reflected in the recent account by bin Laden's son, Omar. See bin Laden, bin Laden and Sasson (2009).
199. Interviews, Kandahar and Kabul, 2008–2010.
200. See Al-Masri (2004) for full details. Al-Masri claims he attended the meeting.
201. Coll (2008), 465.
202. Al-Masri (2004).
203. This observation is a reflection of the authors who have lived and worked in southern Afghanistan and conducted qualitative interviews with individuals as well as engaged in day-to-day dealings with community and tribal leaders. The same observations have been made by other researchers and journalists, both foreign and Afghan (Interviews, Kabul, July 2010).
204. *Qahtan* is a legendary or apocryphal figure from the Arabian Peninsula.
205. Al-Masri (2004); Interview, Kabul, July 2010.
206. Gannon (2006), 35.
207. http://www.pbs.org/newshour/terrorism/international/fatwa_1996.html (accessed 5 August 2010).

208. Fisk (2005), 588.
209. Bowden (2002).
210. http://www.pbs.org/newshour/terrorism/international/fatwa_1996.html (accessed 14 June 2010).
211. Kean and Hamilton (2004), Kindle Electronic Edition: Location 3095–3106.
212. Wright (2006), Kindle Electronic Edition: Location 4275–99.
213. Kepel (2008a), 55.
214. It should be noted that there are disputes within at least one of the groups over the statement and the *fatwa*. Members of the Egyptian groups based in Egypt itself stated publicly that they refused to ratify the document and that a decision had been taken without consulting them. (Ibid., 282–3.)
215. Interview, Kabul, July 2010.
216. Davis (1998), 68.
217. Matinuddin (1999), 88.
218. Davis (1998), 56.
219. Quoted in Stenersen (2010a), 199.
220. Matinuddin (1999), 43.
221. Interview, Kabul, July 2010.
222. 'Islamische Ordnung a la Hekmatyar,' *Mahfel* 45 (March–April 1995), 3.
223. Interview, Kabul, July 2010.
224. Buruma and Margalit (2005), 44–5.
225. Fergusson (2010), 59–62.
226. Interviews, Kabul, 2009–10; Zaeef (2010), 84–5; Zaeef (2012).
227. Interview, Kabul, July 2010.
228. Al-Masri (2004).
229. See Scheuer (2011), Kindle Location number 2062–2083, for more on the various assassination attempts made against bin Laden while he was living in Afghanistan pre-September 11, 2001.
230. Interviews, Kabul and Kandahar, June/July 2010.
231. See FBIS (2004).
232. Interview, London, January 2010.
233. Mutawakil (2007).
234. Interview, Kabul, July 2010.
235. Ibid.
236. Interview, Kandahar, July 2010.
237. Interview, Kabul, July 2010.
238. See bin Laden, bin Laden and Sasson (2009), chapter 20.
239. Burke (2004), 178.
240. Interviews, Kabul and Kandahar, June and July 2010.
241. Rashid (2001a), 53.
242. Zaeef (2011).

243. Al-Masri (2004).

244. Interview, London, January 2010.

245. Interviews, Kabul, June and July 2010. See also http://easterncampaign.word-press.com/2009/11/04/haqqani-network-suffers-defeat-massive-desertion/ (accessed 6 March 2011).

246. Al-Masri (2004).

247. One Taliban interviewee made the point that regardless of these figures' existence, their positions within the movement were, relatively speaking, without actual authority and so their influence could only have ever been minimal. (Interview, Kabul, June 2010).

248. Interviews, Kabul and Kandahar, 2009–10.

249. Bergen (2006), Kindle Electronic Edition: Location 4386–8.

250. Al-Masri (2004).

251. Ibid.

252. See bin Laden, bin Laden and Sasson (2009), 245. Also, interviews, Kandahar, 2009–10.

253. Interviews, Kandahar, July 2010.

254. Interview, London, January 2010. Interview, Kandahar, July 2010.

255. Al-Masri (2004).

256. Interview, London, January 2010.

257. It should be mentioned that this statement does not imply that individuals who came to Afghanistan to train and join the jihad had not already subscribed to the central doctrine and therefore were indoctrinated or brainwashed. The effect of the training camps, however, would reinforce and strengthen the bonds between them and deepen their ideological steadfastness. As Sageman shows in his study, group dynamics played an important role in the process of individuals joining al-Qaeda. (Sageman (2008), 70).

258. For the full statement, see Kepel (2008a), 53–6.

259. Gutman (2008), 129.

260. Al-Masri (2004).

261. Interview, Kabul, July 2010.

262. Cullison and Higgins (2002); Wright (2006), Kindle Electronic Edition: Location 9031–9043.

263. Lia (2009), 287.

264. See, for example, 'Afghan Ambassador to Pakistan Denies Existence of Terrorist Training Camps,' *Rawalpindi Jang*, 17 August 2001.

265. Lia (2009), 284.

266. *Ibid.*, 288.

267. Al-Masri (2004).

268. Coll (2005), Kindle Electronic Edition: Location 7802–7815.

269. Cullison and Higgins (2002).

270. *Bid'a* or innovation is a key development that salafists argue against.
271. Nasiri (2008), 192.
272. Combating Terrorism Center (2007).
273. Al-Zayyat (2004), 57–8.
274. Ruttig (1995), 1–2.
275. Rashid (2001a), 194.
276. Interview, Kabul, July 2010.
277. See Department of State, 'Afghanistan: Meeting with the Taliban,' *National Security Archive*, 11 December 1997, for full details of this meeting. http://www.gwu.edu/~nsarchiv/NSAEBB/NSAEBB97/tal24.pdf (accessed 13 July 2010).
278. Ibid., 5.
279. Note, too, Michael Keating's observation that negotiating with the Taliban was like 'grasping smoke.' (Quoted in Maley (2002), 232).
280. Interview, Kabul, July 2010.
281. AFP (1997b).
282. Zaeef (2011).
283. Feldab-Brown (2010), Kindle Electronic Edition: Location 1578–80.
284. Expressed by a senior Taliban member in 2008.
285. http://www.amnesty.org/en/library/info/ASA11/005/1997 (accessed 22 June 2010).
286. http://edition.cnn.com/WORLD/9709/29/taliban.arrests.update/index.html (accessed 10 August 2010).
287. Mackenzie (1998), 90.
288. http://archives.cnn.com/2001/COMMUNITY/11/09/leno.cnna/ (accessed 18 August 2010).
289. Maley (2002), 243.
290. Interviews, Kabul, 2008–10.

6. A BONE IN THE THROAT (1998–2001)

1. Interview, London, January 2010.
2. Rashid (2008), 60.
3. Interviews, Kabul and Kandahar, spring and summer 2010. Also see Zaeef (2010), chapter 9.
4. Rashid (2001a), 77 and 55 ff.
5. Interviews, Kabul and Kandahar, June/July 2010.
6. Islamic Emirate of Afghanistan (1998).
7. Kean and Hamilton (2004), Kindle Electronic Edition: Location 3090–3098.
8. http://www.pbs.org/newshour/terrorism/international/fatwa_1996.html (accessed 16 April 2010); Wright (2006), Kindle Electronic Edition: Location 5072–5084.

9. Bonney (2007), 125. While Bonney's argument is made on later statements of Osama bin Laden (August 2003), it can be assumed that he held similar views at earlier times.

10. Sami ul-Haq has explained that bin Laden reached out to him following Mullah Mohammad Omar's placing of restrictions on his media appearances; bin Laden asked the Pakistani cleric to ask Mullah Mohammad Omar to allow him at least to talk about Palestine. Sami ul-Haq wrote a letter to the Taliban leader making this request, and some of the restrictions were reportedly lifted shortly after. (See 'I Knew Bin Laden, part 2.' http://www.youtube.com/watch?v=M-3QtQoa04U& feature=relmfu (accessed 12 June 2011)).

11. Wright (2006), Kindle Electronic Edition: Location 306.

12. Coll (2005), Kindle Electronic Edition: Location 7850–51; Bonney (2007), 124.

13. Wright (2006), Kindle Electronic Edition: Location 5072–5084.

14. Interviews, Kandahar and Kabul, June/July 2010.

15. LeVine (2007), Kindle Electronic Edition: Location 5609.

16. Interviews, Kandahar and Kabul, June/July 2010.

17. Interview, Kabul, July 2010.

18. Senior Taliban figures apparently referred to the missiles as 'Monica Lewinsky rockets.' (Interviews, Kabul and Kandahar, June and July 2010.)

19. Interview, senior Taliban political official, Kabul, July 2010.

20. Interview, Kabul, July 2010.

21. See Wright (2006), Mojdeh (2005) and Bin Laden (2009).

22. Bin Laden, bin Laden and Sasson (2009), 245.

23. Ibid., 246–7.

24. Ibid., 247.

25. Ibid., 247. The outlines of this meeting are also confirmed in al-Masri (2004).

26. One interview conducted for this book set out Mullah Mohammad Omar's response as follows: 'This is not a matter of Islam or not. This is a country and we have our own limitations. We want to prevent a situation that might lead to conditions that are unsafe for you. We don't want that so here are our conditions. You can accept them or leave.' (Interview, Kabul, July 2010.)

27. Interview, Kabul, July 2010.

28. National Security Archive (1998a).

29. See National Security Archive declassified communications on these meetings for further details.

30. 'Taliban warns Bin Laden against threats,' The Atlanta Journal and Constitution, 24 August 1998.

31. Coll (2005), Kindle Electronic Edition: Location 7802–7815.

32. Wright (2006), Kindle Electronic Edition: Location 268.

33. Note there are two publicly available accounts of this meeting: one is the interview given by Turki al-Faisal to journalists in subsequent years; and then the other is in Murshed (2006), 300.

34. National Security Archive (1998b).
35. Interview, Kabul, July 2010.
36. As reported in al-Masri (2004).
37. Interviews, Kabul and Kandahar, June/July 2010. Also see National Security Archive (1998b). Mullah Mohammad Omar wrote an open letter to 'all Taliban members, young and old' in June 1998 in which he stated: 'I think that there are no more people who fully trust in good any more. Everyone has trained his followers so that they are only concerned about their own status name and rank, that they have forgotten everything about following orders and respecting their main leader [Mullah Mohammad Omar].' (Authors' copy, dated 13 June 1998).
38. Ibid.
39. Nawaz (2008), 536–7.
40. Sayyed Iftikhar Murshed has stated, though, that Mullah Mohammad Omar told him 'on several occasions [around that time] in [his] capacity as the leader of the shuttle mission for promoting an intra-Afghan dialogue that [Omar] wanted to get rid of Bin Laden but did not know how.' (Murshed (2010)).
41. National Security Archive (1998d).
42. See, for example, al-Bahri (2005), al-Masri (2004), Allix (1998), Bergen (2006), Gannon (2006), Mojdeh (2003), Zaeef (2010) and Zaeef (2011).
43. Interviews, Kabul and Kandahar, 2009–10.
44. Interview, Kabul, 2010; also see bin Laden, bin Laden and Sasson (2009).
45. Interviews, Kabul and Kandahar, June and July 2010. Mullah Mohammad Omar probably spoke some degree of Arabic, however.
46. Interviews, Kabul and Kandahar, June/July 2010; also see bin Laden (2009) and al-Masri (2004).
47. National Security Archive (1998b).
48. Interview, Kabul, July 2010; interviews, London, February–June 2011.
49. See, for example: 'Teach them that there is no Islam without the organized group, and no such group without an emirate where an Amir leads, and no emirate without listening and obeying. And you know Allah has enabled this Umma during these trying times the establishment of an Islamic state that applies the shar'ia of Allah, that upholds the flag of monotheism, and that is the Islamic Emirate of Afghanistan under the leadership of Amir of the faithful Mulla Muhammad Omar, may Allah protect him.' (Bin Laden speech (read out by someone else) at the Deoband Conference in Peshawar on 8–11 April 2011). Also, Scheuer (2011), 105–128.
50. Brown (2010): 1–6.
51. Interviews, Kabul and Kandahar, July 2010. Given the sources, we believe this to be a true confirmation of the fact. The possibility that interviewees had access to and read al-Masri's account, however, cannot be completely ruled out. Nevertheless, the footnote above confirms that bin Laden was at least not pretending that he didn't make the pledge (he publicly affirms and restates that pledge).

52. Mullahs Mohammad Rabbani, Mohammad Hassan, Mutawakil and Zaeef were all removed from Kandahar; distance from Mullah Mohammad Omar was as good an indication of standing within the movement as any.

53. Michael Scheuer provides some evidence and examples of this funding in his biography of bin Laden. Scheuer (2011), Kindle Location number 2359 and 5048.

54. National Security Archive (1999).

55. Coll (2008).

56. Interview, Kandahar, July 2010.

57. Interview, Kabul, July 2010.

58. His remarks are not necessarily credible, but his job did give him extensive access to the Taliban leader.

59. Interview, southern Afghanistan, June 2009.

60. Interview, Kabul, July 2010. Gutman (2008), 120–1.

61. 'BBC News Profile: Mullah Mohammad Omar,' http://news.bbc.co.uk/1/hi/world/south_asia/1550419.stm (accessed 6 March 2011).

62. Interview, southern Afghanistan, June 2009.

63. Al-Masri (2004). This marriage of his daughters is also not mentioned in the account by bin Laden's son and wife (Bin Laden, 2009).

64. Interview, Kabul, July 2010.

65. Interview, Kabul, July 2010.

66. Ibid.

67. Rashid (2001a), 65.

68. http://www.apbspeakers.com/speaker/mavis-leno (accessed 15 June 2010),

69. http://www.msmagazine.com/news/uswirestory.asp?id=2590 (accessed 10 June 2010).

70. http://www.msmagazine.com/news/uswirestory.asp?id=3526 (accessed 7 March 2011).

71. Associated Press (1998).

72. Coll (2005), Kindle Electronic Edition: Location 5927–5939.

73. Bridas is an Argentinean oil and gas company that has been involved in Central Asia since the early 1990s.

74. http://www.worldpress.org/specials/pp/pipeline_timeline.htm (accessed 1 June 2010).

75. http://web.archive.org/web/20020808053241/www.unocal.com/aboutucl/history/index.htm (accessed 18 August 2010).

76. Coll (2005), Kindle Electronic Edition: Location 6019–6069.

77. Rashid (2001a), 233.

78. Interview, Khost, January 2006.

79. Interview, Kabul, July 2010.

80. Interviews, Kabul, June/July 2010.

81. 'From 3,276 tonnes of opium in 2000, production fell dramatically to 185 tonnes in 2001.' (MacDonald (2007), 78).

82. Interviews, Kandahar and Kabul, summer 2010.
83. Interview, Kabul, July 2010; for a translation of Mullah Mohammad Omar's letter to President Clinton, dated 6 September 1999 see Murshed (2006), 310.
84. Murshed (2006), 310–11.
85. Credit to Thomas Barfield for this characterisation (Barfield (2010)).
86. Interview, Kabul, July 2010; interview, Kandahar, June 2010.
87. Interviews, Kabul and Kandahar, 2008–2010.
88. National Security Archive (1998a).
89. Amnesty International (1999).
90. Zaeef (2010), 128–30.
91. Clark (2001).
92. See Gannon (2006), 61–5, for full details of this visit.
93. Ibid.
94. Interviews, Kabul and Kandahar, June/July 2010.
95. Interviews, Kabul and Kandahar, spring and summer 2010.
96. Ibid.
97. Zaeef (2010), 136–9; Zaeef (2011).
98. Resolution 1267 (1999) Adopted by the Security Council at its 4051st meeting on 15 October 1999. http://daccessdds.un.org/doc/UNDOC/GEN/N99/300/44/PDF/N9930044.pdf?OpenElement (accessed 10 May 2005).
99. Interviews, Kabul and Kandahar, June/July 2010.
100. Regardless of the number of jihadi actors during this period, bin Laden was always seen by the Taliban (and the other jihadis) as the de facto central figure, as we already saw in the way Zarqawi's request was purportedly handled by Mullah Mohammad Omar (see above).
101. Lia (2009), 233–4. He claimed to be living just 12km away from the frontline, and would hear the 'bombs and artillery shells exploding' every morning.
102. Ibid., 281. Al-Suri was referring specifically to geographical centralisation in his criticism; the camps, he argued, were too easy a target, especially in an age where missiles could strike at any point around the world. He would be vindicated again following the September 11 attacks, when al-Qaeda adopted many of his recommendations on this point and heavily decentralised their operations.
103. Ibid., 282.
104. Ibid., 235.
105. Ibid., 285.
106. Interview, Kabul, July 2010; Juma Namangani and Tahir Yuldash, the founders of the Islamic Movement of Uzbekistan, were running camps and consolidating their organisation in Afghanistan from 1998 onwards. As with many other groups, they are believed to have been close to al-Qaeda but were operating as a distinct and separate entity with primarily nationalist goals at the time.
107. http://www.ctc.usma.edu/aq/pdf/AFGP-2002-601402-Trans.pdf (accessed 18 August 2010).

108. Interview, Kabul, July 2010.
109. See al-Suri and al-Uyayri (date unknown) for excerpts from both reports.
110. Ibid., 2.
111. The points listed in the report were as follows: 'Quburiyyah, Irja' in Takfir, Sufi-yyah and Deobandiyyah, Ta'assub and Taqlid, and joining the United Nations' (Ibid, 2).
112. Al-Suri and al-Uyayri (date unknown).
113. http://www.ctc.usma.edu/aq/pdf/AFGP-2002–601693-Trans.pdf (accessed 18 August 2010), 2.
114. This is the practice of designating someone as a *kafir* or non-believer.
115. http://ctc.usma.edu/aq/pdf/AFGP-2002–003472-Trans-Meta.pdf (accessed 18 August 2010), 6.
116. This was also to limit exposure to Arabs.
117. Sirrs (2001).
118. For example: 'Massoud's intelligence sources reported that no Afghans were per-mitted in Derunta, only Arabs.' (Coll (2005), 77.).
119. They were also not—strictly speaking—allowed inside the Arabs' compounds in the south (Interviews, Kandahar, spring and summer 2010).
120. 'The two were completely separate, whether it came to outposts, vehicles, weap-ons, night patrols, this was all separate.' (Interview, Kandahar, June 2010).
121. Interview, Kabul, July 2010.
122. Interview, Kabul, June 2010.
123. Gutman (2008), 205.
124. Interview, Kabul, May 2009; the outer layer of Taliban security checkpoints seems to have been a later measure, implemented as part of the Taliban's attempt to control bin Laden.
125. Interviews, Kabul and Kandahar, 2009–10; an article (Sirrs (2001)) reveals some details about the presence of foreign fighters based on interviews with some of those captured by Massoud, but doesn't reveal enough to be able to draw wider conclusions as to the total numbers or exact nature of this foreign fighter dimen-sion to the conflict in northern Afghanistan.
126. Interviews, southern Afghanistan, 2009–10.
127. In July 2001, for example, a senior US diplomat reportedly announced that 'the Taliban and al-Qaida are one enterprise' at a conference organised by the Brit-ish Foreign Office. (Fergusson (2010), 90).
128. See Gutman (2008), 192–3, and Mojdeh (2003) for full detail.
129. Ibid.
130. The Chechen delegation are reported to have gone on a tour round Afghanistan on behalf of the Taliban, even receiving four 'Stinger' missiles in Herat in recog-nition of their fighting against Russian troops (Mojdeh (2003)).
131. There was also a comment in 1998. The Taliban leader commented on the unfold-ing scandal over Monica Lewinsky, saying: 'Clinton is a confessed sinner and a

bad person. [...] It is absolutely not possible to negotiate with such a person and he should be removed (from power) and stoned to death. He is of bad character.' (*The News* (Islamabad), 31 August 1998).

132. 'Taleban Leader Urges Jihad Against US, Security Council "Atheists,"' *Al-Quds al-Arabi*, 21 December 2000.

133. See, for example, remarks by the United Nations Secretary-General in a December 2001 report: 'it became clear over the year that the tone of Mullah Mohammad Omar's decrees and statements had evolved from concern with just Afghan issues to notably greater support for a global jihad, as promoted by Bin Laden.' (Quoted in Maley (2002), 257.)

134. Several of the senior former and current Taliban members interviewed for this book even claimed that Mullah Mohammad Omar had never made these comments.

135. National Security Archive (1998c).

136. Interview, Kabul, July 2010.

137. Borchgrave (2010).

138. Rashid states that they had already fired rockets at the heads of the Buddha statues on 18 September 1998. Rashid (2001a), 76; Coll (2005), 554.

139. Bergen (2006), 247–249.

140. Maley (2002), 241.

141. Gutman (2008), 241.

142. Interviews, Kabul and Kandahar, June and July 2010; Zaeef (2011).

143. Gutman (2008), 239; http://www.aan-afghanistan.org/index.asp?id=1538 (accessed 23 May 2011).

144. In early 2000, for example, Mawlawi Abdur Razaq passed on a message to the United States via *The New Yorker* writer William Vollman: 'We fought against Russia for years, and the Americans helped us. And we ask them and their government to help us again. As Afghanistan is destroyed, we expect help in reconstruction, and facilities for widows and orphans.' (Vollman (2000)).

145. 'Rocca fails to convince Zaeef on Osama charges,' *The News* (Islamabad), 3 August 2001.

146. Gutman (2008), 238.

147. Ibid.

148. Interviews, Kabul and Kandahar, spring and summer 2010.

149. Giovanni (2001); this cites meeting minutes from 3 and 4 March 2001 between foreign Islamist groups and the Taliban leader suggesting they convinced him to change his mind.

150. A statement issued by the Taliban's media office on 12 March 2001, 'on the occasion of the visit of delegates from the Organisation of the Islamic Conference,' for example, noted that 'the delegation agreed with the legality of the [destruction of the Buddha] [...] but they expressed some reservations as to the timing of the destruction.' (Authors' copy of the statement).

151. Interviews, Kabul and Kandahar, June–July 2010.
152. Gutman (2008), 241; Mojdeh (2003).
153. Hegghammer (2010), Kindle Electronic Edition: Location 1170–71. Both al-Shu'aybi and al-Fahd published several statements to this end.
154. 'Pakistan: Taleban unconcerned about backlash from statue destruction,' *The Age* (Islamabad), 16 March 2001.
155. http://www.un.org/News/dh/latest/afghan/un-afghan-history.shtml (accessed 1 March 2010).
156. Gutman (2008), 229.
157. Maley (2002), 245–50. There was, however, an emergency provision of wheat food aid from the United States (distributed by the World Food Programme) in early 2001; see http://reliefweb.int/node/75552 (accessed 7 June 2011) for more.
158. Interview, Kabul, July 2010.
159. As stated in 2008 to the authors.
160. Interviews, Kandahar, 2008–10.
161. 'Afghan Opposition Says Not Responsible For Blast,' Agence France-Press, 25 August 1999. Omar bin Laden's autobiographical account of the period claims two of Omar's wives and two of his brothers were killed in the explosion along with many members of his staff.
162. Feldab-Brown (2010), Kindle Electronic Edition: Location 1575–1589.
163. Riedel (2008), Kindle Electronic Edition: Location 1210.
164. Al-Masri (2004).
165. Al-Suri and al-Uyayri (date unknown). This is an unlikely tale.
166. Hegghammer (2010), Kindle Electronic Edition: Location 1481.
167. Murshed has written that a previous initiative proposed by Mullah Mohammad Omar also failed: 'Subsequently, Omar proposed that a small group of ulema from Afghanistan, Saudi Arabia and a third Islamic country should decide Bin Laden's fate but this was rejected by Washington and Riyadh. Eventually the Taliban established a judicial commission under their chief justice to hear evidence against Bin Laden so that he could be punished. The evidence was provided to Mulla Jalil, the Taliban deputy foreign minister, by US Under-Secretary of State Thomas Pickering during a secret meeting at the Foreign Office in Islamabad on the night of 27 May 2000. Jalil promised that Bin Laden would be brought to justice after the evidence was examined. These facts, which demonstrate Taliban duplicity, need to be exploited by the Karzai government in its reintegration programme for driving a wedge between the armed Afghan opposition and their Al Qaeda backers.' (Murshed (2010)).
168. Interviews, Kabul, spring and summer 2010.
169. Interviews, Kabul, June and July 2010.
170. Interview, Kabul, July 2010.

171. Kean and Hamilton (2004), section 5.3.

172. Mohamedou (2007), 52.

173. The opium ban was, at least on one level, for this purpose, and the political wing of the movement still felt that their offer of an external tribunal had not been seriously considered.

174. Coll (2008), Kindle Electronic Edition: Location 7791–98.

175. Hegghammer (2010), Kindle Electronic Edition: Location 1371.

176. 'Bin-Ladin Offers To Leave Afghanistan Following Stormy Meeting with Mola Omar,' al Sharq al Awsat, 30 August 2000.

177. Summarising an article published in the *Washington Post* (see 'Weekly Intelligence Notes' briefing by the Association of Former Intelligence Officers, http://www.afio.com/sections/wins/2000/2000–31.html (accessed 7 March 2011)).

178. Lia (2009), 293–6.

179. http://100years.upi.com/sta_2001–06–14.html (accessed 18 August 2010).

7. SEPTEMBER 11, 2001

1. Bergen (2001), Kindle Electronic Edition: Location 3355.

2. Al-Masri (2004), chapter 2.

3. National Commission on Terrorist Attacks Upon the United States (2004).

4. See the 1998 declaration entitled 'The World Islamic Front's Declaration to wage Jihad Against the Jews and Crusaders' (Ibrahim (2007), Kindle Electronic Edition: Location 541ff). Also see al-Qaeda's reply in February 2002 to a letter drafted by sixty American thinkers entitled 'Why We Are Fighting You,' published online in October 2002 (Ibid., Location 3383ff).

5. The treaty printed in Ibrahim's Al-Qaeda Reader (Ibid, Kindle Location 2535ff) outlines al-Qaeda's ruling on suicide operations, as well as the legitimacy for bombing the infidels if Muslims, women and children, or *dhimmis* are intermingled with them.

6. http://www.nato.int/docu/review/2006/issue2/english/art2.html#, nato_contribution.doc (accessed 4 June 2010).

7. Interview, senior political Talib involved in foreign affairs, Kabul, June 2010.

8. See, for instance, 'Lou Dobbs Moneyline,' aired on CNN on 13 November 2001. http://edition.cnn.com/TRANSCRIPTS/0111/13/mlld.00.html (accessed 11 September 2010).

9. See chapter 5 and 6, as well as documents released by the National Security Archive relating to the 1994–2001 period.

10. Woodward (2003), Kindle Electronic Edition: Location 587–88.

11. See Bergen (2009a).

12. See Riedel (2008) as an illustration of this.

13. Kean and Hamilton (2004), Kindle Electronic Edition: Location 5233. Note that the report is vague but does claim in one paragraph that Mullah Mohammad Omar was opposed to a major al-Qaeda operation directly against the United States. Khalid Sheikh Mohammad is quoted in the next paragraph saying that Mullah Mohammad Omar preferred for al Qaeda to attack Jews, not necessarily the United States. (Khalid Sheikh Mohammad appears to be the main, if not only, source for much of the section that relates the story in the 9/11 Commission's report. It should be noted that he was subject to severe interrogation techniques, including dozens of water-boardings.) Furthermore, there is no later statement reported that saw Mullah Mohammad Omar in agreement with such attacks.

14. Interviews with former senior political Taliban, Kabul, June and July 2010.

15. Reeve states that it was only eleven airplanes. (Reeve (1999), 90).

16. Wright (2006), Kindle Electronic Edition: Location 4285–87.

17. Kean and Hamilton (2004), 345; a British documentary filmmaker uncovered evidence suggesting the very first inspiration for using the plane itself as a weapon came when Abdul Hakim Murad and Ramzi Yousuf were talking outside the Hard Rock Cafe in Manila which has a replica of a plane crashing into a building. (Interview, London, May 2011 and http://news.bbc.co.uk/1/hi/programmes/correspondent/2975842.stm (accessed 12 June 2011)).

18. Reeve (1999), 74–5.

19. McDermott (2005), Kindle Electronic Edition: Location 3113–20.

20. Ressa (2003); Atran (2010); Reeve (1999).

21. Kean and Hamilton (2004), Kindle Electronic Edition: Location 3040–50.

22. Coll (2005), Kindle Electronic Edition: Location 4892–93.

23. Kean and Hamilton (2004), Kindle Electronic Edition: Location 3040–50. See, for example, the 1993 World Trade Center attack which he helped to fund, and then his activities in the Philippines from 1994.

24. Kean and Hamilton (2004), 76.

25. Bergen (2001), Kindle Electronic Edition: Location 757–68; Reeve (1999), 78–9. Bin Laden had apparently also asked Yousuf to assassinate American President Clinton (Reeve (1999), 76), but Yousuf estimated that the security would be too tight successfully to carry this out.

26. The Abu Sayyaf Group (ASG) was founded by Abdurajal Janjalani who had fought during the 1980s in Afghanistan under Sayyaf. While in Afghanistan he allegedly established ties with bin Laden. A number of sources claim that the groups' formation was helped along by Mohammad Jamal Khalifa, bin Laden's brother-in-law. The ASG fights for an independent Islamic State in the Philippines. See Ressa (2003).

27. Reeve (1999), chapter 4.

28. Vizcarra (1994).

29. Wright (2006), Kindle Electronic Edition: Location 4289.

30. Coll (2005), Kindle Electronic Edition: Location 5388.

31. McDermott (2002).

32. Brzezinski (2001).

33. Coll (2005), Kindle Electronic Edition: Location 4933.

34. Fineman and Paddock (2002).

35. Kean and Hamilton (2004), 76.

36. CBC News, 'Bin Laden claims responsibility for 9/11,' 29 October 2004. http:// www.cbc.ca/world/story/2004/10/29/binladen_message041029.html (accessed 3 September 2010).

37. Riedel (2008), Kindle Electronic Edition: Location 950.

38. http://www.rediff.com/news/1999/dec/24onkar.htm (accessed 24 June 2010).

39. http://www.rediff.com/news/1999/dec/25akd.htm (accesssed 24 June 2010).

40. BBC News (1999a).

41. Air Hijack, National Geographic documentary.

42. The National Geographic documentary states that the hijackers originally sought to fly to Kabul, but there was no facility for performing a night-landing so they decided on the UAE instead.

43. http://www.rediff.com/news/1999/dec/26ia12.htm (accessed 24 June 2010). This account suggests it was the to-and-fro of security forces in Amristar that provoked the stabbing.

44. http://www.liveindia.com/news/zzzzu.html (accessed 24 June 2010).

45. http://www.rediff.com/news/1999/dec/31ia12.htm (accessed 24 June 2010).

46. http://www.rediff.com/news/2000/aug/03pak.htm (accessed 24 June 2010).

47. This was repeated by bin Laden's former bodyguard in an interview aired on Al-Jazeera in May 2011; al-Bahri said that bin Laden hosted Azhar and some Taliban leaders 'two or three days' after the end of the hijacking. (See 'I Knew Bin Laden, part 2' for more. http://www.youtube.com/watch?v=M-3QtQoa04U& feature=relmfu (accessed 12 June 2011)).

48. Gul (2010), 251–3; Hussain (2008), 63–6.

49. Sageman (2008), 9.

50. http://www.rediff.com/news/2000/jun/21hijack.htm (accessed 24 June 2010).

51. http://www.rediff.com/news/2000/jan/09cbi.htm (accessed 24 June 2010).

52. http://www.rediff.com/news/2000/jan/10jake.htm (accessed 24 June 2010).

53. One traveller interviewed for this book who passed though the airport frequently at the time noted the lack of rigorous security checks. (Interview, Washington D.C., March 2010).

54. Other passengers recall seeing at least two pistols. (http://www.rediff.com/ news/1999/dec/26ia16.htm (accessed 24 June 2010).

55. http://www.rediff.com/news/1999/dec/26ia11.htm (accessed 24 June 2010).

56. http://www.rediff.com/news/2000/jan/09cbi.htm (accessed 24 June 2010); http://www.rediff.com/news/1999/dec/26ia17.htm (accessed 24 June 2010).

57. http://www.rediff.com/news/2000/jan/10onkar.htm (accessed 29 June 2010); http://www.rediff.com/news/1999/dec/28intel.htm (accessed 29 June 2010).
58. http://www.rediff.com/news/1999/dec/26nepal.htm (accessed 29 June 2010).
59. Harakat ul-Mujahedeen ran a training camp at Rishkhor (outside Kabul) and their fighters were among those killed in the August 1998 cruise missile strikes targeting bin Laden in Khost. They had links to the Taliban independent of bin Laden, as illustrated by the split in hierarchies of control over non-Afghan fighters (with bin Laden as head of the non-Pakistanis and various Pakistani groups, especially Harakat ul-Mujahedeen, in charge of the Pakistanis. (See Abou Zahab and Roy (2004), 48).
60. http://in.rediff.com/news/1999/dec/30josy1.htm (accessed 29 June 2010).
61. http://www.rediff.com/news/2000/jan/10jake.htm (accessed 29 June 2010).
62. BBC News (1999a).
63. Interview, Kabul, July 2010.
64. http://www.rediff.com/news/1999/dec/26ia20.htm (accessed 29 June 2010); http://www.rediff.com/news/1999/dec/27hijak.htm (accessed 29 June 2010); http://www.rediff.com/news/1999/dec/27ia9.htm (accessed 29 June 2010).
65. Reuters (1999a).
66. http://in.rediff.com/news/1999/dec/25ia1.htm (accessed 29 June 2010).
67. Air Hijack, National Geographic documentary.
68. Air Hijack, National Geographic documentary.
69. Ibid.
70. He was a Taliban spokesman. BIO
71. AFP (1999a).
72. http://www.rediff.com/news/1999/dec/29ia3.htm (accessed 29 June 2010).
73. http://www.rediff.com/news/1999/dec/27us1.htm (accessed 29 June 2010). "'We just do not want any catastrophe to happen on our land,' says Abdul Hakim Mujahid. [...] "Besides, we don't encourage this kind of act, we do not support hijacking or violence against innocent people." Echoing his government's decision that the plane should leave Afghanistan, he said: "We will take any measure that is necessary to make sure the plane leaves our soil."' (Reuters (1999c)).
74. http://www.rediff.com/news/1999/dec/28ia9.htm (accessed 29 June 2010); Gul (2000).
75. Reuters (1999b).
76. Rashid (2001), 74–5.
77. http://www.rediff.com/news/2000/jan/03iype.htm (accessed 29 June 2010).
78. Reuters (1999b).
79. NNI (2000a); BBC (1999b); AFP (1999b).
80. AFP (2000).
81. Reuters (1999d).
82. Interview, Kabul, July 2010.

83. NNI (2000b).
84. Rashid (2008), Kindle Electronic Edition: Location 3767–70; The FBI later concluded that Daniel Pearl had been executed not by Omar Sheikh but by three Arabs, one of whom was Khalid Sheikh Mohammed, the principal organiser of the September 11 attacks. Mohammed admitted killing Pearl in a March 2007 hearing in Guantánamo Bay, although the reliability of his confession was questioned, as there was little doubt that it came after he had been subjected to 'enhanced interrogation techniques' by the CIA and would have had motive to claim attacks in which he had played no role. See ibid., Kindle Electronic Edition: Location 3767–70; and McDermott (2010).
85. Interview, Kabul, July 2010.
86. See Shahzad (2003) and Mir (2005).
87. Interview, Kabul, July 2010.
88. Abou Zahab and Roy (2004), 27–8.
89. Interviews, Kabul, June 2010.
90. Interview, Kabul, July 2010.
91. Zaeef (2010), 116–8.
92. Interview, Kabul, July 2010.
93. 'No Pakistani Organization Being Given Terrorism Training in Afghanistan: Afghan Ambassador,' *Rawalpindi Jang*, 17 August 2001.
94. This was confirmed by one interviewee. He met with Massoud Azhar some months after the 1999 hijacking (Interview, Kabul, July 2010).
95. Interviews, Kabul, June and July 2010.
96. Singh (2007), 204.
97. Note especially the hijacking of an El Al plane on July 22, 1968, that was held for 39 days; the 12 Israeli passengers whom the hijackers held hostage were exchanged for 15 Palestinians jailed in Israeli prisons. This was carried out by the Popular Front for the Liberation of Palestine. See Napoleoni (2005), Kindle Electronic Edition: Location 663–67; and Hoffman (2006), 63–66.
98. Qazi (2000); West (1999); http://www.rediff.com/news/1999/dec/25ia5.htm (accessed 29 June 2010); http://www.rediff.com/news/2001/dec/07ter1.htm (accessed 29 June 2010).
99. Kean and Hamilton (2004), 153.
100. Note, however, that Abu Jandal, bin Laden's 'bodyguard,' stated in an interview with al-Jazeera in 2006 that bin Laden planned the attack in order to free Azhar. See AFP (2006).
101. One senior Taliban political figure extensively involved in the 1999 hijacking case remarked that there were three parts of the Taliban government involved: 'the army (under Osmani), the airport staff (technical staff), and the diplomatic corps as represented by the ministry of foreign affairs.' (Interview, Kabul, July 2010.)

102. Interviews, Kabul, June and July 2010.

103. Interviews, Kabul and Kandahar, June and July 2010.

104. http://www.rediff.com/news/1999/dec/28josy4.htm (accessed 29 June 2010).

105. Coll (2004).

106. Mojdeh (2003).

107. Coll (2005), Kindle Electronic Edition: Location 11160.

108. Ibid.

109. Ibid., Location 11163.

110. Junger (2001).

111. Anderson (2002), 186–7.

112. Cullison and Higgins (2001).

113. Coll (2005), Kindle Electronic Edition: Location 11299.

114. *Ibid*, Location 11296.

115. Wright (2006), 189–90.

116. See Kean and Hamilton (2004).

117. Vidino (2006), Kindle Electronic Edition: Location 151; Nasiri (2008), Kindle Electronic Edition: Location 4311–12.

118. Anderson (2002), 192–3.

119. Nasiri (2008).

120. Mojdeh (2003), 86.

121. Ibid.

122. McDermott (2010).

123. Abbreviation for Khalid Sheikh Mohammad.

124. Kean and Hamilton (2004), 252.

125. Wright (2006), Kindle Electronic Edition: Location 6615–19.

126. Gutman wrote: 'As the assassins waited, bin Laden approached the Taliban *shura* and gave formal notice that an attack would take place in the coming weeks. Some members objected, but bin Laden countered that Mullah Omar had no authority to prevent al Qaeda from conducting jihad outside Afghanistan.' Gutman's summary refers back to the 9/11 Report. The report itself, however, does not state that bin Laden officially informed the Taliban shura about imminent attacks; the phrasing of the report is unclear regarding the details of the discussion that is reported to have been taken place between bin Laden and Mullah Mohammad Omar. In the report, it is never stated that an imminent or a concrete operation was discussed between the two, but states that: 'There is evidence that Mullah Omar initially opposed a major al Qaeda operation directly against the United States in 2001.' It continues by stating that Mullah Mohammad Omar's opposition was based on ideological grounds. It should be noted that while the report states that he 'initially opposed' an operation, it later on does not state that he changed his mind. It should also be mentioned that the information presented in the section is solely based on detainee interrogations, largely sourced

to Khalid Sheikh Mohammad and unnamed detainees. Due to the interrogation techniques employed, one should treat the information with considerable caution. See Kean and Hamilton (2004), footnote on 181–184 and 250–252; also Gutman (2008), 252.

127. There is even a report that bin Laden wrote a letter to Mullah Mohammad Omar (dated 13 September 2001) urging him to go on the offensive. This would seem to suggest that the Taliban hadn't done so yet. (Astor (2006)).
128. Interviews, Kabul and Kandahar, June and July 2010.
129. Coll (2005), Kindle Electronic Edition: Location 9031; Zaeef (2010), 87–90.
130. Interviews, Kabul and Kandahar, June and July 2010.
131. Coll (2005), Kindle Electronic Edition: Location 11309.
132. http://www.afghanistannewscenter.com/news/2001/september/sep11y2001.html (accessed 10 May 2010).
133. http://www.afghanistannewscenter.com/news/2001/september/sep8y2001.html (accessed 10 May 2010).
134. Zaeef (2011).
135. Interviews, Kabul, July 2010.
136. Interview, Kabul, June 2010.
137. Coll (2005), Kindle Electronic Edition: Location 4309–10.
138. Interview, Kabul, June 2010.
139. McDermott (2005), Kindle Electronic Edition: Location 3593–98.
140. Interview, Kabul, July 2010.
141. McDermott (2005), Kindle Elec[141] McDermott (2005), Kindle Electronic Edition: Location 3593 98.
142. See part 2 (Afghanistan) of Nasiri (2008).
143. Their arrival in Kandahar was not part of any grand strategy by Mohammad Atef, Khalid Sheikh Mohammad or bin Laden himself. It was pure chance.
144. McDermott (2010).
145. Kean and Hamilton (2004), 148–9.
146. Ibid.
147. Ibid., 148.
148. Ibid.
149. Kean and Hamilton (2004), 149; Rashid (2008), Kindle Electronic Edition: Location 5136–41.
150. Kean and Hamilton (2004), 154.
151. McDermott (2005), Kindle Electronic Edition: Location 3058–59.
152. Kean and Hamilton (2004), 149.
153. Kean and Hamilton (2004), 154; McDermott (2005), Kindle Electronic Edition: Location 3058–59.
154. Ibid., Location 3028–30. Kean and Hamilton (2004), 149 and 154.
155. McDermott (2005), Kindle Electronic Edition: Location 3070–72.

156. Ibid, Location 3067–3079.
157. Kean and Hamilton (2004), 248.
158. McDermott (2005), Kindle Electronic Edition: Location 3660–62.
159. Kean and Hamilton (2004), 153.
160. McDermott (2010).
161. Ibid.
162. Kean and Hamilton (2004), 155. These accounts should be treated with great care; the entire description derives from interrogations of Khalid Sheikh Mohammad and is not corroborated by a second source. The overall description, however, fits into the general profile of Khalid Sheikh Mohammad as well as bin Laden himself.
163. McDermott (2005), Kindle Electronic Edition: Location 3058–59.
164. McDermott (2005), 178.
165. McDermott (2005), Kindle Electronic Edition: Location 6998.
166. Ibid, Location 1573–85; Kean and Hamilton (2004), 161.
167. Sageman (2004), 86.
168. Nasiri (2008).
169. The 'muscle hijackers' characterisation is taken from the 9/11 Report (p. 227).
170. McDermott (2005), Kindle Electronic Edition: Location 3058–59.
171. McDermott (2005), Kindle Electronic Edition: Location 3578–79.
172. Ibid, 3981–84.
173. Kean and Hamilton (2004), 236.
174. Ibid, 251.
175. Wright (2006), 264.
176. Kean and Hamilton (2004), chapter 7.
177. Ibid, 251.
178. Ibid., 532n180.
179. Brown (2010), 1–6.
180. Interview, Kabul, July 2010.
181. See Fazul Abdullah Muhammad, *Harb ala'l-Islam* 1 (2009), 392, in Brown (2010), 5.
182. Brown (2010), 5.
183. Kean and Hamilton (2004), 532n180.
184. Kean and Hamilton (2004), Kindle Electronic Edition: Location 3468.
185. McDermott (2005), Kindle Electronic Edition: Location 114.
186. Ibid, locations 3898–3900 and 3903–5; Coll (2005), Kindle Electronic Edition: Location 10988–11005.
187. McDermott (2005), Kindle Electronic Edition: Location 3951–2.
188. See Rotella and Meyer (2002); Carroll (2002).
189. McDermott (2005), Kindle Electronic Edition: Location 3820–22; Lia (2009), 208.

190. Ibid, 3380.
191. Kean and Hamilton (2004), Kindle Electronic Edition: Location 8573. By 1998, bin Laden had stopped using his satellite telephone and was frequently on the move. This made tracking him considerably more difficult.
192. Kean and Hamilton (2004), 250.
193. Clark (2002).
194. Interview, Kabul, May 2010.
195. Tawil (2010a), 13–14.
196. Riedel (2008), 6.
197. Al-Masri (2004).
198. Interviews, Kabul, June and July 2010.
199. A recent account, based on observations and recollections told to Camille Tawil, suggests that certain figures within the Taliban's leadership did in fact have a vague idea that some kind of attack against America was being prepared, but that they lacked the precise details of what would happen. This account claims that figures within the leadership tried to warn the United States of this impending attack. See Tawil (2010a).
200. Interviews, Kandahar and Kabul, spring and summer 2010.
201. Ibid.
202. Quoted in Murshed (2006), 301.
203. Interview, Kabul, May 2009.
204. Zaeef (2010), 143–4.

8. COLLAPSE (2001–2003)

1. See 'US will be expelled from Afghanistan: Mullah Omar,' *Hindustan Times*, 24 November 2003. http://www.afghanistannewscenter.com/news/2003/november/nov272003.html (accessed 1 September 2010).
2. Caroe (1964), 397.
3. Gopal, Mahsud and Fishman (2010a).
4. See, for instance, the remarks made by Nigel Inkster in 'The al-Qaeda-Taliban Nexus' (http://www.cfr.org/publication/20838/alqaedataliban_nexus.html (accessed 8 October 2010)).
5. Peters (2009).
6. Giustozzi (2007), 13–14.
7. Woodward (2003), Kindle Electronic Edition: Location 2230–2.
8. Woodward (2003), 27.
9. Ibid, 34.
10. Woodward (2003), 33; Rashid (2008), 56. Bill Clinton had stated that 'the ties of Pakistanis to the Taliban and Al-Qaeda' were one of the biggest security issues when he handed over the presidency to George W. Bush.

11. Woodward (2003), 43. Another document recently declassified shows and states that there was 'no inclination in Washington to engage in a dialog with the Taliban.' (National Security Archive (2001a)).

12. Woodward (2003), 32 and 43; Rashid (2008), 61.

13. Woodward (2003), Kindle Electronic Edition: Location 1299.

14. Rashid (2008), 62.

15. Johnston (2006).

16. http://www.september11news.com/PresidentBushSpeech.htm (accessed 11 September 2010).

17. Rashid (2008), 24, 27.

18. Rashid (2008), 27.

19. Ibid., 29.

20. Ibid., 28.

21. Porter (2008).

22. National Security Archive (2001b).

23. Rashid (2008), 65.

24. Afghan Islamic Press (2001); Associated Press (2001).

25. Maley (2002), 262; Rashid (2008), 70.

26. Gannon (2006), 93–4.

27. Rashid (2008), 30.

28. Al-Masri (2004), 248; Rana and Gunaratna (2007), 52, where a letter is quoted; allegedly sent to religious affiliates of the Taliban by Mullah Mohammad Omar after America had identified bin Laden as the prime suspect in the September 11 attacks, it states: 'If I want to bargain and accept the US conditions and hand over bin Laden to them (US), I can get whatever I want. I can become richer than the Arab Sheikhs, but of what worth such material wealth that makes me bow before the infidel West.' Also see Dorronsoro (2005), 321.

29. 'They had left with the impression that Mullah Omar, and other Taliban clerics, had no sense of the military might of the United States, nor of the outrage in America after the Sept. 11 attacks. "You tell them they may die, and the Taliban with them, and they are unmoved," one officer said.' (Burns (2001b)).

30. Zielenziger and Tamayo (2001).

31. Interviews, Kabul and Kandahar, June/July 2010; Mutawakil (2007).

32. Frantz and Rohde (2001).

33. Interview, Kabul, June 2010.

34. Interview, Kandahar, July 2010.

35. Whitaker (2001).

36. Ibid.

37. Burns (2001a).

38. Ibid.

39. 'Afghan Clerics' Decisions Delivered to Osama: Taliban Envoy,' People's Daily

(Online), 28 September 2001. http://english.people.com.cn/english/200109/28/eng20010928_81241.html (accessed 12 October 2010).

40. Interview, Kabul, June 2010.

41. Interviewees state that they had a good idea about the general direction and parts of the country he was travelling in and between.

42. Ibn Mahmud (date unknown), 39–40.

43. Interview, Kabul, July 2010.

44. Traynor and Younge (2001).

45. Hersh claims that the United States had not planned to destroy the Taliban entirely but had wanted to undermine them. (Hersh (2002)).

46. Another interviewee (Kabul, June 2010) stated that Mullah Mohammad Omar had told a 'secret meeting' of senior Taliban members in 2000 that non-Muslims were planning to take over Afghanistan and destroy the Islamic Emirate there.

47. Interview, Kabul, July 2010.

48. Interview, southern Afghanistan, May 2009.

49. Schroen (2005), Kindle Electronic Edition: Location 1362.

50. Woodward (2002).

51. Rashid (2008), 77.

52. Mullah Abdul Hai Mutma'in, Taliban spokesman, Kandahar, 11 September 2001. http://www.satp.org/satporgtp/usa/taliban_opinion.htm (accessed 5 March 2010).

53. Mullah Mohammad Omar, Kandahar, 14 September 2001 (as read out by Mullah Zaeef in Islamabad). http://www.satp.org/satporgtp/usa/taliban_opinion.htm (accessed 5 March 2010)

54. 'A Statement from Amir-ul-Momineen on the possible American Agression [sic] against Afghanistan,' dated 15 September 2001. (Authors' copy).

55. Mullah Mohammad Omar, Kandahar, 19 September 2001. http://www.satp.org/satporgtp/usa/taliban_opinion.htm (accessed 5 March 2010).

56. Mullah Mohammad Omar, Kandahar, 25 September 2001. http://www.satp.org/satporgtp/usa/taliban_opinion.htm (accessed 5 March 2010).

57. See Zaeef (2010) for more.

58. Kean and Hamilton (2004), Kindle Electronic Edition: Location 5492–5520.

59. Bergen (2006), 308.

60. Ibid, 314.

61. http://www.september11news.com/PresidentBushSpeech.htm (accessed 13 September 2010). In President Bush's address, he thanks and mentions various memorials that were held around the world in the days after 11 September.

62. See also the account of popular support in Zaeef's book: Zaeef (2010), chapter 16.

63. Hussain (2008), viii.

64. Hussain (2008), 47.

65. 'TNSM supporters head for Afghanistan,' Dawn (Pakistan), 28 October 2001.

66. Hussain (2008), 43.

67. Rashid (2008), 63.

68. Wright (2010), 93ff.

69. Interviews, Kabul and Kandahar, 2006–10.

70. A dissenting view on this has been expressed by Noman Benotman (see Tawil (2010a)): 'What I know and what I have seen (through taking part in the infamous Kandahar meetings, which lasted for more than a week in the summer of 2000) is that the main group in al-Qaeda, which includes bin Laden, felt certain that U.S. forces would not wage a ground war and would not fight them face to face. This was the al-Qaeda view ever since it returned to Afghanistan (from the Sudan) in 1996. To them, the idea that the U.S. forces would establish a presence on the ground in Afghanistan was unthinkable.' (p. 10).

71. Bergen (2006), 322.

72. Rashid (2008), 61; Rashid makes reference to the 055 brigade at this point (although he states that it is the '555' brigade). There is considerable debate among experts as to the existence of the 055 brigade: some claim it was an al-Qaeda unit and others state that it did not exist. There were many foreign fighters in Afghanistan post-September 11, but it is by no means clear that those were al-Qaeda troops. Moreover, al-Qaeda's general organisational structure, tactics and goals fuel doubts about straightforward guerrilla units for conventional insurgency or guerrilla warfare (as the 055 brigade is claimed to have been).

73. Tawil (2010b), 168–9. This passage quotes from an account by Benotman, stating, 'Bin Laden duly promised to stop launching military operations from Afghanistan, because of the risk they posed to the Taliban. But there was one operation, he said, for which preparations were almost complete, and which he could not abandon under any circumstances.'

74. Benotman (2010).

75. These differences ranged from ideological to tactical issues and regarding whom they regarded as their enemy.

76. Wright (2006), 3–6.

77. Ibrahim (2007), Kindle Electronic Edition: Location 4405.

78. Ibid., Location 4278. ('This battle is not between al-Qaeda and the U.S.. This is a battle of Muslims against the global Crusaders.'); Riley-Smith (1999); Asbridge (2010).

79. http://www.september11news.com/OsamaSpeeches.htm (accessed 12 September 2010).

80. CBC News (2004).

81. Benotman (2010).

82. Interview, Kabul, May 2009; Interview, Kandahar, July 2010.

83. See, as an example of this, the lead editorial of the Sarasota Herald Tribune (USA) on 8 October 2001.

84. Woodward (2003), 33.

85. Woodward (2003), Kindle Electronic Edition: Location 3702.

86. Woodward (2003), 226.

87. See http://query.nytimes.com/gst/fullpage.html?res=9E02E1D71F30F931A
1575AC0A9649C8B63&scp=9&sq=bush+doctrine&st=cse&pagewanted=p
rint and http://www.defense.gov/news/newsarticle.aspx?id=28921.

88. Woodward (2003), Kindle Electronic Edition: Location 3154–7.

89. http://www.nato.int/docu/pr/2001/p01–124e.htm (accessed 8 October 2010).

90. http://www.nato.int/cps/en/natolive/official_texts_17120.htm (accessed 8
October 2010).

91. Woodward (2003), Kindle Electronic Edition: Location 4950–4961.

92. Interviews, Kabul, July 2010.

93. Interviews, Kabul and Kandahar, June and July 2010.

94. Interview, southern Afghanistan, May 2009.

95. Interviews, Kabul and Kandahar, June and July 2010.

96. See, for example, the events reported in Rashid (2008), 72–3.

97. See http://articles.cnn.com/2001–10–07/us/ret.retaliation.facts_1_bin-tali-
ban-foreign-ministry-taliban-offer?_s=PM:US and http://www.guardian.co.uk/
world/2001/oct/14/afghanistan.terrorism5 from October 2001.

98. Zaeef (2010), 154–5; Rashid (2008), 76–9.

99. Zaeef (2010), 147. He recalls a conversation with General Mahmoud Ahmed in
which he assured Mullah Zaeef that, 'We want to assure you that you will not be
alone in this *jihad* against America. We will be with you.' See also Rashid (2008),
27–30.

100. 'TNSM supporters head for Afghanistan,' *Dawn*, 28 October 2001, in Haroon
(2007), 212.

101. Rashid (2008), 28–30; Lieven (2011), 410–14.

102. Al-Masri (2004). Kathy Gannon also notes that 'no obvious preparations were
made in Kabul for an attack.' (Gannon (2006), Kindle Electronic Edition: Location 1070–1.)

103. Ibid.

104. Zaeef (2010), 149.

105. As multiple commentators have pointed out (both Talibs and other Afghans),
bin Laden had a good reputation among many Afghans and the Taliban might
have faced internal repercussions if they had handed him over to the United
States.

106. Al-Masri (2004).

107. See Scheuer for examples of bin Laden's value for the Taliban in terms of their
appeal to the wider Muslim world. Scheuer (2011), Kindle Electronic Edition:
Location 2331 and 5015.

108. Bergen (2006), 315.

109. Ibid.
110. Ibn Mahmud (date unknown), 38.
111. http://www.independent.co.uk/news/world/americas/president-bush-announces-operation-enduring-freedom-631702.html (accessed 8 October 2010).
112. http://www.pbs.org/newshour/updates/october01/international_10–7.html (accessed 8 October 2010).
113. Hersh (2001).
114. Ibrahim (2007), Kindle Electronic Edition: Location 3336–3349; this statement was almost certainly pre-recorded.
115. Wright (2010).
116. Omicinski (2001).
117. Chayes (2006), Kindle Electronic Edition: Location 382.
118. Ibid., Location 394.
119. Shirzai was one of the few options available to the United States and his tribal backing (Barakzai) as well as his father's reputation seemed to be good signs.
120. Wright (2010), 106.
121. Ibid., 102 figure 14.
122. Chayes (2006).
123. Gannon (2006), Kindle Electronic Edition: Location 1094.
124. Wright (2010), 69–71; Woodward (2003), Kindle Electronic Edition: Location 2453–61 and 3461–70.
125. Wright (2010), 69; Interview, Washington D.C., February 2010; Woodward (2003), 174 and 210–16 and 220.
126. Wright (2010), 86.
127. http://www.pbs.org/wgbh/pages/frontline/darkside/etc/script.html (accessed 12 March 2011).
128. Interviews, Kandahar and Kabul, June and July 2010.
129. See also Yong (2011) for supporting research along these lines.
130. Conversations, Anand Gopal, Winter 2010/11; Interviews, Kandahar, 2010.
131. Interviews, Kabul and Kandahar, May–July 2010.
132. Al-Masri (2004); Tawil (2010a), 15–24.
133. Al-Masri (2004).
134. http://www.isaf.nato.int/history.html (accessed 10 March 2011); http://www.history.army.mil/brochures/Afghanistan/Operation%20Enduring%20Freedom.htm (accessed 10 March 2011).
135. Everett (2006).
136. See, for instance, Kaim (2007).
137. Rana and Gunaratna (2007), 53.
138. 'TNSM supporters head for Afghanistan,' Dawn, 28 October 2001, in Haroon (2007), 212.

139. Interviews, Kabul and Kandahar, June–July 2010.
140. Interview, Kandahar, July 2010.
141. Interviews, Kandahar, 2008–10.
142. Maley (2002), 262–8.
143. Wright (2010), 88.
144. Interview, New York, January 2010; Interview, Washington D.C., February 2010; Interviews, Kandahar, June 2010.
145. Burns (2001c).
146. Gertz (2001); Rashid (2008), 221.
147. Franco (2009), 272.
148. Mullah Mohammad Omar was negotiating with Mullah Naqibullah, in a twist of irony given that the latter had contributed significantly to the Taliban taking Kandahar City in 1994. (Source: recording of radio conversation between Mullah Naqibullah and Mullah Mohammad Omar made during the Taliban's final week in Kandahar, authors' copy.)
149. Mawlawi Abdur Rahman Akhundzada, interviewed by Newsweek, late summer 2009. http://www.newsweek.com/2009/09/25/the-taliban-in-their-own-words. print.html (accessed 1 November 2009).
150. Ratnesar (2001).
151. Steele (2001).
152. Ibn Mahmud (date unknown), 37.
153. 'The negotiations for the surrender of Kandahar over several days last week appear to have been dominated by Mullah Omar's efforts to save his own skin. The deal included an amnesty clause that would have allowed the top Taliban leaders, including Mullah Omar, to "live in dignity" in Kandahar. This clause was incorporated into the Bonn agreement at the last moment, with a condition that Mullah Omar should publicly denounce terrorism.' (Mather and Peters (2001)).
154. Gopal (2010b)
155. Interviews, Kabul and Kandahar, June–July 2010.
156. Interview, Kandahar, July 2010.
157. Hussain (2008), 122.
158. 'Most of the Arabs who flocked to Afghanistan after the events of 11 September headed directly to Northern Afghanistan through Taliban leaders in Kabul. None of them joined al-Qaeda and they did not even see bin Laden, who was then preparing himself and those around him from al Qaeda for a battle in the mountains of "Tora Bora" in Jalalabad.' (Taken from a dialogue between Abu al-Walid al-Masri and Australian analyst Leah Farrall; http://allthingsct.wordpress.com/my-dialogue-with-abu-walid-al-masri/arabic-and-english-versions-of-abu-walids-answers-to-my-questions/english-trans-abu-walids-fifth-reponse/ (accessed 18 December 2010)).
159. Bergen (2009a); Stenersen (2010b).

160. Interview, Kabul, June 2010.
161. Korgun (2005); Al-Masri (2004).
162. Al-Masri (2004).
163. Interviews, Kabul and Kandahar, 2010.
164. Al-Masri (2004); Bergen (2006), 395.
165. A number of foreign jihadists and leaders fled to Iran.
166. Bergen (2009b).
167. UNI (2001).
168. Bergen (2009b).
169. Ibid.
170. Ibid.
171. Ibid.
172. Bergen (2006), 332–3.
173. Kerry (2009); Berntsen (2006); Fury (2009); Bergen (2009b); Bergen (2006), chapter 10; http://gulfnews.com/news/world/usa/yemeni-describes-bloody-siege-on-al-qaida-1.200180 (accessed 10 March 2011).
174. Rashid (2008), 77–9; Lieven (2011), 407–414.
175. Rashid (2008), 80 and 90; Hussain (2008), 33–7 and 40–42.
176. Suskind (2006), 58; Rashid (2008), 89.
177. Rashid (2008), 77–78.
178. Rashid (2008), 80 and 90.
179. Rashid (2001b); McGirk (2002).
180. Hersh (2002); Rashid (2008), 91–3.
181. Interview, Kandahar, June 2010; Interview, Kabul, July 2010.
182. Interviews, Kabul and Kandahar, June and July 2010.
183. Interviews, Afghanistan, 2005–10; Rashid (2008), 130.
184. 'In fact, some farmers in Helmand province later alleged that Afghan anti-Taliban forces had promised to let them grow poppy in exchange for their help in toppling the Taliban regime.' (Feldab-Brown (2010), Kindle Electronic Edition: Location 1684.)
185. Gopal (2010).
186. Woodward (2004), chapter 2.
187. The United States had 4000 troops in Afghanistan in February 2002. By June it had increased to 7000, and by September 2003 it was at 9800. *Afghanistan Index*, Brookings Institution, 23 February 2005. http://www.brookings.edu/~/media/Files/Programs/FP/afghanistan%20index/index20050223.pdf (accessed 7 October 2010).
188. ISAF's expansion from Kabul would happen in four stages over the course of three years. In 2004, ISAF would expand to the north in stage 1, then move to the west in 2005 in stage 2, onwards to the south in July 2006 in stage 3 and finally into the east in autumn 2006 in stage 4 which completed ISAF's expan-

sion. ISAF, *ISAF Key Facts and Figures Placemat*, 16 September 2006. http://www.reliefweb.int/rw/fullmaps_sa.nsf/luFullMap/08733FF8CF4216848525 71F40051E492/$File/nato_PRG_afg160906-a.pdf?OpenElement (accessed 8 October 2010).

189. For more on the impact of the DDR process see Thruelsen and DIIS (2006).
190. Rashid (2008), 128–9.
191. Rashid (2008), 125–9.
192. 'New Afghan government sworn in,' *CNN.com* (Online), 22 December 2001. http://articles.cnn.com/2001–12–22/world/gen.afghan.government_1_afghan-national-anthem-pashtun-leader-hamid-karzai?_s=PM:asiapcf (accessed 21 October 2010).
193. Wright (2010), 109.
194. Rashid (2008), 129.
195. Vendrell (2009), 30–2.
196. Rashid (2008), chapter 7.
197. See, for example, how Ismael Khan was shifted from Herat to Kabul, or how Gul Agha Shirzai was moved from Kandahar to Nangarhar.
198. 'NATO's role in Afghanistan,' 30 September 2010. http://www.nato.int/cps/en/natolive/topics_8189.htm (accessed 8 October 2010).
199. Interviews, June–July 2010, Kandahar and Kabul; Gopal (2010b).
200. It is also used in Pashtu, however, as a loan term.
201. Gopal (2010b).
202. The command structure thus partially mirrors the command structure of the warlord networks in northern Afghanistan as outlined by Giustozzi in *Empires of Mud* (2009).
203. Rashid (2008), 240–45.
204. Rashid (2008), chapter 10.
205. See Zaeef (2010).
206. http://www.dawn.com/2002/02/10/top8.htm (accessed 2 August 2010). See also Mutawakil (2007).
207. Interview, Kabul, July 2010.
208. Qarhani (2002).
209. Spillius (2002).
210. *Interfax News Bulletin*, 12 June 2002.
211. Nadia Abou el-Magd, 'Alleged Mullah Omar Statement Aired,' *Associated Press*, 12 September 2002. There is a qualitative difference between using the term 'infidels' and 'invaders.' While the Taliban leadership has rarely issued statements referring to 'infidels,' in particular in the last few years, some Taliban fighters on the ground interviewed refer to the 'infidels' they are fighting.
212. Interviews, Kabul and Kandahar, June and July 2010.
213. Yousafzai (2003).

214. Ibid.
215. This then went on to inform their sense of righteousness and justice which pervades much of the movement's rhetoric towards the Afghan government.
216. Interview, Kabul, July 2010 (with a senior Taliban political figure who attended the meeting).
217. Conversation, Ali Jalali, June 2010. There does seem to have been another meeting in late 2003/early 2004 with a similar purpose (and seeking 'protection and space for political activities') which resulted in a Taliban representative being dispatched to Kabul to meet with government authorities.
218. Ruttig (2009a), 66; also see Ruttig's paper, *The Ex-Taliban on the High Peace Council* (Kabul: Afghanistan Analysts Network) available at http://aan-afghanistan.com/uploads/20101020TRuttig_ExT_in_HPC.pdf (accessed 12 June 2011).
219. Giustozzi (2007), 135–6;
220. For details, see the list of articles at http://www.afghanistannewscenter.com/news/2004/november/nov82004.html (accessed 8 October 2010).
221. Ruttig (2010), 21; Gopal (2010b).
222. Interviews, Kandahar and Kabul, 2009–10.
223. Foreigners may not have intended to pick favourites, but this was often how it was perceived by local communities (whether the foreigners recognised this or not). See Shane, Mazzetti and Filkins (2010) for more on corruption within the Afghan government.
224. Interviews, Kandahar, Khost, Mazar-e Sharif, Herat, Badakhshan, Badghis, Faryab, Helmand, 2006–10.
225. Jones (2010), Kindle Electronic Edition: Location 2388–89.
226. Gopal (2010b); Coghlan (2009); MacKenzie (2010).
227. Giustozzi (2007), 19–21.
228. Interviews, Kandahar, 2008–9; Giustozzi (2007), 55–6.
229. Interviews, Kandahar, 2008–9.
230. Gopal (2010b).
231. Interviews, Kandahar, 2009–10.
232. Gopal (2010); Forsberg (2009).
233. Interviews, southern Afghanistan, 2006–11.
234. Giustozzi (2007), 2.
235. Ibid., 103.
236. Ibid., 3.
237. Dorronsoro (2005), 339.
238. There are no comprehensive assessments available on how many people have died in the Taliban's assassination campaign, in part because identifying who was responsible—it is not always related to the Taliban/insurgency—is extremely difficult. One source is that compiled in Kandahar by a local news group and

researcher; the results are available at http://www.surgar.net/english/include/
print.php?id=1023&fd=Hot-News (accessed 10 March 2011).

239. Fergusson (2010), 125.
240. Giustozzi (2007), 3.
241. Interviews, Kandahar, 2009–10.
242. See chapters 2 and 3 for the role of mullahs in rural society, in particular among
Pashtun communities, and also for the general attitude of mullahs towards the
central government and authority.
243. Giustozzi (2007), 43–46.
244. RFE/RL Newsline, 'Taliban Announce Creation of Council to Help "Evict"
Leadership in Afghanistan,' RFE/RL (Online), 25 June 2003. http://www.rferl.
org/content/article/1142945.html (accessed 10 October 2010).
245. Giustozzi (2007), 47.
246. See the report of a meeting between Mullahs Dadullah, Akhtar Mohammad
Osmani, Obaidullah and others in 2003 in Yousafzai (2009).
247. Rubin (2006).
248. Yousafzai (2009).
249. Farrall (2009).
250. Some of these were set up in cooperation with Pakistani jihadist groups (Hussain (2008), 127–8).
251. Gul (2010), 11–12 and 43–44.
252. Hussain (2008), 213.
253. Ibid., 120.
254. Yousafzai (2009).
255. http://www.pbs.org/newshour/terrorism/international/binladen_10–7.html
(accessed 27 July 2010).
256. http://www.september11news.com/OsamaSpeeches.htm (accessed 28 July
2010).
257. Bin Laden and Lawrence (2005), 148–9.
258. Sude (2010), 5. Not all of these were directly ordered by the central leadership
(who were now firmly in hiding) and some were undoubtedly planned before
the September 11 attacks.
259. Bergen (2006), 316.
260. Gul (2010), 11–12, 13, 43–44.
261. Ibid., 24.
262. Even Bangladesh: 'A Saudi-owned vessel was reported to have smuggled 150 Al-
Qaeda and Taliban to the Bangladeshi port of Chittagong.' (Hussain (2008),
122.)
263. Gul (2010), 24–25.
264. Abu Zubayda, for instance, was staying in a house rented by a member of Lashkar-e Taiba at the time of his arrest in Faisalabad in 2002. (Hussain (2008), 60.)

265. Pipes (2001). The general argument used in this article is suspect, although some of the evidence cited is useful.
266. Interviews, Kabul and Kandahar, June and July 2010.
267. Interview, Kandahar, July 2010.
268. Gul (2010), 16.
269. The creation of the 'Muttahida Jihad Council,' for example, was one such prominent result. (Gul (2010), 17).
270. Hussain (2008), 52.
271. Hegghammer (2010), Kindle Electronic Edition: Location 235–37.
272. RAND Database of Worldwide Terrorism Incidents, http://smapp.rand.org/rwtid (accessed 21 October 2010).
273. Ruttig (2009a), 66.
274. 'Had he wanted to, Haqqani could have handed the United States the entire Al-Qaeda network.' (Gannon (2006), Kindle Electronic Edition: Location 1094.)
275. Ruttig (2009a), 67.
276. Solomon (2007). Also, interview, Anand Gopal, Washington D.C., June 2010.
277. Interview, Kabul, July 2010.
278. The way the Taliban disintegrated and remerged after October 2001 is another demonstration of the sort of coalition-nature of the movement that had integrated entire groups into its structure while capturing more territory during the 1990s. Even the core group was a patchwork of smaller groups, with a core group around Mullah Mohammad Omar himself.
279. Hegghammer (2010), Kindle Electronic Edition: Location 1737.
280. See Nathan (2009) for more details.
281. Tohid (2003).
282. Yousafzai (2009).
283. Schmidle (2009), Kindle Electronic Edition: Location 1113–17; Kapisthalam (2004). There are repeated claims made in media outlets that Mufti Nizamuddin Shamzai and the Binori Town madrassa served to hide a wounded bin Laden as well as Mullah Mohammad Omar at the same time in early 2002, but this seems more myth than fact. (Raman (2004)).
284. Interviews, Kabul and Kandahar, June–July 2010.
285. Exact figures are impossible to come by, but the length of the battle indicates that those present were at least trained fighters. 5000 is the uppermost estimate of the numbers involved, but the actual figure is probably far less and closer to the lower end of the scale.
286. Naylor (2005).
287. Ruttig (2009a), 79. Ruttig writes that the battle that unfolded in Shahi Kot was led by Saifurrahman, the brother of Nasrullah Mansur, and included his and Haqqani's fighters along with a number of foreigners (Arabs, Uzbeks, Tajiks and Chechens). The battle also reportedly included Jalaluddin Haqqani's brother,

Ibrahim Omari, who, according to an article by Kathy Gannon (cited in the book), surrendered to General Gul Haidar.

288. See Naylor (2005) and Ruttig (2009a), 79.

9. REDUX (2003–2009)

1. Coghlan (2009), 126.
2. Interview, Panjwayi Taliban commander, Rob Densmore, 2006.
3. 'Afghanistan—Timeline,' *BBC News* (Online), 5 October 2010. http://news.bbc.co.uk/1/hi/1162108.stm (accessed 10 October 2010); Johnson and Leslie (2005).
4. For Kandahar, see Gopal (2010b).
5. Yousafzai (2009).
6. 'Interview with Mullah Omar—Transcript,' *BBC News* (Online), 15 November 2001. http://news.bbc.co.uk/1/hi/world/south_asia/1657368.stm (accessed 10 October 2010)).
7. 'Everyone knows that the Soviets and British had been defeated in Afghanistan and this will be the fate of the Americans.' (statement made on 13 October 2001— http://www.satp.org/satporgtp/usa/taliban_opinion.htm (accessed 10 March 2011).
8. Giustozzi (2007), 5.
9. It was during 2004 that Mullah Dadullah was appointed commander of the Taliban's military forces, and Mullah Akhtar Osmani as head of liaison between the Taliban and the tribes.
10. Reuter and Younus (2009), 104.
11. Ibid., 183.
12. Interview, Kabul, June 2010; Interview, Kandahar, July 2010.
13. Note that not all of these may be said to be al-Qaeda-planned or actioned, but all retained ties to the central group whether through inspiration or motivation from certain figures from within it. RAND Database of Worldwide Terrorism Incidents, http://smapp.rand.org/rwtid/ (accessed 21 October 2010).
14. Hussain (2008), 141–44.
15. Hussain (2008), 144.
16. Hussain (2008), 142.
17. Gul (2010), 28.
18. Hussain (2008), 135–7.
19. Kepel (2008b), chapter 3.
20. Al-Qaeda's campaign in the Kingdom of Saudi Arabia was swiftly rooted out by Saudi security. See Hegghammer (2010).
21. Rohde and Sanger (2007).
22. Woodward (2003), Kindle Electronic Edition: Location 881–897.
23. Figure cited in Margesson, Bruno and Sharp (2009).

24. Interviews, Kabul and Kandahar, June and July 2010.
25. Gul (2010), 136.
26. There is a report of a statement faxed to al-Jazeera from Taliban leader Mullah Mohammad Omar, but the authenticity of this document has never been confirmed. In the fax, he allegedly stated the following: 'America is harboring terrorism and using it as a justification to launch war against Iraq, and Afghanistan is facing more hostility, chaos and destruction now than ever.' ('Mullah Omar accuses US of faking excuses to launch war against Iraq,' Associated Press, 4 December 2002.)
27. http://www.kavkazcenter.com/eng/content/2003/09/30/1725.shtml (accessed 28 August 2010).
28. http://www.afghanistannewscenter.com/news/2003/november/nov272003.html (accessed 28 August 2010).
29. http://www.memri.org/report/en/0/0/0/0/0/0/3351.htm (accessed 10 October 2010).
30. Gehriger and Yousafzai (2007).
31. http://hotair.com/archives/2006/07/07/video-london-bomber-shehzad-tanweer/ (accessed 10 October 2010).
32. 'Al-Zarqawi group claims allegiance to bin Laden,' CNN.com (Online), 18 October 2004. http://edition.cnn.com/2004/WORLD/meast/10/17/al.zarqawi.statement/ (accessed 10 October 2010).
33. See Hegghammer (2010) for more.
34. Hegghammer (2008).
35. Scheuer (2006).
36. Corera (2005).
37. He stated this in a 2004 letter to bin Laden: 'Targeting and striking their religious, political, and military symbols, will make them show their rage against the Sunnis and bear their inner vengeance. If we succeed in dragging them into a sectarian war, this will awaken the sleepy Sunnis who are fearful of destruction and death.' (cited in http://www.jamestown.org/single/?no_cache=1&tx_ttnews[ttnews]=27304 (accessed 28 August 2010)).
38. Nash (2006).
39. For more on the Madrid bombings, read Lia (2009), 332–9.
40. Yousafzai and Moreau (2005).
41. Ibid.
42. Interviews, Kabul and Kandahar, June–July 2010.
43. Yousafzai (2009).
44. Tom Vanden Brook, 'Use of Humvees restricted in Afghanistan,' USA Today, 8 September 2010. http://www.marinecorpstimes.com/news/2010/06/gns_humvee_restriction_063010/ (accessed 10 October 2010).
45. Feifer (2009), 117; Braithwaite (2011), 132.

46. Stratfor, 'Afghanistan: Another Round in the IED Game,' 31 March 2010.

47. The Taliban also exploit public opinion in the wake of IED attacks in which civilians are injured or killed; there is often a perception among those present that the party at fault in these instances is the foreign forces (e.g. for driving through the city) rather than the Taliban for planting the IED. (Interviews and authors' observations, Kandahar, 2006–11).

48. Giustozzi (2007), 83–4.

49. Conversation, Kandahar, June 2010.

50. In a night letter distributed in southern Afghanistan in September 2010, the head of the assassination unit listed two phone numbers for complaints and mediation giving rise to the impression, as noted by other commentators, that the Taliban have a dedicated mediation commission.

51. 2010 Layeha, author copy.

52. Interviews, Kandahar, 2009–10.

53. Interviews and authors' observation, Kandahar, 2008–10.

54. Interview and authors' observation, Kandahar, 2009–11.

55. Interviews, Kandahar, 2009–10.

56. 'Taleban "turn on ex-minister,"' BBC News (Online), 21 October 2010. http://news.bbc.co.uk/1/hi/world/south_asia/3209584.stm (accessed 13 October 2010).

57. 'Ex-Taleban chief's brother killed,' BBC News (Online), 4 July 2005. http://news.bbc.co.uk/1/hi/world/south_asia/4649827.stm (accessed 10 March 2011).

58. Witte (2006).

59. http://theunjustmedia.com/Islamic%20Perspectives/June10/An%20English%20Translation%20of%20the%20Questionnaire%20of%20the%20Members%20of%20Ansar%20al-Mujahideen%20Arabic%20Forum%20with%20the%20Commander,%20Sheikh%20Sirajudeen%20Haqqani.htm (accessed 13 October 2010).

60. Witte (2009).

61. 2010 Layeha, author copy, section 6.

62. Freeze (2009); Barfield (2006)

63. Interviews, Kandahar, 2010. Such courts existed as of August 2010.

64. The approval for 'phase three' was granted on 8 December 2005 in Brussels, and by 28 September 2006, approval was granted for a NATO expansion into fourteen additional provinces.

65. Interviews, Kandahar, 2006.

66. See, for example, the speech made by President George W. Bush at the US Naval Academy in Annapolis, Maryland, during which he stated: 'Across the world, our military is standing directly between the American people and the worst dangers in the world, and Americans are grateful to have such brave defenders.' (http://www.presidentialrhetoric.com/speeches/05.27.05.html (accessed 14 March 2011)).

67. Hutt (2009); David Richards also remarked that, 'I think of my own daughters in London and the risk they would be in' during a speech on 9 July 2006 (http://www.timesonline.co.uk/tol/news/article685013.ece (accessed 14 March 2011)).
68. Interviews, Kandahar, summer 2006; interviews, Kandahar, summer 2007.
69. Interview, Panjwayi Taliban commander, Rob Densmore, 2006.
70. Al-Jazeera Interview, 20 July 2005. Read an English translation/transcript at http://forum.pakistanidefence.com/index.php?showtopic=47059&mode=threaded&pid=659870 (accessed 14 March 2011).
71. It was also around this time that the Taliban had started to increase the output on their website, translating articles into Arabic, Urdu and English as well as Dari and Pashtu. See Giustozzi (2007), chapter 4.
72. See, for instance, Shahzad (2007) and the Taliban statement made on 4 February 2007 (http://www.afghanwire.com/article.php?id=4039 (accessed 12 March 2011)).
73. Statements referenced here were made on 29 December 2006, 18 December 2007, 2 December 2008 and 8 December 2008. (Authors' email copies).
74. Rashid (2008), 359.
75. Smith (2012).
76. See chapter 3 for more.
77. See Smith (2012) for more.
78. Rashid (2008), 363–4.
79. Human Rights Watch (2006).
80. For example, 'Taleban in rare frontal assault,' BBC News (Online), 7 August 2007. http://news.bbc.co.uk/1/hi/world/south_asia/6935590.stm (accessed 21 October 2010).
81. Rashid (2008), 398–9, Fergusson (2010), 184.
82. Fergusson (2010), chapter 7.
83. Note that an official Taliban-endorsed detailed biography of Dadullah published in Al-Somood magazine in July 2007 stated that Dadullah was born in Deh Rawud. A series of articles by Waliullah Rahmani in the Jamestown Foundation's Terrorism Monitor newsletters about the Dadullah brothers stated that the family was originally from Arghandab district of Kandahar province. (http://www.jamestown.org/programs/gta/single/?tx_ttnews%5Btt_news%5D=707&tx_ttnews%5BbackPid%5D=239&no_cache=1 (accessed 1 August 2010)).
84. Translated by the NEFA Foundation. See http://www.nefafoundation.org/miscellaneous/FeaturedDocs/nefasamooddadullahbiography.pdf for the full translation.
85. Dadullah was allegedly also single-handedly responsible for baking bread for mujahedeen during the 1988 siege of Arghandab: 'Mullah Mansur, his second brother, adds in this issue and says: "Once, the Russians imposed a siege on the county Agnadab [sic] from the land and the air and gathered great forces in this county.

The jihad warriors were found in the big siege and Dadullah was among the jihad warriors and spent all the day in a hard fight against the Russians, and in the night he used to bake bread and to prepare food for the jihad warriors until the dawn, when he kneaded 150 kilograms of flour and baked it to bread by himself, and he didn't include anyone in this work.'" (page 2)

86. http://www.nefafoundation.org/miscellaneous/FeaturedDocs/nefasamooddadullahbiography.pdf (accessed 29 September 2010); Zaeef (2010); Rashid (2008), 242; http://www.jamestown.org/programs/gta/single/?tx_ttnews%5Btt_news%5D=707&tx_ttnews%5BbackPid%5D=239&no_cache=1 (accessed 21 August 2010).

87. http://www.nefafoundation.org/miscellaneous/FeaturedDocs/nefasamooddadullahbiography.pdf (accessed 29 September 2010); interviews, Kabul and Kandahar, June and July 2010.

88. 'Mullah Dadaullah, a senior Taliban commander, was assigned command of a strike force that set off from Bamyan on 8 June and advanced to central Yakaolang. There the Taliban established their headquarters in Nayak. On 10 June the Taliban forces burned down the old bazaar of Yakaolang. According to human rights reports, Dadaullah then carried out what the Taliban's official news agency termed a "mopping up operation"; over a two-day period, his troops allegedly burned over four thousand houses, shops, and public buildings in central and eastern Yakaolang, including a medical clinic, twelve mosques and prayer halls, and the main madrasa, or Islamic seminary, which was Shi'a and therefore considered heretical. Over the next two weeks, troops under Dadaullah reportedly moved through the district, burning villages and summarily executing civilians. Some civilians were killed while trying to escape, and a number of detainees were held for a period of forced labor.' (UN Human Rights Abuses report, October 2010. http://www.flagrancy.net/salvage/UNMappingReportAfghanistan.pdf (accessed 10 October 2010)).

89. Maley (2002), 240.

90. Ibid., 241.

91. Legend has Dadullah riding away on horseback, reportedly allowed to pass through by Northern Alliance commanders allied to Dostum in return for Dadullah releasing some of their commanders captured in previous years, although cash seems to have also played a role. See http://www.jamestown.org/programs/gta/single/?tx_ttnews%5Btt_news%5D=707&tx_ttnews%5BbackPid%5D=239&no_cache=1 (accessed 21 August 2010). Also interview, New York City, February 2010.

92. See http://www.jamestown.org/programs/gta/single/?tx_ttnews%5Btt_news%5D=707&tx_ttnews%5BbackPid%5D=239&no_cache=1 (accessed 21 August 2010).

93. Tohid (2003).

94. Fergusson (2010), 129.

95. See http://www.abc.net.au/news/stories/2003/08/26/931846.htm and Rashid (2008), 247.

96. Reportedly the first time a Taliban member had been interviewed for al-Jazeera. See van Dyk (2004).

97. See Rashid (2008), 449n51.

98. See http://www.atimes.com/atimes/South_Asia/IA10Df02.html (accessed 15 July 2010).

99. See http://www.jamestown.org/programs/gta/single/?tx_ttnews%5Btt_news %5D=707&tx_ttnews%5BbackPid%5D=239&no_cache=1 (accessed 13 February 2010); originally sourced to an interview with al-Jazeera.

100. Gopal, Mahsud and Fishman (2010b), 9.

101. http://www.nefafoundation.org/miscellaneous/FeaturedDocs/nefasamood-dadullahbiography.pdf (accessed 29 September 2010)

102. See Smith (2009), 194.

103. Interviews, Kabul and Kandahar, June–July 2010.

104. 'The analyst Kovanen compared the first 29 weeks of 2008 against the same period in 2007 and found a slight decline in suicide bombs in Kandahar, while other types of attack increased dramatically.' (Smith (2009), 194.)

105. Interviews, Taliban commander, Helmand (by phone); low-level fighters, Kandahar City, summer 2007.

106. Rashid (2008), 399; Elias (2008), 49; Coghlan (2008), 138.

107. See, for example, Bergen (2009a).

108. Conversation, Graeme Smith, Summer 2007; Interviews, Kandahar, 2007 and 2009.

109. See below for details on this.

110. Interview, al-Jazeera, 20 July 2005.

111. Coghlan (2008), 138–9.

112. Gehriger and Yousafzai (2007).

113. 'Taleban sack military commander,' BBC News (Online), 29 December 2007. http://news.bbc.co.uk/1/hi/7164277.stm (accessed 13 October 2010).

114. Khan (2007).

115. Note, though, that there are 'relatively few' examples of wills of suicide bombers in comparison to other conflict arenas, as in Iraq, for example. (Nathan (2009), 31.)

116. Robinson (2007).

117. Wright (2006), 217–8.

118. Hussain (2008), 99.

119. For this data, see Fair (2007), 39.

120. Gul (2010), 32.

121. Six attacks in 2006, 56 attacks in 2007, 61 attacks in 2008 and 87 attacks in 2009. (Gul (2010), 129.)

122. This was reportedly as a direct result of Mullah Mohammad Omar's intervention. (Wattie (2009), 43–45).

123. Interviews with Afghan graduates of madrassas in Pakistan, Kandahar, 2006–10 and Fair (2007), 85–91.

124. Authors' observation and interviews, Kandahar, spring and summer 2010.

125. In 2008 there was also reportedly an edict issued by Mullah Mohammad Omar calling for an end to the use of beheadings as a method of execution. (Hashimzada and Noorzai (2008)).

126. Interviews, Kandahar, 2010.

127. ISAF translation, manuscript copy.

128. See v1.theglobeandmail.com/talkingtothetaliban/ (accessed 12 March 2011).

129. The responses were very similar, even to the extent of matching in the exact phrases used.

130. Interview, Kabul, Rob Densmore, 2006.

131. Cited in Smith (2009), 203 and 210n12. Also Pedwell (2006).

132. Russian General Staff (2002), 243.

133. Barker (2010), 1.

134. Figures taken from ibid., 4. Note that this dataset includes suicide IEDs.

135. See, for example, Williams (2007).

136. For example, neither explosively formed projectiles (EFPs), shaped charges, massive-sized bombs designed specifically for mass casualties, nor 'chemically-enhanced' IEDs have passed back to Afghanistan. (See Barker (2010), 14 and 17.)

137. Ibid., 17.

138. Yousafzai (2009).

139. Barker (2010), 18.

140. Hussain (2008).

141. Interviews, Mansera, Murree and Muzafferabad, January 2006; Hussain (2008), 86–7.

142. Rashid (2008), 146–7.

143. Ali and Ansari (2006).

144. Gul (2010), 136–7.

145. Ibid., 39.

146. Gul (2010), 18.

147. Gul (2010), 67; Schmidle (2009).

148. Gul (2010), 68.

149. Interviews, Kandahar, summer 2006 and 2007.

150. Gall (2009).

151. Gopal, Mahsud and Fishman (2010a).

152. Gul (2010), 62–4.

153. Authors' observation/conversations, Kandahar, 2008.

154. Ajami (2009).

155. Bumiller and Landler (2009).

156. 'Karzai protests civilian deaths,' *The New York Times*, 25 January 2009. http://www.nytimes.com/2009/01/25/world/asia/25iht-25karzai.19659063.html?_r=1&pagewanted=print (accessed 13 October 2010).

157. Woodward (2010).

158. Mashal (2010).

159. Special Inspector General for Iraq Reconstruction, 'Quarterly Report to the United States Congress,' 30 October 2009.

160. http://www.cfr.org/publication/18952/obamas_strategy_for_afghanistan_and_pakistan_march_2009.html (accessed 13 October 2010). This was repeated with almost exactly the same wording in his December 2009 speech at West Point.

161. In July 2009, for example, a local Taliban commander in Panjwayi district postponed a planned attack campaign when this was requested from him by local village elders. He ordered his men to help with the grape harvest since the grapes would otherwise have rotted on the vines. (Interviews, Kandahar, July 2009.)

162. Woodward (2010).

163. Interview conducted by Anand Gopal, January 2010.

164. For more, see Franco (2009), 269–91.

165. 'One of Baitullah Mehsud's senior commanders informed a newspaper that after hectic efforts, four bodies were brought back to Makeen in South Waziristan through unfrequented routes. He said dozens of Mehsud's tribal militants, led by Commander Khan Ghafoor, had gone to Afghanistan to fight against the US-led forces there. Around two dozen militants had been sent to retrieve the remaining bodies.' (Gul (2010), 40.).

166. Ibid., 20.

167. Van Bijlert (2009).

168. Possibly via crop eradication and the demanding of bribes to forestall this.

169. Interviews and authors' observations, Afghanistan, 2006–11.

170. Interviews and conversations, Kandahar, 2008–10.

171. Interviews, Kandahar, 2008–10.

172. Ibid.

173. For example, http://theunjustmedia.com/Afghanistan/Statements/Dec09/Obama,%20following%20Bush%20Steps.htm (accessed 12 March 2011).

174. This sense of disappointment is speculation, but it does come across from reading the statements written in reaction to various early announcements by Obama on Afghanistan-related policy.

175. See http://theunjustmedia.com/Afghanistan/Statements/Dec09/Statement%20of%20the%20Islamic%20Emirate%20of%20Afghanistan%20Regarding%20Obama%E2%80%99s%20New%20Strategy.htm (accessed 17 October 2010) and http://theunjustmedia.com/Afghanistan/Statements/Dec09/Obama,%20following%20Bush%20Steps.htm (accessed 17 October 2010).

176. Interviews, Kabul and Kandahar, 2009–10; Taliban statements 2008–10.
177. Carnegie Endowment for International Peace, *What's Really Happening in Afghanistan: a Report From the Front*. (Washington D.C.: Carnegie Endowment for International Peace, 2009), 9. http://carnegieendowment.org/files/0911 carnegie-afghanistan2.pdf (accessed 17 October 2010).
178. The exact background to the first *layeha* and those that followed are still somewhat unclear, especially in terms of who was involved. It seems that Mullah Berader was behind the first version, but the 2009 and 2010 versions brought in a wider group of people, including Mullah Zakir and Amir Khan Mottaqi. See Clark (2011b) for more.
179. Interview, Mullah Rahmatullah, Kandahar, Robert Densmore, 2006.
180. This was most likely in reaction to a series of executions associated with Mullah Dadullah filmed and released in a video in 2006.
181. The reality inside Afghanistan is much more complex than the 'ideal' outlined in the *Layeha*.
182. Interview, Kabul, April 2010; interviews and authors' observations, Kandahar, 2010–11.
183. Interviews, Kandahar and Kabul, 2009–10.
184. Interviews, Kabul and Kandahar, April 2010.
185. Authors' observation, Kandahar, 2010; also interview, Kabul, July 2010.
186. Bay (2010).
187. There is an inherent tension between this desire for a sustainable (and replaceable) leadership and the type of charismatic leadership that Mullah Mohammad Omar cultivates.
188. http://iwpr.net/report-news/taleban-try-hearts-and-minds-tactics-0 (accessed 13 October 2010); Ruttig (2010), 20.
189. Ruttig (2010), 22.

10. THE FORGE (2010)

1. Feldman (2008), 195–6.
2. Horne (2006), 5.
3. Gul (2010), 14.
4. Kelly (2009).
5. Woodward (2010).
6. Afghanistan is a difficult research environment where real and false information is a commodity. Intentions and the meaning of actions are difficult to decipher. The account that follows leaves out any material regarding individuals involved in the current conflict that could be used to take deliberate actions against them or to contact them. This is a descriptive and analytical effort that seeks to identify trends and processes, rather than give details about individuals involved.

7. See, for example, the report of the United States Government Accountability Office on 'Afghanistan's Security Environment,' 5 May 2010. http://pdf.usaid.gov/pdf_docs/PCAAC053.pdf (accessed 5 October 2010).
8. Giustozzi and Reuter (2010); Giustozzi (2010).
9. Rubin (2010a).
10. Partlow (2010b).
11. Zoroya (2010).
12. Nordland (2010b). The monitoring group counted 630 insurgent attacks in August 2009, which would amount to a 114% increase in attacks.
13. Roadside bombs wounded or killed 6,200 allied troops and Afghan forces in fiscal year 2009 compared with 3,800 in 2008. Casualties are even higher this year.
14. For example, the attack on the Herat PRT on 30 May 2011, or that in the Kabul Military Hospital on 21 May 2011.
15. This happened on 28 January 2011. (http://www.bbc.co.uk/news/world-south-asia-12307463 (accessed 12 June 2011)).
16. See Woodward (2010) for a detailed exposition of these different approaches to Karzai.
17. Kaplan (2009a).
18. Authors' observation and interviews, Kandahar, 2009–10.
19. McChrystal's assessment is available for download at http://media.washington-post.com/wp-srv/politics/documents/Assessment_Redacted_092109.pdf (accessed 5 October 2010).
20. Authors' observation, Kandahar, 2009–10; interviews, Kabul and Washington, 2010.
21. http://www.nato.int/isaf/structure/bio/rc_s/carter.html (accessed 22 October 2010); He spent six months as Director of Plans of the US-led Combined Joint Task Force 180 in Afghanistan in mid-2002, and three months in the Cross Government Iraq Planning Unit based in the British Foreign Office leading up to and during the invasion of Iraq in 2003. He commanded 20 Armoured Brigade, based in Germany, from January 2004 until December 2005, including a tour in Iraq in command of British Forces in Basra.
22. Hastings (2010).
23. Partlow (2010a).
24. Meyer (2009).
25. Woodward (2010), Kindle Electronic Edition: Location 284.
26. Sude (2010).
27. See van Bijlert (2010).
28. http://unama.unmissions.org/Default.aspx?tabid=4482 (accessed 5 October 2010).
29. See Waldman (2010c) and UK Foreign Affairs Committee Testimony available at http://www.publications.parliament.uk/pa/cm201011/cmselect/cmfaff/514/10101303.htm (accessed 16 March 2011).

30. Maclean (2010); Conversations, London, Washington D.C and New York., 2008–11.
31. Kaplan (2009b).
32. Authors' observations and conversations, Kandahar, 2010.
33. Arnoldy (2010); Gopal (2010a).
34. The distinction between the two is more theoretical than actual, and perhaps means more for international actors and observers than for the insurgency.
35. See Nixon (2011) for a useful outline of Afghan views on the subject.
36. This, however, should not be understood to mean that the different entities cooperate or interact.
37. Interviews, Kabul and Kandahar, June–July 2010.
38. AFP (2010a).
39. National Commission on Terrorist Attacks Upon the United States (2004), 9.
40. Farrall (2010b).
41. For more on the idea of al-Qaeda as a franchise operation, see McLaughlin (2010).
42. Farrall (2011).
43. See, for example, the pledge of allegiance in al-Zawahiri's statement issued in February 2007 (CNN, 'Purported al Qaeda message: Unite with Taliban,' CNN.com (Online), 12 February 2007. http://edition.cnn.com/2007/WORLD/meast/02/12/zawahiri.video/index.html?section=cnn_latest (accessed 6 October 2010)).
44. Hoffman (2008).
45. Sageman (2008).
46. Temple-Raston (2010).
47. See, for example, a recent edition of Inspire. http://www.theunjustmedia.com/Islamic%20Perspectives/Oct10/Inspire%20Magazine%20Issue%202.htm (accessed 19 October 2010).
48. Wali Khan Amin Shah is the one exception of an Afghan who was closely associated with core al-Qaeda figures.
49. Weiser and Moynihan (2010); Wilson (2009); New York Daily News, 'Najibullah Zazi reveals chilling details on Al Qaeda training and terrorist plot to blow up subways,' New York Daily News, 23 February 2010. http://www.nydailynews.com/news/ny_crime/2010/02/23/2010–02–23_najibullah_zazi_reveals_chilling_details_on_al_qaeda_training_and_terrorist_plot.html (accessed 18 October 2010).
50. Rahman (2010).
51. Farrall (2010a).
52. http://counterterrorism.newamerica.net/drones (accessed 19 October 2010); note that it seems to have been different for more senior command and control leadership of al-Qaeda who were often based in urban centres.
53. For more on the history of these tribal borderlands, read Knudsen (2009).
54. Gul (2010).

55. Van Dyk (2010).
56. Gul (2010).
57. Van Dyk (2010), Kindle Electronic Edition: Location 2266.
58. Gul (2010), 171.
59. Waldman (2010b); Interview, Kabul, July 2010.
60. Pakistan's security establishment fostered groups primarily to use them in the ongoing conflict with India over Kashmir (Jamal (2010b)).
61. This is a shorthand term to refer to a variety of different (and competing) interests within Pakistan's ruling circles, military hierarchies and intelligence agencies, and should not be taken to imply consensus.
62. Rubin (2010b); see also the testimony of Marvin Weinbaum to the US House Committee on Foreign Affairs, http://foreignaffairs.house.gov/111/wei031110.pdf (accessed 5 October 2010).
63. Chalk (2010).
64. Roggio (2010b); Roggio (2010a).
65. Bergen (2009a); ISAF Joint Command, 'IJC Operational Update,' 6 June 2010. http://www.dvidshub.net/news/50929/ijc-operational-update-june-6 (accessed 19 October 2010); ISAF continues to claim to be killing Taliban commanders associated with al-Qaeda. Suicide bombing is often cited as a tactic closely tied to al-Qaeda; while there is indication that al-Qaeda or individuals associated with al-Qaeda provided the initial expertise in constructing suicide bomb vests, claims about training involvement seem doubtful. Except for some high profile operations, suicide bombings are poorly executed in southern Afghanistan. Furthermore, the majority of suicide bombings are carried out in vehicles.
66. See 'Bin Laden behind Cheney hit,' Daily Telegraph (Australia), 26 April 2007. http://www.dailytelegraph.com.au/news/world/bin-laden-behind-cheney-hit/story-e6frev00-1111113416035 (accessed 1 October 2010).
67. Ibid.
68. Gopal, Mahsud and Fishman (2010b), 11.
69. Filkins (2009).
70. Talk at New America Foundation, 24 June 2010. http://www.newamerica.net/events/2010/captive (accessed 19 October 2010).
71. Farrell (2010).
72. There remain claims, however, of al-Qaeda involvement in the conflict (AFP, (2010c)).
73. Loyd (2010).
74. Whitlock (2010).
75. Ibid.
76. Dressler (2010), 1.
77. Interview, Anand Gopal, Kabul, July 2010.
78. Waldman (2010b), 5–7.

79. Interviews, Kabul and Kandahar, June–July 2010.
80. Interviewee #7, Kandahar, July 2010.
81. Wikileaks data available for download as a spreadsheet from http://image.guard-ian.co.uk/sys-files/Guardian/documents/2010/07/25/Afghanevents1.xls (accessed 5 October 2010).
82. The other reports suggest that single-sourcing was a common occurrence. The Wikileaks documents are generally unanalysed reports from a single source that were passed on to higher-level intelligence, where they would be vetted and synthesised with other sources. Many of these therefore have the quality of rumour and hearsay, though being leaked as 'secret documents' gives then an aura of truth among the general public.
83. Ibid.
84. At least one interviewee claimed that Mullah Mohammad Omar was moving between Pakistan and Afghanistan. Interview, Kabul, July 2010.
85. As of 6 October 2010. Data taken from New America Foundation's Drones Monitoring Project (see http://counterterrorism.newamerica.net/drones (accessed 6 October 2010)).
86. Bergen and Tiedemann (2010).
87. Smith (2010).
88. Rohde (2009). Jere van Dyk has stated, however, that his captors did not fear the drone attacks as much.
89. New America Foundation and Terror Free Tomorrow, Public Opinion in Pakistan's Tribal Regions. (Washington D.C.: New America Foundation, 2010). http://www.newamerica.net/sites/newamerica.net/files/policydocs/FATApoll.pdf (accessed 6 October 2010). As always, considerable scepticism should be brought to bear on this data given the problems with conducting opinion polls in Afghanistan and Pakistan in the midst of a conflict environment.
90. Meyer (2009).
91. Ruttig (2010), 18.
92. Ibid.
93. Part of the problem with the characterisation of the Taliban as 'they' is their fragmented nature, and questions posed to low-ranking fighters or commanders will not necessarily represent the senior political figures within the movement.
94. http://theunjustmedia.com/Afghanistan/Statements/Sep10/Message%20of%20Felicitation%20of%20the%20Esteemed%20Amir-ul-Momineen,%20on%20the%20Eve%20of%20Eid-ul-Fitr.htm (accessed 9 September 2010).
95. Layeha (2010 edition), author copy; interviews, Kandahar and Kabul, 2010.
96. Interviews, Kunduz, Balkh and Baghlan, November 2009.
97. This has been the case with a number of suicide bomb attacks that took place in Kandahar province. While the official national-level Taliban spokesman denied Taliban involvement, local Taliban commanders privately claimed responsibility. Authors' conversations/observations in Kandahar, 2009.

98. Night letter, September 2010, Kandahar.
99. Interviews and conversations, Kandahar, Kabul, Khost, Kunduz, Mazar-i Sharif, 2006–2010.
100. Authors' observation, Kandahar, 2007–10; Boone (2009); http://news.bbc.co.uk/1/hi/world/south_asia/8221233.stm (accessed 16 March 2011).
101. For example, 'the historic hatred of foreigners exhibited by rural Pashtuns' as suggested by Mark Urban in Urban (2008).
102. Interviews, Kandahar, 2009–10; Interviews with individuals who travelled/worked in Afghanistan in the mid-1960s, email, October 2010; Gopal (2010b), 3; Rohde (2010), chapter 1; conversation, individual who travelled in Afghanistan during the late 1960s, New York, February 2011.
103. McGregor (2009).
104. Interviews, Kandahar, 2005–10.
105. Almost all foreign actions are reduced to the characterisation of 'the United States.'
106. Interviews and conversations, Kandahar, 2007–10.
107. Ibid.
108. Conversations and interviews, Kandahar, 2008–2010.
109. See Peters (2010) for related details.
110. See chapters 2 and 3.
111. Mullah Mohammad Omar, 'Message Of Felicitation Of The Esteemed Amir-Ul-Momineen Mullah Mohammad Omar Mujahid, On The Eve Of Eid-Ul-Fitr,' theunjustmedia.com, 8 September 2010. http://theunjustmedia.com/Afghanistan/Statements/Sep10/Message%20of%20Felicitation%20of%20the%20Esteemed%20Amir-ul-Momineen,%20on%20the%20Eve%20of%20Eid-ul-Fitr.htm (accessed 5 October 2010).
112. Interviews, Kabul and Kandahar, 2008–10.
113. Ibid.
114. Associated Press (2010).
115. It begins as follows: 'Jihad in the path of Almighty God is a such a great worship [ebadat] and a great obligation which, in fulfilling it will bring dignity and raise up God's testament of faith [qaliamah]. Jihad for Muslim's success and prosperity is such a significant instrument that with its blessings, the shamla [pride, literally the tip of the turban which points upwards] of the Islamic umma [the global community of believers] can rise. Nations who have made jihad have achieved the blessings of living in independence and freedom. On the contrary, nations who sheath their swords in their scabbards and quit the path of jihad have not achieved any benefits other than to put the chains of slavery and captivity on their own necks' (2010 version, authors' copy).
116. Note that there are surprisingly few categorical pronouncements of death sentences in the rule book. Many of the more serious 'crimes' are simply referred up the chain of command for action.

117. ISAF translation, manuscript copy.
118. Barnes (2010a).
119. Moreau and Yousufzai (2010).
120. Jackson (2011); http://aan-afghanistan.com/index.asp?id=1322 (accessed 17 March 2011).
121. Authors' observation, Kandahar, 2009–10. This applies to the group of people who have the option to leave, many of whom had returned after the Taliban government's fall.
122. Giustozzi (2010), 9–10.
123. Email conversation, Anand Gopal, 4 October 2010.
124. Giustozzi and Reuter (2010).
125. Ibid., 4.
126. Ibid., 2; Azarbaijani-Moghaddam (2009), 257.
127. Giustozzi and Reuter (2010), 2.
128. Ibid., 1 and 5–6.
129. One example of several given in Baghlan was that, 'during the 2009 elections, the police were ordered to surrender to the Taliban in all instances, even when outnumbering them' (ibid., 6). The exact reasons for government reticence towards the insurgency remain, however, unknown, but the incidents themselves are suspect.
130. Interviews, northern Afghanistan, October 2009.
131. Gebauer (2011).
132. Interview, Kandahar, February 2011.
133. UPI (2010).
134. Flintoff (2010).
135. Hazem (2010).
136. The reasoning for the strategy is that a government which provides services and projects will be supported by the population. The correlation of services and development to local support, however, is doubtful.
137. Ackerman (2011).
138. MacKenzie (2010); Chandrasekeran (2011).
139. Carlstrom (2010). ('The security situation in the south remains grave: Insurgent attacks in Kandahar and Helmand have increased by 40 per cent and 219 per cent, respectively.'); Pitman (2010).
140. Grant (2010).
141. McChrystal (2009).
142. See U.S. Army/Marine Corps Counterinsurgency Field Manual, FM 3–24. http://www.fas.org/irp/doddir/army/fm3-24fd.pdf (accessed 19 October 2010). A cable published by Wikileaks has seemed to underscore this idea: 'The US intelligence community has long hoped that a rising tide of chaos and violence, caused by increased Nato operations, would help the military campaign.

According to a US state department cable released by Wikileaks, in December 2008 a top US spy briefed Nato ambassadors that the alliance should put intense pressure on the Taliban "in order to bring out their more violent and radical tendencies. This will alienate the population and give us an opportunity to separate the Taliban from the population," the cable concluded.' (Boone (2011)).

143. Capaccio and O'Leary (2010).
144. '"It's no longer about whack-a-mole," another senior Isaf officer said in reference to killing Taliban, only for others to appear elsewhere. "We're whacking all the moles all the time in all the places."' (Boone (2010)).
145. Shanker and Rubin (2010).
146. Partlow (2010b).
147. 'In the past 3 months, ISAF conducted 3279 special operations resulting in 293 insurgent leaders killed/captured and 2169 insurgents captured.' (10 October. http://twitter.com/#!/USFOR_A/statuses/26941509487 (accessed 10 October 2010)).
148. These figures were provided to a Frontline PBS documentary film crew researching the subject. http://afpak.foreignpolicy.com/posts/2011/05/10/kill_capture_a_live_chat_with_pbs_frontline (accessed 13 June 2011).
149. Filkins (2010).
150. Data presented by Sami Kovanen, Incidium Consulting.
151. See Clark (2011a) for more details of one such incident.
152. Dozier (2010).
153. Interview, Kabul, July 2010, and London, November 2010.
154. Coughlin (2010).
155. Interviews, Kandahar, 2008–2010.
156. Authors' observation and interviews, Kabul and Kandahar, 2008–10.
157. For the significant problems with intelligence gathered in Afghanistan, see Flynn, Pottinger and Batchelor (2010).
158. Authors' observation, Kandahar, 2009–10.
159. See, for example, Peters (2010), 98.
160. Authors' observation and interviews, Kabul and Kandahar, 2009–10.
161. For example, Richter (2010).
162. 'Taliban Allegedly Threatens Tribal Elders In Southern Afghanistan,' *Radio Free Europe/Radio Liberty*, 30 July 2010. http://www.rferl.org/content/Taliban_Allegedly_Threatens_Tribal_Elders_In_Southern_Afghanistan/2114127.html (accessed 19 October 2010).
163. Interviews, Kandahar, July 2010.
164. Yousufzai and Moreau (2010a).
165. This has mostly taken place in private, or at occasional moments when a commander or political figure has let their guard down with a journalist.
166. Yousufzai and Moreau (2010b).

167. Agencies, 'Mullah Omar spotted in Pakistan: Karzai,' *The Times of India*, 29 November 2003. http://timesofindia.indiatimes.com/world/Mullah-Omar-spotted-in-Pakistan-Karzai/articleshow/330758.cms (accessed 5 October 2010).

168. This is speculative, but it is based on interviews with a variety of actors based in Pakistan, Afghanistan and the United States.

169. This letter was, however, never authenticated and the circumstances surrounding it are suspect. http://www.longwarjournal.org/archives/2010/07/mullah_omar_orders_t.php (accessed 19 October 2010).

170. 'Taleban sack military commander,' *BBC News*, 29 December 2007. http://news.bbc.co.uk/2/hi/7164277.stm (accessed 5 October 2010).

171. See Smith (2009), 203.

172. See, for instance, the remarks made by a commander in Helmand (MacKenzie (2010), 12).

173. For example, 'About New Militias,' 1 February 2009. http://theunjustmedia.com/Afghanistan/Statements/Feb09/About%20new%20militias.htm (accessed 19 October 2010).

174. Interviews, Kandahar, 2009–10.

175. Taken from 'The Reintegration Approval Form' that was being distributed in Helmand province in summer 2010 (in English and Pashtu versions), authors' copy.

176. See U.S. Army/Marine Corps Counterinsurgency Field Manual, FM 3–24. http://www.fas.org/irp/doddir/army/fm3–24fd.pdf (accessed 19 October 2010); Islamic Emirate of Afghanistan, 'Can we call this reconciliation?' *TheUnjustMedia.com* (Online), 6 February 2010. http://theunjustmedia.com/Afghanistan/Statements/Feb10/Can%20We%20Call%20This%20Reconciliation.htm (accessed 22 October 2010). Also, Interviews, Kabul and Kandahar, June–July 2010.

177. Waldman (2010a); Semple (2009).

178. 'Former Taliban group commander assassinated at home by militants,' *Trend* (Online), 29 July 2010. http://en.trend.az/regions/world/afghanistan/1727810.html (accessed 19 October 2010).

179. Nordland (2010a).

180. Barnes (2010b).

181. Ruttig (2009b).

182. Interview, London, August 2009; Borger and Walsh (2010).

183. Interviews, Kabul, June and July 2010; Gopal, Mahsud and Fishman (2010b).

184. http://theunjustmedia.com/Islamic%20Perspectives/June10/An%20English%20Translation%20of%20the%20Questionnaire%20of%20the%20Members%20of%20Ansar%20al-Mujahideen%20Arabic%20Forum%20with%20the%20Commander,%20Sheikh%20Sirajudeen%20Haqqani.htm (accessed 22 October 2010).

185. Anand Gopal interview with Seraj Haqqani, March 2010.

11. CONCLUSION

1. Interview in United States on ABC's 'This Week' (Schifrin (2010)).
2. Interview on National Public Radio, quoted in Thier (2010).
3. Interview, Kabul, July 2010.
4. The Taliban consider the 1980s *jihad* as a key part of their identity and narrative. Their official website during the 1990s included a long historical reminiscence entitled 'A Reminding Glimpse of the Islamic Jihad.' (http://web.archive.org/web/19981206133219/www.taleban.com/jihad.htm (accessed 16 December 2010)).
5. 'Afghan Arab' was the name by which the foreign jihadis in Afghanistan came to be known during and after the 1980s *jihad* against the Soviet Union.
6. These were the *Harakat-i Inqilab-i Islami*, led by Mawlawi Muhammad Nabi Muhammadi and the *Hizb-e Islami* faction led by Mawlawi Yunus Khalis. Today's Haqqani Network in Waziristan and south eastern Afghanistan is led by former fighters of Khalis' party.
7. See UNAMA Press Release (http://unama.unmissions.org/Default.aspx?tabid=1760&ctl=Details&mid=2002&ItemID=8252 (accessed 12 September 2010)) and Pannier (2010). There are a number of individuals affiliated with *Hizb-e Islami* currently holding positions in the government or parliament.
8. The authors do not mean to imply that any of the Taliban interviewed for this book have fundamentally changed their stance on issues regarding *shari'a* law and human rights, or women's rights. Rather, there appears to be a growing understanding and awareness among political Taliban that the handling of these issues have a significant impact on foreign relations and are important to the international community with regards to Afghanistan.
9. Islamic Emirate of Afghanistan, 'Can we call this reconciliation?' 6 February 2010. http://theunjustmedia.com/Afghanistan/Statements/Feb10/Can%20We%20Call%20This%20Reconciliation.htm (accessed 12 July 2010).
10. http://www.uruknet.info/?p=60059 (accessed 21 October 2010).
11. http://theunjustmedia.com/Afghanistan/Statements/Ma11/West%20Admits,%20Afghanistan%20has%20no%20Military%20Solution.htm (accessed 20 March 2011).
12. Human Rights Watch (2010).
13. Interviews and conversations in Kandahar, Helmand, Kabul, Khost, Baghlan, Kunduz, Ghazni, Paktya, Nangarhar, Wardak, Mazar-e Sharif, Herat, Badghis, Faryab and Badakhshan, 2005–10.
14. Giustozzi and Reuter (2010); interview, Kandahar, February 2011.
15. Haleem and Jianhua (2011).
16. Their short-term priorities are to some extent determined by international statements of intent and goals.

17. Bergen (2010); Gen. David Petraeus testified there were 'under 100' in March 2011 (Shanker (2011)).
18. Al-Qaeda's leadership also senses that any deal with the Taliban would threaten their sanctuary. For this reason they are significant possible spoilers to any negotiating process, possibly with assassinations.
19. There is, of course, always the possibility of using Pakistan as a partner for a negotiated settlement, a party with real leverage over regional insurgent groups, as recently suggested by one prominent expert. See Dorronsoro (2010).
20. AP/MSNBC, 'Saudi Arabia wants Taliban to expel bin Laden,' 2 February 2010. http://www.msnbc.msn.com/id/35196297/ (accessed 1 September 2010).
21. The failure to provide assurances and guarantees that insurgency members will not be detained (and that government members will not be 'judged' and killed) has always been a major barrier to starting discussions between different parties. This is a reflection of the lack of trust on all sides.
22. The tendency to play out internal U.S. conflicts and political one-upmanship through the prism of the Afghan conflict has also been extremely destructive, and should be avoided in the future.
23. There may have to be an agreement that public statements are not necessarily connected to ongoing discreet discussions, since domestic considerations may dictate what is said by all parties in the short-term.
24. Even Mawlana Fazlur Rahman has stated that, in the context of a peace settlement, 'Al Qaeda will have to fall in line or leave the region.' (MacDonald (2010)).
25. Again, this is not to say that they don't see it as an important issue to be settled, but it is—relatively speaking—seen as one on which there is some consensus within the political cadre of the movement as to the lessons of 11 September and it is less difficult for them to agree to some level of distancing themselves from internationalist jihadism.
26. Dressler (2010).
27. Landler and Shanker (2010).
28. See Van Dyk (2010) and Rohde (2009).
29. Solomon (2007); interview, Anand Gopal, Washington D.C., June 2010.
30. '...a war of necessity, as Cameron told the troops at Camp Bastion in July [2010].' 'We are paying a high price for keeping our country safe, for making our world a safer place.' http://thinkstrat.wordpress.com/2011/01/05/afghanistan-the-conservatives-and-the-national-interest/ (accessed 31 May 2011).
31. The other exception is Wali Khan Amin Shah.
32. Interviews, Kabul, Kandahar and Khost, 2006–10; of course, the 1996–2001 period also saw the Taliban's leadership undergo an analogous learning process with regard to international relations.
33. See, for instance, a poll released by CNN/Opinion Research Corp. in September 2009 showing that only 39% of Americans were in favour and 58% against the

war in Afghanistan. http://edition.cnn.com/2009/POLITICS/09/15/afghan.war.poll/ (accessed 12 September 2010).

34. Ashley Tellis stated India's goals in Afghanistan as follows: '1) prevent return of the Taliban in Afghanistan; 2) a reasonably independent Afghan state; 3) restore long-standing reach to Pashtun communities; 4) strengthen economic integration between India and Afghanistan.' (June 2010).

35. Rather, it might be more useful to see Afghanistan as the issue that could first be addressed, using progress on this external problem to build confidence which could then be focused on Kashmir. Thanks to Stephen Cohen for this idea. For an alternative position, read Coll (2010).

36. In a workshop held in Washington in the summer of 2010, over 90% of the participants (experts, practitioners, researchers and journalists concerned with Afghanistan) agreed that Afghanistan was heading towards civil war, or a situation comparable to the early 1990s.

37. See, for example, the al-Jazeera interview and report from Nuristan in June 2010. http://english.aljazeera.net/news/asia/2010/06/20106682427762407.html (accessed 13 September 2010).

38. Chick (2010).

39. Chivers, Rubin and Morgan (2011); http://theunjustmedia.com/Afghanistan/Statements/Ma11/America%20salutes%20Kunar,%20the%20proud%20land%20of%20our%20Mujahid%20forefathers!!.htm (accessed 21 March 2011).

40. AFP (2010b).

41. The possibility that he dies or is killed does exist, but it should not be seen as a goal nor can it be planned for. Moreover, an active targeting of the Taliban leader as part of the military campaign (especially if it results in his death) could have serious negative consequences for any negotiations.

42. Interviews, Kandahar and Kabul, winter 2009–10.

43. International Crisis Group (2010b).

44. International Crisis Group (2010a).

45. See, for example the statement on 2 September 2010, entitled, 'Karzai in Vortex of Corruptions [sic].' http://theunjustmedia.com/Afghanistan/Statements/Sep10/the%20Islamic%20Emirate%20of%20Afghanistan%20Karzai%20in%20vortex%20of%20corruptions.htm (accessed 13 September 2010).

46. There was an initial comment made by Zabiullah Mujahed on 2 May: 'We have not received any word from our leadership on Osama's death. I can't confirm that he is dead or alive. Because of some security problems, the Taliban has not had much contact with Osama bin Laden for the past 10 years.' (http://www.time.com/time/world/article/0,8599,2069101,00.html (accessed 9 June 2011)).

47. http://www.alexstrick.com/2011/05/the-afghan-taliban-react-to-bin-ladens-death/ (accessed 13 June 2011).

48. http://shahamat-english.com/index.php?option=com_content&view=article&id=7078:statement-of-the-leadership-council-of-the-islamic-emirate-of-afghan-

istan-regarding-the-martyrdom&catid=4:statements&Itemid=4 (accessed 13 June 2011).

49. http://shahamat-english.com/index.php?option=com_content&view=article&id=7232:the-martyrdom-of-sheikh-osama-will-not-benefit-america&catid=2:comments&Itemid=3 (accessed 13 June 2011).

50. Gilles Kepel and Jean-Pierre Milelli, eds. (2008), Al Qaeda in its own words. (Cambridge: Belknap Press of Harvard University Press), part 2.

51. Sami Yousafzai (2011), 'Exclusive: Taliban leader details final visit with bin Laden,' The Daily Beast (Online), 13 May. http://news.yahoo.com/s/dailybeast/20110513/ts_dailybeast/14074_talibancommanderosamabinladenwasnotisolated (accessed 13 June 2011).

52. http://www.treas.gov/press/releases/tg782.htm (accessed 12 September 2010).

53. Interviews, Kabul and Kandahar, July and August 2010.

54. Interviews, Kandahar, July and August 2010.

55. See Waldman (2010a) for more.

56. Saudi policy is—from the outside—not entirely coherent and beyond its enmity with al-Qaeda it is difficult to tease out specific details of their engagement with Afghanistan. See Christopher Boucek's essay in Tellis and Mukharji (2010) for more.

57. See, for instance, Lord Robertson at the Atlantic Council stating that 'if the Taliban and their allies can defeat the most successful defense alliance in history, why should they stop at Afghanistan? They won't.' (http://www.acus.org/new_atlanticist/lord-robertson-if-we-lose-afghanistan-they-will-be-back-over-here (accessed 13 September 2010)); and David Cameron told MPs in June 2010 that the Afghan war had made the United Kingdom safer (http://www.dailymail.co.uk/news/article-1286437/The-Afghanistan-war-safer-says-David-Cameron.html (accessed 13 September 2010).

DEFINITIONS

1. Oxford Dictionary of Islam (2006), 88.

2. Mandaville defines Islam as: 'a particular tradition of discourse and practice that is variously defined across multiple social and historical settings. There is no connotation of normativity implied in our usage, for example, of the term "Islamic."' (Mandaville (2007), 5.)

3. This distinction, originally derived from a *hadith* report found in the anthology of al-Nasa'i, is frequently disputed; dissenters—from Mohammad Abdul Salam Faraj to Abdullah Azzam—claim the *hadith* is a forgery.

4. See Hegghammer (2009) for a more intensive discussion of the use of the term 'jihadi.'

5. Mandaville's definition is: 'anyone who identifies him or herself, at least in part, with Islam—regardless of how the latter may be understood.' (Mandaville (2008), 5).
6. Oxford Dictionary of Islam (2006), 275.
7. Oxford Dictionary of Islam (2006), 288.
8. Oxford Dictionary of Islam (2006), 333.

DEFINITIONS

'**Alim**: Singular version of *Ulemaa'*. Literally 'one who has knowledge'; it refers to a religious scholar (primarily used for the Sunni clergy) who has been educated in the religious 'sciences' (the *Qur'an*, the *Sunna* and the *Hadith*s etc). See *Hadith*, *Qur'an*, *Sunna* and *Ulemaa'*.

Ahl-e Hadith: Literally translates as 'People of the traditions of the Prophet,' and refers to a branch of Salafi Muslims who seek to emulate the traditions practiced by the Prophet (rather than the various actions referred to as accretions that had been added since). The *Ahl-e Hadith* tradition is antithetical, for instance, to the ideas and practice of Sufism.

Al-Qaeda: An Arabic-language term literally translated as 'base' or 'foundation,' *al-Qaeda* was also a group founded in August 1988 by a group of Islamists closely associated with Osama bin Laden. The term had been used during the 1980s in jihadi discourse (notably by Abdullah Azzam), but the group founded in 1988 was conceived as a different entity.

Al-Shu'aybi: This is a loose reference to the so-called 'al-Shu'aybi' school of religious practice and thought that emulated the teachings of Hamoud al-'Uqlaa' al-Shu'aybi, a Saudi Salafi cleric noted for issuing several *fatwas* in support of the Afghan Taliban.

Amir: Literally translated as 'prince' or 'commander,' the word amir has a specific meaning in the context of the Afghan conflict post-1979. The *mujahedeen* in southern Afghanistan, and indeed throughout most of the country, were organised into fronts and *otaq*s (literally, 'room') that had specific commanders associated with them, who would then be tied to a specific *amir* or chief, who would usually be fundraising across the border. The *amir*, in turn, would be affiliated with one of the seven *mujahedeen* parties officially sanctioned by the ISI, and therefore could gain access to funds, weapons and training.

Amir ul-Mu'mineen: An Arabic-language phrase literally translated as 'Commander/Prince of the Faithful,' first applied to the second of the *rashidun* caliphs who succeeded the Prophet Mohammad, Omar ibn al-Khattab, and used by many who followed him. It fell out of use in the mid-thirteenth century but was invoked in 1996 by Mullah Mohammad Omar.

Andiwaal: Literally translated as 'friend,' this term can also refer to groups (usually four or larger) that meet together regularly (e.g. once every week on a Thursday evening is common in the case of Kandahar).

Barelvi: Also known as *Ahl al-Sunna wal-Jama'a* ('People of the Sunna and the Community'), Barelvi Muslims are named after a madrassa founded in 1880 in the town of Bareilly. The Barelvi tradition is broadly rural-based and commonly found in Indian and Pakistani Muslims, and as such includes strong provision for the role of saints in religious life.

Bayat: An Arabic-language term used to refer to an oath or pledge of loyalty made to one's leader (in whatever context).

Bid'a: An Arabic-language term literally translated as 'innovation,' this refers to a change in traditional or accepted religious practice. This can be on a small issue or a larger doctrinal debate. *Bid'a* is often cited by Salafi writers and followers who see many widely-accepted traditions or activities as being un-Islamic accretions or 'innovation.'

CIA: Acronym for the US 'Central Intelligence Agency' (formed in 1947).

Da'wa: An Arabic-language term literally translated as 'invitation,' this refers to the offering of an invitation to non-Muslims (or non-practicing Muslims) to convert or to resume practice of the faith.

Dastarbandi: Literally 'turban-tying.' Refers to ceremonies held at madrassas in which religious scholars or *ulema* tie turbans around the heads of graduate students. Common in Pakistan and Afghanistan.

Deobandi: Deobandi refers to a small religious seminary in India (established in 1867) that has had a profound impact on the religious and ideological education/upbringing of generations of Muslims in south Asia. It is frequently cited as one of the major external influences on the Taliban's world view (since many were educated in Deobandi madrassas) but the precise extent of this has yet to be delineated.

DEFINITIONS

Fard 'Ayn: An Arabic-language phrase that literally translates as 'individual obligation.' As such, it is distinguished from *fard kifaya* ('collective obligation') in the context of specific activities, for instance in the case of jihad; both terms carry *shari'a* legal connotations.

Fatwa: Legally authoritative opinion issued by Islamic religious scholars. This term is best known from the *fatwa* issued by Ayatollah Khomeini in Iran in 1989 calling for the execution of author Salman Rushdie following the publication of his book, *The Satanic Verses*.

Fiqh: See *shari'a*.

Fitna: An Arabic-language term that literally translates as 'sedition' or 'temptation,' but with the various consequences also implied (e.g. disorder/chaos). It is often used as the antonym to a state of peace. As such, it takes on an Islamic context with the suggestion that dissent or conflict (e.g. within the *umma*) is un-Islamic.

Fundamentalism: 'Fundamentalism' is historically rooted in the Protestant religious tradition, but for this book the term refers to a body of thought that advocates returning to the 'fundamentals' of Islam (however these are defined) without any claimed accretions; the precise definition of these accretions varies, from claims that Sufism is a corruption of Islam, to televisions or toothbrushes as inconsequent developments. The idea of 'the text' is very important to fundamentalism, and it accordingly figures prominently in Esposito's definition: 'defines belief in an absolutist and literalist manner.[...] involves an effort to purify or reform adherents' beliefs and practices in accord with self-defined fundamentals of faith, and a self-conscious effort to avoid compromise, adaptation, or critical reinterpretation of basic texts and sources of belief.'[1] 'Fundamentalist' is the adjectival form of fundamentalism.

GID: Acronym referring to the 'General Intelligence Directorate', Saudi Arabia's intelligence services.

Hadith: A report of the words and actions of the Prophet Mohammad as determined and authenticated by a chain of evidence and proof (known as *asnad*). It is an important part of the oral tradition of Islam, and these reports survive in written form in collections codified by religious scholars.

Hajji: A title technically given only to those who have been on the *Hajj*, the Islamic pilgrimage to Mecca which is one of the five pillars of the Muslim faith, but also is a title which in Afghanistan (and throughout the Muslim world) is sometimes used merely as a term of respect for the middle-aged and elderly.

Hanafi: One of the four main Islamic schools of legal thought, it is predominant in Afghanistan (and also is the largest in terms of adherents globally). Named after the legal scholar Abu Hanifa (d. 767), it advocates a more liberal approach to the Islamic law or *shari'a*. See *shari'a*.

Hanbali: One of the four main Islamic schools of legal thought or *fiqh*. Named after the legal scholar Ahmad ibn Hanbal (d. 855), the so-called *Sheikh ul-Islam*, the Hanbali school is considered more conservative than other schools.

ISI: 'Inter-Services Intelligence' is the main Pakistani military intelligence wing. Especially prominent in the funding and supplying of weapons to the Afghan *mujahedeen*, ISI has become synonymous with the strong involvement of Pakistan's military in political affairs.

Intifada: *Intifada* is an Arabic-language term literally translated as 'shaking off.' It is closely associated with the Palestinian conflict, for example, the 'first *intifada*' of 1987–1993.

Islam: Islam refers to a religion: an ethical and philosophical system of belief coupled with a set of prescribed rituals. It is, by implication, as useful or ethically 'good' a system as it is applied (i.e. by Muslims). Islam is found in multiple and varied forms around the world (a result of local cultural accretion and a natural evolving process), but when using the term 'Islam' this book refers to the general meaning of the basic set of traditions common to all the different global variations.

Islamic: Islamic (the adjectival form of the noun 'Islam') is a term used to refer back to the set of principles and customs that make up 'Islam' and that are used to define those who call themselves 'Muslim.' As Mandaville notes,[2] there is no normativity implied in our use of the term.

Islamism: The term 'Islamism' refers to an attempt to use Islam as the basis for a totalising system to regulate all facets of life (often impinging on politics, but not always). An 'Islamist' is used for someone (or a group, when the word is used adjectivally) who seeks to implement such a system.

Islamist: See Islamism.

Ja'afari: A major *shi'i* school of legal thought or *fiqh*. It is named after the legal scholar Ja'afar al-Sadiq (702–765) and is followed by most *shi'i* Muslims around the world. It places a strong emphasis on the concept of *ijtihad* (the use of reason to interpret the traditions and laws).

Jahiliyya: An Arabic-language term literally translated as a state of 'ignorance,' often used in the context of 'religious ignorance' (such as the period prior to the birth of the Prophet Muhammad).

Jihad: The Arabic-language term *jihad* is derived from an Arabic root meaning 'to struggle,' 'to exert oneself,' or 'to strive.' As such, the word can mean different things depending on the context: sometimes a struggle against evil inclinations (the so-called 'greater *jihad*'),[3] or at other times a reference to legally-sanctioned (by the Islamic legal code) war. The term has a rich history of meanings (both theoretical and practical), some of which is explored in this book.

Jihadi: Jihadi is often used to refer simply to 'someone who does *jihad*,' but for the purposes of this book, the term jihadi refers to a person (or a strand of thought) taking up arms for what he says is *jihad*. Again, here the definition is concerned not so much with the objective reality but rather with the self-perception of the person.[4]

Jirga: *Jirga* is a Pashtu-language term meaning 'council' or 'consultative gathering.' It is to be distinguished from the word *shura*, although the two are sometimes used indistinguishably in a loose sense.

Kafir: Refers to a person believed to be in a state of *kufr* or 'unbelief.' See *kafir* and *kuffar*.

KhAD: An abbreviation of *Khedamat-e Ittla'aat-e Dawlati*, or 'State Security Service.' President Najibullah changed its name to WAD, but it is still commonly used to refer to the internal state security apparatus.

Khan: A tribal chief and/or head of a community. It is an honorific title often also used to describe those who own large portions of land. The title is usually placed after the name of a person. See *malik*.

Kuffar: Plural form of *kafir*. See kafir and kufr.

Kufr: The verbal noun form of this word literally translates from the Arabic to mean 'unbelief.' In Afghanistan, the communist regime was frequently spoken of as embodying *kufr*. The openly anti-religious policies of the PDPA were swiftly written off as coming from a state of *kufr*.

Madrassa: Religious school common in southern Afghanistan and Pakistan as the first choice for education (especially for the rural poor). Schools are by and large for boys only, although girls are educated in some, and the syllabus mainly constitutes a full outline of the religious sciences, often including the expectation that graduates will learn various holy books by heart (notably, the *Qur'an* itself).

Malik: Localised versions of *khan*s. The title is used to denote the local strongman on the district or sub-district level, and this often also means that that

DEFINITIONS

person is somehow employed by the government to give some outreach for micro-management of particular issues. See khan.

Mawlawi: A title used by graduates of madrassas who have received further religious education as well. It is the equivalent of postgraduate study for scholars of Islam. A *mawlawi* is a member of the *Ulema'*, the Islamic clergy.

Mehdi: A religious figure commonly portrayed in messianic and eschatological tones. For *shi'i* Muslims, the *Imam-e Mehdi* is identified with the 'twelfth Imam,' who is believed to have gone into a state of hiding or occultation (*ghayba*) in the 9th Century. The mehdi, therefore, is alive right now, and will emerge toward the end-times to rid the world of oppression and injustice. He is not mentioned in the *Qur'an*.

Mujahed: The active participle *mujahed* (plural *mujahedeen*) is a term used to refer to someone who is or was engaged in *jihad* (this almost always implies combat). It is used both as a noun ('a *mujahed* was killed') and adjectivally ('*haghe yaw mujahed saray wu*' in Pashtu; 'he was a *mujahed*-type man'). The plural form is generally reserved for reference to those Afghans who fought in the 1980s against their government and the Soviet soldiers inside Afghanistan. This usage is inherited and common among scholars. See *mujahedeen* and *jihad*.

Mujahedeen: The plural version of *mujahed*, which literally translates from the Arabic as 'one who engages in *jihad*' or 'one who struggles.' Often translated as 'holy warrior,' the term does not necessarily have a connection with the practice of war, but rather can be used to refer to spiritual inner struggle (to be a better person and so on). See *mujahed* and *jihad*.

Mullah: Religious functionary or cleric extremely prevalent outside the cities in Afghanistan. They will usually be the single religious authority (having attended a madrassa during childhood, or maybe because they can read some Arabic and thus the language of the *Qur'an*) in a particular village. As such their authority is usually limited to religious matters.

Murid: See *Pir*.

Muslim: The term 'Muslim' refers to whoever uses the word for him/herself[5] regardless of what this means in practice. This inevitably results in the inclusion of many different shapes and types of Muslims. What counts is self-perception rather than outside perception (which might seek, for example, to argue that someone isn't actually a real Muslim).

NGO: Acronym for 'Non-governmental organisation.'

Otaq: See *amir*.

432

Pir: *Pir* refers to a religious figure in a Sufi context. Between 945–1273, a disciple-master theme developed in Sufism, where Sufi masters (or *Pirs*) would engage so-called *murids* and instruct them in 'the way.' By the 11th century, a new pattern of mass piety had developed, with a pantheon of the old Sufi 'classic' heroes but at the same time a glut of new figures. This was followed by the institutionalisation of the *pir-murid* relationship in the form of Sufi *tariqaat* and a new focus on the practice of *dhikr*. A *tariqa* was a Sufi order—much as Christian brotherhoods were often formed into monastic 'orders'—which offered a system of spiritual development as well as a place to stay while undergoing his/her instruction.

Purda: *Purda* refers to the separation between male and female sexes, although it can also be used literally to mean 'curtain' or 'veil.'

Qadiriyya: Qadiriyya are the followers of the Qadiri tradition of Sufism. Mysticism initially grew out of the Sunni orthodoxy, though, with figures like Ghazali (d.1111) in Khurasan and Baghdad displaying their mastery of the shari'a as well as a mystical belief system. Between 945–1273, a disciple-master theme developed in Sufism, where Sufi masters (or *Pirs*) would engage so-called *murids* and instruct them in 'the way.' Sufi masters became objects of massive popular respect as a result of their charismatic preaching and moral purity. This in turn fuelled the growth of hagiographic accounts of the Sufi masters. In Baghdad, Sheikh 'Abd al-Qadir Gailani (1077–1166) was one such preacher whose popularity relies largely on these hagiographic biographies, even though he developed a whole system of teaching and a mystical philosophy.

Qibla: *Qibla* is an Arabic-language term that refers to the direction in which Muslims around the world pray (i.e. towards the *ka'aba* in Mecca (Saudi Arabia)). The *qibla* was originally oriented towards Jerusalem but this changed to the *ka'aba* in the year 623.

Qur'an: The holy *Qur'an* is the religious book of Muslims around the world, literally translated as 'recitation' since Muslims believe it is the result of the direct revelation of God to the Prophet Muhammad starting in 610.

Salafi: A 'Salafi' is someone who follows the principles of Salafism; 'Salafi' can also be used adjectivally to refer to actions which conform to the principles of Salafism (and are intended to do so). Note that there is a certain interchangeability between the terms Salafi and wahhabi: certain wahhabis reject the term because it suggests they are followers of Mohammad ibn Abdul Wahab himself rather than God; they prefer the term salafi. See Salafism.

Salafism: This book follows Esposito's definition of 'Salafism' as a 'name (derived from *salaf*, 'pious ancestors') given to a reform movement led by Jamal al-Din al-Afghani and Muhammad Abduh at the turn of the twentieth century. Emphasised restoration of Islamic doctrines to pure form, adherence to the *qur'an* and *sunna*, rejection of the authority of later interpretations, and maintenance of the unity of umma. Prime objectives were to rid the Muslim umma of the centuries-long mentality of *taqlid* (which they held to be unquestioning imitation of precedent) and stagnation and to reform the moral, cultural, and political conditions of Muslims. Essentially intellectual and modernist in nature. [...] In the late twentieth century, the term came to refer to traditionalist reformers.'[6]

Salafist: 'Salafist' is the anglicised noun/adjectival form of 'Salafi' and may be used interchangeably. See Salafi and Salafism.

Sayyed: Sayyeds are descendants of the Prophet Muhammad who live in Afghanistan. They are seen as a tribe unto their own by Pashtuns, but a better word to describe this status is *qawm*. In Afghanistan, the word Sayyed is sometimes also used for healers and holy men in general. Sayyeds are highly respected by the rural population.

Shari'a: For *shari'a* this book follows Esposito's definition as 'ideal Islamic law.'[7] There is a large body of thought which asks people to distinguish between *shari'a* and *fiqh* (human efforts to codify 'Islamic' law in the absence of a specific injunction in the *Qur'an* or the sunna), arguing that the former is 'ideal' and the latter is tainted and flawed. For this book, the term *shari'a* is generally used to refer not only to the prescriptions and proscriptions themselves, but also the system surrounding it—the scholars and clerics whose role it is to interpret the law, as well as the *hadith* and *sunna* repository. There are five prominent schools of Islamic law: Hanafi, Hanbali, Maliki, Shafii and Ja'fari.

Shi'i: Distinguished from the sunnis, the *shi'i* are the so-called 'partisans of Ali' (coming from the Arabic phrase *shi'at 'Ali*). Shi'i Muslims identify the fourth of the *rashidun* caliphs, Ali, as the head of a line of leadership that they consider legitimate over the sunni clerics that followed.

Shura: *Shura* is an Arabic-language term meaning 'consultation' used extensively in the Afghan context to mean 'council' or 'consultative gathering.' It is to be distinguished from the word *jirga*, although the two are sometimes used indistinguishably in a loose sense.

Sufism: The so-called 'mystical' side of Islam, Sufism focuses on the vertical relationship between the believer and God, seeking to personalise and individualise that connection through prayer, training and discipline. This basic principle is common among rural Muslims in Afghanistan, and its importance is attested to by the prevalence of *ziarat*s or shrines built over the graves of alleged 'holy men and women.' In the absence of real medicine or doctors, many villagers place their faith in a culture of miracles and signs instead.

Sunna: The established custom or precedent established and based on the example of the Prophet Muhammad. It offers a separate set of principles of conduct and traditions which were recorded by the Prophet's companions. These customs complement the divinely revealed message of the *Qur'an*. A whole field of jurisprudence has grown up alongside the study of the *Sunna*. The *Sunna* is recorded in the *ahadith* (pl. of *hadith*). The Sunna represents the prophetic 'norm.' See *hadith*.

Sunni: This term refers to someone who follows the *sunna*. It is used to distinguish them from *shi'i* Muslims. See *sunna* and *shi'i*.

Tablighi: A member of the *Tablighi Jamaat*, an Indian reform movement founded in 1927 that emphasises religious elements of Islam over the political, and which advocates the mission of *da'wa* or conversion.

Takfir: *Takfir* is an Arabic-language term and verbal noun that refers to the process by which someone is declared a *kafir*. See *kafir* and *kufr*.

Talib: Singular version of *Taliban*. See *Taliban*.

Taliban: Dari/Pashtu plural form of *Talib*. Used to refer to religious students, mainly those who are graduates of madrassas. The term gained notoriety in the mid-1990s because of the movement that took the word as its name on account of its large number of madrassa student supporters. See *madrassa* and *Talib*.

Taqlid: *Taqlid* is an Arabic-language term referring to the imitation of religious traditions. For example, the traditions of one particular religious scholar or legal school may be followed since their religious authority is deemed sound.

Tasawwuf: See Sufism.

Tawhid: *Tawhid* is an Arabic-language term literally meaning 'unity' and in an Islamic context refers to the belief that God is one/a single entity. It is a core principle of the Islamic faith.

Topakiyaan: This is a Pashtu neologism dating back to the early 1990s. It literally translates as 'the men with guns' (*topak* is the singular term for 'gun' or 'firearm') and is closely associated with the period of civil war following the fall of the Najib government.

Ulemaa': Plural version of *'Alim*. Literally 'those who have knowledge'; it refers to religious scholars (primarily used for the Sunni clergy) who have been edu-

DEFINITIONS

cated in the religious 'sciences' (the *Qur'an*, the *Sunna* and the *Hadith*s etc). See *Hadith*, *Qur'an* and *Sunna*.

Umma: *Umma* is an Arabic-language term referring to the community of Muslims around the world. It is sometimes used in a secular form to mean 'nation' (as in the Arabic version of 'the United Nations,' *al-Umam al-Muttahida*).

Umra: *Umra* is approximate to the *hajj* pilgrimage to Mecca, but may be performed at any point or time of the year. It is optional for Muslims.

Wahhabi: Wahhabi is the verbal noun and adjectival form relating to Wahhabism. See Wahhabism.

Wahhabism: 'Wahhabism' is a fundamentalist and Islamist interpretation of Islam as advocated by Mohammad ibn Abdul Wahhab, a Hanbali scholar living in what we now know as Saudi Arabia during the eighteenth century. He emphasised *tawhid* (oneness) and 'proposed a return to an idealised Islamic past through reassertion of monotheism and reliance on *Qur'an* and *hadith*, rejecting medieval interpretations of Islam and jurisprudence.'[8] It gained many advocates internationally as a result of a Saudi programme where funds were provided for global propagation. Note that there is a certain interchangeability between the terms Salafi and wahhabi: certain wahhabis reject the term because it suggests they are followers of Mohammad ibn Abdul Wahhab himself rather than God; they prefer the term salafi.

Wahhabist: Wahhabist is the verbal noun and adjectival form relating to Wahhabism. See Wahhabism.

Ziarat: A holy place where a certain deceased 'saint' or other such holy person is buried. In the conception of Islam practiced by many in southern Afghanistan, people visit these tombs in order to pray that the holy men will intercede on their behalf. Certain *ziarat*s, for example, are popular among women wanting to become pregnant. Southern Afghanistan and the border areas of Pakistan have many of these shrines.

BIOGRAPHIES

Abd al-Haq: Abd al-Haq (1958–2001) was a Pashtun mujahedeen leader prominent in eastern Afghanistan, particularly Nangarhar province. He was killed on 26 October 2001 by Taliban forces after he entered Afghanistan in an attempt to encourage resistance against the Taliban.

Abd ul-Rabb al-Rasul Sayyaf: Abd ul-Rabb al-Rasul Sayyaf (1946–), a Kharoti Ghilzai Pashtun from Paghman, is an Islamic scholar educated in Al-Azhar (Egypt) who founded his own political party, the *Ittehad-e Islami baraye Azadi-ye Afghanistan* ('Islamic Union for the Freedom of Afghanistan') in Peshawar in 1981. He speaks fluent Arabic and his party was very closely aligned with Arab donors during the 1980s. As a consequence, his party received a large proportion of the funding, prompting many commanders in southern Afghanistan to switch from whatever party they were affiliated with to Sayyaf's *Ittehad* in order to receive more supplies. Sayyaf continues to play a role in Afghan politics.

Abdel Bari Atwan: Born in 1940 in Gaza, Abdel Bari Atwan is a journalist and editor-in-chief of the London-based *Al-Quds al-Arabi* newspaper. He has interviewed bin Laden several times and is the author of 'The Secret History of al-Qa'ida.'

Abdel Rahman Pasha Azzam: Abd al-Rahman Pasha Azzam (1893–1976) was an Egyptian nationalist diplomat who served as the first Secretary-General of the Arab League following its founding in 1945. His grandson was Ayman al-Zawahiri (via al-Zawahiri's mother).

Abdellatif al-Derbas: Also known as Abu Haza'a, Abdul Latif Derbas was Kuwaiti and the brother-in-law of Abu Mohammad Asem Maqdisi (they were married to two sisters). Derbas was involved in the 1979 Mecca siege and was a close supporter of Juhayman al-Utaybi, spending years in a Saudi prison after the siege.

Abdul Aziz bin Baz: Abdul Aziz bin Baz (c. 1909–1999) was a prominent cleric who served as Grand Mufti of Saudi Arabia from 1993 until his death in 1999. He supported Azzam's *fatwa* that characterised the 1980s Afghan war as *fard kifaya* or a communal obligation and later earned the ire of bin Laden when he issued a *fatwa* of his own authorising the presence of US troops on Saudi soil during the 1991 Iraq war.

Abdul Hai Mutma'in: Abdul Hai Mutma'in served as a Taliban spokesman during the 1990s. Since the fall of the Emirate he has been a senior propagandist. He was captured in Ghazni by ISAF forces in late July 2010.

Abdul Hakim Murad: Abdul Hakim Ali Hashim Murad (b. 1968) is a Pakistani who was involved in the Bojinka plot and a close associate of Ramzi Yousuf. He trained as a pilot in several American flight schools during the 1990s but was arrested in Manila in January 1995. He was transferred to the United States in April 1995 and received a life sentence in May 1998.

Abdul Latif Mansour: Mullah Abdul Latif Mansour served as Taliban Minister of Agriculture during the 1990s. He continues to be active in south-east Afghanistan, serves on the Miram Shah Shura and is rumoured to be the current head of the Peshawar Shura. A Taliban statement issued in May 2009 referred to him as the head of the Taliban's political commission; he does not hold that position any more.

Abdul Rashid Dostum: An Uzbek commander notorious for switching sides numerous times during the war in Afghanistan. During the 1980s, he led a mostly-Uzbek militia who fought for the Soviets, only to change sides and be awarded a position in the mujahedeen government. His militia was the most well-known and feared of the Afghan armed forces during the 1980s. He continues to play a prominent role in Afghan politics, both in Kabul and in the north.

Abdullah Anas: Abdullah Anas is a prominent figure among the former 'Afghan Arabs' who fought in Afghanistan during the 1980s and who were involved in the discussions and events of the 1990s. He is involved in mediation efforts to try to work for a political settlement in Afghanistan. He founded the organisation, Taruf. See taruf.org for more.

Abdullah Azzam: Abdullah Yusuf Mustafa Azzam (1941–1989) was born near Jenin in Transjordan. He joined the Muslim Brotherhood in the mid-

1950s as a teenager. In 1963 he travelled to Syria and studied at the Islamic law school of Damascus University from which he obtained a diploma in *shari'a* studies in 1966. Azzam had already formed relationships and took part in discussions with a number of Islamists during his time in Damascus, many of whom would rise to prominence later. Shortly after the June 1967 war, now married, he fled with his family to Jordan where he later joined the Palestinian *jihad*. In 1968 he attended Al-Azhar and obtained a master's degree in Islamic law, followed by a doctoral fellowship in 1971. He returned to Amman where he taught at university. His lectures in and outside the university gained him wide recognition and led many to call him the Jordanian Sayyid Qutb. He was elected to the advisory council of the Jordanian Muslim Brotherhood. Growing tensions in Jordan and a dispute with a local publication caused him to decide to go to Saudi Arabia where he taught at the King Abdul Ibn Saud University in Jeddah were Muhammad Qutb was also teaching. It is likely that bin Laden heard or even attended Azzam's lectures; details, however, are not known and disputed in academic circles. In the early 1980s, Azzam went to Pakistan to join the Afghan *jihad* against the Soviet Union. He had been supplied with contacts to mujahedeen leaders by Sheikh Kamal al-Sananiri. In Pakistan he helped facilitate Arab volunteers and funding for the Afghan mujahedeen, becoming the main link between the Afghan *jihad* and Islamic groups in the Middle East. Together with bin Laden, he established the Services Office, an organisation that aimed to help Arab volunteers to join the Afghan *jihad*. While bin Laden established a pure-Arab fighting force, Azzam, who did not agree with this, continued to fundraise and look for Arab volunteers. Azzam is believed to have raised several hundred million dollars between 1985 and 1989 for the Afghan *jihad*. After the withdrawal of the Soviet Union, the Afghan Arabs debated how to proceed. On 24 November 1989, Azzam, along with two of his sons, died in a bomb explosion in Peshawar. Five main theories have been put forward about the identity of his murderers, accusing Zawahiri, the US, Afghan mujahedeen groups and others; it is not certain who carried out the attack. Abdullah Azzam is a central figure of pivotal importance for the developments within radical political Islam and the Afghan *jihad*. His books remain key reading for Islamists around the world to this day. He published over 100 books, articles and recorded conferences.

Abdur Rahman: Abdur Rahman (1840–1901) was the King of Afghanistan from 1880–1901 and was known as the 'Iron Amir' for his heavy-handed manner of ruling. He is well-known for resettling Pashtuns to northern Afghani-

BIOGRAPHIES

stan and offers one example of what a strong central state in Afghanistan looks like. He died in 1901 and was succeeded by his son, Habibullah Khan.

Abdur Rasheed Ghazi: Abdur Rasheed Ghazi (c. 1964–2007) was a Pakistani cleric and brother of Abdur Rasheed Ghazi. The two led the group that took over the Lal Masjid in Islamabad in July 2007. He was killed on 10 July 2007, when Pakistani security forces stormed the mosque in an attempt to end the siege.

Abu Bakr: Abu Bakr (573–634) was the father-in-law of the Prophet Mohammad. He was the first Caliph (following the death of Mohammad) and ruled from 632–634. He died of an illness in 634.

Abu Bara al-Yemeni: Abu Bara al-Yemeni was originally selected by bin Laden to take part in the September 11 attacks but was unable to obtain a visa for the United States so did not participate.

Abu Faraj al-Libi: Abu Faraj al-Libi is a Libyan militant and senior figure within al-Qaeda. He is believed to have fought in Afghanistan during the 1980s, moved to Sudan with bin Laden during the early 1990s and worked together with Pakistani groups upon their return to South-East Asia in the second half of the decade. He was captured in May 2005 following a raid in Mardan, Pakistan. He was believed to be running al-Qaeda's operations (following the arrest of Khalid Sheikh Mohammad) and was eventually brought to Guantánamo where he continues to be held.

Abu Hafs al-Masri: Abu Hafs al-Masri (1950s-2001) was an Egyptian senior member of al-Qaeda and served as its military chief until his death in 2001. He is also known as Mohammad Atef. He grew up in Egypt and was exposed to local jihadist groups from an early age. He fought in Afghanistan during the 1980s, meeting Azzam, bin Laden and al-Zawahiri there. He participated in the founding meeting of al-Qaeda. He spent time in Africa (including Sudan from 1992) during the early 1990s. He was appointed as the group's military chief following the death of Abu Ubaida in 1996. His daughter married bin Laden's eldest son, Mohammad, in Afghanistan in January 2001. Abu Hafs was killed by an airstrike in November 2001.

Abu Hajer al-Iraqi: Abu Hajer al-Iraqi (1958–) is a senior affiliate of al-Qaeda. He is also known as Mamdouh Mahmoud Salem. He is believed to have fought in Afghanistan during the 1980s, and even attended the founding meetings of al-Qaeda in 1988. He travelled to Sudan in the early 1990s and is believed to have been a key ideological influence on bin Laden during this period. He is cited in the US indictment relating to the 1998 Embassy bombings in Africa. He was arrested in Germany in September 1998, however, and is currently being held in US custody following extradition.

Abu Hamza Rabia: Abu Hamza Rabia (c. 1970s–2005) was a senior Egyptian al-Qaeda leader. He was killed in a drone strike in December 2005. At that time he was believed to have taken over the role of al-Qaeda's senior representative in Pakistan following the arrest of Abu Faraj al-Libi in May that year.

Abu Hani: Abu Hani (also known as Abd al-Rahman al-Masri) was an Egyptian who was associated with Sayyaf's *Ittehad-e Islami* during the 1980s *jihad*. He is believed to have been a senior affiliate of al-Qaeda, and is cited as having been present in Somalia during the 1990s, for example. He played an important role in logistical assistance for the 2001 assassination of Ahmed Shah Massoud.

Abu Jandal: Abu Jandal (1973–) was a Yemeni bodyguard who protected bin Laden during the 1990s. He fought in Bosnia, Somalia and Tajikistan prior to meeting bin Laden in 1996. He was arrested in Yemen following the September 11 attacks but released some months later and remains there under what amounts to house arrest. He gave an account of his time together with the al-Qaeda leader, entitled 'Al-Qaeda from Within,' which was serialised in *Al-Quds al-Arabi* newspaper in mid-2004. He has also appeared in a documentary film of his life, entitled 'The Oath.'

Abu Khabab: Abu Khabab (1953–2008) was an Egyptian al-Qaeda affiliate best known for his work at the Darunta training camp in Afghanistan that operated during the 1990s. He was knowledgeable about explosives and reportedly taught courses in the subject at Darunta. He is also known as Mihdat Mursi. He was killed on 28 July 2008, in a drone strike in Pakistan.

Abu Khabib: Abu Khabib ran the offices of Sayyaf's *Ittehad-e Islami* in Quetta during the 1980s and was well-known for this role among Afghan and Arab fighters alike. Arabs who fought in southern Afghanistan during this period would almost certainly have passed through Abu Khabib's office on their way to the fronts.

Abu Muhammad 'Asaam Maqdisi: Abu Muhammad 'Asaam Maqdisi (1959–) is a Palestinian Islamist writer. He spent his early years in Kuwait, Iraq and Saudi Arabia, travelling to Pakistan and Afghanistan during the 1980s. He returned to Jordan in 1992 and began preaching and writing against the government, at which point he was arrested. He spent several years in prison together with Abu Musa'b al-Zarqawi and is often cited as having been a prominent ideological influence on him. Maqdisi remained in Jordan, was later arrested but was released again in 2005. He was subsequently arrested again and (as of early 2011) was put on trial in Jordan on charges of recruiting people to travel to Afghanistan to fight with the Taliban.

Abu Muhammad al-Zayyat: Abu Muhammad al-Zayyat was a senior member of al-Qaeda. He is reported to have objected—from his position as head of the group's Security Committee, and later in 2000 as head of the Military Committee—to the plans for the September 11 attacks, believing they were illegitimate as long as permission was not requested from or granted by Mullah Mohammad Omar.

Abu Mus'ab al-Suri: Abu Mus'ab al-Suri (1958–) is a Syrian Islamist writer and al-Qaeda affiliate, also known as Mustafa bin Abd al-Qadir Setmariam Nasar. He is a veteran of the 1980s *jihad* against the Soviets, and one of the most outspoken strategic thinkers of the Arab jihadis who—during the 1990s—sought to outline a direction for the next phases of *jihad*. After several years of involvement in the jihadi debates in Europe, as well as of playing an important role in discussions over activities in Algeria, al-Suri returned to Afghanistan with his family. He had followed bin Laden's activities and the discussions surrounding his announcement of the 'World Islamic Front' in 1998. This was and could become a new stage in the *jihad*, al-Suri believed, and Afghanistan was a good base from which to prepare—albeit one that had the potential for being mishandled. He soon fell out with bin Laden over these strategic issues and worked together with the Taliban as a media advisor. He also helped organise the visits of several international journalists to interview bin Laden. He fled to Pakistan following the start of US operations in Afghanistan in late 2001. He was arrested in Quetta on 31 October 2005 and continues to be held in US custody.

Abu Mus'ab al-Zarqawi: Abu Mus'ab al-Zarqawi (1966–2006) was a Jordanian Islamist militant and affiliate of al-Qaeda, most famous for his activities in Iraq following the American invasion. He travelled to Pakistan in 1989 with a number of other Jordanians and met Abdullah Azzam there. He trained at Sada camp under Mohammad Atef, where he made many contacts. He was also introduced to al-Maqdisi there. They left for Jordan in 1993, and carried out some attacks there but were arrested. Following his release in 1999, he returned to Afghanistan and set up his own camp near Herat (following a disagreement with bin Laden). He refused to take the oath to bin Laden at this time. When the United States launched its air war inside Afghanistan on 7 October 2001, al-Zarqawi joined forces with al-Qaeda and the Taliban. He fought together with his group in and around Herat and Kandahar. By December 2001, however, he left Afghanistan once again and entered Iran. Saif al-Adel encouraged him to go to Iraq and provided contacts there. Once he arrived in northern Iraq, he cooperated with the separatist militant Islamist group *Ansar al-Islam*. In the summer of 2003, three months after the American invasion, al-Zarqawi moved to the Sunni areas of Iraq. He became well-known quite quickly. On 7 August, he allegedly was responsible for a car-bomb attack at the Jordanian embassy in Baghdad. Twelve days later, he was linked to the bombing of the United Nations headquarters in which twenty-two people died. On 29 August, in what was then the deadliest attack of the war, he is believe to have been behind the attack on a well-known cleric, Ayatollah Muhammad Baqr al-Hakim, in a car bombing in Najaf. The suicide bomber in that attack was Yassin Jarad, from Zarqa. He was al-Zarqawi's father-in-law. He received recognition from bin Laden in December 2004 (having pledged *bayat* two months earlier) as an al-Qaeda affiliate group following months of difficult negotiations. The relationship between the al-Qaeda leadership and al-Zarqawi and his al-Qaeda in Iraq franchise remained conflicted over Zarqawi's sectarian attacks. He was killed on 7 June 2006, when discovered by US forces.

Abu Qatada: Abu Qatada (1960   ) is a Palestinian cleric currently held in the Long Lartin prison in Worcestershire, UK. While born in Bethlehem in 1960, he is a Jordanian national. He arrived in the United Kingdom in September 1993 and received asylum. He went into hiding in December 2001 but was caught ten months later and held in Belmarsh prison. He was released in March 2005 on bail, but returned to jail five months later pending extradition to Jordan. The extradition request to Jordan was halted in April 2008 when it was overturned by three appeal court judges. Two months later he was again released on bail. By November he was back in jail for having allegedly violated the bail conditions. In February 2009 it was ruled by law lords that he could be extradited to Jordan. He has made a number of speeches and statements calling for *jihad* or militant action to be taken.

Abu Turab al-Urduni: Abu Turab al-Urduni was a Jordanian al-Qaeda affiliate. The 9/11 Report states that he was one of five individuals around bin Laden who knew the full operational details of the September 11 plots. It also claimed that he was the 'trainer' of the so-called muscle hijackers from 2000–2001.

Other reports have claimed that he married one of al-Zawahiri's daughters pre-2001. He is believed to have been killed in Kandahar during the initial bombings of Operation Enduring Freedom in October 2001.

Abu Ubaida: Abu Ubaida (1950–1996) was an Egyptian Islamist and senior al-Qaeda member. He fought in Afghanistan during the 1980s alongside Ahmed Shah Massoud, earning him the epithet 'Al-Banshiri' (in the Arabic pronunciation). He served as al-Qaeda's senior military commander until his accidental drowning in Lake Victoria (Africa) in 1996.

Abu Yahya al-Libi: Abu Yahya al-Libi (1963–2009) was born in Libya. His real name is Muhammad Hasan Qaid but he is also known as Yunus al-Sahrawi. He is a senior member of al-Qaeda. In the late 1980s or early 1990s he travelled to Afghanistan and lived in Lowgar province for a period of time. He was involved in the Libyan Islamic Fighting Group (LIFT) then, too, and in 1992 he travelled to Mauritania to pursue further/advanced Islamic studies. He is believed to have returned to Afghanistan in 1996. Around 2001–2 he is also alleged to have taken up a position in Karachi as web administrator for the Taliban's website. He was captured in May 2002 and held in Bagram (from which he escaped on 10 July 2005). Al-Libi has produced a number of propaganda videos and was regarded by some as a rising star within al-Qaeda and a possible successor to bin Laden; however, on 11 December 2009, he was most likely killed in a drone strike in Pakistan. His death has, however, not been confirmed. Al-Libi had wide ranging contacts and a considerable public profile.

Abu al-Walid al-Masri: Abu al-Walid al-Masri (1945–) was born in Sharqiyya, Egypt. He enrolled in the Muslim Brotherhood in 1951 and graduated from the University of Alexandria in 1969 with a mechanical engineering degree. He moved to Kuwait following his marriage and then to Abu Dhabi (where he owned a car repair garage). In 1975 he had an 'Islamic conversion' experience and began to seek out Muslim Brotherhood and Palestinian Islamic Jihad representatives in Abu Dhabi. In 1978 he joined Fatah/PLO and fought in Lebanon and received training there as well. In 1979 he returned to Abu Dhabi and (following an invitation from Haqqani via a friend of al-Masri) then went to Afghanistan. He fought in Paktya together with Haqqani for much of the 1980s and early 1990s. In 1984 he met Abdullah Azzam in Peshawar. In 1989 he arranged the meeting between al-Zarqawi and al-Maqdisi in Peshawar. He fell out with bin Laden during this time over the Jalalabad operation. He fought in the siege of Khost in 1990 (writing a lengthy account). His daughter, Asma, was married to Saif al-Adl in 1991/2. By 1993 he was training jihadis as part of the 'Furqan Project,' especially those from Central Asia. He travelled to Khartoum in 1995 but returned to Afghanistan in 1996 together with bin Laden. From 1997–2001 he was, variously, the editor of several Taliban publications, an al-Jazeera correspondent, and a trainer in al-Farouq camp. Following the September 11 attacks, he fled to Iran with Saif ul-Adl, where he remains under house arrest. Since that time he has been a prolific author, releasing several books online that criticise bin Laden and others within the militant Islamic universe.

Adel Tebourski: Adel Tebourski (1963–) is a Tunisian journalist who allegedly provided journalist accreditation and funds to the two Arabs who assassinated Ahmed Shah Massoud. He was arrested for this role in November 2001, sentenced to six years of jail time in May 2005 and released in July 2006, after which he returned to Tunisia.

Adnan Basha: Adnan Basha was the Secretary General of the International Islamic Relief Organization during the mid-1990s and has stated that the organisation gave over $60 million to the Taliban.

Ahmed Khalfan Ghailani: Ahmed Khalfan Ghailani (1974–) is a Tanzanian believed to have assisted in preparations for the 1998 al-Qaeda attacks on the two American embassies in Africa. He flew to Karachi (Pakistan) prior to the attacks. He married an Uzbek woman during this period. He remained in Pakistan until his arrest in Gujrat in July 2005, at which point he was brought to Guantánamo. He was sentenced to life imprisonment in January 2011 for his role in the 1998 bombings by a US District Court judge.

Ahmed Omar Saeed Sheikh: Ahmed Omar Saeed Sheikh (1973–) was born in London on 23 December 1973. He grew up in an upper-middle class environment there, but his family returned to Lahore in 1987 where he was enrolled in a private college. His family returned to London in 1990 when the business venture in Pakistan failed, and Omar went back to the Forest School which he had attended before going to Pakistan. He himself confided to his cellmate in India in the late 1990s, Peter Gee, that he had been subject to bullying and racism in school in London which had radicalised him. After school he was accepted by the LSE where he took courses in applied mathematics, statistical theory, economics, and social psychology. He joined the school's Islamic Society. He was also a professional arm-wrestler and competed in two international championships representing the UK. The war in Bosnia affected Omar and he volunteered for the Convoy of Mercy that delivered aid and clandestine support to the Muslim fighters. He did not make it to Bosnia, falling ill on the way, but met Abdur Rauf, a Pakistani veteran of the Afghan *jihad*. Rauf provided Omar with a letter of introduction to the *Harakat ul-Mujahedin* (HUM) and soon after Omar returned to London, he fled to Pakistan. In August 1993, he arrived in Khalid bin Waleed camp, where he met Mawlana Masood Azhar. He returned to England in January 1994 but was heading on to Afghanistan by May once again. Some HUM leaders had been arrested in India, and Omar was asked to kidnap five foreigners (Westerners) in order to exchange them for the leaders of the HUM. When no one noticed the disappearance of the foreigners, Omar delivered photos of the hostages. The police, however, managed to find and free one of the hostages. Omar was wounded in a gun battle, and taken prisoner. He was imprisoned in India where he met Peter Gee. He was exchanged in December 1999 along with the HUM leader, Mawlana Masood Azhar, in exchange for 154 passengers of an Indian airplane that was hijacked by HUM members. After his release, he stayed in Pakistan, married and had a child. Nothing was heard about him until after the September 11 attacks, even though he remained active in radical Islamist circles. He was arrested in 2002 and received a death sentence for his alleged involvement in the kidnapping and beheading of Daniel Pearl.

Ahmed Shah Massoud: Born in Panjshir in 1953, Ahmed Shah Massoud was one of the most famous resistance commanders of the 1980s *jihad* against the Soviets, and played a prominent role in the politics and fighting of the 1990s prior to his assassination just days before the attacks on the World Trade Center in 2001. He served as Minister of Defence in 1992, and led the 'Northern Alliance' against the Taliban in the late 1990s. He was known as the 'Lion of Panjshir.'

Ahmed Wali Karzai: Half-brother of Hamid Karzai, the current president of Afghanistan, Ahmed Wali lives in Kandahar City and is head of the Provincial Council. He is often cited as having links to the drugs trade, but he has not been prosecuted or found guilty of this, either inside or outside Afghanistan. He was assassinated by one of his close associates on 12 July 2011 in Kandahar.

Akbar Agha: Akbar Agha (Sayyed by tribe and in his early-mid forties) is a Kandahari who led an offshoot group to the Taliban post-2001 which was responsible for the kidnap of three UN staff in 2004. He was arrested in Pakistan in December 2004, handed over to the Afghan government, and sentenced to 16 years imprisonment following a trial in Kabul. He was released in late 2009 following a presidential pardon. He lives in Kabul and continues to claim his innocence.

BIOGRAPHIES

Akhund of Swat: The Akhund of Swat (1793–1878) or Abdul Ghaffur was a Safi-Mohmand tribesman from upper Swat (Pakistan). He was a Sufi cleric and rose to prominence in 1835 after the Afghan Amir Dost Mohammad appealed for his help in fighting against the Sikhs (led from Lahore by Ranjit Singh) in Peshawar. As a reward Abdul Ghaffur was given land in Swat, Lundkhwar and Mardan. He was succeeded by a notable line of Sufi clerics.

Ali: Ali ibn Abi Talib (598–661) was the cousin and son-in-law of the Prophet Mohammad. He ruled as Caliph from 656–661. He was the fourth of the so-called *Rashidun* caliphs that ruled after the death of the Prophet Mohammad. Shi'a Muslims also regard Ali as the first Imam. He was assassinated by a Kharijite in Kufa in 661.

Ali Abdul Aziz Ali: Ali Abdul Aziz Ali (1977–) is a nephew of Khalid Sheikh Mohammad and helped facilitate the September 11 attacks. The 9/11 Report concluded that he helped in transferring funds as well as in providing other logistical support from the United Arab Emirates. His wife is Aafia Siddiqui, an American-educated Pakistani who was arrested in Ghazni in July 2008. He was arrested in May 2003 in Pakistan, transferred to various CIA so-called 'black sites' and ended up in Guantánamo in September 2006 where he continues to be held.

Ali Abdullah Saleh: Ali Abdullah Saleh (1946–) is the President of Yemen, an office he took in 1978 following two decades of civil war. Despite a modest background, he rose through the Yemeni Army. He is an ally of the United States, with whom he cooperates on their counterterrorism agenda. His government has been plagued by internal problems, however, facing two insurgencies and the presence of Al-Qaeda in the Arabic Peninsula (AQAP).

Amanullah: Amanullah Khan (1892–1960) ruled Afghanistan from 1919–1929. He played a prominent role in asserting the country's independence from British interference and attempted to implement a reform agenda. He moved too fast too soon, however, and was met with uprisings in response. He abdicated in early 1929 and went into exile in India. He spent his remaining days in Europe (Italy and Switzerland), dying in Zurich in 1960.

Amanullah Zadran: Amanullah Zadran is the brother of Padshah Khan Zadran, a signatory of the Bonn Conference, and a strongman in Paktya province. He was appointed Minister of Borders in the post-Bonn interim government in 2002, but only held the office for a few months.

Amina Qutb: Amina Qutb was the sister of Sayyed Qutb. She married the cleric, Kamal al-Sananiri, in 1974 following his release from prison. He was killed in the very early 1980s while being interrogated by Egyptian officials. Amina died in January 2007.

Amir Abdullah: Amir Abdullah (apparently a pseudonym) was targeted in a 2010 US Treasury Department sanctions order. He is believed to come from Loya Paktya. The Treasury Department document stated that he was the former treasurer to Mullah Berader, former deputy to the Taliban governor of Kandahar, and that he had travelled to Kuwait, Saudi, Libya and the United Arab Emirates in order to raise funds for the Taliban. In 2001, he also reportedly helped Taliban fleeing from Afghanistan to resettle in Pakistan.

Amir Khan Muttaqi: Amir Khan Muttaqi (c. 1968–) is best known as the Taliban's minister for information and culture during the mid-late 1990s. His family was originally from Loya Paktya (probably from Zurmat) but they had resettled to Kunduz. He studied at the Akora Khattak madrassa in Pakistan and served together with Nabi Mohammadi during the 1980s *jihad*. He played a prominent role in the Taliban's government post-1996. In July 1997 he was trapped in Kunduz under siege from forces opposed to the Taliban. He served as Minister for information and cultural affairs from 1996 (when the Taliban took Kabul) until his dismissal in October 1999 when he was relegated to the Ministers' Council. In November 1999 his car exploded outside the Wazir Akbar Khan mosque, although Muttaqi was unhurt. In 2000 he was a key interlocutor between the United States and the Taliban in discussions over the issue of bin Laden and also in the UN discussions with the Northern Alliance. He also served as Minister for Education during that same year. In recent years he has served as head of the Taliban's information and culture committee (handling, for example, the movement's propaganda) but is increasingly sidelined over ideological and strategic differences of opinion within the senior leadership. He wrote a book in 2004 which is believed to have discussed issues that the Taliban leadership preferred not to be publicly aired, and it was, in fact, banned by the Taliban upon completion.

Amrullah Saleh: Amrullah Saleh (1972–) was Afghanistan's Intelligence Chief from 2004–2010. Pre-2001 he worked for Ahmed Shah Massoud in Dushanbe as a liaison figure. He resigned from his position in the Afghan government in 2010 following disagreements with President Karzai. Since his resignation he has been an outspoken opponent of attempts to bring the Taliban into the Afghan government.

Andrei Gromyko: Andrei Gromyko (1909–1989) served as Soviet Minister of Foreign Affairs from 1957–1985. As such, he played a key role in many crises of the Cold War, including in averting the Cuban Missile Crisis. He was known as 'Mr No' among Western diplomats and media outlets.

Anwar al-Sadat: Anwar al-Sadat (1918–81) was the President of Egypt from 1970–81. He also served as President of the United Arab Republic from 1970–71 following the death of Gamal Abd al-Nasser. He is best known for his role in the peace treaty between Egypt and Israel formalised in the Camp David Accords 1978 and signed in Washington D.C. in 1979. He was assassinated on 6 October 1981, in part in reaction to the peace treaty with Israel. He was succeeded by Hosni Mubarak.

Atatürk: Mustafa Kemal Atatürk (1891–1938) was the founder of the Republic of Turkey, and as such he served as its first President (from 1923–1938). He is widely remembered for his reformist agenda which sought to create a modern secular nation-state.

Ayman Sabri Faraj: Ayman Sabri Faraj is an Egyptian former Afghan Arab who wrote an account of his time fighting in southern Afghanistan during the 1980s and early 1990s. His account was published in 2002 under the penname Abu Ja'far al-Masri al-Kandahari and titled *Zikriyat Arabi Afghani* ('Memories of an Afghan Arab'). This book is one of the few accounts of the Afghan Arabs' presence in southern Afghanistan, with a particular focus placed on Kandahar. He is believed to be alive and living in Egypt.

Ayman al-Zawahiri: Ayman al-Zawahiri (1951–) was born into a wealthy family in Cairo. His uncle, Mahfouz Azzam, introduced him to the work of Sayyed Qutb and by the age of 14 he had joined the Muslim Brotherhood. He graduated from Cairo University and served three years as a surgeon in the Egyptian military. He joined *al-Jihad* or Egyptian Islamic Jihad group during this time. In 1985, he travelled to Saudi Arabia and soon after went on to Peshawar, Pakistan. Egyptian Islamic Jihad had suffered a severe blow during the 1980s after a coup attempt had been uncovered. In Pakistan, al-Zawahiri worked to reestablish the group. He moved to Sudan in the early 1990s, although was involved in various activities in different countries as well, and organised the bombing of the Egyptian Embassy in Islamabad in 1995. Al-Zawahiri was expelled from Sudan (together with bin Laden) in 1996. It is believed that he travelled widely at this time, including spending several months in Russia, but the details of his trips are subject to disagreement. He was a signatory on the February 1998 declaration of a 'World Islamic Front Against Jews and Crusaders,' although this was controversial within his group, Egyptian Islamic Jihad. That same year he announced that Egyptian Islamic Jihad had merged together with al-Qaeda, a claim much disputed, again, by other members of his group. He was sentenced to death in absentia in Egypt in 1999. He is a prominent theorist and ideologue within al-Qaeda and long functioned as bin Laden's deputy until being chosen to lead al-Qaeda in June 2011 following bin Laden's death. He is believed to be hiding in Pakistan.

Barack Obama: Barack Obama (1961–) is the current serving President of the United States. He took office in January 2009 and has been highly involved in trying to forge a new US policy for Afghanistan.

Basil Mohammad: Basil Mohammad is the Saudi author of 'The Arab Helpers in Afghanistan,' published in 1991.

Beitullah Mehsud: Beitullah Mehsud (1974–2009) was the head of *Tehrik-e Taliban Pakistan* (TTP) and a senior militant based in Waziristan. He played a prominent role in the mid-late 2000s following the death of Nek Mohammad. He was killed in a drone strike on 5 August 2009.

Benazir Bhutto: Benazir Bhutto (1953–2007) was a well-known Pakistani political figure, heading the Pakistan Peoples Party (in the wake of her father's execution in 1979), and serving as Prime Minister from 1988–90 and 1993–1996. She returned from exile to Pakistan to great fanfare in October 2007, only to be killed leaving a PPP rally in Rawalpindi on 27 December.

Bill Clinton: Bill Clinton (1946–) served as President of the United States between 1993 and 2001. His presidency is often associated with the US interventions in Somalia and Bosnia, as well as the scandal regarding the White House intern, Monica Lewinsky.

Bouraoui el-Ouaer: Bouraoui el-Ouaer (1972–2001) was one of the two assassins who killed Ahmed Shah Massoud on 9 September 2001. El-Ouaer was a Tunisian living in Belgium. He travelled to Afghanistan in May 2000 and was recruited as part of the plot to kill Massoud. El-Ouaer was killed instantly in the explosion.

Brigadier Muhammad Yousaf: Brigadier Muhammad Yousaf ran the Afghan desk of Pakistan's ISI from 1983–87 (during the war against the Soviets). He wrote two accounts of his work and time spent together with the Afghan mujahedeen, one together with Mark Adkin entitled 'The Bear Trap' and another entitled 'Silent Soldier.'

Brigadier-General Daniel Ménard: Brigadier-General Daniel Ménard (1968–) served as the senior commander of Canadian military forces in Afghanistan from November 2009 until June 2010 when he was removed from his post following allegations that he had had sexual relations with a subordinate. He quit the military in December 2010 and was court-martialed in 2011.

Burhanuddin Rabbani: Born in 1940 in Faizabad (Badakhshan province in the north-east of Afghanistan). He was educated in Kabul and at Al-Azhar in Cairo, before returning to Afghanistan in 1968. He was head of one of the major political parties of the 1980s *jihad*, the *Jamiat-e Islami*. He served as president of Afghanistan between 1992 and 1996, until the Taliban took Kabul. He continues to play a role in Afghan politics in Kabul, currently as head of the government's official High Peace Council responsible for reconciliation with the insurgency.

Christina Rocca: Christina Rocca was alleged to have worked for the CIA's Operations Directorate since 1982 and was nominated for appointment as US Secretary of State for South Asia in April 2001. Some sources suggest she was closely involved with the funding and arming of the anti-Soviet mujahedeen during the 1980s. She left government service in January 2009.

Clare Short: Clare Short (1946–) is a British politician. She served as Secretary of State for International Development under Blair's Labour government from 1997–2003. She resigned in May 2003, two months after the start of the Iraq War (prior to which she had said that she would resign if Britain backed the US invasion).

Colin Powell: Colin Powell (1937–) was a four-star general in the US Army, serving as Chairman of the Joint Chiefs of Staff from 1989–1993 (including during the First Gulf War) and later as Secretary of State from 2001–5 under President George W. Bush. He famously delivered a speech at the United Nations Security Council in New York on 5 February 2003, outlining the case for war in Iraq.

Dahmane Abd el-Sattar: Dahmane Abd el-Sattar (1962–2001) was born in Tunisia. He moved to Belgium in 1987 and studied communications at Brussels University. He became a Belgian citizen when he married Samia, a Belgian girl of Moroccan descent, in 1991. The marriage was arranged by the Centre Islamic Belgians. Even though el-Sattar frequently drank alcohol, he grew more religious and started to attend the mosque regularly in 1997. He and Tarek Maaroufi organised an exhibition about the war in Chechnya in 1999 with the alleged aim to encourage young Muslims to join the *jihad*. He travelled to Afghanistan in May 2000. He volunteered for a suicide mission. His second wife Malika el-Aroud joined him in Afghanistan. He applied for a visa at the Afghan embassy in Islamabad in August 2001 under the name of Karim Toussani.

He used forged documents that Tarek Tebourski provided for him, and had with him a recommendation letter from Yasser el-Sirri, director of the Islamic Observation Center in London. He travelled to Afghanistan alongside Bouraour el-Ouaer. They posed as Belgian journalists wanting to produce a television report about Afghanistan and Massoud. On 9 September 2001, the two men managed to get an interview with Massoud. Bouraoui el-Ouaer detonated the bomb, killing himself and fatally wounding Massoud. El-Sattar was killed trying to escape a short while after.

Dick Cheney: Dick Cheney (1941–) is a US politician who served as Vice President under President George W. Bush from 2001–2009. He was also Chairman and CEO of Halliburton from 1995–2000.

Donald Rumsfeld: Donald Rumsfeld (1932–) is an American politician who served as Secretary of Defense from 2001–6 under President George W. Bush, but also from 1975–77 under Gerald Ford. He resigned in November 2006 and published a memoir in early 2011 entitled 'Known and Unknown.'

Dr Fadl: Dr Fadl or Sayyed Imam al-Sharif (1950–) is an Egyptian religious scholar and leading theoretician of the Egyptian Islamic Jihad group. He was based in Peshawar during the 1980s *jihad* against the Soviets, where he was head of the Kuwaiti Red Crescent Hospital in the city. He wrote a number of highly influential works during this period. He later travelled to Sudan and Yemen and was arrested there prior to the September 11 attacks. He was transferred to Egyptian authorities in February 2004, where he continues to be held. In recent years he has written works critical of bin Laden, al-Zawahiri and al-Qaeda as a whole.

Dr Safar al-Hawali: Dr Safar bin Abdul Rahman al-Hawali (1950–) is a Saudi religious scholar. He graduated from Umm al-Qura University in Mecca in 1986 and is strongly associated with the Saudi *sahwa* or 'awakening' movement. He was arrested for his involvement in these activities (along with Salman al-Auda), an action that bin Laden claimed help turn him against the Saudi royal family. He is alive and lives in Mecca.

Dr Zafar Iqbal: Dr Zafar Iqbal (1955–) is a Pakistani religious figure closely associated with jihadi groups started during the 1980s. He was at the University of Engineering and Technology of Lahore in 1986 when he founded *Markaz Da'wa wal Irshad* together with his colleague Hafiz Mohammad Said and the Palestinian cleric Abdullah Azzam. He has continued to be involved in this group (and its offshoots, some renamed), particularly the *Jama'at ul-Da'wa* group based in Muridke. He is also known as Abu Hamza.

BIOGRAPHIES

Emma Bonino: Emma Bonino (1948–) is an Italian politician who was elected several times to the European Parliament. She was outspoken in her condemnation of the Taliban's government during the 1990s.

Engineer Mahmud: Engineer Mahmud (unknown–1996) was the political figure closely associated with Hajji Abdul Qadir, the former Afghan vice president, and Nangarhar province and its shura. He was one of the few present at bin Laden's arrival in Afghanistan in May 1996, but he was killed a few weeks later in unclear circumstances—either in a tribal dispute or by forces associated with the then-growing Taliban movement. He was killed in an ambush together with Mawlawi Saznour.

Faqir of Ipi/Mirza Ali Khan: Mirza Ali Khan, also known as the Faqir of Ipi, (1897–1960) was a Pakistani Pashtun religious cleric based in North Waziristan who led a campaign against British troops from 1936 until their departure at the creation of Pakistan in 1947. He fought a guerrilla campaign organised along tribal lines which he promoted as a *jihad*. He died in 1960, but his life story remains a strong cultural and historical symbol for many who inhabit the Afghanistan-Pakistan border region.

Farag Foda: Farag Foda (1946–1992) was an Egyptian secularist intellectual and author. He was not especially prominent within Egypt but had a large following outside the country, and wrote many outspoken articles opposing the implementation of the *shari'a* and so on. He was assassinated by *al-Gama'a al-Islamiyya* members on 8 June 1992, the first attack in a new wave that would afflict Cairo and Egypt.

Fazl Omar Mujaddidi: Fazl Omar Mujaddidi (d. 1956) was a religious cleric and respected figure from within the Mujaddidi family (descended from Sheikh Ahmad Sirhindi). He is also known, variously, as Noor ul-Mashayekh, Sher Agha or Hazrat Saheb of Shor Bazaar. He was an active participant in the *jihad* against the British in 1919 but, having initially been supportive of Amanullah, soured against the government in the mid-1920s, initially over the Durand Line discussions but also on account of Amanullah's reform programme. He assumed the honorific title of 'Hazrat Saheb of Shor Bazaar' in 1925 following the death of his brother, Shah Agha or Shams ul-Mashayekh. He left Afghanistan in 1926 on the hajj but didn't return and instead went into exile in India, from where he opposed the government. Several members of his family and his religious followers were arrested and/or executed in the second half of 1928 for opposing the constitutional reforms proposed by Amanullah. Fazl Omar was instrumental in supporting Nadir Khan's push to oust Bacha-ye

Saqao (who ruled in the place of Amanullah when he fled in January 1929) in June 1929. Amanullah rewarded Fazl Omar with the position of Justice Minister, which he held until his resignation in December 1931 (only accepted in December 1932), stating that the emergent situation had now normalised. Fazl Omar supported calls for *jihad* in Kashmir during the first Kashmir war of 1948 despite an official pronouncement from the government-sanctioned *Jamiat-i Ulema'* that stated the opposite.

Gamal Abd al-Nasser: Gamal Abd al-Nasser (1918–70) was an Egyptian politician who served as President of Egypt (and President of the short-lived United Arab Republic) from 1956–1970. He was the central figure of the pan-Arab movement that flourished during the middle of the last twentieth century.

Gary Schroen: Gary Schroen is a former CIA officer who postponed retirement to lead the CIA's activities in Afghanistan post-September 11 which contributed to the fall of the Taliban government. He wrote an account of his experiences, 'First In,' which was published in 2005.

General David Petraeus: David Petraeus (1952–) was the senior commander of ISAF in Afghanistan from 2010 to 2011, and became Director of Central Intelligence at the CIA in 2011. He has previous held other senior military positions, including as commander of CENTCOM. He is widely credited as leading the refocus on counterinsurgency within the US military, even heading the effort to develop the US Army/Marine Corps Counterinsurgency Manual, FM 3-24, and led the US implementation of that strategy in the Iraq war.

General Khattak: Major General Niaz Mohammad Khattak (1954–) is a deputy to Ahmed Shuja' Pasha, ISI's Director-General. He has served in the Pakistani army since 1973.

General Mahmud Ahmed: General Mahmud Ahmed (b. 1941) served as Director General of ISI until 8 October 2001, when he retired. He is still alive. He was in Washington on 11 September 2001 and worked together with the US government following the attacks in New York and Washington.

General Mirza Aslam Beg: General Mirza Aslam Beg (1931–) is a Pakistani military officer. He served as Chief of the Army from 1998–1991 and has remained involved in political and military affairs since his official retirement.

General Naseem Rana: Major General Naseem Rana (1942–) is a former head of Pakistan's Inter Services Intelligence group. He served in that position from 1995–October 1998.

BIOGRAPHIES

General Nasirullah Babar: Major General Nasirullah Babar (1928–2011) was a Pakistani (Pashtun) military officer and politician. He served as Interior Minister between 1993–1996 under Prime Minister Benazir Bhutto. He is strongly associated with the Pakistan People's Party (PPP). He was heavily involved in the formulation and implementation of Pakistan's policies towards Afghanistan from the 1980s onwards, during both the 1980s *jihad* and the Taliban's rise to power.

General Stanley McChrystal: Stanley McChrystal (1954–) served as commander of ISAF from 2009–10. Prior to this, he was commander of the US Joint Special Operations Command (JSOC) from 2003–6, credited with successes in the capture of Saddam Hussein and in the killing of Abu Mus'ab al-Zarqawi in Iraq. He resigned as ISAF commander following a profile of him and his team in *Rolling Stone* magazine.

George Tenet: George Tenet (1953–) served as Director of Central Intelligence at the CIA 1997–2004. He resigned in June 2004 citing 'personal reasons.' In 2007, he published a memoir of his years at the CIA entitled 'At the Center of the Storm.'

Ghulam Mohammad Niazi: Ghulam Mohammad Niazi was born in Ghazni. He studied at al-Azhar University in Cairo, Egypt, gaining a postgraduate degree there before returning to Afghanistan in 1957. He taught as a professor at Kabul University but before long was appointed Dean of the Islamic Studies faculty. He began organising meetings at the Abu Hanifa madrassa in Paghman, where those involved would translate Qutb and Mawdudi, amongst others. This group was originally called *Jawanan-e Musulman* (modelled on the Egyptian Muslim Brotherhood) but morphed into what became the *Jamiat-e Islami*. In 1973, Rabbani was elected as chairman of the leadership in secret; Niazi remained the de facto head, however. He was jailed in 1974, and executed on 28 May 1979.

Glyn Davies: Glyn Davies is a long-standing officer of the US Foreign Service, serving in Australia and Zaire as well as in various positions in Washington. He is best known for his statement that there was 'nothing objectionable' about the domestic policies pursued by the Taliban. As of February 2011, he is the Permanent Representative of the US to the International Atomic Energy Agency and the United Nations Office in Vienna.

Gordon Brown: Gordon Brown (1951–) is a British politician (Labour Party) who served as Prime Minister from 2007–2010 following the resignation of Tony Blair. He was Chancellor of the Exchequer from 1997–2007.

BIOGRAPHIES

Gretchen Peters: Gretchen Peters is an American author and journalist. She covered Afghanistan and Pakistan for the Associated Press and later for ABC News. She wrote 'Seeds of Terror' (2009) about the role opium has played in the war in Afghanistan and Pakistan.

Gul Agha Shirzai: Gul Agha Sherzai is originally from Kandahar province and is the son of one of Kandahar's most famous 1980s mujahedeen commanders, Hajji Latif, the so-called 'Lion of Kandahar.' He served as the governor of Kandahar in the early 1990s following the fall of the Najibullah regime in Kabul, as well as from 2001–2003 after the fall of the Taliban. He is currently the governor of Nangarhar.

Gulbuddin Hekmatyar: While Hekmatyar's parents were originally from Qarabagh district of Ghazni province, he was born in northern Afghanistan in 1948. Hekmatyar attended military school for two years before being expelled for political activism, at which point he enrolled (in 1970) in the engineering faculty of Kabul University, then a hotbed of political debate and conflict. After a brief flirtation with the Communist Parchamis, Hekmatyar was involved with the Islamists around the university's *shari'a* faculty. He was jailed in 1972, however, for killing a Maoist student on campus, only to take refuge in Pakistan in 1974. Initially siding with *Jamiat-e Islami* figures, Hekmatyar helped found *Hizb-e Islami* in 1976 following a feud with Rabbani (and Massoud). Hekmatyar received a large portion of the funding distributed by outside powers during the 1980s war; he was also implicated in the killings of various civil society actors in Afghanistan and Pakistan. As part of the Peshawar Agreement and the subsequent deal in Kabul of April/May 1992, Hekmatyar was appointed Prime Minister although the swift outbreak of fighting between the different political parties precluded his active participation in this government. After outside funding ran dry in 1989, Hekmatyar is rumoured to have involved himself in the narcotics and arms trade. He had a poor relationship with the Taliban and his forces were involved in clashes with the Taliban as they advanced from the south. At the time of the 9/11 attacks, Hekmatyar was staying in Iran, but he was forced to leave in February 2002. Between this time and the present day, Hekmatyar has remained in hiding, issuing public statements on his website, *Shahadat*. His son-in-law was in Kabul in March/April 2010 with a delegation from *Hizb-e Islami* for discussions with the government and United Nations.

Habibullah Khan: Habibullah Khan (1872–1919) was the eldest son of Abdur Rahman Khan and ruled as Afghan King from 1901–19, when he was assassinated. He was involved in modernisation and reform initiatives inside Afghanistan during this period.

Hadda-i Sahib: Sheikh Najmuddin Akhundzada (d. 1901) was also known as Hadda-i Sahib or the Hadda Mullah. He was a prominent Afghan religious cleric and pir (initiated into multiple Sufi orders) born in Ghazni. He studied under the Akhund of Swat during his early years. He became the most influential pir in eastern Afghanistan, establishing his own network of clerics. The King of the time, Amir Abdur Rahman, sought to influence and control him—Abdur Rahman even engineered an attempt on Sheiikh Najmuddin's life—but these efforts failed. Sheikh Najmuddin travelled to Pakistan where he remained in Mohmand agency. He was an important force behind anti-British disturbances in 1893, 1897 and 1899.

Hafez Mohammad Saeed: Born in Sarghoda approximately in 1950, Hafez Mohammad received a religious education but early on was appointed by Zia ul-Haq to the Council on Islamic Ideology. This allowed Saeed to travel, and he was educated in Saudi Arabia at Medina University—he also received a degree from King Saud University in Arabic language—before returning to teach at the University of Lahore at the Engineering Faculty. In 1986 he co-founded *Markaz Da'wa wal Irshad* (MDI), reportedly with Saudi funding and assistance from when he was studying there. In 1990 he established *Lashkar-e Taiba*, the militant arm of MDI. He is often cited as having travelled to Saudi Arabia and Sudan to visit bin Laden during these years. He had had extremely ambivalent relationship with the Pakistani authorities: first arrested in December 2001, then released in March 2002, then arrested May 2002, then released October 2002, then arrested August 2006, then released October 2006. He has always denied any involvement with *Lashkar-e Taiba*, and retains a low profile within Pakistan today.

Hafiz Abdul Majid: The life and background of Hafiz Abdul Majid are not well known. Noorzai by tribe and originally from Sperwan (Panjwayi district, Kandahar), he was close to Hajji Bashar. During the Taliban's rule over Afghanistan, Majid was an omnipresent figure in meetings (along with Mullah Ghazi) that Mullah Mohammad Omar attended or held. Majid was Kandahar's intelligence chief during this period. He was one of the few Taliban members who refused to surrender in late 2001 and was connected to the Arabs who held out at Mirwais Hospital until January 2002. Since the fall of the Taliban's government, he has been cited as personal emissary to Mullah Mohammad Omar and as head of recruitment and as tribal liaison in southern Afghanistan. He has several brothers who are also in the insurgency. *The New York Times* reported his capture in 2004 but sources have seen him active in Quetta in recent years. His brother, Mullah Qasim, was active in Maiwand district as a Taliban commander.

Hafiz Abdul Rahman Makki: Hafiz Abdul Rahman Makki (1948–) is a Pakistani cleric and Islamist figure strongly associated with the *Markaz Da'wa wal Irshad* group and its successor, *Jama'at ud-Da'wa*. He was born in Bahawalpur (Punjab province, Pakistan) and was one of the co-founders of *Markaz Da'wa wal Irshad* in 1985. He spent several years in Saudi Arabia teaching at Medina University but returned to live in Pakistan. He is the *Jama'at ud-Da'wa's* political affairs head. He is also the brother-in-law of Hafiz Mohammad Saeed (Talha Saeed, Hafiz's son, married Makki's daughter). He continues to teach in the *Jama'at ud-Da'wa* headquarters at Muridke and was targeted by the US Department of the Treasury for reportedly raising funds for *Lashkar-e Taiba*.

Hafizullah Amin: Hafizullah Amin (1929–1979), born in Paghman to Kharoti Ghilzai Pashtuns, was appointed Minister of Foreign Affairs following the Saur coup. He ousted Noor Mohammad Taraki in September 1979, but was himself assassinated in December that year after falling foul of his Soviet sponsors. He was replaced by Babrak Karmal of the Parcham faction.

Hajji Bashar: Hajji Bashar (Noorzai by tribe) was born in Maiwand district of Kandahar province in around 1960. During the 1980s war Hajji Bashar was an Amir of a front near Sangisar for Khalis' *Hizb-e Islami*. Mullah Mohammad Omar was reportedly one of his commanders for that front. By 1994, Hajji Bashar was the district administrator of Keshkinakhud in Maiwand, Kandahar, and he was one of the first non-Talibs to support and submit to the Taliban—he shaved his head in the public square. He donated weapons, vehicles and fuel in the early days of the movement. He has houses in Quetta, Pakistan, the UAE and Afghanistan. In December 2001, he was reportedly one of the contenders for the handover of Kandahar along with Mullah Naqib. In January 2002 he handed over a collection of weapons to American forces, and also apparently persuaded Wakil Ahmed Mutawakil to surrender to the Americans. He had strong ties to Mullah Mohammad Omar and the Taliban through which he increased his involvement in the opium trade. Following the ousting of the Taliban, Hajji Bashar tried to align himself to the US. In an attempt to prove his loyalty to them, Hajji Bashar travelled to New York where he spent several days in a hotel in Lower Manhattan answering questions from US government agents. He cooperated with them and hoped to prove that he would be a vital asset to the American and Afghan governments. He was, however, subsequently arrested on the basis of a sealed indictment against him. After a short trial in late September 2008 he was found guilty of an 'international drug trafficking conspiracy.' On 1 May 2009 he was sentenced to life in prison.

Hajji Latif: Hajji Latif (Barakzai by tribe) was one of the key figures of the 1980s *jihad* in Kandahar. He was the father of Gul Agha Sherzai, the current governor of Nangarhar, and was well-known for fighting in the Mahalajat area of Kandahar. Hajji Latif was poisoned and died on 8 August 1989. He was affiliated with Gailani's *Mahaz-e Milli* party.

Hajji Qadir: Hajji Qadir (1951–2002) was one of the top figures in eastern Afghanistan during the early 1990s. He served as vice-president (and Minister for Urban Development) in the post-Bonn interim government until his assassination on 6 July 2002. During the 1980s he was associated with Khalis' *Hizb-e Islami*. He was governor of Nangarhar province from 1992–6 until the Taliban took the area. His younger brother was Abd al-Haq.

Hamid Karzai: Hamid Karzai (Popolzai by tribe) is originally from Karz (Dand district, Kandahar province) and was born there in 1957. His father was the leader of his tribe and a well-known figure (also serving as an MP during Zahir Shah's reign). Karzai was studying in India at the time of the Soviet invasion. During the 1980s he worked in Pakistan as a liaison for the mujahedeen. He considered joining the Taliban government in 1994, but ended up trying to mobilise opposition to them. Following the fall of the Taliban in 2001 he eventually came to be selected as President in 2002 and was elected again in 2004 and 2009. As of August 2011 he is still serving as Afghan President.

Hassan al-Banna: Hassan al-Banna (1906–1949) was a prominent Islamist activist and the founder of the Muslim Brotherhood movement in Egypt. He was born into a religious family in a village on the Nile Delta in Egypt. He was initiated into the Hasafiya Sufi order at an early age. He trained as a teacher and taught in a local government school in Ismailiyya. Al-Banna regarded education as a holistic undertaking and soon began lecturing outside of school at meeting halls and mosques. His reputation as a public speaker grew and he was invited to speak in private homes. In 1928, he formed the Muslim Brotherhood. Al-Banna was a practitioner, an activist and organiser who regarded the traditional religious establishment with scepticism. Al-Banna sought to reform the state through what he termed 'social Islam.' While he wanted society to return to Islam he did not necessarily regard the government or state as the primary agent for the Islamisation of society. The Brotherhood grew and al-

BIOGRAPHIES

Banna moved to Cairo in 1932 where he established the central secretariat. At the beginning, al-Banna was primarily interested in establishing a social organisation that would engage society. The growth of the Muslim Brotherhood, however, soon gave him considerable political weight. By the late 1930s he was openly calling on the government to initiate an Islamisation of society. He also established a militant wing of the Brotherhood. After the assassination of the Prime Minister in 1948 the Egyptian government cracked down on the Brotherhood. Al-Banna was killed a year later. As founder of the Muslim Brotherhood, al-Banna has influenced almost every Islamic organisation in the world. In particular, his unique style of organisational structure was emulated by many groups throughout the Middle East and beyond.

Hassan al-Turabi: Dr. Hassan Abdullah al-Turabi (b. 1932 approx) is an Islamist politician in Sudan. His party, the National Islamic Front, came to power in 1989 following a coup d'etat by Omar al-Bashir. He was an ideologue with considerable influence on al-Bashir, and was responsible in many ways for encouraging the arrival of Islamist groups in Sudan during the 1990s. He is still alive and based in Sudan.

Hosni Mubarak: Hosni Mubarak (1928–) served as Egyptian President from 1981–2011. He was vice president to Anwar al-Sadat, but assumed the presidency himself following the latter's assassination. He resigned in February 2011 following days of demonstrations on the streets of Egypt.

Ibn Taymiyya: Taqi al-Din Ahmad ibn Taymiyya (1263–1328) was a prominent medieval Islamic scholar of the Hanbali school. He was born in the border area of Turkey-Syria. He lived in Damascus during the Mongol invasions; Baghdad had been captured in 1258. His writings have formed much of the foundations behind the Wahhabi-Salafi impulse in the past two centuries, and he is frequently cited by contemporary militant Islamist fighters.

Ilyas Kashmiri: Ilyas Kashmiri was born in Kashmir and passed the first year of a public relations degree at university in Islamabad before becoming involved with jihadi matters to the exclusion of most other things. In 1980 he left his studies at Karachi's *Jamia Uloom al-Islamia* with two fellow students and set up the group that would become *Harakat ul-Jihad ul-Islami*, one of the most important and earliest Pakistani jihadist groups spawned out of the Soviet invasion of Afghanistan. He was reportedly an active participant and trainer (with a specialism in 'mine warfare') of Afghan and Pakistani mujahedeen during the 1980s, and lost an eye at one point. He was active during the mid-1990s as well, launching the al-Hadid operation in Delhi to release some of his jihadi colleagues which involved the kidnapping of foreigners. Kashmiri was arrested and imprisoned for two years by the Pakistani government but managed to escape, at which point he returned to Kashmir to continue his activities there. He is often cited as a key military implementer for the broader ideological and strategic plans of 'al-Qaeda,' and the '313 Brigade' is especially important in this regard. His network and group affiliates are often cited as having played a role in actions in Pakistan and the wider region (including most recently in the bomb-blasts in Daghestan in April 2010) but these links are difficult to confirm. He was arrested by the Pakistani government in 2003 following an assassination attempt on Pervez Musharraf but later released. Kashmiri surfaced again recently in connection to David Headley and the Chicago plot, in which he reportedly played an advisory role. He is ideologically closer to the international jihadis, but retains ties to Afghanistan, primarily through the Haqqanis. He is claimed to have been killed in a drone strike on 3 June 2011.

Imam Khomeini: Ruhullah Musavi (1902–89) is also known as the Grand Ayatollah Ruhullah Khomeini and was the first supreme leader of Iran following the revolution in 1979. He spent a long time in Najaf, Iraq, studying in exile but returned to Iran in February 1979 (from France, where he had been living for several months). He was a prolific writer and speechmaker and is perhaps best remembered for the concept of *velayat-e faqih* ('guardianship of the jurist') which provided part of the basis for his model of government that continues to this day in Iran.

Ishtaique Parker: Ishtaique Parker was a South African Muslim convert involved in the Bojinka plot. He later became an informant for the US government, passing on information that led to the capture of Ramzi Yousuf. He reportedly received a reward of $2 million (which had been publicly advertised) and was offered a new identity in the United States.

Ismael Khan: Ismael Khan was born in 1946 in Shindand (near Herat). He fought in western Afghanistan against the Soviets and was affiliated with *Jamiat-e Islami*. He continues to play a role in Afghan politics, serving until recently as Minister of Power.

Jalaluddin Haqqani: Mawlawi Jalaluddin Haqqani (c. 1950–) is a prominent mujahedeen commander with a traditional stronghold in south-east Afghanistan. He was strongly associated with Khalis' *Hizb-e Islami* during this period, and hosted many of the foreign fighters who fought inside Afghanistan. He played a role in the Taliban government after they moved into Loya Paktya in 1995, but he was sidelined from a senior position—those were mostly held by a Kandahari core. He is believed to currently be based out of Miram Shah, Pakistan, and at the head of the eponymous 'Haqqani Network,' although operational details have passed to his son, Serajuddin.

Jamal al-Din al-Afghani: Jamal al-Din al-Afghani (1838–97) was a Muslim intellectual and political philosopher. After a childhood in Iran and Afghanistan, he spent much of his adult life travelling. He was an important reformist thinker and influenced many of the reformists who followed him, such as Mohammad Abduh in Egypt.

Jamil ul-Rahman: Jamil ul-Rahman is a Safi Pashtun from the Pech Valley, Kunar province. His real name was Mohammad Hussain. He was active in Kunar during the 1980s, establishing a de facto 'Islamic Emirate' there (complete with a full cabinet). He was originally affiliated with *Jamiat-i Islami* but switched to *Hizb-e Islami* in 1978. Many foreign fighters were present in Kunar during the time of his 'Emirate,' established under the name *Hizb ul-Da'wa wal Jihad* ('The Party of Islamic Invitation and *Jihad*') in 1985; this party had a specifically Salafi orientation. He was killed in Peshawar by an Egyptian, Abdullah al-Roumi, who had fought in southern Afghanistan.

Jaswant Singh: Jaswant Singh (1938–) is an Indian politician who served as Minister for External Affairs from 1998–2002. During the December 1999 Indian Airlines hijacking crisis, he was responsible for escorting and releasing the Pakistani prisoners (Massoud Azhar and others) in response to the hijackers' demands. He also served the finance and defence minister. He is the current Prime Minister of India (and has been since 2009).

Jere van Dyk: Jere van Dyk (1945–) is an American journalist and author. He spent time with the Haqqanis during the 1980s and travelled to Kandahar as well. He wrote 'In Afghanistan' based on his experiences of that period. He returned to Afghanistan post-2001 but was kidnapped by Pakistani Taliban fighters in 2008 and held for 45 days. His account of that time was published as 'Captive: My Time as a Prisoner of the Taliban.'

Jimmy Carter: James 'Jimmy' Carter (1924–) was president of the United States from 1977–81. He received the Nobel Peace Prize in 2002 for his work in finding 'peaceful solutions to international conflicts.' Since leaving office, he has written and published 21 books.

Juhayman al-Utaybi: Juhayman al-Utaybi (1936–80) was from Saudi Arabia and led the siege of the Grand Mosque in Mecca in late 1979. His group believed that the return of the Mehdi was imminent (due to take place on the

BIOGRAPHIES

first day of the new year, 1400, in the Islamic calendar). They took over the Grand Mosque in the expectation that this would take place. His writings continue to be read by jihadists. He was executed on 9 January 1980, by Saudi authorities.

Juma Namangani: Juma Khojiyev Namangani (1969–2001) was an Uzbek paratrooper who fought in Afghanistan during the 1980s. After he returned to his hometown of Namangan in Uzbekistan, he met the Islamic ideologue Tahir Yuldashev. After Uzbekistan gained its independence Namangani and Yuldashev founded a group called *Adalat* ('Justice'). The group assumed local authority, implementing the *sharia* and imposing its rule over part of the Ferghana Valley. *Adalat* challenged Uzbek President Karimov and demanded that he implement *sharia* across Uzbekistan. Subsequently, the group was outlawed. Namangani and Yuldashev both fled to Tajikistan to avoid being arrested. Namangani's fighting experience made him valuable to the Islamic Renaissance Party of Tajikistan, for whom he commanded active combat forces during the Tajik civil war from his base in the Tavildara Valley. After the peace agreement was signed, Namangani and Yuldashev founded the Islamic Movement of Uzbekistan in 1998. Namangani increasingly oriented himself towards Afghanistan and away from the Islamic Renaissance Party even though he kept his base in Tavildara Valley. In 1999, Namangani and the IMU carried out a number of raids into Kyrgyzstan. The IMU was also widely credited with a series of explosions in Tashkent as well as an attempt on President Karimov's life. In 2000, more operations followed as well as excursions into Kyrgyzstan. The raids were carried out from Namangani's base in the Tavildara Valley. Namangani and his men were flown out by Russians back to Afghanistan as part of an agreement. Namangani was appointed as head of the foreign fighters by Mullah Mohammad Omar in 2001 in preparation for the defence of the country following the September 11 attacks. He was killed in an airstrike in November 2001.

Karam Zuhdi: Karam Zuhdi is an Egyptian Islamist and senior figure with the group *al-Gamaa al-Islamiyya*. He met Mohammad Abd al-Salam Faraj in 1979/80 at around the time *al-Jihad* group was formed. Following the assassination of Anwar al-Sadat, however, he split from the group and helped found *al-Gamaa al-Islamiyya*. He was imprisoned for life in 1984. He was instrumental in *al-Gamaa al-Islamiyya*'s move away from violence during the 1990s. In the aftermath of the Luxor massacre of 1997 which was carried out by members of *al-Gamaa al-Islamiyya*, Zuhdi made a public apology to the families

463

of their victims and called on other groups, including al-Qaeda, to do the same. He was released from prison in September 2003.

Karl Inderfurth: Karl Inderfurth (1946–) is a former American diplomat. He served as Assistant Secretary of State for South Asian Affairs from August 1997 to January 2001. Prior to his work as a diplomat, he was Moscow correspondent for ABC News from 1981–91. As of 2011, he was a professor at George Washington University's Elliott School of International Affairs.

Khaled al-Islambouli: Khaled Ahmed Showqy al-Islambouli (1955–1982) was an Egyptian militant jihadist responsible for the assassination of Egyptian President Anwar al-Sadat (see above). He was a keen reader of the writings of Juhayman al-Utaybi and a member of the Egyptian *al-Jihad* group. He was executed on 15 April 1982.

Khalid Sheikh Mohammad: Khalid Sheikh Mohammad (1964–) is a Kuwaiti operational manager closely associated with al-Qaeda and various terrorist plots, including the September 11 attacks. He grew up in Kuwait but traces his lineage back to Baluchistan. He joined the Muslim Brotherhood when he was 16 years old and is believed to have been introduced to militant *jihad* at desert youth camps. After he graduated from secondary school in Kuwait he enrolled in Chowan College (now Chowan University), a small private Baptist institution in North Carolina in the United States. Khalid gained a degree in mechanical engineering in December 1986. In 1987, he travelled to Pakistan for the first time, where his brother Zahid introduced him to the Afghan mujahedeen leader, Abdul Rasul Sayyaf. Sayyaf provided Khalid with training facilities at the Sada camp. Khalid claims he fought for several months alongside bin Laden before starting to work with Abdullah Azzam. He worked for a communications company next and then ran an NGO from 1988–1992 in Peshawar and Jalalabad, sponsored by Sayyaf. In 1992, he reportedly went to Bosnia to fight alongside other Islamist groups. After returning to Pakistan he moved with his family to Qatar where he became project manager for the Qatari Ministry of Electricity and Water. He worked at the Ministry until 1996 when he fled to Pakistan from US authorities. Khalid was involved in the 1993 World Trade Center bombing, wiring money to co-conspirator Mohammed Salameh. In 1994, Khalid and his nephew Ramzi Yousef were both involved in planning the Bojinka plot in Manila (Philippines). After the failure of the Bojinka plot and the arrest of Yousef, Khalid allegedly travelled to Yemen, Sudan, Malaysia and Brazil. Khalid settled in Afghanistan in mid-1996 where he arranged for a meeting with bin Laden through Mohammad Atef. The meeting would establish the working relationship between the two men. The first meeting concluded without firm plans and Khalid continued to travel to India, Indonesia and Malaysia where he met with Hanbali. Khalid moved to Karachi in 1997. Sometime in late 1998 or early 1999, bin Laden gave him the green light for the September 11 plot. He moved to Kandahar and took over al-Qaeda's media operations along with the planning of the September 11 attacks. Khalid Sheikh Mohammad was captured in Rawalpindi, Pakistan, on 1 March 2003. Much of the information about him and his involvement in the September 11 plot in general came from interrogations, during which Khalid was subject to 'intensive interrogation techniques'; he was waterboarded 183 times. Accordingly, parts of his testimony are highly contested. He continues to be held by the US in Guantanamo Bay.

Khalid al-Mihdhar: Khalid al-Mihdhar (1975–2001) was one of the Saudi Arabian airplane hijackers of the September 11 attacks. He was originally selected by bin Laden to be a pilot during the operation but he was not able to successfully obtain the necessary pilot licence so he participated in the operation as one of the other hijackers. He was on board American Airlines Flight 77 which crashed into the Pentagon. He reportedly fought in Bosnia during the 1990s as well as in Afghanistan against the anti-Taliban opposition forces in the north.

Khalil Abu Mulal al-Balawi: Khalil Abu Mulal al-Balawi (1977–2009) was a Jordanian Islamist responsible for the suicide attack on CIA personnel of December 2009. He was educated as a doctor (in Kuwait, Jordan and Istanbul). He carried out the attack as a double agent, pretending to grow close to the CIA operatives but remaining loyal to al-Qaeda affiliates and members. The attack, on 30 December 2009, reportedly killed seven CIA operatives, including the base's head.

Khattab: Khattab (1969–2002) was a Saudi Islamist fighter, originally named Samir Salih Abdullah al-Suwailem. He was born in Saudi Arabia to a Saudi father and a Circassian mother but left during the 1980s to fight in Afghanistan. He is believed to have spent significant periods during the early 1990s in Afghanistan, and was instrumental in bringing Chechens back to Afghanistan to train in the camps there. He fought in the first and second Chechen wars and commanded groups of foreign fighters during this time, even to the extent that his reputation was larger than that of bin Laden. He made a pledge of allegiance to the al-Qaeda head after the September 11 attacks, however. He was killed in March 2002 by a poisoned letter.

King Abdullah: King Abdullah bin Abdul-Aziz (1923–) became King of Saudi Arabia in 2005. He served as Regent from 1996–2005 and prior to that in the National Guard as a Commander.

King Faisal: King Faisal bin Abdul Aziz al-Saud ruled Saudi Arabia from 1964–75, succeeding his elder brother, Saud. He also served as Crown Prince and Prime Minister during the 1950s. As King, Faisal embarked on a lavishly-funded programme of encouraging Pan-Islamism. He was assassinated by his half-brother's son, Faisal bin Musa'id, on 25 March 1975.

Madeleine Albright: Madeleine Albright (1937–) served as US Secretary of State from 1997–2001—the first woman to hold that office. Prior to this she was US Ambassador to the United Nations (1993–97).

Mahmud Beg Tarzi: Mahmud Beg Tarzi (1865–1933) was an Afghan writer and public intellectual. Born in Ghazni, he was a Mohammadzai Pashtun and lived for much of his early life in Turkey (following his father's exile from the country). He returned in 1901 following an invitation from King Habibullah and played a key role in the reform and modernisation agenda of those early years of the twentieth century inside Afghanistan. In 1929 he went back into exile in Turkey following the coup d'etat that deposed Amanullah. He died in Istanbul in 1933.

Major General Nick Carter: Major General Nick Carter is a senior British military officer who has served in the British Armed Forces since 1978. He was deployed to Bosnia in 1998, to Kosovo in 1999, and also commanded British forces in Basra in 2004. He was head of ISAF's Regional Command-South from 2009–10.

Malika el-Aroud: Malika el-Aroud (1960–) is a Moroccan-Belgian woman who was married to Dahmane Abd el-Sattar, one of the two assassins of Ahmed Shah Massoud. She is an active public commentator and has stated several times her devotion to bin Laden. As a result of this outspoken nature, she has been detained and put on trial several times in Europe post-2001. She was arrested again in December 2008 on suspicion of having 'terrorist links.'

Mansour Dadullah: Mansour Dadullah (also known as Bakht Mohammad) is the brother of Mullah Dadullah who was killed in May 2007. They are both believed to come from Char Chino (Uruzgan province). Mansour initially replaced his brother in the Taliban's command structure, but he was publicly sacked (in a message from Mullah Mohammad Omar posted on the Taliban's website) in late December 2007. This dismissal was in part an attempt by the senior Taliban leadership to regain control over their command structures but also on account of ideological differences; Mansour followed his brother's footsteps in advocating for a global *jihad*. He is believed to have been captured by Pakistani security services.

Massoud Azhar: The son of a well-known religious scholar, Massoud Azhar was born in 1968 and was educated at Binori Town's Deobandi madrassa in Karachi. A significant number of prominent Afghan and Pakistani Islamists passed through this institution, from which he graduated in the 1980s. He taught religious students for several years in Karachi before, by his own account, being 'recruited for *jihad*' by a *Harakat ul-Mujahedeen* member. At this point the facts are difficult to ascertain—some allege that Azhar was already operating together with/for Osama bin Laden (training jihadis in Yemen, suggests one source)—but by 1993 Azhar had risen to a significant status within *Harakat ul-Mujahedeen*. In June, following the dispatch of a prominent Saudi Deobandi Sheikh to contain inter-jihadist squabbles, Azhar played a prominent role in the merger of *Harakat ul-Mujahedeen* and *Harakat ul-Jihad ul-Islami* to form *Harakat ul-Ansar*. His involvement in the jihadist universe was important, and he has been cited as having played key roles in the expansion and sending of Pakistani jihadis to Somalia, Chechnya and Central Asia. Kashmir was their focus, however, and as a result of these activities he was arrested in February 1994 by Indian security forces. While in prison he wrote and published several books and articles, contributing to Pakistani debates from afar. In December 1999, following the hijacking of an Indian Airways flight, he was released along with several other prominent jihadi figures and later reappeared in Pakistan. By January 2000, he announced the formation of a new organisation, *Jaish-e Mohammad*, that received the blessing of the prominent Deobandi scholars (including that of Mufti Nizamuddin Shamzai). Many members of other Pakistani jihadi organisations shifted over to *Jaish-e Mohammad*. Azhar was subsequently arrested and rereleased in February and April 2000 by Pakistani forces, and has maintained a low profile since then. He was reportedly arrested in 2008 following the Mumbai attacks, but Pakistani officials have denied this. He remains a key point of interaction between al-Qaeda affiliates and the Pakistani jihadis.

Mavis Leno: Mavis Leno (1946–) is the wife of US talk show host, Jay Leno. She played a key role in activism and promotion of the women's rights agenda while the Taliban were in power during the 1990s.

Mawlana Abdul Aziz: Mawlana Abdul Aziz is a Pakistani cleric. He led the group which took over the Lal Masjid in Islamabad in July 2007 together with his brother, Abdur Rasheed Ghazi. He was arrested while attempting to flee disguised in a burqa on 4 July 2007. He was freed on bail in April 2009 pending his trial.

Mawlana Abdul Samad Sial: Mawlana Abdul Samad Sial is a Pakistani cleric who co-founded a group called *Jamiat Ansar ul-Afghaneen* ('Party of the Friends of the Afghan People') which was later renamed as *Harakat ul-Jihad ul-Islami*. He founded these groups together with Qari Saifullah Akhtar and Ilyas Kashmiri. He is also known as Matiur Rehman. He is currently (as of February 2011) believed to be the senior operational commander of *Lashkar-e Jhangvi* group. He is frequently tied to the training of international militants who return to America and other countries to carry out attacks, such as Najibullah Zazi.

Mawlana Fazlur Rahman: Mawlana Fazlur Rahman (born 1953) is the head of a section of the *Jamiat-e Ulema-ye Islam* political party. He has served in Pakistani politics (including in the National Assembly) and also ran against Musharraf for the presidency.

Mawlawi Abdul Kabir: Mawlawi Abdul Kabir (Zadran by tribe) is originally from Zadran (Paktya). He was governor of Jalalabad during the Taliban's rule, and also head of the eastern military zone. The UN 'travel ban' list states that he was born between 1958 and 1963. News agencies reported that he had been captured in Pakistan in July 2005, but other sources (including a statement issued by Mullah Mohammad Omar) indicated that this wasn't the case and that he is now Eastern Zone (Nangarhar, Laghman, Kunar and Nuristan provinces) commander for the Taliban. He allegedly attended the '*iftaar* meeting' hosted by the Saudi King in Mecca in September 2009 in which negotiations with the Taliban were reportedly discussed. He serves as the sometime-head of the Peshawar *Shura* and is believed to have been detained by Pakistani authorities in February 2010.

Mawlawi Abdul Rahman: Mawlawi Abdul Rahman Agha fought in Kandahar during the 1980s in Panjwayi province (in part under Mohammad Ayyub Agha, a relative of his). During the early 1990s he remained in Sangisar and taught religious classes at a madrassa there. He was a judge during the Taliban's rule of the 1990s.

Mawlawi Ahmad Jan: Mawlawi Ahmad Jan was originally from Zurmat district of Paktya province. He was close to Nasrullah Mansour, the head of an alternative '*Harakat*' political party. He is currently believed to be heading the Taliban's education committee.

Mawlawi Faqir Mohammad: Mawlawi Faqir Mohammad (1970–) is a Pakistani militant associated with the *Tehrik-e Taliban Pakistan* in Bajaur. He is Mohmand by tribe. He is believed to have become involved in the activities of this group in the early 1990s. He was close to Pakistani jihadi leader Sufi Mohammad. He is reported to have pledged loyalty to Mullah Mohammad Omar and bin Laden in 2010.

Mawlawi Mohammad Ali: Mawlawi Mohammad Ali lived in Pashmol in Panjwayi district (Kandahar province). He was one of the first to issue a *fatwa* in his area in 1979 sanctioning *jihad* against the Afghan government.

Mawlawi Mohammad Ataullah Faizani: Mawlawi Mohammad Ataullah Faizani (1923–c.1979) was a Herat-born religious cleric who led a group opposing the communist influence in Afghan politics during the late 1960s and 1970s. He was arrested in 1973 for this work and is believed to have been executed in or around 1979 in Kabul.

Mawlawi Nabi Mohammadi: Born into a Pashtun family (either Ahmadzai or Stanikzai by tribe) in the early 1920s, Nabi Mohammadi studied religious subjects in the traditional manner, both with his father and with other well-known scholars in Lowgar province. After he completed his studies, he himself began teaching in Lowgar, but increased activism by communist supporters led him to run for parliament, to which he was elected in 1969. He was well-known as a bulwark against the communists during this period—famously assaulting Babrak Karmal badly enough to put him in hospital. After Daud dissolved the parliament, Nabi Mohammadi returned to Lowgar (and later Helmand) to teach. He fled to Pakistan in 1978, setting up the political party *Harakat-e Enqelab-e Islami* as an umbrella organisation for all the mujahedeen in September. Rabbani and Hekmatyar, the two main figures of that time, both signed up. His party had started to fragment by 1979, however, and a failed uprising in Kandahar served to confirm to many that Nabi Mohammadi wasn't up to the task. He decided to keep the party as a grouping for religious scholars (*Ulemaa'*) and students (*taliban*), although they received little outside funding. In 1992, Nabi Mohammad was appointed Vice-President of the mujahedeen government, but by March 1995 he had aligned himself with the then-nascent 'Taliban movement.' He died of tuberculosis in Pakistan on 21 April 2002, and was brought back to Lowgar for burial.

Mawlawi Nazar Mohammad: Mawlawi Nazar Mohammad (Noorzai by tribe) was originally from Sia Chuy, and was the first Taliban judge in Kandahar at the beginning of the *jihad* period. He was replaced by Mawlawi Pasanai Saheb. Known as 'Titi Mawlawi Saheb' (literally 'small' Mawlawi Saheb) on account of his short stature and hunchback, he was uneducated and sentenced many to death. He had grey hair, and was killed in early fighting in Pashmol.

Mawlawi Nuruddin Turabi: Mullah Nuruddin Turabi (Achekzai by tribe) was originally from Tirin Kot (Uruzgan province) and fought with Harakat, and then later with Sayyaf's *Ittehad*, during the 1980s *jihad*. He commanded a hundred fighters, and was later appointed Minister of Justice under the Taliban. He is still alive.

Mawlawi Pasanai Saheb: Mawlawi Pasanai Saheb (Ismaelkhel by tribe) was the senior Talib judge following the death of Mawlawi Nazar Mohammad. Originally from Shah Juy (in Zabul province), he died after the 2001 invasion, probably in 2002 of old age. He was well-known in Kandahar for having rejected (and continuing to reject) reports of Massoud's assassination in September 2001. He was the most famous of the older generation of Taliban judges.

Mawlawi Qalamuddin: Born in Barak-i Barak district of Lowgar province, Mawlawi Qalamuddin was best known for his position as head of the Taliban's 'prevention of vice and promotion of virtue' ministry. He was also (in the first years following the Taliban's capture of Kabul) deputy minister of mosques and *hajj*. The ministry was independent of the judiciary or other government organs and reported directly to Mullah Mohammad Omar. He saw it as his goal to reform society and 'make it 100% Islamic.' From 2000–1, Qalamuddin was head of the Taliban's Olympic Committee. He was arrested in Barak-i Barak in April 2004. After his release on 14 September 2004 following tribal petitions to President Karzai, he ran for parliament in the elections, albeit unsuccessfully. He is still alive and living in Afghanistan.

Mawlawi Salam Jan Agha: Mawlawi Salam Jan Agha was from Zangiabad (Sayyed by qawm). He issued a *fatwa* to residents of Panjwayi district (Kandahar province) in 1979 sanctioning *jihad* against the Afghan government.

Mawlawi Saznour: Mawlawi Saznour is an Afghan mujahedeen commander affiliated with Sayyaf's *Ittehad-e Islami*. He reportedly fought together with bin Laden during the 1980s. He is believed to have travelled to Sudan in early 1996 to request that bin Laden come back to Afghanistan. He was killed shortly after the Taliban seized Jalalabad in 1996; Jason Burke writes that this was in 'an ambush almost certainly organized by the Taliban [at which point] Bin Laden swiftly set about building a relationship with the movement.'

Mawlawi Shah Mohammad: Mawlawi Shah Mohammad was a *shari'a* judge in Panjwayi (Kandahar province). He was one of the first to issue a *fatwa* in his area in 1979 sanctioning *jihad* against the Afghan government.

BIOGRAPHIES

Mawlawi Yunis Khalis: Mawlawi Yunis Khalis (1919–2006) was the head of an Afghan mujahedeen political party, *Hizb-e Islami*, and a prominent Islamist cleric. He was born in Nangarhar's Khogiani district and continued to play a prominent role in the politics of that province. When the Taliban moved into Nangarhar in 1996 he gave them his support, although he spent at least as much time in Pakistan as he did in Afghanistan during the 1990s. He died on 19 July 2006.

Milton Bearden: Milton Bearden (1940–) is an American former CIA officer. He served as CIA station chief in Pakistan, Moscow and Khartoum and was involved in the US effort to fund anti-Soviet fighters during the 1980s. He wrote a novel based on his experiences in Afghanistan and Pakistan, entitled 'The Black Tulip.'

Mohammad Abd al-Rahim al-Sharqawi: Mohammad Abd al-Rahim al-Sharqawi was an Egyptian Islamist closely associated with Ayman al-Zawahiri. They are believe to have formed a 'clandestine cell' together in 1968 and also shared a prison sentence following the case against members of *al-Jihad* group in Egypt. He spent three years in Tora Prison. Upon his release at the end of 1984 he travelled with al-Zawahiri to Pakistan. He was in Pakistan following the end of the 1980s *jihad* and was extradited by the Pakistani government to Egyptian authorities. It is unclear what he was involved in during the 1990s, but he was captured again in Pakistan in January 2002 and shows up in lists of US detainees who were subjected to 'intensive interrogation techniques.' In November 2005 he was being held in Poland at a CIA prison.

Mohammad Abd al-Salam Faraj: Mohammad Abd al-Salam Faraj (1952–82) was born in lower Egypt. His father was a member of the Muslim Brotherhood, believed to be more radical than most. He studied electrical engineering in Cairo and found work in Alexandria in that profession after finishing his studies. He rejected the Muslim Brotherhood for its neglect of *jihad* in the face of Israel and joined the *al-Gama'a al-Islamiyya* early on. In 1978, he joined a cell led by Ibrahim Salama as part of al-Jihad group, but managed to cut his ties to them before they were caught. Around 1979, he formed Egyptian Islamic Jihad together with Karam Zuhdi. After the assassination of Anwar al-Sadat, he was arrested. He was executed on 15 April 1982, along with Khalid al-Islambouli, 'Essam al-Qamari and three others.

Mohammad Abduh: Mohammad Abduh (1849–1905) was an Egyptian Islamic reformist scholar. He was strongly influenced by the writings of Jamal al-Din al-Afghani and studied at al-Azhar in Cairo.

471

Mohammad Atta: Mohammad Mohammad al-Amir 'Awad al-Sayyed Atta (1968–2001) was the leader of the 'Hamburg Cell' which formed the core of the September 11 attackers. He was born in Egypt and grew up there, studying architecture at Cairo University before he went to Germany to continue his studies at the Technical University in Hamburg. In Hamburg he frequented the al-Quds mosque. He lived with Marwan al-Shehhi and Ramzi bin al-Shibh. At the end of the 1990s the group became increasingly radical, in particular in their discussions about the United States and *jihad*. Atta was the leader of the September 11 plot and responsible for target selection, coordination and all other operational aspects once inside America. In 1999, the group around Atta decided to go to Chechnya in order to take part in the *jihad*. A chance meeting on a train with Khalid al-Masri, however, set the group on a different path. Al-Masri is believed to have introduced them to Abu Mus'ab al-Suri, an al-Qaeda affiliate who lived in Duisburg, Germany. In a common tale echoed by other jihadis who sought to go to Chechnya, the group was told by al-Suri that they should first go to Afghanistan to train before joining the *jihad* in Chechnya. Atta and Jarrah flew to Karachi and went to Quetta from where they were taken to Kandahar. By the time Ramzi bin al-Shibh arrived two weeks later they had already pledged an oath of loyalty to bin Laden. Ramzi bin al-Shibh took the oath as well. The group then met with Mohammad Atef who told them that they would take part in a secret mission. They were to return to Germany and enrol in flight training. Atta was chosen by bin Laden to lead the group and received additional information including a pre-approved target list. The group returned to Hamburg in early 2000. After their return, the group changed their behaviour noticeably, avoiding radical preachers and changing their appearance, all in an effort to divert any unwanted attention. After enquiring about flight schools in Europe, the group soon learnt that they would have to learn how to fly passenger planes in the United States. Atta was granted a visa to the United States on 18 May 2000. In mid-December 2000, Atta obtained his commercial pilot's licence. Soon after, he began training on large commercial airline simulators. Atta travelled to Germany in early 2001 where he met with Ramzi bin al-Shibh for a progress report, telling him that the other pilots had obtained their licences and were awaiting orders. Atta would pilot American Airlines Flight 11. He boarded the plane with Satam al-Suqami Waleed al-Shehri, Wali al-Shehri and Abdulaziz al-Omari. Not one survived.

Mohammad Da'ud Khan: Mohammad Da'ud Khan (1909–78) was Pashtun and the cousin of the Afghan King Zahir Shah. He served as Prime Minister

(1953–63) and President (1973–78) after seizing power in the 'Saur' coup. He himself was killed in a coup headed by Taraki.

Mohammad Ibrahim Athar Alvi: Mohammad Ibrahim Athar Alvi (1966–) was one of the hijackers of the Indian Airlines flight in December 1999. He is also the younger brother of Massoud Azhar. He is believed to have been arrested in Pakistan on charges of sedition on 31 December 2001. His current location is unknown.

Mohammad Jamal Khalifa: Mohammed Jamal Khalifa (1957–2007, also known as Abu Bara'a) was born in Jeddah (Saudi Arabia) on 1 February 1957. He was the brother-in-law of bin Laden and believed to be involved in numerous organisational and operational tasks related to al-Qaeda. Khalifa was involved in several alleged al-Qaeda fronts, such as the Benevolence International Corporation, founded in the Philippines in 1988, and the Islamic Benevolence Committee (1992) which was renamed the Benevolence International Foundation. He started Khalifa Trading Industries and other companies believed to be front organisations. He was also the director of the International Islamic Relief Organisation (IIRO). Jamal Khalifa is believed to have assisted Abdulrajak Janjalani with founding the Abu Sayyaf group in the Philippines in 1989. He also is believed to have used his position in the IIRO to support the Moro Islamic Liberation Front. He was convicted in absentia in Jordan for alleged involvement in the 1993 and 1994 series of bombings of public places there. During the trial, Jamal Khalifa admitted that he had known the perpetrators of the bombing and had sent them money. Khalifa trained with bin Laden in Afghanistan. He met Mohamed Loay Bayazid, president of the Benevolence International Foundation, in the United States and was arrested on 14 December 1994, on charges relating to the World Trade Center bombing of 1993, but was later released. Khalifa denounced al-Qaeda and bin Laden following the September 11 attacks and continued with his various business interests. He was assassinated on 31 January 2007, while visiting his gemstone mine in Sakamiko in southern Madagascar. There is evidence that puts him close to operatives like Ramzi Yousuf, himself related to Khalid Sheikh Mohammad.

Mohammad Masoom Stanikzai: Mohammad Masoom Stanikzai is an Afghan advisor to President Karzai and former Telecommunications Minister (2002–4). He was one of the main figures behind the Afghan government's official 'Peace and Reintegration' strategy unveiled in June 2010.

Mohammad Qutb: Mohammad Qutb (1919–) is the second eldest son of five children and the younger brother to Sayyed Qutb. He is himself an Islamist thinker and writer, publishing several books and academic articles. Like his brother, Mohammad became a member of the Muslim Brotherhood and one of its ideological leaders. He was arrested on 29 July 1965, days before his brother Sayyed, and charged as one of the main conspirators in an assassination plot to overthrow the government of Egypt. Unlike his brother, he was not executed. He was released by President Anwar al-Sadat in 1972; he moved immediately to Saudi Arabia. There he edited and published the works of his brother alongside his own publications, teaching at several universities including King 'Abdul Aziz University in Jeddah and at the *Shari'a* College at Umm al-Qura University in Mecca. He met Mawlana Mawdudi in Lahore, Pakistan, in December 1978 and supervised the doctoral thesis of Safar al-Hawali, one of the 'Awakening Sheikhs.' During his stay at King 'Abdul Aziz University he taught bin Laden and worked alongside Abdullah Azzam. He was also reportedly visited by Ayman Al-Zawahiri there. In a video statement in 2004, bin Laden recommended his book 'Concepts that should be corrected.' His best known work, however, is 'Jahiliyya in the Twenty-first Century.' Muhammad Qutb, while in Saudi Arabia, re-interpreted his brother's work, in particular the passages regarding Saudi Arabia. He is still alive.

Mohammad Sa'di al-Keilani: Mohammad Sa'di al-Keilani is best known for his involvement in a 1938 plot to depose Afghanistan's King Zahir Shah. Also known as the 'Shami Pir,' al-Keilani was born in Damascus in 1901. He received his education in Germany. While travelling in India in the late 1930s he was asked to use his religious standing—stemming from his connection to the Gailani Sufi family—to challenge the Afghan government. He travelled to Waziristan and, with some help from the Faqir of Ipi and some Qadiri clerics, gathered together a force of around 5000 fighters. He was prevented from following through on his plan just days before their coup attempt by British/Indian intervention.

Mohammad Salah: Mohammad Salah is a writer and journalist for the Lebanese newspaper *Al-Hayat*. He is the author of 'Narratives of the *Jihad* Years: the journey of the Afghan Arabs' (published in Arabic).

Mohammad Taher Aziz Gumnam: Mohammad Taher Aziz Gumnam (Eshaqzai by tribe and originally from Kandahar) is a doctor and writer. He is the author of 'Kandahar Assassins' (1986) and 'Kandahar Heroes' (1996). He is still alive.

Mohammad ibn Abdul Wahhab: Mohammad ibn Abdul Wahhab (1703–92) was a Salafi scholar and founder of the eponymous Wahhabi movement.

He allied together with Mohammad ibn Saud to found the first Saudi state in 1744.

Mufti Nizamuddin Shamzai: Arguably one of the most important Deobandi figures in Pakistan and frequently cited as a key ally by many jihadi groups, Shamzai studied in Karachi at the *Jami'a Farooqia* after which he taught there for over two decades. He then joined the Binori Town madrassa where he remained for the rest of his life. This madrassa graduated many of the leaders of the jihadi groups. In 1979, Shamzai issued a *fatwa* calling for *jihad* following the Soviet invasion of Afghanistan, and reportedly also sent students from his madrassa to Afghanistan to fight. Shamzai is frequently cited as the main link between the senior Taliban and senior al-Qaeda figures; for example, he is alleged to have mediated between Mullah Mohammad Omar and Osama bin Laden in 1995 in order to arrange the latter's travel from Sudan to Afghanistan. This seems somewhat unlikely since bin Laden did not yet know that he would be expelled from Sudan the next year. Shamzai was, however, present at the marriage of bin Laden's eldest son in 2000. He issued a *fatwa* authorising retaliation against the United States in 1998 after the cruise missile strikes on Afghanistan, a *fatwa* that was repeated following the commencement of Operation Enduring Freedom in 2001. Shamzai is again listed as one of the key facilitators for Mullah Mohammad Omar and bin Laden to leave Afghanistan in 2001/2. He was killed on 30 May 2004, in a suicide blast which also killed his son, nephew and driver. His ties with the Pakistani government (including very senior figures like Musharraf) are also important in explaining his stature—as this link, he was even asked to travel to Mullah Mohammad Omar in September 2001 to persuade him to surrender bin Laden.

Mullah Abdul Razaq: Mullah Abdul Razaq Akhundzada (Achekzai by tribe) is the former corps commander for northern Afghanistan. He also served as the Taliban government's Interior Minister.

Mullah Akhtar Jan: Mullah Akhtar Jan (Noorzai by tribe) fought with *Hizb-e Islami* during the 1980s *jihad*. He was the District Chief of Spin Boldak during the Rabbani government. He is still alive.

Mullah Atta Mohammad: Mullah Atta Mohammad (Eshaqzai by tribe) was originally from Sangin and fought with *Jamiat* as a mujahed during the 1980s *jihad*. He was middle-aged at that time, but was killed (by unidentified attackers) in Quetta during the Taliban's rule.

Mullah Berader: Mullah Berader (1968–) is a senior member of the Afghan Taliban. Popolzai by tribe, Berader was born in Uruzgan but fought in Kandahar during the 1980s *jihad*, mainly in the Panjwayi area. He was a founding member of the Taliban movement from 1994 onwards and served in a variety of posts while the Taliban were in power. He was actively involved in the insurgency that developed post-2001 but was arrested in February 2010 in a raid in Pakistan, allegedly as part of a Pakistani government attempt to regain control over peace talks between the Karzai government and the Afghan Taliban. He has since been rumoured to have been released (in late 2010) but this is unsubstantiated.

Mullah Dadullah: Mullah Dadullah (Kakar by tribe) was born around 1966 in a village called Munara Kalay in Char Chino district of Uruzgan province to a Kuchi family, but his family moved to Deh Rawud (Uruzgan) soon after. He was active in the 1980s *jihad* and a strong ally of the Taliban's leader Mullah Mohammad Omar. He lost his leg fighting in western Afghanistan in 1994 but went on to play significant roles in battles in central and northern Afghanistan pre-2001. He rose to prominence in 2006 (particularly in the Western media) as the 'butcher of the south' for videos in which he beheads so-called 'spies.' He was killed by ISAF forces in May 2007.

Mullah Ehsanullah Ehsan: Mullah Ehsanullah Ehsan (Popolzai by tribe) was originally from Kandahar and served in the Taliban's government post-1996 as a member of Mullah Mohammad Omar's shura in Kandahar as well as head of the Afghan Central Bank. He was one of the senior leaders of the movement post-1996, and he was at the head of the first official Taliban delegation to meet with bin Laden in 1996 following their capture of Jalalabad and the surrounding area. He reportedly assured bin Laden that the Taliban would not hand him over to the United States, even if it would mean sacrificing the Taliban. He also was head of the delegation sent to Loya Paktya in early 1995 to negotiate their acceptance of the growing Taliban movement in their provinces and served for a period as the Taliban's senior commander in the Khost area. He also negotiated with Hazara representatives in Ghazni in October 1994, assuring them that the Taliban would not encroach on Hazara areas and that they would respect Shi'a jurisprudence. He was killed in late 1997 in Mazar-e Sharif.

Mullah Fazl: Mullah Fazl (Kakar) was head of the Army Corps under the Taliban. Originally from Tirin Kot (Uruzgan province), he fought as a mujahed during the 1980s *jihad* but wasn't famous as a commander during that time. He was captured in 2001 after surrendering to General Dostum together with Taliban soldiers, and is still being held in Guantánamo prison.

BIOGRAPHIES

Mullah Ghazi: Mullah Ghazi fought in the 1980s *jihad* in the Panjwayi area. He was very close with Mullah Mohammad Omar during the 1990s, and witnesses report that they were often in meetings together.

Mullah Gul Agha: Mullah Gul Agha (Eshaqzai by tribe) is a close friend of Mullah Mohammad Omar and originally from Maiwand district (Kandahar province). He fought in Kandahar and Helmand during the 1980s *jihad* and served together with the Taliban leader during the 1990s. He is believed to have taken over senior operational control of the Taliban since Mullah Berader was arrested in early 2010.

Mullah Khairullah Khairkhwa: Mullah Khairullah Khairkhwa (1967–) served as the Taliban's interior minister from 1996–99 as well as governor of Herat from 1999–2001. He is originally from Arghestan district (Kandahar province) and Popolzai by tribe. He is believed to have been educated in the Haqqaniya and Akhora Khattak madrassas in Pakistan. He was affiliated with the *Harakat-e Enqelab-e Islami* party during the 1980s *jihad* against the Soviets. He served as a spokesman for the movement from 1994–1996. He was arrested in Pakistan in February 2002 and was transferred to Guantánamo jail (after a short initial period of detention in Kandahar) where he remains to this day. He is one of the names suggested by the Afghan government's High Peace Council for release back to Afghanistan and a case was heard by the Federal District Court in Washington D.C. in March 2011 seeking the release of Khairkhwa for 'unlawful detention.'

Mullah Khaksar: Mullah Khaksar was born around 1960 in Kandahar. He received a madrassa education and fought under the *Hizb-e Islami* (Khalis) commander Abdul Raziq in Kandahar during the 1980s (as did Mullah Mohammad Omar). When the Taliban came to power, he was the movement's Intelligence Minister (1994–6) but was reportedly demoted in 1996 over the issue of the foreign militants inside the country. He was then appointed as Deputy Minister of the Interior in 1996, a position he held until 2001. He reportedly met bin Laden in 1998 following the cruise missile attacks and told him to leave the country. Gannon writes that he met with United States officials in 1999 in Peshawar, offering them help dealing with bin Laden, but his offer was turned down. Khaksar broke with the Taliban on 13 November as Kabul fell and by December was reportedly calling on people to support the Northern Alliance along with several other high-ranking Talibs in Peshawar. He ran for parliament in 2004, albeit unsuccessfully. He was shot dead in Kandahar in January 2006, and the Taliban claimed responsibility.

Mullah Khudaidad: Mullah Khudaidad was a well-known Mullah based in Taloqan (Panjwayi district, Kandahar province) who was among the first to issue a *fatwa* sanctioning *jihad* against the Afghan government in 1979.

Mullah Malang: Mullah Sher Mohammad Malang (Popolzai by tribe) was one of Mullah Malang's commanders during the *jihad* period. After the Taliban took control in the south in the mid-1990s, Mullah Sher Mohammad served in a leadership position at the beginning. He was appointed as governor of Nimruz and then later served with the military. He is still alive, although he was arrested and held at the American base at the former house of Mullah Mohammad Omar for a long time.

Mullah Mohammad Hassan: There are two Mullah Mohammad Hassans, both of whom were governor of Kandahar during the Taliban's rule over Afghanistan. Sources frequently confuse and collate the two biographies so it is difficult to offer anything but a composite biographical portrait for 'Mullah Mohammad Hassan.' One of the two has both legs and is Babar by tribe, the other has only one leg and is Achekzai by tribe. He is reported to have studied in Pakistan and Afghanistan, but cut his studies short with the outbreak of fighting in Afghanistan. Both are cited as having fought with *Harakat-e Enqelab* during the 1980s, and also as a commander in Kandahar City for Khalis' *Hezb-e Islami*. Mullah Mohammad Hassan was a close associate of Mullah Mohammad Omar, and briefly served as Foreign Minister (replaced by Mutawakil). From 1994–6 he was governor of Kandahar. In 1996–7 he served as governor of southwestern Afghanistan, and in 1997 he was appointed as the acting head of the interim shura in Kabul. He was a Taliban founding member.

Mullah Mohammad Omar: Born in the early 1960s in southern Afghanistan, Mullah Mohammad Omar grew up in a time of relative peace and stability. He pursued his religious studies from a young age at local institutions and schools, and it was only in the late 1970s that the issues of the outside world began to impinge on his life. He fled to Pakistan along with many members of his family, but began his *jihad* against the Soviet and the Afghan Communist government fighters soon after. He played a prominent role in the clashes in the fertile triangle west of Kandahar City, switching between different political parties as one or the other received more funding and supplies from the foreign powers which were supporting the mujahedeen. When the Soviet troops finally withdrew in 1989, Mullah Mohammad Omar returned to his village along with most of the other clerics who had fought in southern Afghanistan. By 1994, however, the situation had deteriorated to such an extent that these quietist clergymen decided to take a stand—one of Mullah Mohammad Omar's signature moments—and the movement that we now know as 'the Taliban' was born. In 1996 he was declared *Amir ul-Mu'mineen* or 'Prince of the Faithful' at a gathering of religious clerics in Kandahar. This was the point when his fate collided with that of Osama bin Laden. Mullah Mohammad Omar could not ignore the bombings of the American embassies in Africa in 1998, particularly with the cruise missile strikes on Afghanistan and Sudan that followed. Bin Laden had already been relocated to Kandahar (the unofficial seat of the Taliban's government) in 1996, and it was at this point that the relationship takes on a new dimension. Increased international condemnation (especially over women's issues), limited support or acknowledgement from other Muslim nations, and pressure over the Taliban's hosting of bin Laden served to impel the two men together. The September 11 attacks separated the two as they went into hiding, and it seems likely that time and distance apart further encouraged a reappraisal of the relationship. Mullah Mohammad Omar is assumed to be alive and based somewhere in Pakistan.

Mullah Mohammad Rabbani: While Mullah Mohammad Rabbani was born in Pashmol, he had strong ties to the district of Arghestan. He received an Islamic education in a madrassa (whether in Afghanistan or Pakistan is disputed) but fought during the 1980s as a deputy commander for Abdul Raziq in Khalis' *Hezb-e Islami*, commanding a half-dozen groups (c. 120 men), and was well-known for operations in Kandahar and Zabul provinces. When the Soviet troops withdrew, Rabbani engaged himself in further study (reportedly in Zabul, Kandahar and Quetta at madrassas) but joined up with the Taliban in 1994 as they began disarming local commanders on the highways. There are rival accounts of the extent and start date for his early involvement: some hold that he was involved in an early meeting with Pakistani officials; others say he only joined the movement after Mullah Naqib's defection to the Taliban; and there is also one account which asserts Rabbani was head of a separate and independently-established Taliban group operating out of Arghestan district which was then united and set under Mullah Mohammad Omar's group. Mullah Mohammad Rabbani also reportedly travelled to Kabul in September 1994 to ask for pledges of support from Burhanuddin Rabbani and Massoud. He was a prominent player in the operation to take Kabul, even meeting with Massoud in Wardak province in late February 1995 to try to cooperate. Rabbani is widely rumoured to have ordered the execution of the former president Najib, reportedly in revenge for the execution of two of Rabbani's brothers over a decade ago. Rabbani always denied the accusation. The Taliban established their government in Kabul and Mullah Mohammad Rabbani was appointed Prime Minister and head of the advisory council. He retained this second-in-command position until his death. He was constantly rumoured to be unhappy with the presence of bin Laden in Afghanistan, and this seems to have been a key point of friction with Mullah Mohammad Omar. In November 1998, for example, following a series of arrests in Jalalabad a month before, Rabbani was summoned to Kandahar for a reprimand—his loyalty was questioned. By 1998, Rabbani was already making regular visits to Saudi Arabia—he was reportedly 'the favourite' of Prince Turki al-Faisal—to treat the cancer that would eventually kill him. The final two years of his life were reportedly full of conflict with Mullah Mohammad Omar, and in August 2000 he even was seated on the far edge of the stage at a military parade, which many commentators claim was an indication of his having been sidelined. He died on 21 April 2001 in a hospital in Rawalpindi, Pakistan, and his body was repatriated to Kandahar in a United Nations plane.

Mullah Mohammad Sadiq Akhund: Mullah Mohammad Sadiq Akhund (Achekzai by tribe) initially fought with *Harakat* but switched to Sayyaf's *Ittehad-e Islami* when they received large quantities of weapons. He had roughly a hundred mujahedeen fighting with him. He was originally from Tirin Kot (Uruzgan province). Following the fall of the Taliban in 2001, with whom he was fighting, Mullah Mohammad Sadiq Akhund was captured and taken to Guantánamo Bay prison. He was later released and is still alive.

Mullah Mohammad Shafiq: Mullah Mohammad Shafiq was the head of the Wano Pul madrassa in Uruzgan.

Mullah Mujahed: Mullah Abdul Hakim Mujahed (1956–) served as the Taliban's representative to the United Nations and was also closely involved in discussions between the United States and the Taliban government. He was closely associated with Nabi Mohammadi's *Harakat* party during the 1980s *jihad*. He is alive and lives in Kabul.

Mullah Mushr: Mullah Mushr is originally from Kandahar and fought alongside Mullah Burjan. He was a leading commander on the front that advanced towards Kabul from 1995–6.

Mullah Naqibullah: Mullah Naqibullah (c.1950–2007) also known as Mullah Naqib or Mullah Gul Akhund was born in Charqulba village in Arghandab district of Kandahar province. Head of the Alikozai tribe until his death in October 2007, Mullah Naqib was extremely prominent as a mujahedeen commander during the 1980s *jihad*. He fought with his men in his native Arghandab district. He continued to play an instrumental role in the upheavals of the mid-1990s and early-2000s.

Mullah Nasim Akhundzada: Mullah Nasim Akhundzada was a prominent Helmandi mujahedeen commander of the 1980s who fought for Nabi Mohammadi's party. He was closely associated with the drug trade operating out of that province. He was killed in 1990 in an attack that was widely blamed on his *Hizb-e Islami* rival in Helmand, Gulbuddin Hekmatyar.

Mullah Nazir: Mullah Nazir (c. 1975–) is a prominent commander associated with the *Tehrik-e Taliban Pakistan* (TTP) in South Waziristan. He was reportedly closely allied to Gulbuddin Hekmatyar in Afghanistan and is believed to be the current head of Taliban forces in Wana.

Mullah Obaidullah: Mullah Obaidullah (Alikozai by tribe) was originally from Nelgham and was known for being a tough fighter but of a quiet nature. He is believed to have been born in approximately 1968. He acted as Defence Minister during the Taliban's rule. During the 1980s *jihad* he acted as *amir* of the front of Mullah Mohammad Sadiq Akhund. When Karam Khan left the front, Mullah Obaidullah took his place as commander. He is almost certainly still alive and is one of the senior Taliban commanders operating in Pakistan, although there were credible reports that he had been arrested on 26 February 2008 and that he continued to be held in a Pakistani jail.

Mullah Samad Akhund: Mawlawi Abdul Samad (Khunday by tribe) was from Tirin Kot (Uruzgan province) although further back his family was originally from Arghestan district of Kandahar. After the Taliban took power he was first District Chief of Spin Boldak district of Kandahar, then head of the electricity ministry in Kandahar, then head of the agriculture ministry in Helmand. He is still alive.

Mullah Yarana: Mullah Yarana fought on the Taliban fronts in Panjwayi during the 1980s *jihad*. During the early 1990s he was based in Sangisar and taught religious classes there.

Mullah Zaeef: Born in 1968 to a poor family in southern Afghanistan, Mullah Zaeef received a basic religious education in the years before the Soviet invasion. He fled from Kandahar to Pakistan along with much of the rest of the local population after the Soviet invasion, returning in 1983 to begin his *jihad*. He fought alongside many of those who we now know as the senior leadership of the Taliban—at that time there were separate fronts manned by the religious students or 'Taliban'—and the bonds generated by this experience extremely important for him. He went on to play a role in the founding of the

Taliban 'movement' in 1994—he was initially suggested as a possible candidate for the leadership position—and was appointed to a wide variety of administrative positions within the Taliban government (including a brief stint at the Defence Ministry). In 2000 he was appointed Ambassador to Pakistan and in this position he came face-to-face with the issues surrounding Osama bin Laden and the presence of Arabs within Afghanistan. As such, he engaged with the United States and Saudi Arabia and tried to find a solution that would be acceptable to all parties. Mullah Zaeef was often identified as being part of a more 'moderate' faction within the Taliban who felt that the continued hosting of bin Laden was a problem for the movement. In 2001 following the September 11 attacks, Mullah Zaeef became the best-known face of the Taliban through his press briefings, and in 2002 he was handed over by the Pakistani intelligence services to the American government. More than four years of detention followed, including three and a half years spent in Guantánamo, prior to his release in September 2005. He currently lives in Kabul.

Mushtaq Ahmad Zargar: Mushtaq Ahmad Zargar (1967–) was one of the three prisoners released in exchange for the hostages of the Indian Airlines hijacking. He was born in Srinagar in 1967 and joined the Jammu and Kashmir Liberation Front (JKLF) at an early age. He formed his own group, *Al-Omar Mujahedeen*, in December 1989 following disagreements with the JKLF leadership. He was arrested in May 1992 following a series of murders and kidnappings of Indian nationals. He is believed to be still alive, living in Muzaffarabad (Pakistan).

Mustafa Hamza: Mustafa Hamza (1956–) is an Egyptian who was arrested following the assassination of Anwar al-Sadat. Following his release he travelled to Afghanistan (as well as other countries) and played a more prominent role within *al-Gamaʾa al-Islamiyya*. He is, for example, believed to have been behind the organisation of the assassination attempt against Hosni Mubarak in Addis Ababa in June 1995. He took over as head of the group in November 1997 following disagreements with the leader, Rifaʾi Taha, and in the wake of the Luxor massacre. He had been living in Iran but was extradited back to Egypt in May 2004. He is believed to be in Egyptian custody.

Nadir Shah: Nadir Shah (1883–1933) was the king of Afghanistan from 1929–33. He succeeded the interim reign of Habibullah Kalakani (also known as Bache-ye Saqao). He was a Mohammadzai Pashtun and his rule represented a return to the old guard, including an initial abandonment of Amanullah's reform agenda. He was assassinated in 1933 and succeeded by Mohammad Zahir Shah.

Najibullah: Najibullah (Ahmadzai by tribe) succeeded Babrak Karmal and was President of Afghanistan from November 1986 to April 1992. Born in 1947 in Kabul, he was a prominent figure in the Communist PDPA and a member of its Parcham faction. When the Taliban captured Kabul in 1996, they tortured and executed him before publicly displaying his body.

Najibullah Zazi: Najibullah Zazi (1985–) is an Afghan-American who was arrested in September 2009 on suspicion of plotting to attack the New York subway system. He pled guilty in February 2010 to several charges, including that of providing material support to a terrorist organisation. He was born in Paktya province of Afghanistan in 1985, but he left Afghanistan in 1992 for Peshawar and then moved to the United States in 1999, settling near Denver, Colorado.

Nasir Haqqani: Nasir Haqqani is the son of Jalaluddin Haqqani. He was involved in fundraising and liaising with Arab donors for the Haqqani network for many years. He was recently arrested in Pakistan.

Nasrullah: Nasrullah Khan (1874–1920) served as King of Afghanistan for a week in February 1919, deposed in the end by his brother, Amanullah Khan. He was imprisoned (suspected of complicity in the assassination of Habibullah (the former King)) and himself killed in 1920.

Nawaf al-Hazmi: Nawaf al-Hazmi (1976–2001) was one of the Saudi Arabian hijackers of the September 11 attacks. He was originally selected by bin Laden to be a pilot during the operation but he wasn't able to successfully obtain the pilot licence so he participated in the operation as one of the other hijackers. He was on board American Airlines flight 77 that crashed into the Pentagon. He reportedly fought in Bosnia during the 1990s together with his friend Khalid al-Mihdhar (see above) as well as in Afghanistan against the anti-Taliban opposition forces in the north, and in Chechnya in 1998.

Nawaz Sharif: Nawaz Sharif (1949–) is a Pakistani politician. He served as Prime Minister from 1990–3 and 1997–9. He returned to Pakistan in 2007 after spending the previous eight years outside the country. He continues to play a role in Pakistani politics.

Nek Mohammad: Nek Mohammad (1974–2004) was a Pakistani Wazir commander who came to prominence post-2001 for his role in resisting military operations in South Waziristan together with a group of fighters. He had fought against American forces inside Afghanistan in 2001 but retreated back to South Waziristan after the Taliban fell. He was killed in a drone strike in June 2004.

Noman Benotman: Noman Benotman (1967–) is a Libyan who fought in Afghanistan during the late 1980s and early 1990s. He met many of the leading militant Islamists during that period and set up the Libyan Islamic Fighting Group in the early 1990s. In recent years he has taken a public stance against al-Qaeda and its actions, for example releasing an open letter to bin Laden in 2010. As of 2011, he was working at the counter-extremism think-tank, Quilliam, in London.

Omar Abdul Rahman: Sheikh Omar Abdul Rahman (1938–) was born in Egypt and lost his sight to diabetes in early childhood. He developed an interest in the teachings of Ibn Taymiyya and studied the *Qu'ran* in Braille. He is a graduate of al-Azhar University in Cairo and was a senior leader in *al-Gama'a al-Islamiyya*, a radical militant group in Egypt. He is believed to have had close contact with Abdullah Azzam and, according to some reports, travelled to Peshawar in the 1980s. He moved to the United States and was convicted in 1995 for seditious conspiracy (related to the World Trade Center bombing in 1993) and sentenced to life imprisonment in 1996. Abdul Rahman is a leading jihadist scholar and is frequently named alongside compatriots of his like Sayyid Qutb and others.

Omar Nasiri: Omar Nasiri is a pen-name for the author of 'Inside the *Jihad*', a memoir detailing life in the training camps that operated inside Afghanistan during the 1990s.

Omar al-Bashir: Omar al-Bashir (1944–) is the President of Sudan, a position he has held since 1993. A warrant for his arrest was issued by the International Criminal Court in March 2009 indicting him on five counts of 'crimes against humanity.'

Omar bin Abd al-Aziz: Omar bin Abd al-Aziz (682–720) was a caliph of the Umayyad dynasty. He ruled from 717–20 and was known for his cautious foreign policies, preferring instead to implement internal reforms (including those tackling the tax system). Fellow Ummayad nobility disagreed with his reform agenda and he died from poison put into his food.

Omar ibn al-Khattab: Omar ibn al-Khattab (586–644) was the second of the so-called *Rashidun* caliphs who ruled following the Prophet Mohammad's death. Omar succeeded Abu Bakr (see above) in 634 after the latter's death from an illness. He was a convert and a companion of the Prophet. He died in 644 at the hands of a Persian attacker.

Osama bin Laden: Osama bin Laden (1957–2011) was a Saudi national who spent time in southeast Afghanistan during the 1980s *jihad*, followed by years in Saudi Arabia and Sudan, before returning back to eastern, then southern, Afghanistan from 1996 where he organised and planned several terrorist attacks on US interests culminating in those of 11 September 2001; he served as the head and founding member of al-Qaeda until his death in early May 2011 in a US Special Forces raid on his compound in Abbottabad, Pakistan.

Osman: Osman bin 'Affan (579–656) was the third of the so-called *Rashidun* caliphs who took power following the death of the Prophet Mohammad. Osman succeeded Omar ibn al-Khattab (see above) and his rule oversaw a massive expansion of the territory under the control of the Caliphate. He was assassinated in 656.

Pervez Musharraf: Pervez Musharraf (born in Delhi in 1943) was President of Pakistan (2001–2008) following a *coup d'etat* in 1999 displacing Rafiq Tarar.

Pir Gailani: Pir Sayyed Ahmad Gailani (1932–) is the current head of the Qadiriyya Sufi order in Afghanistan and led one of the groups officially sanctioned by Pakistan to operate as jihadi fronts, the National Islamic Front of Afghanistan. He used this spiritual authority along with business clout— reportedly a large share in the narcotics smuggling trade coupled with the sales franchise for Peugeot cars in Afghanistan—and marriage into the Durrani Pashtun clan to establish a large social hierarchy and organisation around him. Still living in Kabul, he currently is as much politician as he is religious leader.

Prince Sultan bin Abdulaziz al-Saud: Prince Sultan bin Abdulaziz al-Saud (1928–) served as Saudi Defence Minister during the 1991 Gulf War. He is currently the Crown Prince of Saudi Arabia and was appointed in 2005. He is first in the line of succession to the Saudi throne.

Qari Saifullah Akhtar: A key figure and founder of *Harakat ul-Jihad ul-Islami*, Qari Saifullah Akhtar has been involved in the jihadi groups since the early 1980s. See the profile of *Harakat ul-Jihad ul-Islami* for details of his activities during the 1980s and 1990s. He was appointed head of *Harakat ul-Jihad ul-Islami* following the death of Mawlana Irshad Ahmed in 1985, but this led to tensions and HUJI members split to set up *Harakat ul-Mujahedeen*, an organisation that Qari Saifullah Akhtar himself became deputy of following a Saudi-initiated truce and rejoining of the two groups. He reportedly was deeply involved in the 1995 coup attempt to topple Benazir Bhutto's government, and later was also tied to the attempt on Bhutto's life on 17 October 2007, in Karachi. In August 2004, Akhtar was detained in Dubai and deported to Pakistan, but released again in May 2007. He was reportedly arrested again in February 2008 in Lahore but freed the next month for 'lack of evidence.'

Like the group that he founded in the 1980s, Qari Saifullah Akhtar is an important point of contact between Afghan jihadi groups (particularly post-2001) and Pakistani/foreign jihadi groups/figures with different agendas. He was arrested again in August 2010 but is believed to have been 'released from protective custody' in late December that year.

Rahimullah Yousufzai: Rahimullah Yousufzai (1954–) is a Pakistani journalist based in Peshawar famous for his interviews conducted with Mullah Mohammad Omar and Osama bin Laden. He continues to cover Afghanistan and Pakistani affairs, currently as Executive Editor of The News International's Peshawar office. He also works with the BBC's Pashtu and Urdu local-language services.

Rahmatullah Hashimi: Rahmatullah Hashimi (1978–) was a Taliban envoy who spent time in the United States in the late 1990s and early 2000s. He also worked in the Taliban's Afghan Embassy in Islamabad in 1998. He was admitted to Yale University in 2005 as a non-degree student, prompting widespread public discussion and condemnation from some quarters. He has since returned to Afghanistan.

Ramzi Yousuf: Ramzi Yousuf (1967–) was the main figure behind the 1993 World Trade Center bombing. Although he was born in Kuwait, his roots go back to Pakistan, where he fled following the 1993 bombing. He was known for his expertise in bomb-making, resulting in the Bojinka plot of 1995, for example. He was arrested in Islamabad in February 1995 and extradited to the United States, where he continues to be held following a life sentence. Ramzi Yousuf is the nephew of Khalid Sheikh Mohammad.

Ramzi bin al-Shibh: Ramzi bin al-Shibh (1972–) was born in Yemen. He worked as a clerk for the International Bank of Yemen. He first tried to leave the country in 1995 but his visa application for the United States was rejected. He went to Germany and applied for asylum, claiming to be a Sudanese citizen. He met Atta in 1998 and they lived in a flat together with Marwan al-Shehhi, a student from the United Arab Emirates. In 1999, the group around Atta decided to go to Chechnya in order to take part in the *jihad*. A chance meeting in a train with Khalid al-Masri, however, set the group on a different path. Al-Masri is believed to have introduced them to Abu Mus'ab al-Suri, an al-Qaeda affiliate who lived in Duisburg, Germany. In a common tale echoed by other jihadis who sought to go to Chechnya, the group was told by al-Suri that they should first go to Afghanistan to train before joining the *jihad* in Chechnya. Atta and Jarrah flew to Karachi and went to Quetta from where they were taken to Kandahar. By the time Ramzi bin al-Shibh arrived two weeks later they had already pledged an oath of loyalty to bin Laden. Ramzi bin al-Shibh took the oath as well. The group then met with Mohammad Atef who told them that they would take part in a secret mission. They were to return to Germany and enrol in flight training. Atta was chosen by bin Laden to lead the group and received additional information including a pre-approved target list. The group returned to Hamburg in early 2000. After their return, the group changed their behaviour noticeably, avoiding radical preachers and changing their appearance, all in an effort to divert any unwanted attention. After enquiring about flight schools in Europe, the group soon learnt that they would have to learn how to fly passenger planes in the United States. Bin al-Shibh's visa request to the United States was rejected, as were his three subsequent attempts. He stayed behind but provided support from afar. He was captured in Karachi on 11 September 2002, and awaits trial.

Rashid Rauf: Rashid Rauf (1981–2008) was a British-born Pakistani and alleged al-Qaeda affiliate. He was implicated in the 2006 Atlantic airlines bombing plot but subsequently managed to reach Pakistan. He is believed to have married into the family of Massoud Azhar in 2002. He was arrested in Pakistan in August 2006, but escaped in December 2007. He is believed to have been killed in a drone strike in North Waziristan in November 2008.

Richard Armitage: Richard Armitage (1945–) is an American career diplomat who served as Deputy Secretary of State from 2001–5 under President George W. Bush.

Richard Smith: Richard Smith was the US Consul General in Peshawar in 1996.

Ridwan Isamuddin: Ridwan Isamuddin (1964–and also known as Encep Nurjaman and Hanbali) was born in West Java. He moved to Indonesia during the 1980s for work. He was involved with *Jemaah Islamiyya*. In 1986 he travelled to Afghanistan and trained in Sayyaf's Sada camp, fighting for around 18 months (according to the 9/11 Report). He met bin Laden during this time. He returned to Indonesia following the end of the Afghan war in the early 1990s, meeting various Islamist figures who passed through. He was involved in starting the company, Konsojaya, in June 1994. It is believed to have been a front company associated with militant activities. 3000 shares of the company were owned by Wali Khan Amin Shah, arrested in connection with the Bojinka plot. Hanbali also met with Khalid Sheikh Mohammad in Karachi to arrange for *Jemaah Islamiyya* recruits to be trained in Afghanistan.

He went underground in 2000 and is believed to have been involved in a wave of bombings of churches. Hanbali provided money to Zacarias Moussaoui along with travel documents in October 2000. He is held responsible for the Bali nightclub bombing that killed 202 people. He was arrested in August 2003. US President Bush later confirmed that he had been transferred to Guantánamo.

Robin L. Raphel: Robin Raphel served as US Assistant Secretary of State for South Asian Affairs under President Clinton from 1993–97, after which she was US Ambassador to Tunisia (until 2000). In August 2009, she was appointed by President Obama as coordinator for non-military assistance to Pakistan.

Sa'ti al-Husri: Sa'ti al-Husri (1882–1968) was an Egyptian writer and political commentator credited with popularising ideas of pan-Arab nationalism in the early twentieth century. He died in Baghdad in December 1968.

Saddam Hussein: Saddam Hussein (1937–2006) was President of Iraq from 1979 until his ouster in 2003 following the American invasion. He was executed by the Iraqi government in December 2006.

Saif al-Adl: Saif al-Adl (1960s–) is an Egyptian and a senior al-Qaeda member. He fought in Afghanistan during the 1980s, after which he is reported to have travelled to Lebanon with other fighters and trained together with Hezbollah during the early 1990s. He is currently believed to be in Pakistan after an extensive amount of time spent in Iran post-2001. He is believed by some to be al-Qaeda's military chief. He has written several public letters and books since fleeing Afghanistan in late 2001.

Sajjad Afghani: Sajjad Afghani was the Pakistani co-founder of *Harakat ul-Mujahedeen*. He was imprisoned by Indian authorities together with Massoud Azhar in February 1994 following a trip to Srinagar. He was killed in 1999 in an attempt to escape jail.

Saleh al-Somali: Saleh al-Somali reportedly served as al-Qaeda's head of external operations towards the end of the 2000s but was killed in a drone strike in December 2009. He is believed to have been associated with the New York subway plot of 2009.

Sami ul-Haq: Mawlana Sami ul-Haq (born 1937) is chancellor of the Haqqania madrassa in Pakistan, a post he took on the death of his father in 1988. He is often referred to as the 'father of the Taliban,' a reference to the large numbers of Afghan Talibs who passed through his madrassa. He leads a section of the *Jamiat-e Ulema-ye Islam* party.

Sayyed Abu al-A'ala Mawdudi: Sayyed Abu al-A'ala Mawdudi (1903–79) was an important revivalist political philosopher and Islamist scholar. He played a prominent role around the time of Pakistani independence, and also founded the *Jamaat-e Islami* political party. He was a prolific writer and is best know for his two works *Jihad* in Islam and *Tafhim ul-Qur'an* (a *tafseer*, or scriptural interpretation, of the *Qur'an*).

Sayyed Ahmad Barelvi: Sayyed Ahmad Barelvi (1786–1831) was a Muslim religious activist strongly influenced by the writings and activities of Shah Wali-ullah (and his son, Abd al-Aziz). He led a movement against the British and Sikh armies inside India, even defeating an army of Sikhs at Balakot in 1826. He established a religious state at that time based on the *shari'a*, but was killed in 1831.

Sayyed Imam al-Sharif: Sayyed Imam al-Sharif (1950–) is a prominent Egyptian Islamist leader, also known as Dr Fadl. He was born in Beni Sueif, Egypt, and was involved in developments within the Islamist movements there from the mid-1960s onwards. He met and associated with Ayman al-Zawahiri, although there was tension between the two over the leadership of groups in Egypt. He worked as a doctor in Pakistan during the 1980s—some say he became the de facto head of Egyptian Islamic Jihad group during this time—and left to Sudan in 1993. He was arrested in late 2001 in Yemen, where he was working as a surgeon, arrested and transferred to Egypt in February 2004. He has been an active writer since his arrest, most famously for the serialisation of a book written in 2007 which undermines the foundations of *jihad* as it is currently being practiced.

Sayyed Qutb: Sayyed Qutb (1906–1966) was born in Asyut, Egypt, attended a state school and had committed the *Qu'ran* to memory by the age of ten. He went to Cairo in 1918 where he attended classes at *Dar al-'Ulum* (House of Sciences), a modernist teacher training institute in 1928–9. After graduation in 1933 he worked for the next 16 years for the Ministry of Public Education. As a journalist and critic, he abandoned party politics in 1945. From 1948–1951 he studied in the United States. Even though trends towards a growing radicalisation had been apparent prior to his studies in America, he returned hardened in his view of the moral bankruptcy of Western society. Only a year after his return he was elected onto the Muslim Brotherhood's leadership council. After the failed assassination attempt against Nasser through a member of the Brotherhood, Qutb was arrested and soon after sentenced to twenty five years in prison. In prison he started drafting the first chapter of what became his influential book 'Milestones.' He was released in 1964 due to the intervention of 'Abd al-Salam 'Arif, the Iraqi President. Following his release, he became central to the Muslim Brotherhood again. 'Milestones' was published in 1964 and banned immediately. President Nasser announced the discovery of a Muslim Brotherhood conspiracy in 1965. Qutb was arrested as the ring leader and executed in 1966. Qutb is a key thinker in modern Islamist thought. He advanced concepts frequently referred to by many radical Islamist groups around the world in subsequent years. He split the world in into that of *jahaliyya* and Islam and advocated for a distinction of modernism and Westernism. He was an advocate of the concept of *takfir*—the justification of waging *jihad* against other Muslims regarded as *kuffar*. He is the author of more than 24 books and numerous articles and essays, ranging from literary criticism to Islamic subjects. His most prominent publications, often described as 'Islamist manifestos' are 'Milestones' and 'In the Shade of the *Qur'an*.'

Seraj Haqqani: Serajuddin Haqqani (1978/9–) is the son of veteran Afghan mujahedeen commander Jalaluddin Haqqani, based in south-eastern Afghanistan. He spent his childhood in Miram Shah, also attending the Haqqaniya Madrassa near Peshawar. In 2001, he fled across the border with his family following the American attack. He reportedly received a visit from Mullah Obaidullah in 2003 in Peshawar asking for his help in starting an insurgency. He is believed to have started taking more operational control of what is known as 'the Haqqani Network' from 2005 onwards. In 2006 he helped arrange a ceasefire in parts of Pakistan together with Mullah Dadullah. In 2007, they both helped set up a new Taliban council for South Waziristan, and he also played a role in the establishment of *Ittehad ul-Mujahedeen*. By 2009 he was reported to be travelling around within Afghanistan to inspect 'the front lines' himself. He is near the top of the ISAF/NATO wanted list.

Shah Waliullah: Shah Waliullah (1703–1762) was a religious scholar and author from Delhi. He was well-known for his writings on the theology of *jihad* and on the importance of reform within Islam. He was also affiliated with the Naqshbandi Sufi order.

Shahabuddin Dilawar: Shahabuddin Dilawar served in the Taliban's diplomatic corps during the 1990s. He was ambassador to Pakistan in 1997–8 but dispatched as the Taliban's representative in Saudi Arabia in late 1998, only to be expelled following Mullah Mohammad Omar's rejection of Prince Turki al-Faisal's appeal that bin Laden be expelled from Afghanistan. By May 2001 he was head of the religious board of the Afghan Supreme Court. A news report in 2011 sourced to Afghan Islamic Press stated that Dilawar had been

BIOGRAPHIES

appointed to the Taliban's Political Committee in order to help with outreach to Pashtun communities.

Sheikh Asim Abdur Rahman: Asim Abdur Rahman is one of the sons of Omar Abdur Rahman, the so-called 'Blind Sheikh' and prominent Egyptian Islamist. He was reportedly very close to bin Laden following the September 11 attacks, and was one of the five Arabs who reportedly received Afghan citizenship in November 2001.

Sheikh Kamal al-Sananiri: Sheikh Kamal al-Sananiri was sent by the Supreme Guide of the Egyptian Muslim Brotherhood to Afghanistan in November 1980. Al-Sananiri, the brother-in-law of Sayyid Qutb, married Qutb's sister, Amina. He spent over twenty years in prison following his arrest during Nasser's crackdown on the Muslim Brotherhood in 1954. He went on a forty-day trip to Pakistan to assess the Afghan *jihad* following his release. The Egyptian Muslim Brotherhood had long-standing ties with the Afghan mujahedeen via al-Azhar. In September 1981, al-Sananiri stopped in Saudi Arabia on his way back from Pakistan, where he met Jordanian-Palestinian friend and Muslim Brother Abdullah Azzam. They planned to travel back to Afghanistan together after al-Sananiri picked up his family in Egypt. In Egypt, however, al-Sananiri was caught up in yet another crackdown and allegedly was tortured to death in prison in 1981.

Sheikh Yusuf al-Uyayri: Sheikh Yusuf bin Salih bin Fahd al-Uyayri (1967–2003) was a Saudi Islamist scholar. He was born in Saudi Arabia to an upper-middle-class family. He was still in secondary school when he went to Afghanistan at the age of 18. He followed bin Laden to Sudan in 1992 but was sent to Somalia together with Abu Hafs al-Masri in 1993. He was imprisoned in Saudi Arabia in 1995 in connection with the Khobar Towers bombing, but later released. He is well-known for his writings—both religious and political-strategic—and knew most major figures within the Arab militant circles around al-Qaeda. He met with Taliban ministers in Mecca during Hajj in late February 2001 to organise a phone conversation between Mullah Mohammad Omar and Sheikh Hamud al-Shu'aybi (of the Shu'aybi school); the call never took place because al-Uyayri was arrested on his way back from *Hajj*. He was killed in June 2003 by Saudi security forces.

Shukri Mustafa: Shukri Mustafa (1942–1978) was an Egyptian Islamist leader. He joined the Muslim Brotherhood when young, but later became the leader of a group called *al-Takfir wal-Hijra*. This group withdrew from society in order to separate themselves from what they saw as *jahiliyaa*. He became a wanted

491

man in 1976, and by the next year the group had kidnapped a former Egyptian government minister, Mohammad al-Dhahabi, in order to influence a trial of *Jama'at al-Muslimeen* members. The Egyptian government increased police measures and al-Dhahabi was killed. Hundreds of Shukris followers, including himself and the entire leadership of the *Jama'at*, were arrested. In November 1977, Shukri was executed after receiving a death sentence.

Sibghatullah Mujaddidi: Sibghatullah Mujaddidi was born in 1925 in Kabul. Educated in Afghanistan as well as at Al-Azhar in Cairo, he led one of the main mujahedeen political parties from Peshawar during the 1980s, and served as interim president in June 1992. He continues to play a role in Afghan politics in Kabul.

Steve LeVine: Steve LeVine is an American author and journalist who covered Afghanistan during the 1990s. His book, 'The Oil and the Glory,' told the story of oil interests in Afghanistan, but he has also written extensively for newspapers and magazines.

Sufi Mohammad: Sufi Mohammad (b. 1933) is the founder of *Tehrik-i Nifaz-i Shari'at-i Muhammadi* (TNSM or 'The Movement for the Application of the *Shari'a* of Muhammad'). TNSM is a Pakistani militant jihadi group founded in Malakand in 1992. He is a former member of *Jamaat-e Islami*. He was arrested 2002 after organising thousands of fighters to travel to Afghanistan and fight in 2001. He was released in 2008, but then rearrested in July 2009.

Sultan Amir Tarar: Colonel Imam (c. 1945–2011), also known as Sultan Amir Tarar, was a Pakistani national who became well-known (particularly in southern Afghanistan) during the 1980s as the main channel of US-Saudi-ISI funding for the mujahedeen in Quetta. He was responsible for training sessions and the distribution of funds/resources. Most commanders in southern Afghanistan knew him.

Sunny Ahmed Qazi: Born around 1971, Sunny Ahmed Qazi was a Pakistani citizen, resident of Defence Area, Karachi.

Tahir Yuldash: Tahir Yuldash (1967–2009) cofounded and led the Islamic Movement of Uzbekistan until his death in August 2009 following a US drone strike in Pakistan. He was a key figure among Central Asian jihadi leaders and was active inside Afghanistan during the 1990s. According to one BBC report, Yuldash had prior knowledge of the September 11 attacks; the article stated that he told then-Foreign Minister Mutawakil about the al-Qaeda plan to attack the United States prior to the attacks.

Tarek Maaroufi: Tarek Maaroufi (1965–) is a Tunisian who later took Belgian nationality. He supplied the fake passports used by the two men who assassinated Ahmed Shah Massoud. He is reported to have been involved in Tunisian and Algerian militant jihadist groups from the mid-1990s onwards. He is currently being held in custody in Belgium.

Tariq al-Fadhali: Tariq al-Fadhali (b. 1960s) fought in Afghanistan with Hekmatyar's forces during the 1980s. He was linked to bin Laden during the 1990s, when the latter reportedly funded his activities. He is still alive.

Tawfiq bin Attash: Tawfiq bin Attash (1979–) is a Yemeni affiliate of al-Qaeda who is believed to have been involved in the 1998 US African Embassy bombings and the September 11 attacks. He is also known as Khallad or Walid bin Attash. He is alleged to have been fighting inside Afghanistan against the Northern Alliance when he lost his leg—he wore a metal prosthesis in its place. He was selected by bin Laden for involvement in the September 11 plot but was restricted to an advisory role following complications. He played a prominent role, however, in the USS Cole bombing of October 2000. He was arrested on 29 April 2003, passed through several CIA so-called 'dark sites' and ended up in Guantánamo, where he remains incarcerated.

Tayyeb Agha: Tayyeb Agha (Naser/Sayyed by tribe) was one of Mullah Mohammad Omar's deputies. He was originally from Jelahor in Arghandab district of Kandahar, and fought with *Harakat* and Khalis' *Hizb-e Islami* during the 1980s *jihad*. He was the brother of the well-known commander Lala Malang. As of 2011, he was believed to be the head of the Taliban's political committee.

Turki al-Faisal: Prince Turki bin Faisal al-Saud (b. 1945) is the former Director General of Saudi Arabia's intelligence services, a post which he held from 1977 until a few days prior to the September 11 attacks in 2001. He was deeply involved in Afghan matters, from the funding of the 1980s *jihad* to intervening with the Taliban during the 1990s regarding bin Laden.

Ustaz Mohammad Yasir: Ustaz Mohammad Yasir is originally from Wardak and was a rising star in the Taliban during the 2006–9 period until his arrest in Pakistan. He was in charge of recruitment for the Taliban and was known for some global jihadist tendencies.

Vahid Mojdeh: Vahid Mojdeh (b. 1960) is a former Taliban Foreign Ministry official, originally from Baglan province. He worked with different mujahedeen factions, including time as editor-in-chief of *Hezb-e Islami*'s newspaper

Shahadat. During the Taliban's rule, he was head of the Foreign Ministry's Publications Department. He lives in Kabul and is a frequent public commentator and analyst.

Vladimir Lenin: Vladimir Ilyich Lenin (1870–1924) was a Russian Marxist political activist and revolutionary thinker. As such, he was heavily involved in the Bolshevik takeover in Russia in 1917 and he served as the first head of the USSR.

Wakil Ahmad Mutawakil: Mawlawi Wakil Ahmad Mutawakil (Kakar by tribe) is originally from Keshkinakhud in Maiwand district of Kandahar. He is not known for being a mujahed during the 1980s *jihad*, but his father, Abdul Ghaffar Barialai, who was killed during Taraki's rule, was (and remains) an extremely famous Pashtu poet in southern Afghanistan. He served as the Taliban's foreign Minister during the 1990s. He surrendered to US forces in 2002 and was released in 2003 to de facto house arrest in Kabul. He was removed from the UN Resolution 1267 sanctions blacklist in January 2010.

Wali Khan Amin Shah: Wali Khan Amin Shah (b. 1967) was an Afghan who is believed to have fought in Loya Paktya during the 1980s *jihad*, even possibly together with bin Laden. He was later involved in the Bojinka plot. He moved to Manila when the Afghan-Soviet war ended. He was arrested in the Philippines in November 1995, escaped four days later, but was recaptured in December 1995 and handed over to US custody. He is serving a life sentence at USP Marion in Southern Illinois, and is due to be released in 2022.

Yasser al-Sirri: Born in the late 1950s, Yasser al-Sirri is the Egyptian director of the Islamic Observation Centre in London. He was arrested in Egypt on accusations of involvement in militant Islamist circles in September 1981, sentenced to death in trial in 1998, but sought asylum in London. He was tangentially tied to the 2001 assassination of Massoud, for which he was arrested in 2001 under suspicion of complicity.

Zahir Shah: Zahir Shah was the King of Afghanistan from 1933 to 1973, when his cousin seized power while he was in Italy for medical treatment. Born in 1914 and the only surviving son of Nadir Shah, he was crowned King when his father was assassinated. His reign is now remembered nostalgically as a time of peace and stability; he died of old age in Kabul in July 2007.

Zia ul-Haq: General Mohammad Zia ul-Haq (1924–1988) was Pakistan's president 1978–1988. He was an important Islamising influence on Pakistan during his rule (which overlapped with the Afghan *jihad*), and was killed in an air crash on 17 August 1988.

BIBLIOGRAPHY

Abdo, Geneive (2000), *No God but God: Egypt and the Triumph of Islam*. (Oxford: Oxford University Press).

Abou el-Magd, Nadia (2002), 'Alleged Mullah Omar Statement Aired,' *Associated Press*, 12 September.

Aboul-Enein, Youssef (2008), *The Late Sheikh Abdullah Azzam's Books: Part III: Radical Theories on Defending Muslim Land through Jihad*. (West Point: Combating Terrorism Center).

Abou Zahab, Mariam and Olivier Roy (2004), *Islamist Networks: the Afghan-Pakistan Connection*. (London: Hurst).

Ackerman, Spencer (2011), 'Assassinations Up 588 Percent in Afghan Province,' *Wired. com* (Online), 9 March. http://www.wired.com/dangerroom/2011/03/assassinations-up-588-percent-in-afghan-province/ (accessed 31 May 2011).

Afghan Islamic Press (2001), 'UAE cuts ties with Taliban,' *CNN.com*, 22 September. http://articles.cnn.com/2001–09–22/world/ret.afghan.taliban_1_taliban-ambassador-taliban-soldiers-afghan-islamic-press?_s=PM:asiapcf (accessed 29 September 2001).

Afghan Mujahedeen (1989), 'AIG's Communique on Anniversary of Russian Invasion of Afghanistan,' *Afghan Jehad*, December 27.

——— (1992), 'Decisions held at the joint council of seven Mujaheddin organizations in Kandahar,' *Afghan Jehad*, August 1992, 35–6.

AFP (1997a), 'Afghanistan: Taleban Declare Afghanistan "an Islamic Emirate,"' 27 October.

——— (1997b), 'Taleban Demand Deployment of UN Monitors at Airfields,' 5 November.

——— (1999a), 'Hijacked airliner parked on Afghan runway, surrounded by jeeps,' 26 December. http://www.afghanistannewscenter.com/news/1999/december/dec26a1999.htm (accessed 29 June 2010).

———— (1999b), 'UN official praises Taliban handling of hijack crisis,' 29 December. http://www.afghanistannewscenter.com/news/1999/december/dec29g1999.htm (accessed 29 June 2010).

———— (2000), 'Indian defence minister alleges Taleban role in Christmas hijacking,' 24 January. http://www.afghanistannewscenter.com/news/2000/january/jan24a2000.htm (accessed 29 June 2010).

———— (2006), 'Osama Guard Says Indian Plane Hijacked for Azhar's Release,' 17 September.

———— (2010a), 'Al-Qaeda threatens attacks on Saudi Royals,' 6 October. http://tribune.com.pk/story/59207/al-qaeda-threatens-attacks-on-saudi-royals/ (accessed 8 October 2010).

———— (2010b), 'US cannot see Mullah Omar playing role in Afghanistan,' 14 October. http://www.google.com/hostednews/afp/article/ALeqM5geyxhk-e9CXDa 19d02MyzAe0Qc_w?docId=CNG.bd6bd0d86d63f1a0e61b464e310712d2.941 (accessed 22 October 2010).

———— (2010c), 'Al-Qaeda "group leader" killed in Afghanistan: NATO,' 16 August. http://www.france24.com/en/20100816-al-qaeda-group-leader-killed-afghanistan-nato (accessed 15 March 2011).

Afsar, Major Shahid, Major Chris Samples and Major Thomas Wood (2008), 'The Taliban: an Organizational Analysis,' *Military Review*, May–June. http://www.humansecuritygateway.com/documents/MILREVIEW_Taliban_Organizational_Analysis.pdf (accessed 13 June 2011).

Ahady, Anwar-ul-Haq (1998), 'Saudi Arabia, Iran and the Conflict in Afghanistan,' in William Maley, *Fundamentalism Reborn? Afghanistan and the Taliban*. (London: Hurst).

Ahmad, Ishtiaq (2004), *Gulbuddin Hekmatyar: an Afghan trail from jihad to terrorism*. (Pakistan: Society for Tolerance and Education).

Ajami, Fouad (2009), '9/11 and the "Good War,"' *The Wall Street Journal*, 11 September. http://online.wsj.com/article/SB10001424052970203440104574402822520657510.html (accessed 10 October 2010).

Al-Bahri, Nasir (2004), 'Al Qaeda from Within, as narrated by Abu Jandal, bin Laden's Personal Guard (part three),' *Al Quds al Arabi*, 3 August.

Ali, Imtiaz and Massoud Ansari (2006), 'Pakistan fury as CIA airstrike on village kills 18,' *The Telegraph*, 15 January. http://www.telegraph.co.uk/news/worldnews/asia/pakistan/1507895/Pakistan-fury-as-CIA-airstrike-on-village-kills-18.html (accessed 13 October 2010).

Allix, Stéphane (1998), *La petite cuillère de Schéhérezade*. (Paris: Editions Ramsay).

Al-Masri, Abu al-Walid (1990), *A Mother's Deep Sorrow*. (Document translated by CTC's Harmony Project; http://ctc.usma.edu/aq/pdf/AFGP-2002–600092-TransMeta.pdf (accessed 20 February 2011).

———— (2004), *The Cross in the Sky of Kandahar. The Night Kandahar Fell: The last Arab resistance!* (Online).

Al-Suri, Abu Mus'ab and Yusuf al-Uyayri (date unknown), *Are the Taliban from Ahl as-Sunnah?* (Online: At-Tibyan Publications).

Al-Zawahiri, Ayman (2001), 'Extracts from Al-Jihad Leader Al-Zawahiri's New Book,' *Al-Sharq al-Awsat*, 2 December.

Al-Zayyat (2004), *The Road to Al-Qaeda: the Story of Bin Laden's Right-Hand Man*. (London: Pluto Press).

Amani, Wahidullah (2005), 'First war, now PR to get bin Laden,' *The Times Union*, 3 September.

Amnesty International (1999), *Afghanistan: Detention and killing of political person-alities*. (London: Online, March). http://www.amnesty.org/en/library/info/ASA11/005/1999 (accessed 16 February 2009).

Anas, Abdullah (2002), *Wildatat al-Afghan al-Arab [The Birth of the Afghan Arabs]*. (London).

Anderson, Jon (1989), 'Menace of mullahs who hate music and mercy,' *The Sunday Times*, 12 February.

Anderson, Jon Lee (2002), *The Lion's Grave: Dispatches from Afghanistan*. (London: Grove Press).

Arnoldy, Ben (2010), 'Pakistan arrests more Afghan Taliban. Why the about-face?,' *Christian Science Monitor*, 18 February. http://www.csmonitor.com/World/Asia-South-Central/2010/0218/Pakistan-arrests-more-Afghan-Taliban.-Why-the-about-face (accessed 5 October 2010).

Asbridge, Thomas (2010), *The Crusades: The Authoritative History of the War for the Holy Land*. (New York: HarperCollins Publishers Inc.).

Assorted Saudi Ulemaa' (1992), 'Verdict of distinguished Saudi Arabian ulama regard-ing the situation in Afghanistan,' *Afghan Jehad*, 5, 3: 36–37.

Associated Press (1998), 'Foreign Workers Leave Afghanistan,' 20 July.

——— (2001), 'Saudi Arabia severs ties with Afghanistan's Taliban,' *The Independent*, 25 September. http://www.independent.co.uk/news/world/middle-east/saudi-arabia-severs-ties-with-afghanistans-taliban-670709.html (accessed 29 September 2001).

——— (2010), 'New Taliban Rulebook: Don't Kill Civilians,' *CBS News*, 3 August. http://www.cbsnews.com/stories/2010/08/03/world/main6739710.shtml (accessed 5 October 2010).

Astor, Michael (2006), 'Ex-Taliban chief details Massood killing,' *Associated Press*, 9 October. http://www.usatoday.com/news/world/2006-09-10-afghan-assassi-nation_x.htm (accessed 31 May 2011).

Atran, Scott (2010), *Talking to the Enemy: Faith, Brotherhood, and the (Un)Making of Terrorists*. (New York: HarperCollins).

Atwan, Abdel Bari (2006), *The Secret History of Al-Qaeda*. (London: Abacus Press).

Azarbaijani-Moghaddam, Sippi (2009), 'Northern Exposure for the Taliban,' in Anto-nio Giustozzi, *Decoding the New Taliban: Insights from the Afghan Field*. (London: Hurst Publications).

Bacevich, Andrew J. (2009), 'Let's Beat the Extremists Like We Beat the Soviets,' 27 September. http://www.washingtonpost.com/wp-dyn/content/article/2009/09/25/AR2009092502011_pf.html (accessed 12 September 2010).

Baker, Aryn (2009), 'Who Killed Abdullah Azzam?,' *Time Magazine* (USA), 18 June. http://www.time.com/time/specials/packages/printout/0,29239,1902809_1902810_1905173,00.html (accessed 20 February 2011).

Barfield, Thomas (2006), *Informal Dispute Resolution and the Formal Legal System in Contemporary Northern Afghanistan*. (Washington D.C.: USIP). http://www.usip.org/files/file/barfield_report.pdf (accessed 10 March 2011).

———— (2010), *Afghanistan: A Cultural and Political History*. (Princeton: Princeton University Press).

Barker, Alec D. (2010), *Improvised Explosive Devices in Southern Afghanistan and Western Pakistan, 2002–2009*. (Washington, D.C.: The New America Foundation).

Barnes, Julian E. (2010a), 'Surge Is Fully Deployed to Afghanistan,' *The Wall Street Journal*, 9 September. http://online.wsj.com/article/SB20001424052748704362404575479750755726446.html (accessed 5 October 2010).

———— (2010b), 'Efforts to Recruit Pashtuns in Afghan South Falter,' *The Wall Street Journal*, 12 September. http://online.wsj.com/article/SB10001424052748704621204575487720827425774.html (accessed 5 October 2010).

Bay, Austin (2010), 'An Afghan Anaconda,' *Strategy Page* (Online), 6 July. http://www.strategypage.com/on_point/20100706233453.aspx (accessed 10 October 2010).

Bays, James (2010), 'The Afghan Peace Plan,' Al-Jazeera Blogs, 3 June. http://blogs.aljazeera.net/asia/2010/06/03/afghan-peace-plan (accessed 11 September 2010).

Bazzi, Mohamad (2001), 'The London connection in the plot that killed Masood,' *The Indian Express*, 10 October. http://www.hvk.org/articles/1001/105.html (accessed 28 August 2010).

BBC Monitoring Service (1990), 'Iranian agency reports fall of Afghan provincial capital to mojahedin,' 6 March.

BBC News (1999a), 'Hijack Negotiations in Dubai,' 24 December. http://news.bbc.co.uk/1/hi/world/south_asia/577635.stm (accessed 24 June 2010).

———— (1999b), 'Analysis: India warms to the Taleban,' 31 December. http://www.afghanistannewscenter.com/news/1999/december/dec31d1999.htm (accessed 29 June 2010).

Beg, General Aslam (1995), 'Wer sind die Taliban?' *Mahfel*, 45 (March–April).

Benotman, Noman (2010), 'Letter to bin Laden,' *The Quilliam Foundation*, 9 September. http://www.quilliamfoundation.org/images/stories/pdfs/letter-to-bin-laden.pdf (accessed 10 September 2010).

Bergen, Peter (2001), *Holy War, Inc: Inside the Secret World of Osama bin Laden*. (New York: Free Press), Kindle Electronic Edition.

———— (2006), *The Osama bin Laden I Know: An Oral History of Al-Qaeda's Leader*. (New York: Free Press).

———— (2009a), 'The Front: The Taliban-Al Qaeda merger,' *The New Republic*, 19 October.

———— (2009b), 'The Battle for Tora Bora,' *The New Republic*, 22 December. http://www.tnr.com/print/article/the-battle-tora-bora (accessed 17 October 2010).

———— (2010), 'Why Bin Laden Still Matters,' *Newsweek*, 4 September. http://www.newsweek.com/2010/09/04/why-osama-bin-laden-still-matters.print.html (accessed 10 September 2010).

Bergen, Peter and Katherine Tiedemann (2010), *The Year of the Drone: An Analysis of U.S. Drone Strikes in Pakistan, 2004–10*. (Washington D.C.: New America Foundation). http://counterterrorism.newamerica.net/sites/newamerica.net/files/policydocs/bergentiedemann2.pdf (accessed 6 October 2010).

Berman, Eli (2009), *Radical, Religious and Violent: The New Economics of Terrorism*. (London: The MIT Press).

Berntsen, Gary (2006), *Jawbreaker: the Attack on bin Laden and Al-Qaeda*. (New York: Three Rivers Press).

Bin Laden, Najwa and Omar bin Laden and Jean Sasson (2009), *Growing Up Bin Laden: Osama's Wife and Son Take Us Inside their Secret World*. (New York: St. Martin's Press).

Bin Laden, Osama and Bruce Lawrence (ed.) (2005) *Messages to the World: The Statements of Osama bin Laden*. (London: Verso).

Blanchard, Christopher M. (2010) *Saudi Arabia: Background and U.S. Relations*. (Washington D.C.: Congressional Research Service). http://www.fas.org/sgp/crs/mideast/RL33533.pdf (accessed 20 February 2011).

Boone, Jon (2009), 'US troop surge met in Afghanistan with cynicism and conspiracy theories,' *The Guardian*, 2 December. http://www.guardian.co.uk/world/2009/dec/02/us-troop-surge-afghanistan-response/print (accessed 22 October 2010).

Boone, Jon (2010), 'Taliban claim success against Nato's night raids,' *The Guardian*, 31 October. http://www.guardian.co.uk/world/2010/oct/31/taliban-success-night-raids-afghanistan/print (accessed 31 May 2011).

Boone, Jon (2011), 'Most Afghan civilian deaths "caused by Taliban attacks, not US forces,"' *The Guardian*, 9 March. http://www.guardian.co.uk/world/2011/mar/09/afghanistan-insurgents-civilian-victims (accessed 31 May 2011).

Bonney, Richard (2004), *Jihad: from Qur'an to Bin Laden*. (New York: Palgrave Macmillan).

Borchgrave, Arnaud de (2010), 'Afghan Peace Solution,' *The Washington Times*, 26 October. http://www.washingtontimes.com/news/2010/oct/26/afghan-peace-solution/print/ (accessed 31 May 2011).

Borchgrevink, Kaja (2010), *Beyond Borders: Diversity and Transnational Links in Afghan Religious Education*. (Oslo: Peace Research Institute Oslo). http://www.prio.no/sptrans/234636690/PRIO%20Paper_%20Borchgrevink_%20Beyond%20Borders%20Diversity%20and%20Transnational%20Links%20in%20Afghan%20Religious%20Education_September%202010.pdf (accessed 31 January 2011).

BIBLIOGRAPHY

Borger, Julian and Declan Walsh (2010), 'US and Afghan governments make contact with Haqqani insurgents,' *The Guardian*, 7 October. http://www.guardian.co.uk/world/2010/oct/06/us-afghan-government-contact-haqqani/print (accessed 22 October 2010).

Bowden, Mark (2002), *Black Hawk Down: A Story of Modern War*. (New York: New America Library).

Braithwaite, Rodric (2011), *Afgantsy: The Russians in Afghanistan 1979–89*. (London: Profile Books).

Brooke, Tom Vanden (2010), 'Use of Humvees restricted in Afghanistan,' *USA Today*, 8 September. http://www.marinecorpstimes.com/news/2010/06/gns_humvee_restriction_063010/ (accessed 10 October 2010).

Brown, Vahid (2010), 'The Facade of Allegiance: Bin Ladin's Dubious Pledge to Mullah Omar,' *CTC Sentinel* 3, 1.

Brzezinski, Matthew (2001), 'Bust and Boom,' *The Washington Post*, 30 December.

Bumiller, Elisabeth and Mark Landler (2009), 'U.S. Envoy Urges Caution on Forces for Afghanistan,' *The New York Times*, 11 November. http://www.nytimes.com/2009/11/12/us/politics/12policy.html?sq=U.S.%20Afghan%20Envoy%20Urges%20Caution%20on%20Troop%20Increase%20&st=cse&scp=1&pagewanted=print (accessed 12 March, 2011).

Burke, Jason (2004), *Al-Qaeda: the True Story of Radical Islam* (London: IB Tauris).

Burns, John F. (1995), 'Terror Network Traced to Pakistan,' *The New York Times*, 20 March. http://www.nytimes.com/1995/03/20/world/terror-network-traced-to-pakistan.html?pagewanted=print&src=pm (accessed 3 March 2011).

——— (2001a), 'Afghans Coaxing bin Laden, But U.S. Rejects Clerics' Bid,' *The New York Times*, 20 September.

——— (2001b), 'Pakistanis Fail in Last-Ditch Bid to Persuade Taliban to Turn Over bin Laden,' *The New York Times*, 28 September.

——— (2001c), 'Taliban Link Fate of Aid Workers to U.S. Action,' *The New York Times*, 6 October. http://www.nytimes.com/2001/10/07/world/a-nation-challenged-kabul-taliban-link-fate-of-aid-workers-to-us-action.html?pagewanted=print&src=pm (accessed 10 March 2011).

——— (2002), 'Villagers Say Errors by U.S. Causing Grief For Innocent,' *The New York Times*, 2 February.

Buruma, Ian and Avishai Margalit (2005), *Occidentalism: the West in the Eyes of its Enemies*. (New York: Penguin Books).

Calvert, John (2010), *Sayyid Qutb and the Origins of Radical Islamism*. (London: Hurst and Company).

Capaccio, Tony and Lizzie O'Leary (2010), 'Petraeus Says Commando Raids on Afghan Taliban Leaders Rising,' *Bloomberg*, 15 April. http://www.businessweek.com/news/2010-04-15/petraeus-says-commando-raids-on-afghan-taliban-leaders-step-up.html (accessed 6 October 2010).

Carlstrom, Gregg (2010), 'Searching for Plan B in Afghanistan,' *Al Jazeera* (Online), 17 September. http://english.aljazeera.net/news/asia/2010/09/201091784454474 302.html (accessed 19 October 2010).

Caroe, Olaf (1964), *The Pathans*. (London: Macmillan).

Carroll, Rory (2002), 'Italian police tapes hint at September 11 attacks,' 30 May.

CBC News (2004), 'Bin Laden claims responsibility for 9/11,' 29 October. http://www.cbc.ca/world/story/2004/10/29/binladen_message041029.html (accessed 3 September 2010).

Chalk, Peter (2010), 'Lashkar-e-Taiba's Growing International Focus and Its Links with al-Qaeda,' *Jamestown Terrorism Monitor*, 29 July. http://www.jamestown.org/programs/gta/single/?tx_ttnews[tt_news]=36683&cHash=634a73cdd0 (accessed 29 October 2010).

Chandrasekeran, Rajiv (2011), *Is NATO's Counterinsurgency Strategy Working in Afghanistan? A Case Study*. (Ottawa: Centre for International Policy Studies). http://www.socialsciences.uottawa.ca/cepi-cips/eng/documents/CIPS_Policy-Brief_Chandrasekaran_Mar2011.pdf (accessed 17 March 2011).

Chayes, Sarah (2006), *The Punishment of Virtue*. (New York: Penguin Press).

Chick, Kristen (2010), 'Petraeus says US has momentum over Afghan Taliban,' *The Christian Science Monitor*, 23 August. http://www.csmonitor.com/layout/set/print/content/view/print/321076 (accessed 13 September 2010).

Chivers, C.J., Alissa J. Rubin and Wesley Morgan (2011), 'U.S. Pulling Back in Afghan Valley It Called Vital to War,' *The New York Times*, 24 February. http://www.nytimes.com/2011/02/25/world/asia/25afghanistan.html?pagewanted=print (accessed 21 March 2011).

Coughlin, Con (2010), 'We may be beating the Taliban, but in this country you'd never know it,' *The Daily Telegraph*, 24 September. http://www.telegraph.co.uk/comment/columnists/concoughlin/8022154/We-may-be-beating-the-Taliban-but-in-this-country-youd-never-know-it.html (accessed 5 October 2010).

Clark, Kate (2001), 'Mullah Mohammad Rabbani,' *The Independent*, 18 April. http://www.afghanistannewscenter.com/news/2001/april/apr18k2001.html (accessed 18 August 2010).

——— (2002), 'Revealed: The Taliban minister, the US envoy and the warning of 11 September that was ignored,' *The Independent* (UK), 7 September. http://www.independent.co.uk/news/world/politics/revealed-the-taliban-minister-the-us-envoy-and-the-warning-of-september-11-that-was-ignored-607124.html (accessed 7 March 2011).

——— (2011a), *The Takhar attack: Targeted killings and the parallel worlds of US intelligence and Afghanistan*. (Kabul: Afghanistan Analysts Network). http://aan-afghanistan.com/uploads/20110511KClark_Takhar-attack_final.pdf (accessed 13 June 2011).

——— (2011b), *The Layeha: Calling the Taleban to Account*. (Kabul: Afghanistan Analysts Network).

Coghlan, Tom (2009), 'The Taliban in Helmand,' in Antonio Giustozzi, *Decoding the New Taliban: Insights from the Afghan Field.* (London: Hurst Publications, 2009).

Coll, Steve (2004), 'Flawed Ally Was Hunt's Best Hope,' *The Washington Post*, 23 February. http://www.washingtonpost.com/ac2/wp-dyn/A62889–2004Feb22?language=printer (accessed 29 June 2010).

—— (2005), *Ghost wars: the secret history of the CIA, Afghanistan, and bin Laden, from the Soviet invasion to 10 September 2001.* (New York: Penguin Group USA).

—— (2008), *The Bin Ladens: an Arabian family in the American century.* (New York: Penguin Press).

—— (2010), 'Kashmir: The Time Has Come,' *The New York Review of Books*, 30 September. http://www.nybooks.com/articles/archives/2010/sep/30/kashmir-time-has-come/?pagination=false&printpage=true (accessed 12 September 2010).

Combating Terrorism Center (2007), *Al-Qa'ida's (mis)Adventures in the Horn of Africa.* (Online). http://www.ctc.usma.edu/aq/aqII.asp (accessed 1 June 2010).

Cooley, John K. (2002), *Unholy Wars: Afghanistan, America and International Terrorism.* (London: Pluto Press).

Corera, Gordon (2005), 'Unraveling Zarqawi's al-Qaeda Connection,' *Jamestown Terrorism Monitor*, 5 May. http://www.jamestown.org/single/?no_cache=1&tx_ttnews[tt_news]=332 (accessed 10 October 2010).

Cullison, Alan and Andrew Higgins (2001), 'Computer in Kabul Holds Chilling Memos,' *The Wall Street Journal*, 31 December.

—— (2002), 'Once-Stormy Terror Alliance Was Solidified by Cruise-Missiles,' *The Wall Street Journal*, 2 August 2002. http://www.freerepublic.com/focus/news/726499/posts (accessed 14 July 2010).

Davis, Anthony (1998), 'How the Taliban became a military force,' in William Maley, *Fundamentalism Reborn? Afghanistan and the Taliban.* (London: Hurst).

Dawisha, Adeed (2003), *Arab Nationalism in the Twentieth Century: From Triumph to Despair.* (Princeton: Princeton University Press).

Dorronsoro, Gilles (2005), *Revolution Unending: Afghanistan, 1979 to the Present.* (London: C. Hurst & Co. Publishers).

—— (2010), *Afghanistan: Searching for Political Agreement.* (Washington D.C.: Carnegie Endowment for International Peace, April). http://www.carnegieendowment.org/files/searching_polit_agreement.pdf (accessed 1 May 2010).

Dozier, Kimberly (2010), 'Petraeus fights time, enemy in Afghanistan,' *Associated Press*, 29 October. http://www.google.com/hostednews/ap/article/ALeqM5gKQgVd-BxfhWneF-UNXpCJfoEDcPgD9IHC3P80?docId=D9IHC3P80 (accessed 5 October 2010).

Dressler, Jeffrey (2010), *Backgrounder: The Irreconcilables: The Haqqani Network.* (Washington D.C.: Institute for the Study of War, 28 June). http://www.understandingwar.org/files/BackgrounderHaqqaniNetwork.pdf (accessed 1 August 2010).

Dupree, Louis (1980), *Afghanistan.* (Princeton: Princeton University Press).

Edwards, David B. (2002), *Before Taliban: Genealogies of the Afghan Jihad*. (Berkeley: University of California Press).

Ehrenfeld, Rachel (2003), *Funding Evil: How Terrorism is Financed and How to Stop It*. (Chicago: Bonus Books).

Elias, Barbara (2002), *The Taliban Biography: Documents on the Structure and Leadership of the Taliban 1996–2002*. (Washington D.C.: National Security Archive). http://www.nsarchive.org/NSAEBB/NSAEBB295 (accessed 19 November, 2009).

Elias, Mohammad Osman Tariq (2008), 'The Resurgence of the Taliban in Kabul: Logar and Wardak,' in Antonio Giustozzi, *Decoding the New Taliban: Insights from the Afghan Field*. (London: Hurst Publications).

Esposito, John L., ed, (2003), *The Oxford Dictionary of Islam*. (Oxford: Oxford University Press).

Evans, Martin and John Phillips (2007), *Algeria: Anger of the Dispossessed*. (New Haven: Yale University Press).

Everett, Colonel Michael L. (2006), *Merging the International Security and Assistance Force (ISAF) and Operation Enduring Freedom (OEF) A Strategic Imperative*. (Carlisle: US Army War College). http://www.strategicstudiesinstitute.army.mil/pdf-files/ksil338.pdf (accessed 10 March 2011).

Fair, Christine (2007), *Suicide Attacks in Afghanistan (2001–7)*. UNAMA (Kabul). http://www.unhcr.org/refworld/pdfid/49997b00d.pdf (accessed 3 June 2010).

Farah, Douglas (2004), *Blood from Stones: The Secret Financial Network of Terror*. (New York: Broadway Books).

Faraj, Ayman Sabri (2002), *Zikriyat Arabi Afghani [Memoirs of an Afghan Arab]*. (Cairo),

Faraj, Muhammad 'Abdus Salam (2000), *The Absent Obligation*, ed. Abu Umamah. (Birmingham: Maktabah al Ansaar).

Farrall, Leah (2009), 'The evolution of command,' *Jane's Strategic Advisory Services*, November. http://allthingsct.files.wordpress.com/2010/03/jsas-11-p16–20-command.pdf (accessed 29 September 2010).

——— (2010a), 'Najibullah Zazi & recruitment,' *AllThingsCT* (Blog), 23 February. http://allthingscounterterrorism.com/2010/02/23/najibullah-zazi-aq-recruitment/ (accessed 8 September 2010).

——— (2010b), 'Death of a hoary old chestnut?,' *All Things CT Blog*, 7 September. http://allthingscounterterrorism.com/2010/09/07/death-of-a-hoary-old-chestnut/ (accessed 8 September 2010).

——— (2011), 'How al Qaeda Works: What the Organization's Subsidiaries Say About Its Strength,' *Foreign Affairs*, March/April. http://www.foreignaffairs.com/articles/67467/leah-farrall/how-al-qaeda-works (accessed 16 March 2011).

Farrell, Stephen (2010), 'Video Links Taliban in Pakistan to C.I.A. Attack,' *The New York Times*, 9 January. http://www.nytimes.com/2010/01/10/world/middleeast/10balawi.html?_r=1&pagewanted=print (accessed 1 October 2010).

FBIS, *Compilation of Usama Bin Laden Statements 1994–January 2004.* (Online: January 2004). http://www.fas.org/irp/world/para/ubl-fbis.pdf (accessed 1 January 2010).

Feifer, Gregory (2009), *The Great Gamble: The Soviet War in Afghanistan.* (New York: Harper).

Feldab-Brown, Vanda (2010), *Shooting Up: Counterinsurgency and the War on Drugs.* (Washington, D.C.: Brookings Institution Press).

Feldman, Noah (2008), *The Fall and Rise of the Islamic State.* (Princeton: Princeton University Press).

Fergusson, James (2010), *Taliban The True Story of the World's Most Feared Guerilla Fighters.* (London: Transworld Publishers).

Filkins, Dexter (2009), 'Qaeda Had Role in Attack on U.N. Staff, Official Says,' *The New York Times*, 31 October. http://www.nytimes.com/2009/11/01/world/asia/01kabul.html (accessed 1 October 2010).

——— (2010), 'Pakistanis Tell of Motive in Taliban Leader's Arrest,' *The New York Times*, 22 August. http://www.nytimes.com/2010/08/23/world/asia/23taliban.html?pagewanted=print (accessed 5 October 2010).

Fineman, Mark and Richard C. Paddock (2002), 'Indonesia Cleric Tied to '95 Anti-U.S. Plot,' *Los Angeles Times*, 7 February. http://articles.latimes.com/2002/feb/07/news/mn-26735 (accessed 5 September 2010).

Fisher, Max (2011), 'In Arming Libyan Rebels, the U.S. Would Follow an Old, Dark Path,' *The Atlantic* (Online), 25 March. http://www.theatlantic.com/international/archive/2011/03/in-arming-libyan-rebels-us-would-follow-an-old-dark-path/73019/ (accessed 21 April 2011).

Fisk, Robert (2005), *The Great War for Civilisation: the Conquest of the Middle East.* (London: Fourth Estate).

Flintoff, Corey (2010), 'U.S. To Pursue "More Nuanced" Operations In Kandahar,' *NPR* (Online), 15 September. http://www.npr.org/blogs/thetwo-way/2010/09/14/129857868/petraeus-u-s-to-pursue-more-nuanced-operations-in-kandahar (accessed 19 October 2010).

Flynn, Major General Michael T., Captain Matt Pottinger and Paul D. Batchelor (2010), *Fixing Intel: A Blueprint for Making Intelligence Relevant in Afghanistan.* (Washington D.C.: Center for a New American Security).

Forsberg, Carl (2009), *Afghanistan Report 3: The Taliban's Campaign for Kandahar.* (Washington D.C.: Institute for the Study of War). http://www.understandingwar.org/files/The_Talibans_Campaign_For_Kandahar.pdf (accessed 10 March 2011).

Foster, Peter (2001), 'Dissident held over Afghan killing,' *The Daily Telegraph*, 31 October. http://www.telegraph.co.uk/news/worldnews/asia/afghanistan/1361047/Dissident-held-over-Afghan-killing.html (accessed 6 January 2010).

Franco, Claudio (2009), 'The Tehrik-e Taliban Pakistan,' in Antonio Giustozzi, *Decoding the New Taliban: Insights from the Afghan Field.* (London: Hurst Publications).

Frantz, Douglas and David Rohde (2001), 'How bin Laden and Taliban Forged Jihad Ties,' *The New York Times*, 22 November. http://www.nytimes.com/2001/11/22/international/asia/22TALI.html?pagewanted=print (accessed 12 October 2010).

Freeze, Colin (2009), 'Taliban religious courts extend their reach into remote regions,' *The Globe and Mail*, 8 June.

Friedman, Thomas L. (2001), 'Foreign Affairs; In Pakistan, It's Jihad 101,' *The New York Times*, 13 November. http://www.nytimes.com/2001/11/13/opinion/foreign-affairs-in-pakistan-it-s-jihad-101.html?pagewanted=print&src=pm (accessed 21 January 2011).

Fury, Dalton (2009), *Kill Bin Laden: A Delta Force Commander's Account of the Hunt for the World's Most Wanted Man*. (New York: St. Martin's Press).

Gall, Carlotta (2009), 'Pakistan and Afghan Taliban Close Ranks,' *The New York Times*, 27 March. http://www.nytimes.com/2009/03/27/world/asia/27taliban.html?ref=baitullah_mehsud&pagewanted=print (accessed 4 January 2010).

Gannon, Kathy (2002), 'Allies in fight against terror at war with each other,' *Associated Press*, 11 September.

——— (2006), *I is for Infidel*. (New York: Public Affairs).

Gayer, Laurent and Christophe Jaffrelot (2009), *Armed Militias of South Asia*. (London: Hurst Publications).

Gebauer, Matthias (2010), 'US to Send 2,500 Soldiers to German-Controlled Area,' *Der Spiegel* (Online), 1 April. http://www.spiegel.de/international/world/0,1518,druck-670085,00.html (accessed 17 March 2011).

Gehriger, Urs and Sami Yousafzai (2007), '"Ours is a Global Struggle": An Interview With Taliban Military Chief Mansoor Dadullah,' *World Politics Review* (Online), 3 July. http://www.worldpoliticsreview.com/articles/899/ours-is-a-global-struggle-an-interview-with-taliban-military-chief-mansoor-dadullah (accessed 13 October 2010).

Gerges, Fawaz (2005), *The Far Enemy: Why Jihad Went Global*. (Cambridge: Cambridge University Press).

Gertz, Bill (2001), 'Taliban leader cites help by China; Beijing officials deny assertion,' *The Washington Times* (USA), 31 October.

Giovanni, Janine di (2001), 'Radicals abroad urged destruction of Bamiyan Buddhas,' *The Times* (London), 24 November.

Giustozzi, Antonio (2007), *Koran, Kalashnikov and Laptop: the neo-Taliban insurgency in Afghanistan*. (London: Hurst).

——— (2009), *Empires of Mud: Wars and Warlords in Afghanistan*. (London: Hurst).

——— (2010), *The Taliban Beyond the Pashtuns*. (Ontario: Centre for International Governance Innovation). http://www.cigionline.org/sites/default/files/Afghanistan_Paper_5.pdf (accessed 5 October 2010).

Giustozzi, Antonio and Christoph Reuter (2010), *The Northern Front: The Afghan insurgency spreading beyond the Pashtuns*. (Kabul: Afghanistan Analyst's Network).

http://aan-afghanistan.com/uploads/20100623NORTH.pdf (accessed 5 October 2010).

Gopal, Anand (2010a), 'Half of Afghanistan Taliban Leadership arrested in Pakistan,' *Christian Science Monitor*, 24 February. http://www.csmonitor.com/World/Asia-South-Central/2010/0224/Half-of-Afghanistan-Taliban-leadership-arrested-in-Pakistan (accessed 5 October 2010).

——— (2010b), *The Battle for Afghanistan: Kandahar*. (Washington D.C.: New America Foundation).

Gopal, Anand and Mansur Khan Mahsud and Brian Fishman (2010a), 'The Haqqanis and al-Qaeda,' *The AfPak Channel* at *Foreign Policy*, 30 June. http://afpak.foreignpolicy.com/posts/2010/06/30/the_haqqanis_and_al_qaeda (accessed 1 August 2010).

——— (2010b), *The Battle for Pakistan: Militancy and Conflict in North Waziristan*. (Washington D.C.: New America Foundation, 2010). http://counterterrorism.newamerica.net/sites/newamerica.net/files/policydocs/northwaziristan.pdf (accessed 29 September 2010).

Grant, Gregg (2010), 'Marines Will Remain in Southern Afghanistan For Years: Conway,' *Defense Tech* (Online), 24 August. http://defensetech.org/2010/08/24/marines-will-remain-in-southern-afghanistan-for-years-conway/ (accessed 19 October 2010).

Gray, John (2003), *Al Qaeda and what it means to be modern*. (London: Faber and Faber).

Griffin, Michael (2001), *Reaping the Whirlwind: the Taliban Movement in Afghanistan*. (London: Pluto Press).

Gul, Imtiaz (2000), 'Taliban foiled India's bid to storm hijacked plane,' *The Friday Times*, 14–20 January. http://www.afghanistannewscenter.com/news/2000/january/jan14c2000.htm (accessed 29 June 2010).

——— (2010), *The Most Dangerous Place*. (New York: Viking).

Gumnam, Mohammad Taher Aziz (1986), *Kandahar Assassins*. (Peshawar).

——— (1996), *Kandahar Heroes*. (Peshawar).

Gutman, Roy (2008), *How we missed the story: Osama bin Laden, the Taliban, and the hijacking of Afghanistan*. (Lahore: Vanguard Books).

Hafiz, Salah al-Din (1992), 'The Rise and Fall of the State of Imbaba,' *al-Ahram*, 16 December.

Haleem, Abdul and Zhang Jianhua (2011), 'Afghans celebrate New Year amid hope for lasting peace,' *Xinhua* (Online), 21 March. http://news.xinhuanet.com/english2010/world/2011–03/21/c_13790524.htm (accessed 21 March 2011).

Haqqani, Husain (2005), *Pakistan: Between Mosque and Military*. (Washington, D.C.: Carnegie Endowment for International Peace).

Haroon, Sana (2007), *Frontier of Faith: Islam in the Indo-Afghan borderland*. (London: C. Hurst & Co. Publishers).

Hashimzada, Janullah and Akram Noorzai (2008), 'Omar to Taliban: Stop beheadings,' *Pajhwok Afghan News*, 3 February. http://www.pajhwok.com/en/2008/02/03/omar-taliban-stop-beheadings (accessed 16 December 2010).

Hastings, Michael (2010), 'The Runaway General,' *Rolling Stone*, 25 June. http://www.rollingstone.com/politics/news/17390/119236 (accessed 18 October 2010).

Hazem, Najeeb (2010), 'An Increase in Pressure Makes Taliban Accept Peace,' *ToloNews.com* (Online), 6 October. http://www.tolonews.com/en/afghanistan/711-an-increase-in-pressure-makes-taliban-accept-peace (accessed 19 October 2010).

Hegghammer, Thomas (2008), 'Saudis in Iraq: Patterns of Radicalization and Recruitment,' *Cultures & Conflits*, English documents, http://conflits.revues.org/index10042.html (accessed 28 August, 2010).

——— (2009), 'Jihadi-Salafis or Revolutionaries? On Religion and Politics in the Study of Militant Islamism,' in Roel Meijer (ed), *Global Salafism: Islam's New Religious Movement*. (London: Hurst).

——— (2010), *Jihad in Saudi Arabia: Violence and Pan-Islamism since 1979*. (Cambridge: Cambridge University Press).

Hersh, Seymour M. (2001), 'King's Ransom,' *The New Yorker*, 16 October. http://www.newyorker.com/archive/2001/10/22/011022fa_FACT1 (accessed 19 October 2009).

——— (2002), 'The Getaway,' *The New Yorker*, 28 January. http://www.newyorker.com/archive/2002/01/28/020128fa_FACT?printable=true (accessed 8 October 2010).

Hertog, Steffen and Diego Gambetta (2009), 'Why are there so many engineers among Islamic radicals?' *European Journal of Sociology*, 50, 2: 201–230.

Hoffman, Bruce (2006), *Inside Terrorism*. (New York: Columbia University Press).

——— (2008), 'The Myth of Grass-Roots Terrorism,' *Foreign Affairs*, May/June. http://www.foreignaffairs.com/articles/63408/bruce-hoffman/the-myth-of-grass-roots-terrorism?page=show (accessed 5 October 2010).

Horne, Alastair (2006), *A Savage War of Peace: Algeria 1954–1962*. (New York: New York Review Books).

Human Rights Watch (2006), *Lessons in Terror: Attacks on Education in Afghanistan*. (New York: Human Rights Watch). http://www.hrw.org/sites/default/files/reports/afghanistan0706.pdf (accessed 21 October 2010).

——— (2010), *The 'Ten-Dollar Talib' and Women's Rights*. 13 July. http://www.hrw.org/node/91466 (accessed 1 August 2010).

Hussain, Zahid (2008), *Frontline Pakistan: The path to catastrophe and the killing of Benazir Bhutto*. (London: I.B. Tauris).

Hutt, Rosamond (2009), 'Soldier's death brings toll to 201,' *The Independent*, 16 August. http://www.independent.co.uk/news/world/asia/soldiers-death-brings-toll-to-201-1772958.html (accessed 10 October 2010).

Ibn Mahmud, Husayn (date unknown), *The Giant Man*. (Online: at-Tibyan Publications). http://www.hoor-al-ayn.com/Books/The_Giant_Man.pdf (accessed 3 January 2010).

BIBLIOGRAPHY

Ibrahim, Raymond (2007), *The Al Qaeda Reader*. (New York: Doubleday).

Inkster, Nigel (2009), 'The al-Qaeda-Taliban Nexus' (http://www.cfr.org/publication/20838/alqaedataliban_nexus.html (accessed 8 October 2010)).

International Crisis Group (2010a), *A Force in Fragments: Reconstituting the Afghan Army*. (New York, 12 May). http://www.crisisgroup.org/en/regions/asia/south-asia/afghanistan/190-a-force-in-fragments-reconstituting-the-afghan-national-army.aspx (accessed 13 September 2010).

———— (2010b), *Exit vs Engagement*. (New York, 28 November). http://www.crisisgroup.org/en/regions/asia/south-asia/afghanistan/B115-afghanistan-exit-vs-engagement.aspx (accessed 21 March 2011).

Isby, David (2010), *Afghanistan: Graveyard of Empires; A New History of the Borderland*. (New York: Pegasus Books).

Islamic Emirate of Afghanistan (1998), 'Aims of the Movement', The Taliban, http://web.archive.org/web/19981205052717/www.taleban.com/moveaims.htm (accessed 7 July 2010).

Jackson, David (2011), 'Gates says there may be some U.S. troops in Afghanistan beyond 2014,' *USA Today*, 7 March. http://content.usatoday.com/communities/theoval/post/2011/03/gates-says-there-may-be-some-us-troops-in-afghanistan-beyond-2014/1 (accessed 17 March 2011).

Jamal, Arif (2010a), 'The Growth of the Deobandi Jihad in Afghanistan,' *Jamestown Foundation Terrorism Monitor*, 8, 2 (14 January). http://www.jamestown.org/single/?no_cache=1&tx_ttnews[tt_news]=35911&tx_ttnews[backPid]=7&cHash=39e7a26547 (accessed 20 January 2010).

Jamal, Arif (2010b), *Shadow War: The Untold Story of Jihad in Kashmir*. (New York: Melville House Publishing).

Jan, Abdullah (1995), 'Die Taliban: Nicht nur Pashtunen,' *Mahfel*, 45 (March–April).

Jansen, Johannes (1986), *The Neglected Duty: the Creed of Sadat's Assassins and Islamic Resurgence in the Middle East*. (New York: MacMillan).

———— (1997), *The Dual Nature of Islamic Fundamentalism*. (New York: Cornell University Press).

Johnson, Chris and Jolyon Leslie (2005), *Afghanistan: The Mirage of Peace*. (London: Zed Books).

Johnston, David (2006), 'At a Secret Interrogation, Dispute Flared Over Tactics,' *The New York Times*, 10 September. http://www.nytimes.com/2006/09/10/washington/ 10detain.html?pagewanted=print (accessed 29 September 2010).

Jones, Seth G. (2010), *In the Graveyard of Empires: America's War in Afghanistan*. (New York: W W Norton, 2010).

Junger, Sebastian (2001), 'Sebastian Junger on Afghanistan's Slain Rebel Leader,' *National Geographic Adventure*, November. http://www.nationalgeographic.com/adventure/0111/junger.html (accessed 29 June 2010).

Kaim, Markus (2007), *ISAF ausbauen—OEF beenden: Zur Debatte um die Bundeswehr-Mandate in Afghanistan*. (Washington, D.C.: SWP Aktuell). http://www.aicgs.org/documents/advisor/kaim0807.pdf (accessed 10 March 2011).

Kapisthalam, Kaushik (2004), 'Learning from Pakistan's madrassas', *Asia Times (Online)*, 23 June. http://www.atimes.com/atimes/South_Asia/FF23Df05.html (accessed 10 October 2010).

Kaplan, Fred (2009a), 'CT or COIN?' *Slate* (Online), 24 March. http://www.slate.com/id/2214515/ (accessed 19 October 2010).

——— (2009b), 'Explaining What Obama Meant About 'Beginning' To Withdraw in July 2011,' *Slate* (online), 2 December. http://www.slate.com/toolbar.aspx?action=print&id=2237263 (accessed 5 October 2010).

Kean, T.H. and L.H. Hamilton (2004), *The 9/11 Report: The National Commission on Terrorist Attacks Upon the United States*. (New York: Saint Martin's Paperbacks).

Kelly, Mary Louise (2009), 'New U.S. Commander In Afghanistan To Be Tested,' *National Public Radio* (Online), 26 May. http://www.npr.org/templates/story/story.php?storyId=104561441 (accessed 22 October 2010).

Kepel, Gilles (2004), *The War for Muslim Minds: Islam and the West*. (Cambridge: Harvard University Press).

——— (2005), *The Roots of Radical Islam*. (London: Saqi).

——— (2006), *Jihad: the Trail of Political Islam*. (London: IB Tauris).

——— (2008a), *Al Qaeda in Its Own Words*. (Cambridge: Belknap Press).

——— (2008b), *Beyond Terror and Martyrdom: The Future of the Middle East*. (Cambridge: Belknap Press).

Kerry, John (2009), *Tora Bora Revisited: How We Failed to Get Bin Laden and Why it Matters Today*. (Washington D.C.: US Senate Committee on Foreign Relations). http://foreign.senate.gov/reports/download/?id=30753123-b747–4b7c-83fb-d350cc0aacef (accessed 10 March 2011).

Khan, Ismail (2007), 'Omar threatens to intensify war: Talks with Karzai govt ruled out,' *Dawn* (Pakistan), 4 January. http://www.dawn.com/2007/01/04/top4.htm (accessed 13 October 2010).

Knudsen, Are (2009), *Violence and Belonging: Land, Love and Lethal Conflict in the North-West Frontier Province of Pakistan*. (Copenhagen: NIAS Press).

Kohlmann, Evan F. (2004) *Al-Qaida's Jihad in Europe: The Afghan-Bosnian Network*. (Oxford: Berg Publishers).

Korgun, Victor (2005), 'Afghanistan's Resurgent Taliban,' *Jamestown Global Terrorism Analysis*, 5 May. http://www.jamestown.org/programs/gta/single/?tx_ttnews[tt_news]=457&tx_ttnews[backPid]=178&no_cache=1 (accessed 12 October 2010).

Landler, Mark and Thom Shanker (2010), 'U.S. May Label Pakistan Militants as Terrorists,' *The New York Times*, 13 July. http://www.nytimes.com/2010/07/14/world/asia/14diplo.html?pagewanted=print (accessed 22 October 2010).

LeVine, Steve (1997), 'Helping Hand,' *Newsweek*, 13 October.

LeVine, Steve (2007), *The Oil and the Glory: The Pursuit of Empire and Fortune on the Caspian Sea*. (New York: Random House).

Lia, Brynjar (2009), *Architect of Global Jihad: The Life of Al-Qaida Strategist Abu Mus'ab al-Suri*. (London: Hurst Publications).

Lieven, Anatol (2011), *Pakistan: A Hard Country*. (London: Allen Lane).

Loyd, Anthony (2010), 'Terror link alleged as Saudi millions flow into Afghanistan war zone,' *The Times*, 31 May. http://www.timesonline.co.uk/tol/news/world/afghanistan/article7140745.ece?print=yes&randnum=1275743867265 (accessed 19 October 2010).

MacDonald, David (2007), *Drugs in Afghanistan: Opium, Outlaws and Scorpion Tales*. (London: Pluto Press).

MacDonald, Myra (2010), 'Afghan settlement would leave no room for al Qaeda—Pakistan,' *Reuters*, 26 November. http://in.reuters.com/article/2010/11/25/idINIndia-53159420101125 (accessed 31 May 2011).

Mackenzie, Richard (1998), 'The United States and the Taliban,' in William Maley, *Fundamentalism Reborn? Afghanistan and the Taliban*. (London: Hurst).

MacKenzie, Jean (2010), *Militancy and Conflict in Helmand*. (Washington D.C.: New America Foundation). http://counterterrorism.newamerica.net/sites/newamerica.net/files/policydocs/helmand.pdf (accessed 5 October 2010).

Maclean, William (2010), 'Afghan exit strategy takes shape ahead of London talks,' 25 January. http://www.reuters.com/article/idUSSGE60N02L20100125 (accessed 5 October 2010).

Maley, William (2002), *The Afghanistan Wars*. (London: Palgrave MacMillan).

Mamdani, Mahmood (2004), *Good Muslim, Bad Muslim: America, the Cold War, and the Roots of Terror*. (New York: Doubleday).

Mandaville, Peter (2007), *Global Political Islam*. (London: Routledge).

Margesson, Rhoda and Andorra Bruno and Jeremy M. Sharp (2009), *Iraqi Refugees and Internally Displaced Persons: A Deepening Humanitarian Crisis?* (Washington D.C.: Congressional Research Service). http://www.fas.org/sgp/crs/mideast/RL33936.pdf (accessed 10 March 2011).

Marsden, Peter (2009), *Afghanistan: Aid, Armies and Empires*. (London: I.B. Tauris).

Mashal, Mujib (2010), 'McChrystal-Karzai Relationship Steers the News in Afghanistan,' *New York Times At War* (Blog), 28 June. http://atwar.blogs.nytimes.com/2010/06/28/mcchrystal-karzai-relationship-steers-the-news-in-afghanistan/ (accessed 21 October 2010).

Mather, Ian and Nick Peters (2001), 'So Far, So Good,' *Scotland on Sunday*, 9 December.

Matinuddin, Kamal (1999), *The Taliban Phenomenon: Afghanistan 1994–1997*. (Oxford: Oxford University Press).

Mayr, Walter (2008), 'The Taliban at the Gates of Peshawar: Pakistan's Deal with the Devil,' *Spiegel Online*, 7 July. http://www.spiegel.de/international/world/0,1518,druck-564345,00.html (accessed 21 January 2011).

BIBLIOGRAPHY

McChrystal, General Stanley (2009), *COMISAF's Initial Assessment*. (Kabul: ISAF Headquarters). http://www.washingtonpost.com/wp-dyn/content/article/2009/09/21/AR2009092100110_pf.html (accessed 12 June 2011).

McDermott, Terry (2002), 'Early Scheme to Turn Jets Into Weapons; Philippines: Police say Khalid Shaikh Mohammed led a cell aiming to blow up planes in '95,' *Los Angeles Times*, 24 June.

———— (2005), *Perfect Soldiers: The 9/11 Hijackers: Who They Were, Why They Did It*. (New York: HarperCollins Publishers Inc.).

———— (2010), 'The Mastermind,' *The New Yorker*, 13 September. http://www.newyorker.com/reporting/2010/09/13/100913fa_fact_mcdermott (accessed 10 September 2010).

McGirk, Tim (2002), 'Rogues no more?' *Time*, 29 April. http://www.time.com/time/magazine/article/0,9171,501020506–233999,00.html (accessed 29 September 2010).

McGregor, Andrew (2009), 'Karzai Claims Mystery Helicopters Ferrying Taliban to North Afghanistan,' *Jamestown Foundation Terrorism Monitor*, 6 November. http://www.jamestown.org/uploads/media/TM_007_dc46ca.pdf (accessed 5 October 2010).

McLaughlin, Captain Joshua (2010), 'The al Qaeda Franchise Model,' *Small Wars Journal*, 31 January. http://smallwarsjournal.com/blog/journal/docs-temp/357-mclaughlin.pdf (accessed 19 October 2010).

Metcalf, Barbara D. (1978), 'The Madrasa at Deoband: A Model for Religious Education in Modern India,' *Modern Asian Studies*, 12, 1: 112.

———— (2002), *'Traditionalist' Islamic Activism: Deoband, Tablighis, and Talibs* (Leiden: International Institute for the Study of Islam in the Modern World (ISIM)).

Meyer, Jane (2009), 'The Predator War,' *The New Yorker*, 26 October. http://www.newyorker.com/reporting/2009/10/26/091026fa_fact_mayer?printable=true (accessed 5 October 2010).

Ministry of Foreign Affairs of Denmark (2005), *Humanitarian and Reconstruction Assistance 2001–5: From Denmark, Ireland, the Netherlands, Sweden and the United Kingdom. A Joint Evaluation*. (Copenhagen, October). http://danida.netboghandel.dk/english/publ.asp?page=publ&objno=16261021 (accessed 12 September 2010).

Mitchell, Richard P. (1969), *The Society of the Muslim Brotherhood*. (Oxford: Oxford University Press).

Mir, Amir (2005), 'The jihad lives on,' *Asia Times* (Online), 11 March. http://www.atimes.com/atimes/South_Asia/GC11Df07.html (accessed 7 March 2011).

Mojdeh, Vahid (2003), *Afghanistan va panj sal-i sultah-i Taliban*. (Kabul).

Mohamedou, Mohammad-Mahmoud Ould (2007), *Understanding Al Qaeda: The Transformation of War*. (London: Pluto Press).

Moreau, Ron and Sami Yousufzai (2010), 'What the Taliban Think of McChrystal's Ouster,' *Newsweek*, 23 June 2010. http://www.newsweek.com/2010/06/23/what-the-taliban-thinks-of-mcchrystal-s-ouster.html (accessed 5 October 2010).

Murshed, Sayyed Iftikhar (2006), *Afghanistan: The Taliban Years*. (London: Bennett & Bloom).

———(2010), 'The quest for an Afghan settlement,' *Asia Despatch*, 9 August. http://www.asiadespatch.com/2010/08/the-quest-for-an-afghan-settlement/ (accessed 6 March 2011).

Mustas'ad, Mullah Mohammad Hussein (2006), *Afghanistan aw Taliban*. (Unknown printing).

Mutawakil, Wakil Ahmad (2007), *Afghanistan and Taliban*. (Kabul).

Napoleoni, Loretta (2005), *Terror Incorporated: Tracing the Dollars behind the Terror Networks*. (New York: Seven Stories Press).

Nash, Elizabeth (2006), 'Madrid bombers "were inspired by Bin Laden address,"' *The Independent*, 7 November. http://www.independent.co.uk/news/world/europe/madrid-bombers-were-inspired-by-bin-laden-address-423266.html (accessed 10 October 2010).

Nasiri, Omar (2008), *Inside the Jihad: My Life With Al Qaeda*. (New York: Basic Books).

Nasr, Vali (1994), *The Vanguard of the Islamic Revolution: The Jama'at-i Islami of Pakistan*. (Berkeley: University of California Press).

———(1996), *Mawdudi and the Making of Islamic Revivalism*. (Oxford: Oxford University Press).

———(2007), *The Shia Revival: How Conflicts Within Islam Will Shape the Future*. (New York: Norton).

Nathan, Joanna (2009), 'Reading the Taliban,' in Antonio Giustozzi, *Decoding the New Taliban: Insights from the Afghan Field*. (London: Hurst Publications).

National Commission on Terrorist Attacks Upon the United States (2004), *Monograph on Terrorist Financing*, (New York: 9/11 Commission). http://govinfo.library.unt.edu/911/staff_statements/911_TerrFin_Monograph.pdf (accessed 14 January 2011).

National Security Archive (1994), *[Excised] to Ron McMullen (Afghanistan Desk), 'Developments in Afghanistan,' 5 December 1994, Unknown Classification, 1 p. [Excised]*, http://www.gwu.edu/~nsarchiv/NSAEBB/NSAEBB227/1.pdf (date unknown).

———(1998a), *U.S. Department of State, Cable, 'Afghanistan: Taliban's Mullah Omar's 8/22 Contact with State Department,' 23 August 1998, Confidential, NODIS, 4 pp. [Excised]*, http://www.gwu.edu/~nsarchiv/NSAEBB/NSAEBB134/Doc%202.pdf (accessed 4 June 2010).

———(1998b), *U.S. Embassy (Islamabad), Cable, 'Afghanistan: Tensions Reportedly Mount Within Taliban as Ties With Saudi Arabia Deteriorate Over Bin Ladin,' 28 September 1998, Secret, 8 pp. [Excised]*, http://www.gwu.edu/~nsarchiv/NSAEBB/NSAEBB227/31.pdf (accessed 4 March 2010).

BIBLIOGRAPHY

———— (1998c), *U.S. Embassy (Islamabad), Cable, 'Afghanistan: Taliban Leader Mullah Omar: Intimations of Radical Pan-Islamic Thinking?'* 22 October 1998, Secret, 8pp. *[Excised]*, http://www.gwu.edu/~nsarchiv/NSAEBB/NSAEBB253/19981 022.pdf (accessed 1 February 2010).

———— (1998d), *U.S. Department of State Cable, 'Osama bin Laden: Taliban Spokesman Seeks New Proposal for Resolving bin Laden Problem'* 28 November, 1998, Secret, 10pp. *[Excised]*, http://www.gwu.edu/~nsarchiv/NSAEBB/NSAEBB253/19981 128.pdf (accessed 4 June 2010).

———— (1999), *U.S. Embassy (Islamabad), Cable, 'Afghanistan: Taliban Seem to Have Less Funds and Supplies This Year, But the Problem Does Not Appear to be that Acute,'* 17 February 1999, Confidential, 2 pp. *[Excised]*, http://www.gwu.edu/~nsarchiv/ NSAEBB/NSAEBB227/32.pdf (accessed 3 August 2010).

———— (2001a), *U.S. Embassy (Islamabad), Cable, 'Musharraf [EXCISED]'* 13 September 2001, Secret—Noforn, 7 pp. *[Excised]*, http://www.gwu.edu/~nsarchiv/ NSAEBB/NSAEBB325/doc04.pdf (accessed 12 October 2010).

———— (2001b), *U.S. Department of State, Cable, 'Deputy Secretary Armitage's Meeting with General Mahmud: Actions and Support Expected of Pakistan in Fight Against Terrorism,'* 14 September 2001, Secret, 5 pp. *[Excised]*, http://www.gwu. edu/~nsarchiv/NSAEBB/NSAEBB325/doc05.pdf (accessed 27 September 2010).

National Security Council (2010), *Afghanistan Peace and Reintegration Program. (Draft Version)* (Kabul, April 2010).

Nawaz, Shuja (2008), *Crossed Swords: Pakistan Its Army, and the Wars Within.* (Oxford: Oxford University Press).

Nawid, Senzil K. (1999), *Religious Response to Social Change in Afghanistan 1919–29: King Aman-Allah and the Afghan Ulama.* (California: Mazda Publishers).

Naylor, Sean (2005), *Not a Good Day to Die: The Untold Story of Operation Anaconda.* (New York: Berkley Books).

Nixon, Hamish (2011), *Achieving Durable Peace: Afghan Perspectives on a Peace Process.* (Oslo: PRIO). http://www.prio.no/upload/halvor/Nixon,%20H%20 (2011)%20Achieving%20Durable%20Peace%20(PRIO%20Paper).pdf (accessed 13 June 2011).

NNI (2000a), 'Taliban role lauded,' 1 January. http://www.afghanistannewscenter. com/news/2000/january/jan1c2000.htm (accessed 29 June 2010).

———— (2000b), 'Afghan official sacked for talking too much to Indian media,' 2 January. http://www.afghanistannewscenter.com/news/2000/january/jan2d2000.htm (accessed 29 June 2010).

Nordland, Rod (2010a), 'Lacking Money and Leadership, Push for Taliban Defectors Stalls,' *The New York Times*, 6 September. http://www.nytimes.com/2010/09/07/ world/asia/07taliban.html (accessed 5 October 2010).

———— (2010b), 'Security in Afghanistan Is Deteriorating, Aid Groups Say,' *The New York Times*, 11 September. http://www.nytimes.com/2010/09/12/world/asia/ 12afghan.html?pagewanted=print (accessed 18 October 2010).

O'Hanlon, Michael and Bruce Riedel (2011), 'Plan A-Minus for Afghanistan.' *The Washington Quarterly*, Winter. http://www.thewashingtonquarterly.com/11winter/docs/11winter_O%27Hanlon_Riedel.pdf (accessed 17 December 2010).

Olesen, Asta (1995), *Islam and politics in Afghanistan*. (Surrey: Curzon Press).

Omicinski, John (2001), 'General: Capturing bin Laden is not part of mission,' *USA Today*, 8 October. http://www.usatoday.com/news/sept11/2001/11/08/pentagon-toll.htm (accessed 29 September 2010).

Ottaway, David B. and Dan Morgan (2001), 'Muslim Charities Under Scrutiny; Saudi-Funded Groups Deny Ties To Terror but Cite Vulnerability,' *The Washington Post*, 29 September.

Packer, George (2007), *The Assassin's Gate: America in Iraq*. (London: Faber and Faber).

Pannier, Bruce (2010), 'Militant Hizb-e Islami Delegation Meets With Afghan President,' *Radio Freedom-Radio Liberty*, 22 March. http://www.rferl.org/articleprintview/1990001.html (accessed 12 September 2010).

Partlow, Joshua (2010a), 'Gen. Petraeus arrives in Afghanistan to take over from Gen. McChrystal,' *The Washington Post*, 3 July. http://www.washingtonpost.com/wp-dyn/content/article/2010/07/02/AR2010070205227_pf.html (accessed 5 October 2010).

——— (2010b), 'Afghan leaders are cutting ties with Karzai,' *The Washington Post*, 23 July. http://www.washingtonpost.com/wp-dyn/content/article/2010/07/ 22/ AR2010072206155.html?wpisrc=nl_headline (accessed 18 October 2010).

Pedwell, Terry (2006), 'Taliban leaders distance themselves from suicide attacks against civilians,' The Canadian Press, 25 August.

Peters, Gretchen (2009), *Seeds of Terror: How Heroin is Bankrolling the Taliban and Al Qaeda*. (New York: Thomas Dunne Books).

——— (2010), *Crime and Insurgency in the Tribal Areas of Afghanistan and Pakistan*. (West Point: Combating Terrorism Center). http://www.ctc.usma.edu/Crime%20 and%20Insurgency_Final.pdf (accessed 16 March 2011).

Pipes, Daniel (2001), 'Bin Laden's Popularity,' *WorldNetDaily* (Online), 22 October. http://www.wnd.com/index.php?pageId=11374 (accessed 8 October 2010).

Pitman, Todd (2010), 'In Afghan town, insurgents vanish after battles,' *Associated Press*, 18 October. http://news.yahoo.com/s/ap/20101018/ap_on_re_as/as_afghan_ chasing_ghosts (accessed 19 October 2010).

Porter, Gareth (2008), 'Bush buried Musharraf's al-Qaeda links,' *Asia Times*, 21 August. http://www.atimes.com/atimes/South_Asia/JH21Df02.html (accessed 29 September 2010).

Qarhani, Badi' (2002), 'Mullah Omar speaks to Asharq Alawsat in his first media interview after the war in Afghanistan,' *Asharq Alawsat* (London), 17 May. http://www. aawsat.com/print.asp?did=103706&issueno=8571 (Arabic; accessed 10 March 2011).

Qazi, M.S. (2000), 'Post-hijacking scenario,' *The Frontier Post*, 11 January. http://www.

afghanistannewscenter.com/news/2000/january/jan11c2000.htm (accessed 29 June 2010).

Qutb, Sayyid (1964), *Ma'alim fii al-Tariq.* (Cairo: Maktabat Wahba).

Rahman, B (2010), 'Terror in NY: A Jem Link?—International Terrorism Monitor—-Paper No. 645,' *South Asia Analysis Group*, 7 May. http://www.southasiaanalysis. org/%5Cpapers38%5Cpaper3800.html (accessed 19 October 2010).

——— (2004), *Al Qaeda Kills its Mentor and Godfather?* (India: South Asia Analysis Group). http://www.southasiaanalysis.org/%5Cpapers11%5Cpaper1018.html (accessed 10 March 2011).

Rana, Muhammad Amir (2004), *A to Z of Jehadi Organizations in Pakistan.* (Pakistan: Mashal Books).

Rana, Muhammad Amir and Rohan Gunaratna (2007), *Al-Qaeda fights back inside Pakistani Tribal Areas.* (Pakistan: Pak Institute for Peace Studies).

Randal, Jonathan C. (2005), *Osama: the making of a terrorist.* (London: I.B. Tauris).

Rashid, Ahmed (1998), 'Pakistan and the Taliban,' in William Maley, *Fundamentalism Reborn? Afghanistan and the Taliban.* (London: Hurst).

——— (1999), 'The Taliban: Exporting Extremism,' *Foreign Affairs*, November/ December. http://www.foreignaffairs.com/articles/55600/ahmed-rashid/the-taliban-exporting-extremism (accessed 16 December 2010)).

——— (2001a), *Taliban: Militant Islam, Oil and Fundamentalism in Central Asia.* (New Haven: Yale University Press).

——— (2001b), 'Intelligence team defied Musharraf to help Taliban,' *The Telegraph*, 10 October. http://www.telegraph.co.uk/news/worldnews/asia/pakistan/ 1359051/Intelligence-team-defied-Musharraf-to-help-Taliban.html (accessed 29 September 2010).

——— (2008), *Descent into Chaos: The United States and the Failure of Nation Building in Pakistan, Afghanistan, and Central Asia.* (New York: Penguin Books).

Ratnesar, Romesh (2001), 'The Hunt for bin Laden,' *Time*, 18/26 November. http:// www.time.com/time/printout/0,8816,185051,00.html (accessed 12 October 2010).

Reeve, Simon (1999), *The New Jackals: Ramzi Yousef, Osama bin Laden and the future of terrorism.* (London: Andre Deutsch).

Ressa, Maria A. (2003), *Seeds of Terror: An Eyewitness Account of Al-Qaeda's Newest Center of Operations in Southeast Asia.* (New York: Free Press).

Reuter, Christoph and Borhan Younus (2009), 'The Return of the Taliban in Andar District, Ghazni,' Antonio Giustozzi, *Decoding the New Taliban: Insights from the Afghan Field.* (London: Hurst Publications).

Reuters (1999a), 'Hijacked India Plane Turned Away From Kabul,' 24 December. http://www.afghanistannewscenter.com/news/1999/december/dec24a1999.htm (accessed 29 June 2010).

——— (1999b), 'Taleban say will storm jet if captives hurt,' 27 December. http:// www.afghanistannewscenter.com/news/1999/december/dec27e1999.htm (accessed 29 June 2010).

———— (1999c), 'Taliban Sees No Progress in Plane Hijack Talks,' 28 December. http://www.afghanistannewscenter.com/news/1999/december/dec28b1999.htm (accessed 29 June 2010).

———— (1999d), 'Hijackers given 10 hours to quit Afghanistan,' 31 December. http:// www.afghanistannewscenter.com/news/1999/december/dec31b1999.htm (accessed 29 June, 2010).

Richter, Paul (2010), 'U.S. government funds may have gone to Taliban,' *Los Angeles Times*, 30 September. http://www.latimes.com/news/politics/la-fg-taliban-payoffs-20101001,0,5088999,print.story (accessed 6 October 2010).

Riedel, Bruce O. (2008), *The Search for Al-Qaeda: its Leadership, Ideology and Future*. (Washington, DC: Brookings Institution Press).

Riley-Smith, Jonathan (1999), *A History of the Crusades*. (Oxford: Oxford University Press).

Robinson, Francis (1984), 'Review of "Islamic Revival in British India: Deoband, 1860–1900" by Barbara Daly Metcalf,' *Modern Asian Studies*, 18, 2: 337–345.

Robinson, Simon (2007), 'The World's Worst Suicide Bombers,' *Time* (Online), 28 July. http://www.time.com/time/printout/0,8816,1647922,00.html (accessed 21 October 2010).

Roggio, Bill (2010a), 'Al Qaeda-linked Taliban leader killed in Kunar,' *The Long War Journal* (Online), 18 September. http://www.longwarjournal.org/archives/2010/09/al_qaedalinked_talib_1.php (accessed 5 October 2010).

Roggio, Bill (2010b), 'ISAF hunts senior al Qaeda leader in Kunar,' *The Long War Journal* (Online), 26 September. http://www.longwarjournal.org/archives/2010/09/isaf_hunts_senior_al.php (accessed 5 October 2010).

Rohde, David and David E. Sangar (2007), 'How a "Good War" in Afghanistan Went Bad,' *The New York Times*, 12 August. http://www.nytimes.com/2007/08/12/world/asia/12afghan.html?pagewanted=print (accessed 10 October 2010).

Rohde, David (2009), 'Held by the Taliban, Part Four—A Drone Strike and Dwindling Hope,' *The New York Times*, 20 October. http://www.nytimes.com/2009/10/21/world/asia/21hostage.html?pagewanted=print (accessed 6 October 2010).

———— (2010), 'Terrorists Without Borders,' *The New Republic*, 23 February.

Rohde, David and Kristen Mulvihill (2010), *A Rope and a Prayer: A Kidnapping from Two Sides* (New York: Viking).

Rotella, Sebastian and Josh Meyer (2002), 'Wiretaps May Have Foretold Terror Attacks,' *Los Angeles Times*, 29 May.

Roy, Olivier (1990), *Islam and Resistance in Afghanistan*. (Cambridge: Cambridge University Press).

———— (1995a), *Afghanistan: from Holy War to Civil war*. (London: Darwin Press).

———— (1995b), 'Die Taliban-Bewegung in Afghanistan,' *Mahfel*, 45, 2 (March–April): 8–10.

Rubenstein, Alvin Z. (1983), *Great Game: Rivalry in the Persian Gulf and South Asia*. (Santa Barbara: Prager/Greenwood).

BIBLIOGRAPHY

Rubin, Alissa J. (2010a), 'U.S. Report on Afghan War Finds Few Gains in 6 Months,' *The New York Times*, 29 April. http://www.nytimes.com/2010/04/30/world/asia/30afghan.html?pagewanted=print (accessed 19 October 2010).

Rubin, Alissa J. (2010b), 'Militant Group Expands Attacks in Afghanistan,' *The New York Times*, 15 June. http://www.nytimes.com/2010/06/16/world/asia/16lashkar.html?pagewanted=print (accessed 5 October 2010).

Rubin, Barnett (2002), *The Fragmentation of Afghanistan: state formation and collapse in the international system.* (New Haven: Yale University Press).

Rubin, Elizabeth (2006), 'In the Land of the Taliban,' *The New York Times*, 22 October. http://www.nytimes.com/2006/10/22/magazine/22afghanistan.html?pagewanted=print (accessed 12 October 2010).

Russian General Staff (2002), *The Soviet-Afghan War: How a Superpower Fought and Lost.* (Kansas: University Press of Kansas).

Ruttig, Thomas (1995), '"Technische Probleme" mit den Taleban,' *Mahfel*, 45 (March–April).

––––––– (2009a), 'The Haqqani Network as an Autonomous Entity,' in Antonio Giustozzi, *Decoding the New Taliban: Insights from the Afghan Field.* (London: Hurst Publications, 2009).

––––––– (2009b), *The Other Side.* (Kabul: Afghanistan Analysts Network, 2009).

––––––– (2010), *How Tribal Are the Taleban? Afghanistan's largest insurgent movement between its tribal roots and Islamist ideology.* (Kabul: Afghanistan Analyst's Network).

Sageman, Marc (2004), *Understanding Terror Networks.* (Pennsylvania: University of Pennsylvania Press).

––––––– (2008), *Leaderless Jihad: Terror Networks in the Twenty-First Century*, (Philadelphia: University of Pennsylvania Press).

Saikal, Amin (1998), 'The Rabbani Government, 1992–1996,' in William Maley, *Fundamentalism Reborn? Afghanistan and the Taliban.* (London: Hurst).

Salah, Mohammmad (2001), *Narratives of the Jihad Years: the journey of the Afghan Arabs.* (Cairo).

Scheuer, Michael (2006), 'Al-Qaeda in Iraq: Has al-Zawahiri Reined in al-Zarqawi?' *Jamestown Terrorism Focus*, 12 April. http://tinyurl.com/37mq9fv (accessed 10 October 2010).

––––––– (2011), *Osama bin Laden.* (Oxford: Oxford University Press).

Schifrin, Nick (2010), 'Afghan President Karzai Steps Up Talks With Insurgents,' *ABC News* (Online), 29 June. http://abcnews.go.com/print?id=11042852 (accessed 21 March 2011).

Schimmel, Annemarie (2003), *The Mystical Dimensions of Islam.* (Lahore: Sang-e-Meel Publications).

Schindler, John R. (2007), *Unholy Terror: Bosnia, Al-Qa'ida, and the Rise of Global Jihad.* (Minneapolis: Zenith Press).

Schmidle, Nicholas (2009), *To Live or to Perish Forever: Two Tumultuous Years in Pakistan*. (New York: Henry Holt and Company).

Schöch, Rüdiger (2008), *Afghan refugees in Pakistan during the 1980s: Cold War politics and registration practice*. (Geneva: Policy Development and Evaluation Service of UNHCR). http://www.unhcr.org/4868daad2.pdf (accessed 1 August 2010).

Schroen, Gary C. (2005), *First In: How Seven CIA Officers Opened the War on Terror in Afghanistan*. (New York: Ballantine Books).

Sciolino, Elaine and Souad Mekhennet (2008), 'Al Qaeda Warrior Uses Internet to Rally Women,' *The New York Times*, 28 May. http://www.nytimes.com/2008/05/28/world/europe/28terror.html?pagewanted=print (accessed 1 June 2009).

Semple, Michael (2009), *Reconciliation in Afghanistan*. (Washington D.C.: United States Institute for Peace).

Shahzad, Syed Saleem (2003), 'When terrorists fall out,' *Asia Times* (Online), 19 July. http://www.atimes.com/atimes/South_Asia/EG19Df04.html (accessed 7 March 2011).

——— (2007), 'Taliban, US in new round of peace talks,' *Asia Times* (Online), 21 August. http://www.atimes.com/atimes/South_Asia/IH21Df03.html (accessed 12 March 2011).

Shane, Scott, Mark Mazzetti and Dexter Filkins (2010), 'Cables Depict Afghan Graft, Starting at Top,' *The New York Times*, 2 December. http://www.nytimes.com/2010/12/03/world/asia/03wikileaks-corruption.html?pagewanted=print (accessed 31 May 2011).

Shanker, Thom (2011), 'General Sees Joint Bases for Afghans After 2014,' *The New York Times*, 15 March. http://www.nytimes.com/2011/03/16/world/asia/16petraeus.html?pagewanted=print (accessed 21 March 2011).

Shanker, Thom and Alissa Rubin (2010), 'Quest to Neutralize Afghan Militants Is Showing Glimpses of Success, NATO Says,' *The New York Times*, 28 June. http://www.nytimes.com/2010/06/29/world/asia/29military.html?pagewanted=print (accessed 19 October 2010).

Sharaf-al-Din, Khalid (1999), 'More on Islamic Jihad Trial Confessions,' *Al-Sharq al-Awsat* (7 March).

Sigler, Rear Admiral John F. (2009), 'Future Force Planning for the Middle East,' *The Journal of International Security Affairs*, number 16, Spring. http://www.securityaffairs.org/issues/2009/16/sigler.php (accessed 20 February 2011).

Singh, Jaswant (2007), *A Call to Honour: In Service of Emergent India*. (New Delhi: Rupa).

Sinno, Abdulkader H. (2008), *Organizations at War in Afghanistan and Beyond*. (Cornell: Cornell University Press).

Sirrs, Julie (2001), 'The Taliban's International Ambitions,' *Middle East Quarterly*, Summer, 61–71. http://www.meforum.org/486/the-talibans-international-ambitions (accessed 7 March 2011).

Smith, Graeme (2009), 'What Kandahar's Taliban Say' in Antonio Giustozzi, *Decoding the New Taliban: Insights from the Afghan Field*. (London: Hurst Publications).

———— (2010), 'Pakistan's deadly robots in the sky,' *The Globe and Mail*, 1 October. http://www.theglobeandmail.com/news/world/asia-pacific/pakistans-deadly-robots-in-the-sky/article1739172/ (accessed 6 October 2010).

———— (2012), *Blood and Dust* (working title). (Toronto: Knopf).

Solomon, Jay (2007), 'Eager for Allies, Army Tries Turning Insurgents; Chaos Embroils Pakistan,' *The Wall Street Journal*, 8 November.

Sonmez, Felicia and Matt DeLong (2010), 'Panetta: 50–100 al-Qaeda remain in Afghanistan,' *The Washington Post*, 27 June. http://voices.washingtonpost.com/44/2010/06/panetta-50–100-al-qaeda-remain.html (accessed 29 July 2010).

Spillius, Alex (2002), 'Bin Laden alive, says Taliban leader,' *The Daily Telegraph*, 18 May.

Steele, Jonathan (2001), 'Mullah Omar: Stand and resist, fleeing fighters told: Leader makes radio appeal to scattered forces,' *The Guardian*, 14 November.

Stenersen, Anne (2010a), *The Taliban insurgency in Afghanistan—organization, leadership and worldview*. (Oslo: Norwegian Defence Research Establishment (FFI)).

———— (2010b), *Al-Qaeda's Allies: Explaining the Relationship between al-Qaeda and Various Factions of the Taliban after 2001*. (Washington D.C.: New America Foundation). http://counterterrorism.newamerica.net/sites/newamerica.net/files/policydocs/stenersen2.pdf (accessed 14 March 2011).

Strick van Linschoten, Alex and Felix Kuehn (2008), *Tribal Solutions for Kandahar*. (Kandahar: Afghanwire, 2008).

Stroobants, Jean-Pierre (2005), 'Vie et mort des assassins de Massoud,' *Le Monde* (in French), 19 April.

Sude, Barbara (2010), *Al-Qaeda Central*. (Washington D.C.: New America Foundation).

Suskind, Ron (2006), *The One Percent Doctrine*. (New York: Simon and Schuster).

Talbot, Ian (1999), *Pakistan: A Modern History*. (Lahore: Vanguard Books).

Tawil, Camille (2010a), *The Other Face of Al-Qaeda*. (London: Quilliam Foundation). http://www.quilliamfoundation.org/images/stories/pdfs/the-other-face-of-al-qaeda.pdf?dm_i=JI3,AZ98,3031IN,UGW9,1 (accessed 8 March 2011).

———— (2010b), *Brothers in Arms: The Story of al-Qa'ida and the Arab Jihadists*. (London: Saqi Press).

Tellis, Ashley and Aroop Mukharji (eds) (2010), *Is a regional strategy viable in Afghanistan?* (Washington D.C.: Carnegie Endowment for International Peace).

Temple-Raston, Dina (2010), 'Bin Laden Told Partners To Plan Mumbai-Like Attacks,' *National Public Radio (NPR)*, 30 September. http://www.npr.org/templates/story/story.php?storyId=130242602 (accessed 5 October 2010).

Thier, J. Alexander (2010), 'Afghanistan's Rocky Path to Peace,' *Current History* 109, no. 726, 131–37.

BIBLIOGRAPHY

Thruelsen, Peter Dahl and DIIS (2006), *From Soldier to Civilian: Disarmament, Demobilisation, Reintegration in Afghanistan.* (Oslo: Chr. Michelsen Institute, 2006). http://www.diis.dk/graphics/Publications/Reports2006/RP2006–7web.pdf (accessed 21 October 2010).

Tohid, Owais (2003), 'Taliban regroups—on the road,' *Christian Science Monitor,* 27 June.

Traynor, Ian and Gary Younge (2001), 'Secret memo reveals US plan to overthrow Taliban regime,' *The Guardian,* 21 September. http://www.guardian.co.uk/world/2001/sep/21/afghanistan.september1112 (accessed 29 September 2001).

Trofimov, Yaroslav (2007), *The Siege of Mecca.* (New York: Doubleday).

UNI (2001), 'Taliban grants Osama citizenship,' *The Hindu,* 10 November. http://www.hinduonnet.com/2001/11/10/stories/03100007.htm (accessed 17 October 2010).

UPI (2010), 'No "military-only solution" in Afghan war,' 21 October. http://www.upi.com/Top_News/Special/2010/10/21/No-military-only-solution-in-Afghan-war/UPI-86611287691870/ (accessed 22 October 2010).

Urban, Mark (2008), 'US general faces new Afghan challenge,' *BBC News* (Online), 17 September. http://news.bbc.co.uk/1/hi/world/south_asia/7619769.stm (accessed 5 October 2010).

US Department of State (1997), 'Afghanistan: Meeting with the Taliban,' *National Security Archive,* 11 December. http://www.gwu.edu/~nsarchiv/NSAEBB/NSAEBB97/tal24.pdf (accessed 13 July 2010).

Van Bijlert, Martine (2009), *Polling Day Fraud in the Afghan Elections.* (Kabul: Afghanistan Analyst's Network). http://www.aan-afghanistan.org/uploads/2009AAN-MvB-pollingfraud.pdf (accessed 12 March 2011).

Van Bijlert, Martine (2010), 'Outsmarted and made to pay,' June 19. http://aan-afghanistan.com/index.asp?id=910 (accessed 3 August 2010).

Van Dyk, Jere (2002), *In Afghanistan.* (San Jose: Authors Choice Press).

——— (2004), 'A war of ugly images,' *Toronto Star,* 12 October.

——— (2010), *Captive: My Times as a Prisoner of the Taliban.* (New York: Times Books).

Vendrell, Francesc (2009), 'What Went Wrong after Bonn,' in *Afghanistan, 1979–2009: In the Grip of Conflict.* (Washington D.C.: The Middle East Institute). http://www.mei.edu/Portals/0/Publications/Afghanistan%20VP.pdf (accessed 8 October 2010).

Vidino, Lorenzo (2006), *Al Qaeda in Europe.* (New York: Prometheus Book).

Vizcarra, Natasha (1994), 'Terrorist group claims responsibility for PAL bombing,' *The Filipino Express,* 25 December.

Vogelsang, Willem (2008), *The Afghans.* (Oxford: Wiley-Blackwell).

Vollman, William T. (2000), 'Letters from Afghanistan: Across the Divide,' *The New Yorker,* 15 May 2000. http://www.smsys.com/wtc/wvollmann.txt (accessed 1 June 2010)).

Waldman, Matt (2010a), *Golden Surrender? The Risks, Challenges, and Implications of Reintegration in Afghanistan*. (Kabul: Afghanistan Analysts Network). http://aan-afghanistan.com/uploads/2010_AAN_Golden_Surrender.pdf (accessed 21 March 2011).

—— (2010b), *The Sun in the Sky: The Relationship between Pakistan's ISI and Afghan Insurgents*. (London: London School of Economics). http://www.crisisstates.com/download/dp/DP%2018.pdf (accessed 1 October 2010); Interview, Kabul, July 2010.

—— (2010c), *Dangerous Liaisons with the Afghan Taliban: The Feasibility and Risks of Negotiations*. (Washington D.C.: United States Institute of Peace). http://www.usip.org/files/resources/SR%20256%20-%20Dangerous%20Liaisons%20with%20the%20Afghan%20Taliban.pdf (accessed 16 March 2011).

Wattie, Chris (2009), *Contact Charlie: The Canadian Army, the Taliban and the Battle that Saved Afghanistan*. (Bolton: Key Porter Books).

Weinbaum, Marvin G. (1994), *Pakistan and Afghanistan: resistance and reconstruction*. (Boulder, Colorado: Westview Press).

Weiser, Benjamin and Colin Moynihan (2010), 'Guilty Plea In Time Square Bombing Plot,' *The New York Times*, June 21. http://www.nytimes.com/2010/06/22/nyregion/22terror.html?_r=1&hp=&adxnnl=1&adxnnlx=1287386481-tGk-ThOZHHTwJK8%20C4yKMEQ&pagewanted=print (accessed 18 October 2010).

West, Julian (1999), 'We'll crash jet, says "bin Laden" hijack squad,' *The Daily Telegraph*, 26 December. http://www.afghanistannewscenter.com/news/1999/december/dec26g1999.htm (accessed 29 June 2010).

Whitaker, Raymond (2001), 'Bin Laden's fate to be decided by 1,000 clerics,' *The Independent*, 20 September. http://www.independent.co.uk/news/world/asia/bin-ladens-fate-to-be-decided-by-1000-clerics-670040.html (accessed 12 October 2010).

Whitlock, Craig (2010), 'Facing Afghan mistrust, al-Qaeda fighters take limited role in insurgency,' *The Washington Post*, 23 August. http://www.washingtonpost.com/wp-dyn/content/article/2010/08/22/AR2010082203029_pf.html (accessed 18 October 2010).

Wiebe, Dietrich (1978), *Stadtstruktur und kulturgeographischer Wandel in Kandahar und Suedafghanistan*. (Kiel: Selbstverlag Des Geographischen Instituts Der Universitaet Kiel).

Williams, Brian Glyn (2007), 'Suicide Bombings in Afghanistan,' *Jane's Islamic Affairs Analyst*, 13 August.

Wilson, Michael (2009), 'From Smiling Coffee Vendor to Terror Suspect,' *The New York Times*, 26 September. http://www.nytimes.com/2009/09/26/nyregion/26profile.html?pagewanted=print (accessed 18 October 2010).

Witte, Griff (2006), 'Taliban Defector Is Assassinated,' *The Washington Post*, 15 January. http://www.washingtonpost.com/wp-dyn/content/article/2006/01/14/AR2006011400983_pf.html (accessed 13 October 2010).

——— (2009), 'Taliban shadow officials offer concrete alternative,' *The Washington Post*, 8 December. http://www.washingtonpost.com/wp-dyn/content/article/2009/12/07/AR2009120704127_pf.html (accessed 10 March 2011).

Woodward, Bob (1987), *Veil: The Secret Wars of the CIA, 1981–1987*. (New York: Simon and Schuster).

——— (2002), 'CIA Led Way With Cash Handouts,' *The Washington Post*, 18 November. http://www.washingtonpost.com/ac2/wp-dyn/A3105–2002Nov17?language=printer (accessed 29 September 2010).

——— (2003), *Bush at War*. (London: Pocket Books).

——— (2004), *Plan of Attack*. (New York: Simon & Schuster).

——— (2010), *Obama's Wars*. (New York: Simon & Schuster).

Wright, Donald P. (2010), *A Different Kind of War: The United States Army in Operation Enduring Freedom October 2001–2005 September*. (Fort Leavenworth: Combat Studies Institute Press). http://s3.amazonaws.com/nytdocs/docs/21/21.pdf (accessed 29 September 2010).

Wright, Lawrence (2006), *The Looming Tower: Al-Qaeda and the road to 9/11*. (New York: Alfred A. Knopf).

——— (2008), 'The Rebellion Within: An Al-Qaeda Mastermind Questions Terrorism,' *The New Yorker*, 2 June. http://www.newyorker.com/reporting/2008/06/02/080602fa_fact_wright?printable=true (accessed 3 March 2010).

Yong, Ed (2011), 'People don't know when they're lying to themselves,' *Discover Magazine*, 7 March. http://blogs.discovermagazine.com/notrocketscience/2011/03/07/people-don%E2%80%99t-know-when-they%E2%80%99re-lying-to-themselves/ (accessed 10 March 2011).

Yousaf, Muhammad and Mark Adken (1992), *The Bear Trap: Afghanistan's Untold Story*. (London: Leo Cooper).

Yousafzai, Sami (2003), 'Periscope: Betrayed by Bin Laden,' *Newsweek*, 17 March.

——— (2009), 'The Taliban in Their Own Words,' *Newsweek*, 26 September. http://www.newsweek.com/2009/09/25/the-taliban-in-their-own-words.print.html (accessed 12 October 2010).

Yousafzai, Sami and Ron Moreau (2005), 'Unholy Allies,' *Newsweek*, 26 September. http://www.newsweek.com/2005/09/25/unholy-allies.html (accessed 29 September 2010).

——— (2010a), 'Not Your Father's Taliban,' *Newsweek*, 17 May.

——— (2010b), 'Taliban in Turmoil,' *Newsweek* (Online), 28 May. http://www.newsweek.com/2010/05/28/taliban-in-turmoil.html (accessed 6 October 2010).

Zaeef, Mullah Abdul Salam (2010), *My Life With the Taliban*. (London: Hurst).

——— (2012), *Taliban: a history* (working title). (London: Hurst).

Zaman, Muhammad Qasim (2007), *The Ulama in Contemporary Islam: Custodians of Change*. (Princeton: Princeton University Press).

Zayyat, Montassir (2004), *The Road to Al-Qaeda: the Story of bin Laden's Right-hand Man*. (London: Pluto Press).

Zielenziger, Michael and Juan O. Tamayo (2001), 'U.S. finds itself relying on information from former Taliban allies,' *Knight Ridder*, 2 November.

Zoroya, Gregg (2010), 'IEDs show troop surge working, U.S. officers say,' *USA Today*, 27 September. http://www.usatoday.com/news/world/afghanistan/2010–09–27-surge27_ST_N.htm?csp=34news (accessed 18 October 2010).

INDEX